THE ENCYCLOPEDIA OF SIXTIES COOL

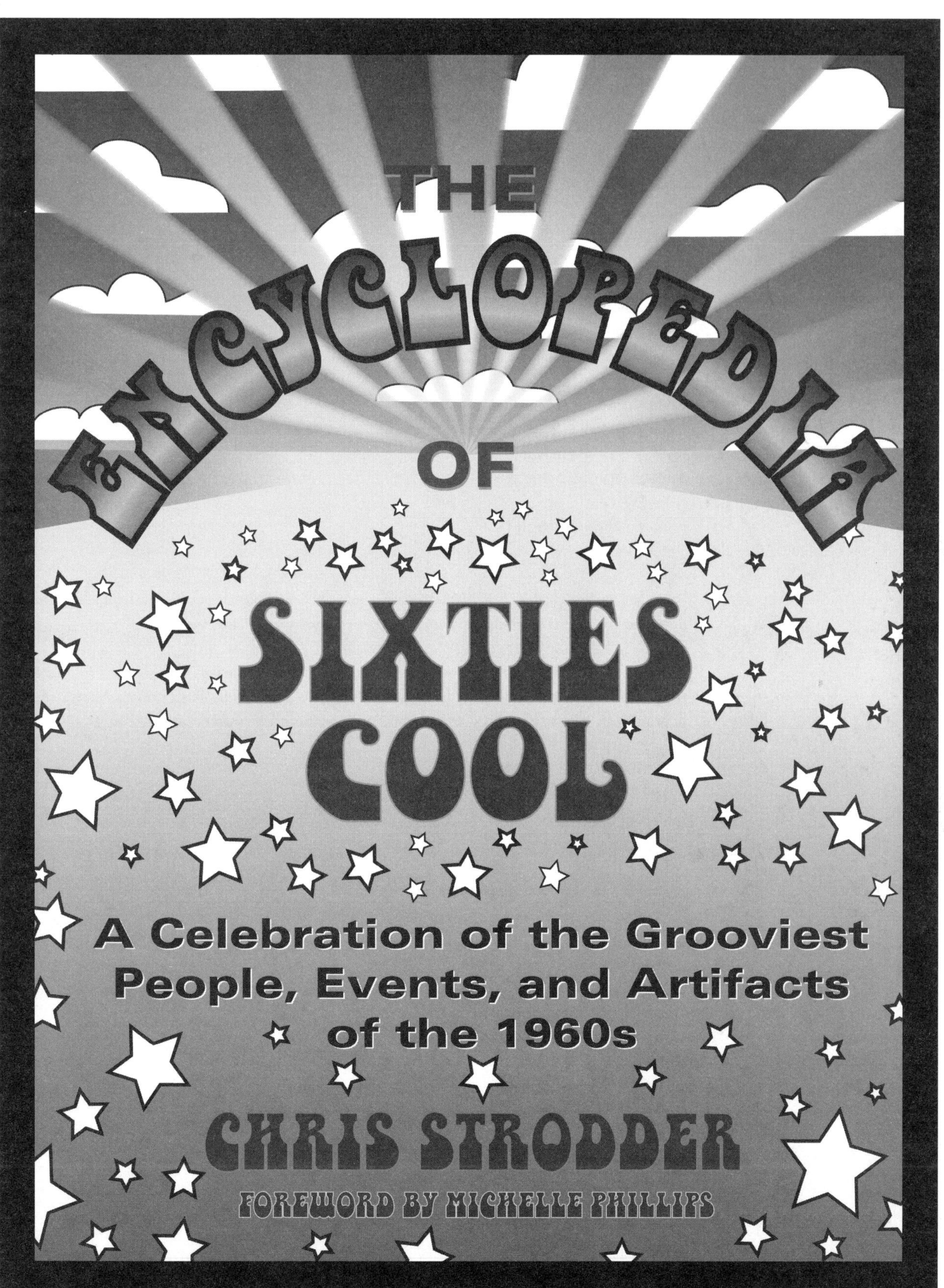
THE
ENCYCLOPEDIA
OF
SIXTIES
COOL
A Celebration of the Grooviest
People, Events, and Artifacts
of the 1960s
CHRIS STRODDER
FOREWORD BY MICHELLE PHILLIPS

Published by: Santa Monica Press LLC
P.O. Box 1076
Santa Monica, CA 90406-1076
1-800-784-9553
www.santamonicapress.com
books@santamonicapress.com

Printed in the United States

Santa Monica Press books are available at special quantity discounts when purchased in bulk by corporations, organizations, or groups. Please call our Special Sales department at 1-800-784-9553.

Although every effort was made to ensure that the information in this book was correct at the time of publication, the author and publisher do not assume and hereby disclaim any liability or responsibility to any person or group with respect to any loss, illness, injury, or damage caused by errors, omissions, or any other information found in this book.

ISBN-13 978-1-59580-017-6
ISBN-10 1-59580-017-4

Library of Congress Cataloging-in-Publication Data

Strodder, Chris
The encyclopedia of sixties cool / Chris Strodder.
p. cm.
Includes bibliographical references.
ISBN-13: 978-1-59580-017-6
ISBN-10: 1-59580-017-4
1. Celebrities--Biography--Dictionaries. 2. Nineteen sixties--Dictionaries. I. Title.

CT120S76 2007
920.02--dc22
2006037119

Cover design by Bryan Duddles
Interior design and production by Future Studio Los Angeles

Contents

January 1, 1959—Batista is overthrown in Cuba with the help of Che Guevara. ☮ January 1, 1960—The Moonglows break up. January 1, 1965—Joe Namath of the University of Alabama is named the MVP of the Orange Bowl. ☮ January 1, 1965—Petula Clark's "Downtown" hits #1. January 1, 1966—Cigarette packs begin to display health warnings from the Surgeon General.

January 1, 1967—The Monkees' "Pleasant Valley Sunday" hits #3. ☮ January 2, 1931—Singer Sam Cooke is born.
January 2, 1938—Fashion photographer David Bailey is born. ☮ January 2, 1960—Senator John F. Kennedy announces he's running for President.
January 2, 1967—Sopwith Camel is the first San Francisco rock band to have a national hit ("Hello Hello").

January 3, 1926—Producer George Martin is born in London.
January 3, 1944—U.S. swimming star Chris Von Saltza is born (she will win three gold medals and a silver at the 1960 Olympic Games in Rome).
January 3, 1945—Singer Stephen Stills is born in Dallas, Texas. ☮ January 4, 1937—Actress Dyan Cannon is born in Tacoma, Washington.

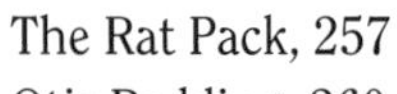

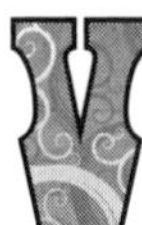

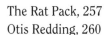

January 5, 1963—*Camelot* closes on Broadway after 873 performances. ☮ January 5, 1964—The Singing Nun appears on *The Ed Sullivan Show*.
January 5, 1988—Basketball star Pete Maravich dies. ☮ January 5, 1998—Sonny Bono dies skiing at Lake Tahoe, California.
January 6, 1931—Actress Capucine is born in Toulon, France. ☮ January 6, 1957—Elvis Presley makes his last appearance on *The Ed Sullivan Show*.

Sidebars

January 6, 1968—Lulu's "Best of Both Worlds" hits the charts. ☮ January 7, 1946—*Rolling Stone* founder Jann Wenner is born.
January 7, 1961—*The Avengers* makes its debut in England (the show comes to America four years later).
January 7, 1966—Sean Connery makes the cover of *Life*. ☮ January 7, 1968—The price of a first-class stamp jumps from five cents to six.

Foreword

As one-fourth of the legendary L.A. group the Mamas and the Papas, Michelle Phillips was at the epicenter of the youthquake that rocked the decade with marvelous music and fab fashions. Here in the 21st century, she's as beautiful and busy as ever, and yes, she's still cool. I asked Michelle to reflect on what that word, and the '60s, meant to her. If anybody would know who and what were cool in the '60s, she would. —C.S.

1. This book is called the *Encyclopedia of Sixties Cool*—how do you define the word "cool"?

MP: "Cool" talent—originality—brave—funny—smart—mysterious—any combination of the above. A good hat helps.

2. What words would you choose that best summarize the 1960s?

MP: Very political—turning away from suburbia and conformity—embracing a credo of no war—progressiveness.

Creatively, many many young people turned to arts and crafts that created whole new fashions such as tie-dye and ribbon shirts, and home decorations with Indian silks and macramé.

An openness to new kinds of spirituality (Subud Transcendental Meditation, the use of peyote, LSD and pot).

3. Who symbolized cool in the '60s?

MP: Bob Dylan, the Kennedys, the Beatles, Cass Elliot, my Daddy, Lenny Bruce, Martin Luther King, Rudi Gernreich, Jean Shrimpton.

4. Who were your own heroes in the '60s?

MP: All of the above plus many foreign film stars like Brigitte Bardot, Sophia Loren, Anita Ekberg, and Marcello Mastroianni. Also foreign directors such as Truffaut, Visconti, Antonioni, and Fellini. And John Phillips.

5. What do you think was the high point of the '60s?

MP: The high points: The civil rights movement. The women's rights movement (including birth control). The anti-war movement and anti-nuclear demonstrations. The new spirituality that included chanting, vegetarianism, and an education in meditation (yoga, etc.). Also the music and fashion revolutions.

The low points were the assassinations of the Kennedys and Martin Luther King. Also, the presidency of Richard M. Nixon, the Vietnam War, and the Manson murders in late '69.

6. What was your favorite band of the '60s? And what were your favorite albums?

MP: Band—the Beatles. Albums—*Meet the Beatles*, *Sgt. Pepper's Lonely Hearts Club Band*, *The White Album* (all by the Beatles); *If You Can Believe Your Eyes and Ears* (the Mamas and the Papas); and the Detroit sound in general.

January 8, 1935—Elvis Aron Presley is born in Tupelo, Mississippi. ☮ January 8, 1937—Singer Shirley Bassey is born in Wales.
January 8, 1939—Promoter Bill Graham is born in Germany. ☮ January 8, 1942—Actress Yvette Mimieux is born in Hollywood.
January 8, 1966—The Beatles' album *Rubber Soul* hits #1. ☮ January 8, 1993—The Elvis Presley stamp is released by the post office.

Twenty Questions with Michelle Phillips

7. What was your favorite concert of the '60s?

MP: The Mamas and the Papas at Carnegie Hall, and the Monterey International Pop Festival.

8. What was your favorite movie of the '60s?

MP: *Breakfast at Tiffany's, Wild Strawberries, Jules and Jim, The 400 Blows, Bonnie and Clyde.*

9. Who was your favorite fine artist or photographer of the '60s?

MP: Richard Avedon.

10. What were your favorite '60s fashions?

MP: For men, long hair. For women, miniskirts.

11. What was the coolest car of the '60s?

MP: The Ford Mustang.

12. What was the silliest fad of the '60s?

MP: Nehru suits.

13. Do you have any favorite '60s slang terms?

MP: Groovy.

14. Where and when was the best party you went to in the '60s?

MP: Our house in August 1967, after our Hollywood Bowl concert.

15. Is there anything you didn't do in the '60s you wish you had done?

MP: Meet John Lennon.

16. Is there anything you regret doing in the '60s?

MP: No.

17. Can you compare the mood of the '60s with the mood of today?

MP: There was less emphasis on materialism in the '60s. There was a great deal more spontaneity. One could wake up in the middle of the night and decide to drive to Mexico and be gone for three weeks. There was more togetherness (such as communal living). There was an innocence to the '60s—everyone hitchhiked, sex became more casual with the introduction of the Pill, there was no fear of AIDS, and we had never heard of Charles Manson.

18. What do you miss most about the '60s that doesn't exist now? And what do you miss least?

MP: We had a belief that the world was changing for the good—that ending hunger and war were within reach. We don't have that now.

I don't miss Nixon and J. Edgar Hoover.

19. What lesson could we learn from the '60s?

MP: To demonstrate in the streets against social injustice. To become very political in college. To teach music and art in school (that, in my opinion, started the music revolution—kids learned to play guitar, piano, and bass and sing in school).

20. What would you say is your own greatest '60s achievement?

MP: Learning to love reading. Learning to sing and blend with John, Cass and Denny.

January 9, 1941—Actress Susannah York is born in London. ☮ January 9, 1941—Singer/activist Joan Baez is born on Staten Island in New York. January 9, 1969—The last original episode of *Star Trek* airs on NBC. ☮ January 10, 1963—Sylvia Plath publishes her only novel, *The Bell Jar*. January 11, 1956—Elvis Presley makes his first RCA recordings (among them is "Heartbreak Hotel").

Introduction

Writing a book called *The Encyclopedia of Sixties Cool* (what I informally named my *Encycoolpedia*) meant making lots of choices. The 1960s were so abundant with cool people, styles, artifacts, and events that not everybody and everything could be included in a single volume. So I had to set limits. One was chronological—while many great stars of earlier decades and later decades were working in the '60s, I tried to pick 250 who peaked in the '60s. Thus '50s kings and queens like Robert Mitchum, William Holden, Lucille Ball, and Jayne Mansfield, and superstars of the '70s like Gloria Steinem, Billie Jean King, Liza Minnelli, and Joni Mitchell, were not included, even though they all did prominent work in the '60s. I realize that some of those I did include—Marilyn Monroe, Jack Nicholson, Toni Basil, to name three—thrived in other decades, but their inclusion was a personal choice because what they did in the '60s was just too significant or interesting or fun to ignore.

In addition, I had to decide what was cool, a word that has a different meaning for everybody. In picking athletes, for instance, I didn't simply choose the best players, I chose those who offered something unique to fans (thus playboy Bo Belinsky is in, while family man Willie Mays is out, even though Willie's the Hall of Famer). In picking which writers and performers to include, I went with those who most influenced the '60s—yes, Hunter Thompson (*Hell's Angels*, '66) and CSN (*Crosby, Stills, and Nash*, '69) were all working back then, but to me they truly belonged to the '70s.

In choosing actresses, I didn't simply pick a cool body (Lara Lindsay—out), I chose a cool body of work, or actresses who had something of special interest (Liz Taylor, Oscar-winner with a notorious lovelife—in). This was a frequent comment I got about my earlier *Swingin' Chicks of the '60s* book—"How could you leave out so-and-so?" Well, sure, so-and-so was beautiful or sexy or whatever she was, but seriously her movie moments were too brief (Carol Wayne), or really she was more '70s than '60s (Ali MacGraw). My apologies to the fans, to Lara, to Carol, to Ali, to anyone else who brought something tasty to the '60s buffet but who didn't make the menu. Maybe a supplemental *Encycoolpedia* for the '60s, and *Encycoolpedias* about the '50s and '70s, will answer all critiques.

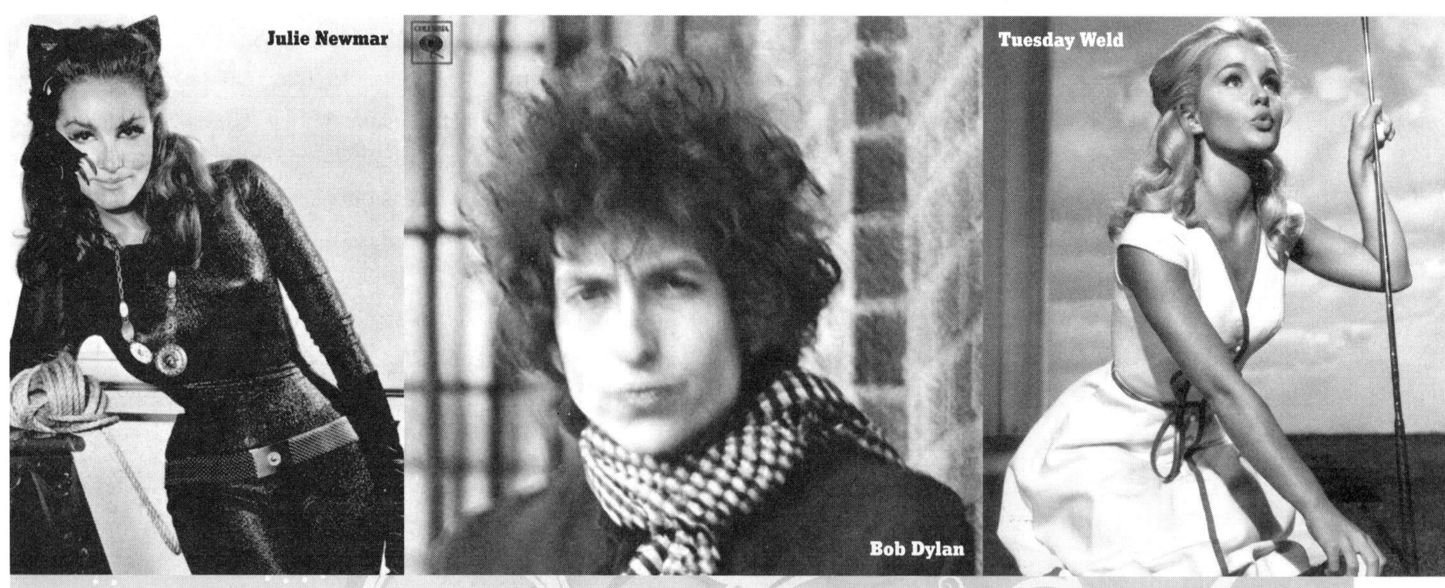

Julie Newmar

Bob Dylan

Tuesday Weld

January 11, 1963—Actress Ann-Margret makes the cover of *Life*. ☮ January 12, 1937—Actress Shirley Eaton is born in London.
January 12, 1966—*Batman* with Adam West debuts. ☮ January 12, 1969—The New York Jets win Super Bowl III.
January 13, 1962—Chubby Checker's "The Twist" hits #1. ☮ January 13, 1962—Actor Ernie Kovacs dies.

Finally, for your edification I've included people either unknown to the masses (Al Fritz) or known but not traditionally thought of as cool (Tiny Tim, anybody?). These entries reward those anonymous specialists who created something cool (Al's awesome Sting-Ray bike) or those unique stars who certainly got our attention (*somebody* bought millions of Tiny's albums—you know who you are). As for some of my more unusual choices (the nuns, for instance, or perhaps a scientist or singer you don't know), well, indulge me, these were interesting people to me so I included them. That's the beauty part about writing a book, you get to do what you want, so I did.

Oh, just to clarify, the subheads for each profile have musical connotations—"Takin' Care of Business," of course, was Elvis's slogan, "Everybody Loves Somebody" is the best-selling Dean Martin song that knocked the Beatles from #1 in '64, and "My Back Pages" is a Dylan classic.

This book was researched and written between September 2005 and March 2006. Research material was gathered through correspondence and phone interviews, supplemented by long hours at the wonderful Marin County libraries and speedy deliveries over my wireless laptop (once you've gone wireless you'll never go back). My thanks go to all the celebrities who spoke with me or replied to my many e-mails and letters. I also am deeply grateful to the friends who helped with photos, either sending me cherished items from their own collections or assisting with recruitment and scanning, especially Annie Helm, Lisa Flood, Russ Lanier, Tara Macia Pollard, Alan Parowski, Dr. Robert Rush, C. Robert Rotter (owner of the amazing photo collection at glamourgirlsofthe silverscreen.com), and Ferenc Dobronyi, just to name a few of the many people who helped. Thanks to publisher Jeffrey Goldman for e-mailing me out of the blue one summer day with a book idea and for answering all my endless questions for the next six months. And to Sheryl Patton, the hardest-workin' woman I have ever known.

—Chris Strodder, Mill Valley, California

Lew Alcindor

Barbara Steele

Sean Connery

January 13, 1964—Bob Dylan's album *The Times They Are A-Changin'* is released.
January 13, 1968—Johnny Cash records his concert at California's Folsom State Prison for a live album.
January 13, 1969—Mike Nichols's *Catch-22* begins production. ☮ January 14, 1936—Actress Linda Lawson is born in Ann Arbor, Michigan.

Don Adams and Barbara Feldon

Agent 86 was bumbling and 99 was beautiful on the beloved spy show where they kept KAOS to a minimum.

TAKIN' CARE OF BUSINESS

Cool sayings from TV shows populated the decade's vocabulary: think "Beam me up, Scotty," "Here comes da judge," and "Danger, Will Robinson!" Delivering some of the most famous phrases, with some of the most famous phrasing, was Don Adams, whose Agent 86 on the hit show *Get Smart* brought "Missed it by *that* much," "Sorry about that, Chief," and "Would you believe . . . ?" to life.

Born Don James Yarmy in New York City, he was a young movie fan who left school at 13, became a theatre usher, and then joined the Marines in time to serve at Guadalcanal and later as a drill instructor (imagine his commands: "Drop and give me 100 push-ups . . . would you believe, 50 push-ups and a jumping jack?"). A successful '54 audition on Arthur Godfrey's *Talent Scouts* (where he first used the name Adams) led to appearances doing impressions on TV and in nightclubs.

With a delivery patterned after William Powell's crisp elocution in *The Thin Man* movies, he got steady TV work in the early '60s and was the enduring voice of cartoon penguin Tennessee Tuxedo. Then he got smart. A new show created by Mel Brooks and Buck Henry, *Get Smart* spoofed all the Bond movies and spy shows thriving as the Cold War heated up. Espionage gadgets, vocabulary, and stratagems were ripe targets, and Don, daring to be idiotic in his natty tuxedo, was so brilliantly inept as Agent 86 he won three Emmy Awards.

Heading the crack supporting cast was sultry-'n'-smart "straight man" Barbara Feldon. Pittsburgh-born Barbara was modeling and doing commercials in New York when *Get Smart* revved up in '65. Barbara, a bright, attractive, elegant actress, picked up two Emmy nominations as patient partner-in-crime-fighting Agent 99. In '67, Barbara brought her charms to *Fitzwilly*, a caper-comedy with Dick Van Dyke, then

in the '68 season of *Get Smart* the two star agents got married (86 + 99 = 185?).

Trying to boost ratings, 99 had twins in '69, but unfortunately *Get Smart* became "Get Cancelled" in '70. Barbara continued, however, with some commercials and TV appearances, plus a dozen TV movies. *Smile* ('75) was her best big-screen role. With that sexy voice, she's always had steady work doing voiceovers and narrations, and late in the '90s she performed a one-woman off-Broadway show. As post-99 screen work came less frequently, she became an astute investor and a stock broker while living in Manhattan.

Meanwhile Don's post-'60s career was mostly an unsuccessful effort to break away from Agent 86. Two early '70s series (*The Partner*, *Screen Test*) failed, so he filled the decade with Vegas gigs and guest spots on lightweight shows like *The Love Boat*. A 1980 Maxwell Smart movie, *The Nude Bomb*, replaced Agent 99 with Agent 34, Sylvia Kristel (of the soft-core *Emmanuelle* movies), but the result was indeed a bomb. In the '80s he found new popularity as the main voice on the *Inspector Gadget* cartoon show. Two more Maxwell Smart efforts—an '89 TV movie that reteamed him with Barbara Feldon, and a '95 sitcom that posited 86 as

January 14, 1941—Actress Faye Dunaway is born in Bascom, Florida. ☮ January 14, 1967—Jefferson Airplane perform at San Francisco's first "Be-In."
January 15, 1929—Martin Luther King is born in Atlanta, Georgia. ☮ January 15, 1961—The Supremes sign with Motown.
January 15, 1966—Petula Clark's "My Love" hits the charts. ☮ January 15, 1967—The Green Bay Packers beat the Kansas City Chiefs in Super Bowl I.

Chief, 99 as a senator, and son Andy Dick as a spy—fell short of the glory days.

EVERYBODY LOVES SOMEBODY

While he was a struggling Miami comic in the '50s, Don was already married with four daughters, but he left them all to restart in New York. There he married a Rockette, who would give him a fifth daughter (they would adopt a son in '69). Unfortunately, a mid-life crisis overtook Don as the *Get Smart* run concluded, and in '77 he married a 20-year-old *Playboy* model. A sixth daughter was born in '79, but the couple separated a year later. Throughout all these traumas Don stayed loyal to his longtime friends, especially Hugh Hefner, and he was a frequent guest at Hef's events. A lung infection finally took Don Adams in 2005 at the age of 82.

Barbara Feldon, before she got famous as an agent with a number for a name, won big on a '50s quiz show. She invested her winnings in a New York art gallery and married her business partner (and kept his last name after their '67 divorce). She was in another relationship into the mid-'70s, then in 2002 she told *Biography* magazine that she hadn't been involved with anyone for two decades. She even wrote a book called *Living Alone and Loving It*, "for anyone who has felt they have to apologize for being alone."

MY BACK PAGES

Smart move: Don accepted a lesser salary ($4,000 per week instead of $12,500) in exchange for part ownership of *Get Smart*, which has enjoyed a long, lucrative run in syndication. . . . Hobbies included painting and studying history. . . . When 86 married 99 on the show, Don's second wife and mother were wedding guests. . . . Barbara admitted that her *Get Smart* hair was nearly always a wig or a fall. . . . *Get Smart* and *I Dream of Jeannie* debuted on the same night on the same network, both in black and white. . . . *Get Smart* (in all its incarnations) is the only show in history to appear on all four major networks—the original version ran for four years on NBC and one on CBS, the '95 TV movie *Get Smart, Again!* was on ABC, and the '97 *Get Smart* was on Fox.

Lew Alcindor

The decade's most dominating college basketball player led UCLA to three straight NCAA titles.

TAKIN' CARE OF BUSINESS

The most overpowering college basketball player of the '60s, Lew Alcindor (as he was known back then) changed the game. So unstoppable was he that the NCAA outlawed dunking for years to try to level the playing field for overmatched opponents. Almost two-feet-tall at birth, Lew was already a seven-footer in high school when he led his New York team to three straight city championships and 71 wins in a row. With his pick of colleges he chose UCLA and its legendary wizard, Coach John Wooden. There, Lew's Bruins won 88 of 90 games and three straight NCAA championships (UCLA was en route to a record seven straight). After the third title, Lew was named the Most Outstanding Player of the Final Four for the third consecutive year, the first and only time anyone has accomplished that feat. He was also Player of the Year twice and an All-American for three years.

Moving on to the pros as the top draft pick, he led the Milwaukee Bucks to the title in '71 and later the L.A. Lakers to five titles in the '80s, winning six MVP awards along the way before retiring in '89 as the NBA's all-time scoring leader. He was also a man of diverse passions: he studied martial arts with Bruce Lee, gathered priceless collections of Persian rugs and jazz records (both destroyed in a fire), and his Muslim studies (begun at UCLA) prompted him to change his name to Kareem Abdul-Jabbar in '71. Movie fans may remember him for his half-dozen screen roles, especially as the shorts-wearing co-pilot in *Airplane!* ('80).

EVERYBODY LOVES SOMEBODY

Lew (as Kareem) was married for most of the '70s until he got divorced. He's got four kids.

MY BACK PAGES

Talk about big man on campus: in '66 Lew's freshman team beat the UCLA varsity, which had just won the NCAA title and was ranked #1 (making the varsity first in the nation but only second on campus). . . . He set a UCLA scoring record of 56 points in his very first varsity game, a record he broke with 61 later that same year. . . . Lew set all his UCLA records despite playing only 20 minutes in many games in which the Bruins built insurmountable leads. . . . In a Bob Hope TV special broadcast from UCLA, Bob announced that the letters stood for University of California at Lew Alcindor. . . . He was enshrined in the Basketball Hall of Fame in '95.

Muhammad Ali

The Greatest fought one of his toughest opponents when he took on the draft board.

TAKIN' CARE OF BUSINESS

Ali—a single name, recognized and respected throughout the world as a hero. While Muhammad Ali's most famous bouts in the ring—his titanic clashes with Joe Frazier and George Foreman—came in the '70s, for many people his reputation was really made in the '60s. Born Cassius Clay, he was training in a gym at 12 years old and had over 100 amateur bouts as a teen, winning several national titles. He got his first global acclaim in '60 when he won a gold medal as a light heavyweight at the Olympic Games in Rome. Parades greeted him back home, but so did the segregation he'd grown up with, and amazingly a restaurant in his own hometown wouldn't serve him.

Teaming with trainer Angelo Dundee in Miami, he learned to dance his way out of trouble and use his lightning-quick reflexes and long reach to land devastating punches without getting hit. Working his way up through the heavyweight ranks, he started making brash predictions about his fights, getting the nickname "the Louisville Lip" for his sassy repartee with the media (Ali later said he boasted to draw crowds to his fights). In '64 his life changed in two important ways: he TKO'd the heavily favored Sonny Liston for the heavyweight crown, and he joined the Nation of Islam (briefly taking the name Cassius X). A high-profile win over Floyd Patterson in '65 preceded five straight wins around the world in '66.

But in '67, now a Muslim minister with the name Muhammad Ali, he refused on religious grounds to be inducted into the Army. The furious response was immediate—much of the public was hostile, he was stripped of his heavyweight title, his boxing license was suspended all across America, and he didn't fight for about three years. But as always, Ali kept talking, visiting colleges to speak defiantly against the Vietnam War.

In '70 he began his comeback by beating Jerry Quarry; a year later he took on, but lost to, Smokin' Joe Frazier at Madison Square Garden, Ali's first pro defeat. The Supreme Court soon granted him an even bigger victory, however, by upholding his claim as a conscientious objector and reversing the earlier conviction that could've sent him to jail for half a decade. His biggest boxing matches followed: a loss and a win against Ken Norton, two wins in rematches with Frazier (the "Thrilla in Manila" was instantly hailed as one of the greatest fights ever), the legendary "Rumble in the Jungle" triumph over powerful George Foreman in Zaire in '74, and the upset loss and win against young Leon Spinks (making Ali the first heavyweight in history to win the title three times). He finished his pro career in '81 having won 56 of 61 fights, with two-thirds of his victories coming by knockout.

January 17, 1942—Boxer Muhammad Ali is born in Louisville, Kentucky. ☮ January 17, 1944—Singer Françoise Hardy is born in Paris.
January 17, 1966—The Simon and Garfunkel album *Sounds of Silence* is released.
January 17, 1996—After 32 years as editor in chief, Helen Gurley Brown resigns from *Cosmopolitan* magazine.

Unfortunately his long career took its toll, and in '84 Ali was diagnosed with pugilistic Parkinson's syndrome, a neurological disorder exacerbated by blows to the head. Ali's greatness—as an athlete and an activist—was celebrated in the '90s and 2000s when he topped several millennium "best" lists, was inducted into the International Boxing Hall of Fame, was named Sportsman of the Century by *Sports Illustrated*, and was given the Presidential Medal of Freedom. In Louisville, the Muhammad Ali Center, a shrine to boxing, peace, and respect, opened in 2005. He is today one of the few, maybe the only, celebrities that all other world-famoushj celebrities will humble themselves to, and he remains the most well-known person on the planet.

EVERYBODY LOVES SOMEBODY

Muhammad Ali first got married in '64, a union that lasted until '66. He remarried in '67 but divorced a decade later. Ali married again in '77 for another decade, and in '86 he married his current wife. He has nine children (seven daughters, two sons). One of his daughters, Laila, became a successful boxer in '99.

MY BACK PAGES

Ali first used his "float like a butterfly, sting like a bee" line at the weigh-in for the '64 fight against Sonny Liston. . . . Capitalizing on his popularity, he recorded an album called *I Am the Greatest* in '64, and five years later he starred and sang in a short-lived Broadway musical, *Buck White*. . . . An unimpressed Ali clowned with the Beatles for photographers in '64. . . . The '74 upset of Foreman, in which Ali employed his surprise "rope-a-dope" strategy that let Foreman tire himself out, was considered Ali's most brilliant tactical fight. . . . At the '96 Olympics in Atlanta, Ali shocked everyone, even the announcers, when he lit the Olympic torch. . . . Ali has been in movies (playing himself), has been the subject of movies (most recently *Ali* starring Will Smith), and has even been at several Academy Award shows to present Oscars.

10 Great Boxers

Nino Benvenuti–middleweight champ, '67–'70
Jimmy Ellis–heavyweight champ, '68–'70
George Foreman–Olympic gold medal, '68
Joe Frazier–Olympic gold medal, '64
Emile Griffith–welterweight champ, '61–'65
Ingemar Johansson–heavyweight champ, '60
Sonny Liston–heavyweight champ, '62–'64
Floyd Patterson–heavyweight champ, '60–'62
Ernie Terrell–heavyweight champ, '65–'67
Dick Tiger–middleweight champ, '62–'65

Woody Allen

One of America's most prolific cinematic auteurs first gained fame as a successful stand-up comedian.

TAKIN' CARE OF BUSINESS

On his live comedy album Woody Allen declared his first name was Heywood, but actually he was born Allan Stewart Konigsberg. Growing up in Brooklyn, he instantly fell in love with the movies upon seeing Disney's *Snow White*. Though he would later play uncoordinated bespectacled characters, he was actually a decent ballplayer as a kid and didn't start wearing glasses until he was 18 (even then they were his trademark heavy black frames). While in high school, he started submitting jokes to New York columnists as Woody Allen; he entered New York University in '53 but soon left and moved to Hollywood in '55 to write for TV. He returned to New York in '56 to write for comedians until he started to perform his own jokes at the turn of the decade, a nervy decision referenced in *Annie Hall*.

Despite almost crippling performance anxiety, his

successes in small Greenwich Village comedy clubs led to national media attention (*Time* and *Variety* both raved about him in early '63). Soon followed his first TV appearances on talk shows and game shows, plus writing jobs on *Candid Camera* and other lightweight TV fare. His live album in '64 (where he based most of the bits on his own life) brought him a job as a writer/supporting actor for *What's New, Pussycat?* ('65), a screwball sex comedy starring Peters O'Toole and Sellers.

When *Pussycat* purred its way to blockbuster status, offers poured in, and Woody began a remarkable run in which he turned out new projects annually for the rest of his career. Here at the beginning, cinematic patterns were already establishing themselves. He toyed with the whole concept of filmmaking in *What's Up, Tiger Lily?* ('66), dubbing hilarious new English dialogue into an obscure Japanese spy film and directly addressing the camera (he did the same kind of experimenting in *Annie Hall* a decade later).

Two weeks after *Tiger Lily* premiered, his first major play, *Don't Drink the Water*, opened on Broadway to favorable reviews. Woody, meanwhile, was already onto his next project—in the '67 Bond-spoof *Casino Royale*, he wrote his own lively scenes as youthful villain Jimmy Bond. Within two years he had another Broadway hit, *Play It Again, Sam* (which he wrote and starred in) and his first directorial effort, *Take the Money and Run*.

Again these projects foreshadowed later successes: *Sam*, with Woody consulting Humphrey Bogart's ghost for dating advice, presaged *The Purple Rose of Cairo* ('85), which also brought fantasy characters from the movies into the "real world"; *Take the Money* (a mock-documentary about an inept criminal) led to the masterful *Zelig* in '83 (a mock-documentary about an insecure "chameleon man"). *Money* was also the first of many movies in which he wore three hats as the writer, director, and star. And already he was gathering around him the players who would populate his later movies: his Broadway co-stars were Diane Keaton and Tony Roberts (she would be in eight of his movies, he in six), and one of the actresses doing voiceovers in *Tiger Lily* was Louise Lasser (six Woody movies).

Somehow he also found time to publish a dozen *New Yorker* stories in the '60s (most of them included in the '71 *Getting Even* compilation). He also appeared in zany *Playboy* pictorials, did print ads for vodka, sunglasses, and shirts, continued to hit the talk shows, and had his own primetime special. Woody Allen was not the most famous entertainer of the '60s, but he may have been the busiest.

Likewise, his post-'60s career represents one of the most productive outpourings of movies in Hollywood history. Between *Bananas* in '70 and *Scoop* in 2006, he wrote and directed (and often starred in) some 35 movies. Though the films are uneven in quality, the highlights are the triumphs of an innovative artist eager to stretch himself: the literary *Love and Death* ('75), the nonlinear breakthrough *Annie Hall* ('77), the bittersweet *Manhattan* ('79), and many many more including a musical, mysteries, slapstick comedies, heartfelt romances, period movies, futuristic movies, intimate family dramas, movies with sad endings/happy endings/Hollywood endings. And he's done all this while also working for other directors, writing for magazines, and turning out new plays.

His prodigious talents have made him the record-holder for most Oscar-nominated screenplays (14, plus six directing nominations, another for Best Actor, and two for Best Picture) and liberated him to work on any project he wants with any actor he asks. The shy comic who began his performing career in the '60s as a lovable loser is continuing it four decades later as the renaissance genius of American movies.

EVERYBODY LOVES SOMEBODY

Woody's private and professional lives have always been intertwined, beginning with his first wife, a 17-year-old Brooklyn girl who had been his first real girlfriend. They were married in '56 while he was working in L.A.; after their '62 divorce, she became the unnamed ex- in his stand-up material (she later sued him, settling out of court).

He married his New York neighbor, Louise Lasser, in '66; in '70 she would be his leading lady in *Bananas* (later she'd star in the TV show *Mary Hartman, Mary Hartman*). By the time *Bananas* came out, though, Woody was with Diane Keaton. While he and Diane worked together into the '90s, they were romantic only a few years and never married.

Mia Farrow, the waifish star of *Rosemary's Baby* ('68), was his next love. She starred in 13 of Woody's films, picking up three Golden Globe nominations along the way. Not only did they never marry, they never lived together, retaining their own apartments on opposite sides of Central Park for the 10 years they were a couple, but they did adopt two kids and have a son of their own. They abruptly broke up after Mia exposed Woody's relationship with Mia's adopted daughter, the 21-year-old Korean-born Soon-Yi Previn. Woody and Soon-Yi married in '97, adopted two daughters, and have stayed together ever since. She's had bit parts in several of Woody's films and co-starred as herself in the documentary *Wild Man Blues* ('97).

MY BACK PAGES

Dancing next to Woody during the closing credits of *What's Up, Tiger Lily?* was China Lee, *Playboy* magazine's Miss August '64 and wife of comic Mort Sahl. . . . Unlike Woody's post-'60s movies, which were often set in a highly romanticized Manhattan, his '60s films were shot in Paris (*What's New, Pussycat?)*, London (*Casino Royale*), and San Francisco's Bay Area (*Take the Money and Run)*. . . . An original cut of *Take the Money and Run* ended with a machine-gun slaying reminiscent of *Bonnie and Clyde*. . . . Woody's later movies would use old jazz songs as soundtracks, but *Take the Money and Run* and *Bananas* both had new scores written by Marvin Hamlisch. . . . Woody made the cover of *Time* in '72, '79 (the cover line—"A Comic Genius"), and '92. . . . In 2004 Comedy Central ranked him fourth (behind Richard Pryor, George Carlin, and Lenny Bruce) among the 100 greatest stand-up comics. . . . Other hobbies—magic (a childhood diversion) and music (he played clarinet in a Manhattan hotspot the night *Annie Hall* swept the Oscars). . . . He's usually named *Stardust Memories* or *Husbands and Wives* as his best films.

Herb Alpert

This big-time bandleader was also a big-time business man.

TAKIN' CARE OF BUSINESS

A child trumpeter in the '40s, a member of the USC marching band in the '50s, L.A.-born Herb Alpert first made a name for himself as co-writer of the Sam Cooke hit "Wonderful World" in the '60s. With Jerry Moss he founded A & M Records in '62, which would become a successful record label boasting such famous artists as Cat Stevens and the Carpenters.

But Herb himself was the company's biggest star. With the Tijuana Brass he created an appealing blend of mariachi and pop music that yielded five consecutive #1 albums and a smile-inducing list of familiar hits through the middle of the decade: "The Lonely Bull," "A Taste of Honey," "Spanish Flea," Tijuana Taxi," "Casino Royale," and many more. At one point in '66 the group had four albums in the Top 10 at the same time. Of the singles, the first to top the charts was the one Herb sang, the Burt Bacharach softy "This Guy's in Love with You" ('68).

Grammy nominations and industry awards poured

January 20, 1961—After four-and-a-half years of marriage, Marilyn Monroe is granted a divorce from writer Arthur Miller in a Mexican courtroom. January 20, 1965—LBJ is inaugurated as the 36th President. ☮ January 20, 1968—Actress Sharon Tate marries director Roman Polanski in London. January 20, 1969—Richard Nixon is inaugurated as the 37th President.

in during these years, and Herb and the boys got Emmy nominations for their popular TV specials. At the end of an inconsistent '70s, Herb peaked again with the instrumental "Rise," becoming the first and only artist to take a vocal and an instrumental to the top of the *Billboard* charts. He and Moss sold A & M for something like a half-*billion* dollars at the end of the '80s, then they started Almo Sounds five years later, featuring more of Herb's own records. By now over 70 million Herb Alpert records have been sold over an ongoing 40-year career.

EVERYBODY LOVES SOMEBODY

In the early '70s, Herb married Lani Hall, who had been a singer with A & M's Sergio Mendes and Brasil '66 a few years earlier. Herb produced her '70s solo albums *Sundown Lady, Hello It's Me, Sweetbird,* and *Double or Nothing.* She also sang the theme song for the James Bond movie *Never Say Never Again* in '83, and together they performed the Oscar-nominated "Maniac" at the Academy Awards in '84.

MY BACK PAGES

Herb briefly went by the professional name Dore Alpert in the early '60s. . . . He performed the national anthem at Super Bowl XXII. . . . He was also one of the co-producers of the Broadway hits *Angels in America, Jelly's Last Jam,* and *Broken Glass.* . . . A renaissance man, his paintings and sculptures have been exhibited in prominent museums, galleries, and art fairs around the world.

Ursula Andress

This statuesque Swiss-born goddess decorated several key '60s movies.

TAKIN' CARE OF BUSINESS

A budding star of European movies in the '50s, Switzerland's Ursula Andress was riveting eye candy for a dozen major English-language films in the '60s. Her impact was immediate from the moment her bikini-clad Honey Ryder character emerged from the sea halfway through *Dr. No* ('62). Her voice, certainly her singing, looked dubbed in that movie, but audiences didn't care. Instantly 26-year-old Ursula became one of Hollywood's most desirable actresses, and she was anointed with a Golden Globe in '64 as Most Promising Newcomer.

A remarkable beauty with a remarkable figure (in '63 her stats were listed by *Movie Life Yearbook* as 5′ 6″ and 121 pounds, 36-21-35) she followed up *Dr. No* with Elvis's sexy *Fun in Acapulco* ('63). Audiences got an eyeful of Ursula in

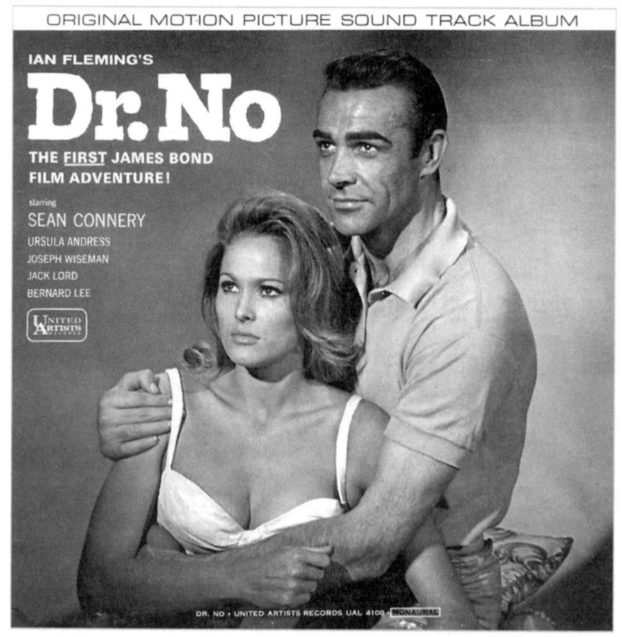

January 20, 1993—Actress Audrey Hepburn dies in Tolochenaz, Switzerland of colon cancer.
January 21, 1966—George Harrison of the Beatles marries model Pattie Boyd in England.
January 21, 1966—S.F.'s three-day Trips Festival (with the Grateful Dead and Jefferson Airplane) begins.

that movie as she again made her entrance by climbing out of the water in a wet bikini. Later in the picture, she flaunted a pair of white pants painted on so tightly you could almost see her veins (supposedly the King was so intimidated by her figure that he told his pallies, "I was embarrassed to take off my damn shirt next to her!").

Other decade highlights for Ursula included a starring role alongside Frank and Dino in *4 for Texas* ('63), the Woody Allen-scripted *What's New, Pussycat?* ('65), the adventure classic *She* ('65), and the Bond spoof *Casino Royale* ('67). *Playboy*, of course, adored her: the dozen pages the magazine devoted to her pictorial in '65 were the most they'd ever given to one woman. Ursula continued to appear onscreen into the '90s, notably in *The Fifth Musketeer* ('79), *Clash of the Titans* ('81), and *Falcon Crest* ('88), plus some foreign films with titles like *Slave of the Cannibal God* ('78). Lately she's added several Bond-themed documentaries to her résumé. In 1999, an appreciative *Playboy* magazine ranked her as one of the century's 100 sexiest stars, with two other vivacious vixens, Kim Novak at #18 and Gina Lollobrigida at #20, forming a delectable Ursula sandwich.

EVERYBODY LOVES SOMEBODY

In *Fun in Acapulco*, Ursula played a vamp who didn't take coffee breaks, she took "man breaks." In real life, she was a married woman from '57-'66; her husband was John Derek, the actor who later married Linda Evans and Bo Derek. Throughout her movie career there were rumored relationships with other stars, including Sean Connery, James Dean, Marlon Brando, Dennis Hopper, Ryan O'Neal, and Peter O'Toole. In the late '70s and early '80s she lived with one of her co-stars in *Clash of the Titans*, actor Harry Hamlin, who is 15 years her junior; in '80, at 44 years old, she gave birth to his son. Ursula now lives in Italy.

MY BACK PAGES

On some films she was credited as Ursula Parker. . . . Elvis's nickname for her was "Ooshie". . . . The most common joke about her name was to mispronounce it as Ursula Undress. . . . The *Mad* magazine spoof called her Bond movie *Dr. No-No* and her character Miss Yes-Yes.

Mario Andretti

Arguably the decade's most famous race car driver won the Indy 500 in '69.

TAKIN' CARE OF BUSINESS

Born in Italy, Mario Andretti and his family spent some post-World War II years in a refugee camp. Immigrating to the U.S. in '55, Mario grew up in Joe Namath's hometown, Nazareth, Pennsylvania. Abandoning plans to become a welder, he took up amateur racing, driving a Hudson around dirt tracks in '59. Within five years he was an acclaimed driver of midget and sprint cars, and in '66 he came in third at the Indy 500 and was named Rookie of the Year. Showing his remarkable versatility, by the end of the decade he'd won virtually every major American race, including Indy (where jubilant owner Andy Granatelli kissed him in '69), the Daytona 500, and Sebring.

Throughout the '70s, Mario went Formula 1 and competed in all the Grand Prix races around the world, winning Long Beach in '77 and the World Championship in '78. He continued driving into the '80s, competed against his two sons and nephew in the same Indy 500 race in '91, and finally retired in '94 with the most recognized racing name in America. Today he's a successful businessman with diverse interests, including his own winery and racing school.

EVERYBODY LOVES SOMEBODY

Mario married his Nazareth sweetheart in '61. He's got three kids, a daughter and two sons, Michael and Jeff, who both became successful race car drivers (both were named Indy's Rookie of the Year).

MY BACK PAGES

After crashing during practice, Mario set 15 new track records when he won at Indy in '69. . . . He was also the first driver to hit 200 mph at Indy ('77). . . . He drove a race car one more time for the Imax film *Super Speedway* ('97).

Indy 500 Winners

1960–Jim Rathmann, USA

1961–A.J. Foyt, USA

1962–Rodger Ward, USA

1963–Parnelli Jones, USA

1964–A.J. Foyt, USA

1965–Jim Clark, Scotland

1966–Graham Hill, England

1967–A.J. Foyt, USA

1968–Bobby Unser, USA

1969–Mario Andretti, Italy

Ann-Margret

This voluptuous rock-'em-sock-'em fireball starred in a dozen major '60s movies.

TAKIN' CARE OF BUSINESS

Ann-Margret had a meteoric rise to international stardom, and that was stardom with staying power. Even though her movie career has slowed, as it did in the late '60s, she has stayed in the spotlight, often with live Vegas shows that have only enhanced her reputation as a dynamic performer.

Born in Sweden, Ann-Margret Olsson and her family moved to America in the late '40s. She landed an agent at 16 and soon had gigs with a Midwestern vocal quartet called the Subtle Tones. When the group got jobs in Hollywood nightclubs, the studios spotted her, tested her, and quickly signed her to record and movie contracts. TV appearances, especially a show-stopper at the '62 Academy Awards, brought her national attention, and *Bye Bye Birdie* ('63), in which she was a 22-year-old playing a ninth grader, got her on the cover of *Life* magazine. JFK certainly appreciated Ann-Margret's exciting talent—she sang for him at his private birthday bash in '63.

A year later *Kitten with a Whip* (in which she went blonde) turned up the heat, but even more electric was her high-powered pairing with the King. In *Viva Las Vegas* ('64), she was as confident and sexy as Elvis (she was even called "the female Elvis"). Off the screen, she headlined Vegas in '67 in a splashy five-week engagement at the Riviera Hotel, toured Vietnam twice with Bob Hope, and recorded albums of jazz, country, and Broadway tunes. After a brief slump and a bout with alcohol, her career revived in '71 with *Carnal Knowledge* and a Best Supporting Actress Oscar nomination. A year later she fell 22 feet while performing on a Tahoe stage—the accident put her in a coma with broken facial bones. Amazingly, within three months

January 25, 1944—Actress Anita Pallenberg is born in Rome. ☮ January 25, 1944—Actress Leigh Taylor-Young is born in Washington, D.C.
January 25, 1961—Disney's *101 Dalmations* opens. ☮ January 25, 1964—Dusty Springfield's "I Only Want to Be with You" hits the charts.
January 26, 1925—Actor Paul Newman is born in Shaker Heights, Ohio. ☮ January 26, 1928—Director Roger Vadim is born in Paris.

she reopened in Vegas to standing ovations.

Throughout the '70s and '80s she continued to headline Vegas, looking more beautiful and drawing bigger crowds than ever. Her film career rebounded too, and she made dozens of movies into the 21st century, including *Tommy* ('75, bringing her a second Oscar nomination) and *Grumpy Old Men* ('93). Her '94 autobiography, *My Story*, became a *New York Times* bestseller, in '99 she got her fifth Emmy nomination, in 2001 and 2002 she toured triumphantly with the hit musical *Best Little Whorehouse in Texas*, and in 2002 she got a Grammy nomination for her gospel album *God Is Love*. Honoring her vivacious curves, *Playboy* put her thirteenth among the 100 sexiest stars of the century, right between Kim Basinger and Anita Ekberg.

EVERYBODY LOVES SOMEBODY

The press romantically linked her with Johnny Carson, Eddie Fisher, Steve McQueen, and Elvis. It was with the King, whom she met on the set of *Viva Las Vegas*, that she got the most attention. She wrote in her autobiography that when she and Elvis met in '63, they simultaneously said the same words to each other: "I've heard a lot about you."

Their on-screen pairing was so hot, the chemistry so obvious, that when the studio released a publicity shot that showed them in wedding clothes, the fan magazines reported that the couple really was married. She later wrote: "We were indeed soul mates, shy on the outside, but unbridled within." After Elvis died in '77, she admitted that she would "never recover from Elvis's death." But she did find true love.

In '61 she met actor Roger *"77 Sunset Strip"* Smith, who was almost 10 years her senior; they hooked up again in '64, and married in Vegas in '67, moving into the Hollywood house formerly owned by Bogie and Bacall. They've been each other's best ally ever since. He nursed her after her '72 accident, and when he was bedridden with a rare degenerative nerve disease, she halted her career for two years to take care of him.

MY BACK PAGES

Ann-Margrock was a character styled to look just like her on *The Flintstones* in '63. . . . Tina Turner's autobiography revealed that Ann-Margret's first date with Roger Smith was to an Ike and Tina Turner concert. . . . She's said that she loves to ride motorcycles, especially Harleys. . . . Whenever she opened a new live show in the '60s and '70s, Elvis always sent a huge guitar-shaped bouquet of flowers. . . . His nickname for her was "Rusty," the name of her character in *Viva Las Vegas*.

January 26, 1944—Activist Angela Davis is born in Birmingham, Alabama. ☮ January 26, 1961—Elvis's "Are You Lonesome Tonight?" hits #1.
January 26, 1962—Robert Kennedy makes the cover of *Life*. ☮ January 27, 1921—Actress Donna Reed is born in Denison, Iowa.
January 27, 1961—John and Jackie Kennedy make the cover of *Life*. ☮ January 27, 1967—The *Apollo 1* fire kills three astronauts.

Michelangelo Antonioni

The master director made *Blow-Up*, one of the coolest, and most confusing, movies of the '60s.

TAKIN' CARE OF BUSINESS

Born in Italy before World War I, Michelangelo Antonioni studied economics and cinema in college during the '30s and '40s. After serving in the Italian Army during World War II, in the late '40s he began making documentaries, and in the '50s he made enigmatic features that brought him a reputation in Italy as a maturing artist.

With the new decade came his first great successes. Written and directed by Michelangelo, *The Adventure* ('60), *The Night* ('61), and *The Eclipse* ('62) formed a highly influential black-and-white trilogy that was extremely light on action but heavy on existential atmosphere and psychological insight. Audiences were either perplexed or lavish with their praise—critics hailed him as a profound visionary, and history has remembered the three movies as cinematic milestones. *The Red Desert* ('64) again studied alienation in modern society while offering little plot.

His breakthrough in America was one of the most bizarre, most analyzed movies of all time. *Blow-Up* ('66), Michelangelo's first film in English, is seen now like a time capsule of what Swingin' London was like in the mid-'60s. Viewers could argue over what the dream-like black-and-white imagery meant (mimes playing tennis with no ball?), but nobody could argue with the movie's coolness factor.

Groovy young David Hemmings tooled around London as an Austin Powers-style fashion photographer who arrogantly chastises his models (including Peggy Moffitt), gets double-teamed by eager young girls (among them singer Jane Birkin), hangs with a topless Vanessa Redgrave, rolls around on the studio floor with the elastic Amazon model Veruschka, strolls through a hip club where the Yardbirds are playing, effortlessly finds perfect parking places for his convertible, and shoots (or doesn't shoot) a photo of a murder that affects (or doesn't affect) him. Meaning was obscure, but not the impact—audiences flocked to see it, and Michelangelo got Oscar nominations for his directing and screenwriting.

Zabriskie Point ('70) at decade's end incorporated American settings and music by the Stones, the Dead, and the Floyd (Pink), to tell an anti-establishment pro-hippie story of free love, but critics and audiences panned it with mocking howls. *The Passenger* ('75), starring Jack Nicholson, is now revered by many as his masterpiece, though reactions were mixed at the time. An '85 stroke severely limited Michelangelo's abilities, but he did contribute to several films over the next two decades. The industry acknowledged his legacy in '95 with an honorary Oscar.

EVERYBODY LOVES SOMEBODY

Michelangelo had two marriages sandwiched around a relationship with actress Monica Vitti. His second wife worked with him on *The Passenger*, appeared in several of his later films, and made a documentary about him in '95.

MY BACK PAGES

Pre-*Blow-Up*, all four of Michelangelo's films of the '60s (including his influential trilogy) starred the great Monica Vitti, better known to English-speaking audiences for the spy spoof *Modesty Blaise* ('66). . . . Perhaps one of the features that made *Blow-Up* popular was its brief nude scene, the first in a movie released by a major studio.

January 28, 1967—Sonny and Cher's "The Beat Goes On" hits the charts. ☮ January 29, 1942—Actress Claudine Longet is born in Paris. January 29, 1942—Actress Katharine Ross is born in Hollywood. ☮ January 29, 1962—Peter, Paul and Mary sign with Warner Bros. Records. January 29, 1964—Stanley Kubrick's *Dr. Strangelove* opens. ☮ January 30, 1922—Comedian Dick Martin is born in Detroit.

Neil Armstrong

What Lindbergh was to the '20s, Neil Armstrong was to the '60s—an aviation hero who riveted the world's attention by doing something nobody else had ever done.

TAKIN' CARE OF BUSINESS

As cool as all the other people are in this book, only a few have museums dedicated to their lives. Neil Armstrong is one of them. He's also got streets, an airport, and a lunar crater named after him. Now that's cool.

If anyone was born to be an astronaut, it was Neil Armstrong. An Ohio kid, he took his first flight (in a Ford Tri-Motor) at age 6, later filled his room with model airplanes, joined the Boy Scouts, was a teenager working in the hangars at the local airport, and took flying lessons before he had his driver's license. After two years at Purdue University, he flew 78 missions in Korea, earning several decorations, and once bailing out of his crippled plane. Stateside, he returned to Purdue for an aeronautical engineering degree (later adding a Master's and several honorary doctorates). Moving to the California desert, he worked as a test pilot through the late '50s, taking up dozens of experimental jets, including the sleek X-15.

In '61, JFK boldly challenged the nation to put a man on the Moon before 1970. At the time, America had sent one man into space for one 15-minute up-and-down flight. Making Kennedy's goal a reality would use up all but five months of the '60s, cost tens of billions of dollars, and take the lives of three *Apollo 1* astronauts who died in a '67 fire. Success came in a carefully planned procession of technical achievements. First, the Mercury program of the early '60s, which got NASA into space; then Gemini in the mid-'60s, which taught NASA how to work and maneuver in space; and finally Apollo, which aimed directly at the Moon.

In '62, with Project Mercury expanding, studious, clean-cut Neil Armstrong became America's first civilian astronaut. Four years later he commanded the near-catastrophic *Gemini 8* mission, an ambitious flight cut short when an errant thruster sent the capsule careening out of orbit. Just before passing out, Armstrong managed to stabilize the tumbling craft, displaying the cool, methodical poise he'd display again while training for the Moon shot, dramatically ejecting from an uncontrollable test vehicle an instant before it exploded.

For the historic *Apollo 11* mission, Neil, Edwin "Buzz" Aldrin, and Michael Collins lifted off in July of '69 and cruised Moonward for 100 hours. As with *Gemini 8*, Neil again took control at the flight's most critical stage, manually steering the spidery lunar lander above looming boulders and finding a safe place to land with under 20 seconds of fuel left. Eager to get outside, the excited astronauts skipped a scheduled four-hour nap and climbed into the 185-pound suits that would insulate them from the 200-degree difference between sunlight and shade on the Moon.

When Neil touched the surface, he uttered one of history's most famous sentences: "That's one small step for man, one giant leap for mankind" (debated later as possibly a mistake, with "a" needed before "man"—Neil himself admitted it didn't come out exactly right). He was on the surface alone for 20 minutes before Buzz joined him. The Moon, Neil declared, had "a stark beauty all its own"; Buzz described it as "magnificent desolation."

For the next 140 minutes they inspected their craft, took a call from President Nixon, set up an American flag and scientific experiments, gathered 50 pounds of rocks, and took photos. After a fitful night's sleep they blasted off, reunited with Collins, and four days later parachuted into the Pacific 11 miles from the U.S.S. *Hornet*. The next three weeks were spent in quarantine (*The Andromeda Strain*, a recent best-seller, had alerted everyone to the possibility of space contamination), followed by a stream of parades, awards, and global praise.

Commander of the most breathtaking, ennobling and coolest technological accomplishment in history, Neil Armstrong was the world's hero. Two years after his *Apollo 11* triumph, Neil retired from NASA to teach at the University of Cincinnati for the rest of the '70s. Through the '80s and '90s he worked in the private sector for different corporations and tried to stay out of the spotlight.

EVERYBODY LOVES SOMEBODY

Neil was a married man from his test pilot days right up to '89, when he and his wife divorced after 33 years together. He remarried in the early '90s and has two sons (a young daughter died in '62 of a brain tumor).

MY BACK PAGES

The Ohio airport where Neil first took flying lessons is now named in his honor. . . . Near Cincinnati, the Neil Armstrong Air and Space Museum showcases many of his awards and interesting artifacts, including the first airplane he ever flew (an Aeronca Champion). . . . Armstrong took two fragments of the Wright Brothers' plane to the Moon with him. . . . He also took a tape of "space music" called *Music Out of the Moon*. . . . Hollywood's Walk of Fame has a special star dedicated to the *Apollo 11* astronauts. . . . Slightly less poetic than Armstrong's first words on the Moon were the last words, spoken by *Apollo 17*'s Eugene Cernan: "Let's get this mutha outta here."

Jane Asher

A stylish sweetheart to Paul McCartney in the mid-'60s, Lady Jane also enjoyed a career as a movie and stage actress.

TAKIN' CARE OF BUSINESS

Overshadowed by her famous Beatle boyfriend, Jane Asher's talent didn't generate the recognition it deserved. She was a London-born child actress who graduated from kid roles in the '50s to grown-up, co-starring parts in the '60s. Key screen credits included the Vincent Price thriller *The Masque of the Red Death* ('64) and a prominent role as Michael Caine's homebody girlfriend in *Alfie* ('66). But her real impact was on young girls of the '60s who read about

February 1, 1946—Singer Chris Clark is born in California. ☮ February 1, 1962—Ken Kesey's *One Flew Over the Cuckoo's Nest* is published.
February 1, 1964—The Beatles score their first #1 hit with "I Want to Hold Your Hand."
February 1, 1967—The Jefferson Airplane album *Surrealistic Pillow* is released.

her in gossip magazines and tried to copy her look (pretty with long bangs and straight auburn hair, she did Breck commercials for awhile).

As early as '64, it was the subject of speculation that she might be the first Mrs. Paul, and his lyrics were analyzed for personal revelations about their relationship. Critics have surmised that some of his best-loved songs, including "And I Love Her," "Here, There, and Everywhere," "All My Loving," "You Won't See Me," "For No One," "Things We Said Today," "I'm Looking Through You," and "We Can Work It Out" were for or about her.

Towards the end of the decade she established herself as a serious stage actress with the Bristol Old Vic, a company that toured the U.S. Continuing to work steadily for the next three decades, Jane made dozens of appearances on popular British TV shows, including *Brideshead Revisited* and *Absolutely Fabulous*. She also wrote a dozen books, most notably a bestselling novel called *The Longing*. Today she's considered the British equivalent of Martha Stewart for her helpful magazine articles, her TV show *Good Living*, and her lifestyle books. Since 1990 she's run Jane Asher Party Cakes, a catering business that helps Londoners lead the good life.

EVERYBODY LOVES SOMEBODY

From '63–'68 Jane was the steady date of the world's most eligible bachelor. They first met after a Beatles concert at London's Royal Albert Hall when Jane, working for a BBC show, interviewed the group. Wrote Cynthia Lennon in *A Twist of Lennon*, "Paul fell like a ton of bricks for Jane." Paul moved into her parents' London home, where he and John soon composed "I Want to Hold Your Hand."

In '66 Paul and Jane moved into a London Victorian home of their own, plus he bought them a fixer-upper farm in Scotland (the subject of "Fixing a Hole"). They seemed like a perfect match and announced their engagement on Christmas Day in '67, but seven months later Jane declared the engagement off (rumors swirled of his indiscretions). She married artist Gerald Scarfe (animator for Pink Floyd's *The Wall*, '82), and today they have three children.

MY BACK PAGES

Jane's brother is Peter Asher, of Peter and Gordon fame (their "Lady Godiva" was a '66 hit). . . . When she played Wendy in Peter Pan at age 14, Jane was the youngest actress to play the role on the London stage. . . . Jane sings in the chorus of "All You Need Is Love". . . . Well known for her charity work, she is President of the National Autistic Society and Vice-President of the Child Accident Prevention Trust.

Claudine Auger

This lithe Parisian beauty swam her way into 007's heart in *Thunderball*.

TAKIN' CARE OF BUSINESS

"Who? She was a Bond girl?," you might ask. Well, yes, she was; and a pretty good one, too. Whereas most of the other actresses in this book bring several formidable films to the discussion, Parisian Claudine's here because of just one movie, the hugely popular *Thunderball* ('65), which she made when she was only 24. Though she did get to kill the movie's crime crumb, Largo, with a spear gun, her impact on audiences was probably diminished by Bond's own infidelity—she was only one of three love interests in *Thunderball*—and also by claims that her voice was dubbed.

Nothing, however, could diminish the film's thunder at the box office, which at the time was tremendous. The follow-up to the mega-hit *Goldfinger*, *Thunderball* topped the box office in '66, helped along by the Tom Jones theme song and the Oscar-winning special effects. As for Claudine's career, pre-Bond she'd been Miss France of '58 and that year's first runner-up for Miss World, and post-Bond she ap-

February 1, 1968—Lisa Marie Presley, daughter of Elvis and Priscilla, is born in Memphis.
February 2, 1937—Comedian Tom Smothers is born in New York. ☮ February 2, 1967—*The Night of the Generals* with Peter O'Toole opens.
February 2, 1972—*Snow Job* with Jean-Claude Killy opens. ☮ February 3, 1918—Comedian Joey Bishop is born in New York.

peared in 15 other '60s movies (nearly all of them French), followed by 30 more foreign flicks into the '90s and some elegant ads for the French Concorde.

EVERYBODY LOVES SOMEBODY

Eminently photogenic, Claudine always looked like the sleek, sexy 5′ 8″ beauty contest winner she was. Her magnificent measurements, given in '66 as 36-23-37, were best displayed in the stunning black-and-white bikini she wore in the last half of *Thunderball*. Info on her personal life is scant, with only some suggestions that she married a businessman.

MY BACK PAGES

Her real name is Claudine Oger. . . . Supposedly Raquel Welch was slated for the Domino role, but she was released from her contract to star in *Fantastic Voyage* ('66). . . . *Thunderball* was remade in '83 as *Never Say Never Again* with Kim Basinger.

Ewa Aulin

This baby-faced Swedish import had two sexy starring roles at decade's end.

TAKIN' CARE OF BUSINESS

Ewa Aulin had little impact on the general movie-going public in the '60s. Her only English-language '60s film, *Candy*, in which she played a sexy nymphet (is there any other kind?) flopped embarrassingly. However, that movie has a definite cult appeal and is seen now as an example of the creativity being found outside of mainstream Hollywood in the late '60s. Ewa herself was a Miss Teen Sweden quickly scooped up by the international film community. First came an Italian sci-fi curiosity in '67 called *Death Laid an Egg,* involving a plot to breed headless chickens. After two more obscure Italian films, she then got *Candy* from strangers. Written by Buck Henry (fresh off *The Graduate*), *Candy* was based on Terry Southern's satirical novel, which itself was loosely based on Voltaire's picaresque classic *Candide* (*Candide, Candy,* get it?).

The film boasted a once-in-a-lifetime cast: Marlon Brando, Richard Burton, Ringo Starr, John Astin (from *The Addams Family*), James Coburn, John Huston, Anita Pallenberg, Walter Matthau, and boxer "Sugar Ray" Robinson. Candy ended up in sexual situations with most of them (even her own father), plus the movie had a hunchback, a glass-bottomed limo, sex on a pool table, dream sequences, cosmic special effects, and a Byrds/Steppenwolf soundtrack. Unfortunately, it also had a novice director who was on his first and last major movie. The result was a confusing mess, entertaining to some, vulgar to most, and a disaster in American theatres, though Ewa would get a Golden Globe nomination as Most Promising Newcomer.

A year later, Ewa reprised her role as a sexually desirable young thing in *Start the Revolution Without Me*, an underwhelming Donald Sutherland/Gene Wilder comedy. It

February 3, 1961—Comedian Lenny Bruce performs at Carnegie Hall. ☮ February 3, 1969—Catherine Deneuve makes the cover of *Life*.
February 4, 1921—Author/activist Betty Friedan is born in Peoria, Illinois.
February 4, 2006—Author/activist Betty Friedan dies of congestive heart failure in Washington, D.C.

would be her last English-language film. For the next three years she appeared in low-budget foreign movies before dropping off the map completely.

EVERYBODY LOVES SOMEBODY

Blonde and beautiful, young and inquisitive, Ewa was presented as a curious child in *Candy*. We can only imagine what it was like being on the European sets of *Candy* as the one cute girl surrounded by Brando, Burton, and everybody else. Internet reports say she has married twice and is the mother of two girls.

MY BACK PAGES

Contending for Ewa's role in *Candy* was a popular *Playboy* Playmate, Connie Kreski. . . . Ringo's appearance in *Candy* was his first role outside a Beatles movie.

Burt Bacharach

The cool composer of dozens of smooth songs.

TAKIN' CARE OF BUSINESS

For the last 50+ years, Burt Bacharach has been everybody's idea of smooth style. Even Austin Powers thinks so: Burt's music appeared in all three of the Mike Meyers movies (and Burt made notable cameo appearances, too). This Kansas City-born piano player grew up loving jazz and first made a name for himself in the '50s as the music man for Vic Damone and Marlene Dietrich.

In '57, he teamed up with lyricist Hal David in New York's famous Brill Building to create one of the most impressive songbooks in music history. Everyone from Aretha Franklin to Tom Jones to Dusty Springfield recorded the pair's songs in the '60s and '70s, yielding over fifty Top 40 hits. Dionne Warwick, of course, was their most famous collaborator; together the team produced such polished landmarks as "I'll Never Fall in Love Again," "Walk on By," and "I Say a Little Prayer." Dionne's voice was mature and controlled (in an era of youthful screaming); Hal's lyrics were sweet and clear (when other lyricists were angry and political); Burt's music was elegant, jazzy, and deceptively sophisticated (as opposed to high-volume guitar-oriented three-chord rock).

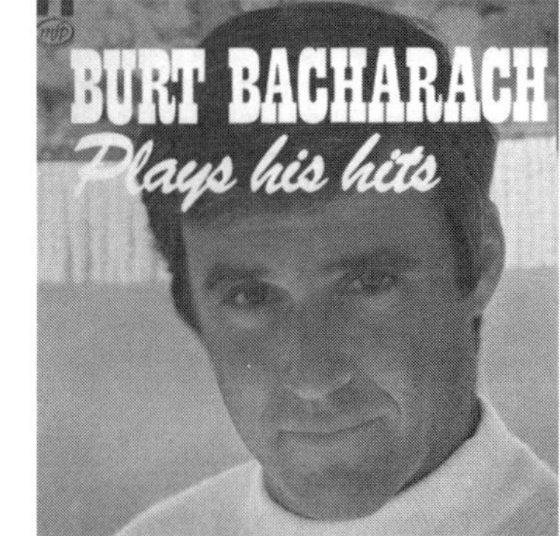

Some of Burt's greatest success came from songs he composed for movies, starting with *The Man Who Shot Liberty Valance* ('62) and continuing through the '60s with songs for *What's New, Pussycat?* ('65), *Alfie* ('66), *Casino Royale* ('67), and *Butch Cassidy and the Sundance Kid* ('69, the score and its single "Raindrops Keep Fallin' on My Head" both winning Oscars and generating top-selling records).

While Burt put out his own solo records (*Reach Out*, '67), his greatest success continued to come with Hal David, and their hits kept comin' into the '70s, highlighted by the Tony Award-winning Broadway musical *Promises, Promises* and the #1 hit "Close to You" for the Carpenters. Burt also continued to write movie music, especially the Oscar-winning "Arthur's Theme" for *Arthur* ('81) and "That's What Friends Are For" for *Night Shift* ('82). Still going strong, the subject of Broadway musicals and tribute concerts, Burt has enjoyed a resurgence of popularity in the last decade and has teamed up with Elvis Costello, Dr. Dre, and others on well-received albums.

EVERYBODY LOVES SOMEBODY

Burt has had four wives: singer Paula Stewart in the '50s, legendary actress Angie Dickinson in the '60s and '70s, lyricist Carole Bayer Sager in the '80s, and Jane Hanson in the 2000s.

February 5, 1966—"California Dreamin'" by the Mamas and the Papas hits the charts.
February 5, 1966—Nancy Sinatra's "These Boots Are Made for Walkin'" hits the charts.
February 5, 1967—*The Smothers Brothers Comedy Hour* debuts. ☮ February 6, 1922—Actor Patrick Macnee is born in London.

MY BACK PAGES

Burt has long been an owner and breeder of championship horses. . . . He's also released over a half-dozen solo records, including one in 2005 for which he wrote both music and lyrics.

Joan Baez

For many people Joan Baez was the female conscience of the '60s, a pure, strong voice singing out for social causes.

TAKIN' CARE OF BUSINESS

Just as Carol King set the tone for female singers in the early '70s, Joan Baez set the tone for female singers in the early '60s. A New Yorker with a Scottish mother and Mexican father, she was exposed to racial taunts as a child and felt like an outsider as she grew up. In her teens she learned the ukulele and guitar and began singing in Boston coffeehouses, where her reputation started to build. Her early concert appearances, most notably at the Newport Folk Festival in '59 and '60, and her first folk records in '60 and '61, were hugely influential, quickly established her as a folk heroine, and landed her as a 21-year-old barefoot guitar-strummer on a '62 cover of *Time*.

Initially she sang traditional folk and children's songs, but soon she applied her pristine three-octave soprano to more topical songs by Bob Dylan and others to promote social change, especially in hopes of ending discrimination (she performed at Martin Luther King's epic March on Washington) and the Vietnam War (she would be arrested several times at anti-war protests). Always a popular live performer, as evidenced by *Joan Baez in Concert* ('63), she teamed up with Dylan and toured England in '65, recording an album of his songs in '68. Broadening her sound and her audience, in the late '60s she recorded a Christmas album with an orchestra, an album of poetry, and a country album, in addition to singing five songs at Woodstock.

A tireless activist, she traveled widely through the '70s and '80s to places as diverse as North Vietnam, the Soviet Union, South America, and Poland, always promoting peace and civil rights. During these years she also recorded some of her bestselling, most pop-oriented records, including the song "The Night They Drove Old Dixie Down" and the album *Diamonds and Rust*, in which she successfully showed off her impressive songwriting skills. She also wrote an honest, articulate autobiography, *And a Voice to Sing With*, which met with critical acclaim.

For over 40 years now she's been wherever people were gathering and statements were being made and things were happening—from Live Aid to *Late Night with David Letterman*, at Grammy Awards ceremonies and Kennedy Center presentations, for American presidents and world leaders, alone or sharing a stage with famous peers like Bruce Springsteen, Sting, Jackson Browne, and U2, Joan Baez has been there, always sincere, always working, always fighting the good fight. She has never *not* mattered.

EVERYBODY LOVES SOMEBODY

Her on-again/off-again relationship with Dylan propelled her music for years. Early on she recognized his unheralded genius and began singing his songs long before he was a house-

February 6, 1932—Director François Truffaut is born in Paris. ☮ February 6, 1933—Actress Mamie Van Doren is born in Rowena, South Dakota.
February 6, 1968—The tenth Winter Olympics open in Grenoble, France. ☮ February 6, 1976—Jazz musician and composer Vince Guaraldi dies.
February 6, 1998—Carl Wilson of the Beach Boys dies of lung cancer in L.A. ☮ February 7, 1961—*Breathless* with Jean Seberg opens.

10 Classic Concerts

1965

June 20–Kiel Opera House, St. Louis, Johnny Carson emcees the Rat Pack

July 25–Newport Folk Festival, Rhode Island, closing night, Dylan goes electric

August 15–Shea Stadium, New York, Beatles, first-ever stadium show, 56,000 people

1967

January 14–Golden Gate Park, San Francisco, "Human Be-In," 30,000 people

June 16–18–Monterey International Pop Festival, California, 200,000 people

1969

July 5–Hyde Park, London, Stones salute the late Brian Jones, 300,000 people

July 31–International Hotel, Las Vegas, Elvis's first concert since '61

August 15–17–Woodstock Music and Art Festival, New York, 500,000 people

August 30–31–Isle of Wight Festival, U.K., 150,000 people

December 6–Altamont Racetrack, California, 300,000 people

hold name; later, she recorded complete albums of his material, toured with him in England (as documented in the film *Don't Look Back*, '67), toured with his famed mid-'70s Rolling Thunder Revue, appeared in his surreal movie *Renaldo and Clara* ('78), wrote songs about their relationship ("Diamonds and Rust"), imitated his vocal delivery on record ("Simple Twist of Fate"), and in 2005 was an articulate commentator in Martin Scorsese's Dylan documentary *No Direction Home*. But she married someone else. In '68 she married anti-war activist David Harris; they had a son but divorced some three years later. In the early 21st century, her long black hair now elegantly short, she was living with her mother near San Francisco.

MY BACK PAGES

Her younger sister, Mimi Farina (1945–2001), was also a singer and '60s scenemaker heavily involved with social causes. . . . For about a decade (mid-'60s to mid-'70s) Joan refused to pay about 60% of her income taxes, because that was the percentage she figured was going to the Vietnam War. . . . Joan was ranked #27 on VH1's list of the 100 greatest women of rock and roll, right between Bessie Smith and Carly Simon.

David Bailey

Swingin' London's swingin'est photographer.

TAKIN' CARE OF BUSINESS

Remember in *Austin Powers* when Austin emulated a groovy fashion photographer who coaxed his beautiful models to "show me love"? It's generally assumed that David Bailey was Austin's inspiration. David was the most famous photographer of the '60s and more than anyone captured the fads, fashions, and feel of swingin' London. A

Londoner himself, he had served with the RAF in the late '50s and was a photo assistant when he signed on as a *Vogue* freelancer. Suddenly operating in celebrity circles, he was taking photos of the biggest rock groups (the Beatles, Stones, Who), top models (Jean Shrimpton, Twiggy, Penelope Tree), and beautiful actors (Mia Farrow, Michael Caine, Terence Stamp). On magazines, in books, for record albums, in commercials and documentaries, David's work was inescapable and made him the coolest photographer of his time.

Antonioni's surreal film *Blow-Up* in '66 made his working technique excessively glamorous—the Baileyesque photographer, played by David Hemmings, sped spontaneously around London in his convertible Rolls with few cares, plenty of women throwing themselves at him, and a knack for being in the hippest place at the most opportune moment. The movie's most telling scene came when he writhed around on the floor with the lanky Veruschka, whipped her into an orgasmic frenzy while shooting pictures, and then nonchalantly retreated. He's continued shooting celebrities for major magazines into the 21st century, has produced many books showcasing his work, and was the subject of major exhibitions in England and America. David was named a Commander of the British Empire in 2001.

EVERYBODY LOVES SOMEBODY

An engagement with Jean Shrimpton, and four marriages, most famously to French actress Catherine Deneuve from '65–'72 (at the wedding David wore a sweater, Catherine wore a black Yves St. Laurent number and smoked). Since '86 he's been married to a former '60s model, Catherine Dyer, and he has three kids.

MY BACK PAGES

David has said that it was Picasso's art that inspired him to pursue photography. . . . Dressed in jeans, Mick Jagger was the best man when David married Catherine Deneuve. . . . Catherine Dyer was the subject of his '95 book, *The Lady Is a Tramp*.

Carroll Baker

This beautiful blonde sex symbol springboarded from a scandalous movie to become a memorable screen siren.

TAKIN' CARE OF BUSINESS

Though she was compared to other screen goddesses of the '50s and '60s, Carroll Baker earned what Marilyn Monroe, Jayne Mansfield, Kim Novak, Gina Lollobrigida, Anita Ekberg, Ursula Andress, and Brigitte Bardot never did—an Oscar nomination as Best Actress. Carroll's came for *Baby Doll,* the sensational '56 film that cast her as a 19-year-old thumb-sucking nymphet who slept in a crib. Her terrific acting, and the subsequent controversy over the movie's "indecency," catapulted the Pennsylvania-born newcomer to stardom at age 25.

Soon followed prominent Westerns, especially *How the West Was Won* ('62). Her natural beauty made her the per-

February 9, 1945—Actress Mia Farrow is born in L.A. ☮ February 9, 1964—*The Scarecrow of Romney Marsh* with Patrick McGoohan debuts.
February 9, 1964—The Beatles perform on *The Ed Sullivan Show* to a record TV audience.
February 9, 1964—The ninth Winter Olympics close in Innsbruck, Austria. ☮ February 10, 1930—Actor Robert Wagner is born in Detroit.

fect frontier woman; *The Carpetbaggers* ('64) made her a goddess. Paramount's highest-grossing movie that year, it presented her as a sexually aggressive bombshell and led to her glamour-queen role in *Harlow* ('65). Here she was a platinum throwback to Hollywood's Golden Age, her lovely face framed by white-gold hair and her vivacious figure packed into sequined gowns.

The studios would have happily typecast her as a sex symbol for the rest of her career, but Carroll wanted more diversity, so she fled to Europe to make 27 foreign films in 20 years. Returning to Hollywood in the '80s, she appeared in another two-dozen movies, including *Star 80* ('83) and *Kindergarten Cop* ('90). A talented writer (as a teen she won a national writing award), she wrote her sizzling autobiography, *Baby Doll*, in '83, followed by two more well-received books. Throughout her long career she's been recognized with many awards (including status as a Kentucky Colonel). Still busy and beautiful, now with over 60 films to her credit, Carroll Baker is that rarest Hollywood goddess: one whose own life story will have a happy ending.

EVERYBODY LOVES SOMEBODY

Close friendships with Elizabeth Taylor, Robert Mitchum, Steve McQueen and Debbie Reynolds, studio antics with Jerry Lewis, dances with Gene Kelly, motorcycle rides with James Dean—Carroll's 1950s and '60s were the stuff that fanzine dreams are made of. For most of this era, Carroll was a married woman. She had a brief marriage in the early '50s, then she got remarried in '55 to writer/director Jack Garfein (*Something Wild*, '61). They had a daughter in '56 and a son in '58, but the marriage broke up at the end of the '60s. She married the British actor and writer Donald Burton in '82 and now lives with him in Southern California.

MY BACK PAGES

Before she was famous, Carroll once worked as a magician's assistant. . . . Her daughter, Blanche Baker, was in *Sixteen Candles* ('84) as Molly Ringwald's about-to-be-married sister. . . . Carroll steamed up the August '68 issue of *Playboy* and ranked #94 (right behind another blonde sex goddess, Fay Wray) on the magazine's millennium list of "The 100 Sexiest Stars of the Century."

Anne Bancroft

Every graduate's favorite older woman was also a Broadway legend.

TAKIN' CARE OF BUSINESS

Anne Bancroft had a long, distinguished career on stage and screen, but she said it was Mrs. Robinson who always defined her in the public's mind. Before *The Graduate* made her a famous movie star, Anna Maria Louisa Italiano from the Bronx was already a two-time Tony Award

winner. In '58 Anne was Best Actress for the comedy *Two for the Seesaw,* and two years later she again took the Tony for her riveting performance as teacher Annie Sullivan in *The Miracle Worker.* Two years after that, her Annie in the movie version won the Oscar.

Several subsequent movie roles led to her role as the graduate-seducer in '67, which brought her another Oscar nomination for her deft portrayal of a woman who was sexy (showing brief flashes of near-nudity), manipulative, and aching. More Oscar nominations (for *The Turning Point,* '77, and *Agnes of God,* '85) punctuated her long, versatile career, which included comedies, dramas, more acclaimed stagework, and six Emmy nominations (two wins, for her own special in '70 and as a supporting actress in a TV movie in '99). Acknowledging the joy she'd brought to audiences for over five decades, the American Comedy Awards gave her lifetime-achievement recognition in '96. When she died of cancer in 2005, she was one of the few actresses to have a Tony, Oscar, and Emmy on her mantle.

EVERYBODY LOVES SOMEBODY

Anne's marriage in the '50s ended with divorce but was followed by one of Hollywood's fabled romances—in '61 she met comedian Mel Brooks, they married three years later, had a son in '72, and were together until her death. Throughout all those years, Mel, her biggest fan, always seemed to introduce her as "the great Anne Bancroft." Theirs was a life of love, laughs, glamour, and success—they were tango partners in his *Silent Movie* ('76), he produced *The Elephant Man* ('80) in which she starred, and together they co-starred in his comedy *To Be or Not to Be* ('83).

MY BACK PAGES

Two other roles Anne almost took—the mom in *The Exorcist* ('72) and Aurora in *Terms of Endearment* ('83). . . . Triple-threat Anne wrote, directed, and starred in the Dom DeLuise comedy *Fatso* ('80).

Tony-Winning Plays and Musicals

1960–*The Miracle Worker; The Sound of Music/ Fiorello!* (tie)
1961–*Beckett; Bye Bye Birdie*
1962–*A Man for All Seasons; How to Succeed in Business Without Really Trying*
1963–*Who's Afraid of Virginia Woolf?; A Funny Thing Happened on the Way to the Forum*
1964–*Luther; Hello, Dolly!*
1965–*The Subject Was Roses; Fiddler on the Roof*
1966–*Marat/Sade; Man of La Mancha*
1967–*The Homecoming; Cabaret*
1968–*Rosencrantz and Guildenstern Are Dead; Hallelujah, Baby!*
1969–*The Great White Hope; 1776*

Brigitte Bardot

The very definition of an erotic French sex kitten, this archetypal nymphet throbbed her way through films and generated international news with her uninhibited sexuality.

TAKIN' CARE OF BUSINESS

Like Marilyn and Cher and Aphrodite, Brigitte Bardot is known throughout the world by just a single name. A beauty even as a young girl, at 15 Paris-born Bardot worked as a model and appeared on the cover of *Elle* in May '49. At 18, a brunette Bardot became famous when she strutted in front of photographers at the '53 Cannes Film Festival. At 22, she became the symbol of sexual temptation when the world saw her nude and lying on her stomach in the first 30 seconds of *And God Created Woman* ('56). That shot, the

movie's later undressing scenes, and the erotic dancing at the climax thrust Bardot into two decades of sexy films and three decades of scandalous news stories. Ironically, her own country didn't immediately accept her—the French censors demanded edits, and the press gave it terrible reviews.

Internationally, however, English and American audiences flocked to see it, and Bardot's career spurted to new heights. Eventually, her near-mythic status as the embodiment of steamy sexual desire would be attributable more to her liberated lifestyle than to her movies—her real talent has always been for attracting men, photographers, and headlines. Even so, for the next few years Bardot was responsible for bringing new attention to the French cinema, and if not a great actress, she was always riveting, able to seduce audiences with both untrammeled sexuality and an appealing naiveté. Her '60s movies included *The Truth* in '60 (her favorite), *A Very Private Affair* in '61 (based on experiences from her own life), *Contempt* in '63 (one of her most versatile performances), *Dear Brigitte* in '65 (the Jimmy Stewart comedy in which she had a single scene), *Masculine-Feminine* in '66 (directed by Jean-Luc Godard), and *Shalako* in '68 (a Sean Connery Western).

While she was adept at costumed roles, the best outfit for her 35-23-35 measurements was usually just a towel or a sheet, a look enhanced by her smooth tan (like Liz Taylor she advanced tanning to new heights). Her wild honey-colored hair, pouty lips, big eyes, and casual sexuality made her perfect for *Playboy*, the magazine that never met a sex symbol it didn't like; they did two pictorials on her in '64 and '69. She also released five French record albums and dozens of singles during the decade.

In '73 she finally retired from the movies, though she has continued to speak in public and appear in documentaries to promote animal rights (a major animal-rights advocate, she fills her home with pets). She's also written two volumes of memoirs. For many people, she will always be the truest definition of the 20th-century woman. Simply, and eternally, Bardot.

EVERYBODY LOVES SOMEBODY

She's had four marriages: director Roger Vadim, '52–'57 (he later married Jane Fonda); actor Jacques Charrier, '59–'62 (with whom she had a son); playboy Gunter Sachs, '66–'69; and politician Bernard d'Ormale in '92. When she wasn't allowed to marry older Roger Vadim (she was 15), she tried to asphyxiate herself; she was allowed to marry him three years later. Bardot made nine films that he either wrote or directed, and he's the one who told her to pout and put her in sexy outfits.

It's believed that she attempted suicide at least four times, including a foiled attempt on her 26th birthday. "I really wanted to die at certain periods in my life," she has said. "I took pills because I didn't want to throw myself off my balcony and know people would photograph me lying dead below." Living in real life the kind of uninhibited roles she played in movies, she had well-publicized relationships with a veritable all-star team of '60s celebrities—Brando, Beatty,

February 11, 1964—The Simon and Garfunkel album *Wednesday Morning, 3 A.M.* is released.
February 11, 1965—Ringo Starr of the Beatles marries Maureen Cox in London.
February 12, 1964—The Beatles play New York's prestigious Carnegie Hall, a first for a pop group.

Jagger, Connery, Belmondo, and many more. The press stalked her capricious movements, the public watched in fascination, and the sexual revolution pounded on.

MY BACK PAGES

Before Bardot was a model she was a dancer-in-training from age 5, and at 13 she studied alongside future dance legend Leslie Caron. . . . Asked what was the best day of her life—"a night," a line Fellini later gave to Anita Ekberg in *La Dolce Vita*. . . . The man she admires most—"Sir Isaac Newton, he discovered that bodies attract each other". . . . At the millennium *Playboy* ranked her fourth, between Raquel Welch and Cindy Crawford, on its list of the century's sexiest stars, and *Time* magazine named her one of the 20th century's 20 most beautiful stars.

Dr. Christiaan Barnard

The decade's swingin'est surgeon, Dr. Barnard made medical headlines and squired famous movie starlets.

TAKIN' CARE OF BUSINESS

Christiaan Neethling Barnard was born in South Africa in 1922. His family was poor, the town was small, his prospects meager. But he was a hard-working student who earned a University of Cape Town medical degree in '46. Ten years later he went to the University of Minnesota to study new techniques in heart surgery. At the time, transplants were being tried on dogs, with little success. After two years Barnard returned to South Africa, performed the country's first kidney transplant in '59, and continued to operate into the '60s in preparation for his landmark operation of '67.

His patient, a diabetic 55-year-old man, lived for only 18 more days after surgery. But he did it while the heart of a young girl who'd died in an auto accident beat inside him. That heart was put there by Dr. Barnard and his 30-person surgical team in the world's first heart transplant. The surgical technique itself, he claimed later, was "basic." And to him, the patient wasn't really taking a risk because he had nothing to lose: "For a dying man," he wrote, "it is not a difficult decision because he knows he is at the end. If a lion chases you to the bank of a river filled with crocodiles, you will leap into the water convinced you have a chance to swim to the other side. But you would never accept such odds if there were no lion."

An astonished world disagreed with his prosaic assessments: the accomplishment was universally hailed as being both brilliant and daring. Late in '67, Dr. Barnard's medical success transformed him from a senior cardiothoracic surgeon into a global celebrity. "On Saturday, I was a surgeon in South Africa, very little known. On Monday, I was world renowned," he said. He was whisked off to do TV and magazine interviews, he was on the cover of *Time*, and his dashing good looks transplanted international beauties onto his arm. There was more surgery, too. Quickly the team tried again, with the patient this time living for a year-and-a-half. Soon dozens of heart transplants were being performed all over the world, Dr. Barnard himself did another 73, and by the '90s several thousand patients were getting replacement hearts every year.

The heart transplant he pioneered in '67 today adds an average of five years to a patient's life, a remarkable achievement by any measure. Discouraged by the high rejection rate for transplanted hearts, in the '70s he experimented with adding the donor heart into the patient's chest without removing the patient's own heart, thus theoretically doubling his blood-pumping power. In the '80s medical advances made this procedure unnecessary, and Barnard, hampered by years of rheumatoid arthritis, retired from the surgical life. He published an acclaimed textbook, several novels, and an autobiography while living on his 32,000-acre South African farm. Dr. Barnard died from a fatal asthma attack while on vacation in Cyprus at age 78.

February 13, 1933—Actress Kim Novak is born in Chicago. ☮ February 13, 1942—Actress Carol Lynley is born in New York.
February 13, 1942—Peter Tork of the Monkees is born in Washington, D.C.
February 13, 1969—Woody Allen's *Play It Again, Sam* opens on Broadway.

EVERYBODY LOVES SOMEBODY

Barnard was husband to a nurse when he became a celebrity surgeon in '67. Unfortunately, the 21-year-long marriage broke up in '69 when he got involved with Italian actress Gina Lollobrigida. "Intoxicated" by fame (as he later wrote), he also had relationships with Sophia Loren and Miss South Africa, among many others. Ultimately he married two more times ('70–'82, '88–2000), but those also ended in divorce, and he was single when he died. He had five kids, one of whom died from a rumored drug overdose.

MY BACK PAGES

In an early display of his surgical skill, Barnard grafted a second head onto a dog in the late '50s. . . . At the height of his fame, Dr. Barnard was listed in the *Guinness Book of World Records* for receiving the most fan mail on the planet. . . . Of Dr. Barnard's own heart-transplant patients, the one who survived the longest after the operation lasted 23 years. . . . Nelson Mandela was among those who publicly praised Barnard after his death. . . . From *Time* just before his death: "At almost 79, people ask me: where do you go from here? I say to them I'm on the waiting list. I don't know exactly where I am on that list or where I'm going, but I'm on it."

George Barris

George's cool cars stole TV and movie scenes.

TAKIN' CARE OF BUSINESS

If you watched '60s sitcoms, you knew George Barris's work. He and his brother, both California kids, opened their custom car shop in L.A. in the '40s and started building hot rods. Tom Wolfe wrote about their eye-catching creations in *The Kandy-Kolored Tangerine-Flake Streamline*

More Cool Screen Cars

"Aerocar" (combination small plane and car), *The Bob Cummings Show* ('61)

Alfa Romeo Spider (driven by Dustin Hoffman), *The Graduate* ('67)

Aston Martin DB-5 (with ejection seat and weapons), *Goldfinger* ('63)

"Black Beauty" (a modified Chrysler Imperial), *The Green Hornet* ('66)

Chevy Corvette (a '59, then a new model each season), *Route 66* ('60)

Dodge Charger (chased by Steve McQueen), *Bullitt* ('68)

Flying jalopies, *The Absent-Minded Professor* ('61) and *Chitty Chitty Bang Bang* ('68)

Ford Mustang GT 390 (driven by Steve McQueen), *Bullitt* ('68)

"Leslie Special" (fictitious amalgam of different classic cars), *The Great Race* ('65)

Lotus Elan (driven by Diana Rigg), *The Avengers* ('66)

Rolls-Royce Phantom II (with twenty coats of paint), *The Yellow Rolls-Royce* ('64)

Sunbeam Tiger (driven by Don Adams), *Get Smart* ('65)

Baby, and Hollywood came calling, most notably with a request for an old jalopy with a platform for a granny in a rocking chair. *The Beverly Hillbillies* was a national hit, and so was George. Jobs and ideas proliferated: a gold limo for Elvis, a little deuce coupe for the Beach Boys, a hip dune buggy Monkeemobile, a rockin' Munsters hearse, a Love Bug named Herbie. The ultimate was the sleek orange-pinstriped Batmobile (a redesigned Lincoln Futura) for the Caped Crusader. After the '60s, George souped up the Trans Am for *Smokey and the Bandit,* enhanced General Lee for *The Dukes of Hazard* and K.I.T.T. for *Knight Rider,* greased Grease Lightning for *Grease,* ectoed Ecto-1 for *Ghostbusters,* and transformed the time-traveling DeLorean for *Back to the Future.*

EVERYBODY LOVES SOMEBODY

George's wife of 40+ years, who helped run his business, passed away in 2000; his adult daughter and son now work with him at Barris Kustom Industries in North Hollywood.

MY BACK PAGES

Currently held by L.A.'s Petersen Museum, Batmobile #1 is considered the ultimate pop culture car. . . . Seventeen cars he's worked on have won the title America's Most Beautiful Roadster. . . . George's current car is a Jaguar XK8 convertible with a jaguar painted on the hood and the license plate BKUSTM.

Toni Basil

This dazzlin' dancer was along for the ride in *Easy Rider.*

TAKIN' CARE OF BUSINESS

Philly's Antonia Christina Basilotta was dancing before she was walking. In grammar school she started a cheerleading squad before the school even had any sports teams, and in high school she was a cheerleader at Las Vegas High. Heading to Hollywood she established herself as an imaginative, ambitious go-go dancer and soon choreographed the moves performed by others (and sometimes by Toni herself) on such seminal '60s productions as *Shindig* and *Pajama Party* ('64). Her own '60s dance highlight was probably her duet with Davy Jones in the Monkees' *Head* ('68). Toni's acting highlight came in the landmark biker epic *Easy Rider* ('69), appearing in the last 20 minutes as pretty Mary, the New Orleans brothelette who dropped acid and disrobed in the cemetery.

After the '60s, Toni danced more than acted, though she did land parts in some prominent movies and TV shows, especially Jack Nicholson's *Five Easy Pieces* ('70). She created the choreography for the classic *American Graffiti* ('73) and helped stage David Bowie's "thin white duke" '74 concerts. In '82, she released her own album of danceable songs called *Word of Mouth* with a catchy single called "Mickey." The exuberant video, directed by and starring Toni, featured her as a bouncy cheerleader in red, white, and blue, surrounded by actual cheerleaders from L.A.'s Carson High. The song became a staple of cheerleading routines, the album went gold, and by the winter of '82 "Mickey" was #1. Two years later, Toni tried to follow up "Mickey" with "Over My Head" and an eponymous album, but her moment on the pop charts had come and gone.

As the MTV juggernaut built steam, Toni directed videos for the Talking Heads and Bette Midler, appeared in a few more movies, and did choreography for *That Thing You Do* ('96), among others. Showing her versatility, she also cho-

February 15, 1963—Tenley Albright becomes the first U.S. figure skater to win the world championships.
February 15, 1965—*The Greatest Story Ever Told* with Carroll Baker opens. ☮ February 15, 1965—Singer Nat "King" Cole dies in L.A. of cancer.
February 15, 1968—Pattie Boyd, George Harrison, and John and Cynthia Lennon fly to India.

reographed the popular Gap commercials that had khaki-clad dancers workin' out some swing moves. Nominated for a Grammy and an Emmy during her career, she won an American Choreography Award in '97.

EVERYBODY LOVES SOMEBODY

One story has her dating Dean Stockwell (*Married to the Mob*) in the late '60s; another story pairs her with Devo bassist Jerry Casale in the mid-'70s. Toni herself told TV's *Biography* about her L.A. life as a dancer in the mid-'60s: "The whole lifestyle was exciting. . . . We were in the thick of it. And that's what was so much fun about it. We were in the thick of it."

MY BACK PAGES

Supposedly "Mickey" was originally going to be called "Kitty," sung by a man to a woman. . . . In 2001 VH1 named "Mickey" the #1 one-hit wonder of all time. . . . It also received one of the greatest kudos possible for a song—a parody version by "Weird Al" Yankovic, this one called "Ricky" and working on *I Love Lucy* themes.

Shirley Bassey

"Bassey the Belter" knocked out three theme songs for Bond movies, including one of the best of the whole series.

TAKIN' CARE OF BUSINESS

Best known for belting out the Goldfinger theme, Shirley Bassey has enjoyed such a long career as a popular British singer that the Queen bestowed the regal title of Dame upon her at the end of the 20th century. Born in Wales, Shirley was singing professionally as a teen in '50s Britain, and she made the Top 10 with "The Banana Boat Song" in '57. She had her first #1 hit, "As I Love You," in '59 and built a reputation in America as an energetic, glamorous live performer. *Goldfinger* ('64), one of the top two or three best Bond movies ever, took her name global with its powerful, instantly identifiable theme song (led off by Shirley's rousing "GoldFINGaaaah!").

So successful was the Bond-Bassey pairing, she sang the themes to two more 007 adventures, *Diamonds Are Forever* ('71) and *Moonraker* ('79). The '70s cemented her stature in concert and on record, especially in Europe, where her interpretations of love songs and show tunes, as on the album *And I Love You So* ('72), have never fallen out of favor. She had her own show on the BBC in the late '70s, was named Britain's Best Female Solo Singer of the last five decades, and came out of semi-retirement in the '80s and '90s to record still more albums and thrill still more live audiences.

EVERYBODY LOVES SOMEBODY

Married and divorced twice, Shirley has kids (her own and adopted) and grandkids. Tragically, a daughter drowned in 1985. After living for years in Switzerland, she now resides in glamorous Monaco.

MY BACK PAGES

She's still the only singer to sing three Bond themes. . . . Among her many TV appearances on talk shows, award shows, and documentaries was a fun turn on *The Muppet Show* in '80.

February 16, 1935—Singer/songwriter Sonny Bono is born in Detroit. ☮ February 16, 1958—Actress Lisa Loring is born in the Marshall Islands.
February 16, 1964—The Beatles make their second appearance on *The Ed Sullivan Show*.
February 16, 1968—Elvis Presley receives a gold record for his gospel album, *How Great Thou Art*.

Batmen

The cool, cartoony TV show was bat-tabulous fun.

TAKIN' CARE OF BUSINESS

It's hard now for 21st-century audiences to understand why *Batman* was such a popular show. The plots were obvious, the dialogue was silly, the special effects were high schoolish, the acting was hammy, the jokes were adolescent, the camera was often tilted at annoying angles. But somehow the show came along at exactly the right time to work as a cool, campy Pop Art attraction, and for three years it was one of the hottest things going.

So hot that new episodes were broadcast on consecutive weeknights; so hot that it made the cover of *Life*; so hot that some of its phrases ("same Bat-time, same Bat-channel") entered into the national vocabulary; so hot that esteemed stars of the day (and yesterday) all wanted to play flamboyant villains or make tiny cameos; so hot that audiences were willing to overlook the gaping plot holes (how were the two heroes able to start down the Batpole in street clothes and finish in costume?) just to be able to play along. Corny? Definitely. Cool? Batsitively.

Batman began, of course, in '39 as a mysterious, brawny crime fighter in comic books. Two *Batman* film serials came out in the '40s starring little-known actors and produced with budgets so low that the Batmobile was just a normal car. In the '60s, the show was originally going to be more like the '50s *Superman* show with George Reeves—heroic action for kids—until studio execs decided to aim for adults with a fun show more spoofy than serious.

Immediately they got the tone right—an enthusiastic narrator, cliffhanger endings (*à la* the '40s serials) that left the heroes dangling in peril on a Wednesday night with justice prevailing on Thursday night, the Ka-Pow! cards during fights, wild costumes, one of the coolest cars of all time, a simple-but-cool theme song, a cute sidekick (Batgirl) in the third season, and a straight-arrow Dynamic Duo who would forever be identified by these roles.

As Batman, Billy West Anderson from Walla Walla used one of the most identifiable vocal deliveries this side of William Shatner. After working as a DJ and serving in the Army, he joined a kiddie TV program in Hawaii. Changing his name to Adam West, he hit Hollywood in the late '50s and got roles in TV Westerns. In the first half of the '60s he was getting movie roles, too, until *Batman* in '66 defined him once and for all. While he didn't have the powerful build usually associated with the role (especially in later movie versions), he did have a commanding presence that added dignity to the otherwise cartoony proceedings.

After the *Batman* movie ('66) reinforced his image, and after the show was cancelled in '68, Adam found it difficult to escape the character, and for several years he helped pay the bills by making paid appearances in costume. In the '70s and '80s, he kept busy with regular screen work (*The Happy Hooker Goes Hollywood*, '80), but the acclaimed new *Batman* movies inaugurated by Tim Burton in '89 sadly ignored him.

In the '90s, Adam seemed to have come to terms with his legacy at last, and he found a new audience that laughed with—not at—his Caped Crusader. His familiar voice has been heard on many animated series (including *The Simpsons* and *The Family Guy*), and his autobiographical *Back to the Batcave* in '94 was a nostalgic hit.

Meanwhile Batman's partner in crime-fighting, Robin the Boy Wonder, ran into career limitations of his own. Herbert Gervis, Jr., better known as Burt Ward, was a novice actor who made his debut with *Batman*. Younger than Adam by almost two decades, he was a fit, energetic kid with whom teens could identify, with hair short enough for parents to love during the hirsute '60s. Unfortunately, he found himself typecast even more tightly than Adam and was never able to establish a durable post-*Batman* screen career. In the '80s, he

February 17, 1936—Football star Jim Brown is born in Georgia. ☮ February 18, 1922—*Cosmo* editor Helen Gurley Brown is born in Green Forest, Arkansas. February 18, 1933—Artist Yoko Ono is born in Tokyo, Japan. ☮ February 18, 1950—Actress Cybill Shepherd is born in Memphis. February 18, 1960—Opening ceremonies for the Olympic Games in Squaw Valley, California are held.

40 Bat-tastic Guests on *Batman*

Steve Allen–"Allen Stevens"
John Astin–"The Riddler"
Tallulah Bankhead–"Black Widow"
Anne Baxter–"Olga, Queen of the Cossacks"
Milton Berle–"Louie the Lilac"
Art Carney–"The Archer"
Chad and Jeremy–Themselves
Dick Clark–Himself
Joan Collins–"The Siren"
Sammy Davis, Jr.–Himself
Phyllis Diller–Unnamed scrubwoman
Zsa Zsa Gabor–"Minerva"
Teri Garr–Unnamed girl
Lesley Gore–"Pussycat"
Frank Gorshin–"The Riddler"
Van Johnson–"The Minstrel"
Carolyn Jones–"Marsha, Queen of Diamonds"
Eartha Kitt–"Catwoman"
Liberace–"Chandell"
Gypsy Rose Lee–Unnamed newswoman
Jerry Lewis–Himself
Art Linkletter–Himself
Ida Lupino–"Dr. Cassandra"
Roddy McDowall–"The Bookworm"
Burgess Meredith–"The Penguin"
Ethel Merman–"Lola Lasagne"
Julie Newmar–"Catwoman"
Paul Revere and the Raiders–Themselves
Otto Preminger–"Mr. Freeze"
Vincent Price–"Egghead"
Rob Reiner–Unnamed delivery boy
Cliff Robertson–"Shame"
Edward G. Robinson–Himself
Cesar Romero–"The Joker"
George Sanders–"Mr. Freeze"
Jill St. John–"Molly" (Riddler's assistant)
Rudy Vallee–"Lord Marmaduke Fogg"
Eli Wallach–"Mr. Freeze"
Shelley Winters–"Ma Parker"
Henny Youngman–"Manny the Mesopotamian"

developed an early-education program called Early Bird, later started a visual-effects company, and also has a company that rescues Great Danes.

EVERYBODY LOVES SOMEBODY

Before *Batman*, Adam had been married twice, once in the early '50s and again in the late '50s–early '60s. He married his current wife in '71 and has a large family. One of his daughters, Nina West, hosted the *Real Estate* show on TV Land.

Burt was already married pre-*Batman*; he had a child, too, but he got divorced the same year the show debuted. The next year he married Kathy Kersh, a model who had been on dozens of '60s TV shows, including two turns on *Batman*. After they broke up in '69, Burt remarried in '90, and they're still together, with a child. Burt's autobiography, *Boy Wonder: My Life In Tights*, revealed many sexual shenanigans enjoyed with eager female fans during the '60s.

MY BACK PAGES

Before the show was cancelled, it was so expensive to produce that the studio considered making severe budget cuts (eliminating some of the regular characters, for instance) before finally pulling the plug. . . . The *Mad* magazine parody—"Bats-man"—had Sparrow the Boy Wonderful trying to kill his mentor so he could use the car to date girls. . . . Sharp-eyed fans may recall an early '60s Nestle's Quik commercial that Adam did. . . . So popular was Burt in his heyday, he recorded a single during the first *Batman* season under the

February 18, 1966—*The Silencers* with Stella Stevens opens. ☮ February 18, 1970—Guilty verdicts for the Chicago Eight are delivered for inciting riots. February 19, 1924—Actor Lee Marvin is born in New York. ☮ February 19, 1963—Betty Friedan's *The Feminine Mystique* is published. February 19, 1964—*The Umbrellas of Cherbourg* with Catherine Deneuve opens.

tutelage of Frank Zappa (the A side was "Boy Wonder, I Love You"). . . . Both stars voiced their famous characters for the animated *New Adventures of Batman* ('77).

The Beach Boys

Brian and the boys set the California lifestyle to music.

TAKIN' CARE OF BUSINESS

Other groups in the '60s created distinctive sounds; the Beach Boys created a distinctive genre. Their influential beach music perfectly captured a time (early and mid-'60s) and a place (the sunny California coast), which is why movies (everything from *Muscle Beach Party* to *American Graffiti* to *Forrest Gump*) have used the Beach Boys on their soundtracks to evoke instant atmosphere.

In the '60s, the topics started out as surfers and girls (or surfer girls), moved to hot rods and lost romance, and graduated to spiritual themes and adult issues. The music grew from simple guitar-based pop to complex layers of unusual instruments and sound effects. And always there were the vocals, the angelic, rich harmonies that were much-imitated but never equaled by a male rock group. Play an old unfamiliar Beach Boys song today and you'll still know its origin by heart: Brian (or Brian and Mike) thought of it, Brian arranged it, the boys sang it, the world listened/ danced/partied/kissed/cried to it.

The band's turbulent story has been retold many times in books and movies because it has so many dramatic elements: the three Wilson brothers, cousin Mike Love and neighbor Al Jardine teaching themselves in '61 to play and sing in a living room ten miles from the nearest L.A. beach; the father, the stern disciplinarian Murry Wilson, pushing them to organize and practice, getting them onto the radio in '62, driving them to early gigs, hooking them up with Capitol Records, and then signing almost everything away as he fought with his kids; insecure Brian, the tormented genius overcoming crippling shyness and personal problems to write and play bass on lush songs about a sport and lifestyle he knew little about, then recording his work in mono because of his hearing defect; guitarist Carl, the baby-faced diplomat, keeping the group together as family, when artistic, and legal issues threatened to fracture them permanently; rugged Dennis, the band's drummer and only surfer, the playboy brother whose soulful side wasn't fully revealed until his '77 solo record *Pacific Ocean Blue*; outgoing frontman Mike, balding and often wearing a hat, not properly credited for cowriting the famous songs until the 21st century; and Al, the cheerful and reliable rhythm guitarist, a mainstay when the others were divided.

The early songs were so good, so popular, and so numerous, a bestselling double-album of greatest hits was released in '74 with not a single post-'65 song on it. Classics poured from the group in a steady stream in the early '60s—"Surfer Girl," "Surfin' USA," "Little Deuce Coupe," "In My Room," "Help Me, Rhonda," "California Girls," "Fun, Fun, Fun," "I Get Around," and many more smile-inducing radio staples. The songs were derivative at first (Brian acknowledged debts to the Four Freshman, Chuck Berry, and Phil Spector's girl groups, among others), but by '65, when a nervous breakdown led to his retirement from the road, Brian's studio wizardry was so advanced he was single-handedly America's answer to the Beatles at their most sophisticated. His achingly beautiful landmark *Pet Sounds* in '66 (named for what he heard in his head and hoped to capture on vinyl) was a worthy rival to the masterful *Rubber Soul* (Paul McCartney declared "God Only Knows" one of his all-time favorite songs) and offered sufficient challenge to inspire the Fab Four's innovative *Revolver.*

Unfortunately Brian's reply, the long-gestating *Smile*, was aborted as Brian succumbed to drugs and mental illness, with only the complicated "Good Vibrations" and a few other songs to suggest what might have been. (Mythologized as the

February 19, 1968—Paul McCartney, his girlfriend Jane Asher, Ringo Starr, and his wife Maureen Cox arrive in India.
February 20, 1927—Actor Sidney Poitier is born in Miami.
February 20, 1941—Singer/songwriter Buffy Sainte-Marie is born on the Piapot Reserve near Regina, Canada.

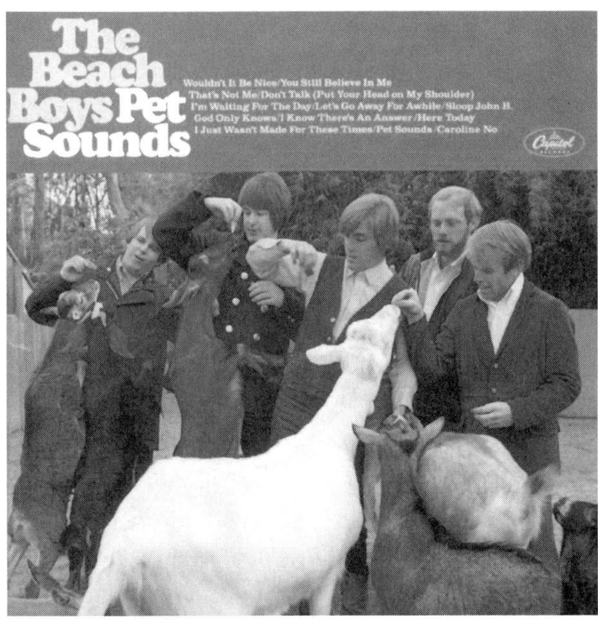

greatest album never completed, *Smile* was finally resurrected and released in 2004 to critical acclaim.) By the end of the decade the band's striped shirts, combed hair, and clean-shaven smiling faces had yielded to love beads, long wrangly hair, and thick beards, Brian had taken to his bed permanently, and new members were being drafted to help with touring and recording as the group struggled anew to find an audience.

Later decades would be just as uneven as the first one had been. "Sail On Sailor" in '72 and the *Endless Summer* compilation in '74 were hits, but as the group fluctuated between its traditional sound and R & B influences, sales and reviews for new albums were mostly disappointing. The group became a huge mid-decade stadium draw, but drinking and squabbling led to concert embarrassments, and Nancy Reagan's intervention was required for them to play at the National Mall in Washington, D.C. in '85.

Brian's return to the group was trumpeted on the *15 Big Ones* LP ('76), but a few years later he was pretty much gone for good and under the care of a full-time live-in psychologist. Still the band staggered on, releasing albums of varying interest, overcoming the deaths of Dennis (drowning) and Carl (lung cancer), and splintering into different touring bands led by Mike and Al. The group made more headlines in the '90s and 2000s with its lawsuits than its records, although Brian did score with audiences and critics when he mounted solo tours of the *Pet Sounds* and *Smile* material. Ultimately, the story of the Beach Boys is the story of all families—some wonderful ideas, messy squabbling, beautiful moments, regrettable failures, and enduring memories.

EVERYBODY LOVES SOMEBODY

Brian got married in '64 and divorced in '79. His two daughters from this marriage, Carnie and Wendy, grew up to be two-thirds of the group Wilson Phillips, which had a hit in '90 with "Hold On." He married again in '95.

Carl got married in '66, divorced in '80 with two kids, then was married to Dean Martin's daughter for the last decade of his life. Dennis was married five times and had four wives; the wife he married twice in the '70s, actress Karen Lamm, was previously the wife of one of the founders of the group Chicago. His last wife was said to be the illegitimate daughter of Mike Love. Near the end of his life, Dennis also had an intense romance with Christine McVie of Fleetwood Mac, and when he died he left behind at least four kids. Mike, rival to Dennis as the group's biggest player, has been married numerous times, while Al married a local girl in '63 and was with her for two decades, with a second marriage in the '80s.

MY BACK PAGES

The Beach Boys were inducted into the Rock and Roll Hall of Fame in '88, their first year of eligibility. . . . So personal was Brian's *Pet Sounds*, "Caroline, No," (originally called "Carol, I Know") was released as a solo single credited only to Brian, not the group. . . . "Good Vibrations," Brian's three-and-a-half minute "pocket symphony," was at the time the most expensive pop song ever recorded (Brian recorded it in pieces at three different studios over a couple of months). . . . Dennis had a brief acting career and co-starred with James Taylor in the car

February 20, 1962—Astronaut John Glenn orbits the earth in *Friendship 7*. ☮ February 20, 1962—*Walk on the Wild Side* with Jane Fonda opens.
February 20, 1963—*How the West Was Won* with Jimmy Stewart opens.
February 20, 2005—Actress Sandra Dee dies of kidney disease in Thousand Oaks, California.

saga *Two-Lane Blacktop* ('72). . . . His "Never Learn Not to Love" on '69's *20/20* album was co-written by Charles Manson, whom Dennis had briefly befriended. . . . Mike's brother Stan was a pro basketball player in the '70s. . . . Mike was in India studying Transcendental Meditation with the Beatles in '68. . . . Al sang lead on only a few of the songs, among them "Surfin' Safari". . . . He temporarily left the band in '62 to study dentistry, replaced by another Wilson neighbor, David Marks. . . . Other musicians who played with the band (especially after Brian stopped touring) included Glen Campbell and Daryl Dragon, who later performed as the Captain with wife Toni Tennille. . . . One of the joys of the '60s records is hearing how handmade (and thus adorably imperfect) they were—random sounds, coughs, and conversations punctuate the backgrounds (and sometimes the foregrounds) of many songs. . . . As classic as the '60s songs were, the group's biggest-selling song of all time came in '88 with "Kokomo."

Rolling Stone Magazine's 10 Greatest Albums of All Time

1. ***Sgt. Pepper's Lonely Hearts Club Band*** ('67)–The Beatles
2. ***Pet Sounds*** ('66)–The Beach Boys
3. ***Revolver*** ('66)–The Beatles
4. ***Highway 61 Revisited*** ('65)–Bob Dylan
5. ***Rubber Soul*** ('65)–The Beatles
6. ***What's Going On*** ('71)–Marvin Gaye
7. ***Exile on Main Street*** ('72)–The Rolling Stones
8. ***London Calling*** ('79)–The Clash
9. ***Blonde on Blonde*** ('66)–Bob Dylan
10. ***The Beatles*** (AKA *The White Album*, '68)–The Beatles

The Beatles

They were the "most": the most studied, most loved, and most important rock band of all time.

TAKIN' CARE OF BUSINESS

Compared to other '60s groups—especially the Rolling Stones—the Beatles' career was relatively short, only about eight years from the time Ringo joined to the break-up in '70. And their output was surprisingly small—under 11 hours of music as a group. But in those eight years, and with those 11 hours that began with *Introducing . . . The Beatles* ('63), the Beatles changed pop culture forever. Musical styles, fashions, hairstyles, drugs, psychedelic art, Eastern religions, Love—if the Beatles advocated/tried/pursued it, millions of people followed right behind.

So eagerly did people look to them for meaning, sometimes "messages" were found that were never intended (the dozens of album clues that "proved" Paul was dead, or the hidden instructions in "Helter Skelter" that steered Charles Manson). But that's how people looked at the Beatles in the '60s—they were the style-setters, the rule-makers, the coolest of the cool and the best of the best, so whatever they did had to be right. And right it was for a long time, until significant changes came in '66.

Up until then, they had traveled a long, hard path from anonymity in Liverpool to global conquest. Their early history is so well-known it's folklore by now. The Liverpool childhoods; John's teen band the Quarrymen playing early rock-and-roll covers; the arrival in '57 of the younger Paul McCartney and, six months later, of the even younger George Harrison; the rough, naughty trips to Hamburg in '60 and '61; their years struggling with various drummers until they invited amiable Ringo Starr to join in '62; Cavern Club grunge and the suit-up ordered by manager Brian Epstein; the fresh new image as Fab Four mop-tops with short, exuberant songs like "Please, Please Me" credited to the songwriting team of

February 20, 2006—Broadcaster Curt Gowdy dies. ☮ February 21, 1965—Malcolm X is assassinated in New York.
February 21, 1967—*One Million Years B.C.* with Raquel Welch opens. ☮ February 22, 1942—Model Christine Keeler is born.
February 22, 1965—The Beatles begin filming *Help!*, their second movie, in the Bahamas.

Lennon and McCartney; the mesmerizing appearances with Ed Sullivan in '64; the never-duplicated stranglehold on the first five positions of the *Billboard* charts; Beatlemania and the wildly successful world tours; the Oscar-nominated *A Hard Day's Night* ('64) and *Help!* ('65); the first stadium concert ever (Shea Stadium, '65); *The Beatles* cartoon and the hundreds of pieces of Beatles merchandise; the successful musical departures (feedback on "I Feel Fine," the string quartet on "Yesterday," the sitar on "Norwegian Wood," the folk-rock on the *Rubber Soul* album) in collaboration with producer George Martin; and, ultimately, the unquestioned status as the world's most popular, most written-about, most widely acclaimed musicians.

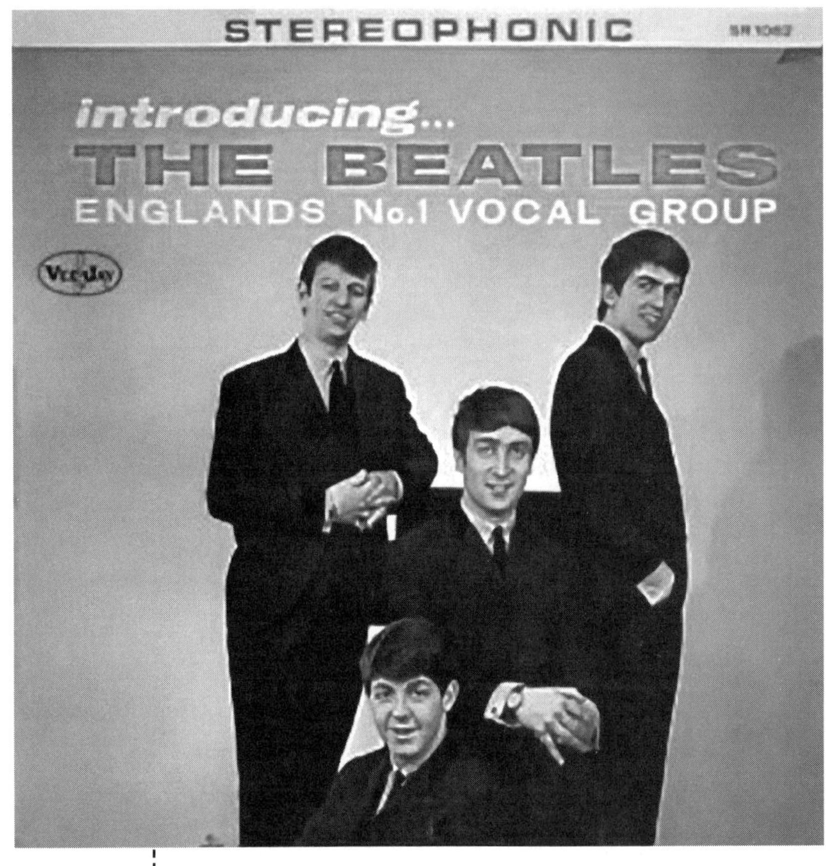

But '66 was a turning point. Exhausted by their grueling touring schedule, angered at the threats they'd recently received in the Philippines after they unknowingly snubbed an official invitation, and unable to hear themselves on stage, the Beatles decided to quit touring so they could focus on recording. The decision was quickly validated by *Revolver*, still honored decades later as one of the greatest and most daring albums of all time. Enigmatic lyrics, psychedelic sounds, an artsy cover, the Beatles photographed on the back indoors in sunglasses—everything about this record was different, and it established the band as rock's pre-eminent studio wizards. Also in '66, the first individual musical project appeared when Paul wrote the soundtrack for a Hayley Mills film, *The Family Way*. And in '66 their run of mistake-free behavior (at least in public) ended when John's inadvertent remark about Jesus resulted in millions of their records being burned.

From then to the end of the decade the Beatles would have hits and misses as they became increasingly independent and headed to their final dissolution: Apple and the Apple boutique in '67 were noble efforts that were soon mired in problems; *Sgt. Pepper's* and a global broadcast of "All You Need Is Love" in '67 were unqualified triumphs, but Brian died that year of a drug overdose, and the band instantly fell on its face with its next project, the amateurish self-made *Magical Mystery Tour* film; the *Yellow Submarine* animated film in '68 was well-received, but that year's hopeful spiritual quest to India backfired embarrassingly; the ambitious *White Album* in '68 was something of an artistic breakthrough, but the band wasn't even playing together on the songs anymore; John and George got busted for drugs, Paul admitted to using LSD, and Ringo briefly quit; the *Let It Be* album and movie were so troublesome they weren't released until after Paul officially announced the end in April of '70; the inspired *Abbey Road* was the last album they made together and was a fitting coda, but already Ringo was star-

February 22, 1976—Florence Ballard, an original member of the Supremes, dies of a heart attack in Detroit.
February 22, 1987—Artist Andy Warhol dies after a gall-bladder operation in New York. ☮ February 23, 1940—Actor Peter Fonda is born in New York.
February 23, 1963—The Chiffons' "He's So Fine" hits the charts. ☮ February 23, 1966—*Harper* with Janet Leigh opens.

The Beatles by the Numbers

73,000,000: The record-setting number of TV viewers in America (40% of the population) who watched the Beatles' first appearance with Ed Sullivan

600,000: The dollars spent by United Artists to make *A Hard Day's Night*

250,000: The number of copies of "I Want to Hold Your Hand" sold in the U.S. in the first three days of release

160,000: The record-setting dollars paid to the Beatles for their 30-minute Shea Stadium concert in '65 (approximately $90 per second)

55,600: The attendance at the Shea Stadium concert, at the time a world's record

45,000: The number of tickets sold when the Beatles played Shea Stadium a year later

10,000: The dollars earned by the Beatles for appearing on Ed Sullivan's show in '64

4,000: The approximate number of fans on hand when the Beatles landed at JFK in '64

1,400: The approximate number of live shows played by the various incarnations of the Beatles

910: "One After 909," a song that John and Paul wrote in '59 but didn't record until 10 years later for *Let It Be*

728: The number of people in the live audience for the Beatles' first appearance on Ed Sullivan's show

700: The approximate number of hours the Beatles spent in the studio working on *Sgt. Pepper's*

500: In dollars, John's fine after his '68 drug bust

495: Length, in seconds, of the Beatles' longest song ("Revolution 9," 8:15)

187: Average length, in seconds, of each song on *The White Album* (30 songs, 3:07 each)

136: In pounds, the weight of Ringo in '64 (George: 142, Paul: 158, John: 159)

132: Average length, in seconds, of each song on *Meet the Beatles* (12 songs, 2:12 each).

94: As in 94 Baker Street, the London address of the Beatles' Apple boutique

68: In inches, Ringo's height (5' 8"; John, Paul, George all about 5' 11").

64: "When I'm Sixty-Four," a song written in '59 but not recorded until '67

62: The number of identifiable celebrities standing behind the Beatles on the cover of *Sgt. Pepper's*

50: The percentage of tickets unsold for the Beatles' final concert in San Francisco

39: The number of episodes of the *Beatles* cartoon show, running on ABC for three seasons (seasons two and three were repeats of season one)

33: The number of minutes the Beatles were on stage at their final concert in San Francisco

31: The number of shows the Beatles played each week while in Hamburg in the fall of 1960 (four shows each weeknight, 11 shows on weekends)

30: The percentage of the audience comprised of police and security personnel when the Beatles played Japan's 10,000-seat Budokan in '66

25: In English pounds, the weekly wage successfully offered to lure Ringo away from Rory Storm and the Hurricanes in August, '62

February 23, 1967—Julie Newmar makes her last appearance as Catwoman on *Batman*.
February 23, 1968—Figure skater Peggy Fleming makes the cover of *Life*. ☮ February 24, 1941—Singer Joanie Sommers is born in Buffalo, New York.
February 24, 1943—George Harrison of the Beatles is born in Liverpool. ☮ February 24, 1967—Liz Taylor makes the cover of *Life*.

23: The length, in seconds, of the Beatles' shortest song ("Her Majesty" on *Abbey Road*)

22: The number of Bible Belt radio stations that banned Beatles records after John's "we're more popular than Jesus" misquote in August, '66

21: The age of Stuart Sutcliffe, ex-bass player for the young Beatles and John's best friend, when he died of a cerebral hemorrhage in '62

20: Number of songs to hit #1 on the *Billboard* charts

19: The number of weeks "Hey Jude" was on the U.S. charts, the longest of any of their singles

17: The highest position reached on the British charts in late '62 by the Beatles' first single, "Love Me Do"

15: George's age when he joined the Quarrymen in '58 (Paul and John were almost 18)

14: The number of songs the Beatles had simultaneously on the *Billboard* Hot 100 in April, '64

12: The number of different songs played by the Beatles during their final stadium concerts in America

11: The number of Elvis Presley-recorded songs played by the Beatles at their early-'60s shows

10: As in 10 Mathew Street, Liverpool, the address of the original Cavern Club where the Beatles played approximately 300 shows and established a cult following in the early '60s

9: Considered by John and Yoko to be their lucky number, hence the experimental "Revolution 9" (named the least popular Beatles song ever in a '71 *Village Voice* poll) and John's later "#9 Dream"

8: The number of names used before the group settled on the Beatles–the Quarrymen, Johnny and the Moondogs, the Nerk Twins (just John and Paul performing together), the Silver Beetles, the Silver Beatles, the Silver Beats, the Beetles, the Beatals)

7: The Beatles' ranking in the *New Musical Express* national poll of 1962's Best British Small Groups

6: The number of drummers who performed live with the group: Colin Hanton ('57-'59), Tommy Moore ('60), Norman Chapman ('60), Pete Best ('60-'62), Ringo Starr ('62-'70), Jimmy Nicol (summer '64, for five concerts when Ringo had tonsillitis)

5.75: In dollars, the cost of a ticket to the Beatles' Shea Stadium concert in '65 (cheap seats were $4.50)

5: The number of Quarrymen members in early '58 (John Lennon, Paul McCartney, Len Garry, Eric Griffiths, Colin Hanton)

4: The number of Top 10 positions held by the Beatles in VH1's 2001 ranking of the greatest albums of all time (1. *Revolver*, 6. *Rubber Soul*, 8. *Abbey Road*, 10. *Sgt. Pepper's*)

3: The number of Beatles who used stage names in their careers (Paul went by Paul Ramon and George went by Carl Harrison in '60, while Richard Starkey went by Ringo Starr his entire Beatles career)

2: Number of weeks their last #1 song, "The Long and Winding Road" was atop the charts in '70

1: Position in "greatest bands of all time" ranking by *Spin* magazine, position in "bestselling bands of all time" ranking by the *Guinness Book of World Records*, position in "greatest album covers of all time" ranking by *Rolling Stone* (*Sgt. Pepper's*)

February 25, 1961—Fresh out of the army, Elvis plays his first concert (a charity performance in Memphis).
February 25, 1964—Muhammad Ali beats Sonny Liston for the heavyweight title. ☮ February 26, 1932—Singer Johnny Cash is born in Arkansas.
February 26, 1945—Actress Marta Kristen is born in Norway. ☮ February 26, 1947—Rocker Sandi Shaw is born in Essex, England.

ring in movies and John, Paul, and George were working on solo albums as quarreling gave way to lawsuits.

In the '70s and beyond, each member had long solo careers of varying success, and by the 2000s they'd won virtually every honor there was to win—just to name one of the many lists they top, they have the #1 album (*Sgt. Pepper's*) on the *Rolling Stone* list of all-time great albums (and two of the top three, and three of the top five). When one of them has died—John from an assassin's bullet in '80, George from brain cancer in 2001—the news has dominated headlines and the world has mourned. Still loved, still copied, still best-sellers, the eternal Beatles are still the most dominating and defining band in pop music.

EVERYBODY LOVES SOMEBODY

While the boys kept their public image as cheeky, fun-loving rascals intact during the early '60s, subsequent biographies have found plenty of evidence to show that different band members were ravenously promiscuous, involved with random hookers, and responsible for unwanted pregnancies. All the Beatles got married during the '60s; three of the marriages (John's, Ringo's, and Paul's) were with already-pregnant girlfriends.

John was a husband and a father when Beatlemania hit, and in fact his '62 marriage to fellow art student Cynthia Powell and their son Julian were kept out of the public eye for years. After John met Japanese artist Yoko Ono in '66 all their lives changed. Yoko, already on her second marriage and mother to a daughter, was to many people a dark, inscrutable "dragon lady" creating esoteric conceptual art that was pioneering to some, baffling to others. By '68 she and John were inseparable, and by '69 they were both divorced and married to each other. Yoko later gave birth to John's son Sean, worked with John on numerous albums and artistic endeavors, built his wealth into a megafortune, and emerged as a dignified, respected survivor after his death. Cynthia went on to remarry several times and write books about her life with John.

Like Cynthia, Maureen Cox was more comfortable in the background, just a-lovin' her Beatle, with no pretensions of a music or movie career. A pretty, dark-haired Liverpudlian, she worked as a hairdresser until she met Ringo. Like Cynthia and Linda McCartney, Maureen was already pregnant when she married Ringo (son Zak was born seven months after the February '65 wedding, two more kids came in '67 and '70). She stayed married to Ringo until their '75 divorce, then she remarried in '89 to one of the co-owners of the Hard Rock and House of Blues chains. After three decades occasionally in but mostly out of the spotlight, Maureen died in '94 of leukemia, with her family and Ringo at her bedside. In '81 Ringo married Barbara Bach, the glamorous actress who was the Bond girl in *The Spy Who Loved Me* ('77).

George was the third married Beatle. His wife was Pattie Boyd, an adorable and successful British model for all the new Carnaby Street fashions that put the fun in functional. George and Pattie met on the set of *A Hard Day's Night*, in which she had a cute bit part. George was quickly smitten, and their romance stayed a secret until they went to Ireland later in '64 and the press invaded the castle where they were staying. A year later, George and 21-year-old Pattie were married; Paul was the only Beatle to attend, and the bride and groom wore matching fur coats designed by Mary Quant. Pattie went from model to muse: inspired by their love, George wrote some of his best songs to/about/for her, among them "I Need You," "For You Blue," and the classic "Something," which no less an expert than Frank Sinatra once called "the greatest love song in the last fifty years." Still inspired by her in the '70s, George wrote "So Sad" as he and Pattie were splitting up and another rock star was entering her life. Eric Clapton's feelings for Pattie were expressed in his most famous song, "Layla" ("I'm begging darling please," he wailed in '70). In '77, George and Pattie divorced. George remarried in '78 and had a son. Pattie and Eric married in '79 for a decade.

Paul's long relationship with aristocratic Jane Asher was well-chronicled in the '60s; she was the girl everyone as-

February 27, 1932—Actress Elizabeth Taylor is born in London. ☮ February 28, 1940—Race car driver Mario Andretti is born in Italy.
February 28, 1942—Brian Jones of the Rolling Stones is born in Cheltenham, England.
February 28, 1960—The eighth Winter Olympic Games close at Squaw Valley.

sumed he'd marry—they traveled together, and they were engaged for the first half of '68. After their sudden split, Paul met and married Linda Eastman, an American divorced single mother who had made a name for herself in the mid-'60s as a photographer of rock stars (contrary to rumors, she was not related to the Eastman family of camera fame). Together Paul and Linda had three kids, among them fashion designer Stella McCartney; also together Paul and Linda created/recorded with/toured with the group Wings, scoring many hits (and sharing an Oscar nomination for co-writing "Live and Let Die"). A woman of many diverse interests, Linda created her own line of vegetarian frozen food in the '90s. She died of cancer in '98—her funeral was the only public post-Beatles reunion of Paul, George, and Ringo. Paul married a former model, Heather Mills, in 2002, and had a daughter with her in 2003. They shared homes in England and L.A. until they announced in 2006 that they were getting divorced.

MY BACK PAGES

Though Lennon and McCartney are considered rock's greatest composers, the early albums supplemented their own compositions with the band's versions of country, rockabilly, Broadway, blues, and folk songs. . . . Musicologists and biographers have decided that only about 30 songs credited to Lennon and McCartney were actually written jointly by the pair—most songs were written by one or the other, with the composer usually the lead vocalist (for "A Day in the Life," a joint composition, John and Paul each sang his own section). . . . "Yesterday" was the group's most-covered song with about 2500 versions, followed by George's "Something" with about 1000 different versions. . . . Ringo wrote only one of the group's hit songs, "Octopus's Garden". . . . One of the current topics the Beatles weren't allowed to address in interviews was the Vietnam War, though John later became a vocal anti-war activist. . . . During the '60s, the Beatles' top-selling albums were, in order, *The White Album*, *Abbey Road*, *Sgt. Pepper's*.

Warren Beatty and Faye Dunaway

One of the sharpest and most committed movie idols pulled together a landmark '60s film that made a star of its beautiful lead actress.

TAKIN' CARE OF BUSINESS

Henry Beaty at birth, this Virginian attended Northwestern and then studied with legendary acting teacher Stella Adler. Warren first made a Hollywood splash as a rich kid on the *Dobie Gillis* TV show and then found success (and a Tony nomination) on Broadway. His Hollywood breakthrough was the role of Natalie Wood's handsome heartthrob in *Splendor in the Grass* ('61). Though the film was not a blockbuster, it brought enough attention to Warren's movie-idol looks and distinctive charisma to bring him steady work, if not award-winning movies, for the next few years.

The watershed was *Bonnie and Clyde*, a film he produced and tried for several years to get made with different directors. The finished film revised history somewhat (Clyde was given a performance problem, C.W. was a composite char-

February 28, 1968—The Cavern Club, the Liverpool nightclub where the Beatles first got famous, closes its doors.
February 29, 1960—The first Playboy Club with Bunnies opens in Chicago.
February 29, 1968—At this night's Grammy Awards, the Beatles' '67 album *Sgt. Pepper's Lonely Hearts Club Band* wins four awards.

acter), and the violence was considered shocking, but it was undeniably stylish and riveting. Somehow the studio initially dismissed *Bonnie and Clyde* and dumped it into drive-ins, but a rerelease later in '67 brought a new wave of attention and acclaim. Not the least of the film's attractions was its leading lady, the sleek, high-cheekboned Faye Dunaway.

A runner-up in the Miss University of Florida contest of '59, Faye was a stage actress who didn't start appearing onscreen until the mid-'60s. With only a few TV and movie credits behind her, but five years of prominent New York theatre work on her résumé, she landed the choice role of Bonnie Parker. Supposedly Carol Lynley, Natalie Wood, Tuesday Weld, and Shirley MacLaine had also been considered, but 28-year-old Faye turned out to be the perfect fit. It was a remarkable performance—she made the gun-toting killer a sympathetic three-dimensional character complicated by inner torments and desires.

The role brought her the first of many Oscar and Golden Globe nominations, as well as the covers of *Newsweek*, *Look* and *Life* magazines (ironically, while audiences everywhere saw her Bonnie as a tall, slender, distinctive beauty with a model's poise, she thought she looked ugly and tried not to throw up when she first saw the film). Her gun-moll look dramatically influenced international fashions, with Faye's beret, blonde 'do, and sleek styles sparking a retro-'30s trend that lasted 'til the end of the decade.

Warren, meanwhile, got rich from his percentage deal, *Bonnie and Clyde* got 10 Oscar nominations (including a Best Actor nod for him and a Best Picture for his movie), and his career was set. When other actors might have cashed in with a string of dumb, profitable action movies, Warren ultimately revealed himself to be more movie artist than movie star—from the '70s onward he has dedicated himself to intelligent projects he's been passionate about (*Shampoo*, '75, *Bugsy*, '91) and established himself as one of the industry's most versatile talents (winning an Oscar for directing *Reds*, '81, and twice getting nominations for producing, directing, writing, and acting in the same year). Even his flops (*Ishtar*, '87) and lightweights (*Dick Tracy*, '91) have been ambitious and carefully considered. Impressed Oscar voters anointed him with the Thalberg career-achievement award in 2000.

Faye, suddenly one of Hollywood's hottest actresses after *Bonnie and Clyde*, went glamorous for *The Thomas Crown Affair* ('68), Western for *Little Big Man* ('70), and royal for *The Three Musketeers* ('73). Her streak continued with the classics *Chinatown* ('74, an Oscar nomination) and *Network* ('76, an Oscar win). Her busy '80s swung from the over-the-top *Mommie Dearest* ('81) to the risky role of the downtrodden Wanda in *Barfly* ('87). She suffered a TV debacle when her attempt at a sitcom quickly bombed, followed by a Broadway debacle when she was rejected for the lead role in *Sunset Boulevard* after she said Andrew Lloyd Webber himself had given it to her. Ever resilient, in the '90s she added an Emmy to her mantle and a well-received autobiography to her bookshelf, and in 2005 she starred in a new reality show, *The Starlet*. Her impact on film history is undeniable. On the American Film Institute's list of the hundred best American movies ever made, three of them starred Faye Dunaway: #19 *Chinatown*, #27 *Bonnie and Clyde*, #66 *Network*.

EVERYBODY LOVES SOMEBODY

More space than what's available here is necessary to chronicle Warren's legendary career as a ladies' man. Biographies and tabloids have placed him in the company of co-stars, models, musicians, older women, younger women, royals and unknowns. Probably his most famous relationships were with Natalie Wood, Julie Christie, Diane Keaton, and Madonna. At 55, he married two-time Oscar-nominee Annette Bening and with her has four children.

For Faye, '60s success brought introductions to some of Hollywood's most famous names. She was reputedly romanced by Marlon Brando, Michael Caine, Steve McQueen, and Jack Nicholson, and she had a long tempestu-

March 1, 1917—Journalist Ralph Gleason is born in New York. ☮ March 1, 1944—Roger Daltrey of the Who is born in England.
March 1, 1961—The Ken doll is introduced by Mattel. ☮ March 1, 1964—*Kissin' Cousins* with Elvis opens.
March 1, 1965—Tom Jones's "It's Not Unusual" hits #1 in the U.K.

ous affair with Marcello Mastroianni. She married Peter Wolf, the lead singer of the J. Geils Band, in '74, divorcing him in '79. She was married again from '83 to '87 and has a son who's now a model.

MY BACK PAGES

Warren's older sister is Shirley MacLaine. . . . He's said to have turned down the lead roles in *PT 109*, *Butch Cassidy* (Sundance), *The Godfather* (Michael), *The Sting*, *The Way We Were*, *The Great Gatsby*, *Mars Attacks!* and *Kill Bill*. . . . His well-known involvement in politics (he's been considered a possible gubernatorial and presidential candidate) first flourished when he backed Robert Kennedy's '68 campaign, followed by a '72 push for George McGovern. . . . To further her filmmaking ambitions, Faye told *Parade* magazine that she watches three movies a day to study the techniques of other directors. . . . The important lesson she learned from the driven Warren: "If you have a vision, the only way to protect it is to fight body and soul, to go to the mat time and again". . . . The American Film Institute ranked *Bonnie and Clyde* as the 27th greatest movie ever, right behind another '60s classic, *Dr. Strangelove*. . . . The movie's rollicking music became a popular LP. . . . "Balmy and Clod" was the *Mad* magazine parody.

Bo Belinsky

If Frank's Rat Pack had included athletes, Bo, who lit up the baseball world with his fastball and his fast living, would've been a charter member.

TAKIN' CARE OF BUSINESS

"Bo knows show." At least he did in '62, when the handsome southpaw took over L.A. as a jaunty playboy pitcher equally at home on the mound or in a nightclub. While his overall career was disappointing—he won only 35% of his games, leaving with a 28–51 record—he enjoyed his moment in the neon like few others have. "I've gotten more mileage out of winning 28 games," said Bo, "than most guys do winning 200."

Born Robert Belinsky, Bo grew up in the tough sections of Manhattan and New Jersey. A hard-throwing lefty, he was signed by the Pittsburgh Pirates in '56 but was soon sent to the Baltimore Orioles and then to the minors. When the L.A. Angels claimed him in late '61, he already had an attitude: he rejected the initial contract offer, announcing he could make more as a pool shark. He opened the Angels' season with five straight wins, among them a no-hitter against the Orioles. It wasn't just the no-hitter itself that made Bo's reputation, it was when and how he accomplished it—it was the first no-hitter ever pitched in star-loving L.A., and Bo audaciously bragged that he'd picked up a woman on the Sunset Strip the night before and had slept in.

Rewarded for his on-field achievements by a local car dealer, Bo tooled around Hollywood in a new candy-apple red Caddy, lived in a Hollywood penthouse, and flashed his stylin' threads to the delight of single women and gossip columnists everywhere. Unfortunately, Bo's fall came almost as quickly as his rise. He won only five more games and lost 11 over the

March 1, 1968—NBC makes a surprise on-air announcement that its cult hit *Star Trek* will return for one last TV season.
March 1, 1968—Johnny Cash and June Carter get married. ☮ March 1, 1969—Jim Morrison is arrested after a concert in Miami.
March 1, 1969—Murph the Surf is sentenced for murder. ☮ March 2, 1943—Guitarist Lou Reed is born in New York.

rest of the '62 season while leading the league in walks. The next year he won only two of eleven, and the year after that he punched out a 64-year-old sports reporter in the middle of the season, leading to a suspension, a minor-league banishment, and a trade to the Phillies.

For the last half of the '60s, he bounced between the majors and the minor leagues, going from the Phils to the Astros, Pirates, and Reds, piling up more losses than wins and calling it quits in '70. He himself half-jokingly blamed the girl he'd been with the night before his no-hitter; despite searching for her later, he never found his "good luck charm" again.

Bo then tumbled into a bleak world of alcohol and drug dependency. Bottoming out in '76, he moved to Hawaii to clean up, eventually counseling others with similar problems. Bo spent his last decade in Vegas, where he worked for a car dealership, found religion, and did charity work. Hampered by a hip replacement and heart trouble, he died in Vegas of bladder cancer at age 64.

EVERYBODY LOVES SOMEBODY

Few athletes have ever grabbed the celebrity lifestyle as eagerly as Bo did in the early '60s. He was a regular in the gossip pages from his dates with young starlets and his engagement to blonde bombshell Mamie Van Doren. "Our life was a circus," said Mamie in 2001. "It was a wild ride, but a lot of fun." Later, he wasn't just a playboy pitcher, he was a *Playboy* husband: his first wife was popular '60s Playmate Jo Collins. After they divorced, he married heiress Jane Weyerhaeuser (of the paper company). He had three daughters, two of them twins, and at different times was estranged from all of them.

MY BACK PAGES

Bo's nickname derived from middleweight boxer Bobo Olson, with whom he shared the same brawling style. . . . Like other handsome L.A. ballplayers of the early '60s (Sandy Koufax and Don Drysdale, to name two), Bo dabbled in movies and TV during the off-season, making appearances on shows like *77 Sunset Strip* and landing a role in a teenybopper musical called *C'mon, Let's Live a Little* ('67). . . . Besides his no-hitter, Bo was involved in another baseball landmark—pitching in relief for the Phillies, he served up Hank Aaron's 400th home run in '66.

George Best

One of the greatest soccer players in history, George Best had the looks and lifestyle of a rock star.

TAKIN' CARE OF BUSINESS

If Pelé is commonly regarded as the greatest footballer ever, George Best is a close second (Pelé himself called Best the best). Born in Belfast, George's glory years came while playing for England's Manchester United Football Club in the mid-'60s. The flashy winger joined the team as a teen and led them to two league championships in '65 and '67, plus the European Cup in '68. His heralded dribbling and passing skills made him the sport's consummate showman and deadliest scorer (he once scored six goals in a match). He'd challenge refs, anger opponents, entertain audiences, and never fail to do the unexpected.

His popularity (10,000 fan letters a week) and his shaggy good looks (he was sometimes called "the fifth Beatle") brought him the same kind of off-the-field business opportunities that Joe Namath enjoyed in America, including many endorsement deals and ownership of boutiques and nightclubs. Unfortunately, by the time he was 25 George Best had peaked and begun a long, sad decline. In the '70s and early '80s, he played for lesser teams in smaller venues, was jailed for drunk driving and assaulting a policeman, and ultimately had a liver transplant after his decades as an alcoholic. Following a long illness, he died in late 2005.

EVERYBODY LOVES SOMEBODY

George had the perfect description of his social life back when he was squiring beautiful women around in his Jaguar: "I used to go missing a lot—Miss Canada, Miss United Kingdom, Miss World." He was married twice, once in the late '70s-early '80s and again from '95–2004, with one son. Supposedly George's first wife took their young child and left because she said she couldn't take care of two babies.

MY BACK PAGES

British fans voted George the best soccer player of all time, and he's been the subject of many books and documentaries. . . . After football George worked as a radio/TV commentator. . . . The British theatrical film about his life, *Best*, came out in 2000, and George has written three well-titled autobiographical books: *Scoring at Halftime*, *The Best of Times*, and *The Good, the Bad, and the Bubbly*. . . . Famous quote: "I spent all my money on booze, birds and fast cars. The rest I just squandered."

Daniela Bianchi and Luciana Paluzzi

These two sexy Italians were in Bondage for two of the decade's best thrillers.

TAKIN' CARE OF BUSINESS

Unless you're talking with true Bond fans, few people would know the name Daniela Bianchi: "Bianchi? That's a red wine, right? Sweet, full-bodied, good legs, fine nose, yeah a '63 Bianchi, that was some year." Only the red wine part would be wrong. Born in Rome, Daniela was modeling when she was tapped for *From Russia with Love* ('63), one of the best of the long series (and the one that most closely paralleled the book on which it was based).

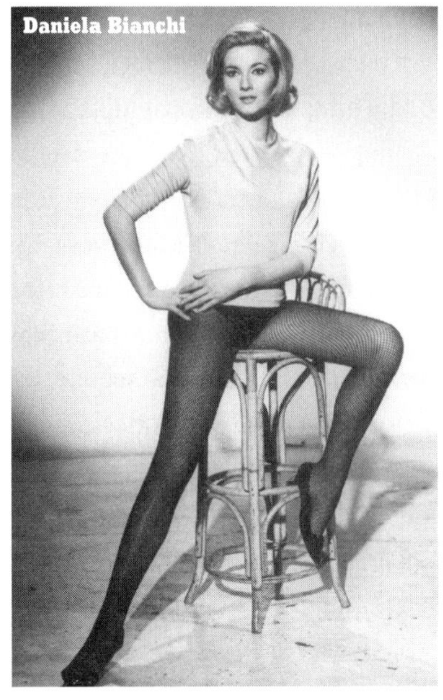
Daniela Bianchi

As Tatiana "Tanya" Romana, she was the stereotypical Bond girl—easy on the eyes, but not expected to do much besides looking scared or laughing at Bond's jokes (a stereotype that didn't get seriously challenged until the majestic Diana Rigg showed up in *On Her Majesty's Secret Service* in '69). Like Mie Hama in *You Only Live Twice* ('67), Daniela got to pose as 007's wife and travel with him for half the movie. It was also the only film in English she made during the decade (some say her voice was dubbed throughout the entire film because she barely spoke English). Away from 007, she put in some TV appearances and made a dozen foreign flicks, among them *Operation Kid Brother* ('67), a lame-brained Italian Bond rip-off that starred Sean's younger brother. A year later she made her last movie.

Luciana Paluzzi

Just two years after *From Russia with Love*, *Thunderball* rolled into theatres. While Claudine Auger was the movie's sexy heroine, some

James Bond fans think Luciana Paluzzi was even more memorable as the sexy villainess. Her scenes were scintillating—seducing Bond, trying to kill him, and then paying for her wicked ways with her life (shot by her own man, she died in 007's arms on the dance floor). A voluptuous Italian screen goddess in the Loren/Lollobrigida tradition, Luciana never attained their status but she did enjoy a busy career from the '50s to the '70s. Lots of these were European films, naturally, and sometimes Luciana was billed with alternative spellings of her name. She landed a co-starring role in an American spy show, "Five Fingers," from '59–'60, and from there many English-speaking parts followed, usually in spy or war dramas. Drive-in fans may remember her as the rich temptress in *Muscle Beach Party* ('64); one of her last highlights was a key role in *The Greek Tycoon* ('78).

EVERYBODY LOVES SOMEBODY

From Russia with Love boasted some of 007's trademark quips: when Daniela's character told Bond she had a small mouth, he said, "It's the right size—for me, that is." Her love scenes with Bond were pretty daring for the times, because two enemy agents were watching and filming as she and Bond hit the rack. In real life, Daniela married an Italian shipping magnate in the '80s. Meanwhile Luciana married actor Brett Halsey in '60; a year later both appeared in *Return to Peyton Place*. After their son was born, they divorced in '62. Married again in '80, she and her husband now live in the toney hills of L.A.

MY BACK PAGES

Daniela was Miss Italy of '60 and first runner-up at the Miss Universe pageant. . . . In *Operation Kid Brother*, Daniela was in bed with Neil Connery and announced, "Your brother was never like this!". . . . Luciana showed off her expansive Bel-Air mansion to HGTV in 2004. . . . When Luciana's character got killed on the dance floor in *Thunderball*, Bond set her down at a table and told the diners she'd sit this one out, "she's just dead."

Jacqueline Bisset

This British beauty played a Bond girl and memorable movie love interests for Frank Sinatra and Steve McQueen.

TAKIN' CARE OF BUSINESS

Jacqueline Bisset's got one of the most perfect faces in movies—a timeless look that transcends fashion, considered by no less than Steve McQueen to be the most beautiful actress he worked with. *Newsweek* agreed, naming her in '77 as the most beautiful actress, not just of the year, but *ever*. Standing over 5′ 6″, she was also curvy, leggy, and athletic (the rare triple), a great look revealed to stunning effect in '77's *The Deep,* by itself justification enough when *Playboy* ranked her #86 on its millennium list of the century's sexiest stars. More than just a pretty face, Jacqueline has been nominated for top acting honors (three Golden Globes and an Emmy) and has enjoyed a long screen career of over 60 movies.

She was born Winnifred Jacqueline Fraser-Bisset (that last pronounced BISS-et) in England. Working as a London model, she got a bit part in *The Knack . . . and How to Get It* ('65), which led to a burst of two films a year for the rest of the '60s. As Miss Goodthighs in the boisterous *Casino Royale* ('67) she had three minutes to simultaneously seduce and drug Peter Sellers, and in Audrey Hepburn's *Two for the Road* ('67) she was a memorable sexy-but-sick traveler. Jacqueline's part in *The Detective* ('68) was supposedly Mia Farrow's until Frank Sinatra, playing the shamus, told his young wife to am-scray. *The Sweet Ride* ('68) brought Jacqueline a Golden Globe nomination as the Most Promising Newcomer, while the Steve McQueen thriller *Bullitt* ('68) propelled her to stardom for the great decade to come.

The '70s got her off to a high-flyin' start with the role as Gwen, the sexy stew who had Dean Martin's love child in *Airport* ('70); that same year she received critical acclaim for her dramatic performance in *The Grasshopper*. Later roles in-

cluded *Day for Night* ('73), *The Deep* ('77) with its legendary wet T-shirt action, *The Greek Tycoon* ('78), *Class* ('83), and *Dangerous Beauty* ('98). Not just a gorgeous star, Jacqueline's also listed as producer of *Rich and Famous* ('81).

EVERYBODY LOVES SOMEBODY

Young and stunning, she was romantically linked to several '60s superstars, including Frank, Dean, Steve McQueen, Terence Stamp, and Marcello Mastroianni. In '68 she moved in with actor Michael Sarrazin, the shooter in *They Shoot Horses, Don't They?* ('69). For most of the '80s Jacqueline was with Alexander Godunov, the dancer who defected to the U.S. in '79 and died at age 46 in '95. In 2002 she told columnist Liz Smith why she never married: "I'm afraid if I married, I might become lazy about everything. I would start nagging. I nag enough as it is."

MY BACK PAGES

Jacqueline is Angelina Jolie's godmother. . . . "Miss Goodthighs" was one of three Bond characters with a "good" name: see also Holly Goodhead (Lois Chiles) in *Moonraker*, and Mary Goodnight (Britt Ekland) in *The Man with the Golden Gun*. . . . In an interview, Jacqueline said she disliked the name Goodthighs because it brought attention to what she felt were two of her weakest attributes. . . . In '99 Jacqueline reportedly had an audience with the Pope, who had enjoyed an advance screening of the Biblical movie *Jesus*, in which she played Mary.

Honor Blackman

A formidable film femme who starred in several '60s hits.

TAKIN' CARE OF BUSINESS

Long before *Goldfinger* was even a gleam in producer Cubby Broccoli's eye, London-born Honor Blackman was appearing in dozens of movies in the '40s and '50s, among them *A Night to Remember* ('58). British audiences also knew her as Mrs. Catherine Gale, karate-chopping leather-wearing partner to John Steed on the pre-Diana Rigg *The Avengers* TV series. Playing Cathy Gale, Honor was probably the first TV star to wear black leather clothes, often accessorizing with long leather boots while riding her motorcycle. *The Avengers* was so popular in England that Honor and Patrick Macnee, who played Steed, were deemed worthy to cut a single, "Kinky Boots"/"Let's Keep It Friendly," plus Honor did an album, *Everything I've Got,* but none of the records caused a ripple on the music seismograph.

March 6, 1944—Singer Mary Wilson is born in Detroit. ☮ March 6, 1964—Liz Taylor divorces for the fourth time; her latest ex- is singer Eddie Fisher.
March 6, 1964—Muhammad Ali makes the cover of *Life*. ☮ March 6, 1968—*Psych-Out* with Jack Nicholson opens.
March 7, 1947—Actress Donna Loren is born in Boston. ☮ March 7, 1967—Sandra Dee and Bobby Darin get divorced.

It didn't matter, though—she'd already decided to let her *Avengers* contract run out and go for the gold. *Goldfinger*, that is. This James Bond classic presented Honor at her peak as a sexy, assured aviatrix in command of five female pilots. Athletic, glamorous, beautiful, and smart, she was able to roughhouse successfully and believably with Bond, tossing him, and then falling for him, in the hay in Auric Goldfinger's barn. Her great riding outfit and jump suits all managed to show off her great figure (her measurements then were listed as 36-24-37). Her other big movie role was as Hera, Queen of the Gods, in Ray Harryhausen's *Jason and the Argonauts* ('63).

After the '60s, Honor worked in various screen projects throughout the '90s: the female lead in *The Age of Innocence* ('74), a regular role in the British TV series *The Upper Hand* ('90–'93), and the part of Joy Adamson in *To Walk with Lions* ('93). She also performed a one-woman show called *Dishonorable Ladies*. Versatile and durable, Honor Blackman is today regarded as something of an English national treasure.

EVERYBODY LOVES SOMEBODY

Honor was married to actor Maurice Kauffman from '61 to '75, she's got a daughter and a son, and entering the new millennium she was still single.

MY BACK PAGES

Avengers alums Honor, Diana Rigg, and Patrick Macnee all starred in Bond films—Diana in *On Her Majesty's Secret Service* ('69) and Patrick in *A View to a Kill* ('85). . . . When Honor left *The Avengers*, there was one post-Honor episode filmed where Steed's partner was played by actress Elizabeth Shepherd, but the producers weren't pleased with her portrayal, so Diana Rigg was quickly brought in, and the show zoomed to whole new levels of popularity. . . . Though "Kinky Boots" floundered when it was released in '64, astonishingly it resurfaced to became a Top 10 hit in the U.K. in '90.

Craig Breedlove

Nobody was faster on land in the '60s than this record-breaking innovator.

TAKIN' CARE OF BUSINESS

Craig Breedlove was a car kid with a need for speed. Born and raised in L.A., at 13 he bought his first car, at 16 he souped up a '34 Ford and got it to go over 150 MPH. After learning engineering skills at his Douglas Aircraft job, at 22 he bought a surplus jet engine, wrapped a three-wheeled bullet-shaped car around it, dubbed it *Spirit of America,* and four years later set a new land speed record of 407 MPH at Bonneville, Utah's famed Salt Flats. For the next three years he and Art Arfons, driving his *Green Monster,* traded the speed record back and forth, with Craig being the first man to take it to 400, then 500, then 600 MPH. Unfortunately, the run past 500 MPH in '64 ended disastrously when the steering, brakes, and chutes failed and the car rocketed into a pond at 200 MPH, though Craig escaped serious injury. In the '70s he set some distance records and worked on a new rocket car powered by the engine of a lunar module. Twenty years later, he was designing another *Spirit of America* iteration, this one with a

March 7, 1999—Director Stanley Kubrick dies in England. ☮ March 8, 1936—Actress Sue Ane Langdon is born.
March 8, 1943—Actress Lynn Redgrave is born in London. ☮ March 8, 1945—Micky Dolenz of the Monkees is born in L.A.
March 8, 1963—Actress Jean Seberg makes the cover of *Life*. ☮ March 9, 1942—John Cale of the Velvet Underground is born in Wales.

45,000 horsepower engine from a Navy F-4 Phantom jet that he hopes will go 800 MPH. He was inducted into the International Motorsports Hall of Fame in 2000.

EVERYBODY LOVES SOMEBODY

Smart, daring, handsome, and only 26, Craig Breedlove was a celebrity the moment he set his first speed record. Revered as a hero for bringing the speed record back to America (British drivers had held it for three decades), he went on national tours and talk shows. Craig's wife at the time, Lee, was also a driver at Bonneville, hitting 308 MPH in '65 for the women's record. Craig and Marilyn Breedlove now live in a converted car dealership in Northern California.

MY BACK PAGES

The '64 accident landed Craig in the *Guinness Book of World Records* for the longest skid marks (five miles). . . . One of the cameramen filming Craig's record runs in the '60s was young George Lucas, who was inspired to create the pod race sequences in *Star Wars: Episode I*. . . . Gary Gabelich broke Craig's record in '70 with his *Blue Flame*. . . . England's Andy Green currently holds the record, the supersonic 763 MPH, set in '97 in the *Thrust SSC*.

May Britt

The Swedish beauty who gave up her budding acting career for marriage to a rat-packin' entertainment legend.

TAKIN' CARE OF BUSINESS

This blonde Swede was a photographer's assistant when Carlo Ponti (Sophia Loren's mentor) discovered her in '52. After making several Italian films, May Britt's strong performances in World War II dramas *The Young Lions* ('58) and *The Hunters* ('58) brought her the lead in

the critically-pounded remake of Marlene Dietrich's *The Blue Angel* ('59). Forsaking showbiz for song-and-dance legend Sammy Davis, Jr., her only '60s movie was the well-received gangster saga *Murder, Inc.* ('60). After her marriage broke up in '66, May moved to L.A. and got some TV work, but an eight-year gulf between Hollywood projects was too much to overcome and the business passed her by. In 2001, she popped up in a *Parade* magazine story that said she's now a painter in L.A. and was declining offers to write about her ex-husband.

EVERYBODY LOVES SOMEBODY

May first got married in '58, followed by a "Mexican divorce" soon after. Sammy first met her in '59 at the studio commissary (she had to pronounce her name for him—"May," not "My"). He flew her and her mother to Vegas for a Rat Pack show at the Sands, they courted through '60 and announced their engagement that October. The marriage was set for early November, before the presidential election. When hate mail, bomb threats, protests, and cruel jokes greeted Sammy and May wherever they went, they postponed the wedding until after the election so as not to hurt Kennedy's chances (Sammy was a big supporter and didn't want to cost JFK critical votes in what became the tightest race in history).

After Sammy and May finally got married, Kennedy showed his thanks by inviting them to the January inaugural, but JFK's advisors convinced him to reconsider, even though Sammy was scheduled to perform and best friend Frank was organizing the gala (31 states still had laws preventing interracial marriage). Eight months after the wedding, May gave birth to a daughter; a few years later May and Sammy adopted two sons. The family lived in New York while Sammy starred on Broadway in *Golden Boy* in '65, but she basically raised the kids on her own. Announcing "Sammy, I love you but I hate our life," in '66 May moved the children to L.A. while Sammy stayed behind. In '68 she was granted a divorce and got custody of the three children.

MY BACK PAGES

Sammy's nickname for her was Peanuts, hers for him was Charlie Brown (the same nickname Mia Farrow had for Frank). . . . Though they were disinvited from JFK's inaugural, Sammy and May were invited to his funeral in '63.

Helen Gurley Brown

Though Helen Gurley Brown didn't invent sex, she sure made it more fun for generations of women.

TAKIN' CARE OF BUSINESS

Helen Gurley Brown is arguably one of the most influential women of the '60s, perhaps even the century. Since the early '60s she's been instructing, helping, advising, liberating, promoting, and cheering for women, giving them new role models and a new manual for the sexual revolution. Like many revolutionaries who seek out better lives and new worlds to conquer, she came from humble beginnings. She was born in Arkansas to parents who were both schoolteachers. Tragedy came early: Helen's father died in an accident when Helen was young, and her sister, a victim of polio, was an invalid at 19.

As a young working woman, Helen herself was the embodiment of the "mouseburger" she would later emancipate. Working as a secretary for a prominent ad agency in the '50s, she impressed her boss with her entertaining letters and was moved to the copywriting department. By the early '60s she was one of the country's highest-paid ad copywriters. Her big breakthrough came in '62 with the publication of *Sex and the Single Girl*, a bestseller

March 11, 1958—Actress Anissa Jones is born in West Lafayette, Indiana. ☮ March 11, 1966—Adam West makes the cover of *Life*. March 12, 1941—Actress Barbara Feldon is born in Butler, Pennsylvania. ☮ March 12, 1946—Actress Liza Minnelli is born in Hollywood. March 12, 1967—The Velvet Underground's debut album, *The Velvet Underground and Nico*, is released.

that became a Natalie Wood movie in '64.

She wrote three more advice books in the '60s, but more importantly she joined the editorial staff of *Cosmopolitan. Cosmo* in '65 was a struggling, underachieving literary magazine trying to find its voice in an era of rapid change. Helen seized the reins for the July '65 issue and, as editor in chief, immediately established *Cosmo* as a powerful advocate for women's sexual liberation. Suddenly women everywhere had a new best friend. *Cosmo* rooted endlessly and unconditionally for women, educated them with underlined insider information, encouraged self-analysis with monthly quizzes, offered them glamorous *Cosmo* girls to emulate, and (thanks to the newest birth-control technology, the Pill) encouraged them to take control of their sexual destinies. Gone was the old double standard that kept women virginal while men were predatory, replaced by frank discussions of how women could maximize their pleasure. Probably the closest parallel is Hugh Hefner, who did for men in the '50s what Helen was doing for women in the '60s, with equal passion and commitment.

For the next 32 years she continued at the magazine's helm, guiding it to spectacular circulation figures and making it the most successful woman's magazine ever. Stylish and witty and positively bubbling with spunky personality, she was a natural for talk shows and has been a frequent visitor to everything from *60 Minutes* to *Entertainment Tonight*. For awhile she had her own show on the Lifetime Network and her own weekly spot on *Good Morning America*. She's also continued to write books, following up her four '60s tomes with updated advice every decade.

In '97, Helen left the *Cosmo* office in New York to oversee the magazine's international editions, which now number 55. And she picked up awards, too. Among them are the 1996 American Society of Magazine Editors' Hall of Fame Award and the 1995 Henry Johnson Fisher Award from the Magazine Publishers of America (the first time this award was ever given to a woman). She was even declared a "living landmark" by New York's Landmark Commission. And as she always did, she still looks chic and sophisticated, poised and professional, a woman who instantly commands respect whether she's meeting with a famous writer or a pompous *maitre d'*. Mouseburger? Maverick. Marvelous!

EVERYBODY LOVES SOMEBODY

Talk about marrying well. Since the '50s Helen's been married to David Brown, the successful producer of big-time movies like *The Sting*, *Jaws*, and *Driving Miss Daisy*. What an ally—at his urging she wrote *Sex and the Single Girl* and took the *Cosmo* job. For over 30 years he even composed the coverlines that accompanied the sensational *Cosmo* cover photos. They've lived a fast-paced jet-set life together for five decades now.

MY BACK PAGES

One of the most famous *Cosmo* issues appeared in April '72 with Burt Reynolds as the first nude male pin-up (second was John Davidson). . . . Helen describes herself as a health nut, a feminist, a workaholic, and someone who's passionately interested in the man–woman relationship, which she has called "the most exciting, dramatic thing in the world."

Jim Brown

The NFL's baddest football player retired early to go Hollywood.

TAKIN' CARE OF BUSINESS

Fast. Nimble. Powerful. Jim Brown was the perfect running back. He's got the records and rep to prove it. Jim was born in Georgia, starred in five different sports at his Long Island high school, and was an All-American in football and lacrosse at Syracuse University. Playing for the Cleveland Browns from '57–'65, he led the NFL in rushing eight of his nine years, averaging over five yards per carry

March 12, 1969—Paul McCartney of the Beatles marries Linda Eastman. ☮ March 14, 1923—Photographer Diane Arbus is born. March 14, 1933—Actor Michael Caine is born in London. ☮ March 14, 1968—The last original episode of *Batman* airs. March 15, 1941—Mike Love of the Beach Boys is born in L.A. ☮ March 15, 1962—*The Day the Earth Caught Fire* with Janet Munro opens.

and scoring more touchdowns than any player before him. A Rookie of the Year and two-time MVP, he led the Browns to the NFL championship in '64. And tough? No one tackler could bring him down, and he missed exactly zero games during his career.

Stunningly, the game's all-time rushing leader decided to retire at only 30 years old, choosing film over football. He made a couple of key action movies in the '60s, *The Dirty Dozen* ('67, Jim's final dash was referenced worshipfully in *Sleepless in Seattle*) and the submarine spectacular *Ice Station Zebra* ('68). Some three-dozen films followed over the next three decades, usually with Jim in tough-guy roles—notably *The Running Man* ('87), *Mars Attacks!* ('96), and *Any Given Sunday* ('99). More importantly, he's worked for over 40 years to help solve difficult inner-city problems, co-founding the Negro Industrial Economic Union and establishing the Amer-I-Can program for troubled kids.

EVERYBODY LOVES SOMEBODY

The violent player has at times been in violent relationships—on at least four occasions women have accused him of some physical act, including tossing a model over a balcony, hitting his fiancée, and smashing his wife's car windows, though in most cases he was acquitted or the charges were dropped. He was married throughout the '60s with three kids, divorced in the '70s and remarried in the late '90s.

10 Legendary Running Backs

Mel Farr–
Detroit Lions, NFL Rookie of the Year '67

Cookie Gilchrist–
Buffalo Bills, AFL Player of the Year '62

Abner Haynes–
Dallas Texans, AFL Player of the Year '62

Calvin Hill–
Dallas Cowboys, NFL Rookie of the Year '69

Paul Hornung–Green Bay Packers, NFL MVP '61

Floyd Little–Denver Broncos, AFL All-Star '68

Lenny Moore–Baltimore Colts, NFL MVP '64

Johnny Roland–
St. Louis Cardinals, NFL Rookie of the Year '66

Gayle Sayers–
Chicago Bears, NFL Rookie of the Year '65

Jim Taylor–Green Bay Packers, MVP '62

MY BACK PAGES

Jim has been inducted into three Halls of Fame: pro and college football, and lacrosse. . . . On ESPN's millennium list of the greatest athletes ever, he was the highest-rated football player, coming in at #4 (behind Ali, ahead of Gretzky). . . . He posed nude for *Playgirl* in September, '74.

March 15, 1962—*No Strings* starring Diahann Carroll opens on Broadway.
March 15, 1964—The decade's most famous affair culminates in marriage for Richard Burton and Elizabeth Taylor.
March 16, 1961—Disney's *The Absent-Minded Professor* opens. ☮ March 16, 1966—*Gemini 8* lifts off.

Lenny Bruce

One of the most influential comics of all time, Lenny Bruce broke new ground before dying young.

TAKIN' CARE OF BUSINESS

Coming in ahead of Woody Allen on Comedy Central's list of great comics is Lenny Bruce. While not as well-known today as he was in the early '60s, he is still widely respected for breaking new ground in subject matter and vocabulary (today's edgiest comedians, such as Chris Rock and Sarah Silverman, are particularly indebted).

Born Leonard Alfred Schneider, he was in the Navy during World War II, then started doing impressions and jokes in small New York clubs. By the '60s, his act had evolved into searing riffs against racism, Fascism, censorship, religious hypocrisy, and any injustice in his path. He swore, he dressed casually (at least one show he did while wearing only a raincoat and socks), he grew a beard, and he got in the faces of the establishment, the Pope, and the police, all at a time when most comedians wore suits on stage and did clean-cut monologues about wacky relatives.

A triumphant Carnegie Hall show in '61 was followed by five years of legal trouble. Several times he was arrested on stage for his raw language, he was banned from clubs, and he was convicted of using obscenities. *Playboy* and the literati championed him as a hero of the First Amendment, but Lenny, bankrupt, depressed, and exhausted from court battles, couldn't sustain the fight. In '66, he died at age 40 from a drug overdose. A year later the Beatles paid him a hip tribute: they included his picture in the photo collage on the cover of their landmark *Sgt. Pepper's* album. Over the decades reissues of his old material (such as *The Sick Humor of Lenny Bruce*, '84) have helped re-introduce him to modern audiences. And today the words that got him sent to jail are heard regularly on cable TV.

EVERYBODY LOVES SOMEBODY

The love of Lenny's life was a stripper who worked under the name Honey Harlowe. Honey had already been in prison as a teen and had tried to make it as a nightclub singer when Lenny married her in '51. With uneven success he tried to incorporate her into his act. By '57 Lenny had a daughter, a pot bust, heroin problems, and a divorce. Honey remained his staunchest ally until her death in 2005.

MY BACK PAGES

Lenny's name has been invoked in songs by Bob Dylan, John Lennon, Paul Simon, R.E.M., and many others. . . . In '74 Bob Fosse's film *Lenny*, starring Dustin Hoffman and Valerie Perrine, was nominated for Best Picture, Best Actor, Best Actress, and Best Director at the Oscars. . . . In 2003 N.Y. Governor Pataki pardoned Lenny's 1964 obscenity conviction.

Michael Caine and Terence Stamp

Two gods of swingin' London.

TAKIN' CARE OF BUSINESS

They were two of the hottest, sexiest scenemakers in mid-'60s London, and they happened to make some pretty cool movies, too. The man now lauded as Sir Michael

March 16, 1968—Robert F. Kennedy announces he's running for president. ☮ March 16, 1968—Otis Redding's "Dock of the Bay" hits #1.
March 17, 1944—Model Pattie Boyd is born in Somerset, England. ☮ March 17, 1951—Actor Kurt Russell is born in Massachusetts.
March 17, 1966—Actress Julie Newmar debuts as Catwoman on *Batman*. ☮ March 17, 1966—*The Singing Nun* with Debbie Reynolds opens.

Caine was born Maurice Micklewhite into a working-class London family. After returning from Army service he changed his name (inspired by a marquee announcing Bogart's *The Caine Mutiny*) and started working his way up through the theatre ranks.

His breakthrough was *Zulu* ('64), in which he played a dignified stiff-upper-lipped British officer. That film made his name, but the next two made him a star: the spy thriller *The Ipcress File* ('65), in which he wore heavy black glasses, and the knowing comedy *Alfie* ('66), in which he endeared himself to viewers by speaking directly to them. Suddenly hot, and boosted by an *Alfie* Oscar nomination, he starred in an average of three movies a year from the mid-'60s into the mid-'70s, often playing rascals or military men; highlights included *Gambit* ('66), *The Battle of Britain* ('68), *Get Carter* ('71), *Sleuth* ('72, his second Oscar nomination), and *The Man Who Would Be King* ('75). So respected is he, the industry and audiences have shrugged off his flops (*Jaws: The Revenge*, '87) because his successes (*Hannah and Her Sisters* in '86, his first Oscar, and *The Cider House Rules* in '99, his second Oscar) have been so triumphant.

Terence Stamp

Meanwhile Michael's roommate for part of the '60s was another Londoner, Terence Stamp. An academy-trained dramatic actor, Terence burst onto the cinematic scene with dyed blonde hair in *Billy Budd* ('62), a powerful debut that brought him an Oscar nomination. Through the mid-'60s he was the handsome star of a number of significant British films, including William Wyler's disturbing *The Collector* ('65), Joseph Losey's spy comedy *Modesty Blaise* ('66) and John Schlesinger's melodrama *Far from the Madding Crowd* ('67), plus he worked for international masters Fellini and Pasolini. One role he was offered but rejected—*Alfie*, which he had already done on Broadway. One role he accepted but had taken away at the last minute—*Blow-Up*, with David Hemmings his replacement. After a long sabbatical that lasted into the '70s and took him around the world, including a stay at an ashram in India, Terence returned to acting with many memorable roles, among them the villainous General Zod in *Superman* ('78) and *Superman II* ('80) and tough guys in *Wall Street* ('87), *Young Guns* ('88) and *The Limey* ('94).

EVERYBODY LOVES SOMEBODY

Michael was married for three years in the '50s to actress Patricia Haines, with one child. He and Patricia met through their theatre work; she went on to appear in dozens of British TV shows, including *The Avengers*, in the '60s. When Michael was smitten upon seeing 1967's Miss Guyana in a TV commercial, he contacted her, and she became Shakira Caine in '73. Together they have one child. Shakira appeared as the beautiful Roxanne at the end of *The Man Who Would Be King*.

When actress Julie Christie was dating Terence Stamp in the early '60s, his London flatmate was Michael Caine. "It was like being with two blond gods of London," she told *Pre-*

miere in '98. Besides Julie, Terence was linked with several other goddesses of the '60s: Brigitte Bardot, Jacqueline Bisset, Peggy Lipton, and, especially, model Jean Shrimpton. Supposedly the end of this last relationship was one of the reasons he started his self-imposed exile from England and movies. His life as a bachelor ended when he finally married in 2002.

MY BACK PAGES

Michael has written two entertaining books about his life and movies, and he remains one of the most quotable of movie stars, as with this sample: "I have never seen [*Jaws: The Revenge*], but by all accounts it is terrible. However, I have seen the house that it built, and it is terrific". . . . He's also a successful restaurateur with a half-dozen brasseries in London and Miami. . . . Terence's younger brother Chris was the manager for the Who in the '60s. . . . *The Limey* included footage from Terence's earlier film *Poor Cow*, thus showing how his '94 character had looked in '67. . . . Though he played Supreme Chancellor Valorum in *The Phantom Menace* ('99), Terence turned down appearances in the next two *Star Wars* films. . . . Terence has written a three-volume autobiography and also a cookbook based on his line of wheat-free, dairy-free foods called the Stamp Collection.

Dyan Cannon

An alluring actress with a sexy charm, Dyan Cannon had one starring role that brought her international fame: Mrs. Cary Grant.

TAKIN' CARE OF BUSINESS

Born in Tacoma, Washington, Samile Diane Friesen had the high school nickname Frosty, was sometimes billed as Diane Friesen, and took her stage name from a producer who supposedly said, "You need a name that's explosive—Boom! Bang! Cannon!" Dyan's screen career began in the '50s when she appeared on *Playhouse 90* and in several TV Westerns. In the early '60s, she was in a few minor movies and TV shows, but by '62 she was already seeing Cary Grant, and her screen appearances came to a screeching halt in '64. After their bitter '68 divorce, she made a huge Hollywood splash in '69 as Alice in the controversial *Bob & Carol & Ted & Alice*. Dyan's disheveled sultriness made her look like one of the decade's wild things, with long blonde movie-star hair giving her a recklessly sexy style. In photos she also flashed a great bare midriff, revealing herself to be an honors graduate of the Navel Academy.

B&C&T&A brought her Oscar and Golden Globe nominations, positioning her for a long memorable screen career. She capitalized quickly on her sudden momentum with four movies in '71 alone and three dozen more by the end of the century. Highlights included another Golden Globe nomination for *Such Good Friends* ('71), another Oscar nomination for *Heaven Can Wait* ('78), *Deathtrap* ('82), and *Christmas in Connecticut* ('92). Proving herself to be a versatile talent, she's also written, produced, and directed her own projects, including the Oscar-nominated short *Number One* ('76) and the full-length autobiographical drama *The End of Innocence* ('91). Still a hard-workin' actress, she continued to make movies through the '90s and became a regular on TV's *Ally McBeal*. In a departure from her screen career, in the 2000s Dyan has hosted weekend Christian-fellowship meetings in Studio City, California.

EVERYBODY LOVES SOMEBODY

She was born in 1937 (according to most sources, though dates vary); Cary Grant was born in 1904. Thus was the fascination with their marriage, which was one of the most-discussed movie matches of the decade. They hooked up in '62, and Dyan was pregnant when they were married three years later at the Desert Inn in Vegas. Daughter Jennifer was born seven months later, but for Dyan and Cary problems and dif-

March 18, 2001—John Phillips of the Mamas and the Papas dies of heart failure in L.A. ☮ March 19, 1928—Actor Patrick McGoohan is born in New York. March 19, 1936—Actress Ursula Andress is born in Berne, Switzerland. ☮ March 19, 1945—Lisa Baker, Playmate of the Year for '67, is born in Texas. March 20, 1964—*The Pink Panther* with Capucine opens in wide release.

ferences already existed. The union would last only 32 months. He got physical with her, as she charged in their divorce hearing, for reasons as insignificant as her wearing a miniskirt. For years they continued to tangle over their daughter, and it took Primal Therapy for Dyan to recover. Long after they were divorced, she said, "If I'd stayed in that marriage I'd be dead today, dead, dead, dead, dead, really dead, in a grave, dead." Dyan married again in '85, but that ended in divorce in '91, and today she's single and living in West Hollywood.

MY BACK PAGES

Jennifer Grant is an actress and played Celeste on *Beverly Hills 90210*. . . . Dyan's also deeply involved with Operation Lookout, an organization that helps locate kidnapped children. . . . According to oxygen.com, Dyan bounces on a trampoline at night to help get to sleep. . . . There's one other regular role Dyan plays on TV, though this one is in real life: after Jack Nicholson, she's the second-most-visible L.A. Lakers fan.

Truman Capote

This Southern literary genius and social-climbing jet-setter penned bestselling novels and threw the decade's biggest party.

TAKIN' CARE OF BUSINESS

Truman Capote knew his impact: "There's never been anybody like me," he once told a biographer, "and after I'm gone there ain't ever gonna be anybody like me again." He was right. In '65 Truman revolutionized 20th-century literature with his "nonfiction novel," *In Cold Blood.* The subject was the senseless murder of the Clutter family on a Kansas farm in '59. Between the capture of the two killers and their deaths in '65, Truman stayed in Holcomb, Kansas for long stretches, conducted hundreds of interviews, compiled 6,000 pages of notes, and then attended the executions. *The New Yorker* published chapters of In *Cold Blood* in '65, and the completed book came out later that same year, quickly becoming a bestseller and one of the landmarks of modern nonfiction (it was made into a startling black-and-white film in '67).

But even if he'd never written *In Cold Blood,* Truman still would've been one of the titans of the '60s. Early in the decade he was riding high on the success of his novella *Breakfast at Tiffany's,* which became a charming Blake Edwards/Audrey Hepburn movie in '61. After the monumental success of *In Cold Blood,* Truman starred in the documentary *A Visit with Truman Capote* in '66 and then semi-retired to live off his fame. Capitalizing on his connections and status, Truman pulled off the decade's most memorable party, the infamous, exclusive, legendary Black and White Ball at Manhattan's Plaza Hotel in '66.

Thrown for *Washington Post* publisher Katherine Graham, the party started at 10 PM and lasted until breakfast. Among the hundreds of stars in attendance—all wearing the requisite exotic masks—were his "swans" (the elegant ladies he socialized with), plus Frank Sinatra and Mia Farrow, George Plimpton, model Penelope Tree, Walter Cronkite, Candice Bergen, Joan Fontaine, and Tallulah Bankhead. "An extraordinary thing in its way," commented Truman later, "but as far as I was concerned it was just a private party and nobody's business." *The New York Times* disagreed and published his entire guest list.

Such social success was quite an accomplishment for someone with his humble beginnings. He was born Truman Streckfus Persons in New Orleans, his dad a con man frequently in trouble. When his mom got divorced and split for New York, Truman was raised by an Alabama aunt near where Harper Lee (*To Kill a Mockingbird*) grew up (that book's summer visitor, Dil, was supposedly based on Truman). When his mom remarried, 8-year-old Truman went to live with her in Manhattan and took her new last name, Capote.

March 20, 1968—"The Forget-Me-Knot," Diana Rigg's, and Emma Peel's, last episode of *The Avengers*, airs in the U.S.
March 20, 1969—John Lennon and Yoko Ono get married in Gibraltar.
March 20, 1969—The Chicago Eight are indicted after arrests at the Democratic Convention.

In '42 Truman got his first job as a copy boy at *The New Yorker*, he got his first story published in *Mademoiselle* in '45, and in '47 *Life* profiled him as an up-and-coming writer. His first novel, the gothic *Other Voices Other Rooms* ('48), was one of the first to deal with gay themes, but it was more famous for the provocative back-cover photo of precocious Truman reclining invitingly on a couch.

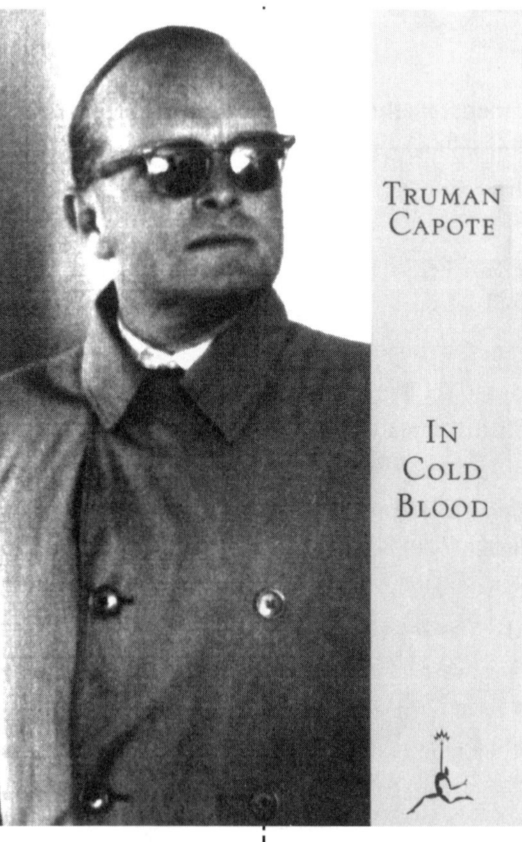

An influential and prominent member of the gay community in the '50s, Truman hob-nobbed with the rich and famous through the Eisenhower years as a 5′ 3″ "boy wonder" who always knew the latest gossip. His breakthrough work, *Breakfast at Tiffany's*, was published in '58, and the next year Truman began researching *In Cold Blood*. After the '60s, Truman spent many nights hanging with Andy Warhol, Liza Minnelli, and the whole Studio 54 crowd.

Meanwhile his older, established jet-set friends, angry that he was writing about them in his ever-forthcoming but never-finished tell-all book, *Answered Prayers*, ostracized him as a "tiny terror" and excluded him from their society events. He did take on an acting role, receiving a Golden Globe nomination for *Murder by Death* ('76), but he disparaged his skill and said he had no real desire to act. Unfortunately, Truman's continued drinking and drug-taking became public knowledge when he was arrested for drunk driving in '76; two years later he made a rambling, incoherent appearance on live TV, the beautiful boy of the '40s now barely recognizable. In '82 doctors told him his brain was shrinking and gave him six months to live. "Sometimes oblivion is a nice place to be" he said before he died from prolonged alcohol/drug abuse in '84.

EVERYBODY LOVES SOMEBODY

Truman never tried to hide his homosexuality or lavish tastes—a person's style was "simply there," he said, "like the color of your eyes." He traveled with royalty, vacationed with the social elite, and partied with Hollywood legends (even though he claimed that "in California you lose a point off your I.Q. every year"). In private, he had a 35-year relationship with another writer, Jack Dunphy, whom he had met in '48. They lived together in New York, Switzerland, and in the Hamptons (*Breakfast at Tiffany's* was dedicated to Dunphy).

MY BACK PAGES

Truman's quick wit: on *The Tonight Show* he said a man had once dropped his pants and asked for an autograph right *there*—Truman calmly told him he didn't think it was big enough to autograph, but perhaps he could *initial* it. . . . In *Music for Chameleons* Truman named some of the things he could do—ski, skateboard, tap dance, and shoot a pistol accurately. . . . He also listed some of the things he couldn't do—recite the alphabet, do anything mathematical, read a prepared speech. . . . The phrase Truman thought should be inscribed on his tombstone: "I tried to get out of it, but I couldn't". . . . Some of Truman's ashes were scattered over a Long Island lake, the rest are in the same Westwood, California mausoleum where Marilyn Monroe is interred.

March 21, 1966—"Land of a 1000 Dances" by Wilson Pickett hits #1. ☮ March 21, 1967—*Thoroughly Modern Millie* with Mary Tyler Moore opens.
March 21, 1968—Dyan Cannon and Cary Grant get divorced after less than three years of marriage.
March 22, 1931—Actor William Shatner is born in Canada. ☮ March 22, 1933—Actress May Britt is born in Sweden.

Capucine

This exotic, regal French beauty rose from the modeling ranks to star with some of Hollywood's top leading men in the first half of the '60s.

TAKIN' CARE OF BUSINESS

As an actress, Capucine was usually someone to watch rather than hear, and the film industry usually asked her just to look her parts rather than act them. After leaving her hometown in France for Paris when she was 17, Germain Lefebvre worked as a model through the early '50s. She had, according to *Cosmo* editor Helen Gurley Brown, "a face that was caressed by angels," and by '56 the 25-year-old Germain was a top fashion model for Givenchy. In '57 she headed for America to conquer New York, was soon spotted by a Hollywood agent, and was whisked westward for a studio screen test.

Using a stage name taken from the French word for a nasturtium, Capucine (pronounced CAP-oo-seen) made her Hollywood debut in the Oscar-winning biopic about composer Franz Liszt, *Song Without End* ('60). Her role as a princess in that movie set a royal precedent that would repeat several times in her career: she played Princess Dominique in *The Honey Pot* ('67), and Lady Litton in two *Pink Panther* sequels, *Trail of . . .* ('82) and *Curse of . . .* ('83). Among her '60s highlights were the John Wayne Western *North to Alaska* ('60), the William Holden African melodrama *The Lion* ('62), the bordello curiosity *Walk on the Wild Side* ('62, in which Capucine was romantically pursued by Barbara Stanwyck), the Peter Sellers comedy *The Pink Panther* ('63, Capucine played Clouseau's wife), and the Woody Allen-scripted *What's New, Pussycat?* ('65).

Despite this early promise, her Hollywood career never really took off, and by the late '60s she was back in Europe making foreign-language films with less frequency. Of her later work, only Fellini's *Satyricon* ('69) and Joan Collins' *Sins* TV mini-series ('86) will stand out for most American viewers. Broke, alone, and chronically depressed, 59-year-old Capucine threw herself out of an eighth-floor window in Lausanne, Switzerland in '90.

EVERYBODY LOVES SOMEBODY

Much about Capucine's private life remains a mystery. In '50 she married a French actor for seven months, and after they divorced she never married again. In the early '60s, she had a passionate two-year affair with Hollywood legend William Holden, who was already married. When Holden died in '81, he supposedly left Capucine $50,000 in his will (some say she was also mentioned in the wills of Peter Sellers and studio chief Darryl Zanuck). Throughout her career, Capucine was rumored to be homosexual, bisexual, or even transsexual. Quotes from Capucine herself—"I used to think I needed a man to define myself; no more"—fueled persistent speculations. In Paris in the mid-'70s she took a male lover who was only half her age, but after a few years they broke up, and she moved to Switzerland. A year after her suicide the young lover she'd known in Paris also killed himself.

MY BACK PAGES

In '52 she worked for two weeks doing fashion shows on board a French cruise ship—her cabinmate was 17-year-old dancer Brigitte Bardot. . . . In *The Pink Panther,* there's a bubble-bath scene that used a sudsing agent so strong it burned Capucine and Robert Wagner's skin, and he was reportedly blinded for almost a month.

Claudia Cardinale

The Italian version of Brigitte Bardot gained international stardom with several classic movies.

TAKIN' CARE OF BUSINESS

While she's not a household name in most American households (unless there's a Cardinale living in it), Claudia Cardinale has enjoyed a 40-year career that includes over 90 films with some of the world's greatest directors, legendary names like Luchino Visconti, Abel Gance, Federico Fellini, and Sergio Leone. Unfortunately, most American moviegoers probably couldn't pronounce most of the titles of her movies.

When she was voted the Most Beautiful Girl in Tunisia in '57, Claudia won a trip to the Venice Film Festival, and acting became her life, she made dozens of Italian movies in the late '50s. Her American breakthrough came with her role as the fantasy girl in Fellini's *8½* ('63), with Visconti's *The Leopard* that same year and Blake Edwards's *The Pink Panther* ('64) establishing her as a rising talent with international appeal.

To Americans, she might've been too similar to other classy well-tanned European hourglasses such as Sophia Loren to distinguish herself, but to international audiences she was one of the world's most beautiful and popular actresses, as verified by all the awards she won in the first half of the decade, including Italy's top movie award in '62, the European *Prix Orange* for popularity in '64, and France's Best Foreign Actress award in '64 and '65.

A sexy pantheress, Claudia's dark smoldering beauty and 37-22-36 measurements translated into any language, which is why she could star in French, Spanish, Italian, German, and American movies (who doesn't know what "Wow!" means?). So universal was her appeal that since '58 she's graced almost 900 magazine covers in over two dozen different countries.

In the second half of the '60s, she made some marvelous English-language films—especially the rugged *The Professionals* ('66) and Leone's epic *Once Upon a Time in the West* ('69)—that cemented her image stateside as a stunning star. Her look changed movie by movie: for elegant roles she would wear her long hair up (as in *8½*, where she was a sultry vision in white), for some of her movies her hair was cut short, and then for playful movies she would let it wrangle and tangle so it looked like she'd just rolled out of bed.

Her career continued in later decades, punctuated by *Escape to Athena* ('79), Werner Herzog's artsy *Fitzcarraldo* ('82), TV movies like *Princess Daisy* ('83), and the feeble *Son of the Pink Panther* ('93), with still more in the 2000s. None was a classic by itself, but taken together with her '60s work they all add up to an impressive *oeuvre,* and in '99 Italy presented her with its Rudolph Valentino Lifetime Achievement Award.

March 25, 1942—Singer Aretha Franklin is born in Memphis. ☮ March 25, 1954—Audrey Hepburn wins the Best Actress Oscar (*Roman Holiday*).
March 25, 1964—Disney's *The Misadventures of Merlin Jones* with Tommy Kirk opens.
March 25, 1964—*Muscle Beach Party* with Frankie Avalon opens. ☮ March 25, 1967—"Somethin' Stupid" by Frank and Nancy Sinatra hits the charts.

EVERYBODY LOVES SOMEBODY

At 19 Claudia had a son, but because the child was the product of a rape, the father was never named, and for years Claudia presented her son as her younger brother. Early in her career she was guided by producer Franco Cristaldi, who was 15 years her senior. As Vadim had done a decade before with Bardot, Cristaldi reshaped Claudia's image and took her from a novice actress to a major international sex symbol. They married in '66, divorced in '75, and he died in '92. Later she took up with, but didn't marry, an Italian film director and had a daughter.

MY BACK PAGES

Quadrilingual, she can speak French, Italian, English, and Spanish, and even a little Arabic. . . . In '66 she appeared, unidentified, in the foldout of the first edition of Bob Dylan's classic *Blonde on Blonde* album, but she didn't appear in subsequent editions, with no explanation as to why she was in there or why she was removed. . . . Claudia made waves in the '60s when she wore a miniskirt for a meeting—with the Pope!

Corky Carroll

The world's most famous surfer of the late '60s.

TAKIN' CARE OF BUSINESS

Orange County preteen Charles Curtis Carroll was surfing just as the sport's "Golden Age" was dawning. The '50s were becoming the '60s, and surf music and surf movies were igniting a surf craze that would draw millions of enthusiasts to the California coast. After 16-year-old Corky took the national junior title in '63, the rising star was signed to surfing's first endorsement deal. Riding longboards in the first half of the decade and short boards towards the end, Corky claimed over 100 championships, including world titles for both big waves and small waves.

In '66, Bruce Brown's epic *The Endless Summer* brought a new wave of attention to the sport, and in '68 Corky won his most glamorous crown yet when a '68 *Surfer* magazine poll anointed him the world's best surfer. Retiring at only 24, Corky started recording beach-themed albums in the '70s, getting a gold record for "Tan Punks on Boards" in '80 and a decent-selling album, *A Surfer for President*, that promoted his brief presidential bid. Another dozen or so albums followed into the 21st century, plus diverse careers as a tennis pro, ski instructor, bartender, developer of his own surfwear line, and author. Now a member of the Surfing Hall of Fame, he currently owns two eponymous surf schools and sells Huntington Beach real estate.

10 Surf Stars

Bruce Brown–
Made (and narrated) *The Endless Summer,* '66

Dick Dale–"King of the Surf Guitar"

Mickey Dora–
Did the surf stunts in many teen surf movies

Joyce Hoffman–Trail-blazing surf queen, voted world's best in '66

Mike Hynson–With Robert August, stars of *The Endless Summer*

Greg Noll–Big-wave king, caught biggest wave in history, '69

Jack O'Neill–Pioneered wetsuits and surf shops

John Severson–Surfer, artist, photographer, founder of *Surfer* magazine

The Surfaris–Prolific guitars/sax/drum group with hit "Wipeout," '63

Dewey Weber–
Most popular surfboard manufacturer

EVERYBODY LOVES SOMEBODY

Early marriage and a son; Corky lives with his current wife and daughter in Huntington Beach, California (with another beachfront home in Ixtapa, Mexico).

MY BACK PAGES

TV audiences first saw Corky as a young panelist on *What's My Line* in '67—years later everybody knew his line when he did some popular beer commercials. . . . He told an interviewer his likely epitaph: "Died laughing (probably at himself)."

Diahann Carroll

This classy actress/singer dazzled the Broadway critics and then won over TV audiences with a groundbreaking sitcom.

TAKIN' CARE OF BUSINESS

Before she was Julia, Diahann Carroll was a musical star. A Bronx-born student at New York's distinguished High School of Music and Art and then at NYU, she was working as a part-time model and nightclub singer when she made her movie debut as one of Dorothy Dandridge's sidekicks in the musical *Carmen Jones* ('54). After earning a Tony nomination for *House of Flowers* in '54, Diahann returned to Hollywood and made another musical, *Porgy and Bess* ('59), followed by the jazzy *Paris Blues* ('61).

On Broadway in '62 she won a Tony Award for the musical *No Strings*, then an Emmy nomination for a '63 appearance on *Naked City* and a couple of solid movie dramas set her up for *Julia* ('68–'71). The first show to star an African-American actress, the gentle comedy/ drama injected reality into the otherwise lightweight primetime network TV shows. The top 40 Nielsen-rated shows of the '68–'69 season included such nutty comedies as *Bewitched*, *Green Acres*, and *Here's Lucy*; *Julia* countered all this slapstick with the story of a single mom whose husband had been killed in 'Nam.

Nothing especially powerful happened on the show (Diahann herself said it was only "slightly controversial"), but it was pleasing and polished, and it finished in the top 10 of the '68–'69 ratings, with Diahann winning Golden Globe and Emmy nominations. What's more, her character was popular enough to generate a line of dolls in her image, Mattel's Talking Julia. During this time Diahann continued to pursue her musical career with several big Vegas engagements. After *Julia* left the air in '71, Diahann returned to films and starred in *Claudine* ('74), earning an Oscar nomination for her portrayal of a welfare mom with six kids. *The Diahann Carroll Show* ran for one season in '76, followed by *I Know Why the Caged Bird Sings* in '79.

The next decades brought lots of TV shows and TV movies, among them a glamorous three years on *Dynasty* in the late '80s, an Emmy-nominated guest appearance on *A Different World* in '89, and *The Court* in 2002. She also found time to write an honest, insightful autobiography, *Diahann!* Still making music, she has now released over a dozen albums; still making musicals, in the mid-'90s she played Norma Desmond in *Sunset Boulevard*; and still blazing trails, in '97 she became the first African-American woman with her own line of wigs, clothes, lingerie, and accessories. Happily, in '97 she won a much-publicized fight against breast cancer, yet another triumph that would inspire others.

EVERYBODY LOVES SOMEBODY

"I'm always getting involved in the wrong relationship," Diahann said in a TV bio, "I do that very well." In '59, while they were both making *Porgy and Bess*, Diahann and Sidney Poitier fell in love. Both of them were married at the time, she since '56 to a Broadway casting director, with a daughter born in '60. In '61 Diahann and Sidney told their spouses of their relationship, by '64 Diahann and Sidney were each divorced and engaged to each other, but four years later they

March 27, 1963—*Come Fly with Me* with Dolores Hart opens. ☮ March 27, 1965—The Supremes' "Stop! In the Name of Love" hits #1.
March 28, 1963—*The Birds* with Tippi Hedren opens. ☮ March 28, 1964—"Stay Awhile" by Dusty Springfield hits the charts.
March 28, 1966—*The Avengers* debuts in the U.S. ☮ March 29, 1916—Senator Eugene McCarthy is born in Minnesota.

broke up. Diahann wrote that the split represented her maturation into a strong adult. She got engaged to interviewer David Frost in '72 but called it off the following February. Within two weeks, Diahann married a Vegas businessman, then divorced him that summer. She married again in '75, this time to a man who was about 15 years her junior. Their troubled union ended two years later when he died in a car accident. Late in the '80s Diahann married singer Vic Damone, and together they performed a stage act before divorcing in '96.

MY BACK PAGES

Her real name is Carol Diahann Johnson, changed at 16 at an audition. . . . In the late '60s Diahann dressed glamorously, made several "best-dressed" lists, and was a much-photographed target of the paparazzi. . . . Unfortunately, the stress of shooting *Julia* took a toll on her, causing her weight to drop under 100 pounds and twice sending her to the hospital, but she bounced back more glamorous and beautiful than ever. . . . "All I ever wanted to do was sing," wrote Diahann in her book, "what happened was more."

Johnny Carson

The King of Late Night reigned with *The Tonight Show.*

TAKIN' CARE OF BUSINESS

Surely Carnac the Magnificent predicted this: it's been about 15 years since his last show, and more than two years since he passed away, yet much of America probably still expects to see him at 11:30 each weeknight. That's how entrenched Johnny Carson is in the national memory. His three-decade run on *The Tonight Show* established him as one of the most beloved entertainers in history—his show is still the standard other talk shows are measured against, and the catch phrases ("I did not know that," "How hot was it," "Heeeeere's Johnny!") still bring affectionate smiles.

Johnny's pre-'60s career had an all-American quality to it: his Iowa birth, Nebraska upraising, "Great Carsoni" magic act as a teen, the mid-'40s Navy years, the early radio jobs, and the '50s gigs hosting various TV quiz shows and talk shows. He was paired with announcer Ed McMahon for the first time on a game show called *Who Do You Trust?* in '57; a year later Johnny substituted for Jack Paar on NBC's *The Tonight Show* (Paar himself had replaced Steve Allen).

When censorship controversy drove Paar to leave, Johnny took over full-time in '62—the band played his new theme song (which he co-wrote with Paul Anka), Groucho Marx handled the first TV intro, and Johnny's first words were a joke about the Vice-President. Throughout the decade, Johnny was on five nights a week (in '72 he switched to four nights, with guest hosts on Mondays), and shows usually lasted for 90 minutes (in '80 he cut the show to an hour). The '60s broadcast originated in New York (the move to Burbank came in '72), with Skitch Henderson the bandleader until he left in '67, to be followed by the flamboyantly dressed trumpeter Doc Severinsen.

Some of the most famous TV moments of all time oc-

March 29, 1944—Pitcher Denny McLain is born. ☮ March 29, 1962—*State Fair* with Ann-Margret opens.
March 29, 1968—Actress Jane Fonda makes the cover of *Life*. ☮ March 29, 1985—The Singing Nun commits suicide in Belgium at age 52.
March 30, 1930—Actor John Astin is born in Baltimore, Maryland. ☮ March 30, 1937—Actor Warren Beatty is born in Richmond, Virginia.

curred on *The Tonight Show* during the '60s—Ed Ames throwing a tomahawk into the groin of a wooden cutout, and Tiny Tim's live wedding, to name two. Young comedians (Woody Allen, Joan Rivers, Flip Wilson) did their routines, Hollywood stars stopped by to chat and sip drinks, musicians performed, animals clowned, and kids charmed. Johnny was always affable, quick-witted Johnny, relaxed enough to smoke during interviews, nattily dressed to match the times (remember the huge ties and Nehru jackets?), able to gently tease Ed and current leaders without being cruel, and allying himself with the audience when the jokes bombed (as they often did, but his escape was always better anyway).

Within 10 years of starting on the show Johnny was the highest-paid TV star in history. Outside of *The Tonight Show*, Johnny wrote a memoir, *Happiness Is a Dry Martini*, in '65, and that same year he emceed a Rat Pack show in St. Louis when regular emcee Joey Bishop was injured. He also made other '60s screen appearances, among them the Connie Francis musical *Looking for Love* ('64), game shows like *The Match Game*, a *Get Smart* episode, and a half-dozen quickies on *Laugh-In*.

But always there was his late-night kingdom, and so closely was he identified with his program that many people called it "The Johnny Carson Show," or simply "Johnny." After 5,000 shows and over 23,000 guests, his final appearance in '92, which everyone knew was coming because he'd given a year's notice, brought tears; his death from emphysema in 2005, which came with no warning, brought shock and grief as the public dealt with the loss of a cherished lifelong friend.

EVERYBODY LOVES SOMEBODY

Since his relationships were tracked in the tabloids anyway, Johnny's marital travails occasionally surfaced as comedy material on the show. He was married four times, three of them to women with similar names. Joan, his wife from '49–'63, was his college sweetheart. They had three kids, one of whom was killed in a car wreck. After their divorce he married Joanne, whom he divorced in '72. That same year he married Joanna secretly, but their expensive '85 divorce was very public. His fourth wife, Alexis, was with him from '87 until his death.

MY BACK PAGES

By far the most frequent guest host when Johnny was away: Rat Packer Joey Bishop (177 times). . . . In the '80s Joan Rivers and then Jay Leno had long stints as permanent guest hosts, then Jay took over after Johnny retired. . . . Johnny's hobbies—magic, drums, astronomy, tennis, sailing. . . . During the '60s he got no Emmy recognition, but from the mid-'70s onward he was an Emmy fixture with a dozen nominations, five wins, and a Governor's Award. . . . He was inducted into TV's Hall of Fame in '87, then won the Presidential Medal of Freedom in '92 and the Kennedy Center Lifetime Achievement Award in '93. . . . Unfortunately, most of the tapes of Johnny's first 10 years on *The Tonight Show* were accidentally destroyed by NBC, so as of '72 Johnny made sure that master tapes were saved of every show, and they're now stored in an earthquake-proof, fireproof, climate-controlled Kansas salt mine.

Johnny Cash

Professionally and personally, the Man in Black had a rocky but ultimately successful '60s.

TAKIN' CARE OF BUSINESS

"Johnny Cash was more like a religious figure to me," said Bob Dylan in 2005. "Just the fact he'd sing one of my songs was unthinkable." Such was Johnny Cash's impact on other great musicians. However, the '60s were turbulent years for Johnny, and he wore the experiences all over his craggy, handsome face. He came into the decade having overcome tragedy (the terrible, bloody death of his older brother when Johnny was only 12) and struggle (for years he had worked the cotton fields of his family's Arkansas farm) to establish himself in the mid-'50s as a star of country music.

Recording in Memphis for Sun Records, his hits included a song he'd written while serving in the Air Force in the early '50s ("Folsom Prison Blues") and an ode to fidelity written to calm his nervous wife who worried about his on-tour behavior ("I Walk the Line"). Switching to Columbia Records, more classics, and bold musical experiments, would pepper his '60s as he released an average of three albums every year. "Ring of Fire" and "A Boy Named Sue" were just two of his radio hits during the decade; his raw live albums recorded at Folsom and San Quentin prisons were huge bestsellers, and several departure albums that included his spoken narration and protest songs showed him to be an authentic, important artist. In '69, he even had his own network show.

Unfortunately, while his career was soaring, demons were dragging him into a personal hell. Alcohol and amphetamines were ruining his personal life, culminating in '65 with a drug bust in El Paso and banishment from the Grand Ole Opry after a frenzied, destructive episode there. Troubles piled up quickly—his decade-long marriage ended, one of the longtime members of his band died in a fire, he grappled with depression and detox, and he had to pay a huge fine for accidentally setting fire to a large section of California wilderness and wiping out 80% of the endangered condor population.

A religious epiphany while alone in a Tennessee cave in '67 and marriage to June Carter in '68 brought new purpose and clarity to his life, and many of his later songs and appearances became more spiritual. Though he lost favor with younger listeners and Columbia Records, he also found success in the '80s and early '90s recording and touring with Kris Kristofferson, Waylon Jennings, and Willie Nelson as the rough-hewn Highwaymen. Another bout with addiction, this time to prescription painkillers, sent him to the Betty Ford Clinic in the '80s.

For decades he was a sturdy actor in movies and on TV, often playing outlaws: *A Gunfight*, '71, plus a recurring role on *Dr. Quinn, Medicine Woman*, dozens of appearances in documentaries and specials, and the role of a baritone coyote on *The Simpsons* in '97. The '90s generated awards and acclaim—his two albums, *American Recordings* and *Unchained,* both won Grammys (he also received two career-achievement Grammys this decade), the Kennedy Center honored him in '96, and modern stars acknowledged their profound debt to the man and the massive catalog of songs that spanned genres and styles.

One of the century's most influential performers, in '80 Johnny was inducted into the Country Music Hall of Fame—at the time he was the youngest living member. When he was inducted into the Rock and Roll Hall of Fame in '92, he was one of only a handful of superstars who were members of both Halls.

EVERYBODY LOVES SOMEBODY

Johnny Cash was a man who knew personal triumphs and pain. Married in '54, he had two kids at home (one of whom, Roseanne, later became famous as a singer) when he met singer June Carter in '56; according to legend he introduced himself by announcing he was going to marry her, even though she was already married. They toured together and courted all through the '60s as June got divorced and married again. After Johnny's wife filed for divorce in '66, he proposed to June during the middle of a concert and they finally married in '68, with a son, singer John Carter Cash, born in '70. For the rest of their lives they performed together and stayed passionate partners and best friends. They died within four months of each other in 2003, she after heart surgery, he from diabetes.

MY BACK PAGES

While he had an outlaw image as someone who'd done hard time, Johnny never did go to prison, though he did get arrested several times. . . . Running for two years, Johnny's '69 TV show featured many prominent musical guests, including the Monkees, Cass Elliot, Eric Clapton, Merle Haggard, Liza Minnelli, and Bob Dylan. . . . Johnny penned Grammy-winning liner notes for Dylan's *Nashville Skyline* LP in '69 and sang on the album. . . . Johnny wrote two popular autobiographies and a novel, *Man in White* ('86). . . . Johnny's black clothes—originally they were worn to match the outfits of the Tennessee Two, but later he wore them to remind audiences of how hard life is for many people.

Catwomen

Three cat-tastic actresses played Batman's coolest villainess.

TAKIN' CARE OF BUSINESS

Sexy and smart and unrelentingly evil, the Catwoman character brought some grown-up sexual intrigue to the otherwise cartoony Batman universe. Most of the other Batvillains were absurd males (the Joker, the Riddler, the Bookworm, etc.), but the slinky Catwoman added a whole new dimension because she was often trying to seduce Batman as much as defeat him.

In the '60s three actresses donned the tight catsuit, two on TV and one in the *Batman* movie ('66), starting with L.A.'s Julie Newmar. This graceful goddess brought style, glamour, and nimble comedic skills to dozens of shows and movies. After studying ballet and graduating high school at only 15, Julie started getting dance parts in various '50s films; *Li'l Abner* ('59) presented her as the show-stoppin' Stupefyin' Jones. She was also starring on Broadway during the '50s as the Tony-winning bombshell in *The Marriage-Go-Round*.

In the '60s, she was a welcome and reliable TV presence who stole any sitcom she was on. *My Living Doll* ('64–'65) was her one-season wonder where she played a lifelike robot; Julie was nominated for a Golden Globe as the year's Best TV Star, poising her for the part that would send fans into a feline frenzy. When negotiations with Suzanne Pleshette

Julie Newmar

April 1, 1939—Actress Ali MacGraw is born in Pound Ridge, New York. ☮ April 1, 1961—"Runaway" by Del Shannon hits #1.
April 1, 1963—*The Doctors* and *General Hospital* both debut. ☮ April 1, 1966—Actress Sophia Loren makes the cover of *Life*.
April 1, 1968—"Stand by Your Man" and "D-I-V-O-R-C-E" by Tammy Wynette are released. ☮ April 1, 1969—*Sweet Charity* with Shirley MacLaine opens.

broke down, Julie was offered the part of the Catwoman on *Batman*, the month-old hit that Julie herself hadn't ever seen.

In '66 she made the first of a dozen co-starring appearances as the purr-fect foil to the Caped Crusader. Always humorous (whether she won or lost a battle on the show), always using her flexible voice to great advantage, Julie seemed to be having the best time of anyone in any given episode. Her look established once and for all the stereotype of the female super-villain. A lithe 5′ 10″ tall, with 38-23-38 curves, she radiated an intimidating sexuality in her black vinyl with the zipper up the back, her belt slung low across her hips. Fans will recall that for a few episodes she had an assistant named Pussycat, played by Lesley Gore, who sang the huge hit "It's My Party" in '63. Midway into the second season Julie left *Batman* to make the Gregory Peck Western *Mackenna's Gold* ('69).

After the '60s she made many TV appearances, plus a dozen minor movies, and she also toured in major musicals. Additional credits on her long résumé include ads and TV commercials (in the late '60s she was a sensuous Mother Nature for Dutch Masters cigars), poses on several romantic album covers, the creation in the '70s of her own line of pantyhose (Nudemar), and success in real estate. Her cult immortality was confirmed when she was deified in *To Wong Foo, Thanks for Everything, Julie Newmar* ('95).

Julie's replacement on *Batman* was South Carolinian Eartha Kitt, who had worked her way up from poverty to become a '50s cabaret star in Europe. An exciting entertainer of diverse talents, she was nominated for two Tony Awards, and VH1 ranked her #89 on its list of great women in rock. She did three *Batman* episodes in a smaller catsuit (she was a half-foot shorter than Julie) and gave the role an exotic dimension; additional TV appearances included an Emmy-nominated turn on *I Spy*, many appearances on talk shows and game shows, dozens of movie roles, and acclaimed vocals for the animated *The Emperor's New Groove* (2000).

The last '60s Catwoman was Lee Meriwether, who was one of four villains in the *Batman* movie ('66). Julie Newmar was still playing Catwoman on the show, but other commitments led to the signing of 1955's Miss America. Lee was already a popular TV veteran before becoming a curvaceous Catwoman who posed as a heavily accented Russian journalist (Lee definitely won the evening-gown competition with some glamorous scenes that showed off her voluptuous figure); her long, ongoing screen career has been highlighted by some other '60s favorites (she was a *Time Tunnel* scientist) and her Emmy- and Golden Globe-nominated role on *Barnaby Jones* in the '70s.

EVERYBODY LOVES SOMEBODY

Early in her career Julie was engaged to Western writer Louis L'Amour, but she left him when she made her break for New York in '54. Julie married a lawyer in '77, but they divorced two years after she gave birth to a son who was diagnosed with Down's syndrome. Julie intentionally slowed down her career to spend more time with her son, keeping him at home in Brentwood, California rather than turning him over to an institution. Meanwhile, Eartha was married and divorced in the '60s, with one child who grew up to become Eartha's manager. Lee has been married twice and is the mother of actress Kyle Aletter and stuntwoman Lesley Aletter.

MY BACK PAGES

In '97 *TV Guide* listed the best TV episodes of all time, and among them were Julie's first two Catwoman appearances. . . . When *Playboy* published its list of the "100 Sexiest Stars of the Century" in '99, Julie was ranked #88. . . . Eartha's antiwar comments at the White House resulted in job offers drying up in the late '60s, so she took her act overseas until the mid-'70s. . . . She has written three successful autobiographies. . . . Lee's Miss America triumph was especially memorable because it was the first one televised. . . . Lee did appear on the *Batman* series in '67, playing the sexy daughter of a kidnapped Gotham City socialite.

April 1, 1970—Pitcher Denny McLain is suspended from baseball. ☮ April 1, 1984—Singer Marvin Gaye dies of gunshot wounds in L.A.
April 2, 1928—Singer Serge Gainsbourg is born in Paris. ☮ April 2, 1939—Singer Marvin Gaye is born in Washington, D.C.
April 2, 1968—Stanley Kubrick's *2001: A Space Odyssey* opens. ☮ April 3, 1924—Actress Doris Day is born in Cincinnati, Ohio.

Richard Chamberlain

He wasn't really a handsome doctor, he just played one on TV, with spectacular results.

TAKIN' CARE OF BUSINESS

Young, clean-cut, too-perfect-to-be-true Richard Chamberlain always looked like someone destined to play Cinderella's charming prince (which he later did). Born George Richard Chamberlain in Beverly Hills, he was an athlete in high school, a sergeant in Korea, and an L.A. stage actor in the '50s. After a couple of years working his way up the TV acting ladder, in '61 Richard beat out dozens of other actors for the title role in *Dr. Kildare,* a new drama series based on the popular movies of the late '30s-early '40s that starred Lew Ayres.

Almost immediately Richard, and the show, were national sensations—he won a Golden Globe as TV's top male star, *Photoplay* named him Most Popular Male Star three years straight, and he received something like 50,000 fan letters a month. With the show leaping up the ratings, MGM capitalized by bringing him into the recording studio to cut several well-received albums of show tunes and ballads (including his own show's theme, "Three Stars Will Shine Tonight").

After five years and a couple of movies away from the show—*Twilight of Honor* with Joey Heatherton ('63), *Joy in the Morning* with Yvette Mimieux ('65)—he decided to leave *Dr. Kildare* and pursue more serious acting challenges. Richard Lester's *Petulia* with Julie Christie ('68) got him to England, where he then took on, and succeeded with, classic stagework, especially an acclaimed turn as Hamlet.

Lester's *The Three* and *Four Musketeers* in the mid-'70s and a villainous role in *The Towering Inferno* ('74) led to Richard's long reign over the mini-series kingdom (*Centennial, The Thorn Birds, Shogun*), dozens of memorable TV movies (*The Count of Monte Cristo*, '75), and some dashing Indiana Jones-style adventure movies in the '80s. For years he's also worked to advance environmental causes, and the artistic ambitions of his youth have blossomed into gallery-exhibited paintings. In 2005, *TV Guide* ranked him seventh on the list of all-time great teen idols.

EVERYBODY LOVES SOMEBODY

In 2003 Richard published *Shattered Love,* a candid, humble memoir that revealed his spiritual side while also discussing his decades of concealing his homosexuality from his fans. He's been with his partner, actor/director Martin Rabbett, for a quarter-century, their home a Hawaiian estate.

MY BACK PAGES

Like *The Twilight Zone* and other popular dramas, *Dr. Kildare* boasted a long list of past and future screen stars among its guests, including William Shatner, Lee Marvin, Carroll O'Connor, Robert Redford, Carolyn Jones, James Caan, Robert Culp, Peter Falk, Charles Bronson, Barbara Eden, Lauren Bacall, Jack Lord, Gena Rowlands, Claude Rains, Douglas Fairbanks, Jr., Walter Matthau, Angie Dickinson, Leslie Nielsen, Teri Garr, Fred Astaire, Basil Rathbone, James Earl Jones, Jack Nicholson, and George Kennedy. . . . Always an elegant TV presence, Richard has appeared on dozens of talk shows and been a presenter (or host) at major awards shows.

Wilt Chamberlain

The Big Dipper was the most unstoppable individual player in NBA history.

TAKIN' CARE OF BUSINESS

Wilt's numbers were so high, they may never be seriously challenged—a fifty-points-per-game average for an entire season, for instance. A seven-foot-tall, multi-sport star at his Philly high school, he went to the Uni-

April 3, 1963—Elvis Presley's *It Happened at the World's Fair* opens. ☮ April 3, 1965—Petula Clark's "I Know a Place" hits the charts.
April 3, 1968—The Simon and Garfunkel album *Bookends* is released. ☮ April 4, 1959—*Rio Bravo* with Angie Dickinson opens.
April 4, 1960—At the Oscars, Simone Signoret wins the Best Actress Oscar (*Room at the Top*), and *Ben-Hur* is Best Picture.

versity of Kansas, where he was a two-time All-American and led the Jayhawks to the '57 NCAA title game. After a stint with the Harlem Globetrotters, he was drafted by the Philadelphia Warriors and quickly established himself as the game's most dominant player. He was Rookie of the Year and MVP in his first season, was MVP four times, scored an unthinkable 100 points in a game, set the single-game rebounding record (55), and at different times led the league in scoring, shooting percentage, rebounding, assists, and minutes played, all while never once fouling out of a game. His record-setting 76ers won the NBA title in '67, and he won another title with the Lakers in '72. He also raced cars, was an awesome volleyball player, could cook gourmet meals, bench-pressed over 500 pounds, was one of the fastest players in the NBA, was a frequent talk-show guest, and co-starred in *Conan the Destroyer* ('84). And oh yes, there was one more thing he could do. . . .

NBA Champions (and Runners-Up)

1959–'60–Boston Celtics (St. Louis Hawks)
1960–'61–Boston Celtics (St. Louis Hawks)
1961–'62–Boston Celtics (L.A. Lakers)
1962–'63–Boston Celtics (L.A. Lakers)
1963–'64–Boston Celtics (S.F. Warriors)
1964–'65–Boston Celtics (L.A. Lakers)
1965–'66–Boston Celtics (L.A. Lakers)
1966–'67–Philadelphia 76ers (S.F. Warriors)
1967–'68–Boston Celtics (L.A. Lakers)
1968–'69–Boston Celtics (L.A. Lakers)

EVERYBODY LOVES SOMEBODY

In *A View from Above*, the second of his two autobiographies, Wilt claimed to have slept with 20,000 women as of '92. The astonishing statistic sent readers scurrying to calculators (approximately 500 per year, that's *three different women every two days for forty years*). If anybody could do it, it would've been Wilt, who never married.

MY BACK PAGES

So gifted was he as an all-around athlete, he was offered a contract to play pro football in '66. . . . Wilt's famous house up on Mulholland Drive in L.A. was custom-built to his scale—everything was taller and higher than usual, plus he asked for no right angles in any of the corners.

Ray Charles

Brother Ray explored musical styles, and defeated one of his biggest demons, in the '60s.

TAKIN' CARE OF BUSINESS

Like Johnny Cash, another genre-jumping genius of American music, Ray Charles already had several classic records behind him when the '60s started. With "I Got a Woman," "Mess Around," "What'd I Say," and other songs, Ray had already mixed gospel and blues into an original, exuberant, heart-stirring sound for Atlantic Records in the '50s. And he'd done it while overcoming brutal Southern poverty, the tragic accidental death of his brother, the loss of his sight by age 7, and the early deaths of both parents.

In '48, having played piano in Florida bars and dance halls, he rode a bus to Seattle, got established as a jazzy pianist/crooner in local clubs, and recorded his first records, with only minor success. During these years he also tried heroin for the first time. Signing with Atlantic he then wrote/arranged/created his distinctive early sound with songs that were sometimes deemed too controversial for radio.

At only 20 years old he switched to another record label in '59 and began recording (and owning, a business breakthrough) the great songs of the early '60s that would forever cement his reputation as an innovator and a legend. "Hit the Road, Jack," "Georgia On My Mind," "Busted," "I Can't Stop Loving You," and more were songs that blended country music, jazz, blues, and gospel into something that appealed to all audiences (his landmark LP, *Modern Sounds in Country and Western Music,* would ride the top of the album charts for over two months in '62).

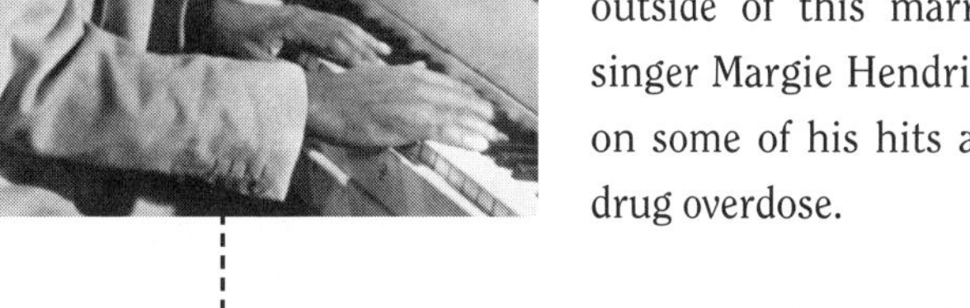

Joining in with the burgeoning civil rights movement, he bravely stopped performing in segregated clubs, earning himself bans in his home state of Georgia. Unfortunately, his heroin use had swelled into a longtime heroin addiction, and he was busted mid-decade for possession. Recognizing the depth of his problem, he voluntarily entered rehab, and defeated his addiction in '66.

While he never again enjoyed the chart success that he had in the early '60s, for the next 30+ years he was a fixture on the American scene, touring constantly (hundreds of shows every year), recording prolifically (over 75 albums and over 75 hit songs when he died in 2004), performing on many music shows and at two presidential inaugurations, appearing in movies (*The Blues Brothers,* '80) and commercials (Diet Pepsi), getting inducted into the Rock and Roll and the Blues Halls of Fame, and winning lifetime-achievement recognition from the Grammy Awards (he won a dozen Grammys in his life, including eight posthumously for his final album). And like Johnny Cash, who died nine months before him, Ray was the subject of a major movie that came out after his death. Having fought his way up from nothing to the pinnacles of musical achievement, Ray is remembered now as one of the key influences and inspirations of the 20th century.

EVERYBODY LOVES SOMEBODY

When it came to women, handsome, charming Ray was gifted. He had two wives, but he also had a long reputation for womanizing (it was said that "let Ray" was required to be a Raelette). He also had 12 children, most of them with women he wasn't married to. After a brief marriage in the early '50s, Ray married a gospel singer, Della Beatrice Howard, in the mid-'50s. She stayed with him through all his trials and triumphs until they divorced in '77. One of his most important relationships outside of this marriage was with the singer Margie Hendrix, who sang backup on some of his hits and died young of a drug overdose.

MY BACK PAGES

At birth Ray's last name was Robinson, but he changed it in the '50s to avoid confusion with the famous boxer. . . . Relying on his extraordinary hearing, Ray never used a guide dog or a cane to make his way through the world. . . . In '79 the state of Georgia officially apologized to Ray and declared "Georgia On My Mind" their official song. . . . *Rolling Stone* ranked him tenth among the greatest rock artists of all time. . . . Ray was also a major fund-raiser for charities that supported African-American education and arts programs.

April 5, 1961—*Danger Man* with Patrick McGoohan debuts. ☮ April 5, 1963—*Bye Bye Birdie* with Ann-Margret opens.
April 5, 1965— At the Oscars, Julie Andrews is Best Actress (*Mary Poppins*) and *My Fair Lady* is Best Picture.
April 6, 1929—Actress Joi Lansing is born in Salt Lake City, Utah. ☮ April 6, 1966—*The Ghost in the Invisible Bikini* with Susan Hart opens.

Julie Christie

The trendsetting star of several major movies, Julie Christie is lionized today as one of the great symbols of the swingin' '60s.

TAKIN' CARE OF BUSINESS

Does any actress represent the '60s as well as lovely Julie Christie? So perfectly does *Darling* capture the decade's zeitgeist, watching that landmark film is like watching a documentary that explains what the swingin' '60s were all about. And to see 24-year-old Julie Christie at her best, all youthful beauty and style and intelligence, is to see the incarnation of the mod ideal. "She is marvelous, absolutely adorable, enchanting, sexy, alive, vibrant, astute, clever and knowledgeable," praised Laurence Harvey, her *Darling* co-star; "the most poetic of actresses," according to Al Pacino.

Born in India, as a 20-year-old she first got noticed on TV and then appeared in several minor films, the strongest impression coming in John Schlesinger's *Billy Liar* ('63). *Darling* ('65) catapulted her to fame. Her character, Diana Scott, was described in the movie as someone who thinks sexual fidelity means "not having more than one man in bed at the same time." Julie's portrayal brought her an Oscar as Best Actress. Her stardom rocketing to even greater heights, later that same year came the much-coveted role of the luminous Lara in David Lean's epic *Doctor Zhivago*.

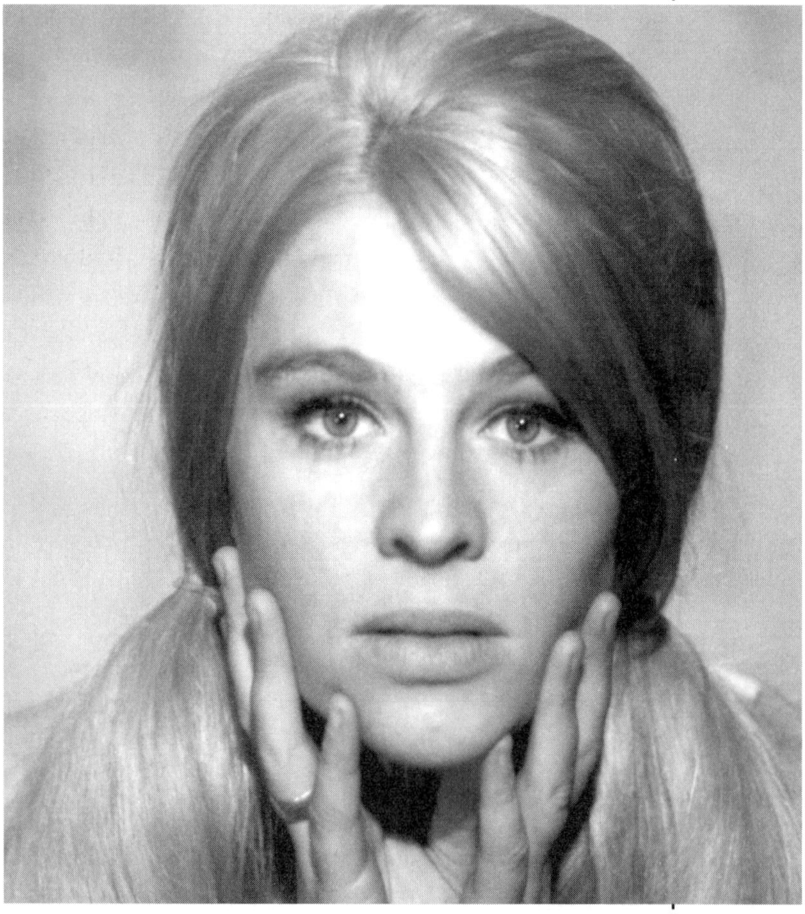

Truffaut's fascinating *Fahrenheit 451* ('66), Schlesinger's underrated *Far from the Madding Crowd* ('67), and Richard Lester's masterful *Petulia* ('68) set her up for the triumphs that would come in the '70s. She got a second Oscar nomination for *McCabe and Mrs. Miller* ('72), while *Don't Look Now* ('73), *Shampoo* ('75), and *Heaven Can Wait* ('78) showed her off as one of the world's most beautiful and appealing actresses. She's worked continuously ever since, often in films that focused on political issues. *Afterglow* ('97, another Oscar nomination), and *Finding Neverland* (2004) reconfirmed her stature as a cinematic treasure.

EVERYBODY LOVES SOMEBODY

Julie's tried to keep her private life away from prying eyes. Unfortunately, when you're that beautiful and that famous, you *will* get noticed, so here's the skinny: for the first half of the '60s she had a steady boyfriend, an artist whom she met (the

April 6, 1998—Singer Tammy Wynette dies of a blood clot in Nashville, Tennessee.
April 7, 1967—Pioneering radio DJ Tom Donahue begins at KMPX, San Jose.
April 7, 1970— At the Oscars, Maggie Smith is Best Actress (*The Prime of Miss Jean Brodie*) and *Midnight Cowboy* is Best Picture.

Oscars for Best Actress

1960–Elizabeth Taylor (*BUtterfield 8*)
1961–Sophia Loren (*Two Women*)
1962–Anne Bancroft (*The Miracle Worker*)
1963–Patricia Neal (*Hud*)
1964–Julie Andrews (*Mary Poppins*)
1965–Julie Christie (*Darling*)
1966–Elizabeth Taylor (*Who's Afraid of Virginia Woolf?*)
1967– Katharine Hepburn (*Guess Who's Coming to Dinner*)
1968–Katharine Hepburn (*The Lion in Winter*)/ Barbra Streisand (*Funny Girl*)
1969–Maggie Smith (*The Prime of Miss Jean Brodie*)

story goes) when he made a delivery as a part-time mailman. Once fame came knocking mid-decade, she spent her free time in the '60s, according to a '65 *Cosmo* interview, going to dance clubs—"most of the time I muck around with my friends."

Among those she mucked around with later in the '60s were some of the decade's most eligible bachelors, including Omar Sharif, Terence Stamp, and Warren Beatty, all of whom were co-stars. Beatty, whom she met in the summer of '67, was her co-star in three '70s films and lover into the mid-'70s. She has been living with an English writer for over two decades now. She's never married; "men don't want any responsibility," she once said, "and neither do I."

MY BACK PAGES

Her childhood nickname—Bugs. . . . At the '66 Oscars (the first televised in color), Julie made a stunning appearance in a gold miniskirt from Carnaby Street. . . . Beatty dedicated *Reds* to her: "For Jules". . . . As further proof that the British had truly invaded, two of the other Best Actress nominees in '66 were also British (Samantha Eggar, *The Collector*, and Julie Andrews, *The Sound of Music*), as were two of the five Best Actor nominees, and half of the 10 Best Supporting Actor/ Actress nominees.

Chris Clark

This blue-eyed soul singer had a Motown hit, a Motown job, and a Motown movie.

TAKIN' CARE OF BUSINESS

A post-war California girl, Chris Clark was one of the few Caucasian artists signed by Motown in the '60s (Bobby Darin was another). Only 18 when Berry Gordy signed her in '64, she had a minor hit with "Love's Gone Bad" in '66 and made a couple of albums of R & B and Beatles songs, *Soul Sounds* ('67) and *CC Rides Again* ('69), that were bigger in England than America. In '69 she became a Motown V.P., which led to *Lady Sings the Blues* in '72. Motown's most successful film, the acclaimed Diana Ross vehicle brought Chris an Oscar nomination as co-writer. She left Motown in the late '80s, lived in Arizona in the late '90s, and is now in Sonoma County, California, still playing live occasionally and making plans for a new album she describes as "Motown revisited."

EVERYBODY LOVES SOMEBODY

Chris married Ernest Tidyman, the novelist (*Shaft*) who won an Oscar for scripting *The French Connection* ('71). Their three-year marriage ended with his death in '84.

MY BACK PAGES

An imposing stage presence as a 6′ blonde, she's also sometimes credited as one of the first singers to popularize go-go boots. . . . Chris's sister Jane is a longtime recording engineer who's worked on many gold records.

April 7, 1970—Composer Burt Bacharach wins two *Butch Cassidy* Oscars.
April 7, 1970—Goldie Hawn wins the Best Supporting Actress Oscar for *Cactus Flower*.
April 8, 1963— At the Oscars, Anne Bancroft and Patty Duke win acting Oscars (*The Miracle Worker*) and *Lawrence of Arabia* is Best Picture.

Dr. Eugenie Clark

"The Shark Lady" was the decade's coolest ichthyologist.

TAKIN' CARE OF BUSINESS

Other people in this book have airports (JFK), highways (Patsy Cline), and craters (Neil Armstrong) named after them: only Dr. Eugenie Clark has four different fish named after her. Born in New York City, she was interested in fish as a child and was a frequent aquarium visitor. After earning a Ph.D. in zoology at NYU in '50, she began a long career of teaching and writing about sharks. Her books made the Book-of-the-Month Club, her dozens of documentaries were hits on PBS, and her profile was so high that she was written about in magazines as diverse as *Look, Mademoiselle,* and *Sports Illustrated.* The Florida marine institute she founded in '55 and ran until '67 is today a popular public aquarium and successful research center, and even in her 80s Dr. Clark has continued to make important discoveries. Her National Geographic documentary *The Sharks* ('82) earned the highest ratings ever on PBS, and *Search for the Great Sharks* was a successful IMAX film ('95).

EVERYBODY LOVES SOMEBODY

Dr. Clark has been married six times to five husbands (two marriages were to the same man). With her second husband she had four kids, all born in the '50s.

MY BACK PAGES

Dr. Clark has made research dives in exotic waters all around the world, mostly with scuba gear but also in deep-sea submersibles. . . . Her *Reefwatch* in '88 was the first-ever live underwater documentary from the Red Sea. . . . She's received dozens of prestigious honors and awards from scientific organizations including the National Geographic Society, the Explorers Club, and the Underwater Society of America, plus awards for her nature films and recognition as Diver of the Year and Ocean Hero, and at least four biographies have been written about her.

Petula Clark

A cheerful clear-voiced British belter who went from child star in the '40s to pop star in the '60s, Pet had mid-decade hits and movie roles.

TAKIN' CARE OF BUSINESS

When people think of the British Invasion, they usually think of the Beatles, the Stones, and other "boy bands." But Petula Clark was right there with them at the vanguard of a musical revolution. "Downtown" in '64 made her the first British female singer to hit #1 on the American charts, and it brought Petula her first Grammy Award in the same year the Fab Four won their first Grammy. That was just one more highlight for her in a long career already filled with them. Petula was a star from childhood on.

Before she was 10 she was appearing regularly on British radio programs; before she was 12 she had her own BBC show, *Pet's Parlour*. She started appearing in movies as a teen, making dozens in the '40s and '50s and becoming so well-known that her life was the subject of a popular comic strip. Her first '60s hit was "Sailor," which hit #1 in the U.K. in '61. Within a year, 30-year-old Petula had million-selling songs in England, France, and Germany. Her U.S. breakthrough, of course, came when she took an energetic trip "Downtown." Additional well-crafted numbers—including "I Know a Place" (bringing her a second Grammy), "My Love," and "Don't Sleep in the Subway"—quickly followed, giving her eight Top 20 hits in the U.S. between '64 and '67.

Wearing a kicky strawberry blonde 'do and fab fashions that perfectly suited the times, she was on many music shows during the decade, including *Shindig* and *Hullabaloo*. On her own '68 special she made a controversial gesture for racial equality: while singing "On the Path of Glory" with Harry Belafonte, she touched his hand. Despite NBC's efforts to cut the image, she made them keep the shot when the show aired. Late in the decade she had starring roles in two big-budget musicals, *Finian's Rainbow* ('68, a Golden Globe nom-

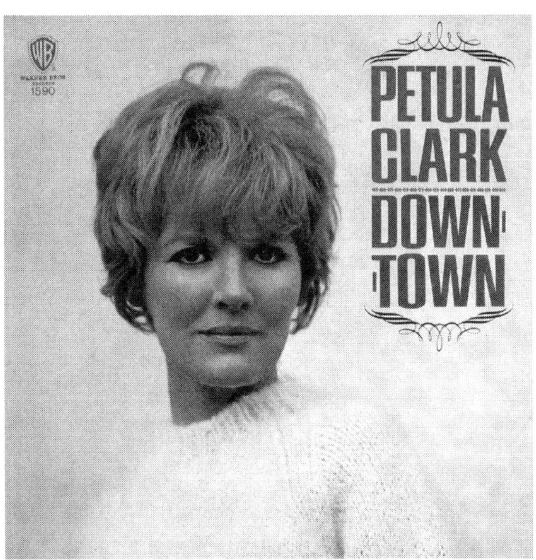

20 Mid-'60s British Invaders (and U.S. Hits)

Animals ("House of the Rising Sun")

Billie J. Kramer and the Dakotas ("Bad to Me")

Chad and Jeremy ("A Summer Song")

Cream ("Sunshine of Your Love")

Dave Clark Five ("Glad All Over")

Freddie and the Dreamers ("I'm Telling You Now")

Gerry and the Pacemakers ("Don't Let the Sun Catch You Crying")

Herman's Hermits ("I'm Into Something Good")

Hollies ("Bus Stop")

Honeycombs ("Have I the Right?")

Kinks ("You Really Got Me")

Moody Blues ("Nights in White Satin")

Peter and Gordon ("Lady Godiva")

Sandi Shaw ("Girl Don't Come")

Small Faces ("Itchycoo Park")

Them ("Gloria")

Tremeloes ("Here Comes My Baby")

Troggs ("Wild Thing")

Yardbirds ("For Your Love")

Zombies ("She's Not There")

April 10, 1965—Actress Linda Darnell dies in a Chicago house fire.
April 10, 1967—At the Oscars, Elizabeth Taylor is Best Actress (*Who's Afraid of Virginia Woolf?*) and *A Man for All Season* is Best Picture.
April 10, 1968—Katharine Hepburn is Best Actress (*Guess Who's Coming to Dinner*) and *In the Heat of the Night* is Best Picture.

ination as Best Actress) and *Goodbye, Mr. Chips* ('69). While neither one thrived at the box office, they did establish Petula as one of the few stars popular and talented enough to make the transition from the recording studio to the big screen.

She's continued to make music ever since, and even though she's had no more glittering U.S. hits to match the rich vein of gold she tapped into in the mid-'60s, she's still a major global star. By now she's sold somewhere in the neighborhood of 70 million albums around the world, and with over 1,000 recorded songs in five languages (English, French, German, Italian, and Spanish) to her credit, she's the most popular British female singer in history.

She still performs benefit concerts, and in '96 she made it to Broadway with *Blood Brothers*. Late in the century she toured the U.S. as Norma Desmond in *Sunset Boulevard*. Currently, she's writing songs and working on an autobiographical one-woman show full of stories and songs from her wonderful career. In recognition of her longevity and accomplishments, in '97 the Queen bestowed the title Commander of the British Empire upon her.

EVERYBODY LOVES SOMEBODY

Being a child star, she acknowledged to the *Daily Mail* in a '98 interview, wasn't easy: "Because of the circles I mixed in, professionally, I knew about things that children in those days were shielded from. Yet, at the same time, I was still very young in my own experiences of life. It was all rather peculiar and confusing." In '61 Petula married a French P.R. man who later became her manager. They're still married, have three kids, and now divide their time between a Swiss estate and a French chalet.

MY BACK PAGES

Her nickname—Pet, and she was also dubbed "The English Shirley Temple" as a child. . . . Petula's #85 (between Laurie Anderson and Yoko Ono) on VH1's list of rock's 100 greatest women. . . . In '99 she told *People*, "You can't minimize the '60s by saying it was just about fashion and music, nothing was the same after the '60s."

Patsy Cline

This incomparable songstress with the big voice and big heart recorded extraordinary early-'60s hits before her career was abruptly cut short.

TAKIN' CARE OF BUSINESS

Patsy Cline was one of the true legends in American music, a stylist who transcended genres and generations. Here are just some of the awards and tributes she received posthumously: election to the Country Music Hall of Fame in '73 and the National Cowgirl Hall of Fame in '94; the Patsy Cline stamp in '93; a lifetime-achievement Grammy in '95; a 55-foot bell tower at the Virginia cemetery where she's buried; a Virginia highway named in her honor; an annual festival in her hometown of Winchester, Virginia; a big-budget Hollywood movie about her life (Jessica Lange's *Sweet Dreams*, '85); a flower named after her (the soft-pink Patsy Cline Hybrid Tea Rose); and legions of professional impersonators. Patsy would've loved it all.

April 10, 1968—*Belle de Jour* with Catherine Deneuve opens. ☮ April 10, 1969—*Goodbye, Columbus* with Ali MacGraw opens.
April 11, 1961—Singer Bob Dylan makes his first performance in New York. ☮ April 11, 1962—Elvis Presley's *Follow That Dream* opens.
April 12, 1932—Singer Tiny Tim is born in New York. ☮ April 12, 1961—Cosmonaut Yuri Gagarin becomes the first man in space.

She was starstruck from her very first viewing, at age 4, of a Shirley Temple movie. At 13, she walked into a local radio station and sang for a live band for free, then for the next few years she helped support the family by singing professionally in local clubs. Struggling to bust out nationally, she finally made her debut on the *Grand Ole Opry* radio show in '55 and had her first big seller, "Walkin' After Midnight," in '57. Then came her great run of hits, none of which she wrote but all of which she made her own, especially the heartbreaking classics of the early '60s, "I Fall to Pieces" and Willie Nelson's "Crazy" (the number-one jukebox hit of all time).

A popular live performer on stage and on TV, she had a pleasing rootin'-tootin' style that was country-glamour, true to her roots and true to her dreams. Patsy survived a horrific head-on car crash in '61 that plunged her through a windshield and put her in critical condition for two days with serious cuts and fractures; after the accident she had plastic surgery and wore her bangs down over her forehead to conceal the scars.

Still the awards tumbled in—*Billboard* magazine's favorite female country/western artist, '61–'63; *Cash Box* magazine's "most-programmed female country/western vocalist," '62–'63; the *Music Reporter* "star of the year," '62. And then, unthinkably, in '63 this titanic force of American music was gone, killed with several other performers in a plane crash near Nashville. Her shocking death at age 30 still stands as one of the entertainment world's saddest losses.

EVERYBODY LOVES SOMEBODY

Patsy had it tough: it's likely she was abused by her father as a preteen, and her second husband occasionally hit her. She was engaged at 17, married at 20, divorced at 25. Once her career was established, she was constantly on the road, where she worked hard and played hard, even though she was remarried from '57 until her death and had two kids in the '60s. She and her second husband both fooled around on the side, what Patsy called "runnin', jumpin', an' playin'." At the time of her death she was allegedly having an affair with her manager, who was piloting the plane Patsy died in.

MY BACK PAGES

The name game—Virginia Patterson Hensley at birth, Ginny as a child, Patsy as a teen (a shortened version of her middle name), Cline was her first husband's name, but she called herself simply "the Cline". . . . She's #11 (between Debbie Harry and Carole King) on the VH1 list of great women in rock history. . . . Briefly, the final flight: Patsy had a premonition of a sudden death coming soon, the pilot was not trained to navigate by instruments, they were flying in a small private plane through a terrible rainstorm, vision was hampered by fog and approaching darkness, the crash dismembered the bodies on impact. . . . Long after her death her songs have continued to sell impressively, and "Walkin' After Midnight" was used in a popular computer commercial in '98. . . . Patsy was the life of any party and could swear, joke, drink, and smoke like one of the boys, in fact there are stories that she once pushed her husband out of a car and on another occasion beat up a man.

James Coburn

America's answer to 007 was Our Man Coburn.

TAKIN' CARE OF BUSINESS

Cool repetitions mark the long, impressive career of James Coburn. After studying acting at UCLA and in New York in the early '50s, and after working in many TV Westerns of the late '50s, his first break came when director John Sturges made him a near-silent, expert knife-thrower alongside Steve McQueen and Charles Bronson in *The Magnificent Seven* ('60). All four worked together again in *The Great Escape* ('63), in which James played the Aussie with the

April 12, 1968—Martin Luther King, Jr. makes the cover of *Life* magazine. ☮ April 12, 1989—Activist Abbie Hoffman commits suicide in Pennsylvania.
April 13, 1923—Comedian Don Adams is born in New York. ☮ April 13, 1933—Actress Shani Wallis is born in London.
April 13, 1962—Actress Liz Taylor and actor Richard Burton make the cover of *Life*.

big suitcase who got away by bicycle (he wasn't born Down Under—James was from Nebraska).

Suddenly recognized as an athletic action star with versatile abilities and the biggest smile in town, he averaged two movies a year through the rest of the decade. Among his best-remembered works were a daring, highly regarded black comedy that he both produced and starred in, *The President's Analyst* ('67), and a great pair of pre-Austin Powers spy spoofs, *Our Man Flint* ('66) and *In Like Flint* ('67). These last two took silly-but-smart aim at the very English James Bond movies: Flint was America's top spy (thus "our man"), an over-the-top, incredibly successful playboy who was an expert in literally everything (he could even speak dolphin!?).

His next successful repetition came when he reteamed with Sam Peckinpah, his director on the Charlton Heston Civil War movie *Major Dundee* ('65); their *Pat Garrett & Billy the Kid* ('73) has become a much-studied cult Western, with James a dark, deadly Sheriff Pat and Bob Dylan a mysterious Alias. Working with Peckinpah again he starred in *Cross of Iron* ('76); with Bronson he co-starred in *Hard Times* ('75); with Heston, *Midway* ('76).

Overcoming a painful, debilitating bout with rheumatoid arthritis in the '80s, James stayed amazingly active with another five dozen movie and TV projects, playing good guys (*Young Guns II*, '90), bad guys (*Hudson Hawk*, '91), appealing guys (his popular TV commercials, especially the "like a rock" Chevy truck ads). In the last years of his life he was doing some of his most acclaimed work, winning an Oscar as Best Supporting Actor for *Affliction* ('97). It was, to say the least, a popular choice for this ever-popular star. A heart attack claimed James Coburn in 2002, but he is fondly recalled as a durable, eminently watchable star, ultimately his best career repetition of all.

EVERYBODY LOVES SOMEBODY

James was married twice, the first time for two decades, with two kids. He was at home with his second wife when he died. In between his marriages he was in a relationship with Lynsey De Paul, a British singer/actress of the '70s and '80s, and he co-wrote several songs that she recorded.

MY BACK PAGES

Like Steve McQueen, James loved fast cars, dabbled in hallucinogens, and was a friend (and trainee) of martial arts expert Bruce Lee—when Lee died both stars were pallbearers. . . . When Paul McCartney was making *Band on the Run* in '73, James and others were in England making a movie, and they ended up on McCartney's album cover. . . . Another of James's passions—Cuban cigars.

Judy Collins

This clear-voiced big-eyed singer and social activist put her angelic vocals to a decade full of folk classics.

TAKIN' CARE OF BUSINESS

With her angelic voice and impeccable musical taste, Judy Collins "inspired a whole generation who had the same kinda dreams," according to Bill Clinton. She was born in Seattle, and music was always her passion: she was taking piano lessons at age 4 and debuted with the Denver Symphony at 13 (incredibly, she was so overcome and disappointed she attempted suicide).

At 17 she became a folksinger and started playing guitar, winning a four-state contest a year later. Her popularity as a 20-year-old folkie in small Colorado clubs led to bigger gigs until she was spotted in '61 by a record exec, who signed her and cut her first album, *Maid of Constant Sorrow*, in only five hours. Her crystalline soprano, exquisite song selection, and rep as "the singer's singer" made her one of the decade's most memorable and respected vocalists.

Albums of other people's material dominated, with

In My Life in '66 her first gold record. At Leonard Cohen's urging, *Wildflowers* in '67 was her first album with her own compositions (though the biggest hit was Joni Mitchell's "Both Sides Now," bringing Judy a Grammy). Her tenth album, *Whales and Nightingales*, included one of her signature songs, "Amazing Grace," recorded in St. Paul's Chapel in New York. Always a beautiful stage presence with the biggest, bluest eyes in the biz, she appeared with Dylan, Donovan, Baez and others in the Oscar-nominated documentary *Festival* in '67 and had a role in the N.Y. Shakespeare Festival's *Peer Gynt* in '69.

Judy made three Spanish films in the early '70s and got an Oscar nomination in '75 as co-director of *Antonia: A Portrait of a Woman*, which was about her childhood piano teacher. Her music career gained new momentum in the '70s as she broadened her audience by covering show and cabaret tunes, scoring a hit with Sondheim's "Send in the Clowns" in '75. Still touring and recording, she has now released over 30 albums. She wrote a novel in '95, which was praised for its realistic portrayal of rock's seamy side, and three autobiographical books. While she still plays dozens of concerts every year, "I would rather be writing than anything," she said in a TV interview.

EVERYBODY LOVES SOMEBODY

Judy met her first love in '55, married him in '58 while pregnant, and gave birth to a son in '59. When her career took off in the early '60s, she traveled half of every month while her husband stayed home with their son. They divorced after seven years and Judy lost a bitter fight for child custody.

Later, she had an intense relationship with singer Stephen Stills, who was one of the studio musicians on her '68 album *Who Knows Where the Time Goes*. Stills wanted her to move in with him, but she declined; he was "brilliant," she wrote in her autobiography, but their relationship was "volatile." In a TV interview she admitted "the legacy of our relationship is certainly in that song," referring to his '69 classic "Suite: Judy Blue Eyes."

She almost married actor Stacy Keach, but careers and marriage anxiety split them up in '74. Plagued with drug and alcohol problems, in '78 she entered rehab and learned to cope with depression through meditation and exercise. Tragically, her son went into rehab in '84, relapsed in '91, and finally killed himself in '92. Devastated, Judy toured to try to heal herself. "My son is with me all the time," she said in a TV interview. Thankfully, she had a strong relationship of her own to help her—in '78 she'd met designer Louis Nelson and after a single date they were together forever, with a wedding in '96.

MY BACK PAGES

Always *au courant*, early in the '60s she wore the classic beatnik/folk look of black pants, black turtleneck, and black hat, then later she eased into the fairy/hippie/vintage look, perfect for her gentle style. . . . She posed nude with her back to Francesco Scavullo's camera for the cover of her '78 album *Hard Times for Lovers*. . . . Arrested in the '60s while marching for civil rights in Mississippi, Judy was again arrested in '73 for protesting the Vietnam War. . . . She performed at Bill Clinton's '92 inaugural. . . . At Clinton's request, Judy has long worked for UNICEF, as Audrey Hepburn had once done. . . . She received an honorary doctorate from NYU in '99. . . . "I'm so grateful for this life. Somehow I won the lottery, I dunno how. . . . I'm very fortunate," she said in her *Intimate Portrait* TV bio.

April 14, 1969—At the Oscars, Barbra Streisand (*Funny Girl*) and Katharine Hepburn (*The Lion in Winter*) win Best Actress Oscars, and *Oliver!* is Best Picture. April 14, 1969—Stanley Kubrick wins the Oscar for *2001* special effects. ☮ April 15, 1933—Actress Elizabeth Montgomery is born in L.A. April 15, 1938—Actress Claudia Cardinale is born in Tunisia.

Sean Connery

Sir Sean, everybody's pick for Best Bond Ever.

TAKIN' CARE OF BUSINESS

He was going bald in his 20s and has often worn toupees on-screen, even in Bond films. He has a tattoo on each arm—"Mum and Dad" and "Scotland Forever"—that he got as a teen. He was in the Royal Navy, worked as a coffin polisher, lifeguard, and model, made a dozen mostly forgotten films in the '50s, and crooned a gentle tune in the Disney movie *Darby O'Gill and the Little People* ('59). But in the '60s, Sean Connery's inauspicious past added up to the man who would become the world's deadliest, sexiest, and smoothest spy: the definitive Bond, James Bond, for over 40 years now, is the man most men have wanted to be, the man most women have wanted to be with.

Born in Edinburgh, Sean was lifting weights as a teen and bulked up enough to be a Mr. Universe contestant in '50 (he came in third). A decade of bit parts and supporting roles in movies followed. In the early '60s, when producers were looking for someone to play author Ian Fleming's sophisticated 007, many top British actors (David Niven, Cary Grant, Richard Burton) were considered before the part was given to the relatively unknown but eminently watchable Sean.

Quickly he made the part his, displaying the right looks for a tuxedo, the right athleticism for the many fight scenes, and the right charm for the dazzling women who paraded past. While he made 15 other movies during the decade (including the D-Day epic *The Longest Day* in '62, Hitchcock's *Marnie* in '64, the Western *Shalako* in '68), it's the batch of five Bond films from '62–'67 that cemented his global reputation forever.

Dr. No, *From Russia with Love*, *Goldfinger*, *Thunderball*, and *You Only Live Twice* established the recipe that has lasted into the 21st century, through at least five more Bond actors (Lazenby, Moore, Dalton, Brosnan, Craig): put a handsome, dashing actor in exotic locations, surround him with memorable villains and beautiful women, add the coolest car (in the '60s, an Aston Martin) and the greatest gadgets (a jet pack in *Thunderball*, a gyrocopter in *You Only Live Twice*), sprinkle in dry quips, top off with a polished theme song sung by a distinctive vocalist (Shirley Bassey, Tom Jones, and Nancy Sinatra for Sean's Bonds), and after two hours of viewing, audiences are full with a delicious, satisfying adventure.

As the Bond films progressed through the decade, the budgets got bigger, the sets became more incredible (think of the Japanese crater with monorail in *You Only Live Twice*), the audiences swelled (*Goldfinger* and *Thunderball* both broke records), and Sean's take increased to make him the highest paid actor of the time. No longer wanting to be typecast as 007, he skipped *On Her Majesty's Secret Service* ('69), was wooed back for *Diamonds Are Forever* ('71), then turned the franchise over to Roger Moore until a one-shot return for *Never Say Never Again* (the '83 remake of *Thunderball*,

April 15, 1966—A *Time* magazine cover story proclaims "swinging London" the city of the decade.
April 16, 1927—Actress Edie Adams is born in Kingston, Pennsylvania. ☮ April 16, 1939—Singer Dusty Springfield is born in London.
April 16, 1947—Lew Alcindor is born. ☮ April 17, 1918—Actor William Holden is born in Illinois.

Bond's Conquests, '62–'67

***Dr. No*:**
Ursula Andress ("Honey Ryder")
Eunice Gayson ("Sylvia Trench")
Zena Marshall ("Miss Taro")

***From Russia with Love*:**
Daniela Bianchi ("Tatiana Romanova")

***Goldfinger*:**
Honor Blackman ("Pussy Galore")
Shirley Eaton ("Jill Masterson")

***Thunderball*:**
Claudine Auger ("Domino")
Luciana Paluzzi ("Fiona Volpe")
Molly Peters ("Patricia Fearing")

***You Only Live Twice*:**
Karin Dor ("Helga Brandt")
Mie Hama ("Kissy Suzuki")
Akiko Wakabayashi ("Aki")

Eunice Gayson

reputedly one of his favorites of the '60s Bonds).

From the '70s onward he's been one of the most regal and acclaimed actors alive, usually playing kings, military leaders, or convincing adventurers in dozens of great movies, among them *The Man Who Would Be King* ('75), *Robin and Marian* ('76), *The Untouchables* ('87, with an Oscar as Best Supporting Actor), *Indiana Jones and the Last Crusade* ('89), *The Hunt for Red October* ('90), and *The Rock* ('96). Now in his 70s and aging better than any man on the planet, he can still believably woo the prettiest girls, kick any bad guy's butt, and always be the coolest guy in the room. *People* magazine named him the "Sexiest Man Alive" in '89 and "Sexiest Man of the Century" a decade later; the Queen dubbed him Sir in 2000. One of the true icons of the '60s—Connery, Sean Connery.

EVERYBODY LOVES SOMEBODY

For most of the '60s Sean was married to Australian actress Diane Cilento, a Broadway star in the '50s who played lusty Molly in the Oscar-winning *Tom Jones* ('63). Their son Jason was born in '63; he's enjoyed a long career in movies and on TV, and during the late '90s he was married to actress Mia Sara, who played Ferris's girlfriend in *Ferris Bueller's Day Off* ('85). Sean meanwhile remarried a French-born artist named Micheline Roquebrune, whose paintings have been exhibited around the world.

MY BACK PAGES

Two days before he was assassinated, JFK saw his last movie—*From Russia with Love* (the President had earlier claimed that Fleming's books were among his favorites). . . . Not only did Sean sing in *Darby O'Gill*, he sang in a Bond film, too, joining in with Ursula Andress as she sang on the beach in *Dr. No*. . . . Features of Bond's Aston Martin DB5—ejector seat, front machine guns, oil slick spray, radar, rear bulletproof shield, rear water jets, rotating license plates, smoke screen. . . . The title *Never Say Never Again* is believed to come from Sean's own "never again" comment after he made *Diamonds Are Forever*.

Mike Connors

The regular-guy star of one of the coolest detective dramas.

TAKIN' CARE OF BUSINESS

On *Mannix*, Mike Connors played a modern TV character right out of old Raymond Chandler stories. Unlike superhero cops and secret agents who glided through their screen adventures relatively unscathed, Joe Mannix took many beatings, was frequently shot at, sometimes got wounded, and was often run off the road in what was surely one of the decade's most violent shows.

But Mike Connors kept his cool. Born Krikor Ohanian in Fresno, California, Mike was a World War II Air Force vet and UCLA basketball player who started getting supporting roles in movies in the '50s and early '60s (*The Ten Commandments*, '56, *Stagecoach*, '66), plus many TV appearances. *Mannix* in '67 made him a star. Playing an L.A. detective who carried a .38 snubnose (no fancy new gun for Joe) and regularly plunged through windows and from rooftops, Mike worked with a crack cast, including Joseph Campanella as his boss, Gail Fisher as his occasionally kidnapped secretary, and pre-Brady Robert Reed as a fellow gumshoe. The show was a frequent award nominee—Mike himself was up four times for an Emmy and won one Golden Globe, and Gail Fisher was the first African-American actress to win an Emmy. After the show ended in '75, Mike turned up frequently in TV movies and series. Today he does much charity work, golfs often, and remains as popular with fans as ever.

Mike Connors with Celeste Yarnall

EVERYBODY LOVES SOMEBODY

Mike's been married for over 50 years to the same woman, and he has two kids.

MY BACK PAGES

Mannix was created by the man behind *Mission: Impossible*, and composer Lalo Schifrin did the great music for both shows. . . . Unlike many other TV detectives (*Cannon, Columbo, Kojak,* for instance), Joe Mannix was athletic enough to run after and catch a taxiing airplane. . . . He drove a cool car, too—a Toronado 425 custom convertible in the first season, then Dodge Dart and Plymouth Barracuda convertibles in later seasons. . . . *Seinfeld* got it right—when George pitched a hare-brained scheme of physical derring-do, Jerry scoffed, "Who are you, Mannix?"

Sam Cooke

Though he died young, Sam is stilled remembered as one of the decade's coolest soul singers.

TAKIN' CARE OF BUSINESS

Born in Mississippi and raised in Chicago, Sam Cooke sang in soul and gospel groups as a kid. At 19 he joined the Soul Stirrers and sang gospel, but a few years later he made a secular record, "Lovable," under the name Dale

April 17, 1961—Actress Hayley Mills receives a special Juvenile Oscar for *Pollyanna*.
April 17, 1964—Lee Iacocca, creator of the Ford Mustang, makes the cover of *Time*. ☮ April 17, 1998—Linda McCartney dies.
April 18, 1946—Actress Hayley Mills is born in London. ☮ April 18, 1960—Golfer Arnold Palmer dramatically wins the Masters.

Cooke, which led to his departure from the Soul Stirrers so he could go solo.

Mainstream acceptance came quickly with "You Send Me," a #1 hit he co-wrote that knocked Elvis's "Jailhouse Rock" from the top. In the late '50s-early '60s, a long string of smooth R & B hits—including "Only Sixteen," "Chain Gang," "Wonderful World," "Another Saturday Night," "Cupid," "Twistin' the Night Away"—showed off his versatility and established him as one of the most popular artists of the pre-Beatles rock era; live albums such as *Sam Cooke at the Copa* ('64) proved him to be an appealing concert attraction.

He was also one of the most successful artists of the early '60s, having founded his own record label, SAR Records. Unfortunately his thriving career was cut short when he was shot and killed in '64. After his death more of his songs were released, including the protest anthem "A Change Is Gonna Come." Sam was inducted as a charter member of the Rock and Roll Hall of Fame in '86.

EVERYBODY LOVES SOMEBODY

Handsome and successful, Sam Cooke enjoyed a social life of swingin' excess and fathered several children with different women in the '50s. For several years he was married to a woman who died in a car crash in '57; two years later he married his high school sweetheart, with whom he had three kids. His death was bizarre—drunk and half-dressed, he was shot by the manager of an L.A. motel after he'd been arguing with an alleged prostitute. The shooter got off with a verdict of justifiable homicide. When Sam was buried a week later, hundreds of thousands of fans turned out to pay their respects. Sam's widow remarried one of the artists on the SAR label, Bobby Womack.

MY BACK PAGES

Sam had a tremendous influence on other singers, including Rod Stewart, Otis Redding, Smokey Robinson, Simon and Garfunkel, James Taylor (Garfunkel and Taylor sang "Wonderful World"), and Cat Stevens (who made "Another Saturday Night" a '70s hit). . . . He wrote the song "Somewhere There's a Girl" in honor of his first wife. . . . He also appeared on many talk shows, and his songs were later used in popular movies like *Animal House* and *The Blues Brothers*. . . . Supposedly Sam's last words were "Lady, you shot me!"

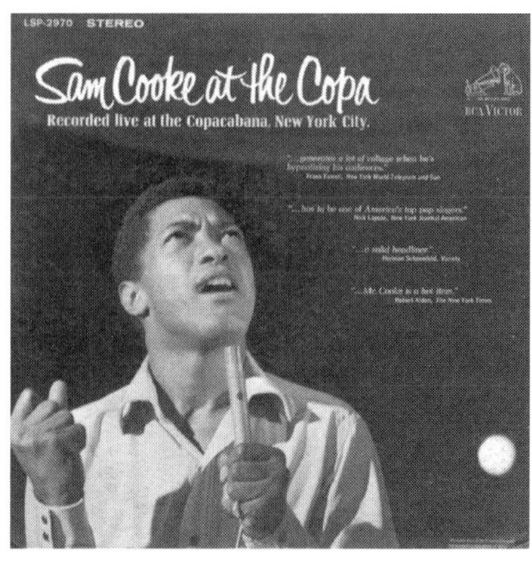

Yvonne Craig

This personable actress livened up the big and small screens with dozens of energetic appearances.

TAKIN' CARE OF BUSINESS

Looking over her credits one may think, "Dang, this girl was in everything." Yvonne Craig brought a wholesome appeal and exuberant energy to her varied roles. With short hair and youthful features, she had an amazing versatility—not many other '60s actresses could successfully sport a bikini, Batgirl vinyl, and hillbilly duds as well as she did.

As an Illinois youth Yvonne studied ballet, moving to L.A. in hopes of a dancing career. But at 22 she got a supporting part in the first, best *Gidget* movie ('59), and her Hollywood momentum built rapidly, bringing her parts in a decade's worth of movies—Bing Crosby's *High Time* ('60), two Elvis movies (*It Happened at the World's Fair*, '63, and *Kissin' Cousins*, '64), Frankie and Annette's *Ski Party* ('65), *In Like Flint* ('67)—and most of the decade's top TV shows—*The Big Valley*, *Wild Wild West*, *Star Trek* (as a sultry green alien), *The*

April 18, 1962—Bo Belinsky makes his first regular-season appearance. ☮ April 18, 1963—Actress Jane Asher meets Paul McCartney.
April 18, 1965—*She* with Ursula Andress opens.
April 18, 1966—At the Oscars, Julie Christie is Best Actress (*Darling*), Lee Marvin is Best Actor (*Cat Ballou*), and *The Sound of Music* is Best Picture.

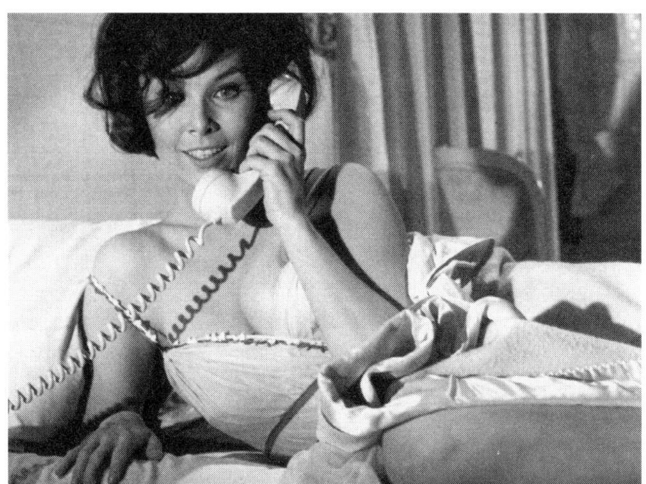

Mod Squad, *77 Sunset Strip*, *My Three Sons*, *Dr. Kildare*, *McHale's Navy*, *Mannix*, and many more. In the second season ('67–'68) of the campy *Batman*, Yvonne's Batgirl character was a librarian named Barbara Gordon, daughter of the Gotham City Police Commissioner and a crime-fightin', motorbike-ridin', cape-flarin', high-heel-boots-wearin' ally to the Dynamic Duo. Though her only appearances were in the show's last season, it's still her most popular role.

More TV appearances followed in the '70s, then later Yvonne built a career in L.A. real estate (successful, no doubt, because who wouldn't want to buy their house from Batgirl). Her candid autobiography, *From Ballet to the Batcave and Beyond*, came out in the spring of 2000.

EVERYBODY LOVES SOMEBODY

A rumored romance with Elvis, then two marriages, first for two years in the early '60s to singer Jimmie Boyd ("I Saw Mommie Kissing Santa Claus"), and then in the late '80s to her current husband, a real estate developer.

MY BACK PAGES

In *It Happened at the World's Fair*, Elvis sang the sexiest song of his movie career, the seductive "Relax" as he leaned over Yvonne. . . . Yvonne has proudly said that she did her own motorcycling on *Batman*.

Bobby Darin

This finger-snappin' smoothie transitioned to Hollywood and folk music before his untimely death.

TAKIN' CARE OF BUSINESS

Everybody's idea of an early '60s swinger, Bobby Darin was also a composer, actor, and successful folk singer during the decade. He was born Walden Robert Cassotto in the Bronx, his childhood marred by a rheumatic fever that scarred his heart. Always interested in music (he could play several instruments), he sang and composed songs as a teen and, using the last name Darin, had a sudden hit with "Splish, Splash" in '58. "Mack the Knife" the next year validated him with Grammy Awards for Best Record and Best New Artist.

Bobby's splashy concerts and slick tuxedoed style made him the quintessential Vegas showstopper into the mid-'60s, plus he continued to write songs such as "Dream Lover" and "Queen of the Hop" (as showcased on *The Bobby Darin Story*, '61). Heading to Hollywood, Bobby found a new career and a new marriage with *Come September*, the movie where he met 16-year-old Sandra Dee. *Hell Is for Heroes* ('62) and *Captain Newman, M.D.* ('63, for which Bobby got an Oscar nomination) were the best of the dozen movies that followed.

As his show-bizzy musical style fell out of favor, he reinvented himself as Bob Darin, covered songs by Dylan and the Stones, went quieter with "If I Were a Carpenter," and went silent with a retirement to Big Sur. He returned in the '70s with a new solo album, a contract with Motown, and his own TV variety show, but poor health plagued him until his death following open-heart surgery in '73. His towering musical accomplishments got him elected into the Rock and Roll Hall of Fame in '90 and into the Songwriters Hall of Fame in '99.

EVERYBODY LOVES SOMEBODY

After an intense relationship with singer Connie Francis in the late '50s, Bobby met the love of his life on the Italian set of *Come September*. Teenage Sandra Dee, according to a *Parade* magazine article in late '57, had never dated or even kissed "except in the line of duty." By '59, thanks to her years as a successful model and two hit movies—the beachy-keen *Gidget* and the classic romance *A Summer Place*—sweet-looking, 90-pound Sandra was America's perfect prom date.

The March '61 issue of *Motion Picture* magazine reported that when he mistakenly addressed her for the first time as Tuesday Weld, she fired back with "I always buy your records, Fabian." They were engaged in two months and eloped a month later. Sadly, a few weeks into the marriage she miscarried. She got pregnant during the filming of *Tammy Tell Me True* and a son was born in late '61.

Sandra starred in three mildly entertaining comedies with Bobby, but with her popularity diminishing her Universal contract ran out in '68, making her the studio's last contract player. Meanwhile she and Bobby separated in '63, and later she suffered another miscarriage. They finally divorced in '67. "It ended with a suddenness I still can't explain," she told *People* in '91. In '73 Bobby wed a woman he'd been living with for three years. They were married for only four months, splitting up two months before he died.

MY BACK PAGES

One story has it that he took the name Darin from the word Mandarin on the sign of a Chinese restaurant. . . . #68 on the VH1 list of shocking moments in rock history was the news that hit Bobby in the late '60s—throughout his life his true mother had been posing as his sister, and his deceased grandmother had been posing as his mother. . . . Sandra was memorialized in the musical *Grease*, which featured the song "Look at Me, I'm Sandra Dee". . . . In a '62 *16 Magazine* interview Sandra said her greatest extravagance was buying clothes and jewelry, and her favorite role was Gidget. . . . *Beyond the Sea*, starring Kevin Spacey and Kate Bosworth, came out in 2004 to mixed reviews.

Catherine Deneuve

This elegant French beauty with the bearing of a queen starred in several memorable '60s movies.

TAKIN' CARE OF BUSINESS

Unlike many other beautiful actresses, Catherine Deneuve didn't play gumsmackers in cheesy flicks that exploited her incredible looks for audience attention. She was usually in serious French films with artistic intentions, which means the mass American audience hasn't always appreciated her in the same way international audiences have.

Like Grace Kelly's in the '50s, Catherine's cinematic rep has usually been that of an elegant ice queen, beneath whose beautiful, cold exterior lurks a passionate sexuality. In her prime (which was like what, 40 years long?), she had one of the world's most exquisite faces, a face born to be photographed, a face often heralded by the press as the most beautiful in the world.

By age 17, Paris-born Catherine was a leading lady in French films, thanks to her early-'60s work with Roger

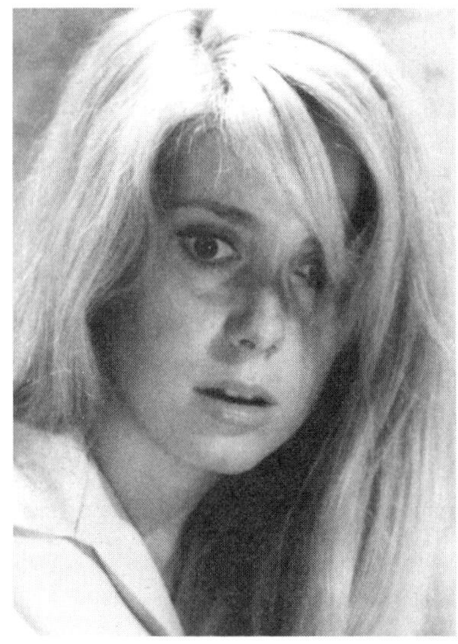

Vadim. By '64 she was an international star when her offbeat *The Umbrellas of Cherbourg* was the triumph of the Cannes Film Festival. And by now she's been in over 90 films, a remarkable cinematic output that has made her one of France's most prestigious and prominent global exports.

During her busy '60s (she made five movies in '65 alone), she explored a range of themes, from the terror of Roman Polanski's *Repulsion* ('65) to the cheery romance of the *Umbrellas* sequel, *The Young Girls of Rochefort* ('68), while always looking beautiful. Sexy, too: watch her in the fascinating mystery *Belle de Jour* ('67), where she changed from sheer nightgowns to adorable tennis whites to a "precocious schoolgirl" uniform and was never less than ravishing (quite an accomplishment considering that in one scene she took a bullet in the face).

She went on to star in over 50 more films, including Truffaut's *The Last Metro* ('80), the wonderful *Indochine* ('92, bringing her an Oscar nomination), and *Les Voleurs* ('96, showing her 50-something body in a discreet nude scene). While she was averaging two movies a year during the '70s, she also did popular perfume commercials for Chanel, and a decade later she launched her own perfume, Deneuve.

But Catherine's true impact has always been as more than just an actress or a celebrity, and only one other '60s actress can claim what she can: in '85 her image was chosen to succeed Brigitte Bardot's as "Marianne," the very symbol of the French Republic. Paying attention was *Playboy*, which featured her in October '65 in a pictorial called "France's Deneuve Wave" and 25 years later positioned her at #45, right behind Mae West, on its list of the century's sexiest stars.

EVERYBODY LOVES SOMEBODY

In '65, Catherine began a seven-year marriage with the decade's most famous fashion photographer, David Bailey. Catherine also took up with—but didn't marry—two of the decade's prominent celebs, director Roger Vadim (pre-Bailey) and actor Marcello Mastroianni (post-Bailey) and had children by both.

MY BACK PAGES

Her sister was French actress Francoise Dorleac, who was killed in a car wreck soon after she starred with Catherine in *The Young Girls of Rochefort*. . . . In the 2000s she said that she still went out salsa dancing with her daughter. . . . In 2005 she told *Vanity Fair* that Nature was the love of her life, and her motto was "With a valiant heart, nothing is impossible."

Pamela Des Barres

A spirited, optimistic star lover, pretty Pamela was famous as a much-loved rock groupie.

TAKIN' CARE OF BUSINESS

"You'd hang out with the band, it was very simple." Thus was the strategy that made Pamela Des Barres the personification of the free-spirited, free-lovin' '60s. Born Pamela Miller in the San Fernando Valley she was a teen rock fan devoted to Elvis in the '50s and to the Beatles and Dylan in the '60s.

At 17, she visited the Sunset Strip one night in '65 and was overwhelmed by the colorful excitement of the flamboyantly dressed, festive kids on the street; calling the new counterculture "a whole new world," she dove into the fashions, fads, and music. She split from her boyfriend, graduated from high school in '66, took various jobs to support her club-hopping, clothes-buying lifestyle, and began seriously pursuing and romancing rock stars.

In '68, Frank Zappa formed Pamela and her girlfriends into the first all-girl rock band, Girls Together Outrageously. The GTO's got a tepid reaction from critics when they performed for the first time: the concert was more like performance art, with spoken dialogues in between the strange, otherworldly songs (none of the girls could really sing or play instruments). Immediately after that concert Zappa had them cutting a record, with Jeff Beck and Rod Stewart on backup. The album *Permanent Damage*, 24 minutes of music and speech, came out in January '69 and got mixed reviews, at best. A month later, Zappa broke up the band when some of the girls dabbled in drugs and got arrested.

In '70, Miss Pamela began studying acting and got cast in Zappa's *200 Motels* ('71). Savaged by critics, the film was a flop, and with no job forthcoming Pamela became Zappa's nanny, taking care of his kids Dweezil and Moon Unit. She got a few more parts in mostly unseen movies, including Stallone's *Paradise Alley* ('78).

In the mid-'80s, she poured through her diaries and wrote *I'm With The Band: Confessions of a Groupie*, an instant bestseller that she followed with two more critically acclaimed books: *Take Another Little Piece of My Heart*, about her marriage and meetings with more rock stars, and *Rock Bottom*, a compendium of "horror stories" about overindulgence in the rock world. Today, a vivacious redhead as lithe and pretty as ever, she teaches writing in L.A. and is working on a new book.

EVERYBODY LOVES SOMEBODY

Pamela's first rock star boyfriend was Jim Morrison of the Doors, whom she briefly dated in '66. She lost her virginity in '67 to a member of Steppenwolf, then hooked up with the bassist for the Jimi Hendrix Experience. In '69 she fell hard for Jimmy Page when she got into a Led Zeppelin after-concert party; she was 21, he was 24, and they began some torrid dating. Unfortunately, he was also seeing a teenage girl simultaneously; Pamela was heartbroken but later that year she met Mick Jagger at a club, and she and the lead Stone then had a brief affair.

A year later Pamela chased (and was chased by) 32-year-old married country star Waylon Jennings, and they had what she told us was "an on-again/off-again fling for two years." When she started acting in the early '70s, she met the Who's drummer Keith Moon, and they too got intense, but he eventually returned to England and his wife and daughter.

Young actor Don Johnson entered her life in mid-'71, and they cohabitated for a year until he left for 15-year-old Melanie Griffith. In '73 Pamela met 26-year-old English rocker Michael Des Barres on a film set; he courted her, moved to L.A. to be with her, and married her in '77. A year later she gave birth to a son and settled into a life as a homemaker; her husband's drug and infidelity problems led to a divorce in '91.

MY BACK PAGES

Pamela remains unapologetic about her sexually active and unique life: "I had fun, I had an amazing time, it was a great life, and I knew some amazing people," she said in a TV interview. . . . In 2001 VH1 ranked the publication of *I'm With the Band* at #58 on the list of all-time most shocking moments in rock history. . . . Plans for a film of the book were announced in 2002. . . . Previous films were contemplated with Ally Sheedy, Drew Barrymore, or Christina Applegate playing Pamela.

Jackie DeShannon

Versatile Jackie DeShannon has enjoyed a long career as both a successful singer and composer.

TAKIN' CARE OF BUSINESS

Famous for her '60s hits, Jackie helped steer the course of music history as a pioneer of American folk-rock. A contemporary of the great Carole King and Joni Mitchell, she was one of the first successful female composers and so paved the way for the popular female singer/songwriters of the '70s. Other performers have long recognized her talent, as proven by the too-numerous-to-count cover versions of her songs. She's written with such luminaries as Van Morrison, Randy Newman, and Jimmy Page; she's recorded with Elvis, Barry White, and Dr. John; and she's shared stages with the Beatles, the Beach Boys, Neil Diamond, Glen Campbell, and many more.

Born in Kentucky and raised in Illinois, teenager Sharon Lee Myers cut '50s country records using the names Sherry Lee, Jackie Dee, and then Jackie Shannon (the name DeShannon appeared in '59, "from Shannon" a tribute to Irish folk songs and the Irish location). In '60, as she was starting to compose her own music, Jackie took the advice of rockabilly star Eddie Cochran and moved to L.A., where she quickly got a recording contract and made a string of promising, yet unsuccessful, records. Simultaneously, her songwriting career began to blossom, especially when she teamed up with Cochran's ex-girlfriend, Sharon Sheeley. Together they wrote minor-but-memorable hits for other artists, notably the Fleetwoods ("The Great Imposter") and Brenda Lee ("Dum Dum").

In '63 Jackie got significant airplay with her own "When You Walk in the Room." Her biggest exposure came when she was chosen as one of the opening acts on the Beatles' first American tour. Her fame spreading, she went to England for an appearance on the show *Ready, Steady, Go!* and writing sessions with Jimmy Page. Returning to the U.S., in '65 she recorded her first Top 10 single in the U.S. Ironically, it was a song written by others—"What the World Needs Now Is Love," penned by Burt Bacharach and Hal David.

She continued releasing albums throughout the decade, her versatile talent taking her from folk to rock to soul. *Laurel Canyon* in '68 cast Jackie in a gentle hippie mode that would influence '70s soft rockers. In '69, she co-wrote and recorded the masterful "Put a Little Love in Your Heart," the million-selling single that would be a Top 5 hit (and is still her personal favorite). Later that same year she had her last Top 40 hit with "Love Will Find a Way."

Meanwhile, as if conquering the music world weren't enough, Jackie, blonde, pretty, and slender, was appearing in youthful movies—especially *Surf Party* ('64) and *C'mon, Let's Live a Little* ('67)—and on many popular TV series and variety shows. After the '60s Jackie continued to write songs, most famously "Bette Davis Eyes," a monster hit in '81 for Kim Carnes. Throughout the '80s and '90s her songs continued to hit the charts and turn up in major movies, and among those singing her songs were Annie Lennox and Bruce Springsteen. In 2000, she released an acclaimed new album and played live to packed houses. By now she's got 600 songs, two dozen original albums, a dozen more compila-

April 27, 1962—Natalie Wood and Robert Wagner get divorced. ☮ April 27, 1963—*The Day of the Triffids* with Janette Scott opens.
April 27, 1967—*Two for the Road* with Audrey Hepburn opens. ☮ April 27, 1967—The first "Twiggy in New York" TV special airs.
April 28, 1929—Actress Carolyn Jones is born in Amarillo, Texas. ☮ April 28, 1941—Entertainer Ann-Margret is born in Valsjobyn, Sweden.

tions albums, and a Grammy on her résumé. Jackie DeShannon is still putting a little love in everybody's heart.

EVERYBODY LOVES SOMEBODY

After dating Elvis Presley in the early '60s, Jackie married a record exec in '66. Later she married Randy Edelman, who played keyboards on her '71 album *Songs* and later composed the scores for dozens of films, TV movies, and TV shows. Their son is involved in the management side of the music business.

MY BACK PAGES

A mid-'60s article about her gave the following likes and dislikes: her favorite artists were Edith Piaf, Bach, Chopin, and the Beatles, her favorite color was "all of them," her favorite beverages were coffee and tea, her favorite food was a BLT with cheese on wheat toast, her likes were "foreign films, great black and white photography, collecting magazines, originality," and her dislikes were "phonies, waiting around before performing, trusting people and being disappointed, and too much or too little of anything."

Donna de Varona

This sleek, blonde aquamaiden won two Olympic gold medals.

TAKIN' CARE OF BUSINESS

Like Peggy Fleming in skating, Donna de Varona defined her sport in the '60s and brought it global attention. Even before her most glorious moments at the Tokyo Olympics, she had a strong enough impact to make the cover of *Life* magazine. A California girl with a name that translates as "lady from Verona," Donna was a swimming star who made the U.S. Olympic Team for the 1960 Rome Games at only 13 years old.

Before the '64 Tokyo Olympics, Donna had already broken 18 world records and 10 American records and was a star at UCLA. In Tokyo she set the Olympic record and won the gold medal in the 400-meter individual medley, and she set a world record and again won gold with the 400-meter freestyle relay team. For her accomplishments she was named America's Outstanding Woman Athlete for '64. A year later she became the first female network sportscaster for ABC Sports, and at the '68 Mexico City Olympics she was a prominent TV commentator (a career she continued for decades).

More importantly, she worked tirelessly on behalf of women's athletics and helped get Title IX of 1972's Equal Education Amendment Act passed, which gave women and men athletes equal financial support. She was also instrumental in getting the Amateur Sports Act of 1978 passed, thus making training facilities and money more accessible to women athletes. In '74 she and Billie Jean King founded the Women's Sports Foundation (Donna was president and chairperson), she served on President Gerald Ford's Commission on Olympic Sports, and she worked with a federal anti-poverty program to help inner-city kids learn to swim. So enduring is her impact on sports, she's been inducted into the International Swimming Hall of Fame and the International Women's Sports Hall of Fame.

EVERYBODY LOVES SOMEBODY

Donna's married, has two kids, and lives in Connecticut.

MY BACK PAGES

In addition to the *Life* cover, Donna made the covers of *Time*, the *Saturday Evening Post*, and *Sports Illustrated* (twice). . . . Donna authored the book *Hydro-Aerobics—Swim Your Way to Total Fitness*, and she narrated a video called *Swimming for Fitness*. . . . Her sister is actress Joanna Kerns, the mom on *Growing Pains* who's also been in dozens of TV movies.

'60s Athletes in the U.S. Olympic Hall of Fame

Muhammad Ali (boxing)
Bob Beamon (track)
Ralph Boston (track)
Willie Davenport (track)
Glenn Davis (track)
Donna de Varona (swimming)
Lee Evans (track)
Peggy Fleming (figure skating)
George Foreman (boxing)
Dick Fosbury (track)
Joe Frazier (boxing)
Bob Hayes (track)
Rafer Johnson (track)
Debbie Meyer (swimming)
Billy Mills (track)
Al Oerter (track)
Wilma Rudolph (track)
Don Schollander (swimming)
Bill Toomey (track)
Wyomia Tyus (track)
U.S. Men's Team, '60, '64 (basketball)
U.S. Men's Team, '60 (hockey)

Angie Dickinson

Combining brains and beauty, style and independence, Angie starred in several '60s classics.

TAKIN' CARE OF BUSINESS

Always popular and always working, Angie Dickinson made an average of two movies a year through the '60s and is today correctly regarded as one of cinema's enduring treasures. A North Dakota girl, she began her career by entering and winning TV's *Beauty Parade* in '53, which led to secretary-type roles in minor movies in the mid-'50s. *Rio Bravo* in '59 made her a star and confirmed her strengths as a spunky, beautiful, self-assured woman who wasn't intimidated by a cast fulla tough guys. After the stylin' Rat Packer *Ocean's 11* ('60), she won a Golden Globe as the Most Promising Newcomer ("newcomer"—she'd already been in a half-dozen movies). Strong roles in 16 '60s flicks followed, including *Captain Newman, M.D.* ('63), *The Killers* ('64), and Burt Reynolds's *Sam Whiskey* ('69). Best was *Point Blank* ('67), the hard-boiled cult classic where she smacked Lee Marvin around. From the '70s right up into the 2000s she has had some great credits, especially her influential *Police Woman* TV series (which brought her a Golden Globe as Best Actress) and the erotic *Dressed to Kill* ('80). When *Playboy* published its list of the "100 Sexiest Stars of the Century" in '99, the magazine ranked Angie in the top 50 between two more screen legends, Clara Bow and Hedy Lamarr.

EVERYBODY LOVES SOMEBODY

Angeline Brown married semi-pro football player Gene Dick-

April 29, 1966—Actress Julie Christie makes the cover of *Life*. ☮ April 29, 1967—"Respect" by Aretha Franklin debuts on the charts.
April 30, 1966—"Good Lovin'" by the Rascals hits #1. ☮ April 30, 1970—Actress Inger Stevens commits suicide with a drug overdose in L.A.
May 1, 1923—Joseph Heller is born in Brooklyn, New York. ☮ May 1, 1924—Terry Southern is born in Alvarado, Texas.

inson in '51. As she got more involved with her career, they split up amicably in '55 and divorced in '60. Affectionate rumors have linked her with several famous names—the only relationship she's acknowledged was her on-again/off-again decade with Frank Sinatra, which continued even though they were at times married to other people. She married handsome composer Burt Bacharach in '65; they tied the knot in Vegas after a whirlwind three-month romance and split up in the late '70s when her schedule got too chaotic with *Police Wo-man*. Single and still dazzling in the 21st century, she's a prominent guest at glamorous Oscar parties and other exclusive events.

MY BACK PAGES

Angie's often played screen characters with great names, including Lucky Legs, Feathers, Ruby, Pepper, and Lindy. . . . In the mid-'60s, she and Burt Bacharach appeared in suave commercials for Martini & Rossi. . . . Wearing a slinky black pants outfit, she once crooned "I'll Never Fall in Love Again" on *The Dean Martin Show*. . . . In '63 Universal Studios had her legs insured for a million dollars, then two decades later those same legs were shown off in a memorable billboard for California Avocados. . . . Angie has campaigned for Alzheimer's research by speaking before Congress for additional funding to fight Alzheimer's disease. . . . She turned down the role of Krystle Carrington in *Dynasty* (it went to Linda Evans), and she rejected an offer from *Playboy* to be featured in a photo spread, which came when she was over 50 years old.

Tom Donahue

The pioneering DJ who opened up radio to cool possibilities.

TAKIN' CARE OF BUSINESS

Like it when an FM station plays a cool album all the way through, or pulls out some lost nugget from a rare bootleg? Thank Tom Donahue. The big man of radio was big in every way—in stature (well over 200 pounds), in ambition (he took on traditional AM radio), in impact (he was inducted into the Rock and Roll Hall of Fame in '96). At 21, he was a DJ in South Carolina, moved up the coast to Philly and D.C., and then headed west in '61.

For the first half of the decade he was a fast-talking star at San Francisco's KYA, an AM station that played, in the style of other Top Forty stations around the country, the same narrow list of quick teenybopper pop hits over and over, punctuated by snappy patter from hepped-up DJs. Tom finally tired of it all in '65 and started up his own label, Autumn Records, scoring a big hit with "Laugh Laugh" by San Francisco's Beau Brummels. He also co-produced the Beatles' last stadium concert, held at Candlestick Park in '66.

But radio was where he would stage his revolution. Eager to play "album-oriented rock" by the Who, Led Zeppelin, and other bands that explored concepts deeper than what could be found in a breezy two-minute pop tune, Tom wrote an article for *Rolling Stone* in '67; "AM Radio Is Dead and Its Rotting Corpse Is Stinking Up the Airwaves" was as confrontational as its title implied and advocated DJs taking playlists back into their own hands.

May 1, 1939—Singer Judy Collins is born in Seattle. ☮ May 1, 1958—Elvis Presley's *King Creole* opens.
May 1, 1961—The Pulitzer Prize is given to *To Kill a Mockingbird*. ☮ May 1, 1967—Elvis Presley marries Priscilla Beaulieu in Las Vegas.
May 1, 1970—Diana Ross leaves the Supremes. ☮ May 2, 1946—Singer Lesley Gore is born in Tenafly, New Jersey.

Presenting his idea of "underground radio" to Bay Area FM stations, he found a home at what had been a Spanish-language station, KMPX in San Jose, and the cool-talk-cool-rock revolution was on, with Tom as the authoritative leader. He worked the evening shift, sometimes played live music, made off-the-cuff political announcements, and became a well-liked big daddy to the community.

In '68 he took the format to what was formerly a classical-music station, KSAN-FM in San Francisco, and soon he'd founded two more "free-form" FM stations in L.A., KMET and KPPC. Stations around the county picked up on the trend, and within a few years bands that never got played on AM stations—Aerosmith, Pink Floyd, Boston, Yes—were becoming huge sellers on the strength of their FM exposure. Tom was general manager of KSAN when, at only 46 years old, he died of a heart attack in '75.

EVERYBODY LOVES SOMEBODY

Tom and Raechel Donahue were married in '69. They'd met when she was a 17-year-old staffer at his Autumn Records label. She too became a DJ, and after he died she relocated to L.A. where she became a star at KMET. In the '80s, she was at the forefront of alternative music with KROQ in Pasadena and then joined the Rick Dees laff-fest at KIIS-FM. She's now a writer and documentary filmmaker based in Denver.

MY BACK PAGES

One of the employees at KSAN in the '60s was Howard Hesseman, who later played DJ Johnny Fever on the show *WKRP in Cincinnati*. . . . Raechel did voiceovers in many movies and came up with the "jive talk" for Barbara Billingsley in *Airplane* ('80).

'60s DJs in the Radio Hall of Fame

Dick Biondi (KRLA, Los Angeles)
Karl Haas (WJR, Detroit)
Hal Jackson (WLIB, New York)
"Murray the K" Kaufman (WINS, New York)
Herb Kent (WVON, Chicago)
Larry Lujack (WLS, Chicago)
Robert W. Morgan (KHJ, Los Angeles)
"Cousin Brucie" Morrow (WABC, New York)
Gary Owens (KMPC, Los Angeles)
Wolfman Jack (XERB, Tijuana)

Donovan

The serene singer/songwriter was a popular, well-connected '60s troubadour.

TAKIN' CARE OF BUSINESS

Donovan Leitch was born in Scotland into a working-class family. He grew up with a love of poetry and song, singing songs in public at age 6 and playing drums in a band before he was a teenager. In the early '60s Donovan dropped out of college and dropped into the folk music scene around London. He pursued bohemian interests—poetry, music, girls, and travel—and it was while playing guitar and singing in small pubs that he was spotted and signed by a record company in '64.

A string of popular appearances on the British music show *Ready, Steady, Go!* led to his first record—the self-penned "Catch the Wind," an instant hit on both sides of the Atlantic. More hits followed all decade long, most of them wistful ballads with gentle themes (though the up-tempo diversion "Mellow Yellow," the jazzy "Sunshine Superman," and the dark "Season of the Witch" showed off his eclectic talents).

May 2, 1962—Bo Belinsky no-hits the Orioles. ☮ May 2, 1965—"For Your Love" by the Yardbirds hits the charts.
May 2, 1969—Singer Judy Collins makes the cover of *Life*. ☮ May 3, 1933—Singer James Brown is born in Barnwell, South Carolina.
May 3, 1939—Singer Mary Hopkin is born in Wales. ☮ May 4, 1922—Marine biologist Dr. Eugenie Clark is born in New York.

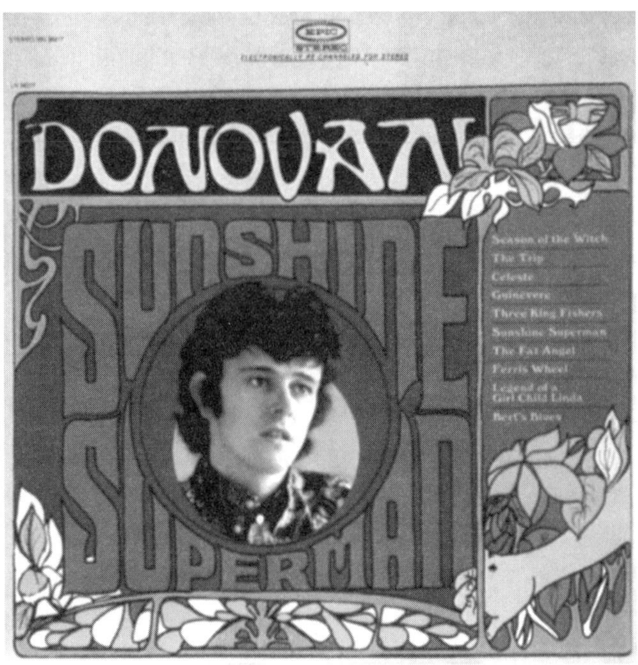

A major concert draw in the '60s, as a singin'-songwritin'-solo-performin' poet he filled the void left by Dylan when the American folk legend swapped his acoustic guitar for an electric and got a band. The mid-'60s Donovan was a pacifist flower child, playing anti-war anthems and psychedelic love songs while decked out in robes and surrounded on stage by incense and flowers.

Experimenting with sounds and styles later in the decade, he worked with various Beatles, Stones, and future Led Zeppelins (Jimmy Page and John Paul Jones played on "Hurdy Gurdy Man"); experimenting with media, he wrote songs for the films *Poor Cow* ('67) and *If It's Tuesday, This Must Be Belgium* ('69); and experimenting with lifestyles, he was alongside the Beatles when they embraced Eastern religion in India in '68. In '70 he decided to stop all the global touring, settled down in England, and wrote the soundtracks for two '72 films, *The Pied Piper of Hamlyn* (he also played the title character) and Zeffirelli's *Brother Sun, Sister Moon*.

In the '70s he released more records and played more concerts, though his soft songs were getting drowned out by the louder, faster punk era. In the '80s, Donovan relocated to the California deserts for some sporadic recording of lesser impact; in the '90s he moved again, this time to Ireland, where he taught spiritual subjects and continued to make music, his reputation boosted by reissues, boxed sets, and acclaimed new albums in '96 and '04.

EVERYBODY LOVES SOMEBODY

On the set of *Ready, Steady, Go!* in '65, Donovan met Linda Lawrence, the woman he'd call his muse. His '66 LP *Sunshine Superman* was dedicated to her, but unfortunately she was with Brian Jones of the Rolling Stones and was already the mother of his son. Meanwhile, Donovan had a son of his own in '69, Donovan Leitch, Jr. (later an actor—*I Shot Andy Warhol*, '96), followed two years later by a daughter, Ione Skye (later an actress—*Say Anything*, '89). After Brian Jones's death in '69, Linda sought out Donovan in '70, and later that year they got married. They added two daughters to the family in the '70s.

MY BACK PAGES

As shown in the '67 documentary *Don't Look Back*, Donovan palled with Dylan, and jammed informally with him, when Dylan made his celebrated tour of England in '65. . . . Yardley used his "Wear Your Love Like Heaven" in its mid-'60s cosmetics commercials. . . . In '67 Donovan was in the studio with the Beatles as they recorded "A Day in the Life". . . . He would've played the Monterey International Pop Festival if not for a pot bust that briefly kept him out of the U.S. . . . In the late '60s, Pattie Boyd (George Harrison's wife) and her sisters briefly ran a London fashion boutique called Juniper, named after the Donovan song "Jennifer Juniper"—that song was inspired by Pattie's sister Jenny, who had spent time with Donovan in India in '68. . . . For decades Donovan's songs have been used in dozens of movies, everything from the hard-edged *GoodFellas* ('90) to the goofy *Dumb and Dumber* ('94).

May 4, 1929—Actress Audrey Hepburn is born in Brussels, Belgium. ☮ May 5, 1942—Singer Tammy Wynette is born in Redbay, Alabama. May 5, 1961—Astronaut Alan Shepard is the first American in space. ☮ May 5, 1966—*Arabesque* with Sophia Loren opens. May 5, 1972—Gymnast Cathy Rigby makes the cover of *Life*. ☮ May 6, 1963—The Pulitzer Prize is awarded to Barbara Tuchman (*Guns of August*).

Donna Douglas

This likable Southerner played curvaceous Elly May Clampett on *The Beverly Hillbillies.*

TAKIN' CARE OF BUSINESS

Of '60s TV actresses, Donna Douglas was one of those who was probably the closest in real life to the role she played on TV. A Loozeeana-born, farm-raised, critter-lovin' tomboy named Doris Smith, she got her start in beauty pageants and won the '57 Miss New Orleans title. The exposure led to small roles in movies and TV shows until her career was made with *The Beverly Hillbillies.*

The most-watched show of the '60s, the homey hillbilly comedy debuted on her birthday in the fall of '62 and within three months topped the Nielsen ratings, a position it maintained until '65. So popular was *The Beverly Hillbillies*, it set ratings records that lasted for decades, it inspired a spin-off, *Green Acres*, and its theme song was a radio hit. On the show, Donna, wearing tight jeans and big blonde hair, had an undemanding role that was pretty much limited to looking attractive, out-wrasslin' Jethro, and bringing home lost animals (among them a bear, bobcat, chimpanzee, eagle, lion, ostrich, and skunk).

While the show was at its peak, Donna landed one of the title roles in an energetic, entertaining Elvis flick, *Frankie and Johnny* ('66). Though Donna has a fine singing voice, her vocals were dubbed in her duet with the King, "Petunia, the Gardener's Daughter." Back on TV, the Clampetts moved from the hills of Beverly to the hills of syndicationland in '71. Donna put in a couple more TV appearances, her last hurrah coming with the slight TV movie *The Return of the Beverly Hillbillies* ('81). From the mid-'70s into the '80s she sold real estate and later established herself as a gospel singer. Unlike other actresses who prefer to forget their earlier roles, Donna has embraced hers and still occasionally makes public appearances dressed like Elly May.

EVERYBODY LOVES SOMEBODY

Elly had a movie-star boyfriend named Dash Riprock (the character's stage name, his real name was Homer Noodleman). Meanwhile, Donna was married in '49 while still in high school and within five years had a son and a divorce. Despite a few weak suggestions that she and Elvis were an item during *Frankie and Johnny*, it's more likely their relationship was limited to spiritual discussions (all sources confirm her as a devout Christian). She married and divorced one of the directors of *The Beverly Hillbillies* in the last half of the '70s.

MY BACK PAGES

Donna made one other memorable contribution to the show: she delivered the enthusiastic "This has been a Filmways presentation!" coda after each episode. . . . Even as a supporting char-

May 6, 1967—Jefferson Airplane's "Somebody to Love" hits the charts.
May 6, 1969—Neil Armstrong narrowly escapes death in the crash of a lunar test vehicle. ☮ May 7, 1931—Singer Teresa Brewer is born in Toledo, Ohio.
May 7, 1966—"Monday Monday" by the Mamas and the Papas hits the charts. ☮ May 7, 1966—The Beach Boys' album *Pet Sounds* is released.

Top Nielsen-Rated Shows

1960–'61: *Gunsmoke*

1961–'62: *Wagon Train*

1962–'63: *The Beverly Hillbillies*

1963–'64: *The Beverly Hillbillies*

1964–'65: *Bonanza*

1965–'66: *Bonanza*

1966–'67: *Bonanza*

1967–'68: *The Andy Griffith Show*

1968–'69: *Rowan and Martin's Laugh-In*

1969–'70: *Rowan and Martin's Laugh-In*

acter, Elly May was popular enough for Kellogg's to offer an Elly doll on cereal boxes (she came wearing either a skirt or jeans, both tied with a rope belt). . . . Cult fave: Donna did a great *Twilight Zone* episode called "The Eye of the Beholder" in which she was deemed "ugly" in a society populated by disfigured people.

Patty Duke

Broadway, movie, and TV audiences were all wowed in the '60s by this talented teen.

TAKIN' CARE OF BUSINESS

How many other teens had a 12-inch doll of themselves in the '60s? Patty did, and it shows how strong her impact was on the decade. Not only was she a major star from the get-go, she was a role model. During the '60s, Milton Bradley sold the Patty Duke Game (a board game filled with teenage dilemmas such as balancing homework with parties), plus there were paper-doll books, storybooks, and coloring books that cashed in on her fame. All this while she was still just a teenager.

A Manhattan-born child actress with a ready smile, Patty had been doing commercials and small TV parts when she made a stunning Broadway debut as the young Helen Keller in *The Miracle Worker* in '59. Reprising the role for the '62 film, she won the Oscar for Best Supporting Actress, making her the youngest actress ever to win an Academy Award until Tatum O'Neal a decade later. That same year Patty also won a Golden Globe as Best Newcomer.

In '63, she became the youngest actress to have her own TV series. Patty's dual roles as the identical cousins Cathy (who, according to the theme song, "adores a minuet") and Patty ("a hot dog makes her lose control") brought her the first of nine Emmy nominations. Firmly entrenched as one of the most popular and prodigiously talented teens in America, she started making music, and from '65–'67 released four hit albums. When *The Patty Duke Show* left primetime in '66, Patty returned to the big screen with several strong roles, including a descent into the campy *Valley of the Dolls* ('67) as pilled-up Neely O'Hara. The touching lead in the sensitive *Me, Natalie* brought her a second Golden Globe in '70. She then became one of the queens of the TV movie (among them a '79 remake of *The Miracle Worker* with Patty in the Annie Sullivan role and Melissa Gilbert as Helen).

Hail to the Chief ('87) was just one of the three TV sitcoms she starred in during the '80s and '90s. Signifying her long contributions to the medium, in '99 *TV Guide* ranked her #40 on its list of the Top 50 TV Stars ever. More than just a popular star, however, she has become a bright light in the dark, misunderstood world of manic-depression, thanks to her two bestselling books (including *Call Me Anna*, '87) that illuminated her struggles with the mental disorder.

EVERYBODY LOVES SOMEBODY

As she later wrote, Patty's "childhood was one of outward glory and inner torment." Her father left the family when

May 8, 1963—*Dr. No*, the first James Bond movie with Sean Connery, opens.
May 8, 1966—The book *Valley of the Dolls* hits #1 on the *New York Times* bestseller list.
May 9, 1936—Actress Glenda Jackson is born in Cheshire, England. ☮ May 9, 1946—Actress Candice Bergen is born in Beverly Hills.

Patty was 6; her mother was given to bouts of severe depression. Named Anna at birth, Patty received her new name from her managers, whom she called "tyrannical" in her autobiography. She moved in with them when she was 16, and according to her they controlled her life, giving her pills and liquor, subjecting her to sexual abuse, and wreaking psychological damage that later resulted in depression, fits of rage, substance abuse, anorexia, and suicide attempts.

Her first beau was Frank Sinatra, Jr., whom she met in '64. In '65 she married an assistant director on *The Patty Duke Show* who was 14 years her senior. It didn't last; spiraling into a morass of drugs and alcohol, she experienced hallucinations and displayed bizarre, impulsive behavior, which included a turbulent two-week marriage with someone she had just met. In '70 a budding romance between 24-year-old Patty and 17-year-old Desi Arnaz, Jr. was ix-nayed, Patty later wrote, by a forceful Lucille Ball.

In early '71, Patty gave birth to Sean, son of actor John Astin, who played Gomez on *The Addams Family* (Sean played Sam in *The Lord of the Rings* trilogy). Patty and John married in '72, and another son, Mackenzie (later a regular on *Facts of Life*), was born in '73. In '85 she and John divorced, and she remarried the next year. All of these topics and more she has courageously and candidly discussed in her books; now living in Idaho, she has emerged in the 21st century as a successful writer, a TV legend, and one of Hollywood's most honest, candid stars.

MY BACK PAGES

Patty won TV's *$64,000 Challenge* in '58, but when news leaked that the quiz show was rigged, Patty testified to the investigating committee that she had been fed the answers. . . . Respected by her peers, Patty was for a time the president of the Screen Actors Guild, the first woman to hold that position. . . . She has also crusaded for women's rights, famine relief, AIDS research, and nuclear disarmament.

Bob Dylan

Just as Sinatra and Elvis had done in the '40s and '50s, Bob Dylan defined/catalyzed/inspired the '60s.

TAKIN' CARE OF BUSINESS

Back then Bob Dylan was the rock star the Beatles wanted to meet; today he is widely regarded as the single most influential musician of the '60s. Sure, there were plenty of singers with smoother voices, and composers who wrote more hummable melodies, and guitar gods who reinvented what guitars could do, but for the first half of the '60s nobody was writing lyrics like Bob's. He was rock's first true wordsmith, and from his challenging artistry came the sophisticated songs of the mature Beatles, the introspective works of Joni Mitchell, Paul Simon, Jackson Browne, and thousands of other rock poets, and most importantly, a whole new vocabulary of metaphor and allusion for songwriters. Reduced to the most basic terms: before him, rock music was simple and broad; after him, rock music was complex and personal.

He arrived in New York in the '60s with a hobo's hazy past (he's always been an elusive biographical subject). Robert Zimmerman of Minnesota had played guitar in various high school bands, attended the University of Minnesota as an art student, and soaked up traditional folk and classic blues songs while playing in coffeehouses with a name borrowed from his favorite poet, Dylan Thomas. Bob's pilgrimage to his hospitalized hero, Woody Guthrie, got him to Greenwich Village in '61, where his career as a folk singer began. He strummed his guitar to other people's songs then, his face soft with baby fat, his reputation slowly building in folk circles.

A nice write-up in the *New York Times* landed him a record contract and his first album of folk songs. A year later he had his first hit album, *The Freewheelin' Bob Dylan*, and the first of his signature anthems, "Blowin' in the Wind." Artistic leaps came with every subsequent album for the next three years. *The Times They Are A-Changin'* ('64) was an am-

bitious collection of mature, articulate songcraft that made him the spokesman of the protesters, though he never pursued or claimed the title.

Later that year he partially separated himself from his "serious" image with *Another Side of Bob Dylan,* which presented whimsical favorites ("All I Really Want to Do") alongside collages of imagery ("My Back Pages"). His first successful forays into electrified rock ("Subterranean Homesick Blues") came on *Bringing It All Back Home* in '65—this album's breakthrough material got him excoriated at that summer's Newport Folk Festival by folk fans who heard betrayal in his new music.

Kicked off with what sounded like a defiant gunshot, the all-electric *Highway 61 Revisited* in August '65 was dramatic and exciting—it's hailed as one of rock's greatest albums ever (his highest-ranking LP, #4, on the *Rolling Stone* list of the all-time best albums, right between *Revolver* and *Rubber Soul*), and it showcased what was, at the time, rock's longest hit single, the epic "Like a Rolling Stone" (ranked #1 on the *Rolling Stone* list of all-time best songs). Nine months later the #9 album on the *Rolling Stone* list, the double-LP *Blonde on Blonde,* cemented Bob's repu-

30 Artists (of Thousands) Who Have Recorded Dylan's Songs

Eddie Albert	**Bette Midler**
Beach Boys	**Willie Nelson**
Harry Belafonte	**Elvis Presley**
Michael Bolton	**Telly Savalas**
Debbie Boone	**William Shatner**
Johnny Cash	**Bobby Sherman**
Cher	**Simon and Garfunkel**
Bobby Darin	**Nancy Sinatra**
Marlene Dietrich	**Sting**
George Harrison	**Supremes**
Goldie Hawn	**Tiny Tim**
Isaac Hayes	**U2**
Jimi Hendrix	**Lawrence Welk**
Guns 'n' Roses	**Mae West**
Billy Joel	**Stevie Wonder**

May 10, 2001—Actress Deborah Walley dies of cancer in Arizona. ☮ May 11, 1941—Singer Eric Burdon is born in Newcastle, England.
May 11, 1963—Peter, Paul and Mary's "Puff" hits #1 on the *Billboard* "easy listening" charts.
May 11, 1967—*Turn On, Tune In, Drop Out* with Timothy Leary opens. ☮ May 12, 1928—Composer Burt Bacharach is born in Kansas City, Missouri.

tation as an endlessly inventive artist.

Words were overflowing from the prolific writer these years—coating the backs of several '60s albums were hundreds of lines of poetry, and in '66 he completed his stream-of-consciousness book, *Tarantula*. A mysterious mid-'66 motorcycle accident sent him into a long seclusion until the end of the decade—when records did surface (*John Wesley Harding*, '67, and *Nashville Skyline*, '69), they were once again in a new musical direction, this time towards a gentler sound.

Bob's '70s output, like that of the solo Beatles, was met with a range of reactions; bracketing the decade were disappointments (*Self-Portrait*, '70, *Street Legal*, '78), but in between were some of his biggest triumphs (the achingly passionate *Blood on the Tracks*, '75, and immensely popular tours in '74 and '76). Declaring himself a born-again Christian, he released religious-themed albums in the '80s, continued to tour tirelessly, teamed up with other superstars such as the Traveling Wilburys, and won a Grammy with, surprisingly, an old-fashioned folk record (*Good As I Been to You*, '92).

An Oscar in 2001 for "Things Have Changed" and two masterful double albums, the ruminative *Time Out of Mind* ('97) and the playful *Love and Theft* (2001), took him into the 21st century with multiple Grammy Awards, more acclaim, a growly voice, and vast new audiences who correctly revered him as music's pre-eminent sage.

EVERYBODY LOVES SOMEBODY

Through the first half of the '60s Bob was in an on-again/off-again relationship with singer Joan Baez. However, another girlfriend, Suze Rotolo, was shown all cozy on the cover of *The Freewheelin' Bob Dylan* (his manager's wife was shown with Bob on the cover of *Bringing It All Back Home*). In '65 he secretly married a former model and Playboy Bunny, Sara Lownds, who would be the subject of several of his songs, including "Sad Eyed Lady of the Lowlands," "Wedding Song," "I'll Be Your Baby Tonight," "On a Night Like This," "If Not For You," and "Sara." They had four children together—one of them, Jakob, would grow up to be a rock star with the Wallflowers. The mid-'70s break-up with Sara would yield the material for one of his most personal and acclaimed albums, *Blood on the Tracks*. A decade later, Bob married his backup singer; they had a daughter before divorcing in the '90s.

MY BACK PAGES

When Bob and the Beatles did meet in '64, he introduced them to marijuana. . . . His musical influence on them turned up almost immediately on the folksy, poetic *Rubber Soul* ('65). . . . Bob has been the subject of numerous landmark documentaries, especially *Don't Look Back* ('67), an intimate, no-holds-barred chronicle of his '65 British tour, and *No Direction Home* (2005), Martin Scorsese's detailed look at his pre-'66 career. . . . Bob's also made his own feature films, though they've been too experimental to garner much praise (*Renaldo and Clara*, '78, *Masked and Anonymous*, 2003). . . . Interviewers have usually found him to be a contrary, evasive subject who spars with, rather than answers, their questions, and only in recent years has he openly reflected on his life (his autobiographical *Chronicles, Volume 1* came out in 2005).

Shirley Eaton

Beautiful Shirley Eaton became an international sex symbol with one brief but memorable movie role.

TAKIN' CARE OF BUSINESS

Shirley's versatility enabled her to appear in adventure films, comedies, mysteries, even sci-fi, playing good girls, bad girls, military girls, and science girls. When you look that good, directors will find a place for you, no matter what kind of movie they're making. A child actress in the late '40s, London-born Shirley graduated to lots of movie ac-

tivity in the '50s, especially in Britain's popular *Carry On . . .* comedies. She appeared in films through most of the '60s, but none were nearly as big as *Goldfinger* ('64), which for awhile was in the *Guinness Book of World Records* as the fastest-grossing movie ever.

On the Bond Market it is still perhaps the most highly regarded of all time, and after three decades of Bond movies, hers are still among the best, sexiest Bond scenes ever filmed, though there are only seven minutes of them. Shirley's character surrendered to Bond's charms within about ten seconds of meeting him (but she had the decency to wait until that night to bed down with him and then start wearing his shirt).

It was while she was nuzzling his neck that Connery talked to Felix Leiter on the phone and delivered one of the best Bond quips ever: "Something big's come up." Minutes later, Shirley's character was killed with skin-suffocating gold paint, the best costume ever worn by any Bond actress and still one of the classic images of '60s cinema.

Later she starred in the classy *Ten Little Indians* ('66) and a handful of decent adventure flicks, but regrettably for movie audiences she left the biz in the '70s to spend more time with her family. An accomplished painter, sculptor, and singer, she's found time to write her autobiography, perform charity work, and make frequent appearances on live British television. For Bond fans worldwide, she will always be a golden memory from the '60s.

EVERYBODY LOVES SOMEBODY

Shirley was married to a building contractor from '57 until his death from cancer in the mid-'90s. She's now got two grown kids and currently lives near London.

MY BACK PAGES

At 17, Shirley made her movie debut doing the horseback-riding scenes for Janet Leigh in *Prince Valiant* ('54). . . . Shirley was actually wearing a G-string for her big paint scene in *Goldfinger*, and a patch of skin on her stomach was left exposed so she wouldn't die during filming. . . . The "gold paint" was actually thick skin lotion loaded with millions of real gold particles; real paint would've dried and cracked under the hot lights.

Barbara Eden

This ever-smilin' dreamgirl became a TV legend when she played a bare-midriffed wish-granter.

TAKIN' CARE OF BUSINESS

Always fun, always watchable, Barbara Eden has stolen every scene she's ever been in. Born in Arizona and raised in San Francisco, teenage Barbara Jean Moorhead moved to Hollywood to break into show biz. Within a

May 13, 1965—*The Yellow Rolls-Royce* with Shirley MacLaine opens. ☮ May 14, 1936—Singer Bobby Darin is born in the Bronx, New York.
May 14, 1969—*The Love Machine* by Jacqueline Susann is published. ☮ May 14, 1998—Singer Frank Sinatra dies in L.A.
May 15, 1963—Peter, Paul and Mary win a Grammy for "If I Had a Hammer." ☮ May 15, 1965—Actress Angie Dickinson marries composer Burt Bacharach.

few years she was in *Will Success Spoil Rock Hunter* ('57) and was also on one of the last episodes of *I Love Lucy*. In '58 she became a TV sitcom star, playing Loco Jones, the glasses-wearing-Monroe-style bombshell, on *How to Marry a Millionaire*.

One of the best Elvis movies, the song-light, tension-heavy *Flaming Star*, followed in '60, with lots more cool movies close behind: *Voyage to the Bottom of the Sea* ('61), *Five Weeks in a Balloon* ('62), *Ride the Wild Surf* ('64), *The 7 Faces of Dr. Lao* ('64), and *The Brass Bottle* (also '64). The latter was notable as a retelling of the classic "genie in a bottle" story, but in this one the troubled master was Tony Randall and the genie was Burl Ives, not exactly a genie with a cute bare midriff. That job was Barbara's.

I Dream of Jeannie debuted in '65, lasted five years, brought Barbara a Golden Globe nomination as Best Actress, and made her one of the most popular TV stars ever. Yet she wasn't even close to being the studio's first choice, as she disclosed to *People* magazine. The creators "had tested every brunette in town, every Miss Greece, Miss Italy, Miss Israel," but once the show debuted with 31-year-old Barbara starring as the 2,000-year-old genie Jeannie, the results were magical. Cute 'n' giggly 'n' subservient to her "master," she appealed to every teenage boy in America; smart 'n' sassy 'n' confident, she was popular with women, too, as she engaged in a playful battle of the sexes with the male lead (Larry Hagman).

So successful was the show, it became one of the first to have a complete merchandising program, including a board game, dolls, and books. Throughout the show's five-year run, Barbara and the creators would playfully experiment with the characters, costumes, and situations. Barbara sometimes played Jeannie's wicked sister, and in '69 Jeannie married Cap'n Tony (Q: What does a genie wear to her wedding? A: White pantsuit).

In the '70s Barbara made a TV movie almost every year, and she had a big-screen hit with the surprisingly successful *Harper Valley P.T.A.* ('78). Her '80s featured a sitcom version of that film and more TV, especially *I Dream of Jeannie: 15 Years Later* in '85 (Wayne Rogers played Tony because Larry Hagman was busy doin' *Dallas*).

Another Jeannie TV movie (*I Still Dream of Jeannie* in '91), and some memorable TV commercials in the late '90s proved that she was a perennial public-pleaser. She has occasionally performed a terrific nightclub act in Vegas, surprising everyone with her great singing voice, plus she's done more theatre and had a recurring role on *Sabrina, the Teenage Witch*. Here it is the 21st century, and we're all still dreamin' of Jeannie.

EVERYBODY LOVES SOMEBODY

Barbara spent the '60s married to actor Michael Ansara, who was featured with her in *Voyage to the Bottom of the Sea* and also in *I Dream of Jeannie* (as an evil genie). She said later it was love at first sight—they were married in '58 after knowing each other just six weeks. Just as *I Dream of Jeannie* was starting to shoot, Barbara learned she was pregnant, and in '65 she gave birth to a son. Divorced in '72, she remarried in '77 and moved to Chicago, then she divorced in '83 and wed again in '91. She and her husband now live in one of the stylish canyons up in the L.A. hills.

MY BACK PAGES

When Barbara first appeared on *I Dream of Jeannie*, she was speaking some exotic language with subtitles—not until the astronaut wished her to speak English did we understand her. . . . Her bare midriff generated debates among the network censors in the '60s, and she never showed her belly-button on *I Dream of Jeannie* until the '91 TV movie (until then it was covered by fabric or a jewel). . . . The navel battle didn't matter to *Playboy*, which ranked her #58 (ahead of supermodel Claudia Schiffer) on its list of the century's sexiest stars. . . . Barbara's performed charity work for the Make-a-Wish Foundation, the March of Dimes, and the American Heart Association, among other organizations.

Anita Ekberg

The immensely endowed Swedish sexpot decorated two movies a year during the '60s.

TAKIN' CARE OF BUSINESS

Even though she was never the star of her movies, Anita Ekberg made a huge impression on anyone who saw her or squeezed through a doorway with her face-to-face. As a 19-year-old Miss Sweden in '50, she competed in the Miss Universe pageant, which led to her first screen credit as scenery in *Abbott and Costello Go to Mars* ('53). For Anita, another 20 movies followed in the '50s, two with Jerry and Dean.

The '60s got off to a great start with Fellini's *La Dolce Vita* ('60), the memorable movie that had her cavorting in a low-cut black dress and a shimmering Trevi Fountain. She seemed to be having the best time of anyone in that three-hour epic, and it proved to be one of her best roles. Other '60s films included Bob Hope's *Call Me Bwana* ('63) and *4 for Texas* ('63, Frank, Dino, and Ursula Andress were the other three).

However, Anita was always more of a '50s goddess than a '60s mod and so her helium-chested impact got lighter as the decade got later. After the '60s, she made a dozen more movies that took her right up through the '90s. Throughout a career that has lasted almost 40 years, she did win one major acting award, a Golden Globe in '56 as the Most Promising Newcomer, but acting wasn't this actress's forte. "Anita Ekberg might not have been much of an actress," wrote Roger Ebert, "but she was the only person who could play herself." With hair like spun sugar and pneumatic pecs, *Playboy* loved her, naturally, showing off her assets in '56 and '61 and then ranking her fourteenth, right behind Ann-Margret, on the millennium list of the century's sexiest stars.

EVERYBODY LOVES SOMEBODY

As you'd guess about a statuesque Swedish beauty queen, she was pretty popular. She was married twice from '56–'59 and '63–'75, and as one of the endowed crowd she allegedly had affairs with Frank, Gary Cooper, and Marcello Mastroianni. She currently lives in Italy, the setting for her most famous movie. "I like three things," she said in *La Dolce Vita*, "love, love, and love."

May 17, 1967—*Don't Look Back* with Bob Dylan opens. ☮ May 17, 1967—The Grateful Dead's first album is released.
May 18, 1937—Singer Fran Jeffries is born in San Jose, California. ☮ May 18, 1938—Actress Joan Blackman is born in San Francisco.
May 18, 1941—Diane McBain is born in Cleveland, Ohio. ☮ May 18, 1995—Actress Elizabeth Montgomery dies of cancer at age 62.

MY BACK PAGES

Sandra Bernhard used Anita's "love, love, and love" line as the title of her '93 book. . . . Bob Dylan included her name in the song "I Shall Be Free". . . . Bob Hope wrote several jokes about her 40-22-36 figure in his '63 book, *I Owe Russia $1200*, including "her parents got the Nobel Prize for architecture!"

Elvis's Actresses

The King's movies always showed off beautiful young actresses, among them Anne Helm, Julie Parrish, and Deborah Walley.

TAKIN' CARE OF BUSINESS

Elvis Presley starred in 27 movies during the '60s. This prodigious output—coupled with the kind of sexy roles he played, usually along the lines of a singin' race car driver, a singin' boat skipper, or a singin' whirlybird pilot—demanded an enormous bevy of beautiful actresses for Elvis to chase, dance with, sing to, or rescue. Occasionally legendary stars like Barbara Stanwyck and Angela Lansbury would grace the King's movies, but more typically his supporting cast was well-rounded out by young, pretty actresses better suited for the raucous clambakes, lu-wows, and pool parties called for by the movies' slim plots. Presented here are profiles of three worthy representatives of all the actresses who were helping the King take care of big-screen business.

Early in her teens Anne Helm and her mother moved from Canada to New York, where Anne studied ballet and began modeling. Success came quickly: at 16 she was a showgirl at the Copa (Sinatra was the headliner), followed by roles on and off-Broadway. She made her first TV appearance in the late '50s and was a guest on all the top dramas for the next decade. A starring role as a pretty princess in the fantasy flick *The Magic Sword* ('62) led her to the King. *Follow That Dream* was one of the most heart-warming and sincere of Elvis's movies—Anne played the sweet 19-year-old babysitter Holly Jones who got serenaded at movie's end with one of the King's prettiest screen ballads, "Angel."

Anne Helm

The immediate years A.E. (After Elvis) brought three more '62 movies for the busy Anne—*The Interns*, *The Couch*, and *The Iron Maiden*. Later she did some cornball classics such as *Honeymoon Hotel* ('64) and *Nightmare in Wax* ('69). A year on *General Hospital* and the TV movie *A Tattered Web* ('71), James Caan's *Hide in Plain Sight* ('80), and a role in one of the best episodes of Steven Spielberg's *Amazing Stories* TV series highlighted her subsequent screen work. In the '90s she successfully pursued other careers away from the camera. A talented artist, her paintings have been exhibited in Southern California art galleries, and currently she writes, paints, and teaches art to seniors.

While not a major star, Julie Parrish was certainly a durable one, appearing in a wide variety of popular '60s projects. Lovely and slim, Julie (born Ruby Joyce Wilbar in Kentucky) got started as a model and as a Michigan teen won the Miss Cinerama beauty contest. A few years later she won the "Young Model of the Year" contest, with the first prize a small role in Jerry Lewis's *It's Only Money* ('62). She graduated to a classroom role in Jerry's *The Nutty Professor* ('63), and her screen career was rolling. In addition to starring in the teeny-boppin' *Winter a Go Go* ('65), *Fireball 500* ('66), and Elvis's *Paradise, Hawaiian Style* ('66), she was busy all decade with roles in dozens of

May 19, 1939—Actress Nancy Kwan is born in Hong Kong. ☮ May 19, 1945—Pete Townshend of the Who is born in England.
May 19, 1960—*Pollyanna* with Hayley Mills opens.
May 19, 1962—Marilyn Monroe sings a sultry version of "Happy Birthday" to President John F. Kennedy at his Madison Square Garden "Birthday Salute."

Elvis's '60s Movies (with Co-Starring Actresses)

1960

G.I. Blues–Juliet Prowse

Flaming Star–Barbara Eden

1961

Wild in the Country–Hope Lange, Tuesday Weld

Blue Hawaii–
Joan Blackman, Nancy Walters, Pamela Austin

1962

Follow That Dream–Anne Helm

Kid Galahad–Joan Blackman

Girls! Girls! Girls!–Stella Stevens, Laurel Goodwin

1963

It Happened at the World's Fair–
Joan O'Brien, Yvonne Craig

Fun in Acapulco–Ursula Andress

1964

Kissin' Cousins–
Pamela Austin, Yvonne Craig, Cynthia Pepper

Viva Las Vegas–Ann-Margret

Roustabout–Joan Freeman, Sue Ane Langdon, Mariana Hill, Raquel Welch

1965

Girl Happy–
Shelley Fabares, Mary Ann Mobley, Chris Noel

Tickle Me–
Julie Adams, Jocelyn Lane, Francine York

Harum Scarum–Mary Ann Mobley, Fran Jeffries

1966

Frankie and Johnny–
Donna Douglas, Sue Ane Langdon

Paradise, Hawaiian Style–
Julie Parrish, Mariana Hill

Spinout–
Shelley Fabares, Deborah Walley, Diane McBain

1967

Easy Come, Easy Go–Pat Priest

Double Trouble–Annette Day

Clambake–Shelley Fabares

1968

Stay Away, Joe–Quentin Dean, Katy Jurado

Speedway–Nancy Sinatra

Live a Little, Love a Little–
Michele Carey, Celeste Yarnall

1969

Charro!–Ina Balin

The Trouble with Girls–
Marlyn Mason, Sheree North, Nicole Jaffe

Change of Habit–
Mary Tyler Moore, Barbara McNair

Diane McBain

May 19, 1968—Don Adams wins his second Emmy for *Get Smart*. ☮ May 19, 1994—Jacqueline Kennedy Onassis dies of cancer at the age of 64.
May 20, 1927—Actor David Hedison is born. ☮ May 20, 1946—Cher is born in El Centro, California.
May 20, 1964—Elvis Presley's *Viva Las Vegas* opens. ☮ May 21, 1928—Radio DJ Tom Donahue is born.

Julie Parrish

cool TV shows, among them the popular "Menagerie" episode of *Star Trek* and a lead in the underrated *Good Morning, World* series which came and went in '67.

Julie also made many appearances on TV talk shows, on game shows, and in numerous late-'60s commercials. For the rest of her life she appeared in dozens of stage productions, movies, TV shows, and commercials, including leads on the series *Return to Peyton Place* in the early '70s, on the series *Capitol* in the '80s, and with the Joan Diamond role on *Beverly Hills 90210* in the '90s. A dark-haired beauty who only seemed to get more attractive as she got older, Julie always radiated intelligence, no matter what role she was playing. Sadly, after battling cancer through the '90s, Julie died in 2003 at age 62.

Deborah Walley

Deborah Walley, all smiles and energy, romped through a dozen '60s movies. Born in Connecticut to parents who were professional ice skaters, Deborah started skating with them at age three and continued until she was bitten by the acting bug as a teen. When a Hollywood producer spotted her in a Broadway drama, he whisked her westward and her screen career was off and running. She was a perky, enthusiastic supporting actress on TV when she landed the plum title role in *Gidget Goes Hawaiian* ('61), the sequel to Sandra Dee's *Gidget* ('59). Soon came a rush of beachy-keen drive-in movies, including three with "bikini" in the title, often with Deborah filling the lead bikini.

In the King's *Spinout* ('66), she played the tomboyish "Les," the drummer in Elvis's band. She finished the '60s as the cute newlywed Suzie on the Desilu sitcom *The Mothers-in-Law*, a critical fave that disappeared after two seasons. So did Deborah for awhile, leaving the biz and living the Malibu life until *Benji* brought her back in '74. Doing TV work and cartoon voices in the '80s turned into writing books and screenplays in the '90s. She co-founded two film/theater production companies and was dividing her time between L.A. and Arizona when she died of cancer in 2001. Always a respectful admirer of "the inner Elvis," Deborah was working on a celebratory book about him at the time of her death.

EVERYBODY LOVES SOMEBODY

After dating Elvis in the early '60s, Anne married novelist John Sherlock in '67, and had one son with him. In '72 she married actor Robert Viharo, who played the director in *Valley of the Dolls* ('67); they were in *Hide in Plain Sight* together, and with him she had a daughter, Serena, who today works behind the scenes in Hollywood.

Late in the '60s, Julie was involved first with actor James Caan and then with comedian Albert Brooks. In the '70s, she unfortunately became involved in a verbally-abusive relationship, but once she got out she devoted her energies to helping others by counseling at shelters for battered women and speaking at schools in L.A.

In '62 Deborah married teen idol John Ashley, her co-star in *Beach Blanket Bingo* ('65). They'd met on a prearranged "date" set up as a photo op by a movie magazine; she gave birth to their

May 21, 1966—Dusty Springfield's "You Don't Have to Say You Love Me" hits the charts.
May 21, 1966—Herb Alpert has five albums in the *Billboard* Top 20. ☮ May 21, 1969—The MPAA gives *Midnight Cowboy* an X rating.
May 21, 1974—Actress Candy Darling dies of cancer in New York. ☮ May 22, 1942—Actress Barbara Parkins is born in Vancouver, British Columbia.

son in '63, but they divorced in '66. Deborah then got involved with the King during the *Spinout* filming. However, the side she saw of Elvis was a side few people ever did: he was an influential spiritual instructor who gave her many philosophical books and discussed mystical Eastern teachings. Deborah was married twice more and had another son.

MY BACK PAGES

Anne's brother Peter is also an actor with lots of TV appearances and movies on his résumé. . . . Though the Elvis movie was more famous, Annie says *The Magic Sword* is the one most lovingly recalled by fans. . . . Julie's first live performance as a singer came at a packed L.A. Forum—she sang the national anthem before a Kings game in the '70s. . . . A versatile talent, Julie wrote many published essays, articles, and book reviews, and in the '90s she released a collection of country-flavored songs called *When We Dance*. . . . Fit and athletic (she weighed only 95 pounds), Deborah often did her own surf stunts in her beach movies. . . . For Disney's *Bon Voyage* ('62) Deborah sailed to Europe, and her chaperone on the crossing was Walt Disney himself. . . . Anne, Julie, and Deborah were all friends and occasionally went together to the Elvis Week festivities held every August in Memphis.

Dolores Erickson

Dolores was the remarkably alluring foam-covered model on the cover of one of the decade's bestselling albums.

TAKIN' CARE OF BUSINESS

Hers is one of the most-recognizable and most-imitated images of the '60s. The album she adorned, *Whipped Cream & Other Delights* by Herb Alpert and the Tijuana Brass, was the group's biggest hit to date and was in the Top 10 on the album charts for 61 weeks. The cover, with Dolores covered in whipped cream against a green background, inspired numerous other album and advertising designs that copied its look and stylized fonts (including a wacky parody called *Clam Dip & Other Delights* by Soul Asylum). Dolores herself had an amazingly seductive face, glowing with a tan, framed by a wrangly 'do. She also had the curves to turn whipped cream—actually shaving cream and a white blanket—into one of the great outfits of the decade. Not many models would dare to wear only foam in their photo shoots, and only the gold paint worn by Shirley Eaton in *Goldfinger* could match this great, creative costume.

Dolores started modeling part-time in hometown Seattle when she was only 15. As a teen she won beauty pageants, and at 19 she moved to San Francisco for more modeling work. In '64 she went to New York, signed with the prominent Ford Agency, and started landing top modeling gigs. A year later, A & M Records flew her to L.A. for one day to shoot the *Whipped Cream* cover. Dolores returned to New York and continued her modeling career for a few more years and even did a few more album covers, including a big close-up on Nat "King Cole's *The Touch of Your Lips*. After the '60s,

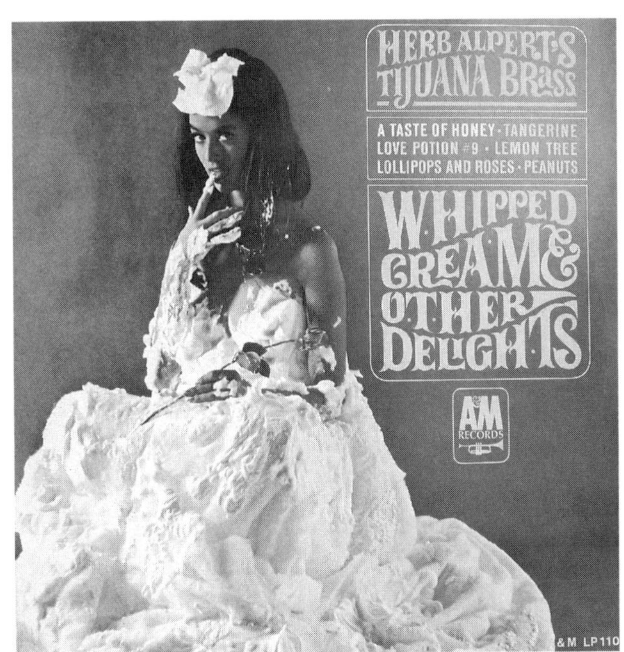

May 22, 1946—Soccer star George Best is born.
May 22, 1966—Actress Mary Tyler Moore wins her second Outstanding Lead Actress Emmy for *The Dick Van Dyke Show*.
May 22, 1969—The X-rated *I Am Curious (Yellow)* opens. ☮ May 22, 1992—Johnny Carson hosts his final show.

Dolores ran her own art studio in Washington for 10 years. She's now a painter living in Kelso, Washington.

EVERYBODY LOVES SOMEBODY

"I've started my life over so many times," Erickson told the *Seattle Times*. She was engaged early in the decade, but that ended and she was Mexico-bound for a year. When she was modeling in New York, she was married, and underneath the *Whipped Cream* she was three months pregnant. In the '70s she was a divorced mother of a son. In '79 she returned to Washington, went back to college, studied art, and married an attorney.

MY BACK PAGES

The only whipped cream she wore in the cover shoot was on top of her head. . . . One of the other memorable Herb Alpert album covers of the '60s was *Going Places*, which featured Herb in the cockpit of a biplane while being served cocktails by a leggy girl who was the wife of Jerry Moss, the M in A & M Records.

John Facenda and Paul Frees

The "voice of God" narrated NFL highlights, and "the man of a thousand voices" provided vocals for dozens of '60s cartoons and popular Disneyland rides.

TAKIN' CARE OF BUSINESS

In a decade of high-pitched vocals (think Beach Boys and Tiny Tim), these deep-voiced legends gave the '60s some memorable gravity. Virginia-born John Facenda was a radio announcer before he became Philadelphia's Channel 10 news anchorman in '52. His mellow baritone, carefully paced delivery, and scholarly integrity made him the area's pre-eminent newscaster for the next two decades. In '65, while watching football highlights on a tavern TV, John began describing the action out loud—incredibly, Ed Sobol, the producer of NFL Films, was within earshot.

Until his death from cancer in '84, John was synonymous with NFL highlights, his mellifluous, dignified voice speaking poetically of "the frozen tundra" and "gridiron gladiators." With a youth movement hitting Philly news, John left his anchor job in '73 and worked on local TV shows. Today his football work is affectionately remembered and much-imitated—John's the one Chris Berman occasionally tries to channel on ESPN.

If you watched cartoons in the '60s or went to Disneyland, you heard Paul Frees, a D-Day veteran who did thousands of radio, TV, and movie voices in a career that stretched from the '40s to his death in the late '80s. Sci-fi fans know him as the narrator of *War of the Worlds* ('53) and as the talking rings in *The Time Machine* ('60). In the '60s he was the voice of many of the decade's coolest cartoon characters, including John and George on the Beatles' cartoon show, Boris Badonov, Professor Ludwig von Drake, the Thing on *The Fantastic Four*, and the narrator and Ape on *George of the Jungle*. Many more movies and cartoons followed into the '80s. Since the late '60s Paul's been heard by hundreds of millions of Disneyland visitors on a variety of landmark rides—he's the Ghost Host in the Haunted Mansion, several buccaneers in Pirates of the Caribbean, the shrinking scientist in the fondly remembered Adventure thru Inner Space, and the narrator of Great Moments with Mr. Lincoln.

EVERYBODY LOVES SOMEBODY

John left behind a wife and son when he died in Philadelphia. For Paul, a wife, a family, a home in Tiburon, California until his death from heart failure.

MY BACK PAGES

Just before he died, John was presented with an award for life-

May 23, 1933—Actress Joan Collins is born in London. ☮ May 23, 1962—*The Miracle Worker* with Anne Bancroft opens. May 23, 1962—*Sex and the Single Girl* by Helen Gurley Brown is published. ☮ May 24, 1941—Singer Bob Dylan is born in Minnesota. May 24, 1945—Actress Priscilla Presley is born in Brooklyn, New York.

A Dozen Disneyland Debuts

May 28, 1960–Mine Train Through Nature's Wonderland (Frontierland)

August 6, 1961–Flying Saucers (Tomorrowland)

November 18, 1962–Swiss Family Treehouse (Adventureland)

June 23, 1963–Enchanted Tiki Room (Adventureland)

July 18, 1963–Great Moments with Mr. Lincoln (Main Street)

May 28, 1966–It's a Small World (Fantasyland)

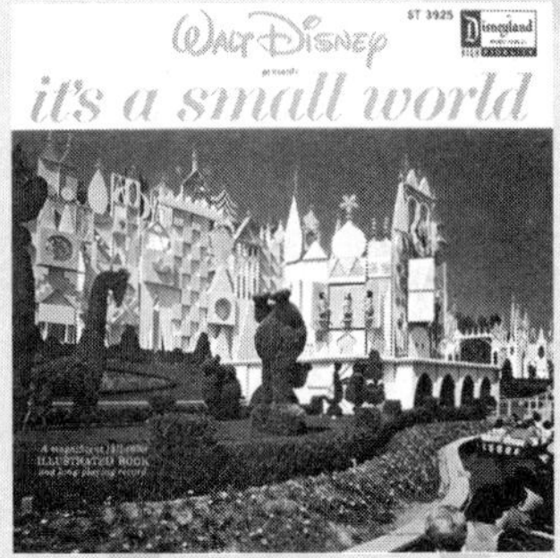

March 18, 1967–Pirates of the Caribbean (New Orleans Square)

June 25, 1967–Circle-Vision 360 Theatre (Tomorrowland)

July 2, 1967–Carousel of Progress, PeopleMover, Rocket Jets (Tomorrowland)

August 5, 1967–Adventure thru Inner Space (Tomorrowland)

August 12, 1967–Flight to the Moon (Tomorrowland)

August 9, 1969–Haunted Mansion (New Orleans Square)

time achievement from the Philadelphia chapter of the National Academy of Television Arts and Sciences. . . . John's signature sign-off at the end of the news—"have a nice night tonight and a good day tomorrow, goodnight all". . . . Paul recorded an unusual album, *Paul Frees and the Poster People*, in which he sang popular '60s songs in the voices of famous actors like Peter Lorre, Humphrey Bogart, and Boris Karloff. . . . On familiar TV commercials he was the Pillsbury Doughboy, Toucan Sam in Fruit Loops ads, and the elf who got the Jolly Green Giant to ho-ho-ho.

Marianne Faithfull

The angel-faced singer was a hit with fans and Mick Jagger.

TAKIN' CARE OF BUSINESS

Marianne Faithfull had it all: looks, talent, connections. Yet several times in her life she almost lost it all. In some ways she is England's version of Edie Sedgwick—another beautiful aristocratic celebrity who ended the decade as a drugged-out symbol of excess.

May 24, 1962—Marilyn Monroe films her famous nude swimming scene for the movie *Something's Got to Give*.
May 24, 1968—Marianne Faithfull and Mick are busted for drugs in their London home.
May 24, 1968—Radio DJ Tom Donahue moves to KSAN, San Francisco. ☮ May 25, 1943—Entertainer Leslie Uggams is born in New York.

After the divorce of her baroness mother and British Intelligence officer father, young Marianne lived in a convent school, but by her mid-teens she was singing in London coffeehouses. At 17 she went to a party attended by several Beatles and Rolling Stones, and her life changed forever. Overnight Mick Jagger and Keith Richards wrote her a song—"As Tears Go By," their first co-writing credit.

Within six months Marianne's gentle rendition of the sweet song was a hit, with other delicate, well-crafted songs quickly following. Taking up with Jagger in '66, she started living the indulgent life of a hard-partying rock star. Her fame and face made her a natural for the big screen, so in the late '60s she made several films, notably *Girl on a Motorcycle* ('68). Unfortunately, use became abuse as drugs soon overtook her (as described in her lyrics for the Stones' song "Sister Morphine") and as a stage actress in '69 Marianne did both *Hamlet* and heroin.

Breaking off with Jagger in '70, her career destroyed, she punched her ticket to junkieville and floundered onto the London streets, crashing in abandoned buildings alongside other addicts. With some help she was able to pull herself together enough to record an album in '71, and from that came the money and strength to enter rehab for eight months. Gradually rebuilding her career, she re-established herself as a solo artist with the wrenching albums *Broken English* ('79) and *Dangerous Acquaintances* ('81). By then her raw-edged voice was a raspy croak adding emotive power to her intense songs. However, a painfully revealing appearance on *Saturday Night Live* in '80, in which Marianne lost her weary voice mid-song, strongly suggested she was using drugs again.

By the mid-'80s she had totally relapsed, so addicted to heroin that she intentionally overdosed to end her miserable life. After another rehabbing, one that finally seemed to take, she continued to bare her soul with autobiographical music and lyrics that confronted, rather than concealed, her troubles. New audiences discovered her in the '90s, thanks to her searing autobiography, *Faithfull*, her startling appearance in a '96 Metallica video, and a deeply introspective '99 album, *Vagabond Ways*. She made a surprising return to the stage in 2004, but the real surprise is that Marianne Faithfull is even alive and working at all.

EVERYBODY LOVES SOMEBODY

Married in '65 to an art student, Marianne was a mother when she found Satisfaction with the ultimate rock icon. Within months of their '66 meeting she was living with Mick, but as a favored courtier among rock's royalty, she also had affairs with other swingin' Londoners, including Brian Jones, Keith Richards, and even Keith's girl, Anita Pallenberg (an experimenter, she was found in bed with another woman on several occasions by Jagger).

But her drug lifestyle was what made her infamous. In early '67 she was rounded up in a drug raid at a party at Redlands, Keith's country manor. Whereas others emerged from the ordeal with their outlaw reputations enhanced, Marianne emerged with her "feminine self. . . . completely besmirched," as she later described. She'd been arrested nude save for a fur rug she'd hastily wrapped around herself. "Naked Girl at Stones' Party" read the headlines, followed by lurid gossip.

In '68 she and Mick were arrested again, she miscarried Mick's baby, and she was plummeting into a drug abyss. Supposedly the first words Jagger said to her when she pulled out of one drug-induced coma in '68 were "wild horses couldn't drag me away," a phrase he turned into a Stones classic. To get rid of him and their life in '70, she overdosed on . . . fatty food! The sudden physical change repulsed him and they split for good.

The tally from her three-plus years with Jagger: a nervous breakdown, heroin addiction, a miscarriage, two arrests, a career-wrecking scandal, and a suicide attempt. For the next few decades, still conducting an on-off affair with heroin, she did try marriage twice more. Unapologetic about her choices, in a televised interview she said she had lived her

May 25, 1947—Actress Karen Valentine is born in Santa Rosa, California. ☮ May 25, 1961—*Gidget Goes Hawaiian* with Deborah Walley opens.
May 25, 1961—JFK announces the goal of going to the moon in a speech to Congress.
May 25, 1964—Actress Mary Tyler Moore wins the Outstanding Lead Actress Emmy for *The Dick Van Dyke Show*.

"life as an adventure, and it's been rather wonderful and I really wouldn't change much about it."

MY BACK PAGES

She was the first person ever to use the f-word in a movie (*I'll Never Forget What's 'is Name,* '67). . . . A movie role she was supposedly up for—Magenta in *The Rocky Horror Picture Show* ('75). . . . Hailed by '60s peers as one of London's most alluring women, only Marianne was able to coax Roy Orbison to take off his trademark sunglasses when they met, as noted by *Biography* magazine.

Mia Farrow

This ethereal young actress made the quantum leap from TV supporting player to a world-famous marriage and starring roles in several prominent movies.

TAKIN' CARE OF BUSINESS

Mia Farrow was born for stardom. Her godfather was Hollywood legend George Cukor, her godmother was famous columnist Louella Parsons, mom Maureen O'Sullivan co-starred in early *Tarzan* movies, and dad John Farrow wrote and directed dozens of movies. After overcoming polio as a child, the L.A. teenager had bit parts in a few '50s movies and got her big break in '64 as Allison Mackenzie on TV's *Peyton Place*; she won the Golden Globe as Most Promising Newcomer but was ambitious for more. More she got when she married Frank Sinatra, but her career stalled during their '65–'68 relationship. She came back strong in '68 with a new Vidal Sassoon haircut and the horror classic *Rosemary's Baby* (in which she played the movie's only sympathetic character), followed a year later by *John and Mary* (another Golden Globe nomination). She made some conspicuous movies in the '70s (*The Great Gatsby,* '74), but it was her work with Woody Allen throughout the '80s and early '90s that brought her the most recognition and acclaim (though she'd now probably hate to admit it).

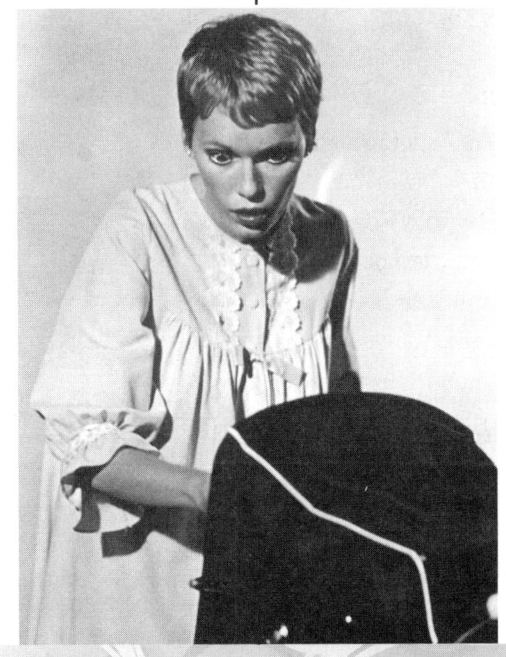

The 13 she made with him included *Broadway Danny Rose* ('84), *The Purple Rose of Cairo* ('85), and *Hannah and Her Sisters* ('86). She averaged a movie a year during the '90s, ranging from starring roles to interesting supporting parts and cameos. Her '97 memoirs, *What Falls Away*, discussed her loves, related stories about chums like Liza Minnelli, Yul Brynner, Michael Caine, Thornton Wilder, and Salvador Dali, and described her lifelong pursuit of that which is truly meaningful. And she's continued to perform into the 21st century: in 2005 she played the lead in the prominent off-Broadway family drama *Fran's Bed*.

EVERYBODY LOVES SOMEBODY

Mia was Frank's third wife, and she hung out with the Beatles—could it get any better in the '60s? Rumors also suggested possible relationships with singer Eddie Fisher, director Roman Polanski, and actor Peter Sellers. On *Late Night with David Letterman* in '99 she described her first meeting with Frank, to whom she was instantly attracted despite the 30-year age difference. She said that she was so nervous she dropped her handbag right in front of him; he helped her scoop up the spilled contents, which embarrassingly included bubble gum, an old donut, and her retainer (she was 20 at the time). Later he handed a

May 25, 1967—*A Guide for the Married Man* with Inger Stevens opens. ☮ May 25, 1967—The second "Twiggy in New York" TV special airs.
May 25, 1967—*Barefoot in the Park* with Robert Redford opens. ☮ May 26, 1942—Drummer Levon Helm is born in Marvell, Arkansas.
May 26, 1965—*The Amorous Adventures of Moll Flanders* with Kim Novak opens.

nine-carat $85K rock to her, and they were married in Vegas in '66, with honeymoons in New York and London.

Meanwhile, back home the pairing generated instant comedy material: "I've got Scotch older than Mia" joked Dean Martin; "Frank didn't have to buy Mia a diamond ring, he gave her a teething ring," guffawed Eddie Fisher; "Frank soaks his dentures and Mia brushes her braces," quipped Jackie Mason; "At his age, he should marry me!," declared Mia's mom. Unfortunately, Mia's desire to act broke up the marriage. Frank confronted her on the *Rosemary's Baby* set and demanded that she leave the film—when she refused, he immediately served divorce papers.

To escape the turmoil, in '68 she went to India, seeking enlightenment at Maharishi Mahesh Yogi's ashram. The Beatles and their women showed up soon after, and Mia became friends with all of them. That summer she and Frank got a quick-but-amiable Mexican divorce. Her later relationships received almost as much attention. After a scandalous pursuit of married conductor Andre Previn, she was married to him through most of the '70s (inspiring Previn's ex-wife Dory to write the song "Beware of Young Girls"). Mia was then the unmarried romantic partner of Woody Allen from the '80s until their acrimonious tabloid-covered split in '92. From these post-Frank relationships she had given birth to, and adopted, a total of 14 children by the turn of the millennium.

MY BACK PAGES

Her full moniker is Maria de Lourdes Villiers Farrow, and her nickname growing up was Mouse. . . . Mia's nickname for Frank: Charlie Brown; his for her: Angel Face, Baby Face, Doll Face, and sometimes, affectionately, "my little boy". . . . She auditioned for the movie role of Liesl in *The Sound of Music*. . . . Supposedly director Roman Polanski wanted Tuesday Weld for *Rosemary's Baby*, but Paramount pushed for Mia, who was "hotter" because of her marriage to Frank. . . . So popular was *Rosemary's Baby*, Mia recorded its gentle lullaby as a single, which briefly lit onto the *Billboard* charts in '68. . . . While Mia was in India with the Beatles, the group wrote some of their *White Album*: "Dear Prudence" was about Mia's sister Prudence, who secluded herself, and "The Continuing Story of Bungalow Bill" was about a character who left the ashram to go tiger hunting; Mia also heard them play "Ob-La-Di, Ob-La-Da" there for the first time. . . . Magazines have always appreciated her appeal—she made the cover of *Vogue* in '67 and was on the cover of the first *People* in '74.

Sally Field

This ever-perky brown-eyed girl-next-door went from high school cheerleading to sitcom stardom.

TAKIN' CARE OF BUSINESS

Best known for her Oscar-winning filmwork, Sally Field enjoyed considerable success in the '60s with two popular TV shows. Back then she wasn't the well-respected dramatic presence that she is now; she came across more like your cute kid sister. The daughter of actress Margaret Field (*The Man from Planet X*, '51) and the stepdaughter of actor Jock Mahoney (lots of Westerns and *Tarzan* movies), adorable Sally was a wholesome all-American L.A. teen in the early '60s,

May 26, 1969—John and Yoko begin their second bed-in, this one at the Queen Elizabeth Hotel in Montreal.
May 27, 1935—Actress Lee Meriwether is born in L.A. ☮ May 27, 1943—Singer Cilla Black is born in Liverpool.
May 27, 1963—The album *The Freewheelin' Bob Dylan* is released. ☮ May 27, 1964—*From Russia with Love* with Sean Connery opens.

cheerleading and starring in school plays.

Everything changed at age 19 when she won the title role on *Gidget*, the sitcom version of the '59 Sandra Dee movie. Sally was a popular, natural actress, lively and personable, and, in fact, on the show she would talk directly to the camera as if viewers were pals spending the night for a slumber party ("Toodles" was her signature goodbye). Bigger success was in the air—literally.

In '67 Sally got a new series that once again keyed on her winning personality and warm charm, though the premise was a little more fanciful. *The Flying Nun* posited Sally as a nun who got airborne, thanks to her 90-pound weight and winged cornet. Occasionally crooning songs on the show, Sally cut an album of gentle songs in '67 (her idol, she said in the liner notes, was Julie Andrews). An interesting development came with the '68–'69 season—Sally got pregnant. Obviously her condition had to be concealed, since she was, after all, playing a celibate nun. She took a quick timeout to deliver a son in November '69 and returned to work in December for the last episodes.

Her two lighter-than-air TV roles in the '60s led to a breezy '73 sitcom, *The Girl with Something Extra*, and some good parts in small movies until her movie career kicked in. The breakthrough was *Sybil* ('76), a disturbing psychological study of a girl with 17 different personalities. The role brought her an Emmy and newfound respect. Soon followed some genuine big-screen hits, especially the entertaining Burt Reynolds adventure *Smokey and the Bandit* ('77), the dramatic *Norma Rae* ('79, bringing her an Oscar), and *Places in the Heart* ('84, another Oscar and the heartfelt "you really like me" speech). Balancing her dramas with comedies, she also starred in *Murphy's Romance* ('85), *Punchline* ('88), *Steel Magnolias* ('89), *Soapdish* ('91), *Mrs. Doubtfire* ('93), and *Forrest Gump* ('94), racking up Emmy and Golden Globe nominations along the way. Lately she's added several directorial gigs to her résumé. From surfer girl to Oscar winner to movie director—what a ride for the girl next door.

EVERYBODY LOVES SOMEBODY

Though she once described herself as having "crippling shyness," in the mid-'60s Sally dated several of Hollywood's prominent young TV and music stars. In '68, only 21 years old, she eloped to Vegas with her high school sweetheart. Within a few years they had two sons, and in '75 they had a divorce. The well-tabloided Burt Reynolds Era lasted for about five years in the '70s. Sally married the producer of *Soapdish* in '84. Within a decade they had a son and a divorce of their own. She sold her Brentwood home in 2004 for about $4,000,000 and moved into the Malibu mountains.

MY BACK PAGES

Sally appeared as a contestant on *The Dating Game* in '65. . . . She wasn't the only future Oscar winner on *Gidget*: in one episode the part of Norman Durfner was played by Richard Dreyfuss, 19. . . . Sally tested for the role of Elaine in *The Graduate*, but her lack of film experience cost her the part. . . . She made the cover of *Playboy*, March '86. . . . Sally has said that on movie sets, she usually does lots of needlework between takes. . . . In an interview she summed up her philosophy with a quote from Rilke, the German poet—"One must always go toward what is difficult."

Peggy Fleming

This exquisite beauty won the hearts of the world—and the only U.S. gold medal—at the '68 Winter Olympics.

TAKIN' CARE OF BUSINESS

Peggy Fleming's figure skating career can be summarized in a word—domination. The elegant teen from San Jose, California won five straight U.S. figure skating championships from '64–'68 and three straight world titles from '66–

May 27, 1965—Model Jean Shrimpton appears on the cover of French *Elle* with the tagline "The Most Beautiful Girl in the World."
May 27, 1965—"(I Can't Get No) Satisfaction" by the Rolling Stones hits #1. ☮ May 28, 1908—Author Ian Lancaster Fleming is born in London.
May 28, 1931—Actress Carroll Baker is born in Johnstown, Pennsylvania. ☮ May 28, 1948—Model Gloria Root is born in Chicago.

'68, culminating with the gold medal at the '68 Winter Olympics. What makes her accomplishments all the more astonishing is the disaster that shook America's Olympic skating team in the early '60s. She'd been skating since she was 9, winning various amateur titles around the country in anticipation of joining the U.S. figure skaters for the '64 Olympics. Tragically, in '61 that entire team, including her own coach, her trainers, and the peers she practiced with, was wiped out in an airplane crash in Belgium.

Rising above the catastrophe (and a high fever), the 14-year-old Olympic rookie finished sixth at the '64 Games in Innsbruck. But she was now poised for her triumph at the '68 Olympics, for which she trained sometimes eight hours per day. Her glorious moment came when Peggy, still a teenager, was unrivaled as the female superstar of the '68 Games in Grenoble, France. These were an especially significant Olympics, because they were the first to be televised globally, live and in color.

Skating to Tchaikovsky's *Pathetique*, Peggy delivered a graceful, impeccable performance, leaving her closest competitor almost 90 points behind and winning America's only gold medal. Her sport surged in popularity: "She made it appear so easy and lovable," said former champion Carlo Fassi, "a lot of little girls fell in love with it." Peggy then turned pro and performed in five TV specials, worked as a commentator for ABC Sports at several subsequent Olympics, and appeared on TV shows and in commercials.

In the '90s she wrote a book and even continued to tour in ice shows. Recognition of her illustrious career and myriad contributions has continued unabated. She was the first skater asked to perform at the White House, she was elected to the U.S. Olympic Committee Hall of Fame in '83, and at the end of the millennium *Sports Illustrated* put her in the top 20 of the greatest female athletes of all time (the magazine praised her looks by saying she had "the face that launched a thousand Zamboni's"). To this day she remains one of the most popular (and most admired) athletes America has ever produced, a glowing symbol of the Olympic ideal and the kind of role model that is sorely missed in 21st-century sports.

EVERYBODY LOVES SOMEBODY

Single during the '60s, in '65 Peggy met her future husband, who was also a skater and later a dermatologist. They married in '70 and are still together, living with their two kids in a toney San Francisco suburb.

MY BACK PAGES

Her mother designed and sewed Peggy's costumes herself, including the chartreuse chiffon mini-dress Peggy wore when she won the gold. . . . Always a competitor, 30 years to the day after she won her gold medal she had successful surgery for breast cancer ("the life Olympics," she called it). . . . Always a contributor, she has done much charity work to support medical research. . . . The quotable Peggy: "The first thing is to love your sport. Never do it to please someone else. It has to be yours."

Jane Fonda

The '60s version of a '50s blonde bombshell, sex kitten Fonda was a smart, liberated, acclaimed actress.

TAKIN' CARE OF BUSINESS

"I've always felt that I wanted my life to make a difference," Jane Fonda said in a televised interview in 2000. A difference, indeed. No matter what people think of her life and views from '70 onward (which is when she generated the controversy that has followed her), there's no escaping the strong impact she had on the '60s. Born in '37 to prominent parents (dad Henry was a screen legend, mom Frances was a popular socialite), Manhattan's Lady Jane left a successful Broadway career to become one of the top international film stars of the '60s. She averaged almost two movies a year throughout the decade, starting in '60 with *Tall Story* opposite gangly Tony Perkins. *Period of Adjustment* (in which she went blonde) and *Walk on the Wild Side* (with Jane as the young temptress Kitty Twist) followed in '62 (along with a Golden Globe as Most Promising Newcomer).

Her big-screen breakthrough, of course, was *Cat Ballou* ('65). The rootin'-tootin' Western got five Oscar nominations, was one of the year's top 10 moneymakers, and made her a star at 28. After *Any Wednesday* ('66) and *Barefoot in the Park* ('67) came the dazzling *Barbarella* ('68), which sent her sexpot image into orbit. By contrast, the grim *They Shoot Horses, Don't They?* ('69) showcased her serious acting talent, bringing her the first of seven Oscar nominations.

Her momentum, and her reputation as an acclaimed actress, increased in the '70s as she starred in some of the decade's most significant films, including *Klute* ('71, her first Oscar win), *Coming Home* ('78, her second Oscar), and *The China Syndrome* ('79). In addition to making more successful films in the '80s—*Nine to Five* ('80), *On Golden Pond* ('81)—Jane won an Emmy for *The Dollmaker* ('84). She also reinvented herself as a health guru in the early '80s, setting up the popular Jane Fonda Workout studio in Beverly Hills and creating bestselling books, records, and tapes. In 2005 she came out of retirement with an autobiography and a costarring role in *Monster-in-Law*. As with everything else she's ever done, she continues to pursue her passions with gusto and commitment.

EVERYBODY LOVES SOMEBODY

Of long-term relationships, Jane Fonda once said, "For two people to be able to live together for the rest of their lives is almost unnatural." She has had three husbands: director Roger Vadim, politician Tom Hayden, and media mogul Ted Turner. She married Vadim in '65 in Vegas; they lived on a farm in France through the '60s and had a daughter in '68. Divorced from Vadim and pregnant with Tom Hayden's child, she married him at her L.A. home in early '73. Their son was born that summer. The marriage ended in '89, and Jane was then married to Turner from '91–2001. True to her image in the '60s and '70s as a liberated modern woman, stories and rumors through the years have placed her with Warren Beatty, Donald Sutherland, Alain Delon, and Huey Newton, among others.

MY BACK PAGES

Her brother Peter starred in the seminal '60s film *Easy Rider*. . . . Figure-atively speaking, she was perhaps the most voluptuous young American actress of the '60s, an image enhanced by her nearly nude appearance in *La Ronde* in '64 (making her one of the first semi-nude American actresses in a major film). . . . Watching was *Playboy*, which featured her in August '66, March/April/July '68, and January/December '69 (she also made the cover of *Life* magazine in '68). . . . In '99 *Playboy* ranked her #28 among the century's sexiest stars, right between Stella Stevens and Mamie Van Doren. . . . She traveled to Russia in '64 and was welcomed warmly by people who knew of her father's career. . . . She visited

Warhol's Factory in '66. . . . Early in her career she was extremely critical of her father, but in '80 she bought the rights to the play *On Golden Pond* so he could star in it and get the Oscar he'd never won (he did). . . . An outspoken critic of America's involvement in the Vietnam War, she earned the derisive nickname "Hanoi Jane" when she flew to North Vietnam in '72. . . . Many Americans have still never forgiven the most troubling part of her legacy—smiling photographs taken while she was sitting at a North Vietnamese anti-aircraft gun used to shoot down American planes. . . . In March 2005, she finally apologized on *60 Minutes*, admitting that her trip to North Vietnam was a "betrayal," "the largest lapse of judgment that I can even imagine."

Peter Fonda and Dennis Hopper

Captain America and Billy rode to counterculture glory in *Easy Rider.*

TAKIN' CARE OF BUSINESS

One of the coolest movies of the '60s, *Easy Rider* was also one of the most influential. Peter Fonda steered the concept (two maverick bikers crossing America) from rambling idea to 20-page story outline (with the help of writer Terry Southern) to hit film (with partner/director/co-star Dennis Hopper). Peter was already a success in '60s movies—the son of Henry and brother of Jane had graduated from supporting roles in early *Tammy* movies to become the star of youth-oriented Roger Corman flicks, including the biker drama *The Wild Angels* with Nancy Sinatra ('66) and the LSD-inspired *The Trip* with Jack Nicholson ('67).

When a top Hollywood exec told him that more *Dr. Dolittle*-type movies were needed these days, Peter responded with *Easy Rider*, his attempt to "shake the cage." Made on a shoestring budget with virtually no special effects, no top stars, often no script, and occasionally no money (just Peter's credit card), the film was one of the biggest moneymakers of the year and helped bring an end to the traditional studio system. Peter was immediately crowned the dashing prince of independent cool.

Flinging off his constraining wristwatch in the first minutes, wearing black leathers all movie long while trying to do right by whomever he met, riding a bitchin' chopper on a spontaneous odyssey away from old-fashioned values with great rock music as his soundtrack—the images of Peter were strong and enduring (so enduring, Peter-on-the-bike footage would be used in commercials in 2005). Nominated for top awards at Cannes and at the Academy Awards, the film catapulted Peter to international stardom, which has brought him a long career of 50+ films stretching into the 21st century, often with Peter playing an outlaw character, sometimes with him directing instead of acting. *Ulee's Gold* ('97) brought him an Oscar nomination for Best Actor, and the TV movie *The Passion of Ayn Rand* ('99) brought him a Golden Globe trophy, showing the respect the industry has for his talent and accomplishments.

Born in Kansas and raised in L.A., Dennis Hopper was a '50s rebel—after appearing in *Rebel Without a Cause* ('55) and *Giant* ('56), he got himself temporarily blackballed for arguing on the set and for years had a rep as being difficult to work with. Relocating to New York, he studied at the Actors Studio and started building a résumé of solid TV work. In '67 he was one of the prisoners in the hit *Cool Hand Luke*, and like Peter Fonda he was in a biker flick, *The Glory Stompers* ('68). He also had supporting roles in two John Wayne Westerns, including *True Grit* ('69).

For the anti-establishment epic *Easy Rider*, not only did he co-star as the brash Billy, as the director he gave the film some of its signature style, including the wide panoramic landscapes and the quick-cutting flash-forwards. Dennis said later he saw *Easy Rider* as a modern Western—two outlaws,

May 30, 1945—Actress Meredith MacRae is born in Houston, Texas.
May 30, 1965—Vivian Malone is the first African-American student to graduate from the University of Alabama.
May 30, 1969—Mario Andretti wins the Indy 500. ☮ May 31, 1929—Actress Elaine Stewart is born in Montclair, New Jersey.

Billy (in buckskins) and Wyatt (wearing spurs), riding across open America, gunned down by the establishment.

Unfortunately, his next directorial effort, *The Last Movie* ('71), flopped amidst talk of Dennis's drug and alcohol problems, which led him to a successful stay in rehab. He's always displayed manic intensity in his acting, especially as the revved-up photographer in *Apocalypse Now* ('79), as the vulgar villain in *Blue Velvet* ('86), as the drunk ex-hoopster in *Hoosiers* ('86, winning him an Oscar), and as the bus-terrorizing psycho in *Speed* ('94). As a director, *Colors* ('88) is his best-known movie. As an art collector, he owns a prized collection of modern masters.

EVERYBODY LOVES SOMEBODY

Both men were married for most of the decade. Peter's marriage produced two pre-*Easy Rider* kids and ended in the early '70s. Son Justin works on film crews; daughter Bridget is an acclaimed actress (*Scandal,* '89) married to composer Danny Elfman. Peter remarried in the mid-'70s. He still rides motorcycles and frequently takes cross-country trips (though his are often north-south). Meanwhile Dennis had a daughter with his first wife Brooke Hayward (the daughter of actress Margaret Sullavan and producer Leland Hayward). He then married singer Michelle Phillips of the Mamas and Papas for one tumultuous week in '70, followed by three more marriages and three more children.

MY BACK PAGES

Among the actors in the *Easy Rider* commune scenes were Sabrina Scharf (a former *Playboy* Bunny who was later a California Senator), Dan Haggerty (later "Grizzly Adams"), Peter's wife and daughter, and Carrie Snodgress (future Oscar-winner for *Diary of a Mad Housewife*). . . . Just before the last campfire scene was shot (where Peter says "We blew it") the bikes were stolen, which is why they weren't shown. . . . His "shut up!" while sitting on the cemetery statue was an improvised command to crewmembers who were talking off-camera. . . . Peter inspired a Beatles song ("She Said, She Said") when he told John Lennon "I know what it's like to be dead". . . . He also inspired Bob Dylan to write the lyrics for "The Ballad of Easy Rider," giving Dylan the song's river imagery. . . . In the '50s one of Dennis's best friends was James Dean—later he palled with Elvis when the King was starting his movie career. . . . A talented photographer, Dennis has published several volumes of his work.

Anne Francis

One of the best, and sexiest, TV spies of all time.

TAKIN' CARE OF BUSINESS

Blonde, beautiful Anne Francis got her start as a young New York model and actress who was performing on Broadway before she was in her teens. TV roles in the late '40s led to lots of good supporting roles in movies in the early '50s. Her big-screen breakthrough came in '55 with starring roles as bad girls in *Bad Day at Black Rock* and *Blackboard Jungle,* followed quickly by the science-fiction classic *Forbidden Planet* ('56). No matter the genre or the

part, Anne always looked amazing and managed to steal any scene she was in (especially in *Forbidden Planet,* where she wore one of the first miniskirts).

While she did make more movies into the '60s (including a compelling disaster epic, *The Crowded Sky*, '61), it was on TV where she was busiest and best-known. Anne guested on all the cool TV dramas of the early '60s, especially on suspense thrillers like *Alfred Hitchcock Presents* and *The Twilight Zone* (on the latter, she was a beautiful mannequin in the great "The After Hours" episode). In '66 she landed her signature role on/as *Honey West*, playing a cool karate-chopping, ocelot-owning private eye.

Liberated and sexy, Honey was an American equivalent of England's great Emma Peel, played by Diana Rigg on *The Avengers*, though Honey had more 007-like gadgets (including a dynamite set of earrings—literally). Somehow *Honey West*, popular but perhaps overwhelmed by all the other spy shows on at the time, disappeared after only one season. Anne, however, was nominated for an Emmy and won a Golden Globe for her work, and today *Honey West* is still considered by many viewers as one of the best shows of the '60s.

Anne worked steadily for the next few years, getting co-starring credits in under-appreciated Jerry Lewis, Burt Reynolds, and Don Knotts movies. Her most curious role was the one she had in *Funny Girl* ('68), playing a prominent supporting character who somehow ended up with more footage on the cutting-room floor than on the screen. Anne survived to appear in about 50 TV shows during the '70s and dozens more into the 21st century, everything from *Charlie's Angels* to *The Love Boat* to *Nash Bridges* to good TV movies. Her '82 autobiography, *Voices from Home*, revealed her to be a deeply spiritual person with a passionate yearning for enlightenment (and someone who's had her share of psychic experiences).

EVERYBODY LOVES SOMEBODY

Anne's been married twice, once at age 21, and again for the first half of the '60s. She has a daughter from this second marriage, plus another daughter she adopted later on her own. Today Anne Francis is single, has a grandson, travels frequently, and lives happily in Santa Barbara, California.

MY BACK PAGES

Signed by MGM as a kid, Anne attended the studio's schoolhouse with Elizabeth Taylor, Natalie Wood, and other young MGM stars. . . . Anne and *Forbidden Planet* both got named in the lyrics of the song "Science Fiction/Double Feature" at the beginning of *The Rocky Horror Picture Show* ('75). . . . the Honey West character didn't debut on *Honey West*—Anne played her in a *Burke's Law* episode the previous spring. . . . *Honey West* got mentioned in a scene in *Reservoir Dogs* ('92), and in 2001 Miramax announced that Reese Witherspoon was doing a full-length *Honey West* movie that sadly never came to be.

Frankie and Annette

The Philly singer with two #1 hits and the all-American Disney girl enjoyed busy '60s careers highlighted by long stays on party beaches.

TAKIN' CARE OF BUSINESS

Both were (and are) known by their first names. Both were from the East—he from Philadelphia, she from upstate New York. Neither was a teen for the teen-oriented beach movies. But both were teen sensations in the '50s. Francis Avallone was a skilled trumpeter who played on several '50s albums until, propelled by *American Bandstand* appearances, he busted out nationally as a singer with two #1 hits in '59, "Venus" and "Why." Supporting parts in early '60s movies (*The Alamo*, '60) carried him until he hit the beach with Annette in '63.

She, meanwhile, became a national sensation in '55

June 1, 1967—The Beatles' album *Sgt. Pepper's Lonely Hearts Club Band* is released. ☮ June 1, 1968—*The Prisoner* with Patrick McGoohan debuts. June 2, 1936—Actress Sally Kellerman is born in Long Beach, California. ☮ June 2, 1941—Charlie Watts of the Rolling Stones is born in England. June 2, 1941—Actress Susan Hart is born. ☮ June 2, 1962—"I Can't Stop Loving You" by Ray Charles hits #1.

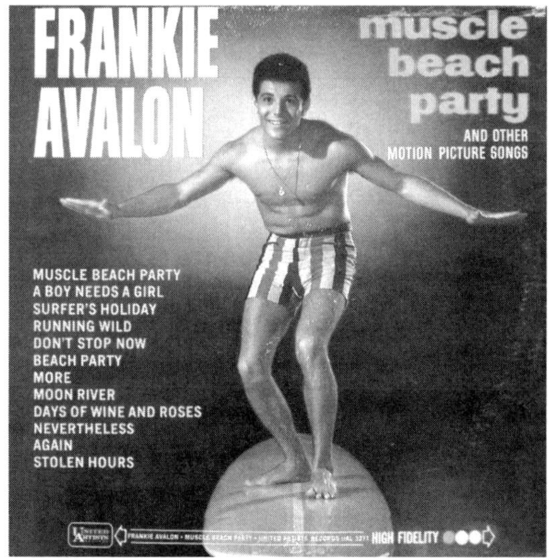

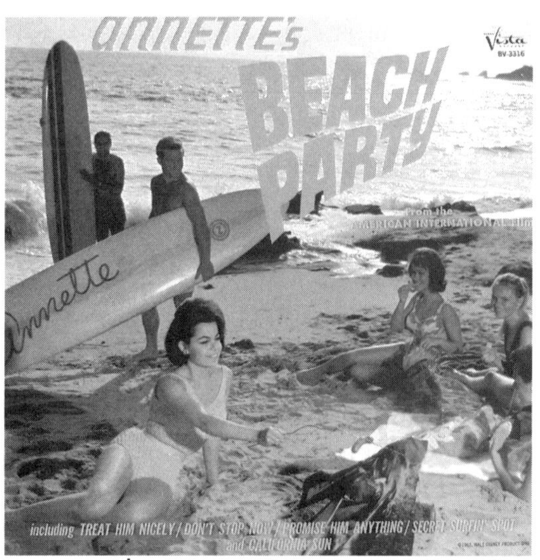

when, at the age of 13, she first appeared on a new afternoon TV show. Her appearances as a pretty, intelligent, talented, and dignified Mousketeer helped make *The Mickey Mouse Club* the most popular children's show of the '50s and soon established her as America's sweetheart, recipient of over a thousand letters a week from boys who adored her and girls who wanted to emulate her. A number of other Disney projects followed, including her own *Annette* show-within-a-show ('58), a role as the starring girlfriend in *The Shaggy Dog* ('59), and the musical *Babes in Toyland* ('61).

It took the series of fun-loving mid-decade beach movies to put her into a bathing suit and more mature situations. *Beach Party* ('63), *Muscle Beach Party* ('64), *Bikini Beach* ('64), *Pajama Party* ('64), *How to Stuff a Wild Bikini* ('65), *Dr. Goldfoot and the Bikini Machine* ('65), and *Beach Blanket Bingo* ('65) all had similar settings, often the same cast, and lightweight plots that were merely excuses for good-looking teens to woo, sing, and dance on camera. Frankie played the good-looking rascally boyfriend, good in a fight or on a surfboard. Annette was the sweet, chaste girlfriend, usually wearing the most conservative clothes of anyone (watch how often she's wearing hostess pants and blouses, or turtlenecks and sweaters, while the girls around her are in skimpy outfits—Walt Disney had requested she not wear bikinis).

Frankie and Annette surfed their surging swell of popularity into more records, usually nice-and-easy for fun-but-innocent parties (you could tell they were for parties because the titles told you so—*Annette's Beach Party*, *Muscle Beach Party*, etc.). Unfortunately, by '67 the wave of '60s beach movies had crested, and their movie momentum had wiped out. But the public still had (and has to this day) a nostalgic affection for their sweetly romantic '50s–'60s images, so in the '70s Annette made lots of happy peanut butter commer-

A Dozen Beach-Movie Cameos

Toni Basil (*Pajama Party*)
Teri Garr (*Pajama Party*)
Boris Karloff (*Bikini Beach*)
Buster Keaton (*Pajama Party*)
Dorothy Lamour (*Pajama Party*)
Elsa Lanchester (*Pajama Party*)
Peter Lorre (*Muscle Beach Party*)
Elizabeth Montgomery (*Beach Party*)
Vincent Price (*Beach Party*)
Mickey Rooney (*How to Stuff a Wild Bikini*)
Brian Wilson (*How to Stuff a Wild Bikini*)
Stevie Wonder (*Muscle Beach Party*)

June 2, 1975—*Rolling Stone* co-founder Ralph Gleason dies of a heart attack at age 58. ☮ June 3, 1925—Actor Tony Curtis is born.
June 3, 1965—The first American astronaut, Ed White, walks in space. ☮ June 3, 1967—Aretha Franklin's "Respect" hits #1.
June 3, 1968—Valerie Solanis shoots Andy Warhol in New York. ☮ June 3, 1969—*Star Trek* shows its final episode ("Turnabout Intruder").

cials while Frankie did lots of TV and performed on some popular nostalgia tours.

In '87 they reteamed for one more beach picture, the bouncy *Back to the Beach*, but while she was making it Annette began to feel symptoms of what would eventually be diagnosed as multiple sclerosis. Bravely maintaining her smile and generous spirit, she stayed cheerfully busy in the '90s by raising money for MS research and pursuing a wide range of interests. She established her collectible teddy bear company, came out with a perfume called Cello, and wrote her autobiography in '94, still with nary a bad word to say about anyone, and with Frankie as her staunchest ally.

EVERYBODY LOVES SOMEBODY

What's nice in this era of tabloid scandals is the lack of indiscreet gossip about either one of them. Frankie is still married to the woman he married in '62, now with eight kids. Annette's first boyfriend was Paul Anka in '57; he wrote "Puppy Love" about their relationship, and she recorded the *Annette Sings Anka* album in '59. Annette lived at home until she married her first husband, who was also her manager, in a big wedding in '65. Exactly nine months later a daughter was born, followed in the '70s by two sons. Annette got divorced in '81 and remarried in '86.

MY BACK PAGES

Her nickname—Dolly. . . . Annette was the final Mousketeer chosen, the only one personally selected by Walt Disney. . . . Frankie was shown wailin' away on his trumpet as a sassy lieutenant in *Voyage to the Bottom of the Sea* ('61). . . . He sang the title song for that movie, too, as well as for *Come Fly with Me* ('63). . . . *How to Stuff a Wild Bikini* ('65) was a turning point for the pair—Frankie was barely in the movie (Dwayne "Dobie Gillis" Hickman was the male lead). . . . Frankie played himself in *Casino* ('95) and laughingly joked about his eight kids ("It was my pleasure!") with Robert De Niro's character.

Aretha Franklin

The Queen of Soul had a run of classic hits that helped make her one of the most influential singers of all time.

TAKIN' CARE OF BUSINESS

Lady Soul has scaled musical heights that no other female singer has ever reached, as proven by her #1 ranking in VH1's list of the 100 greatest women in rock history. She was the first woman to be inducted into the Rock and Roll Hall of Fame, was the youngest award-winner in the history of the Kennedy Center Honors, and according to *Time* magazine she's the "one monarch in music whose title has never rung false and still holds up."

A Memphis-born gospel singer in her father's Detroit church in the '50s, Aretha started recording in '56 for Checker Records. Leaving her two kids with family, she moved to New York, signed with Columbia in '60, and while still a teen began recording jazz/pop albums for the first half of the decade (her one minor hit—"Rock-a-Bye Your Baby with a Dixie Melody"). In '66 Aretha signed with Atlantic, and a year later her breakthrough album, *I Never Loved a Man the Way I Love You*, blasted into the Top 40 with a tougher, more soulful sound.

Her renowned mezzo-soprano voice was (and still is) the marvel—soaring, diving, shrieking, howling, spanning five octaves, and expressing emotion in ways other singers only dream of. Her first mega-hit, Otis Redding's "Respect," became an anthem for women and for African-Americans who were gaining strength and momentum in their long struggles for equality. *Billboard* named her the top vocalist of '67 and would eventually give her over a dozen awards (30 years later, *Rolling Stone* would rank the song #6 of the all-time greatest pop songs, making Aretha the first '60s woman on their list).

More hits poured out of her during a remarkable 18-month streak, including "Chain of Fools." During one eight-year stretch that began in '67, Aretha won at least one Grammy Award every year. In the early '70s, she released some of her

June 3, 1969—Singer Tiny Tim meets future wife Miss Vicki. ☮ June 4, 1944—Michelle Phillips is born in Long Beach, California.
June 4, 1963—*The Nutty Professor* with Jerry Lewis opens. ☮ June 4, 1967—*The Monkees* TV show wins the Emmy for Outstanding Comedy Series.
June 4, 1967—Don Adams wins his first Emmy for *Get Smart*. ☮ June 5, 1928—Director Tony Richardson is born in Shipley, England.

most acclaimed albums and most familiar songs (Carole King's "(You Make Me Feel Like) A Natural Woman"), but her momentum was slowing and her contract with Atlantic ran out at the end of the decade. In '80 she had a brief but memorable role belting out "Think" in *The Blues Brothers* movie. In the mid-80s, wearing outrageous outfits on stage, she had hits with "Who's Zoomin' Who?" and "Freeway of Love" and more, spanning genres from pop to gospel into the late '90s (she's now recorded over 50 albums). She published her autobiography in '99, has continued performing live into the 21st century, and is now praised as being better than she's ever been.

EVERYBODY LOVES SOMEBODY

By age 16, Aretha was a high school dropout and the mother of two kids. She got married in '61 to her manager, but they ended their stormy marriage in '69 after having four sons. She then married actor Glynn Turman (*Cooley High*, '75); they divorced in '84. She also has a son from another relationship.

MY BACK PAGES

All in the family—Aretha's younger sister wrote one of Aretha's hits, "Ain't No Way," and her brother became her manager. . . . Her fear of flying is so intense—resulting from a near-miss in a small plane—she has sometimes skipped important events. . . . Not just a singer, she has written some of her own material, including "Rock Steady" and "Dr. Feelgood," and she plays some mean keyboards. . . . So powerful and influential is Aretha's voice, it was declared one of Michigan's natural resources by the state legislature. . . . Among the impressive events where she has sung: Martin Luther King, Jr.'s funeral, Jimmy Carter's inauguration, Bill Clinton's inaugural gala. . . . Among her answers for the "Proust Questionnaire" in *Vanity Fair*, 2003: her greatest regret was not learning to read music, the one thing she'd change about herself was her weight, in men she liked "straight-up honesty and good taste," in women "honesty, style, and realness," she dislikes bad manners, and her motto is "Live and let live."

Betty Friedan

In '63 this passionate crusader ignited the feminist movement with her revolutionary manifesto.

TAKIN' CARE OF BUSINESS

The author of one of the 20th century's most influential books was born Bettye Naomi Goldstein in Peoria soon after World War I. Outspoken and ostracized in high school, she graduated *summa cum laude* from Smith College in the '40s and then did graduate work in psychology at Cal Berkeley. She briefly worked as a reporter in Manhattan before moving with her new husband to the suburbs, where she raised their family and wrote freelance articles for women's magazines.

Her life changed in '57 when she conducted a survey of hundreds of women—to her surprise, most had not settled into happy suburban lives but were instead haunted by a "nameless, aching dissatisfaction" that led to depression, tranquilizers, even suicide. Six years later her provocative and wildly popular book, *The Feminine Mystique*, would label this

June 5, 1963—*Come Blow Your Horn* with Frank Sinatra opens. ☮ June 5, 1963—*Irma la Douce* with Shirley MacLaine opens.
June 5, 1963—British government official John Profumo resigns. ☮ June 6, 1968—Robert Kennedy is assassinated at the Ambassador Hotel in L.A.
June 6, 1969—The Who's album *Tommy* hits #4. ☮ June 6, 1988—Nico performs her final concert; she'll die in an accident a month later.

dissatisfaction "the problem that has no name." The "mystique" was the supposed fulfillment women "enjoyed" as subservient, career-sacrificing housewives—Betty articulately skewered that notion and made an impassioned 400-page argument for equality in the workplace and in the world. As she told *Life* magazine, she advocated that women of the world unite—"you have nothing to lose but your vacuum cleaners."

Returning to Manhattan, in '66 she and several colleagues started the National Organization for Women, hoping it would do for women what the NAACP did for African-Americans; Betty was NOW's first president and most visible spokesperson. The group's most prominent action was the nationwide Women's Strike for Equality, which included a march by thousands of banner-carrying women through Manhattan exactly 50 years after women had won the right to vote. Betty, who led the group down Fifth Avenue, gave one of the impassioned speeches at the march's endpoint.

A year later she co-founded the National Women's Political Caucus and the first women's bank, but some of her momentum was slipping away—she later struggled (and failed) to get the Equal Rights Amendment passed, and she drew criticism from other feminists who thought she should do more to help minority groups. Over the next decades she continued to write books, speak at international conferences, and appear on talk shows. She was also a visiting professor at top universities, and she championed rights for the elderly. As a world-famous leader who had been at the vanguard of a world-changing revolution, she was lauded with many honors and awards before her death from heart failure on her birthday in 2006. Any modern woman who is a doctor, or in the military, or running her own business, or running for office, or taking maternity leave, or pursuing any goals at all outside the home, owes a debt to Betty Friedan.

EVERYBODY LOVES SOMEBODY

Betty got married in '47 and had three children. The marriage ended in '69—Betty's memoirs would charge him with being physically abusive to her, charges he adamantly denied. When she died Betty had homes in Washington, D.C. and New York City, plus a summer house on Long Island.

MY BACK PAGES

In the mid-'50s Betty was fired from her job when she requested a maternity leave—her replacement was a man. . . . Betty was a delegate to the Democratic Convention in '84 and helped secure the breakthrough nomination of Geraldine Ferraro as vice-president. . . . By the 21st century *The Feminine Mystique* had been translated into over a dozen languages and had sold over 3,000,000 copies.

Al Fritz

You don't know the name, but you know the bike.

TAKIN' CARE OF BUSINESS

With two years of high school and two years of World War II service behind him, in '45 Al Fritz came home to Chicago and took a job as a metal grinder in the

Schwinn bicycle factory. Because of his typing ability, he became the assistant to the company's president, Frank W. Schwinn. In '63 Al took a call from a distributor who described how California kids, emulating the styles of customized motorcycles, were adding banana seats and high-rising "longhorn" handlebars to their bikes. Al built a prototype of a low-rider "muscle bike," rode it around the Schwinn warehouse, and realized immediately how fun and maneuverable it was.

Initially fellow employees laughed, but they quickly applauded once they rode it themselves. By the end of the year the souped-up Sting-Ray bike (Al thought up the name) was in production. Within a year TV commercials made the bike such a sensation that two out of every three bikes sold in America were Sting-Rays. Al, meanwhile, was promoted to V.P. of Engineering, working with R & D to come up with new ideas.

During the decade he added treadless "sliks" to the back wheel and sissy bars behind the seat, came out with Deluxe Sting-Rays, Superdeluxe Sting-Rays, the Fastback, the Mini-Twinn Tandem, the Manta-Ray, and flowered Sting-Rays for girls (all priced about $50-$100). In '68 he introduced the hot new Krate design with Stik-Shift, front forks, and shock absorbers (and he helped give the bikes all their cool colors and names—Grey Ghost, Lemon Peeler, Orange Krate, Kool Red, etc.). During his tenure at Schwinn the company tripled in size (from 900 employees to almost 3,000), Sting-Ray sales were over a million a year, and Al eventually rose to become the Chief Operating Officer. He retired in the '90s when the Schwinn family, struggling to keep up with imports, sold the company. The Sting-Ray, though, lives on as one of the coolest creations of the '60s.

EVERYBODY LOVES SOMEBODY

Al met his wife in the '40s when they were both working in the Schwinn factory (she was one of the company's top welders, having gotten experience during the war years). They married in '49, had three kids, and retired to Florida. Their eldest son worked at Schwinn, got a Ph.D. in engi-

30 Cool Toys (Year Introduced)

Addams Family "Thing" Coin Bank by Poynter Products ('64)
Air Blaster and Gorilla Target by Wham-O ('63)
Astro-Ray Gun by Ohio Art ('62)
Batman Utility Belt by Ideal ('66)
Beatles Bobbing Head Dolls by Carmascot ('64)
Big-Play NFL Electric Football by Gotham ('63)
Booby-Trap game by Parker Brothers ('65)
Easy Bake Oven by Kenner ('63)
Etch-A-Sketch by Ohio Art ('60)
Frosty the Sno-Cone Maker by Hasbro ('61)
Game of Life board game by Milton Bradley ('60)
G.I. Joe by Hasbro ('64)
Hands Down game with "Slap-O-Matic" action by Ideal ('63)
Hot Wheels by Mattel ('68)
James Bond Shooting Attaché Case by Multiple Products ('65)
Monster model kits by Aurora ('64)
Mouse Trap game by Ideal ('63)
Operation by Milton Bradley ('65)
Operation Moon Base by Marx ('62)
Rock 'Em Sock 'Em Robots by Marx ('67)
Sooper Snooper periscope by Marx ('65)
Spirograph by Kenner ('67)
Stratego game by Parker Brothers ('62)
Super-Ball by Wham-O ('65)
Super Stuff by Wham-O ('66)
Thingmaker Fright Factory by Mattel ('66)
Time Bomb game by Milton Bradley ('64)
Trouble game by Kohner Bros. ('65)
Twiggy Fashion Tote Bag by Mattel ('67)
Twister by Milton Bradley ('66)

June 8, 1940—Singer Nancy Sinatra is born in Jersey City, New Jersey. ☮ June 8, 1947—Singer Julie Driscoll is born in London. June 8, 1963—The Crystals' "Da Doo Ron Ron" hits #3. ☮ June 8, 1966—Elvis Presley's *Paradise, Hawaiian Style* opens. June 8, 1966—*Boy, Did I Get a Wrong Number!* with Elke Sommer opens. ☮ June 8, 1969—*Get Smart* wins the Emmy for Outstanding Comedy Series.

neering, and is now regarded as one of the world's authorities on battery-powered vehicles.

MY BACK PAGES

At one time Al was one of the world's fastest typists at 145 words per minute (on a manual typewriter). . . . He's also credited with developing Schwinn's line of stationary bikes and fitness equipment. . . . Popular new versions of the Sting-Ray—plus replicas of the classic '63 Coppertone—came out in 2004.

Serge Gainsbourg and Jane Birkin

This pair created one of the decade's sexiest songs.

TAKIN' CARE OF BUSINESS

Serge Gainsbourg was a distinctive figure on the '60s music scene, especially in Europe. At a time when bouncy, sunny hits were popping off the charts, the drinking, smoking, sultry Serge wrote and sang songs that brought erotic sexuality to the forefront. A Parisian named Lucien Ginzberg, he studied art before working as a piano player in French cabarets. After getting experience singing in front of audiences, he recorded albums using his new name in the late '50s-early '60s, albums that were jazzy and distinctive but poor sellers.

He struck gold when he teamed up (professionally and personally) with sex-kitten Brigitte Bardot, who was already a global movie sensation. With her he recorded some lush, sexy duets with readily identifiable pop themes—"Comic Strip," "Harley Davidson," "Bubble Gum," and "Bonnie and Clyde." One of their hits, "*Je T'Aime . . . Moi Non Plus,*" became a minor classic in '69 when Serge rerecorded the song with new whispers and heavy breathing from his new love, English actress Jane Birkin. The song was so steamy it got banned from some radio stations and was later recorded by '70s disco throbqueen Donna Summer.

From this pinnacle Serge began a slow descent, with songs that got darker and stranger, including some about male prostitutes and one about incest that he sang with his daughter. Branching into film he wrote soundtracks, directed, and appeared in numerous French films before dying (reputedly of a heart attack) in '91, and while some of his compositions won French movie awards none of his later work eclipsed the legacy of his memorable '60s music.

London-born Jane Birkin followed in her mother's footsteps by becoming a stage actress. Mid-'60s stage appearances while she was still a teen brought her roles in two notable '60s films, Richard Lester's *The Knack . . . and How to Get It* ('65) and, more memorably, Michelangelo Antonioni's surreal *Blow-Up* ('66), in which a nude Jane rolled on the floor with another girl and the movie's star, David Hemmings. Moaning out Serge's "*Je T'Aime*" in '69 she hit #1 on the British charts and rode that momentum with more albums (with and without Serge) into the 21st century. She also got deeper into French cinema with numerous movies depicting sexy situations, including one that featured her as the girlfriend of Brigitte Bardot.

American audiences might remember her as Penny Lane in the psychedelic art-house fave *Wonderwall* ('68, with music by George Harrison) and also as one of the many stars in the Agatha Christie mysteries *Death on the Nile* ('78) and *Evil Under the Sun* ('82), but again her audience was mostly on the continent—always popular in France, she's been nominated for several French movie awards. In recent years she's become a successful stage actress and a popular concert draw around the world. Today in France she is something of a cultural icon, and in Britain her long career was recognized by the Queen when she was awarded an O.B.E. (Order of the British Empire).

June 8, 1969—Don Adams wins his third Emmy for *Get Smart.* ☮ June 9, 1963—Barbra Streisand appears on *The Ed Sullivan Show.*
June 9, 1963—Jan and Dean's "Surf City" hits #1.
June 10, 1941—Singer Shirley Owens Alston of the Shirelles ("Soldier Boy") is born in Passaic, New Jersey.

EVERYBODY LOVES SOMEBODY

Slender, leggy, long-haired Jane was married in '65 to composer John Barry, who wrote the music for most of the Bond films and won Oscars for *Born Free* ('66), *The Lion in Winter* ('68), *Out of Africa* ('85), and *Dances with Wolves* ('90). Their daughter is photographer Kate Barry. After John and Jane's three-year marriage broke up, Jane auditioned for (and got) the lead in the French movie *Slogan* ('69); she also got the leading man, Serge Gainsbourg, whom she married in '68 for a dozen years. When they met, Serge had already been married and divorced twice, plus he'd been Brigitte Bardot's lover. Jane and Serge's daughter is the actress Charlotte Gainsbourg (*21 Grams*, 2003). Since '80 Jane has been married to French director Jacques Doillon. Serge had married a fourth wife before he died, leaving behind three children.

MY BACK PAGES

In later years Serge's surprising behavior on live TV created headlines, especially the times when he burned cash (a tax protest) and propositioned Whitney Houston. . . . Serge rests in the famed Paris cemetery where many other French heroes—Sartre, Baudelaire—are buried. . . . Jane's brother is screenwriter Andrew Birkin (*The Name of the Rose*, '86). . . . Created by Hermès in '84, the Birkin Bag is one of the designer's most expensive handbags.

Marvin Gaye

In the '60s, Motown's masterful singer was a smooth romantic stylist.

TAKIN' CARE OF BUSINESS

Arguably Motown's greatest singer ever, in the '60s Marvin Gaye recorded what is arguably Motown's greatest song ever. Born without the "e" he'd later add to his last name, young Marvin was singing in the choir of a Washington, D.C. church and absorbing regular beatings from his abusive father. After a stint in the Air Force, he joined the Marquees, a D.C. doo wop group that later became the Moonglows with several late-'50s records. Music impresario Berry Gordy, Jr. invited Marvin to break out as a romantic crooner at Gordy's Motown Records label, so in '60 Marvin was off to Detroit, where he worked with other Motown stars like Stevie Wonder, the Marvelettes, and Martha and the Vandellas (Marvin played instruments on hits by the first two, and he co-wrote "Dancing in the Streets" for the third). In '62 "Stubborn Kind of Fellow," another song Marvin co-wrote, was his first acclaimed solo record, followed a year later by several other small successes and one unqualified hit, "Pride and Joy."

In '64 he teamed with Mary Wells for the popular *Together* album; singing duets would become a hallmark of Marvin's later '60s, though his partner (platonically) was a different Motown songbird, Tammi Terrell. Their *United* album in '67 believably presented the two as a passionate couple singing passionate love songs like "Your Precious Love" and "Ain't No Mountain High Enough." Another romantic album, *You're All I Need*, followed in '68 with another "Ain't" love song ("Ain't

Nothing Like the Real Thing"). Sadly, Tammi's career ended prematurely when she died of a brain tumor in '70.

Working solo again, in '68 Marvin recorded the song that would become Motown's biggest hit of the decade (quite a feat, considering that the Supremes were Motown's reigning superstars). "I Heard It Through the Grapevine" wasn't written solely by Marvin, and it wasn't even sung first by Marvin, because Gladys Knight had gotten it on the *Billboard* pop chart the year before. But his version, with its eerie instrumentals, was the nation's most popular song for almost two months and was ranked for awhile by *Rolling Stone* as the best rock song *ever*.

After a break from touring and recording, Marvin came back strong in '71 with one of his most personal, and one of rock's all-time greatest, albums. The landmark *What's Going On* was revolutionary as a concept album concerned with social and ecological issues ("Mercy Mercy Me (The Ecology)" was just one of its hits), and by establishing Marvin as a visionary artist it set him on a new, independent course.

For the rest of the '70s and early '80s, he released some of the most striking and sensual music—"Let's Get It On," the Grammy-winning "Sexual Healing"—in the soul canon. Unfortunately, tax problems, prolonged drug use, and depression plagued his last years. His death in '84 was horrible—he was shot by his enraged father. Tributes to his greatness—including "Missing You," a hit by Motown partner Diana Ross in '85, induction into the Rock and Roll Hall of Fame in '87, an all-star tribute album in '99—have never stopped coming.

EVERYBODY LOVES SOMEBODY

Marvin married Berry Gordy's sister in '61. Their changing relationship coincided with his change in musical direction at the end of the decade; by the mid-'70s they were getting divorced, and his album *Here, My Dear* in '78 was a painful, personal look at their past life. In the late '70s Marvin was married again, to a much younger woman, for a few years. When he died he left behind two sons and a daughter, Nona, who would become a singer and actress.

MY BACK PAGES

The song that replaced "Grapevine" as Motown's biggest-seller was the Jackson 5's "I'll Be There" in '70 (the same year that Creedence Clearwater Revival recorded an 11-minute version of "Grapevine"). . . . "Grapevine" also became the California Raisins' theme song in commercials in the late '80s. . . . Before he came out with *What's Going On*, Marvin briefly tried out for the NFL's Detroit Lions, and Lions Mel Farr and Lem Barney sang backup on that LP.

Bobbie Gentry

This Delta darlin' rode the top of the pop charts with "Ode to Billie Joe."

TAKIN' CARE OF BUSINESS

A Mississippi kid in the '50s, Roberta Streeter wrote her first song at 7 years old. In the late '50s her family moved to California, and in the early '60s she was a UCLA student, a secretary, and a nightclub performer. Signed by Capitol Records in early '67, and using the name Bobbie Gentry, she recorded her self-penned "Ode to Billie Joe," originally with only her own guitar accompaniment and a seven-minute length that explained a lot more about what was thrown off the Talla-

June 10, 2004—Singer Ray Charles dies of liver failure in Beverly Hills. ☮ June 11, 1937—Actress Luciana Paluzzi is born. June 11, 1964—Queen Elizabeth commands the Beatles to play at her birthday party. ☮ June 11, 1969—*True Grit* with John Wayne opens. June 12, 1944—Actress Linda Foster is born in Lancaster, England. ☮ June 12, 1960—Rod Serling wins an Emmy for *The Twilight Zone*.

hatchie Bridge. Capitol execs re-recorded it with strings, cut the length almost in half to heighten the mystery and make it more suitable for AM radio, and rereleased it as Bobbie's first single.

That summer "Ode to Billie Joe" hit #1 on the pop charts (bumping aside the Beatles' "All You Need Is Love"), sold three million copies and stayed atop the charts for a month. At the Grammy Awards, Bobbie took home three trophies, plus the song won an additional award. "Ode" generated a movie in '75, has been covered by dozens of artists, and still hasn't revealed its secret.

After this monster hit, her follow-ups were only mild successes at best; she and Glen Campbell got some attention with their version of the Everly Brothers' "Let It Be Me," plus some others, but Bobbie would have no more major solo hits in the U.S., though she did have a #1 hit in the U.K. with her version of Burt Bacharach's "I'll Never Fall in Love Again" and had her own British and American TV shows. By the late-'70s Bobbie was retired from music and reportedly focusing on behind-the-scenes TV production; in 2004, a comprehensive career retrospective CD showed off the full range and depth of her remarkable talents.

EVERYBODY LOVES SOMEBODY

As a Vegas headliner, she married and divorced a Vegas hotelier in '69. After a second marriage in the mid-'70s, in '78 she briefly married singer Jim Stafford, who had his own TV show in '75.

MY BACK PAGES

The name Gentry came from the film *Ruby Gentry*, a '52 Charlton Heston/Jennifer Jones drama about a Southern woman "who wrecked a whole town, man by man, sin by sin". . . . Produced by Max Baer, Jr. (*The Beverly Hillbillies*), the film *Ode to Billy Joe* starred Robby Benson and Glynnis O'Connor, and it showed a doll being thrown off the bridge. . . . Bob Dylan wrote a sarcastic response to "Ode to Billy Joe" called "Clothes Line Saga" on *The Basement Tapes* LP ('75).

Astrud Gilberto

The Girl from Ipanema helped take bossa nova global.

TAKIN' CARE OF BUSINESS

Born in Brazil and married to one of her country's most popular singers, 23-year-old Astrud added soft English-language vocals to a song her husband, João Gilberto, was recording with jazzman Stan Getz in '63. A year later that song, "The Girl from Ipanema," became a major hit and Astrud began a long solo career that has lasted into the 21st century. Though her voice was limited and unexpressive when compared to the vocal queens of the '60s, her talents suited the light, breezy songs on her '60s albums (her appealing looks didn't hurt, either). Albums like *The Shadow of Your Smile* ('65) included Brazilian songs, a movie theme, and gentle renditions of standards such as "Fly Me to the Moon."

During the decade Astrud also dabbled with a screen career and appeared (as herself) on TV and in several movies

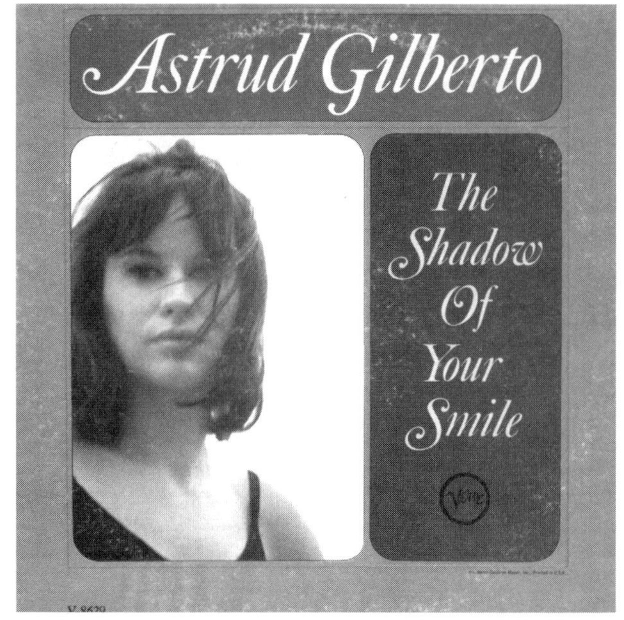

June 12, 1961—Disney's *The Parent Trap* with Hayley Mills opens. ☮ June 12, 1963—*Cleopatra* with Elizabeth Taylor opens.
June 12, 1965—Sonny and Cher make their first TV appearance on *American Bandstand*.
June 12, 1965—The Supremes' "Back in My Arms Again" hits #1. ☮ June 12, 1967—*You're in Love, Charlie Brown* debuts.

(*Get Yourself a College Girl*, '64), plus she sang the theme song for a good Sidney Lumet thriller, *The Deadly Affair* ('66). None of this added up to major success in America, but she was a top star in Brazil for decades, has performed around the world, and today she's still fondly recalled by the easy-listening crowd everywhere.

EVERYBODY LOVES SOMEBODY

Astrud and João Gilberto were married for the first half of the '60s. She has two sons who are musicians, and they have both performed on Astrud's records.

MY BACK PAGES

Fans may remember popular commercials she recorded for Eastern Airlines. . . . Astrud is also a talented artist, creating digital works and acrylic paintings.

Ralph J. Gleason and Jann Wenner

The *Rolling Stone* co-founders took rock journalism national.

TAKIN' CARE OF BUSINESS

These two New Yorkers hooked up in San Francisco in the mid-'60s and together created a new magazine that would be a lasting, influential chronicle of pop culture. Ralph was born during World War I, studied at Columbia, worked in the Office of War Information during World War II, and then headed west. After founding an early jazz magazine, in '51 he started writing a jazz column for the *San Francisco Chronicle,* but within a decade his subject matter also embraced folk, rock, and pop music.

Soon he was writing about '60s issues, too, not just '60s musicians, with articles about the free speech protests in Berkeley and the Haight-Ashbury flower-power scene. He interviewed Elvis, befriended Lenny Bruce, was an early champion of Bob Dylan, and had articles published in *Playboy*, *Variety*, *Esquire*, and all the major newspapers. Ralph also hosted a jazz show, produced numerous music specials, and co-founded the Monterey Jazz Festival.

His most lasting contribution, however, was *Rolling Stone*. In '67 the only magazines that covered rock music were either teenybopper fan rags (more interested in gossip than music) or radical underground newspapers (more interested in blaring their politics than real journalism). Ralph teamed with Jann Wenner to co-found a new San Francisco-based bi-weekly magazine that would be serious in its intentions, occasionally playful in its execution, brilliant in its literary ambitions, and all-encompassing in its coverage of "all the news that fits."

Jann was a post-World War II kid, a U.C. Berkeley student and music fan who became a publishing visionary. He saw the need for a magazine that respected and celebrated the new culture while simultaneously exploring it with risk-taking, investigative journalism. Working out of an old San Francisco warehouse, with funding from his wife's family (and from Ralph, too), Jann landed John Lennon for the cover of the first black-and-white newsprint issue of *Rolling Stone* in November '67, and the new publication was off and running.

Ralph was the magazine's mentor, senior editor, first essayist, and learned scholar; Jann was the idea man, also a writer/editor/interviewer but ultimately more important as a businessman and recognizer of young talent (among his hires were unknown writer Hunter S. Thompson and novice photographer Annie Liebovitz, both of whom became national stars). Articles were long, contributing authors and editors were famous, topics were diverse, and always the energetic magazine felt up-to-the-second current.

Ralph died suddenly of a heart attack in '75, only 58 years old. Jann took the magazine's headquarters to New York in '76, is still editor and publisher, and started up two other successful magazines (*Us* and *Men's Journal*). He has

June 12, 1968—Elvis Presley's *Speedway* opens. ☮ June 12, 1968—*Rosemary's Baby* with Mia Farrow opens.
June 13, 1960—Actress Hayley Mills makes the cover of *Life*. ☮ June 13, 1962—*Lolita* with Sue Lyon opens.
June 13, 1967—*You Only Live Twice* with Sean Connery opens.

also branched out into other media as the producer of movies (*Perfect*, '85) and TV specials (the Rock and Roll Hall of Fame induction specials). Jann was inducted into the Rock and Roll Hall of Fame in 2004, *Rolling Stone* #1000 issue came out in 2006, and an appearance on the magazine's cover is still as important for today's stars as it was for stars of the early '70s, back when "Cover of the Rolling Stone" was a hit record.

EVERYBODY LOVES SOMEBODY

Ralph was married in '40 and had three kids; his widow still lives in the Berkeley house they bought in '70. Married in '67 and the father of three kids, Jann left his wife in the mid-'90s for his fashion-designer boyfriend.

MY BACK PAGES

Ralph's trench coat is in the Rock and Roll Hall of Fame. . . . In the early '70s Ralph was a V.P. at Berkeley's Fantasy Records (home of Creedence Clearwater Revival). . . . For the first years of *Rolling Stone*, Jann was the magazine's primary interviewer of major rock stars like John Lennon, Bob Dylan, Mick Jagger, and Pete Townshend. . . . Jann has appeared in several films, notably as an editor in *Perfect* and as an agent in *Jerry Maguire* ('96), and he also played a regular character on the series *Crime Scene* in the late '80s.

This legendary sportscaster covered the coolest '60s events.

TAKIN' CARE OF BUSINESS

In the '60s, the way you could tell if a sporting event was important was if Curt Gowdy was broadcasting it. He didn't have the smooth delivery of a Vin Scully or a Pat Summerall—he had more of a cowboy twang—but he was always enthusiastic, honest, and professional. "I tried to pretend," he said, "that I was sitting in the stands with a buddy watching the game—poking him in the ribs when something exciting happened."

Born in Wyoming, Curt enlisted in the Army Air Corps to be a World War II fighter pilot. He started calling high school and college football games in the '40s, had a brief stint working for the New York Yankees in '49 and '50, and then in '51 became the main voice of the Boston Red Sox, a high-profile gig that lasted for 15 years. During that time he was one of the few media men to make friends with Ted Williams, and Curt called the Splendid Splinter's last at-bat (a famous homerun) in '60.

In '66, Curt jumped to NBC for a decade to be the lead announcer on the network's prestigious *Game of the Week*. Throughout the decade he was also the main announcer for televised AFL games, and, more memorably, he was hired for some of the decade's most significant sports events—Super Bowls, Rose Bowls, Olympic Games, and every World Series

A Dozen Super Sportscasters

Red Barber–N.Y. Yankees
Jack Brickhouse–Chicago Cubs
Don Dunphy–Boxing
Marty Glickman–N.Y. Jets
Ernie Harwell–Detroit Tigers
Chick Hearn–L.A. Lakers
Jim McKay–Olympics
Lindsey Nelson–N.Y. Mets
Chris Schenkel–College football
Ray Scott–NFL
Vin Scully–L.A. Dodgers
Pat Summerall–NFL

June 13, 1969—Guitarist Brian Jones quits the Rolling Stones, the band he founded some six years before.
June 14, 1928—Cuban revolutionary Che Guevara is born. ☮ June 14, 1962—The Beach Boys' first Top 20 hit, "Surfin' Safari," is released.
June 14, 1964—Ken Kesey and the Merry Pranksters begin their cross-country trip in the bus *Further*. ☮ June 14, 1967—*To Sir with Love* with Lulu opens.

from '66–'75. In '69, he was the sportscaster for two of the biggest upsets in sports history, certainly two of the galvanizing memories of the '60s—the Jets' 16–7 win over the heavily favored Colts in Super Bowl III, and the Mets' four-out-of-five triumph over the powerful Orioles in the World Series.

TV audiences will also recognize him from the *American Sportsman*, the long-running Emmy-winning show about the outdoors which he hosted and co-wrote. National awards punctuated his career, which ended in the '80s: a Peabody, an Emmy for lifetime achievement, and awards from the pro football and baseball Halls of Fame, among many others. Curt continued as a businessman, owning five radio stations until he lost his battle with leukemia in 2006. Today, the Curt Gowdy Award is given by the Basketball Hall of Fame to media superstars.

EVERYBODY LOVES SOMEBODY

Curt and his wife celebrated 50 years of marriage in '99. When Curt died, he also left behind two sons and a daughter.

MY BACK PAGES

The game he said was the best he ever saw—Game Six of the '75 World Series (Fisk's HR beats the Reds). . . . Another best baseball moment—April 8, '74, Hank Aaron's Ruth-eclipsing HR. . . . Curt also appeared as an announcer in several movies, including *Heaven Can Wait* ('78). . . . Curt Gowdy State Park is in Cheyenne, Wyoming.

Vince Guaraldi

This smooth jazzman made the music for the classic Charlie Brown specials.

TAKIN' CARE OF BUSINESS

Even with all its revolutions and rock music, the '60s had a sweet side that offered a gentle counterpoint to everything that was hip and cutting-edge. Perhaps the sweetest and gentlest of all was the Charlie Brown juggernaut —*Happiness Is a Warm Puppy,* a small hardcover version of the Charles Shulz comic strip, was the top-selling book of '63, the *Peanuts* characters were merchandised on everything from jewelry to garbage pails to lunch boxes, and the decade's many Charlie Brown TV specials were instant classics.

The man behind the memorable music of those TV specials was Vince Guaraldi. A San Francisco pianist nicknamed Dr. Funk, Vince played backup on jazz records in the early '50s and was a popular draw in the city's top nightclubs. After forming his own trio, Vince toured and landed a hit and a Grammy in '63 with the timeless "Cast Your Fate to the Wind." His graceful melodies and soothing arrangements pro-

June 14, 1969—John Lennon and Yoko Ono appear on David Frost's British TV show.
June 15, 1942—Xaveria Hollander, author of *The Happy Hooker*, is born in Surabaya, Indonesia.
June 15, 1951—Comedian Lenny Bruce and stripper Honey Harlowe marry. ☮ June 15, 1960—*The Apartment* with Shirley MacLaine opens.

vided perfect accompaniment to *A Charlie Brown Christmas* in '65—unlike other cartoons, which had slapstick, loud music, adult actors, and even laugh tracks, this animated special went sophisticated with a religious message, Vince's quiet music, child actors, and no laugh track.

The show was a monster success, won an Emmy and a Peabody, and spawned dozens of similar Schulz-inspired specials, including the Halloween perennial *It's the Great Pumpkin, Charlie Brown*. Vince's music backed the full-length *A Boy Named Charlie Brown* movie ('69) and more *Peanuts* soundtracks right up to his death from a heart attack in '76 (the day he died he was completing the music for *It's Arbor Day, Charlie Brown*). Meanwhile "Linus and Lucy," the bouncy instrumental the kids danced to on the original Christmas show, has been recorded countless times by other artists, and "Christmas Time Is Here" is a holiday staple.

EVERYBODY LOVES SOMEBODY

Vince was married in '53 and divorced in '70, with a son and a daughter. David, his son, is himself an accomplished jazz musician, and he's produced several recent reissues of his father's music. As a side note, Charlie Brown's love life was dominated by the elusive Little Red-Haired Girl. Never fully shown in the comic strip, she was based on Charles Schulz's first serious girlfriend, a woman who is now a grandmother in Minnesota. *You're in Love, Charlie Brown* gave a quick glimpse of the Little Red-Haired Girl, while *It's Your First Kiss, Charlie Brown* ('77) brought her out into the open with a name (Heather) and lush, long crimson tresses.

MY BACK PAGES

Vince's non-*Peanuts* records explored diverse musical styles and featured his experiments as a singer and guitarist. . . . One of his most unusual gigs was a halftime jazz performance at a Stanford University football game in '63—for most people it was the first time they'd ever heard a live amplified concert in a stadium.

Che Guevara

**A hero in Cuba,
an icon of revolution in America.**

TAKIN' CARE OF BUSINESS

Born in Argentina, Che Guevara became a hero to revolutionaries, first in Cuba, and then around the world. While studying medicine in '51, he and a friend toured South America by motorcycle (the basis for the film *The Motorcycle Diaries*, 2004). Seeing poverty and tyranny wherever he went, Che then dedicated himself to revolutions that would free the third world from oppressive dictatorships.

After finishing his medical studies, in the mid-'50s he hooked up with Cuban exile Fidel Castro in Mexico and became a rebel leader, his outrageous guerrilla tactics helping to bring about the overthrow of the Batista regime in Cuba at decade's end. As a top official in Castro's new government, Che continued to foment revolution in other Latin American countries. Speaking out passionately against what he considered U.S. imperialism, he toured the world in '64 to make speeches and rally support to his socialist ideals.

In '65 Che helped organize insurrections in Africa; a year later he brought his guerrilla warfare to Bolivia, but Bolivian forces (with the support of the C.I.A.) captured and killed him in '67. Supposedly his last defiant words to his executioners were "Shoot, coward, you're only going to kill a man." Back in Cuba the country grieved with three days of mourning.

In America he was adopted as an icon of revolt by the political left, and his handsome, strong, unyielding image, complete with a military beret, ragged beard, and long hair, adorned posters, shirts, and flags as a symbol of protest against the establishment. His global legend as a courageous, poetry-loving intellectual who was willing to sacrifice his own affluent upbringing to fight for the downtrodden has held fast over the decades.

EVERYBODY LOVES SOMEBODY

Che was married twice, first to a Peruvian woman in the '50s (with one child). After their divorce, in '59 he married a Cuban revolutionary and had four more kids into the mid-'60s. He's also thought to have fathered another child outside of his marriages.

MY BACK PAGES

After he was dead, Che's hands were amputated and sent to Castro. . . . In '97 Che's body was exhumed from its Bolivian grave and returned to Cuba, where he was reburied with military honors under a gun-carrying statue. . . . His monument and mausoleum are now popular tourist destinations.

Mie Hama and Akiko Wakabayashi

These perky Japanese dolls had key roles in two cool '60s movies.

TAKIN' CARE OF BUSINESS

Both born in Tokyo during World War II, Mie and Akiko were both cheerful, athletic, attractive presences onscreen. Both hit the '60s as teenagers and quickly found places in the Japanese cinema; by mid-decade 24-year-old Mie had already been in 50 Japanese movies. Six of them were with Akiko, including the Toho Studios classic *King Kong vs. Godzilla* ('63), which climaxed with the giant ape trying to ram a tree trunk down the lizard's throat.

Both girls then turned up in two English-language hits: as Teri and Suki Yaki in Woody Allen's spy-spoof *What's Up, Tiger Lily?* ('66), and as allies in the James Bond movie set in Japan, *You Only Live Twice* ('67). In the latter, Akiko saved Bond's life and was killed off; Mie got a pretend marriage from 007 but a real consummation in a life raft, thus revealing Bond's position on off-shore drilling.

After Bonding, neither actress appeared in any other major English-language films. Some rumors suggest that Akiko was injured during the Bond film and had to retire soon after; meanwhile, in the '70s Mie became a popular TV hostess in Japan, giving her career a chance to live twice. While today they remain anonymous to American audiences, in Japan they're both revered as beloved stars.

EVERYBODY LOVES SOMEBODY

Info is scant, only a suggestion that Mie was married to a Japanese businessman.

MY BACK PAGES

In Cantonese, Mie's first name means "beautiful" and is pronounced to rhyme with the ballet move *plié*. . . . Tough negotiator: when the producers threatened to fire Mie from *You Only Live Twice* because of her poor English, she threatened them with suicide because of the dishonor—they kept her on, but switched her role with Akiko's to give Mie fewer lines to speak.

Françoise Hardy

This beautiful French chanteuse recorded million-selling records and appeared in several '60s movies.

TAKIN' CARE OF BUSINESS

Tall (almost 5′ 11″), slender, and beautiful, Françoise Hardy was, for most American audiences, best known as the sullen jeans-wearing girlfriend of the Italian driver in John Frankenheimer's *Grand Prix* ('66). Overseas, however, she was already a top recording star. Her first album came out in '62, when she was still a teenager; a single, "Tous les Garçons et les Filles," sold over two million copies in the early

June 16, 1963—Russia puts the first woman into space, parachutist Valentina Vladimirovna Tereshkova.
June 16, 1967—Opening night of the Monterey International Pop Festival in California. ☮ June 17, 1961—Russian dancer Rudolf Nureyev defects.
June 17, 1964—*Zulu* with Michael Caine opens. ☮ June 17, 1967—"Don't Sleep in the Subway" by Petula Clark hits the charts.

'60s. Writing many of her own songs, accompanying herself on guitar, and singing in a soft, sultry style, she combined catchy tunes with sentimental lyrics to score many more hits in France and land spots on big-time TV music shows. Going for the international market, she tried singing in English, but only one of her songs charted well in the U.K. ("All Over the World" in '65). Another half-dozen albums in the '60s, and two dozen more into the 21st century, solidified her reputation in France as a durable, popular star.

EVERYBODY LOVES SOMEBODY

Bob Dylan seemed to have had a crush on her—they were photographed together in the mid-'60s and he mentioned her in a long poem on the back of his '64 album *Another Side of Bob Dylan* ("for françoise hardy at the seine's edge . . . i look across to what they call the right bank an envy your trumpet player"). In '67 Françoise married French singer/composer Jacques Dutronc; they soon had a son and married in '73. Their son grew up to become a guitarist who accompanied his mother on one of her records.

MY BACK PAGES

Her nickname—the Yeh Yeh girl. . . . Françoise had bit parts in several other '60s movies before *Grand Prix,* including *What's New Pussycat?* ('65).

Linda Harrison

This pageant beauty played mute Nova in *Planet of the Apes.*

TAKIN' CARE OF BUSINESS

Linda Harrison was one of the loveliest actresses of the '60s, with the teen-modeling and beauty-contest experience to prove it. Competing as Miss Maryland, 20-year-old Linda was the first runner-up in the Miss American pageant held in Long Beach, California, in '65. Though she didn't win, she got noticed by a Hollywood agent, who quickly put her in front of the camera. She did two *Batman* episodes in '66 and had small roles in a couple of films, most notably the five minutes she spent as the jaw-droppingly sexy Miss Stardust in *A Guide for the Married Man* ('67), her waist a concave wonder.

Then came Nova, the part that has kept her signing autographs for 30+ years. *Planet of the Apes* was perfect for a young actress still learning her craft—as the love interest for stogie-chompin' Charlton Heston, Linda just had to look frightened, fascinated, and fabulous as the action unfolded around her. After the movie was a huge Oscar-winning hit, Linda graduated to a regular role on the TV series *Bracken's World* and then reprised Nova for *Beneath the Planet of the Apes* in '70 (this time she did get a line when she got to yell out "Taylor!").

After a brief retirement, she re-emerged in the mid-'70s with some screen time in *Airport '75*, but there was a bigger movie she supposedly got aced out of. As the story's told, her husband, producer Richard Zanuck, wanted her for the plum role of Ellen Brody in *Jaws*, but Sid Sheinberg, who was Zanuck's boss, decided to give his own wife, Lorraine Gary, the part of the police chief's wife. The '80s brought Linda good roles in two *Cocoon* movies, and the '90s kept her busy with travels and appearances at film conventions.

EVERYBODY LOVES SOMEBODY

Linda married producer Richard Zanuck, 10 years her senior and the son of studio kingpin Darryl Zanuck, in '69. They have two sons, with Helen Gurley Brown and her husband David as godparents. Divorced in '78, Linda and Richard are still close friends.

MY BACK PAGES

Linda was the gorgeous cover girl on the January '70 *Cosmopolitan*. . . . There was an additional scene filmed for *Planet of the Apes* that revealed Nova's pregnancy, but the scene was cut. . . . Linda made a brief appearance in Tim Burton's 2001 *Planet of the Apes* remake (Nova is shown trapped in a cage).

Susan Hart

Scintillating Susan dazzled in drive-in favorites.

TAKIN' CARE OF BUSINESS

In the '60s, one of the mainstays of drive-in movies was gorgeous Susan Hart. Often working in the quick, inexpensive flicks churned out by American International Pictures, Susan always managed to steal a scene or two or 10. Born near Seattle and raised in Southern California, she studied acting, was discovered while vacationing in Hawaii, and was soon getting early '60s TV work. A starring role in the horror cheapie *The Slime People* ('63) brought a flurry of prominent roles in *Ride the Wild Surf* ('64), *The City Under the Sea* ('65), and three different mid-decade beach-party movies. By decade's end she'd wrapped up her brief but affectionately remembered movie career to try to make it as a singer. "Is This a Disco or a Honky Tonk" got some airplay in '81.

EVERYBODY LOVES SOMEBODY

That Susan was in so many AIP movies was no coincidence—her husband, who was about twice her age, was the company's co-founder. They had one child before he died of a brain tumor in '72. Susan's been remarried since '81 and now lives in Palm Springs.

MY BACK PAGES

In her last movie, Susan was *The Ghost in the Invisible Bikini* ('66), wearing a blonde wig. . . . Susan had some singing spots in a couple of movies—a song in the short *The Wild Weird World of Dr. Goldfoot* ('65) and a jukebox appearance in AIP's *Chrome and Hot Leather* ('71).

June 18, 1960—Golfer Arnold Palmer charges from behind to win the U.S. Open. ☮ June 18, 1962—*The Music Man* with Shirley Jones opens. June 18, 1967—The Mamas and the Papas perform as the closing act of the three-day Monterey Pop Festival. June 18, 1969—*The Maltese Bippy* with Rowan and Martin opens.

Goldie Hawn

The giggly go-go dancer who regularly stole the show on TV and then won an Oscar in her first major movie.

TAKIN' CARE OF BUSINESS

Goldie Hawn established the lasting archetype of the teen ding-a-ling, and she could've cruised on that persona—what she has called her "zany/ditsy/dingy shtick"—for years, but to her credit she quickly established herself as a talented actress and eventually as a serious film producer. Though she's best known for her comedy roles, she has formal training as a dancer, taking ballet and tap lessons from the age of 3, when she was Goldie Studlendgehawn from Washington, D.C. Early-'60s jobs included work as a teenage can-can dancer at New York's '64 World's Fair and as a chorus girl in Vegas.

In '67 she played a dingbat neighbor on the quickly cancelled *Good Morning World*, and then came *Laugh-In*, the psychedelic laff-fest that ruled the TV ratings of the late '60s. The show and the stars got many Emmy and Golden Globe nominations, but Goldie was the most popular cast member and got the most fan mail. Her lithe figure was ideal for fun bikinis and the funny fake tattoos, and her golden bob, koo-koo smile, and huge blue eyes made hers one of the most memorable faces of the decade. In addition, she displayed natural comic timing as she reacted naively to the chaos swirling around her. This naiveté wasn't an act: as a dyslexic, she really did have trouble reading cue cards, and her resulting befuddlement only amplified the comic return.

In '68 she got her first major role in her first big movie, *Cactus Flower*, and at only 24, she won the Oscar as that year's Best Supporting Actress (an award that Raquel Welch accepted for her because, as Goldie explained later, she forgot to attend the ceremony). After the '60s she became a major Hollywood player, both starring in and/or producing numerous hits with Hollywood's heaviest hitters. Steven Spielberg's *The Sugarland Express* ('74), Warren Beatty's *Shampoo* ('75), *Foul Play* with Chevy Chase ('78), *Private Benjamin* ('80), and *The First Wives Club* ('96) are just some of the movies that have made her one of Hollywood's most durable, and powerful, stars. Today she's as lean, healthy, active, and positive as ever.

EVERYBODY LOVES SOMEBODY

"Marriage is a form of ownership," she once declared, "you lose personal power." Goldie has had three husbands, and three divorces: director Gus Trikonis (married in '69), actor Bruno Wintzell ('73), and entertainer Bill Hudson ('76). With Hudson she had two kids, Oliver and Kate (both of whom are actors). Goldie has said that these marriages broke up because the men couldn't handle her fame. Since '84 she's lived with actor Kurt Russell, whom she first met in '68 when they both had roles in *The One and Only Genuine Original Family Band*. They started dating when they co-starred in *Swing Shift* ('84); later they also co-starred in *Overboard* ('87). Together they have a son, Wyatt.

MY BACK PAGES

One of her ancestors was Edward Rutledge, the youngest person to sign the Declaration of Independence. . . . In '72 she recorded *Goldie*, an album of country-western songs. . . . In '84 she was a *Playboy* cover girl. . . . When Woody Allen directed her in his charming musical *Everyone Says I Love You* ('96), he had to caution Goldie to rein in her dancing talent during her musical numbers—because of her earlier training she was clearly much better than the other

June 19, 1940—Shirley "Cha Cha" Muldowney, the first woman to win drag racing's Top Fuel championship, is born.
June 19, 1963—*Jason and the Argonauts* with Honor Blackman opens. ☮ June 19, 1963—*PT-109* with Cliff Robertson opens.
June 19, 1963—Russia's first woman cosmonaut, Valentina Vladimirovna Tereshkova, successfully lands in central Asia after flying a three-day mission.

actors. . . . In '96 she made *People* magazine's list of the 25 Most Intriguing People. . . . Of her giggly *Laugh-In* dimbulb she once said, "I'm like her only in small ways". . . . Of herself: "I have a light personality and a deep-thinking brain". . . . Her autobiography was published in 2005.

Tom Hayden and Abbie Hoffman

Two student revolutionaries catalyzed anti-war protests in the '60s.

TAKIN' CARE OF BUSINESS

One of the most intense moments of the '60s came when the Democrats held their convention to nominate a candidate for the '68 presidential election. Even before the convention the year had already been scarred with outrage: a wave of violence had rumbled across America following the assassination of Martin Luther King, Jr., students had briefly taken over Columbia University in April, student demonstrators had clashed with police in Paris in May, and the Democrats' most popular candidate, Robert Kennedy, had been assassinated in June. Late in August the convention brought tensions to a boil when thousands of raucous rock-throwing anti-war protesters clashed head-on with tear-gas-throwing baton-wielding policemen in the streets and parks of Chicago, a terrible spectacle that was shown on national TV. The resulting trial of the Chicago Eight (later the Chicago Seven) became a galvanizing event in the history of American revolution.

A prominent two of the Eight were Tom Hayden and Abbie Hoffman. Tom was a University of Michigan student, editor of the student newspaper and a cofounder of the Students for a Democratic Society in '61. His "Port Huron Statement" advocating civil rights and peace became a manifesto of the SDS and the foundation of his early-'60s work in the South (where he was arrested and beaten) and with New Jersey's inner-city poor.

With other student protesters he helped lead the '68 demonstrations in Chicago that got him arrested for conspiracy and inciting riots. Lasting from September '69 to February '70, the long circus-like trial of the Chicago Eight was peppered with numerous outbursts from the defendants, included appearances by celebrity witnesses, and ended with convictions that were overturned in '72.

Venturing into politics, Tom lost his first California election in '76, but later won races for the California State Assembly and the State Senate; during his almost two decades of public service he got over 100 of his measures passed. He also helped organize successful grass-roots campaigns against nuclear power and cancer-causing chemicals. A prolific author, he has written numerous books, has taught college, and today is still fighting against U.S. wars.

While Tom Hayden has spent most of his life working forcefully within the system, Abbott "Abbie" Hoffman spent most of his on the outside, and for most of the '70s he was a fugitive living underground because of a drug bust (he finally surrendered in '80). During the '60s, he co-founded the "Yippie" movement (Youth International Party) and helped organize many anti-war protests (he also led a '67 demonstration at the New York Stock Exchange in which he and others tossed money onto the trading floor, where a wild scramble ensued). Arrested in Chicago in '68, Abbie openly mocked the proceedings with creative antics (wearing judicial robes into court, offering LSD to the judge, etc.). His later writings advocated continued revolution and anti-establishment lifestyles (*Steal This Book* in '71 was a how-to guide for radicals). In '89, at age 52, he committed suicide.

EVERYBODY LOVES SOMEBODY

From '73–'89, Tom was married to actress Jane Fonda. They have two kids. He's now married to Canadian actress-singer Barbara Williams, who's appeared in dozens of movies, TV series, and plays. They have one adopted son and live in Los Angeles. Abbie was married for the first half of the '60s, had two kids, and got divorced in '66. A year later he remarried and had another child before a divorce in '80.

MY BACK PAGES

The other members of the Chicago Eight were Jerry Rubin, David Dellinger, Rennie Davis, John Froines, Lee Weiner, and Bobby Seale. . . . Seale's vocal protests were so vehement in court that the judge sent him to prison for contempt, thus leaving the Chicago Seven. . . . At the '68 convention Tom was the first conspirator arrested—for letting the air out of the tires of a police car. . . . In '69 Abbie attempted to make a statement during the Who's set at Woodstock, but Pete Townshend famously kicked him off the stage.

Bob Hayes

In the mid-'60s, Bullet Bob was the world's fastest man.

TAKIN' CARE OF BUSINESS

Imagine being an NFL cornerback in '65. You're playing the Dallas Cowboys. You line up on defense and see #22 trotting out of the opposing huddle. Facing you is the fastest man on the planet. The touchdown machine who scored every fourth time he caught a pass.

You call a timeout.

Bullet Bob Hayes built his reputation with two incredible runs at the Tokyo Olympics in '64, but he was more than a sprinter. Born in Florida, he was a well-muscled football player at Florida A & M before he was invited to run track in the off-season. As a top collegiate sprinter in the early '60s, he flirted with the world record (10.05 seconds) in the 100-meter dash. In Tokyo, he tied the record when he won the gold medal, beating the world's best runners by 12 feet (a race typically won by inches). Even more impressive was his mind-boggling sprint as the anchor of the 400-meter relay team. Taking the baton 10 feet behind the entire field, he exploded past every other anchorman—the world's fastest runners, remember—and *won* by 10 feet. Trackside viewers said he was literally a blur; two decades later the *L.A. Times* hailed it as "the most astonishing sprint of all time."

It was his last race. The Dallas Cowboys, seeing game-breaking potential in him, made Bob their seventh-round draft pick and lined him up at wide receiver in '65. He was the ultimate deep threat—he could catch up with any long bomb, he led the league in yards per catch, and opposing teams, unable to defend him man-to-man, were forced to devise the first zone defenses. His stellar career—he made three Pro Bowls, and he's still the Cowboy receiver with the most TDs—was capped in '72 when the Cowboys beat the Dolphins 24–3 in Super Bowl VI, making him the first and only player with both a Super Bowl ring and an Olympic gold medal.

Bob's 11-year career in the NFL ended with the 49ers in '76, and his life then spiraled downwards. Battles with alcohol and drugs led to 10 months in prison in '79–'80 (a conviction later overturned). Many experts say his sentence is what has kept him out of the Pro Football Hall of Fame, since his career stats compare favorably with other Hall of Famers. Even the Cowboys delayed inducting him into their Ring of

June 20, 1969—150,000 attend the music festival in Newport, Rhode Island. ☮ June 20, 1969—Sam Peckinpah's *The Wild Bunch* opens.
June 21, 1932—Composer Lalo Schifrin is born in Argentina. ☮ June 22, 1920—Paul Frees, the voice behind many popular '60s cartoons, is born.
June 22, 1947—Basketball star Pete Maravich is born in Pennsylvania. ☮ June 22, 1962—Actress Marilyn Monroe makes the cover of *Life*.

Honor until 2001. In the '90s Bob wrote a candid autobiography, moved back in with his parents in Florida, and in the last years of his life fought liver and prostate problems before finally dying of kidney failure in 2002. He was inducted into the U.S. Olympic Hall of Fame in 2005.

EVERYBODY LOVES SOMEBODY

Bob had two failed marriages, and he left behind five children when he died.

MY BACK PAGES

Bob won his gold medal in borrowed cleats, his own having been misplaced by fellow Olympian Joe Frazier. . . . Bob caught two passes in Super Bowl VI, with Cowboy QB Roger Staubach the MVP. . . . For four decades the Bob Hayes Invitational Track and Field Meet has brought together top high school athletes.

Joey Heatherton

For many men and boys who saw her in the '60s, this scintillating sex kitten is one of their best, most formative memories.

TAKIN' CARE OF BUSINESS

Born to the biz, Joey Heatherton grew up on Long Island as the daughter of a mother who was a Broadway dancer and a father who was TV's "Merry Mailman" on a local kids' show. After studying dance throughout her childhood years, Joey got her big break in '59 when at 15 she made the Broadway cast of *The Sound of Music.* She released her first single ("That's How It Goes"/"I'll Be Seeing You") that same year, with three more 45s to come in the mid-'60s. None of them made much impact, however—Joey's appeal was more visual than aural.

In the early '60s, she started making what would be dozens of TV appearances on everything from Westerns (*The Virginians*) to dramas (*Route 66*) to comedies (*I Spy*) to teen dance shows (*Hullabaloo*) to many variety shows (*Hollywood Palace*). Of all these, the variety shows proved to be her launching pad to stardom because they showcased her, not as a costumed character, but as what she truly was: one of TV's hottest live performers.

Singing and dancing energetically in fringy mini-outfits, with the curves to make 'em really swing, sexy Joey stopped shows, and heartbeats, in living rooms across the country. *Dean Martin Presents The Golddiggers* in '68 gave her regular exposure as a whirling 5′ 3″ sex goddess and

June 22, 1965—*What's New, Pussycat?* with Capucine opens. ☮ June 22, 1966—*Who's Afraid of Virginia Woolf?* with Liz Taylor opens.
June 22, 1993—Pat Nixon, First Lady from '69–'75, dies of lung cancer at 81.
June 23, 1940—Sprinter Wilma Rudolph is born in St. Bethlehem, Tennessee. ☮ June 23, 1963—The Enchanted Tiki Room attraction opens in Disneyland.

showed off the decade's best shag 'do. She also took a shot at movies, playing a murderous teen in the Susan Hayward potboiler *Where Love Has Gone* ('64) and the female lead in the Troy Donahue movie *My Blood Runs Cold* ('65).

But the live stage was where she sparkled, so between gigs she took her brilliant wattage to the darkest corners of Vietnam, touring several times—and always to riotous acclaim—with Bob Hope's USO shows. In '72 she released an album (*The Joey Heatherton Album*) and three singles (including her versions of "Crazy" and "God Only Knows"). She headlined Vegas during the '70s, continued to put in TV appearances on various variety shows and specials, and in '75 had her own one-season sitcom, *Joey and Dad*.

She also made more films, most notably *Bluebeard* ('72) and *The Happy Hooker Goes to Washington* ('77). Always a magazine fave, she was on the cover of *Esquire* in December '65, and in April '97 she was featured in *Playboy* in an array of sexy poses—at age 53! Today she puts in occasional screen appearances (John Waters' *Cry-Baby* in '90) and appears at autograph shows, still titillating those who first saw her over 40 years ago.

EVERYBODY LOVES SOMEBODY

Joey suffered through one of the most agonizing marriages of the late '60s. In '69 she married glamorous Dallas Cowboy wide receiver Lance Rentzel, and for a year or so they were the toast of the town, appearing together at events and on TV. Unfortunately, that marriage ended in '71 when he was arrested for indecent exposure in front of a young girl (an episode he wrote about in his '72 book *When All the Laughter Died in Sorrow*). Though she stayed with him for awhile, they eventually split up. The notoriety seemed to take the spark out of her career, and she was later arrested for cocaine possession and causing a disturbance in an airport. But none of these unfortunate events shake the conviction for many males that Joey Heatherton is still one of the best things to remember about the '60s.

MY BACK PAGES

Joey writhed upon Serta mattresses in several TV commercials of the early '70s (Susan Anton replaced her in '79). . . . Joey turned up on one of David Letterman's Top 10 lists in '88: "Top Ten Fears of Snuggles the Fabric Softener Bear, #5—First wife Joey Heatherton will write book claiming he beat her regularly". . . . *The Simpsons* acknowledged her in several episodes—in one of them, Principal Skinner said he was shot by his fellow soldiers when he tried to cover up Joey at a Bob Hope Vietnam show.

David Hedison

This acclaimed stage actor captained one of TV's super subs.

TAKIN' CARE OF BUSINESS

Rhode Island native Albert David Hedison was a successful Broadway stage actor when he hit Hollywood in the late '50s. Billed as Al Hedison he starred in *The Fly,* the '58 classic sci-fi shocker that put him in a lab coat and a big creepy fly head. After he starred in the cool but short-lived TV series *Five Fingers,* war and adventure movies took him to the great *Voyage to the Bottom of the Sea* adventure series in '64. Irwin Allen's remake of his own '61 movie ran for four years and made David (now going by his middle name) the cool captain of the high-tech *Seaview* as it explored marine mysteries and battled giant sea creatures. Bond fans will recognize him as C.I.A. agent Felix Leiter in two different 007 epics, *Live and Let Die* ('73) and *License to Kill* ('89). Always working, David has continued to enjoy a long career on TV, with many many appearances on popular series and regular roles on *Dynasty II: The Colbys* in the '80s, *Another World* in the '90s, and *The Young and the Restless* in the 2000s.

June 23, 1964—*A Shot in the Dark* with Elke Sommer opens. ☮ June 23, 1965—*Harlow* with Carroll Baker opens.
June 23, 1965—*The Art of Love* with Elke Sommer opens. ☮ June 23, 1967—*The Happiest Millionaire* with Lesley Ann Warren opens.
June 23, 1967—The third "Twiggy in New York" TV special airs. ☮ June 23, 1967—Jim Ryun sets the world record in the mile (3:51.1).

EVERYBODY LOVES SOMEBODY

Tall, dark, and handsome, David's been married to producer Bridget Hedison (*The Last Tattoo*, '94) since '68 and has two kids.

MY BACK PAGES

Early in his career David won a *Theatre World* award as the Most Promising Newcomer. . . . When his deformed character came to a sticky end in *The Fly*, that was a small robotic figure doing the movements in the spider's web as it pleaded "Help meee, help meee" to brick-throwing Vincent Price. . . . *Voyage to the Bottom of the Sea* ran longer than Allen's other '60s sci-fi shows, *Lost in Space*, *The Time Tunnel*, and *Land of the Giants*.

Tippi Hedren

This cool blonde model got her screen career off to a quick start with starring roles in two Alfred Hitchcock movies.

TAKIN' CARE OF BUSINESS

In '63 lovely Tippi Hedren was working as a New York fashion model when Alfred Hitchcock spotted her doing a commercial on *The Today Show*. Hitchcock had cast elegant blonde actresses in most of his movies—including Grace Kelly, Kim Novak, and Eva Marie Saint. Minnesota-born Nathalie Hedren, sleek, modern, and regal with perfect features crowned by upswept hair, had a sophisticated urban look ideal for Hitchcock's intelligent filmmaking. He cast her alongside 3,200 birds in his big-budget thriller *The Birds,* an instant success that brought Tippi the Golden Globe in '64 as the Most Promising Newcomer (an award she shared with two other beautiful newcomers, Ursula Andress and Elke Sommer).

Dazzled by her subtle talent, which he said was "like a dormant volcano we know one day is going to erupt," Hitchcock starred her in his next movie, the psychological thriller *Marnie* ('64). Critics are divided over these two Hitchcock films—some consider them under-appreciated classics, others rank them as two of the master's lesser achievements. Either way, they springboarded Tippi to stardom, and she continued to make movies for the rest of the decade, notably Charlie

June 24, 1942—Actress Michele Lee is born in L.A. ☮ June 24, 1964—*Robin and the 7 Hoods* with Frank Sinatra opens. June 24, 1965—*Cat Ballou* with Jane Fonda opens. ☮ June 25, 1925—Actress June Lockhart is born in New York. June 25, 1963—*8½* with Claudia Cardinale opens. ☮ June 25, 1967—The Circle-Vision 360 Theatre opens in Disneyland.

Chaplin's last film, *A Countess from Hong Kong* ('67).

Pursuing an eclectic mix of screen projects, her post-'60s appearances have ranged from the insubstantial—the TV movies *Return to Green Acres* ('90) and *The Birds II* ('94)—to the memorable—*The Harrad Experiment* ('73) and *Pacific Heights* ('90, both with daughter Melanie Griffith). She produced *Roar*, a movie about saving African animals, in '80, and from that has sprung two decades of work dedicated to saving big cats.

Founder and president of the Roar Foundation, Tippi now oversees (and lives on) a wildlife preserve north of L.A. called Shambala. There she cares for over 50 lions, cheetahs, and other big cats that have been cast off from movie productions, circuses, and zoos. She wrote a heart-wrenching book about the experience, *The Cats of Shambala* ('85). Other humanitarian endeavors include global travels to help feed the hungry and appearances before Congress on behalf of Asian refugees.

EVERYBODY LOVES SOMEBODY

Tippi was married to actor Peter Griffith until '61, then she married actor/producer Noel Marshall in '64, followed by a third husband in '85 and reportedly a fourth in 2002. With Griffith she had a daughter in '57, actress Melanie. Of morbid curiosity to film fans and psychologists is Alfred Hitchcock's bizarre behavior toward Tippi. In *Hollywood Babylon II*, Kenneth Anger said Hitchcock "developed a powerful romantic and sexual obsession for Hedren" who "paid dearly for piquing his passions," and so he terrorized her in *The Birds* with actual birds, not the mechanical birds she was expecting. According to Anger, Tippi's resulting wounds were bad enough to shut down the production for a week.

MY BACK PAGES

Supposedly *Marnie* was going to be Grace Kelly's comeback movie after living for six years as a royal in Monaco, but scheduling problems and disapproval from her subjects caused her to back out. . . . Tippi has received numerous lifetime-achievement awards from international film organizations.

Hugh Hefner

The only celebrity in this encyclopedia with a species of rabbit named after him (*Sylvilagus palustris hefneri*).

TAKIN' CARE OF BUSINESS

In the '60s *Playboy* magazine became the Playboy empire. What had started in a kitchen in '53 as an intelligent, sexy, mostly black-and-white periodical with a "Sweetheart of the Month" and photos of girls who worked in the Playboy offices had blossomed a decade later into a hugely successful, deeply influential publishing juggernaut.

A few '60s landmarks in the magazine's evolution: the centerfold girls, called Playmates as of '54, for the first time included minorities; the first Ian Fleming fiction (the first of many from the James Bond author) ran in '60; the "Playboy Advisor" column began in '60; the *Little Annie Fanny* comic strip and long, in-depth interviews both started in '62 (Miles Davis was the first interviewee); and the line of rabbit-logo merchandise expanded dramatically all decade long.

Simultaneously, exclusive Playboy Clubs, debuting in Chicago in '60, were opening in three dozen cities all around the world. Moving into other media, the company bracketed the decade with two swingin' TV ventures: from '59–'60 *Playboy Penthouse* was a relaxed showcase for stars such as Nat "King" Cole, Ella Fitzgerald, and Lenny Bruce, and then in '69 *Playboy After Dark* used the same sophisticated party atmosphere to interact with hip new stars like Rowan and Martin, Linda Ronstadt, Sharon Tate, and the Byrds.

Hef was insatiably active, pursuing new projects all decade long: a '64 radio show, *Playboy Table Talk*; splashy parties almost nightly with famous friends (all chronicled in

Playmate Stats

Averages

Height ('60s)—5′ 4″
Height ('90s)—5′ 7″

Measurements ('60s)—36-22½-35
Measurements ('90s)—35-23½-34½

Weight ('60s)—115 lbs.
Weight ('90s)—117 lbs.

Record-Setting '60s Playmates

Shortest Playmates ever—4′ 11″
(Sue Williams, April '65; Karla Conway April '66)

Biggest bust of any Playmate ever—41″
(Rosemarie Hillcrest, October '64)

Smallest waist of any Playmate ever—18″
(Michelle Winters, September '62)

Largest hips of any Playmate ever—39″
(Unne Terjesen, July '62)

Lightest Playmate ever—85 lbs.
(Joni Mattis, November '60)

First African-American Playmate—
Jennifer Jackson (March '65)

First Asian-American Playmate—
China Lee (August '64)

Playmates with a Playmate daughter—
Carol Eden (December '60) and
Simone Eden (February '89)

the magazine); the first ventures into movie production (early highlight—Roman Polanski's *The Tragedy of Macbeth*, '71); the move in '71 from being a privately held company (HMH Publishing Co. Inc.) to the publicly traded Playboy Enterprises; and the move in '71 to an extravagant pleasure palace, the Playboy Mansion near Beverly Hills, with travel between the Chicago offices and the L.A. residence in a company-owned black DC-9 (*The Big Bunny*) tricked out with a bar, beds, and disco. By the late '60s, the Playboy dream was a Playboy reality.

Living that reality was the man who'd orchestrated this vast expansion, the magazine's charismatic 40-ish founder and editor-in-chief, Hugh Hefner. Born into a strict, religious Chicago family, Hugh (or Hef, or Ner, as Woody Allen later called him) served briefly in the Army in World War II, studied sociology at the University of Illinois, worked on the staff of *Esquire*, and in the early '50s concocted the idea for an urbane men's magazine called *Stag Party*. Renamed *Playboy* (a rival called *Stag* already existed), the new 50-cent magazine had more than girls on its mind—from the beginning Hef had serious social intentions, which he articulately expressed in his long-running "Playboy Philosophy" column.

The '60s, with the rise of the Pill, women's rights, free speech, and civil rights (all addressed by Hef and promoted through the magazine), saw the full flowering of the seeds he'd planted, or if not planted, nourished, a decade before. Not that the revolution was smooth—Hef was arrested in '63 for "indecent" Jayne Mansfield photos (the jury was hung—insert your own joke here). But the revolution was definitely on.

Hef's triumphs and tragedies, successes and struggles in later decades have all been well-documented, usually by Hef himself—he's often in his own magazine (partying in psychedelic shirts back then, not pajamas); he's made dozens of appearances on game shows, talk shows, variety shows, and documentaries (even befriending a pajamas-wearing Bart on *The Simpsons* in '93); and he's opened up his private life on

June 27, 1969—A police raid in Greenwich Village leads to the Stonewall riots.
June 27, 2002—John Entwistle of the Who dies of a heart attack in Las Vegas. ☮ June 28, 1960—*Murder, Inc.* with May Britt opens.
June 28, 1963—Comedian Judy Carne marries actor Burt Reynolds.

reality shows (the one thing he hasn't done is finish his stalled autobiography).

He battled to keep his magazine classy when similar magazines got sleazy, had a stroke, turned over the company to his daughter, launched overseas editions and lucrative Web sites, produced hundreds of popular adult videos, set up the charitable Playboy Foundation, made the cover of *Time* magazine, and has been lauded as one of the most influential, and most envied, Americans of the 20th century.

EVERYBODY LOVES SOMEBODY

Before he was the *Playboy* publisher, Hef was a husband. He had two kids before his 10-year marriage ended in '59. His legendary bachelor years continued until '89 when he married that year's Playmate of the Year, Kimberley Conrad, who was 37 years his junior. They also had two kids together before amicably splitting up a decade later (amicable, indeed—she continued to live on Hef's property). Between the two wives Hef had hundreds (thousands?) of affairs and numerous steady girlfriends who got spotlighted in the magazine's pages, among them Barbi Benton in the late '60s–early '70s. Hef's never been shy about sharing his good fortune with the world—in the 2000s he had seven girlfriends at once, all of them living with him in the mansion, all of them shown on TV. In 2005, the *The Girls Next Door* show chronicled the mansion lives of three main girlfriends whose *combined* ages were about the same as Hef's.

MY BACK PAGES

Playboy has been published almost continuously since '53—the exception is March '55, when Hef missed the printing deadline and so skipped over that month. . . . The plaque at his front door—*Si Non Oscillas, Noli Tintinnare* ("If you don't swing, don't ring"). . . . A bronze bust of Barbi's bust graced the foyer of the mansion for years. . . . Hef has been portrayed a half-dozen times in movies, most notably by Cliff Robertson in *Star 80*.

Joseph Heller and Kurt Vonnegut

Bracketing the decade were two cool anti-war novels by these two friends.

TAKIN' CARE OF BUSINESS

In a decade of anti-war protests, two authors found fame with anti-war novels that sprang from their own World War II experiences. Born near the islands (Manhattan and Coney), Joseph Heller was an Army Air Corps bombardier who flew over 60 European missions in World War II. Returning to New York after the war, he got his Master's from Columbia, studied at Oxford, and then landed the first of several teaching jobs. While writing ad copy for prominent national magazines in the '50s, he started writing *Catch-18* about his military experiences. The first chapter was published quietly in a magazine, and the completed book, renamed *Catch-22* so as to avoid confusion with Leon Uris's *Mila 18,* came out in '61 with little success.

Some positive reviews in '62, however, jump-started sales, and by mid-decade the book was a sensation and on its way to becoming one of the biggest-selling novels in history. While the subject was a rebellious World War II bombardier, readers found obvious parallels between the futility and insanity of war that Heller comically expressed and America's bedeviling involvement in Vietnam. Filled with puns (Colonel Korn), satirical situations (the men intentionally bomb their own base), and tragic deaths, the book both amused and agitated readers.

Surprisingly, Joseph followed up his masterpiece, not with another novel, but with TV and film work, including such lightweight fare as a *McHale's Navy* episode and the Natalie Wood comedy *Sex and the Single Girl* ('64). At decade's end his play *We Bombed in New Haven* ran for a few months on Broadway. His subsequent books—among them the somber *Something Happened* ('74), the playful *Good As Gold* ('79), the autobiographical *Now and Then* ('98)—sparked interest but failed to recapture the magic and the audience of his first novel.

Like Joseph Heller, Kurt Vonnegut fused wartime settings with a comic sensibility in his masterpiece *Slaughterhouse-Five* ('69). However, Kurt also added science-fiction elements, including a protagonist who had come "unstuck in time" and so jumped uncontrollably back and forth through his life, and intelligent aliens who brought humans to their planet. Compared to *Catch-22*, *Slaughterhouse-Five* was much more unconventional in its telling: the author spoke directly to readers about the book even as they were reading it, and there were doodle-like illustrations (by Kurt) on some pages. Kurt's own experiences informed the entire book.

Born in Indiana, he attended Cornell and then served in the infantry in World War II. Captured during the Battle of the Bulge and held in a prison camp, he witnessed the fire bombing of Dresden, Germany, a terrible, senseless event that killed more civilians than the Hiroshima bombing. After the war he studied at the University of Chicago and became a reporter. His first novels, *The Sirens of Titan* ('59) and *Cat's Cradle* ('63), used science fiction to satirize the modern human condition.

A prolific writer after the '60s, he wrote many novels (including *Breakfast of Champions*, '73, *Slapstick*, '76, *Hocus Pocus*, '87), plus plays, essays, articles, and speeches. When Joseph died, one of the commentaries solicited by the media was Kurt's, who declared the passing of his friend "a calamity for American letters." Both writers saw their most famous works become fascinating, if not wildly successful, Hollywood films. Mike Nichols's *Catch-22* ('70) was the director's next major movie after *The Graduate* ('67); it boasted an inspired cast that included Orson Welles, Alan Arkin, Buck Henry, and Art Garfunkel, but the book was probably too sprawling for a two-hour movie. George Roy Hill's *Slaughterhouse-Five* ('72) was his next movie after *Butch Cassidy and the Sundance Kid* ('69); with no major stars in the cast, it thrives today as a cult classic, and Kurt himself wrote that he was the second-luckiest novelist ever (after Margaret Mitchell) when it came to filmed books.

Kurt Vonnegut

EVERYBODY LOVES SOMEBODY

Both had long marriages and divorces. Joseph's four-decade marriage ended in '84; his second marriage continued from '87 until his death. He had two kids. Kurt had a three-decade marriage that ended in the '70s; he then married photographer Jill Krementz. He has many children, his own and several he adopted.

MY BACK PAGES

Kurt and Joseph did an entertaining interview with *Playboy* in '92, and in it they debated the date of their first meeting, finally settling on April of '68 at Notre Dame. . . . Joseph's *Closing Time* in '94 continued the story of *Catch-22* to show how Yossarian and a few other characters had made out after the war (not happily, it turns out). . . . Kurt announced that *Timequake* ('97) would be his last novel.

June 29, 1960—*Strangers When We Meet* with Kim Novak opens.
June 29, 1967—Actress Jayne Mansfield is killed in a late-night car accident in Louisiana.
June 29, 1969—The Jimi Hendrix Experience plays its last concert in Denver before breaking up.

Jimi Hendrix

Simply the coolest guitar hero of all time.

TAKIN' CARE OF BUSINESS

Jimi was the one all other rock superstars admired. What he did with an electric guitar was unprecedented, much imitated, but never surpassed, and today, almost 40 years after his death, he's still regarded as rock's master virtuoso. Clapton, members of the Who, even some Beatles came to listen and learn when he played in London—they knew that he was changing their world right before their very ears. Amazingly, his entire career lasted just four years.

Jimi's life began as Johnny Allen Hendrix in pre-World War II Seattle (later his father replaced the Johnny Allen moniker with James Marshall). He was a self-taught musician who modeled his acoustic guitar playing on the blues masters. By the late '50s he had switched to an electric guitar and had been in two bands. After some minor troubles with the law, in '61 Jimi joined the Army and a year later became a paratrooper stationed in Kentucky. An injury drove him out of the service and into session work under the name Jimmy James.

For the next couple of years he played with established stars like Sam Cooke and Little Richard. In '65 he formed his own band, Jimmy James and the Blue Flames, in which he played lead guitar. Successful gigs in Greenwich Village led to an invitation in mid-'66 to go to London, where he hooked up with drummer Mitch Mitchell and bassist Noel Redding to form the Jimi Hendrix Experience. The group's first single, "Hey Joe," in '67 was followed by the album *Are You Experienced?*, an instant classic that made "Purple Haze" and other hard-rock anthems staples for radio stations and air-guitarists everywhere.

A show-stopping, guitar-burning turn at the Monterey International Pop Festival in the summer of '67 cemented his reputation as rock's most dynamic performer. *Axis: Bold as Love* (with "If Six Was Nine") was his next album, followed by the ambitious *Electric Ladyland*, a double album that became his first LP to top the American charts. With the break-up of the band (constant touring and drug problems took their toll), Jimi played Woodstock in '69 backed by a group called Gypsy Sun and Rainbows; Jimi's intense, psychedelic solo rendition of the national anthem is hailed today as one of rock's defining moments.

Leading a revamped band called Band of Gypsies, Jimi welcomed the new year with a series of New York concerts that were compiled into a live album in '70. Altering his band's lineup and name once again, Jimi and his new Jimi Hendrix Experience began work on a new album, *First Rays of the New Rising Sun* at his Electric Lady Studios in New York, but he died in his sleep (choking on his own vomit after a drug overdose) in London before the album was released. His tragic death at only 27 years old, along with the sudden passings of Janis Joplin, Jim Morrison, and Brian Jones, signified the end of an era. Dozens of albums have showcased his greatest hits (*Smash Hits*, '69) and unreleased material—some of it recorded live, some of it unfinished, all of it proving what a creative, prolific genius he'd been.

EVERYBODY LOVES SOMEBODY

A legendary player with several girlfriends at once, Jimi never married. He was one of the most-prized catches of the Plaster Casters, a pair of sisters who immortalized him (and many other rock stars) with an intimate plaster sculpture made when they had his full attention.

MY BACK PAGES

When he was 14, Jimi went to see an Elvis concert in Seattle. . . . In late '65 Jimi rented out a London flat owned by Ringo Starr—Jimi painted the entire interior black and ruined the furniture, and Ringo sued him for the damages (they settled out of court). . . . One of the first gigs for the newly formed Jimi Hendrix Experience was as the opening act for the Monkees' American concerts, but the teenybopper audience didn't like Jimi's music, so he and his group soon left the tour. . . . Not all of Jimi's incendiary displays came off smoothly—the first time he burned his guitar on stage, he ended up in the hospital. . . . Jimi's favorite musician—Rahsaan Roland Kirk, a blind jazz saxophonist of the '60s who altered his instruments and sometimes played two or three simultaneously. . . . Jimi's favorite guitar—a Fender Stratocaster. . . . Jimi's favorite amp—the famed Marshall stack that could handle his high-volume feedback. . . . In 2003 *Rolling Stone* named him the greatest guitarist of all time.

Audrey Hepburn

This beloved international sweetheart was a cinema queen.

TAKIN' CARE OF BUSINESS

Audrey Hepburn starred in only 22 major films, but among them are some of Hollywood's best-loved classics. Today she's still spoken of reverentially and regularly appears on prominent movie lists (in June '99 the American Film Institute named the "50 Greatest Screen Legends," and Audrey was third among the actresses).

She was born Edda Kathleen van Heemstra Hepburn-Ruston to wealthy Belgian parents, but her father walked out on the family when she was only 6. Audrey grew up in London but at 10 was evacuated to neutral Holland when World War II broke out. In her early teens Audrey worked for the Resistance by helping to raise funds and passing out anti-Nazi leaflets. By '44, food was desperately scarce—Audrey later confessed to eating flower bulbs—and she was suffering from anemia, asthma, and chronic migraines.

After the war she and her mother relocated to Amsterdam, where Audrey studied dance. When they moved to London in '48, Audrey's grace and beauty started to bring her modeling and acting jobs. A meeting with the writer Colette put 22-year-old Audrey on Broadway as the title character in Colette's *Gigi* ('52). The show was a smash, and Audrey was a star. Days after the show closed, she flew to Rome to film *Roman Holiday*, the movie that would bring her an Oscar as Best Actress in '54. Audrey followed that stunning success with some of the most acclaimed and popular films of the '50s, including *Sabrina* ('54) and *Funny Face* ('57).

At a time when big, brassy blondes like Marilyn Monroe and Jayne Mansfield were dominating the fan mags, Audrey's distinctive ethereal elegance was thrown into high relief (had she not been an actress, she could've been a top fashion model, and in fact she made the cover of *Vogue* in '64 and a *Life* cover in '62). *Breakfast at Tiffany's* ('61) brought 32-year-old Audrey one of her defining roles, spirited Holly Golightly, and her fourth Oscar nomination. It also showed off her singing, as she performed "Moon River" in the movie and on the soundtrack.

Charade in '63 successfully teamed her with another Hollywood legend, Cary Grant. The following year, *My Fair Lady* charmed audiences and critics around the world. Controversy ensued when her performance as Eliza Doolittle wasn't nominated for an Oscar, probably in response to the news that her singing voice was dubbed by Marni Nixon (studio chief Jack Warner downplayed the move, saying "We've been doing it for years, we even dubbed the barking of Rin-Tin-Tin"). After '67's underrated *Two for the Road* and the creepy *Wait Until Dark* (her fifth Oscar nomination), Audrey retired to concentrate on her personal life and have a baby. The romantic *Robin and Marian* ('76) with Sean Connery was her wonderful comeback film. Her film output was sporadic after that, capped by Steven Spielberg's *Always* ('89), in which she played, appropriately enough, an angel. Sadly, the irreplaceable Audrey Hepburn died of cancer in '93. Later that year the Academy of Motion Picture Arts and Sciences gave her the Jean Hersholt Humanitarian Award in recognition of her years of tireless charity work for UNICEF. More than just a magnificent star, Audrey was a magnificent inspiration.

EVERYBODY LOVES SOMEBODY

When her father abandoned Audrey and her mother in '35, Audrey's emotional life was forever changed. She later admitted to being ever-insecure in relationships, with a constant fear of abandonment. In the '50s and '60s, Audrey was romantically linked to several major stars. She was married to actor Mel Ferrer for most of the '50s and through to '68, giving him a son in '60. After their divorce, she married a psychiatrist in '69 and had his son three years later, but that marriage broke up in the late '70s. Her last and most serene relationship was with another actor whom she met in '80, and for the last dozen years of her life he was her live-in companion.

MY BACK PAGES

Multilingual, Audrey could speak English, Flemish, Dutch, and French from childhood. . . . Audrey's co-star in *Breakfast at Tiffany's* was almost Steve McQueen, but he couldn't get out of his contract for the TV show *Wanted: Dead or Alive*. . . . Supposedly whenever Audrey traveled, she took with her as many personal belongings from home as she could, then she'd unpack all the dozens of trunks and suitcases, set up all the mementos in her hotel room, then repack them all and take them with her to the next destination. . . . In a TV bio Richard Dreyfuss, her *Always* co-star, called her "perfectly charming, perfectly loving . . . The best that we can hope to be". . . . Audrey herself told you all you need to know: "The most important thing is to enjoy your life—to be happy—it's all that matters."

Dustin Hoffman

One of the premier actors of the 20th century got his start in the '60s with two classic movies.

TAKIN' CARE OF BUSINESS

Dustin Hoffman was born into a movie-loving family: his dad was a studio prop man and his mom was a fan who enrolled her three kids in music and drama classes (young Dustin took piano). Teenage Dustin was a lonely, sensitive 5′ 6″ student who didn't start to blossom until he studied drama at Santa Monica City College in '55. He left college for the prominent Pasadena Playhouse in '57, then left L.A. altogether with new pal Gene Hackman in '59, determined to start a New York stage career in the tradition of their acting idol, Marlon Brando. Over the next couple of years, Dustin gained another pal, Robert Duvall, took a series of jobs in restaurants, at Macy's, and in a morgue, was accepted to the Actors Studio, got an agent, and made his Broadway debut in '61. TV dramas and commercials were

Dustin Hoffman, Anne Bancroft

coming his way, as were more attention-getting stage roles. Though not really a movie actor, he was about to make the jump to global movie stardom.

Before *The Graduate,* movie heroes looked like John Wayne or Rock Hudson: tall, sturdy, experienced all-American types who took swaggering steps. After *The Graduate,* movie heroes could look like everyman: short, young, offbeat characters who slouched, proclaimed their individuality, and challenged (not defended) authority. One of the prime agents of this change, Dustin was an intense perfectionist who redefined what a hero and heroism could be. In his footsteps walked the great actors of the '70s and beyond who were equally non-traditional anti-heroes, stars like De Niro, Pacino, and Dreyfuss.

That Dustin was even in *The Graduate* at all was a surprise: Charles Webb's provocative '63 novel called for a tall, blonde surfer-type. Director Mike Nichols felt the dark, 29-year-old Jewish Dustin would bring something unique to the role, and his instincts paid off—released in late '67, *The Graduate* quickly became one of the most successful comedies of all time, bringing an Oscar to Nichols and six more nominations, including one for Dustin. The score won a Grammy, the song "Mrs. Robinson" and soundtrack album were top sellers, and the $3,000,000 movie earned over $50,000,000 by '69.

In an unusual but telling career move, Dustin responded to the acclaim with . . . nothing. Refusing to be typecast, for two years he rejected similar roles that would've made him rich; *Life* magazine even ran a photo of him in an unemployment line. When he did take on another movie, it was to stretch himself about as far from clean-cut Benjamin Braddock as he could get. The part of Ratso Rizzo, the crippled hustler in the grungy *Midnight Cowboy,* brought him universal acclaim and another Best Actor Oscar nomination. *Little Big Man,* in which Dustin played a 121-year-old survivor of Custer's Last Stand, was a '70 triumph that landed him on the covers of *Life, Time, Esquire,* and *Look* and confirmed his stature as his generation's leading actor.

After the '60s, he worked steadily on a long string of ambitious projects, most of them popular and acclaimed—*Lenny* ('74), *All the President's Men* ('76), *Kramer vs. Kramer* ('79), *Tootsie* ('82), *Rain Man* ('89)—with Oscar nominations or Oscar wins in every decade through the '90s. Occasional flops (*Ishtar,* '87) and quirky roles (*Hook,* '91, *Meet the Fockers,* 2004) only solidified his reputation as an artist willing to try something new.

He made a triumphant return to Broadway in '84 in *Death of a Salesman* (the TV presentation brought him an Emmy and a Golden Globe), he became a successful movie producer (*A Walk on the Moon,* '99), he narrated dozens of specials and documentaries, and he even played a character on *The Simpsons* (Lisa's substitute teacher in '91). But most of all he worked, an actor's actor who has refused to be stereotyped or pigeonholed, as busy and admired in the new century as he was in the last.

EVERYBODY LOVES SOMEBODY

For much of the '60s, Dustin's girlfriend was a ballet dancer named Anne Byrne (she would later play Michael Murphy's wife in Woody Allen's *Manhattan*). They married in '69, with Dustin adopting her daughter. They had their own daughter in '70 and that year moved to New York's Upper East Side after their Greenwich Village townhouse was destroyed in a fire. During the filming of the divorce drama *Kramer vs. Kramer,* Dustin and his wife were going through their own divorce drama, with Dustin remarrying in '80. He and his wife are still together and have four kids.

MY BACK PAGES

He was named after Dustin Farnum, an actor in 1920s Westerns. . . . *Graduate* screenwriter Buck Henry said that initially the producer's hoped to cast Robert Redford, Candice Bergen, Ronald Reagan, and Doris Day. . . . Other possible Benjamins included Warren Beatty, Charles Grodin, Jack Nicholson, and Burt Ward (of *Batman* fame). . . . Though Benjamin was a recent college grad and Mrs. Robinson had a college-age daughter, in real life Dustin and Anne Bancroft were only about six years apart in age. . . . The American Film Institute ranked *The Graduate* seventh (right behind *The Wizard of Oz*) among the 100 greatest movies of all time, with *Midnight Cowboy* at #36. . . . To give Ratso a consistent limp for *Midnight Cowboy*, Dustin put pebbles in his shoe. . . . His famous "I'm walkin' here!" line, delivered as he's crossing the street, was improvised when he was almost run over by an unaware taxi driver.

Paul Hornung

If Joe Namath was pro football's Beatle, the Golden Boy from Kentucky was the sport's Rat Packer, a celebrity athlete who scored on and off the field.

TAKIN' CARE OF BUSINESS

Handsome and blonde, Paul Hornung was a dazzling mid-'50s college football hero. As quarterback he led Notre Dame in scoring, passing, rushing, punting, and return yardage, and as a defensive back he was among the leaders in interceptions and tackles. When he won the Heisman Trophy for the 2–8 Irish in '56, he became the only winner from a losing team.

He took his versatility to the pros as the #1 overall draft pick in '57, taken by the Green Bay Packers to play quarterback and fullback. Switched to halfback by his new coach, Vince Lombardi, in '59, Paul led the NFL in scoring for the next three years, setting records for most points in a season, in a title game, and in the Pro Bowl. During these years Paul was one-third of a Hall of Fame backfield, with quarterback Bart Starr and fullback Jim Taylor the other cogs in the Packers' efficient offensive machine (Paul also kicked field goals and threw the occasional pass).

During his career with the Packers, the team won four titles and the first Super Bowl, a game Paul missed due to injury. He was also getting rich with endorsement deals for Chevy and Marlboro, plus in one series of ads he and Frank Gifford modeled swimwear. After retiring in '67 as "the best clutch player" Coach Lombardi had ever seen, he went into real estate, broadcasting, and business; today he owns everything from a shopping mall to a soybean refinery. Awards came in pairs: two MVPs, two All-Pros, two Pro Bowls, two football Halls of Fame (college and pro).

EVERYBODY LOVES SOMEBODY

"Never get married in the morning—you never know who you might meet that night." All Paul, who lived, enjoyed, and set new standards for the good life. Beautiful women, all-night parties, rivers of alcohol—any of the skirt-chasing hipsters tearing up Vegas in the early '60s would've felt right at home.

July 4, 1963—*The Great Escape* with Steve McQueen opens. ☮ July 4, 1964—Maria Fraser wins the women's single title at Wimbledon.
July 4, 1965—Golfer Carol Mann wins the U.S. Women's Open Golf Championship.
July 4, 1969—Ann Jones beats Billie Jean King to win the women's singles title at Wimbledon.

Not that he got away with his swingin' lifestyle—in '63 he and the Lions' Alex Karras were suspended for a year for betting on games (both returned to continue their successful careers). Paul stayed out of serious trouble after that, but even in the year he was reinstated ('64) Coach Lombardi fined him twice for missing curfew. He did eventually settle down, though—Paul and his wife celebrated their 25th anniversary in 2005.

MY BACK PAGES

Besides starring in football, Paul also lettered in basketball at Notre Dame. . . . In '61, Coach Lombardi worked out a special arrangement so Paul could complete his Army service during the week and still play games on Sundays. . . . Paul was contrite after the gambling scandal, saying it was just for fun at a time when many other players (whom he refused to implicate) gambled much more seriously. . . . After quitting football, Paul appeared in a William Holden war movie, *The Devil's Brigade* ('68). . . . He's been inducted into the Wisconsin, Kentucky Athletic, and National High School Halls of Fame, and each year Kentucky still gives its best high school football player the Paul Hornung Trophy. . . . He wrote an autobiography, *Golden Boy*, in 2004.

Heisman Trophy Winners

1960–Joe Bellino, Navy, RB
1961–Ernie Davis, Syracuse, RB
1962–Terry Baker, Oregon State, QB
1963–Roger Staubach, Navy, QB
1964–John Huarte, Notre Dame, QB
1965–Mike Garrett, USC, RB
1966–Steve Spurrier, Florida, QB
1967–Gary Beban, UCLA, QB
1968–O.J. Simpson, USC, RB
1969–Steve Owens, Oklahoma, RB

Olivia Hussey

This Argentine teen queen won instant international acclaim as the doomed Capulet in *Romeo and Juliet*.

TAKIN' CARE OF BUSINESS

Born in Argentina, Olivia Hussey moved to England as a child and began studying to become an actress. She had supporting roles in minor British TV and film productions until she was spotted in a West End play at age 15. The spotter was director Franco Zeffirelli, who selected her out of 800 girls to be in his lavish production of *Romeo and Juliet* ('68). The movie was an internationally acclaimed Oscar-nominated hit, and young Olivia was a star. To many viewers she represented the teen ideal of romantic love, her beautiful face perfectly evoking Juliet's innocence and devotion.

Though she won the Golden Globe as the Most Promising Newcomer, her next '60s roles were in minor British films. She overcame the lost potential of *Lost Horizon* ('73), in which she both sang and danced, to star in the creepy *Black Christmas* ('74), then she was the Virgin Mary in the TV mini-series *Jesus of Nazareth* ('74) and one of the all-stars in *Death on the Nile* ('78). Olivia was seen on-screen all

July 5, 1944—Robbie Robertson of the Band is born in Toronto, Canada.
July 5, 1969—The Rolling Stones put on a free London concert in tribute to Brian Jones. ☮ July 6, 1924—Football Coach Darrell Royal is born.
July 6, 1927—Actress Janet Leigh is born in Merced, California. ☮ July 6, 1945—Actor Burt Ward is born in L.A.

through the '90s in various projects, most notably as Norma Bates in *Psycho IV* ('91).

EVERYBODY LOVES SOMEBODY

Olivia's marriage to Dean Martin's son ended in divorce in the late '70s. She then married a British pop star, Paul Ryan, and after they divorced she married another singer for most of the '80s. She married again in the '90s, this time to hard-rocker David Eisley of the group Dirty White Boy, and she now has three kids.

MY BACK PAGES

Her Juliet represented one of the first times that a teenager actually played this teenage role. . . . In '98 *Cosmo* rated *Romeo and Juliet* one of the 10 most romantic films ever. . . . The film's theme song, "A Time for Us," became a #1 hit for Henry Mancini. . . . At the Royal Command Performance of the movie, Olivia was presented to the Queen of England. . . . Before Len Whiting got the role of Romeo, it was reportedly offered to Paul McCartney. . . . The movie was intentionally made more sensual than previous Shakespeare films, in hopes of arousing the interests of a younger, hipper audience, thus there were partial nude scenes and provocative ads.

Martha Hyer and Janette Scott

These two beauties starred in cool sci-fi flicks of the mid-'60s.

TAKIN' CARE OF BUSINESS

Sci-fi fans know Martha from Ray Harryhausen's '64 epic *First Men in the Moon,* a classic Victorian space adventure. Martha was in three other movies that same year, including the titillating melodrama *The Carpetbaggers* and the frothy *Bikini Beach*. Martha's impact might've soared to legendary heights if she'd have gotten one more key role she was up for, but lost—the doomed Marion Crane in Hitchcock's *Psycho*.

Martha Hyer

Throughout the '60s she averaged two movies a year with some of the biggest names in the biz (Robert Mitchum, John Wayne, and Marlon Brando among them), plus many hit TV sitcoms. It was the culmination of a long career that had begun in Texas and taken her to L.A., where she found lots of work in popular '50s movies including *Sabrina* ('54) and *Houseboat* ('58). Her big break came when she got a Best Supporting Actress Oscar nomination for her role as a teacher in Frank and Dino's *Some Came Running* ('58). After the '60s she moved behind the scenes to write the screenplay for *Rooster Cogburn* ('75) and then her autobiography.

Born in Britain, Janette Scott was a child star whose screen career began in the '40s at age 4. As a teen her roles got bigger and more diverse, and by the end of the '50s she was starring in sweeping epics (*Helen of Troy*, '56), musicals (*The Good Companions*, '57), and comedies (*The Devil's Disciple*, '59). Janette is best known for two good sci-fi hits: *The Day of the Triffids* ('63) and *Crack in the World* ('65). The former was based on John Wyndham's masterful '51 novel,

July 6, 1963—Margaret Smith beats Billie Jean King to win the women's singles title at Wimbledon.
July 6, 1964—The Beatles' movie *A Hard Day's Night* premieres in London, with Princess Margaret in attendance.
July 6, 1968—Billie Jean King wins the women's singles title at Wimbledon for the third year in a row. ☮ July 6, 1968—Rod Laver wins Wimbledon.

which didn't include the character Janette played in the movie. In fact, *The Day of the Triffids* was actually two separate films spliced together—the original version was deemed thin, so the studio added additional sequences with Janette, filmed by a different director. As a result of the separate shoots, Janette never even saw her co-star while the movie was being made because his portion had already been completed.

Janette Scott

In *Crack in the World*, she played a heroic, devoted wife who was unable to save her doomed scientist husband, but as a fit blonde beauty she looked great trying. Several veddy veddy British comedies rounded out her '60s résumé. Unfortunately for her fans, once Janette got romantic with Mel Tormé in the mid-'60s, she quit show biz and never appeared in another movie.

Another 15 Sci-Fi Classics

2001: A Space Odyssey ('68)
Alphaville ('65)
The Angry Red Planet ('60)
Fahrenheit 451 ('66)
Fantastic Voyage ('66)
Five Million Years to Earth ('67)
The Illustrated Man ('69)
Marooned ('69)
Planet of the Apes ('68)
Robinson Crusoe on Mars ('64)
Seconds ('66)
The Time Machine ('60)
Village of the Damned ('60)
Voyage to the Bottom of the Sea ('61)
X: The Man with the X-Ray Eyes ('63)

EVERYBODY LOVES SOMEBODY

For three years in the '50s, Martha was married to film director Ray Stahl. Then on the last day of '66 Martha married one of the biggest producers in Hollywood, Hal Wallis, at his Palm Springs estate. She was 42, Wallis was 67, and she was with him until he died 20 years later. Wallis produced over 200 movies in his long, illustrious career, including *The Maltese Falcon* ('41), *Casablanca* ('42), the Martin and Lewis comedies of the '50s, and nine Elvis movies. Janette was married to a songwriter in the '50s, and then in '66 she married the Velvet Fog, Mel Tormé, who was some 13 years her senior. They had two children before divorcing in '77. Janette remarried in '81.

MY BACK PAGES

Martha was given sexy pin-up treatment in several magazines in the '50s. . . . Helping *First Men in the Moon* at the box office was its timing, which coincided with the building momentum of America's own space program. . . . Janette's mom was Thora Hird, a distinguished English screen actress who was awarded the Order of the British Empire in '83 and was later named Dame Thora Hird. . . . Fans of *The Rocky Horror Picture Show* will recall Janette from that movie's opening lyrics: "And I really got hot, when I saw Janette Scott fight a triffid that spits poison and kills."

July 7, 1940—Ringo Starr of the Beatles is born in Liverpool. ☮ July 7, 1962—Karen Susman wins the women's singles title at Wimbledon. July 7, 1968—Golfer Susie Maxwell Berning wins the U.S. Women's Open Golf Championship. ☮ July 8, 1948—Actress Kim Darby is born in L.A. July 8, 1962—Rod Laver wins the Grand Slam. ☮ July 8, 1964—*The Moon-Spinners* with Hayley Mills opens.

Lee Iacocca

The '80s industrialist in a '60s encyclopedia? Meet Mr. Mustang.

TAKIN' CARE OF BUSINESS

At the Ford Motor Company, young Lido Iacocca from Pennsylvania was an automotive engineer in the late '40s, a successful sales leader in the mid-'50s, and a rising star in product development at the cusp of the '60s. As General Manager in '62, he gambled on a sleek new car with in-your-face power that would appeal to young males—the Ford Galaxie. Of this line, the best was the 500XL Sunliner, a long, low, chrome-flashed convertible made "X-tra Lively" by a monster engine. It was the pure expression of sport and speed, all at a reasonable $3,400 price. The Galaxies were instantly successful and helped launch the army of muscle cars that would storm onto the market later in the decade.

But Lee (as he was now known) was already on to the Next Big Thing. Seeing the need for a spirited compact that would appeal to the huge group of baby boomers who were becoming first-time car buyers, he championed the Mustang, the car that would come to define the pony car genre. Combining elements from two previous Ford cars, the Falcon and the Fairlane, the Mustang was a sporty, sophisticated new design, created with only two seats in its first iteration.

By the time it was shown to the public at the New York World's Fair in '64, the Mustang had grown to include four seats and a dazzling array of options that made it a smash hit, not just with young buyers, but with all ages. It was a versatile treat for all tastes: the $2,300 base model could be customized to become a stylin' family car, a fun campus runabout, or a $5,000 hot rod. Exciting TV commercials in early April of '64 built the public's anticipation to a fever pitch; when it was finally made available, demand quickly outstripped supply, and Ford had to commit its plants in New Jersey and California to help the Michigan plant churn out the 1.5 million Mustangs needed. Twiggy drove a Mustang, it was the pace car at that year's Indy 500, and *Motor Trend* magazine anointed it as the Car of the Year. Lee's car was the most successful launch in history, and it's still Ford's fastest-seller ever.

Almost immediately Ford tinkered with it—new engines, new options, and a new fastback model came out over the next couple of years (independent designer Carroll Shelby even modified the fastback into the thunderous GT-350 and GT-500 race cars). When Steve McQueen tore up San Francisco's streets in one for *Bullitt* ('68), the Mustang was cemented in American lore as an automotive icon. The early '70s would bring the Mach 1 and the Boss 429 and 302 variations, then a long slow decline as the Mustang lost ground to foreign imports during the energy-depleted '70s (though the car was still a screen star—two of *Charlie's Angels* drove Mustangs).

By '77 Lee had risen to become Ford's #2 man with a million-dollar salary, but conflicts with Ford's #1 man drove him to Chrysler in '78. In '81 he got a billion-dollar loan to keep the struggling company afloat and throughout the '80s he was one of the most visible businessmen in the country, thanks to his starring role in a series of popular commercials ("If you can find a better car, buy it" was his familiar slogan).

July 8, 1966—Actress Claudia Cardinale makes the cover of *Life*. ☮ July 8, 1967—Billie Jean King wins the women's singles title at Wimbledon. July 9, 1942—Actress Edy Williams is born in Salt Lake City, Utah. ☮ July 9, 1947—Mitch Mitchell of the Jimi Hendrix Experience is born in Ealing, England. July 9, 1963—"Walk Like a Man" by the Four Seasons hits #1. ☮ July 10, 1946—Actress Sue Lyon is born in Davenport, Iowa.

On his watch Chrysler survived with new compacts and the revolutionary minivan. Lee went on to write a bestselling autobiography, act as an instrumental force in the Statue of Liberty renovation, and retire from Chrysler in '92, though he has stayed on as the company's commercial pitchman.

EVERYBODY LOVES SOMEBODY

Lee was married in '56; after his wife died of diabetes in '83, he soon created the Iacocca Foundation to raise funds for diabetes research. Lee subsequently married and divorced twice. He's got two kids.

MY BACK PAGES

The very first Mustang was bought by a Canadian airplane pilot, who traded it back to the company in '66 for another Mustang (the cream-white Mustang #1 is now on view at the Ford Museum). . . . By '68 Ford's stunned rivals had generated their own pony cars—the Chevy Camaro, Pontiac Firebird, Lincoln-Mercury Cougar, and AMC Javelin. . . . Not all of Lee's Ford cars met with universal acclaim—he was also in charge of the Pinto.

Motor Trend Magazine's Car of the Year

1960–Chevrolet Corvair
1961–Pontiac Tempest
1962–Buick Special
1963–American Motors Rambler
1964–Ford Mustang
1965–Pontiac (general award)
1966–Oldsmobile Toronado
1967–Mercury Cougar
1968–Pontiac GTO
1969–Plymouth Road Runner

I Spies

Culp and Cosby broke ground while playing two smooth spies.

TAKIN' CARE OF BUSINESS

Espionage was everywhere in the mid-'60s: on British TV (*The Avengers*), on American TV (*Get Smart, The Man from U.N.C.L.E.*), and on global theatre screens (the Bond movies). Among the classiest—and most significant—spy guys were Robert Culp and Bill Cosby. Not only was *I Spy* the first American show to give a lead role to an African-American, it took TV from the studio to exotic international locales like Acapulco, Hong Kong, and Morocco. Robert helped create the show, along with writers and directors who would go on to such classic cop shows as *McCloud* and *Kojak*.

Robert's character Kelly was a tennis pro, with Bill's Scotty his personal trainer, though actually they were two hip, intelligent Cold War agents who had great chemistry, often questioned their orders, and believably engaged in weekly chases. For all three seasons that the show ran it got nominated as best dramatic series, and each actor got three nominations for Emmy Awards (with Bill winning every year). The film *Hickey & Boggs* ('72) was a more violent reteaming of the pair (directed by Bob), and *I Spy Returns* was a '94 TV movie that brought them out of retirement to help their spy kids.

Bob and Bill both had successful careers before they went a-spying. Oakland-born Bob had his own Western series, *Trackdown*, in the late '50s, with several movie roles (*PT 109*, '63) already establishing him as a handsome, likeable screen presence. After *I Spy* he was the Bob in *Bob & Carol & Ted & Alice* ('69), a breakout movie that helped make him a fixture on TV for the next three decades.

Philly's Bill was a Temple University athlete who began his career telling jokes as a bartender, which led to him becoming the first widely accepted African-American stand-up comedian. His family- friendly routines became bestselling albums all through the '60s (*The Best of Bill Cosby*, '69) and made him a staple in Vegas and on talk shows. *The Bill Cosby Show* in '69, with Bill as a gym teacher, was one of several attempts at his own show, but not until he became kindly Dr. Huxtable in '84 did he score a beloved long-running hit. Popular cartoons based on his Fat Albert and Cosby kids characters, roles in successful movies (*Uptown Saturday Night* in '74, *Let's Do It Again* in '75), best-selling books, and his efforts as an educator have made him one of the most respected all-around entertainers in history.

Robert Culp, Bill Cosby

EVERYBODY LOVES SOMEBODY

Bob's been married at least four times, and at least two of his kids have become actors. His wife in the late '60s was the exotic actress France Nuyen, a Broadway star who made her movie debut as the beauty in *South Pacific* ('58) and who was later a regular on many popular TV shows. His next wife was '70s actress Sheila Sullivan, who was in *Hickey & Boggs*. Bill's been married to the same woman since '64 and has had five kids, one of whom was senselessly murdered alongside a California freeway in '97.

MY BACK PAGES

One later role Bob almost had—J.R. on *Dallas*, as a replacement for Larry Hagman when his contract negotiations stalled (the show would've explained the new J.R. with a story about an accident and plastic surgery). . . . One of Bob's pals—Hef, thus Bob has been a mainstay at mansion parties. . . . Bill had a minor hit record in '67 with the single "Little Old Man" from his album *Silver Throat: Bill Cosby Sings*. . . . "Wonderfulness," an invented *I Spy* word, was the title of Bill's '66 comedy album. . . . *Mad* magazine spoofed the show with a "Why Spy?" parody.

Fran Jeffries

This exotic beauty recorded three stylin' albums and appeared in three prominent movies.

TAKIN' CARE OF BUSINESS

In the early '60s, several stylin' singers jumped effortlessly back and forth from movie studios to recording studios to casino lounges. Fran Jeffries was one of these versatile talents. Fans still collect her albums, hearing in them a smooth sound that recalls a style and sophistication rarely recorded since. She followed a California-Vegas-Hollywood career path, going from San Jose, where she won talent contests as a preteen, to singing in San Francisco clubs at age 17, to mid-'50s gigs in Vegas hot spots. Fran then teamed up with singer Dick Haymes in the late-'50s, and for awhile they toured together. When she went solo in '61, Fran's career took off. She began performing in the country's most prestigious hotels and clubs, including Manhattan's Plaza Hotel, Waldorf-Astoria, and Copacabana, plus San Francisco's Fairmont Hotel.

During the first half of the '60s she released three stylish albums—the lush, romantic *Fran Can Hang You Up the Most*, in which she was backed by an orchestra; *Fran Sings "Sex and the Single Girl,"* an album that included the theme song of the popular '64 movie; and *This Is Fran Jeffries*, defying easy categorization and so gaining little airplay, though *Playboy* reviewed the results as "Frantastic." Meanwhile her Hollywood career heated up with a part in *Sex and the Single Girl* ('64), a show-stopping musical number in *The Pink Panther* ('64), and a lead role in Elvis's *Harum Scarum* ('65).

The late '60s brought a European tour with Sammy Davis, Jr., a Southeast Asian tour with Bob Hope, and several long runs in Vegas. In the '70s and '80s, Fran worked steadily in top clubs, hotels, and lounges around the country. For Fran these decades were golden years of cabaret, when she could hit all the many lounges, rooms, and clubs that were flourishing across America. She opened at casinos for Dean and

Sammy, and she worked top supper clubs with Bill Cosby. More live dates through the '90s led to a new album, the well-received *All the Love* (2000).

EVERYBODY LOVES SOMEBODY

Fran was married to Dick Haymes in the late '50s. They split in '61 and finally divorced in '65. Haymes was some 23 years older and had several hit songs in the '40s, including the Oscar-winning "It Might As Well Be Spring." He'd had four wives, including Rita Hayworth, before he married Fran. With Haymes Fran had a daughter, Stephanie. Fran married again in '65, this time to Richard Quine, who was her elder by about 19 years. Quine was a child actor in the '30s and '40s and a movie director in the '50, '60s, and '70s (*Bell, Book and Candle*, '58, *Paris When It Sizzles*, '64). After a long illness he took his own life in '89.

MY BACK PAGES

Fran has said that daughter Stephanie was the inspiration for the album *All the Love*, which lists Stephanie as executive producer. . . . During her post-'60s years Fran's career got a considerable boost from two prominent *Playboy* appearances in '71 and '82—though the layouts were almost a full decade apart, Fran still looked as beautiful and glamorous as when she had started some 20 years before.

Judy Jetson and Veronica Lodge

Pony-tailed Judy and raven-haired Veronica were two cool cartoon teens.

TAKIN' CARE OF BUSINESS

In the '60s, the cartoon characters of the previous decade, who were often talking animals, were being supplanted by some cool talking humans. While not entirely realistic, many of these new characters were at least normal-looking teenagers and presented situations a little more advanced than goofy cats chasing mice. Bracketing the decade were two attractive teens, Judy Jetson and Veronica Lodge.

The Jetsons ('62) was a committed recycler: the first season, shown in primetime, had only 24 episodes that were repeated endlessly on Saturday mornings for the next 20 years (new episodes weren't created until the mid-'80s). What's more, the show's formula—a wacky suburban family in the future—was Hanna-Barbera's variation on the successful formula of *The Flintstones*—a wacky suburban family in the past—which had debuted two years earlier. But *The Jetsons* did have a great theme song and nifty gadgets, plus it was ABC's first show in color, and so it became a long-running hit.

Judy was the 16-year-old daughter in the Jetson family (the others were George, his wife Jane, his boy Elroy, Astro

July 14, 1969—*Easy Rider* with Peter Fonda opens. ☮ July 15, 1932—Actress Nina Van Pallandt is born in Copenhagen, Denmark.
July 16, 1930—Actress Anne Francis is born in Ossining, New York. ☮ July 16, 1969—*Apollo 11* lifts off for the moon.
July 17, 1928—Jazz musician and composer Vince Guaraldi is born ☮ July 17, 1935—Actress Diahann Carroll is born in the Bronx, New York.

the dog, Rosie the robot maid, and later the slinky-like Orbitty). As a cute, perky student at Orbit High School, Judy's main interests were boys, shopping, boys, the phone, and boys, although in one episode she showed a talent for sculpting. Behind the scenes, her vocals were performed by veteran actress Janet Waldo, who did voices for many other cartoon characters including Josie on *Josie and the Pussycats*. Janet reprised her Judy vocals in the '87 TV movie *The Jetsons Meet the Flintstones*, but in the '90 *Jetsons* movie, Judy's vocals were performed by pop star Tiffany, who also sang three songs.

The lanky vixen Veronica Lodge was the object of Archie Andrews's affections, though she only toyed with Archie while dating others, including snobby Reggie Mantle. Sweet, blonde Betty Cooper was also available, but everybody usually went daffy for Veronica because she was rich and played hard to get. Veronica made her debut into the Archie comic book universe in '42, four months after Archie and Betty. In '68 the comic book characters starred in *The Archie Show*, which ran on Saturday mornings and continued in various incarnations over the next decades.

On the original '68 show, Veronica's voice, Betty's, and even Sabrina's, Big Ethel's, and Miss Grundy's, were all provided by the same actress—Jane Webb, who later played Ginger Grant on *The New Adventures of Gilligan* series ('74). More than just an Archie graphic, though, Veronica was part of the Archie sound: in the cartoon rock band the Archies, Ronnie sang backup, chiming in on the saccharine "Sugar Sugar" with the line "I'm gonna make your life so sweet." Astonishingly, that song, rejected by the Monkees and then recorded by studio musicians, hit #1 for four weeks in '69, the same year that saw hit records by the Who, Led Zeppelin, the Beatles, and Elvis. What's more, all of the vocals on "Sugar Sugar," including those for Veronica and Betty, were performed by one man, veteran studio singer Ron Dante.

But acting and singing weren't the best talents created for the Veronica Lodge character. For any guy's romantic compass, Ronnie was the true north where their needles perpetually pointed. Vain and beautiful, Veronica was more like a '40s vamp, which was appropriate since the comic book started in '41; actually, she looked suspiciously like Betty, and they were almost identical twins except for the hair (she and Betty both had knockout figures, all sleek legs and flat stomachs). Unlike the other girls, who wore teenage sweats and jeans, Veronica usually wore expensive designer fashions. So Veronica was beautiful, rich, well-dressed, and had every guy in Riverdale except Moose and Jughead acting like punch-drunk saps as they competed for her affections. No wonder the girls all hated her.

Another 15 Cool '60s Cartoons (with Debut Year)

Astro-Boy ('63)
The Batman/Superman Hour ('68)
The Bullwinkle Show ('61)
The Fantastic Four ('67)
Fantastic Voyage ('68)
The Hardy Boys ('69)
Iron Man ('66)
Jonny Quest ('64)
Journey to the Center of the Earth ('67)
King Kong ('66)
The Pink Panther Show ('69)
The Road Runner Show ('66)
Shazzan! ('67)
Spider-Man ('67)
Top Cat ('61)

EVERYBODY LOVES SOMEBODY

That Judy lived in the Skypad Apartments in Orbit City throughout the decade was pretty cool, but that she was living there with her parents and little brother wasn't. Judy did get a boyfriend in the "Rosie's Boyfriend" episode, and later she tried to elope with Mr. Spacely's nephew Samuel, who was a student at M.I.T. (the Moon Institute of Technology). She also got three jobs in the "9 to 5 to 9" episode: construction worker, dog-walker, and fast-food server. Meanwhile, Veronica, a student at Riverdale High, also lived at home all decade. But who wouldn't, given that the home was the town's biggest mansion (her dad's favorite magazine was *Moolah Monthly*).

MY BACK PAGES

No year was specified as the setting for *The Jetsons*, but Judy revealed that it was after the millennium when she criticized George's dancing as being "practically 20th century!". . . . Janet Waldo performed hundreds of voices over her long career, but she also appeared on-screen in many TV shows and movies, including a memorable *I Love Lucy* episode in which she played a love-struck teen who chased Ricky. . . . Jane Webb (birth year unknown) had bit parts in '30s movies, left the business for almost 30 years, and returned to voice cartoons in '67. . . . When a new live-action Archie movie was first announced in the late '90s, the part of Veronica was supposedly Shannon Doherty's. . . . Among *Archie* readers, Betty is generally the most popular in head-to-head Internet polls.

Candy Johnson

The greatest go-go dancer of the '60s got showcased in four popular beach movies.

TAKIN' CARE OF BUSINESS

The amazing Candy Johnson was hired to dance—not sing, not act, just dance—in all her movies. So famous were her moves, she even got billing on movie posters (even though she rarely had any lines), and in *Muscle Beach Party* her swingin' hips were used as a "secret weapon" (she'd shake so hard that bad guys would fly off the set). For many fans, Candy's dancing was always the best thing in the lightweight movies she was in—no matter how dopey the plot or how silly the songs, Candy could always be counted on to salvage things with her frenetic dances.

Born in either L.A. or Oklahoma (sources vary), Candy was singing and dancing in hotels in Palm Springs and Vegas in the early '60s. Backing her were the Exciters, a wailin' sax/guitar/drums combo that put out an album with her called *The Candy Johnson Show*. Spotted by producers, she was invited into four mid-'60s beach movies, often playing characters named Candy: *Beach Party*, *Muscle Beach Party*, *Bikini Beach*, and *Pajama Party*. In all these movies Candy had the fastest hips in the West, shown off to best effect when she danced solo, and barefoot, during three minutes of the closing credits of three of the movies. Smilin' and stylin', she looked like she was always having the best time of anybody (even though she was working the hardest), and she always stood out with her blonde hair and brightly colored skirts or pants (all fringed to accentuate her wild dance moves). Unfortunately, when the beach movies lost their momentum, so did her entertainment career, and she disappeared into legend.

EVERYBODY LOVES SOMEBODY

"The lithesome lass has sung and danced her way into the hearts of thousands of people all over the country"—that's from the liner notes on her album. One heart she danced her way into was the band's manager. They married, later divorced, and then the facts get really hard to come by—one rumor places her in Branson, Missouri as a choreographer, another puts her in an L.A. rest home, and the happiest has her retired and married in Palm Springs.

MY BACK PAGES

A movie press kit listed her '60s hobbies as roller skating, ice skating, and swimming. . . . Her nickname in her show (and

July 19, 1969—Mary Jo Kopechne, a passenger in Ted Kennedy's car, drowns at the age of 28 when he drives off the Chappaquiddick Bridge in Massachusetts.
July 20, 1924—Actress Lola Albright is born in Akron, Ohio. ☮ July 20, 1938—Actress Diana Rigg is born in Doncaster, England.

sometimes in her movies)—Miss Perpetual Motion. . . . Songs on her album included "Swing Low," "Yes Sir, That's My Baby," "Fever," "Ooh Poo Paa Doo," "Hound Dog," "Abba Dabba Honeymoon," "Baby Face," and "What'd I Say". . . . Dancing behind Candy in *Pajama Party* was young Teri Garr, who also appeared in the backgrounds of several Elvis movies.

Carolyn Jones

TV's coolest mom was the sinister, sexy Morticia Addams.

TAKIN' CARE OF BUSINESS

Carolyn Jones was not a major star, but she was always an interesting one, versatile enough to play a gangster's moll, a nutty bongo player, a West-taming frontier wife, and a Gomez-seducing, French-speaking, Japanese-singing 'Tish. A Texan born Carol Baker in the year of the stock market crash, Carolyn used her voice before she used her looks and acting talent. While she was still in high school she worked as a disc jockey for a Texas radio station, and she continued with radio as she pursued her Hollywood dreams.

In the '50s she landed small roles in over a dozen prominent movies, including *Road to Bali* ('52), *House of Wax* ('53, she played the Joan of Arc wax figure), and *The Seven Year Itch* ('55). Playing a bongo-bangin' existentialist, Carolyn flashed through *The Bachelor Party* ('57) like a glimmering meteor, but her six minutes were so incandescent that she got nominated for a Best Supporting Actress Oscar and won a Golden Globe as Most Promising Newcomer. Strong movie roles took her to the end of the decade, including a memorable part with the King.

In late '57, Elvis was feeling a draft—Uncle Sam had come knocking, and he was up for Army induction in January '58. Unfortunately, *King Creole* was ready to shoot, with the great Michael Curtiz (*Casablanca*) directing and Carolyn Jones co-starring as a good girl gone bad. Only by grace of a special deferment was Elvis's induction postponed, which meant Carolyn's character could die in Elvis's arms as scheduled. The '60s brought a flurry of minor movies and appearances in TV Westerns, then in '62 she got a coveted role alongside half the stars in Hollywood in the sprawling blockbuster *How the West Was Won*. Still, even with big stars and big movies on her résumé, big stardom eluded her. It took a popular cartoon to make her a legend.

Charles Addams's famous drawings about a macabre family had been appearing in *The New Yorker* since the '30s; in '64 they got reinvented as a TV series, *The Addams Family*. With its sinister sets and skewed perspectives, the show became one of the most stylish comedies of the era. Though it only ran for two seasons, the show firmly cemented its bizarre characters (Lurch, Thing, Cousin Itt) and its signature phrases ("You rang!") into the national consciousness. Carolyn's smooth, seductive, stable Morticia was the perfect partner for joyous, rakishly-

July 20, 1938—Actress Natalie Wood is born in San Francisco. ☮ July 20, 1963—Marvin Gaye's "Pride and Joy" hits #10 on the charts. July 20, 1966—*The Wild Angels* with Nancy Sinatra opens. ☮ July 20, 1968—Jane Asher breaks off her engagement with Paul McCartney. July 20, 1969—Astronauts Neil Armstrong and Buzz Aldrin walk on the moon.

mustachioed Gomez Addams (John Astin), whose eyes twinkled with impulsive ideas and whose heart beat with eternal passion for his beautiful *cara mia*. The long straight black wig suited Carolyn's small face beautifully, and her slinky 5′ 5″ figure was perfect for Morticia's black-widow gown (her real talent may have been her ability to stand up and walk in that bewitching "tube dress").

Just as *Bewitched, I Dream of Jeannie*, and *The Patty Duke Show* put their lead actresses in dual roles, so too did *The Addams Family* have a second character for Carolyn—donning a long blonde wig, she occasionally played Ophelia Frump, Morticia's sister. Though the show left primetime in '66, it has lived on in reruns, in several TV movies, in two animated versions, and two clever '90s movies. Carolyn had a steady career after the show (including five episodes as Marsha, Queen of Diamonds, on *Batman* in '66 and '67), and she was one of the stars on *Capitol* in '82, bravely carrying on though her health was failing. Sadly, Carolyn, only 54, died of cancer in '83. Her early death may have been tragic, but her life was triumphant.

EVERYBODY LOVES SOMEBODY

In '53, Carolyn married Aaron Spelling, who later produced some of the most famous shows in TV history, including *Fantasy Island, Dynasty*, and *Beverly Hills, 90210*. After 12 years of marriage, she and Spelling divorced. She married director Herbert Greene in '68. In the last years of her life she was married to actor Peter Bailey-Britton.

MY BACK PAGES

Carolyn was part Comanche Indian. . . . Her famous line in *The Bachelor Party*: "Just say you love me—you don't have to mean it!". . . . There must have been something slightly sinister in the air back in '64: *The Addams Family* debuted one week before another creepy comedy that gave audiences the TV jeebies, *The Munsters*, and then the two shows aired their final episodes within a week of each other in '66.

Tom Jones

This big-voiced, curly-haired Welshman got famous singing hits and movie themes in the '60s.

TAKIN' CARE OF BUSINESS

After singing in choirs in his native Wales, young Thomas John Woodward left school in the '50s to sing in pubs 'n' clubs as Tommy Scott, with jobs as a laborer helping to pay the bills. Hitting London just when the city was starting to swing in '63, the rechristened Tom Jones soon had a record deal and a year later a hit single, the polished, propulsive "It's Not Unusual," which brought him a Best New Artist Grammy.

In '65 he was a high-profile star, touring with the Stones and singing themes to popular movies including *What's New, Pussycat?* and *Thunderball*. His powerful voice and sexy, Vegas-style shows were appealing alternatives for music fans who weren't jumping aboard the guitar-powered rock and roll express that was speeding through the decade. "Help Yourself," "Delilah," and the album *Green Green Grass of Home* ('67) were additional '60s hits that became fixtures of his rousing live act, an act that included covers of Beatles

July 21, 1998—Alan Shepard, the first American in space, dies of leukemia in Monterey, California.
July 22, 1922—Comedian Dan Rowan is born in Oklahoma. ☮ July 22, 1939—Actor Terence Stamp is born in London.
July 22, 1964—*Marnie* with Tippi Hedren opens. ☮ July 22, 1964—*Bikini Beach* with Frankie Avalon opens.

songs, some sexy, teasing patter, and Tom's tight-pantsed gyrations. His own '69–'72 TV variety show, *This Is Tom Jones*, amplified his popularity, so that by the end of the decade he'd sold over 25 million records.

After a slump in the '70s and an attempt at country music, his career revived in the '80s and '90s on the strength of new hits ("A Boy from Nowhere"), popular videos, and well-received concerts. Collaborations with the Pretenders, Van Morrison, the Cardigans and others showed him to have a timeless, fluid talent that could cross genres, span decades, and reach broad audiences.

As he'd done in the '60s, he again sang movie themes, this time "You Can Leave Your Hat On" for *The Full Monty* ('96) and "Perfect World" for *The Emperor's New Groove* (2000). He also got some screen time in *Mars Attacks!* ('96), on lots of talk shows and awards shows, and even on *The Simpsons* (as himself). The 21st century brought a huge (and hugely successful) world tour, his biggest-selling album ever (*Reload*), and the ultimate recognition—at the end of 2005, the Queen named him as the once and future Sir Tom Jones.

EVERYBODY LOVES SOMEBODY

At 16 Tom got married and soon had a son. Early on he and his wife lived with her parents as he struggled to establish his singing career. In '74 Tom and the family moved to Bel-Air, their new home the mansion formerly owned by Dean Martin.

MY BACK PAGES

Legend has it that he passed out in the recording studio upon hitting the final note of the *Thunderball* theme song. . . . Tom's TV show presented a great time capsule of '60s musical guest stars, among them Joey Heatherton, Diana Ross, Dionne Warwick, Nancy Sinatra, Davy Jones, Steve and Eydie, Aretha Franklin, Diahann Carroll, Liza Minnelli, Burt Bacharach, Mary Hopkin, Peter Noone, Sandi Shaw, and Cass Elliot. . . . A global favorite, he's been named Entertainer of the Year in many different countries.

Janis Joplin

Free-wheelin', whisky-swiggin' Janis gained rock immortality with soul-baring songs, passionate live performances, and a sad death.

TAKIN' CARE OF BUSINESS

Singers know. "Her performance was so in your face and electrifying that it really put you right there in the moment," wrote Chrissie Hynde of the Pretenders, "there you were living your nice little life in the suburbs and suddenly there was this train wreck, and it was Janis." There was simply no white singer in the '60s like Janis Joplin. Nobody could match her growly supercharged voice full of carnality, adrenaline, and Southern Comfort, for one thing. Singer Ethel Merman once said about her, "That girl has problems, bein' heard ain't one of 'em." And nobody could match Janis's pain, either, the result of trying to cram a full life into 27 short years.

Born in conservative East Texas in '43, Janis was a lonely, troubled outcast as a child. She split from home at 17, tried Texas colleges, then hitchhiked randomly around the country, singing folk songs in coffeehouses. In '66 she hit the burgeoning San Francisco scene and joined an already-established local band, Big Brother and the Holding Company. Hooked in deep to the free-love/free-drugs atmosphere of the Haight-Ashbury, wearing funky vintage clothes accessorized by colorful jewels and feather boas, Janis became famous for her gut-wrenching live performances, especially a show-stopping turn at the Monterey International Pop Festival in '67. Big Brother's chart-topping *Cheap Thrills* album in '68 showcased her powerful vocals with such signature songs as "Ball and Chain" and "Piece of My Heart."

Lured by the promise of solo stardom, later that year she quit Big Brother to form the Kozmic Blues Band. With them came the masterful "Try" and another successful rock festival, Woodstock. Finally, working in '70 with a new group called the Full-Tilt Boogie Band, she recorded *Pearl*, though

July 22, 1965—Actress Dyan Cannon marries screen legend Cary Grant. ☮ July 23, 1962—François Truffaut's *Shoot the Piano Player* opens. July 24, 1936—Comedienne Ruth Buzzi is born in Westerly, Rhode Island. ☮ July 24, 1965—Bob Dylan releases "Like a Rolling Stone." July 24, 1965—"In the Midnight Hour" by Wilson Pickett hits #1. ☮ July 24, 1967—*Privilege* with Jean Shrimpton opens.

this classic album (carrying the only #1 song of her career, "Me and Bobby McGee") wasn't released until after her death in '71.

Her sad heroin overdose in a Hollywood motel precluded the future success she might've had. But fans and the music community have never forgotten her impact. Posthumous collections (*Janis Joplin's Greatest Hits*, '73) have been steady sellers, *Rolling Stone* voted *Pearl* the #11 album of all time, in '95 she was posthumously inducted into the Rock and Roll Hall of Fame, and in '99 VH1 put her third on its list of the hundred greatest rock women. Many '60s singers were great; Janis was legend.

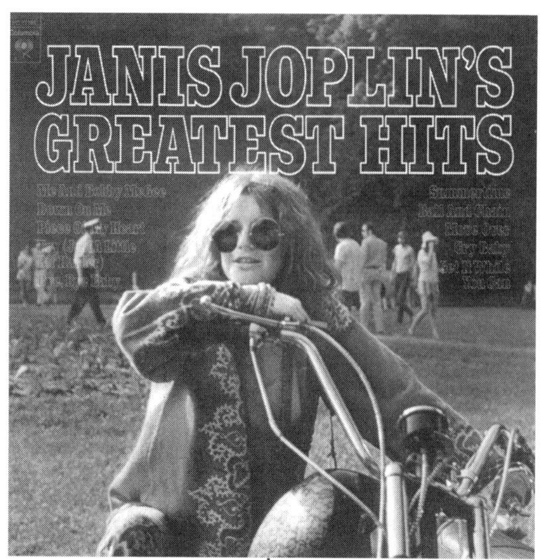

EVERYBODY LOVES SOMEBODY

Rumor has it that in the last five or six years of her life Janis squeezed lots of celebrities onto her dance card, men with last names like Clapton, Morrison, Hendrix, Kristofferson, Namath, plus assorted bandmates, roadies, and even other women. If true, it's an amazing list for someone who died so young, and for someone who was once nominated as the University of Texas's "Ugliest Man on Campus." Never married, she was engaged to a rich Berkeley student in the last months of her life. Even at the time she knew she was living a reckless, dangerous lifestyle—when she heard that Jimi Hendrix had died in September of '70, she said, "Dammit! He beat me to it!" Three weeks later, she too was gone, her ashes scattered from a plane over the coastline of Marin County, California.

MY BACK PAGES

According to the book *They Went That-A-Way*, the Southern Comfort distillery gave her a fur coat in gratitude for all the free publicity Janis gave them by drinking their brand on stage. . . . The liner notes for *Box of Pearls: The Janis Joplin Collection* included tributes written by famous fans who named Janis as an inspiration, including Chrissie Hynde, Joan Jett, Stevie Nicks, and Deborah Harry. . . . After Janis's death, Mimi Farina composed, and her sister Joan Baez recorded, the song "In the Quiet Morning" in her memory. . . . The '79 Bette Midler film *The Rose* was a loose retelling of Janis's life, and several biopics came out in the 2000s. . . . Janis explained it all for you: "Don't compromise yourself, you're all you've got."

Christine Keeler and Mandy Rice-Davies

England's "scandal of the century" brought these two teens to prominence.

TAKIN' CARE OF BUSINESS

Models, party girls, and later authors, Christine Keeler and Mandy Rice-Davies were the two young beauties at the heart of England's Profumo Affair. Christine came from an English village, and Mandy from Wales, to seek excitement in London in the early '60s. Working as a showgirl in '61, Christine had a month-long relationship with John Profumo, a high-ranking British government official who was already married. The ensuing scandal revealed that Christine was also having an affair with a Russian dignitary during these years, that Profumo had lied about Christine to the House of Commons, and that wild parties had been enjoyed by Christine, her friend Mandy, and prostitutes with prominent Londoners and government officials.

Provocative photos of Christine and titillating rumors of orgies and sadomasochism spiked the media coverage to the heights (or depths) seen in today's well-tabloided celebrity trials. Ultimately Christine was convicted and jailed on unrelated charges, Profumo resigned in disgrace in '63, another key figure committed suicide that same year, and the scandal was seen as a contributing factor when Profumo's Conservative Party was voted out in '64.

Christine subsequently wrote numerous books about the controversy, plus an autobiography. Mandy dabbled in music later in the decade, opened a series of eponymous night spots, wrote an autobiography and a novel, and in recent decades has occasionally worked as an actress. Profumo never wrote about or publicly discussed the scandal; he dedicated his life to charity work, was honored for it by the Queen in '75, and died in 2006.

EVERYBODY LOVES SOMEBODY

In '59 Christine had an illegitimate son who died within a week of being born. It was her relationship with an unsavory character, and some ensuing violence in late '62, that drew the press to uncover and expose the Profumo Affair in early '63. She still lives in London. Mandy married in the '60s and today lives in the U.S. Before and after the scandal, Profumo was married to retired actress Valerie Hobson, who had a long film career and played Victor Frankenstein's wife Elizabeth in *Bride of Frankenstein* ('35).

MY BACK PAGES

In the film *Scandal* ('89), Christine and Mandy were played by Joanne Whalley and Bridget Fonda. . . . The most famous photo of the scandal was a shot of Christine, apparently nude and straddling a chair. . . . The most famous line of the scandal was Mandy's—when told in court that Lord Astor denied ever having met her, she replied, "Well, he would, wouldn't he?"

John and Jacqueline Kennedy

Globally respected as American royalty, the graceful Kennedys inspired, charmed, and shaped the world during the '60s.

TAKIN' CARE OF BUSINESS

No other couple had a stronger global impact in the '60s than the regal Kennedys. John and Jacqueline were both born into privilege: both lived their adult lives in the public spotlight and became cherished American icons; both are buried in Arlington National Cemetery, the resting place of heroes.

Every facet of their pre-'60s life has been well-chronicled: John's prominent Massachusetts Irish Catholic family, his three brothers, the bootlegger father who was ambassador to England, John's education at exclusive schools and graduation from Harvard, his World War II *PT-109* saga (a Cliff Robertson movie in '63). In '52, he was elected Senator, and his '50s became a much-photographed pageant of energizing the Democratic Party, sailing, and courting his future wife.

As a young girl, Jacqueline Bouvier, born into a rich New York family, was winning equestrian championships and attending private schools. After being named Debutante of the Year in '47, she attended Vassar and the Sorbonne, graduated from George Washington University in '51, and got a job at the *Washington Times Herald* in '52. She became Senator John Fitzgerald Kennedy's wife in '53, and when he won a close presidential race in '60, she became history's most glamorous First Lady.

Youthful vigor sparked their White House years. JFK, the youngest elected President (and the first one born in the 20th century), optimistically championed the space program, desegregation, and the Peace Corps; he stared down the Russians in the Cuban Missile Crisis and pushed to limit nuclear weapons; and, regrettably, he ordered the Bay of Pigs debacle and escalated involvement in Vietnam. Meanwhile, Jackie's lean, aristocratic beauty was a marked contrast to the elderly Mamie Eisenhower, Bess Truman, and Eleanor Roosevelt who had preceded her.

For the inauguration in '61, she hired designer Oleg Cassini to create her wardrobe, telling him she wanted to dress as if "Jack were President of France." Her glamorous clothes dazzled the nation and inspired a whole look (her pillbox hats were all the rage). Jackie's impeccable grace and communication skills (she spoke four languages) enabled her to charm foreign dignitaries when the couple toured Europe in the early '60s (upon their return, a beaming JFK said, "I am the man who accompanied Jacqueline Kennedy to Paris"). She also undertook a massive restoration of the White House, conducted a nationally televised tour of the building, and brought new attention to the arts. Their White House became Camelot (after the contemporary Broadway musical), American women viewed her as a role model, and handsome JFK symbolized for many the best America could be.

And then, some 1,000 days into his presidency, it was over. On November 22, 1963, while campaigning through Dallas streets in an open-top limo, JFK was killed by two gunshots from Lee Harvey Oswald, perched in a sixth-floor window of the Texas Schoolbook Depository building. The President's death that afternoon sent the world into shock and instantly created where-were-you-when-you-heard memories. While an investigation later concluded that Oswald had acted alone, numerous inconsistencies and improbabilities suggested additional gunmen—if true, this most-analyzed murder of all time is still unsolved, four decades later.

Three days after the shooting JFK was buried, his casket carried through Washington, D.C. on the same carriage that had carried Lincoln's body a century earlier. Throughout the televised event, Jackie, wearing a black veil, mourned stoically and silently, helping the nation ease through this crisis by always maintaining her gallant, proud dignity. A '64 Gallup Poll named her the most-admired woman in America, and for the rest of her life, though she avoided publicity, she was a highly prized target of photographers (*Life* put her on 10 covers).

After the '60s, Jackie worked for a publishing house and raised funds for art-related projects, including the '78 restoration of Grand Central Station. In early '94 she was diagnosed with non-Hodgkin's lymphoma, and in April of that year, knowing she would soon die, she left the hospital to return to her New York apartment, where she could be surrounded by family and friends.

Honoring JFK's charisma and achievements, New York's airport, countless schools, and an aircraft carrier have

July 26, 1945—Actress Linda Harrison is born in Berlin, Maryland. ☮ July 26, 1950—Actress Susan George is born in London.
July 26, 1961—*Tammy Tell Me True* with Sandra Dee opens. ☮ July 26, 1963—Tuesday Weld makes the cover of *Life*.
July 26, 1992—Singer Mary Wells dies of throat cancer in L.A. ☮ July 27, 1944—Singer Bobbie Gentry is born in Chickasaw County, Mississippi.

been named after him, hundreds of books have been written about him, several movies have depicted his life, and it's his profile that's on the 50-cent piece. Inspired by her beauty, style, and dignity, there have been Jackie dolls, a Jackie Broadway play, several Jackie movies, and many Jackie postage stamps from different countries. When *People* magazine put out an issue called "Unforgettable Women of the Century," there was only one photo on the cover—Jackie's.

EVERYBODY LOVES SOMEBODY

Before she married JFK, 23-year-old Jackie was engaged to a New York broker. However, once she met John at a society dinner and they began dating, she got herself unengaged. In *the* social event of '53 they married in Newport, Rhode Island, then moved into a Georgetown home. John was having chronic back pains throughout these years from his fall on the deck of the sinking *PT-109*, and though he had surgery he was never pain-free again.

After a miscarriage in '55 and a stillborn baby in '56, Jackie gave birth to daughter Caroline in '57 and son JFK, Jr. in '60. If later accounts are to be believed, John conducted many extra-marital affairs with prominent actresses, staffers, and others during the Camelot years. Jackie never addressed these rumors in public, preferring to keep them a family matter. Meanwhile, in August '63 she gave birth to another son, Patrick, but he died within two days. Jackie then went on a Mediterranean cruise with her sister to recuperate, and there she met shipping magnate Aristotle Onassis, the world's richest man.

After JFK's death, she moved to New York City for some privacy and to raise her kids as normally, and with as little press attention, as possible. When she married Onassis in '68 on the Greek island of Skorpios, some in the public and press condemned the marriage, seeing her as a gold digger and him as an opportunist trying to gain power and prestige. When his son died in a '73 plane crash, Onassis basically lost the will to live and died of pneumonia two years later.

MY BACK PAGES

Jackie was the older sister of the jet-setting Lee Radziwell and the aunt of Maria Shriver, wife of Arnold Schwarzenegger. . . . Though Jackie was a chain smoker, there are few photos of her with a cigarette, as she requested. . . . JFK won a Pulitzer Prize for his '55 book *Profiles in Courage*. . . . Rat Pack connection—Peter Lawford was JFK's brother-in-law, and Frank Sinatra organized the inauguration celebration (and escorted Jackie). . . . TV helped get JFK elected when his debate with opponent Richard Nixon was televised, to JFK's advantage, and TV was there at the end, with networks for the first time ever switching to 24-hour live coverage of the assassination aftermath. . . . The Sotheby's auction of 5,500 pieces of her jewelry, art, and books in '96 drew widespread attention and raised over $34 million, an amazing $29 million more than was predicted. . . . Among the items sold (for $2.6 million) was the 40-carat engagement diamond she got from Onassis.

Robert Kennedy

JFK's right-hand man was his brother Bobby, to many people the last great hero of the '60s.

TAKIN' CARE OF BUSINESS

Like his older brother John, Robert Francis Kennedy was born into privilege, served in the Navy, and graduated from Harvard (where Bobby played on the football team). After getting his law degree at the University of Virginia in '51, he ran his brother's successful senatorial campaign in '52, worked on committees pursuing communists and racketeers, and managed John's successful bid for the presidency in '60. JFK appointed RFK Attorney General and relied heavily on his counsel during critical events, including the Cuban Missile Crises and the violence surrounding the burgeoning civil rights movement. Bobby also aggressively confronted organized crime

July 27, 1949—Skater Peggy Fleming is born in San Jose, California. ☮ July 28, 1929—Jacqueline Bouvier is born in Southampton, Long Island.
July 28, 1971—Photographer Diane Arbus commits suicide at the age of 48.
July 29, 1965—The Beatles' second movie, *Help!*, premieres, with Queen Elizabeth in attendance.

and labor rackets, which some conspiracy theorists speculate may have led to his brother's shocking murder in '63.

The tragedy was devastating for Bobby and plunged him into intense grief, but within a year he resigned his cabinet post and won himself a seat in Congress as the Senator from New York. In office he continued to battle segregation and poverty, and in '68, speaking forcefully against the Vietnam War (a reversal of his and JFK's earlier position), he ran for president. His proposals embraced minorities, excited America's youth, and promised vast social changes. A strong, healthy man capable of working 16 hours a day during the campaign, he won four of the five spring primaries, including the vital California race in June, and seemed poised to claim the nomination and eventually the White House.

Tragically, just as his brother had fallen to a gunman, Robert Kennedy was shot moments after making a celebratory speech in L.A.'s Ambassador Hotel. And just as inconsistencies swirled around the facts of JFK's assassination, some evidence suggested two gunmen may have fired at RFK. Sirhan Sirhan was a young Palestinian apprehended with a pistol at the scene, and he later confessed to the murder. Bobby was buried in Arlington, near his brother. The death of Robert Kennedy, coming only two months after the death of Martin Luther King, Jr., helped certify '68 as the decade's most violent year.

EVERYBODY LOVES SOMEBODY

In the mid-'40s Bobby was dating Ethel Skakel's sister, and when that relationship ended he started up with Ethel. They married in the summer of '50, lived on a Virginia estate, and had 11 children (the last born after Bobby's death). In addition to the many tragedies that befell the Kennedy family, Ethel endured tragedies of her own—her parents and brother were killed in separate plane crashes. Vague rumors have long swirled around Bobby's social life while his brother was in the White House, including speculation that he was secretly involved with Marilyn Monroe and may have been one of the last people to see her before she committed suicide in '63.

MY BACK PAGES

Like John, Robert was popular with the entertainment community—director John Frankenheimer drove him to the Ambassador Hotel the day he was assassinated, celebrities were in the crowd as he gave his final speech, and Andy Williams sang at the funeral. . . . As with JFK, many schools and structures have been named after RFK, including the stadium in Washington, D.C. and the Department of Justice Building. . . . The words he is perhaps most identified with, originally penned by George Bernard Shaw, delivered once more in the eulogy given by his brother Ted: "Some men see things as they are and say why. I dream things that never were and say why not."

Ken Kesey

The playful writer created iconic books and events.

TAKIN' CARE OF BUSINESS

Writer, wrestler, prankster—only Ken Kesey could've had a '60s business card listing those three titles (though who knows what job they would've qualified him for, or if he would've taken that job anyway). Ken lived a creative life far outside the status quo, a life that incorporated elements of the '50s beat generation with the burgeoning hip-

July 29, 1966—Bob Dylan gets mysteriously injured on his motorcycle in New York.
July 29, 1974—Singer Cass Elliot dies of a heart attack at age 32 in London. ☮ July 30, 1966—The *Batman* movie with Adam West opens.
July 30, 1966—England beats Germany 4–2 to win soccer's World Cup. ☮ July 30, 1966—Petula Clark's "I Couldn't Live Without Your Love" hits the charts.

pie movement of the mid-'60s.

Born in Colorado and raised in Oregon, he was a record-setting wrestler in high school and voted "most likely to succeed." After graduating from the University of Oregon, in the late '50s Ken moved to a bohemian community near San Francisco, soaked up artistic influences in the city, and studied creative writing at Stanford.

While working in the psychiatric ward at a Bay Area hospital, he voluntarily participated in medical research into the effects of hallucinogenic drugs, including LSD, and closely observed patients who were supposedly insane but to him were merely social outcasts. The result was his breakthrough novel, *One Flew Over the Cuckoo's Nest*, in '62. One of the most popular and inventive books of the '60s, it told the darkly humorous, sometimes tragic story of psychiatric patients and their revolt against the strict rules of their caretakers.

Two years later, Ken followed up with another literary success, *Sometimes a Great Notion*, a sprawling masterpiece about a logging family in Oregon. What followed next was one of the wilder ideas of the decade—in June of '64 he and his friends stocked up on Kool-Aid and LSD, piled into a '39 school bus they'd painted in fluorescent colors, and drove from California to New York as the Merry Pranksters, spreading spontaneous, high-spirited freedom and fun across the countryside (Tom Wolfe made their playful, nose-thumbing travels the subject of *The Electric Kool-Aid Acid Test* in '68).

Ken financed and filmed the whole thing, they met Timothy Leary and other cool cats in New York, and two months later everyone returned to his ranch in the Bay Area hills for more partying and performing (what came to be known as the Acid Tests). Ken then helped organize the three-day Trips Festival in January of '66, a colorful, creative, chaotic event in San Francisco that became a seminal '60s happening.

Unfortunately, authorities weren't as amused by these antics as Ken's followers, and two drug busts (one in '65, the other in '66) sent him on the lam to Mexico and eventually to jail in the U.S. Back on an Oregon farm, he continued to challenge the establishment for the rest of his life with creative, often costumed performances and diverse writings—a screenplay, a play, children's books, one last novel (*Sailor Song*, '92), and several collections of stories and articles. When Ken Kesey died in 2001 after undergoing surgery for cancer, he was buried in a coffin painted in the same kind of psychedelic swirls that had decorated his bus.

EVERYBODY LOVES SOMEBODY

Ken was married from '56 until his death. In the '60s he and his wife had three children, one of whom later died in a car accident. He also had another child (named Sunshine) with "Mountain Girl," who would be Jerry Garcia's wife in the '80s.

MY BACK PAGES

Ken claimed that he never saw the Oscar-winning film version of *Cuckoo's Nest* because he was unhappy with the changes it made to his original story. . . . The Merry Pranksters' bus, *Further*, still exists in Oregon, awaiting restoration. . . . Originally it was named *Furthur*, but a later repainting corrected the spelling. . . . The sign on the back of the bus—Caution: Weird Load.

Jean-Claude Killy

This handsome French skier won three Olympic gold medals.

TAKIN' CARE OF BUSINESS

Skiing at his dad's ski resort from the age of 3, dashing Jean-Claude Killy was World Cup ski champion in '67 and '68. He won three glamorous golds—in slalom, giant slalom, and downhill (alpine skiing's "Triple Crown")—at the '68 Winter Olympics held in Grenoble, France. His need for speed also led him to try auto racing in the late '70s, and his movie-idol looks led him to a one-movie career as the star of the crime caper *Snow Job* ('72), in which he played a thief who escaped on skis. Later he ran a successful sports-clothing company, made a skiing video, and served on the executive committees of the Tour de France and the Olympics.

EVERYBODY LOVES SOMEBODY

Jean-Claude was married to his *Snow Job* co-star, Daniele Gaubert, from '72 until her death from TB 15 years later. He's got three kids and has lived in Geneva, Switzerland since '69.

MY BACK PAGES

Controversy surrounded Killy's third gold medal—another skier actually had a faster time, but was disqualified. . . . Hailed as France's greatest skier ever, he did all his own dramatic ski stunts (who else could do them?) in *Snow Job*.

Martin Luther King, Jr.

Only one person in this encyclopedia, and only one American born in the 20th century, has been honored with his own national holiday.

TAKIN' CARE OF BUSINESS

Martin Luther King, Jr., was born in Atlanta to a father who was a pastor and a mother who was a teacher. Exposed to racism as a kid, he sprinted quickly through school and began attending Morehouse College at only 15 years old. When he graduated four years later, he went to a private seminary in Pennsylvania, became the top student at the school, and won a scholarship to get his doctorate in theology.

In '54, Dr. King became the pastor at a Baptist church in Montgomery, Alabama, at the time America's most racially intolerant state. In Montgomery a year later, Rosa Parks refused to give up her bus seat to a white passenger. To support her, Dr. King and others organized a bus boycott. During the year-long battle, Dr. King's house was bombed and he was arrested, but eventually the U.S. Supreme Court struck down the segregation laws for interstate buses, the first of many hard-won victories for the civil rights movement.

In '57, Dr. King co-founded and headed the Southern Christian Leadership Conference, which would organize nonviolent demonstrations to promote civil rights and bring media attention to the cause. The first of these was a "freedom ride" by bus through several Southern states in '61, but violence marred the trip through Alabama. A freedom march in Birmingham in January of '63 ended with vicious harassment from police, producing terrible images that galvanized the nation. Though many of his followers were beaten, and over 1,000 were arrested, Dr. King refused to surrender, maintained his nonviolent stance even as strident activists like Malcolm X became more vocal, and ultimately managed to get several key local desegregation issues resolved favorably.

August 1, 1936—Fashion designer Yves Saint-Laurent is born in Oran, Algeria. ☮ August 1, 1942—Jerry Garcia of the Grateful Dead is born. August 1, 1971—*The Sonny and Cher Comedy Hour* debuts. ☮ August 1, 1975—Actors Liz and Dick remarry. August 2, 1932—Actor Peter O'Toole is born in Ireland. ☮ August 2, 1967—*In the Heat of the Night* with Sidney Poitier opens.

That summer, at a rally in Washington, D.C., in front of 200,000 people, Dr. King improvised the impassioned "I have a dream" speech that is a touchstone in American history, as important in the 20th century as Lincoln's Gettysburg Address had been in the 19th. Named *Time* magazine's Person of the Year at the end of '63, and the youngest-ever recipient of the Nobel Peace Prize in '64, he continued to work tirelessly, crisscrossing the country for the next several years to generate support with his speeches and his writings (he published a half-dozen books in his lifetime).

Many of the issues he targeted—labor equality, voting rights, the end of Jim Crow laws—were formalized with the Civil Rights Act of '64 and the Voting Rights Act of '65. However, his last years were still difficult and controversial—in '66 his attempt to expand the civil rights movement northward into Chicago was not successful; in '67 he spoke out against the Vietnam War, a divisive position that was criticized in the media and by some other civil rights leaders; and in '68 he was calling for extreme measures to address chronic economic injustice.

While in Memphis for an April meeting with other civil rights leaders, Dr. King was assassinated by a single sniper. The tragedy immediately touched off riots across America, followed by a national day of mourning and a funeral attended by 300,000 people. Today he is revered, not as a perfect man (some stories of infidelities and possible plagiarism emerged after his death), but as a hero who, like Gandhi, had fought a war with nonviolence and who, like Lincoln, had been martyred for his triumphs.

EVERYBODY LOVES SOMEBODY

While he was studying in Boston for his Ph.D., Dr. King met a music student, Coretta Scott. When they married in '53, his father performed the ceremony. Dr. King and Coretta had four children (two daughters, two sons). While not as prominent as her husband, Coretta was also a speech-making activist in the '60s; after his death, she continued to champion civil rights and was instrumental in getting a national holiday established in his honor. Martin Luther King Day, first celebrated in '86, is now celebrated nationwide on the third Monday of January.

MY BACK PAGES

The man who shot Dr. King was a career criminal named James Earl Ray—Ray was captured two months after the assassination and soon confessed to avoid the death penalty (he was given a 99-year sentence, briefly escaped from prison in '77, and died there in '98). . . . The motel where Dr. King was shot is now the National Civil Rights Museum. . . . "Pride (in the Name of Love)" is U2's tribute to Dr. King.

Gunilla Knutson and Edie Adams

These two commercial cuties coaxed viewers to "take it off" and "spend a little dime on me."

TAKIN' CARE OF BUSINESS

A former Miss Sweden, at 18 Gunilla Knutson coaxed guys to "take it off, take it all off" in 15 different Noxzema commercials in '66. The ads were popular, sexy, and surprisingly innocent—all that TV audiences saw of Gunilla were close-ups of her face and hands while David Rose's "The Stripper" played. But that didn't stop a Rhode Island Senator from criticizing the commercials as being too adult for TV and asking that they not be shown. Gunilla

August 3, 1964—Writer Flannery O'Connor dies at 39 years old. ☮ August 3, 1965—*Darling!* with Julie Christie opens.
August 3, 1966—Comedian Lenny Bruce dies. ☮ August 3, 1983—Actress Carolyn Jones dies at 54 of cancer.
August 4, 1944—Actress Tina Cole is born in Hollywood. ☮ August 4, 1945—Pin-up girl Jo Collins is born in Lebanon, Oregon.

moved on to became a spokesperson and executive for a skin cream company, an author, a wine taster, and a gym teacher.

More overtly sexy was the commercial starring a sultry, singing Edie Adams for Muriel Cigars. Elizabeth Edith Enke of Pennsylvania studied at Julliard, but it was her stunning looks that first made her famous as "Miss U.S. Television" in '50. She won a Tony in '57 for playing Daisy Mae in *Li'l Abner* and recorded several albums before she hit it big in movies. Her prominent '60s roles included the vengeful secretary in the Oscar-winning *The Apartment* ('60) and a treasure-hunter in *It's a Mad, Mad, Mad, Mad World* ('63). She also played Vegas, and on TV she got Emmy nominations for a regular role on *The Ernie Kovacs Show* and her own variety program.

But it was her TV commercial that brought the most attention. In the early '60s she put on a blonde wig, evoked Marilyn Monroe-style glamour, and purred a sexy rendition of "Hey Big Spender" for Muriel Cigars. The song was from the hit Broadway show *Sweet Charity* and had been a hit for Peggy Lee; here Edie seductively sang the altered lyrics "spend a little dime on me" and "why don't you pick me up and smoke me some time." Afterwards dozens of movies and TV appearances took her long career into the '90s.

EVERYBODY LOVES SOMEBODY

In the 2000s, a travel article presented an informal conversation with Gunilla in which she described the two decades of ski trips she'd been taking with her husband and friends. Meanwhile, Edie's been married three times, most famously to TV star Ernie Kovacs. Their seven-year union ended with his tragic death in a '62 car crash. One of her two kids was killed in another car crash in '82.

MY BACK PAGES

An early proponent of healthy living, Gunilla was a *Life* magazine cover girl for a '70 story about organic food. . . . Gunilla's two books in the early '70s were about massage and nutrition. . . . Edie and Ernie Kovacs would've been paired in *It's a Mad, Mad, Mad, Mad, World*, but he died just before filming began. . . . Kovacs left behind a serious financial debt that Edie stoically worked for years to repay.

Sandy Koufax

The premier pitcher of his day, Sandy enjoyed one of the most dominating five-year runs in baseball history.

TAKIN' CARE OF BUSINESS

Most of the records—for strikeouts, for no-hitters—have been broken now. But what's never left is the image of the graceful lefthander fighting through chronic pain to deliver the sharpest curve and mightiest fastball of the '60s, of the poised gentleman whose dignity earned the undiminished respect of fans, the media, teammates, and opponents, of the deeply spiritual man who refused to play in the biggest game because of a religious holiday. Sandy Koufax is not just a baseball legend—he's a baseball hero.

A strong, natural athlete from Brooklyn, Sanford Braun (he later took the last name of his stepfather) excelled at basketball and baseball in high school and earned a basketball scholarship to the University of Cincinnati. Freshman success on the baseball team brought him an offer to pitch for the Brooklyn Dodgers in '55. His first spring-training pitch sailed over the backstop, and his first appearance in a major-league game didn't come until the season was two months in, but already he was showing flashes of brilliance: his first win was a complete-game shutout.

Sandy's career statistics divide neatly in two. From '55 to '60, he was a wild-throwing young benchwarmer with more losses than wins. Unable to control his pitches, he recorded almost as many walks as strikeouts. By the end of '60, saddled with a losing record over his six-year career, he se-

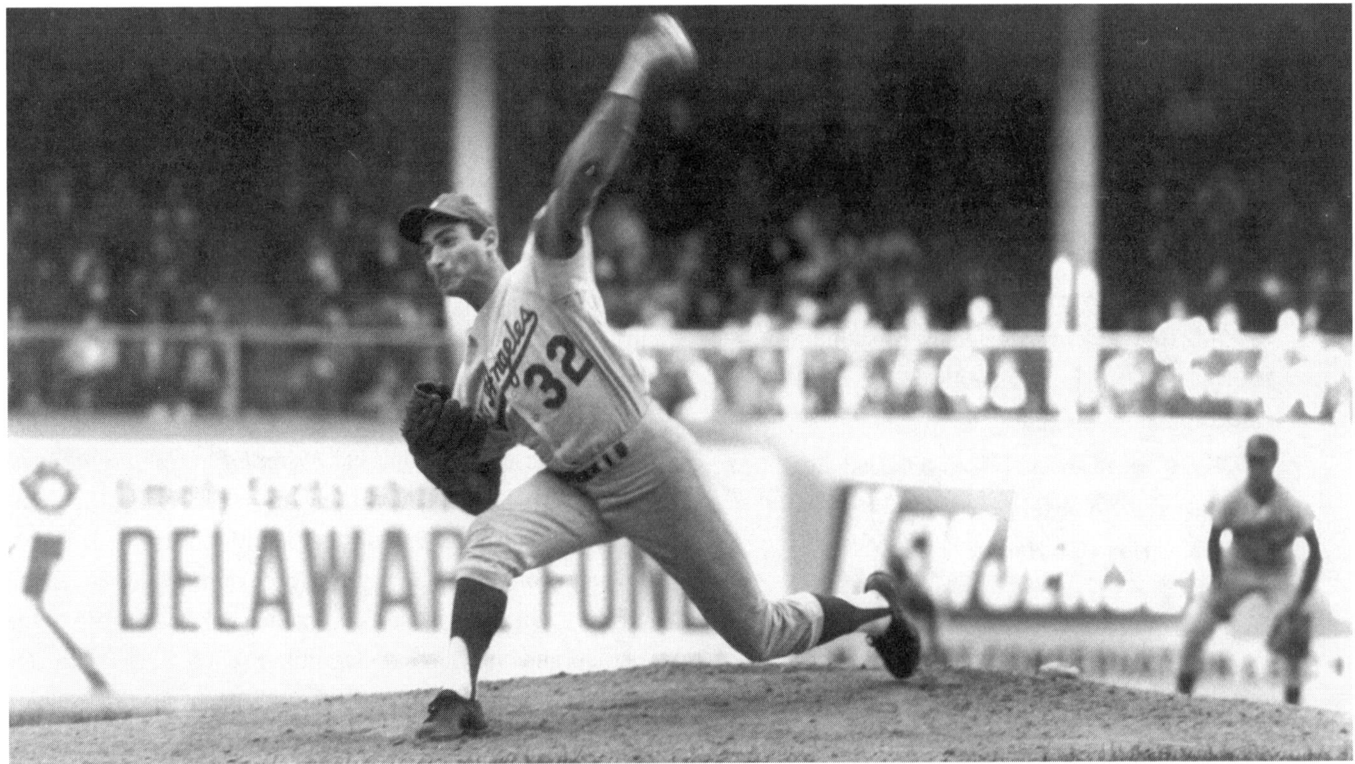

riously contemplated quitting. When he decided to relinquish velocity to gain accuracy, his pitches suddenly found their intended targets with a whole new explosiveness. In '61 hitters began describing Sandy's pitches more by sound than by sight, and his career as the Dodgers' staff ace soared.

From '62 through '66 he led the league in earned-run average and shutouts, set a new major-league record for strikeouts, tossed four no-hitters (one a perfect game), won three Cy Young awards as the game's best pitcher, and led his L.A. Dodgers to three World Series ('63, '65, and '66). Sandy became the modern standard against which all later pitchers—especially lefty fireballers like Sudden Sam McDowell, Steve Carlton, Vida Blue, Ron Guidry, and Randy Johnson—would be measured. Opponents responded to his pitching prowess with either reverent awe or gallows humor (approaching the plate, they'd tell teammates to keep their seats on the bench warm because they'd be right back).

More important than the stats, however, was the style. While other pitchers (including teammate Don Drysdale and Cardinals' ace Bob Gibson) routinely knocked down opposing batters to intimidate them, Sandy was never known for throwing at hitters. When other players (such as Angels' playboy Bo Belinsky) embraced celebrity, Sandy shunned it. When other star athletes eagerly cashed in on their glory with lucrative endorsement deals, Sandy declined most offers. And when baseball's biggest stage, opening day of the World Series, was given to him in '65, he gave it back because the game conflicted with Yom Kippur. Coming back to win two games of the World Series, including the clinching game seven that brought the Dodgers the championship, his baseball immortality was assured.

Unfortunately, injuries were already limiting Sandy's success. A numb finger in '62 and a sore elbow in '64 carved entire months out of those seasons. The worst came in '65 and '66, when an arthritic left arm forced him to pitch with intense pain. Though only 30 years old and still at the top of his

August 5, 1964—*Ride the Wild Surf* with Susan Hart opens. ☮ August 5, 1966—The Beatles' album *Revolver* is released.
August 5, 1984—Actor Richard Burton dies in Switzerland of a cerebral hemorrhage. ☮ August 6, 1928—Artist Andy Warhol is born in Pennsylvania.
August 7, 1962—*The Wonderful World of the Brothers Grimm* with Yvette Mimieux opens. ☮ August 7, 1972—Actress Joi Lansing dies.

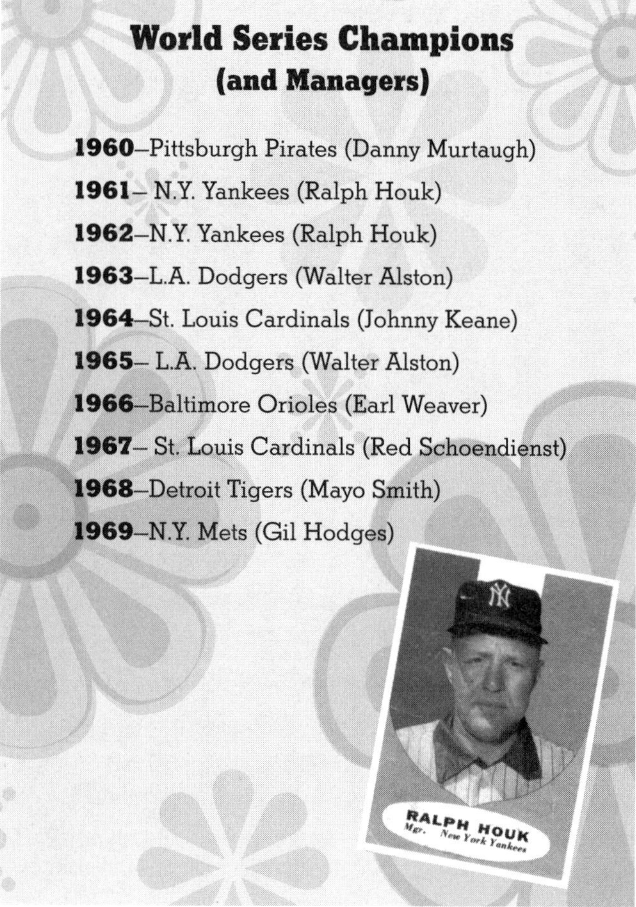

World Series Champions (and Managers)

1960–Pittsburgh Pirates (Danny Murtaugh)
1961– N.Y. Yankees (Ralph Houk)
1962–N.Y. Yankees (Ralph Houk)
1963–L.A. Dodgers (Walter Alston)
1964–St. Louis Cardinals (Johnny Keane)
1965– L.A. Dodgers (Walter Alston)
1966–Baltimore Orioles (Earl Weaver)
1967– St. Louis Cardinals (Red Schoendienst)
1968–Detroit Tigers (Mayo Smith)
1969–N.Y. Mets (Gil Hodges)

game, he retired after the '66 season. Sandy then took a shot at broadcasting, worked as a minor-league pitching coach for the Dodgers, and in the '90s was a consultant at the team's Vero Beach training grounds near his Florida home. But mostly he stayed quietly in the background, fishing and playing golf and taking flying lessons, avoiding the spotlight that still tried to find him.

EVERYBODY LOVES SOMEBODY

He wasn't a saint, but at least he was discreet. He smoked (like Walt Disney and Jackie Kennedy, he wouldn't let his photo be taken with a cigarette), he drank occasionally, and he was known to break curfew once in awhile. As one of America's most eligible bachelors living near Hollywood, he dated starlets through the '60s, but never with any trace of scandal. After leaving baseball, he married twice, with both marriages ending in divorce: the first (to Richard Widmark's daughter) lasted for 16 years, the second for nine.

MY BACK PAGES

The player Sandy replaced on the Brooklyn Dodgers' roster in '55: pitcher Tom Lasorda, who was sent down to the minors. . . . Despite his shyness, in his heyday Sandy did make occasional TV appearances during the off-season, usually playing himself on sitcoms like *Mister Ed* and *Dennis the Menace*. . . . The night Sandy threw his perfect game, the Cubs' pitcher, Bob Hendley, tossed a one-hitter, with the Dodgers' sole run coming on a walk, sacrifice bunt, stolen base, and error. . . . The Associated Press named him the Athlete of the Decade, and on ESPN's millennium list of the top 50 athletes of the 20th century, Sandy was the only pitcher. . . . Today starting pitchers rarely complete a game, but in Sandy's last two seasons he completed a total of 54. . . . On occasion he even pitched complete games in *spring training*, and he once threw 211 pitches in a game (double the usual limit for modern pitchers). . . . Voted into baseball's Hall of Fame in '72 (the first year he was eligible), Sandy was the youngest inductee ever.

Marta Kristen

This statuesque Nordic beauty hit the beach in *Beach Blanket Bingo* and hit the galaxy in *Lost in Space*.

TAKIN' CARE OF BUSINESS

Visually, Marta had quite an impact on any '60s production she was in. She's best-remembered, however, for her role as the sexy mermaid in *Beach Blanket Bingo* ('65) and for Irwin Allen's epic *Lost in Space*. This three-sea-

August 8, 1913—Sportscaster John Facenda is born. ☮ August 8, 1937—Actor Dustin Hoffman is born in L.A.
August 8, 1938—Actress Connie Stevens is born in Brooklyn, New York. ☮ August 8, 1960—"Itsy Bitsy Teenie Weenie Yellow Polkadot Bikini" hits #1.
August 8, 1964—Actress Marilyn Monroe makes the cover of *Life*. ☮ August 8, 1964—The album *Another Side of Bob Dylan* is released.

son TV show cast Marta as svelte Judy, eldest daughter in the *Space Family Robinson* and the only one who made the aluminum-foil costumes look good. Unfortunately, of everyone on the show Marta was given the least to do; even the younger Penny (Angela Cartwright) had more episodes built around her. One of the show's biggest mistakes was not pursuing a romance between young and beautiful Judy and young and handsome Don West (Mark Goddard). Their pairing would've been natural, and they seemed to be on board just for the possible relationship developments that could've been pursued, but regrettably weren't.

Born in Norway to an unwed Finnish mother and a soldier who died in World War II, Marta, then named Birgit Annalisa Rusanen, was only two months old when she was left in an orphanage. Four years later, a Michigan couple adopted her: Marta made the flight from Europe to America by herself, started to learn English, and as a young teen was singing, dancing, and acting in summer stock. For her high school years the family moved to L.A., where Marta was discovered at a restaurant and soon had her first professional roles, making her big-screen debut in Disney's delightful *Savage Sam* ('63), the *Old Yeller* sequel.

When *Lost in Space* blasted off for Planet Syndication in '68, Marta had no major screen credits until some guest-starring roles on classic '70s series. Her most unusual movie came in '74 when she co-starred in *A Gemini Affair* and had some steamy scenes with another actress. Since then Marta has been active in theatre, she had a cameo role as a reporter in the '98 remake of *Lost in Space*, and she and her TV sister Angela Cartwright still occasionally go to fan conventions.

EVERYBODY LOVES SOMEBODY

In '63 Marta, a 19-year-old beach girl, met a surfer/grad student, whom she married six months later. Pregnant with her first child, she traveled alone through Europe in '69 looking for her long-lost relatives, she delivered her daughter in America in '69, then she left her husband in '73. In '74 she met another man, an attorney, to whom she is still married. They now live in California.

MY BACK PAGES

Not until '69 was Marta able to revisit her real mother in Finland, and when she went back she met her older sister for the first time. . . . Marta is an avid traveler who says she loves treks to the Himalayas. . . . In '83 Marta joined with others from her *Lost in Space* family (Angela, June Lockhart, Guy Williams, and Bob May, who played the Robot) to take on members of the *Batman* cast (Adam West, Burt Ward, Yvonne Craig, Lee Meriwether, and Vincent Price) on *Family Feud* (the two teams split two matches). . . . In the '98 big-screen *Lost in Space*, Heather Graham played Judy Robinson, her title upgraded to Dr.

August 9, 1938—Tennis star Rod Laver is born. ☮ August 9, 1961—*Come September* with Sandra Dee opens.
August 9, 1969—Actress Sharon Tate and hairstylist Jay Sebring, among others, are murdered by the Manson Family in L.A.
August 9, 1969—The Haunted Mansion attraction opens in Disneyland.

Stanley Kubrick

The master auteur created cinematic worlds that still astonish.

TAKIN' CARE OF BUSINESS

Alongside Hitchcock, Bergman, and Hawks, Stanley Kubrick stands as the best director never to win a Best Director Oscar. His innovative works tower over most other acclaimed films of any decade, and even today they continue to challenge, disturb, and amaze audiences. And they were *his* movies—though most were based on existing novels, Kubrick usually wrote his own screenplays, created the special effects, did some of the camera work, and nurtured the projects as a producer, director, and father giving life to a personal vision.

Born in New York, Stanley was an indifferent student who first got noticed as a photographer, and he was still in high school when he started working for *Look* magazine. In 1951 he made a boxing documentary, followed by more documentaries and his first features, especially *The Killing* ('56), a nonlinear caper that influenced *Pulp Fiction*, and *Paths of Glory* ('57), a powerful anti-war drama starring Kirk Douglas.

In '59, Douglas invited Kubrick to take over his troubled epic *Spartacus* in mid-shoot, resulting in a Best Picture Golden Globe but an unhappy Hollywood experience for Stanley. He moved his operations permanently to England, where he began work on *Lolita*, despite the overwhelming public opinion that Vladimir Nabokov's novel about a sick, middle-aged man falling for a preteen girl was unfilmable. Casting was cautious—after considering Cary Grant, Errol Flynn, Marlon Brando, David Niven, and Laurence Olivier for the role of monstrous Humbert Humbert, Kubrick settled on the dignified James Mason; the 12-year-old nymphet was turned into a 14-year-old teenybopper played by 16-year-old Sue Lyon. Somehow Stanley made it work, and the result was another Golden Globe nomination for his direction.

In '64 he again showed something unthinkable—the end of the world. *Dr. Strangelove* began as a serious thriller, in keeping with the original novel, Peter George's *Red Alert*. Seeing too many irresistible comic elements, Kubrick recruited satirist Terry Southern to help turn the story of a wayward B-52 into a black comedy that climaxed with a chilling orgy of nuclear explosions. Peter Sellers (brilliant in three disparate roles), George C. Scott (at his funniest), and Slim Pickens (charmingly unaware that he was in a comedy) highlighted a perfect cast in a perfectly realized, totally believable military world gone mad (the movie would've been even wilder if Stanley hadn't cut the pie-fight ending he shot). The movie was up for Best Picture, and Kubrick was Oscar-nominated for his screenplay and direction.

As successful as *Dr. Strangelove* was, though, nobody was prepared for what would come next. Four years in the making, *2001: A Space Odyssey* is still science fiction's masterpiece, named by Lucas, Spielberg, and many other modern filmmakers as a key inspiration. Long, difficult, and abstract, spanning four million years and the deepest reaches of the universe, *2001* was more of a philosophical artwork than a movie. Stanley holed up in New York's Chelsea Hotel with sci-fi titan Arthur C. Clarke to work out a screenplay and novel based on Clarke's short story "The Sentinel." Using that story's core plot point—astronauts discovering an object on the moon—the pair added a lengthy, wordless preamble involving prehistoric ape-men (the alien object they discover propels their survival), the

August 9, 1995—Jerry Garcia of the Grateful Dead dies at a drug-treatment clinic. ☮ August 10, 1924—Actress Martha Hyer is born in Fort Worth, Texas. August 10, 1942—Fashion designer Betsey Johnson is born in Connecticut. ☮ August 10, 1943—Singer Ronnie Spector is born in New York. August 10, 1960—*Ocean's Eleven* with Frank Sinatra opens. ☮ August 10, 1962—Actress Janet Leigh makes the cover of *Life*.

murderous HAL computer (burdened with a secret knowledge of the alien object), and an enigmatic finale that took audiences on a psychedelic tour of interstellar space only to plop them into an elegant hotel room to witness the hero's rebirth as a porcelain star-child.

To realize his vision, Kubrick spent two-thirds of his $10,000,000 budget on the never-before-imagined special effects that would win him his only Oscar. He refused to appease audiences by adding in narration, definitions (the monolith's purpose as a teaching machine is clearer in the book than in the movie), or even dialogue (only 40% of the movie's scenes have dialogue, with none in the first 25 minutes or the final 23). Viewers didn't know what to think: some were enthralled, others outraged, but all were dazzled by the startling visuals. Kubrick and Clarke would have it no other way—theirs wasn't an easily digestible movie with an easily expressed theme. They were grappling with the biggest ideas of all—man's beginnings on Earth, his ultimate destiny, the nature of God. "If you understood *2001* completely," proclaimed Clarke, "we failed. We wanted to raise far more questions than we answered."

When a planned Napoleon movie bogged down, Kubrick jumped from the past to the future, from military biography to savage social commentary. *A Clockwork Orange*, based on Anthony Burgess's '63 novel, continued his run of provocative films, this time confronting audiences with an invented language, graphic violence, brutal sex, and cynical humor. X-rated when it was released, the controversial film took Oscar nominations for Best Picture and Best Director, and Stanley's reputation as the most daring and artistic major filmmaker ever was confirmed.

Another genre shift followed with the Oscar-nominated *Barry Lyndon*, a beautifully crafted historical drama with 18th-century paintings as templates for the visuals. *The Shining* five years later was a hugely popular horror film starring Jack Nicholson as Stephen King's axe-wielding psycho. Through the '70s Stanley's reputation as a demanding perfectionist was cemented by tales of actors doing 100 takes of a single scene. His reputation as a recluse was also advancing, as he rarely granted interviews and his film production dropped to one or two every decade. In '87, *Full Metal Jacket* was a riveting critique of the Vietnam War. In the early '90s, he began *A.I.*, a sci-fi fantasy he turned over to Steven Spielberg (Spielberg dedicated the movie to him). Stanley Kubrick died of a heart attack just as he finished *Eyes Wide Shut*, an erotic Cruise/Kidman vehicle that delivered muddled meanings to disappointed critics.

Oscar-Winning Directors

1960–Billy Wilder, *The Apartment*

1961–Robert Wise/Jerome Robbins, *West Side Story*

1962–David Lean, *Lawrence of Arabia*

1963–Tony Richardson, *Tom Jones*

1964–George Cukor, *My Fair Lady*

1965–Robert Wise, *The Sound of Music*

1966–Fred Zinneman, *A Man for All Seasons*

1967–Mike Nichols, *The Graduate*

1968–Carol Reed, *Oliver!*

1969–John Schlesinger, *Midnight Cowboy*

EVERYBODY LOVES SOMEBODY

Like Woody Allen (one of Kubrick's favorite directors), Stanley put loved ones into his movies. His first wife, whom he met in high school, worked on the crew of *Fear and Desire* ('53). His second wife danced in *Killer's Kiss* ('55). And the woman who would be his third (and final) wife was the *fräulein* singing at the end of *Paths of Glory*. Christine Kubrick would later become an artist, with paintings seen in *A Clockwork Orange* and *Eyes Wide Shut*. Stanley's daughter with Christine, Vivian, played the squirmy little "squirt" who asked for a bush baby in *2001*. Vivian was then seen briefly in

Barry Lyndon, *The Shining*, and *Full Metal Jacket*. Stanley's brother-in-law was executive producer of all his post-*Orange* films. Finally, stepdaughter Katharina made brief appearances in both *A Clockwork Orange* and *Eyes Wide Shut*.

MY BACK PAGES

From childhood on Stanley loved to play chess. . . . More favorites: *The Godfather*, *The Simpsons*, the Yankees, cats. . . . He might've been the most well-read filmmaker ever: a 12,000-word *Playboy* interview in '68 covered astronomy, poli-sci, religion, and cryonics and included his memorized quotes from arcane scientific journals. . . . Many of his movies include sly references to himself or his previous work—a horse in *The Killing* is named Stanley K, in *A Clockwork Orange* the record store has the *2001* soundtrack on display and he's briefly glimpsed in the aisles, and in *Eyes Wide Shut* a pile of Kubrick videos is on a table.

Sue Ane Langdon

This sexy, spirited actress showed off her comedic talents in dozens of movies and TV shows.

TAKIN' CARE OF BUSINESS

Before she was a '60s screen star, New Jersey's Sue Ane Langdon was singing at Radio City Music Hall and on Broadway. In '59 TV execs snapped her up for *Bachelor Father,* and her Hollywood career was on its way. Sue Ane's most memorable '60s roles came in two Elvis movies and one comedy classic. In *Roustabout* ('64) she got to kiss the King while she played a dark-haired gypsy fortune teller, and in *Frankie and Johnny* ('66) she again got a kiss, this time while wearing a pink wig in what was one of Elvis's most energetic musicals. Sue Ane thus became one of the few actresses to star in more than one Elvis movie. The third of Sue Ane's best '60s movies was the Gene Kelly-directed *A Guide for the Married Man* ('67), an urban comedy about infidelity in L.A.; Sue Ane in her sexy shorts almost stole the show from an all-star cast.

Meanwhile she was doing lots of TV these years. In '60 and '61 she was playing Kitty Marsh on John Forsythe's *Bachelor Father*, plus she was guesting on lots of other hit shows, all leading up to her regular role as one of the most famous characters in TV history. Playing opposite the great Jackie Gleason, Sue Ane was Alice in the new "Honeymooners" sketches Gleason did on his show *American Scene Magazine* (the part landed her on the cover of *Life* magazine).

More cool TV shows and juicy movie roles followed for the rest of the decade, including *McHale's Navy*, *The Man from U.N.C.L.E.*, *The Wild, Wild West*, *Ironside*, *The New Interns* ('64), the musical *When the Boys Meet the Girls* ('65), and Sean Connery's *A Fine Madness* ('66). After the '60s, Sue Ane got her most triumphant reviews for her work as a regular on Herschel Bernardi's endearing comedy *Arnie*; the show

August 12, 1944—Author Ian Fleming dies in England of a heart attack at age 56.
August 12, 1970—Singer Janis Joplin gives her last live performance at Harvard Stadium. ☮ August 13, 1967—*Bonnie and Clyde* with Warren Beatty opens.
August 13, 1969—Actress Sharon Tate, murdered by the Manson Family, is buried wearing a blue Pucci miniskirt.

ran for two seasons, and Sue Ane was nominated for a Golden Globe as Best Supporting Actress both years (she won in '72).

In '78 Sue Ane was a regular on another TV series, the short-lived *Grandpa Goes to Washington* with Jack Albertson, followed by yet another sitcom, *When the Whistle Blows*. In the '80s she had good parts in more films, in the '90s she joined the cast of *General Hospital*, and all along she's been doing great stagework and turning up as a frequent and funny talk-show guest.

EVERYBODY LOVES SOMEBODY

Sue Ane has been married for over 30 years to Jack Emrek, who is a longtime writer and director. He and Sue Ane live in what they call a "time warp" ranch in the west end of Southern California's San Fernando Valley, their house filled with authentic Western antiques collected over the years.

MY BACK PAGES

Sue Ane is such an accomplished horsewoman, she's ridden her horses in the Rose Parade on New Year's Day. . . . The unique spelling of her middle name (it's a Swedish variation) has occasionally gotten her into published crossword puzzles. . . . Her great sense of humor has also enabled her to be an emcee at film festivals, rodeos, autograph shows, and other special events.

Joi Lansing

A screen and nightclub star, glamorous Joi was always a riveting presence.

TAKIN' CARE OF BUSINESS

As if *The Beverly Hillbillies* didn't have enough beauties already, what with Donna Douglas in the Clampett clan and Sharon Tate working in Mr. Drysdale's bank office, stunning Joi Lansing added even more va-va-va-voom to a half-dozen episodes of the top-rated show. In them hills of Beverly she sashayed in as the wife of musician Lester Flatt, who was playing himself as half of the Flatt and Scruggs country duo. Never quite a movie star, Joi certainly looked like one with her 38-23-35 measurements and platinum blonde hair swirled around her lovely face.

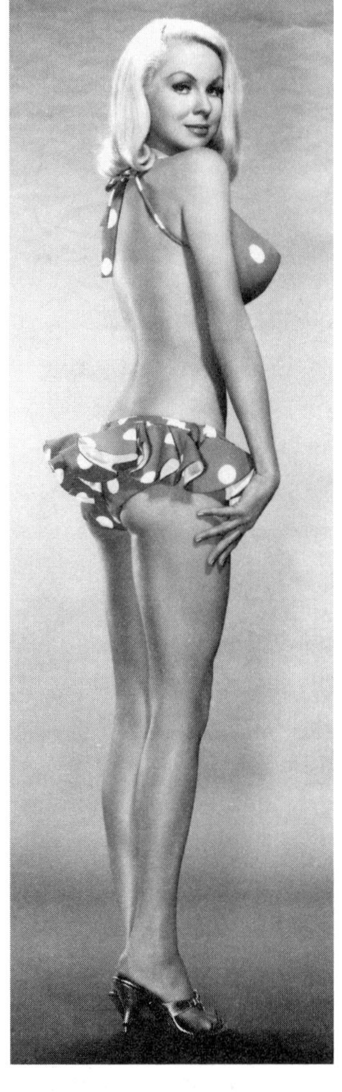

Formerly Joyce Wassmansdorff from Salt Lake City, she'd been a model in the '40s and as an up-and-coming actress made the cover of *Life* in '49. Changing her name in the '50s, she started landing parts on TV and in some significant movies, including Orson Welles's great *Touch of Evil* ('58). The '60s brought her dozens of TV roles, but with her movie career stalling she went musical, recording an album in '65 and developing a popular act that played in top nightclubs and hotels. Joi made two more B movies in the early '70s, but they were released posthumously after her sad passing from breast cancer in '72.

EVERYBODY LOVES SOMEBODY

In '50 young Joi had a brief, tempestuous marriage to a studio executive who was twice her age. A year later she eloped with actor Lance Fuller, who made it into lots of '50s movies; they divorced after two years. At different times rumors put her on the arms of Mickey Rooney and Frank Sinatra. Joi had been married to her manager for over a decade at the time of her death.

MY BACK PAGES

In '50 Joi was voted "Miss Hollywood". . . . That year she almost landed the Marilyn Monroe part as the ingénue in *All About Eve*.

Rod Laver

Perhaps the greatest male tennis player ever bracketed the '60s with his sport's biggest titles.

TAKIN' CARE OF BUSINESS

Australia's Rod Laver accomplished something no other player ever has—he won the Grand Slam (Wimbledon, U.S./Australian/French singles championships) twice. Though under 5′ 9″ and only 145 pounds, he was a powerful lefty with devastating topspin and fierce competitiveness. He had already won the Australian title in '60 and Wimbledon in '61 when he won all four titles in '62 as an amateur. Immediately turning pro, he won many more titles through the decade (including Wimbledon in '68) before he again captured all four crowns in '69. From '61–'70, he won 31 Wimbledon matches in a row, a record that lasted until Bjorn Borg broke it a decade later, and he was ranked the world's #1 player for four different years. Retiring in '74 at the top of his game, and now the author of several instructional tennis books, he was inducted into the International Tennis Hall of Fame in '81.

EVERYBODY LOVES SOMEBODY

Time magazine included a mention of Rod's '66 marriage to a "California accountant" in San Rafael, California.

MY BACK PAGES

In '71, Rocket Rod won almost $300,000 in prize money, the most up to that time, and he was the first player to claim career winnings of a million dollars. . . . Australia put his name on its Australian Open arena in 2000 and his face on a postage stamp in 2003.

Wimbledon Winners

1960–Neale Fraser (Australia)/
Maria Bueno (Brazil)

1961–Rod Laver (Australia)/
Angela Mortimer (England)

1962–Rod Laver (Australia)/
Karen Hantze Susman (USA)

1963–Chuck McKinley (USA)/
Margaret Smith Court (Australia)

1964–Roy Emerson (Australia)/
Maria Bueno (Brazil)

1965–Roy Emerson (Australia)/
Margaret Smith Court (Australia)

1966–Manuel Santana (Spain)/
Billie Jean King (USA)

1967–John Newcombe (Australia)/
Billie Jean King (USA)

1968–Rod Laver (Australia)/Billie Jean King (USA)

1969–Rod Laver (Australia)/
Ann Haydon Jones (England)

August 15, 1936—Actress Pat Priest is born in Bountiful, Utah. ☮ August 15, 1960—Actress Marilyn Monroe makes the cover of *Life*.
August 15, 1962—John and Paul invite Ringo to join the Beatles. ☮ August 15, 1965—The Beatles play Shea Stadium.
August 15, 1969—Fans assemble for the three-day festival of love, peace, and music known as Woodstock Music and Art Fair.

Daliah Lavi

This sexy foreigner with the dark visage and seductive body had key roles in several '60s comedies.

TAKIN' CARE OF BUSINESS

Israel's beautiful Daliah Levenbuch was a star in Europe before she made it in America. In her teens Daliah was studying to be a dancer and had barely begun a film career when she left for three years to serve in the Israeli army. She returned in '60 to make a couple of European films, and her career as an international star was on its way. The sheer diversity of her international movies is impressive: during the '60s she appeared in Swedish, German, French, Italian, Spanish, British, and American productions. Her first starring role in an English-language hit was Peter O'Toole's *Lord Jim* in '65, followed a year later by the Agatha Christie thriller *Ten Little Indians.* In '67 Daliah was one of the stars of *The Silencers,* the first and best of Dino's Matt Helm movies.

Her biggest impact came playing sexy Lady James Bond in *Casino Royale* ('67), the chaotic Bond spoof that didn't feature Sean Connery and played the whole 007 spy thing for laughs with five different directors stirring the soup (aided by a cool soundtrack album). Minor movies took her into the early '70s, at which point she disappeared from movie radar until reappearing in the '90s in some obscure German productions.

EVERYBODY LOVES SOMEBODY

In 2000 Daliah told an interviewer that she was married to a realtor and was living in Asheville, North Carolina.

MY BACK PAGES

So controversial was Daliah's bizarre '63 horror flick *The Whip and the Flesh,* which showed Daliah moaning in ecstasy while being flagellated by a ghost, that before it could be shown in different countries the censors hacked it up, resulting in cinematic mutations that went by other names, including *What!, Son of Satan,* and *The Night Is the Phantom.* . . . In *Casino Royale* she was only one of several performers who played a character named James Bond—others included Peter Sellers, Woody Allen as nephew Jimmy Bond, Terence Cooper, and even a monkey. . . . After the '60s Daliah made a few records—one of her biggest hits was a German version of "Look What They've Done to My Song, Ma."

Linda Lawson

This dark, exotic beauty released a cool '60s album of swingin' standards, then she co-starred in a cult-classic horror flick.

TAKIN' CARE OF BUSINESS

Born Linda Gloria Spazian in Michigan, Linda and her family headed west when she was 5. Fresh out of high school she moved to Las Vegas in '55, quickly landing a gig as a showgirl and then a singer at the venerable Sands Hotel. Two years later Linda returned to L.A., changed her name to Lawson at the suggestion of gossip columnist Louella Parsons, auditioned for record execs, and landed a few small TV roles.

In '58 Blake Edwards, whom she'd met earlier at an audition, wrote an episode of his Peter Gunn TV series for Linda. "Lynn's Blues" it was called, and it featured Linda as a torch singer who knocks out the song "Blue" during the show.

With a vocal style inspired by Lena Horne, she recorded a great album, *Introducing Linda Lawson*, in '60 that has been a durable fave of lounge lovers (the record featured a crack backup band, and the alluring close-up photo of Linda on the cover sure didn't hurt).

Her promising singing career got sidetracked when in '61 she landed her most memorable role: Mora, the beautiful but dangerous carnival mermaid who captivates young Dennis Hopper in the cult classic *Night Tide*. Prominent TV work and several movies took her into the mid-'60s, when the birth of her second daughter in '66 precipitated a semi-retirement. She came back to play a role in one more strong movie, the Paul Newman drama *Sometimes a Great Notion* ('71), then left the biz for good to concentrate on raising her family.

EVERYBODY LOVES SOMEBODY

From '61 until his death in '92, Linda was married to producer John Foreman. Foreman was the producer of many memorable films, including *Butch Cassidy and the Sundance Kid* ('69), *The Man Who Would Be King* ('75), and *Prizzi's Honor* ('85). With him Linda had two daughters.

MY BACK PAGES

As a comely teenager, Linda won the Miss Fontana beauty pageant. . . . On the "I Can Take Care of Myself" episode of *Alfred Hitchcock Presents*, Linda was the only guest star in the long history of that series to sing.

George Lazenby

The post-Connery pre-Moore Bond.

TAKIN' CARE OF BUSINESS

One of the very best James Bond movies in the long-running series starred Sean Connery. Actually, most of the very best James Bond movies in the long-running series starred Sean Connery. But when Connery turned down a sixth Bond movie after making five from '62–'67, the global search was on for a worthy replacement. To everyone's surprise, the man filling the tuxedo in *On Her Majesty's Secret Service* ('69) was a successful Australian male model named George Lazenby. George had the rugged good looks and muscular athleticism but not the reputation in the minds of many viewers—his acting experience had mainly come from TV commercials.

Still, he gave it his all, did most of his own stunts (at the cost of a broken arm), performed believably in fights and on skis (he was an expert at martial arts and skiing), became the only Bond to marry for real (not for pretend) his female lead (Diana Rigg), emoted authentically when his bride died on their wedding day, and ultimately delivered a rousing action-packed hit that stayed #1 at American box offices for a month.

Though the producers wanted him back for more, George walked away, feeling 007 wouldn't last and other opportunities awaited. They did, just not with the same high profile, so he's enjoyed a long if unremarkable screen career of foreign films (many *Emmanuelle* movies) and soap operas. He's also made a fortune in real estate, owning mansions and ranches around the world. Maybe he was no Connery, but nobody else ever has been either.

EVERYBODY LOVES SOMEBODY

George's long post-Bond marriage ended in divorce in the mid-'90s. He married former tennis star Pam Shriver in 2002, and he's got five kids from his various relationships.

MY BACK PAGES

At one point the Bond producers considered an opening sequence that showed Sean going in for plastic surgery and coming out as George, thus accounting for the new Bond. . . . The *Mad* magazine spoof in '70 renamed him George Lazybee. . . . More talents—he's an accomplished golfer, an experienced motorcyclist, a competitive car racer. . . . Marriage to Pam Shriver makes him a relative of the Kennedys and Arnold Schwarzenegger.

Timothy Leary and Owsley

The good doctor advocated "turning on," and Owsley helped people do it.

TAKIN' CARE OF BUSINESS

President Nixon called him "the most dangerous man in America." But to many others Dr. Timothy Leary was a handsome, charming mind-opening guru. He really was a doctor—after a brief, failed stint at West Point, Timothy earned his bachelor's degree at Alabama via correspondence courses while he was in the Army, his Master's at Washington State, and his Ph.D. in psychology at the University of California, Berkeley in '50. He taught at Cal in the '50s, wrote about personality disorders, and joined Harvard's faculty at decade's end.

After traveling to Mexico to experiment with psychedelics, he and some Harvard students began experimenting with hallucinogenic chemicals (including mescaline and LSD), ostensibly to research their effects and find useful applications. Frustrated by his prolonged absences, and nervous about his claims of profound spiritual journeys and "expanded consciousness," Harvard dismissed him in '63, even though LSD was still legal (and would be until '66). Timothy continued his research independently and in '64 co-wrote an influential book, *The Psychedelic Experience*, about his findings, which for him were nearly all positive. Many rock stars agreed, and so several significant songs directly or indirectly pointed to him and his work (among the most famous were "Tomorrow Never Knows" by the Beatles, "Legend of a Mind" by the Moody Blues, and "The Seeker" by the Who).

Timothy's invitation to "turn on, tune in, drop out," delivered barefooted at love-ins and lectures, became a mantra for disaffected kids who were receptive to an ex-Harvard professor's encouragement to find groovy new ways of living with the aid of recreational drugs. Unfortunately, legal problems plagued the second half of Timothy's '60s. In '65 he and his daughter were busted for marijuana while crossing the Mexican border, a conviction that brought him a *30*-year prison sentence (the conviction was later overturned). Timothy continued to preach the gospel of LSD in lectures and documentary films (one, '67's *Turn On, Tune In, Drop Out*, he not only appeared in but also produced and wrote).

Busted and convicted again in '70, Timothy did do time in a California minimum-security prison. When he pulled off a dramatic escape, he and his wife went to Algeria, Switzerland, and Afghanistan, only to be captured in '74. Co-operating with authorities, he turned informer (of debatable significance) and entered the Witness Protection Program in '76. In '82 he surprisingly paired up with G. Gordon Liddy, one of Nixon's most ruthless henchmen and himself an ex-con, for a cross-country tour of conversations and debates.

Throughout the '80s and '90s, Timothy appeared in dozens of movies and documentaries while continuing to lecture (he even tried stand-up comedy). Always at the cutting-edge of new experiences (he called himself a "futurist"), Timothy explored cryogenics towards the end of his life in hopes that he could be frozen until the prostate cancer that was killing him could be cured. He co-wrote his last book, *Design for Dying*, to offer a creative, even humorous look at "the ultimate trip." When he died in '96 his body was cremated; three years later some of his ashes (along with those of Gene Roddenberry, the *Star Trek* creator) were launched into space.

Supplying the LSD that Timothy advocated was Augustus Owsley Stanley III, the grandson of a Kentucky senator. Known as Owsley, he was in the Air Force in the '50s and then an art student at Berkeley in the early '60s. As an underground chemist working in L.A., the San Francisco Bay Area, and Denver, he mass-produced LSD in quantities that may have numbered millions of doses. Owsley tried to exert some quality control over his product, making it as pure as possible and monitoring the strength of the invisible, tasteless drug so that people would reliably know what they were taking. As a self-described "artist" in the LSD community, and not a profit-minded businessman, he gave away much of the LSD that he created.

Mid-decade he worked with several San Francisco bands, including the Grateful Dead and Jefferson Airplane, as a sound man making live recordings. A police raid of his lab in '65 was ineffectual, since LSD wasn't yet illegal; however, a subsequent raid led to a two-year prison sentence in the early '70s for drug possession, manufacturing, and conspiracy. Upon his release he continued working in music (mostly with the Dead, but also some gigs with the Beach Boys and others) and is credited with having recorded all or parts of over a dozen different rock albums. Today he's still an artist, though now his medium is sculpture.

EVERYBODY LOVES SOMEBODY

Timothy was married four times. His first wife, with whom he had two kids, committed suicide in '55. A brief second marriage in the mid-'60s was with the woman who would later give birth to actress Uma Thurman. His third wife—late '60s–mid-'70s—was the one who was on the lam with him when he escaped from prison. He was separated from his fourth wife in the '90s. Timothy's daughter committed suicide in '90; he also had a stepson. Owsley now lives in the Australian countryside with his second wife and their children.

MY BACK PAGES

Timothy was godfather to both Uma Thurman and Winona Ryder. . . . He declared himself a candidate for California governor in '70 (his drug bust ended his campaign). . . . Owsley's acid was often given colorful names—"Owsley Blues," "Monterey Purple," "Purple Haze," and "White Lightning". . . . In *The Electric Kool-Aid Acid Test* ('67) Tom Wolfe wrote about Owsley when he was supplying LSD to Ken Kesey's "Merry Pranksters"—Wolfe called him "the little wiseacre" and "the world's greatest acid manufacturer, bar none."

Janet Leigh

This interesting, versatile dramatic actress took the most famous shower in movie history.

TAKIN' CARE OF BUSINESS

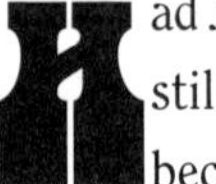ad Janet Leigh done nothing besides *Psycho*, she would still be venerated by film fans. As it is, way before she became a human pegboard in that Bates Motel shower,

August 18, 1965—Disney's *The Monkey's Uncle* with Annette Funicello opens.
August 18, 1965—Photographer David Bailey marries actress Catherine Deneuve in London, with Mick Jagger standing as the best man.
August 18, 1969—Woody Allen's *Take the Money and Run* opens. ☮ August 18, 1969—Jimi Hendrix plays Woodstock.

Jeanette Morrison of Merced, California had a successful career making dramas, adventure movies, comedies, and mysteries. A good student, Janet skipped several grades and graduated high school at only 15. She got discovered when actress Norma Shearer saw her photo at the ski lodge run by Janet's dad. Soon Janet had a screen test at MGM and a film career that included the Orson Welles classic *Touch of Evil* ('58).

In '60, *Psycho* catapulted her to true stardom, even though she was killed off only 45 minutes into the film. But what a 45 minutes—her complex evolution from guilt-ridden criminal to helpless victim brought her an Oscar nomination, a Golden Globe trophy, and lasting fame. Riding the momentum, she landed starring roles in diverse films with some of the decade's most prominent stars: the political thriller *The Manchurian Candidate* with Frank Sinatra ('62), the musical *Bye Bye Birdie* with Ann-Margret ('63), the detective story *Harper* with Paul Newman ('66), and the comedic *Three on a Couch* with Jerry Lewis ('66).

Guest spots on TV shows only added to her rep as a versatile, appealing presence. From the '70s onward she made a dozen TV movies, but writing was her main focus and she produced several well-received books, including an autobiography. In tribute to her long, remarkable career, in '99 she received the highest honor the French government can bestow on an artist, the *Commandeur Des Arts et des Lettres*. Sadly, after months of battling vasculitis (an inflammation of the blood vessels), Janet died in 2004.

EVERYBODY LOVES SOMEBODY

Janet married two times in the '40s. The first one, when she was only 14, was annulled; the second ended late in the decade. In the '50s rumors placed her in the company of billionaire Howard Hughes and later various Rat Packers. But her main relationship through that decade was with movie idol Tony Curtis. Their romance was closely watched in all the fan mags, and in '51 they married, becoming one of Hollywood's most glamorous couples. She and Tony co-starred in five films and produced two daughters, actresses Jamie Lee Curtis and Kelly Lee Curtis. Divorced in '61, a year later Janet remarried, a union that lasted until her death.

MY BACK PAGES

Her intense and interesting appeal, combining beauty with sincerity and intelligence (not to mention a knockout figure), made her a good photographic subject—twice she was on the cover of *Life*, and countless times on the covers of movie magazines. . . . Janet broke her wrist during the filming of *Touch of Evil*, but she refused to stop production and filming continued. . . . Supposedly Martha Hyer, Shirley Jones, Hope Lange, Piper Laurie, Eva Marie Saint, and Lana Turner were considered for the role of Marion Crane in *Psycho*.

August 19, 1933—Actress Debra Paget is born in Denver, Colorado. ☮ August 19, 1940—Actress Jill St. John is born.
August 19, 1967—"Funky Broadway" by Wilson Pickett hits #1. ☮ August 19, 1968—Actress Mia Farrow and singer Frank Sinatra divorce.
August 20, 1918—Writer Jacqueline Susann is born in Philadelphia. ☮ August 21, 1936—NBA star Wilt Chamberlain is born.

Richard Lester

The clown prince of '60s cinema directed several of the decade's biggest comedies.

TAKIN' CARE OF BUSINESS

Richard Lester never won an Oscar—in fact, his only nomination was for a 1959 jokefest that was up for Best Short Subject. But a Lester-less '60s would've been a less-memorable decade. Richard brought an exuberant style to cinema that perfectly captured the buoyant, swingin' zeitgeist of the times. "I'm inclined to be on the side of youth, of rebellion, of playfulness," he told *Playboy* in '65. Youth, rebellion, playfulness—no wonder his most popular hits were the two films that brought the Beatles to the big screen.

Though closely identified with British films, Richard was born in Philadelphia in '32. He graduated high school at 15, the University of Pennsylvania at 19, and was directing live TV shows in Philadelphia at 20. He then hopped the pond and toured Europe in the mid-'50s, earning money as a jazz pianist in nightclubs. His American TV experience landed him a job on British TV, and soon he had his own variety spectacle, *The Dick Lester Show*, which lasted just one episode but attracted a significant fan: Peter Sellers.

The newly formed Sellers-Lester team had British radio and TV hits through the '50s, and in '59 they made an 11-minute short called *The Running, Jumping, and Standing Still Film*, which brought them an Oscar nomination and enough acclaim for Lester to start directing features. *It's Trad, Dad* in '62 was a jazz-themed quickie, followed by *The Mouse on the Moon* in '63—neither was a hit, but they put him on track to make one.

His black-and-white *A Hard Day's Night* ('64) presented a supposedly typical day in the life of the Beatles, which meant lots of sight gags, wacky chases, witty ad-libs, a great soundtrack album, adoring fans, cute girls, and madcap adventures involving theatres, trains, nightclubs, and a helicopter. Lester's techniques for filming the musical numbers (such as the multi-camera concert footage) served as blueprints for future music videos. *Help!* ('65), filmed in color ("Green!" proclaimed John Lennon), inserted the Fab Four into a Bond-style action flick with even more sight gags and songs, plus cult rituals, mad scientists, bombs, and exotic locations (the Alps, the Bahamas). From these movies fans saw what it was like to be a Beatle, and Lester's fast-cutting comedic style became the template for *The Monkees* TV show in '66.

Between his two Beatles movies Lester made *The Knack . . . and How to Get It* ('65), a Michael Crawford comedy that won the *Palm D'Or* at Cannes and two Golden Globe nominations. Lester's hit streak continued in '66 with *A Funny Thing Happened on the Way to the Forum*, a musical/comedy that defined the term zany (again with Crawford, plus a cast full of comedic pros like Zero Mostel, Phil Silvers, and Buster Keaton). Less popular but still important films rounded out Lester's '60s, especially the misunderstood satire *How I Won the War* ('67, with John Lennon) and the intimate drama *Petulia* ('68, with Julie Christie).

While these films struggled at the box office, Richard's romp through the '60s is still remembered fondly as the spirited sprint of energetic youth. He then directed Italian TV commercials until he got his next big break: *The Three Musketeers* ('73), which led to a new run of hits including *The Four Musketeers* ('74), *Robin and Marian* ('76), and *Superman*

Paul McCartney, producer Walter Shenson, Richard Lester

August 21, 1944—Singer Jackie DeShannon is born in Hazel, Kentucky. ☮ August 21, 1961—Ann-Margret's "I Just Don't Understand" hits the charts.
August 21, 1961—Patsy Cline records the single "Crazy." ☮ August 21, 1961—*The Pit and the Pendulum* with Barbara Steele opens.
August 22, 1964—The Supremes' "Where Did Our Love Go" hits #1. ☮ August 22, 1968—Cynthia Lennon files for divorce from Beatle John Lennon.

II and *III* ('80, '83). Interspersed were several lesser movies and a few flops, but Lester's status as a '60s star remains secure, and MTV ultimately recognized his pioneering contributions to the music video art form with a special award.

EVERYBODY LOVES SOMEBODY

When Lester went to England in the '50s and started working on TV, he met a choreographer whom he soon married. They live today in a village near London.

MY BACK PAGES

A '60s scenemaker, Richard filmed *Petulia* in San Francisco and used the Grateful Dead on the soundtrack. . . . Richard was seen twice in *A Hard Day's Night,* once waving the fans onward at the train station, and later backstage while the boys sing "Tell Me Why". . . . He was also in *The Knack,* standing on the street as the bed is pushed by. . . . In a 1970 interview with J. Philip di Franco, Lester ranked *Help!* higher than *A Hard Day's Night, How I Won the War* higher than both, *A Funny Thing Happened on the Way to the Forum* a disappointment, and Buster Keaton as his favorite filmmaker.

The Let's Make a Dealers

***Let's Make a Deal,* our nominee as the decade's coolest game show.**

TAKIN' CARE OF BUSINESS

Let's Make a Deal wasn't really a game show—there was no *game,* just tempting offers and lucky hunches, valuable payoffs and humiliating "zonks." Contestants didn't have to answer any quiz questions, identify a hidden celebrity, or match a partner's answer, as contestants did on other daytime shows. On *Let's Make a Deal,* contestants simply tried to trade up from whatever they already had to bigger unseen prizes. The choices were simple but excruciating—keep your new color TV, or trade it for whatever was behind that curtain? Hold onto the exotic vacation, or swap it for the envelope being extended to you?

The fun was in seeing the outcomes, and also in seeing the contestants, who came to the show dressed in wacky costumes (early in the show's history contestants dressed normally, but when a costumed audience member got chosen for a deal, people started dressing outrageously to get picked). Near the end of the show winners would be confronted with yet another tantalizing choice—keep their winnings (nearly always merchandise) or go for the "Big Deal of the Day" hidden behind one of three doors (decent prizes, not junk furniture or decrepit cars, were behind the other two). What TV viewer didn't take a guess at the doors and then stick around to see them get opened in ascending order?

Choreographing the mayhem on "the marketplace of America" (so named in the intro) was "America's top trader, TV's big dealer," Monty Hall. Born Maurice Halperin in Canada, Monty hosted kids' shows and game shows before starting the new *Let's Make a Deal* show in '63. Though much of what he said was actually scripted, Monty was a master emcee who kept things moving briskly with rapid-fire deals (so fast was the action, Monty was still throwing out deals even when the show was over, offering people $50 for paper clips or bobby pins).

The announcer for the first year was Wendell Niles, who previously had announced in many films since the '30s. In '64 Jay Stewart (born Jay Fixx), who'd already worked on *American Bandstand, The Mike Douglas Show,* and more, took over the announcing chores. Affable Jay was the star of many of the *Let's Make a Deal* joke prizes (or zonks)—the audience would burst into laughter upon seeing, not a new Cadillac, but Jay dressed up as Little Bo Peep, or Jay driving a tiny car.

"The lovely Carol Merrill" (as Monty usually referred to her) had been Miss Azusa and a model in print and in commercials before becoming everybody's favorite prize hostess.

August 22, 1969—New York's Gloria Smith is crowned the second Miss Black America. ☮ August 23, 1930—Actress Vera Miles is born in Boise City, Idaho. August 23, 1934—Actress Barbara Eden is born in Tucson, Arizona. ☮ August 23, 1946—The Who drummer Keith Moon is born near London. August 23, 1962—John Lennon weds Cynthia Powell. ☮ August 23, 1967—*The Trip* with Peter Fonda opens.

On *Let's Make a Deal,* Carol not only pointed to doors, boxes, and prizes, she (like Jay) was also involved in zonks—Carol riding a tricycle, Carol as an old lady (missing a few teeth) who cranked an old-fashioned washing machine (after the show, contestants were given merchandise alternatives to their zonks).

Although she was on thousands of episodes of *Let's Make a Deal,* Carol rarely got to speak, and one of the show's best gags came on the 2,500th show when Monty called on her and as a joke she talked nonstop. Throughout her *Deal* career Carol was always an attractive, wholesome presence whose long legs were shown off to good effect in skirts and even (in '71) hot pants.

In '77 this first, most famous version of the show came to an end; revamped "all-new" versions, sometimes with Monty as the host, sometimes with him as the executive producer, none with Jay or Carol, have run every decade since. All three stars enjoyed long post-*Deal* careers: Monty still works behind the scenes with production and product tie-ins (such as a Vegas slot machine), and he is a successful fundraiser for charities (so successful several hospital wings are named after him); Jay was the announcer on many more TV shows, but physical problems and depression led him to commit suicide in '89; Carol had small roles in movies and TV shows, was a frequent guest on prominent talk shows, and has become a popular advocate of organic food and healthy living.

EVERYBODY LOVES SOMEBODY

Monty's been married to the same woman since '48; among his three grown kids is Tony Award-winning actress Joanna Gleason, who has also appeared in dozens of movies including *Hannah and Her Sisters* ('86) and *The Wedding Planner* (2001). Jay was survived by a wife and family—the death of one of his children contributed heavily to his depression in his last years. Carol and her husband lived in Hawaii and ran a nursery and farm during the '90s, relocating to Australia at the millennium.

MY BACK PAGES

Carol's niece is actress Carla Gugino (*Snake Eyes,* '98). . . . One person the show (and Carol) had an impact on was singer Jimmy Buffett—he included her in a song called "Door Number Three" on his early *A1A* album. . . . There were a couple of "games" on the show that required some skill or knowledge—for instance, contestants would sometimes have to arrange items in order of price. . . . In '68 the show switched from NBC to ABC, and it also ran for several years in primetime. . . . Occasionally celebrities made appearances, among them Zsa Zsa Gabor, Red Buttons, and Milton Berle. . . . The cool theme music was written by Sheldon Allman, a longtime actor who also wrote and sang the *Mister Ed* theme.

John Lindsay

Da Mayor of NYC steered the city through turbulent times.

TAKIN' CARE OF BUSINESS

He called his job the second-toughest in America, but John Lindsay handled it with style and a firm conviction in his own beliefs. A Manhattan native, a Yalie, and a World War II Navy lieutenant, Lindsay practiced law and worked as assistant to the Attorney General in the '50s. In '58 he won a Congressional election, became a vocal advocate of civil rights, and was seen as a Republican version of another young, handsome politician of the time, Robert Kennedy.

In '66 Lindsay was elected Mayor of New York City, one of the youngest ever. A maverick within his party (a *Life* cover story was headlined "Stunning victory of a loner"), he confronted crippling financial problems, transit and sanitation strikes, racial turmoil, and the student occupation at Columbia University; he also revitalized Central Park, improved the city's status as a tourist destination, and drew national

recognition for his civil rights and immigration programs. Unfortunately, a corruption scandal and a brief, failed run at the '72 presidential election led him to quit politics in '73 and return to law (he also became a semi-regular on *Good Morning America*). He wrote memoirs and a novel, but Parkinson's disease, heart attacks, and strokes plagued his last years before his death in 2000.

EVERYBODY LOVES SOMEBODY

A charismatic, dynamic leader, Lindsay was spotlighted in *Playboy*, appeared on *The Tonight Show* several times, played a senator in a movie (*Rosebud*, '75), and had celebrity pals. He was married from '49 to the end of his life, with three daughters and a son.

MY BACK PAGES

While other American cities were aflame with riots in the '60s, New York wasn't, in part because of Lindsay's reputation for caring for all ethnicities (he often walked through the city's toughest neighborhoods, talking with locals). . . . In '72 Mayor Lindsay appealed on John Lennon's behalf when a minor drug conviction brought the threat of deportation.

Peggy Lipton

A slim-bodied, straight-haired, doe-eyed teen, Peggy jumped from small TV roles to big TV stardom on *The Mod Squad*.

TAKIN' CARE OF BUSINESS

Peggy's had quite a career, considering she has overcome a problem with stuttering. A Long Island girl who was a New York model at 15, Peggy landed some TV appearances in her late teens, became a regular on the short-lived *John Forsythe Show* in '65, and was in several minor movies. But when you talk about Peggy Lipton's '60s career, there's really only one thing to talk about. Debuting in '68 and running for five years, *The Mod Squad* was a hip, happenin' police show that was based on the actual experiences of the show's creator, a former undercover cop.

Peggy played pretty Julie, a runaway and vagrant whose probation included an assignment with an unarmed undercover unit, *The Mod Squad* (her partners were curly-haired car thief Michael Cole and ultra-cool rioter Clarence Williams III). Aimed at a young audience and mixing groovy counterculture heroes with slam-bang police action, the show was a sturdy hit with teens, who copied its up-to-the-minute lingo and flashy fashions, and critics, who bestowed an Emmy nomination as Best Dramatic Series.

On the show Peggy was probably a little more mod and a little less squad than your average L.A. cop. She had the bedroom eyes of a bonged-out beauty, the face of an innocent angel, and a long lissome frame adorned with patterned dresses and big bell-bottoms. Plus she had talent to match the looks: she received four Golden Globe nominations (with one win) from '70–'73. The post-*Mod Squad* years brought some failed films (Kevin Costner's *The Postman*, '97); she also recorded an album in '71, composing half the songs herself. Her best work came in the early-'90s as the sanest of the odd squad in David Lynch's quirky *Twin*

August 25, 1969—Crosby, Stills, Nash and Young make their first Los Angeles appearance at the Greek Theater.
August 25, 1984—Author Truman Capote dies at 59 in L.A. ☮ August 26, 1936—Actress Yvette Vickers is born in Kansas City, Missouri.
August 26, 1941—Actress Akiko Wakabayashi is born. ☮ August 26, 1944—Drummer Maureen Tucker of the Velvet Underground is born.

Peaks, reprising this popular TV role for the '92 movie.

EVERYBODY LOVES SOMEBODY

Peggy has written about her brief affairs with such '60s icons as Paul McCartney, Terence Stamp, and Elvis. In '74 she married Quincy Jones, 14 years her senior and the famous conductor/composer who's won dozens of Grammy Awards. With Quincy she had two kids and an '89 divorce.

MY BACK PAGES

The Mod Squad was one of the first hits for producer Aaron Spelling, who later produced dozens of shows ranging from *Charlie's Angels* to *Melrose Place*. . . . Among the guest stars on *The Mod Squad* were David Cassidy, Richard Dreyfuss (twice), Margot Kidder, Bobby Sherman (twice), Robert Duvall, and Sammy Davis, Jr. (playing a priest). . . . In the '99 movie, Claire Danes starred as Julie Barnes, who was now a recovering cocaine addict. . . . Peggy successfully battled cancer in 2004 and published a candid, appealing autobiography, *Breathing Out*, in 2005.

Liz and Dick

Dramatic both on and off the big screen, this closely watched couple shared a passionate, diamond-studded romance.

TAKIN' CARE OF BUSINESS

Elizabeth Taylor and Richard Burton couldn't cough in the '60s without the international papers printing a picture or writing a story about it. They were to the decade what Lady Di and Prince Charles were to the '90s: photogenic royalty. London-born Liz started her career with 29 films in the '40s and '50s, her breakthrough to stardom coming at 12 years old with *National Velvet* ('44). Quickly maturing, at 15 she was dubbed "the most beautiful woman in America" by Hedda Hopper, and a few years later she was co-starring in *Giant* ('56). Then came a remarkable streak in which she was nominated for a Best Actress Oscar four years in a row: *Raintree County* ('57), *Cat on a Hot Tin Roof* ('58), *Suddenly, Last Summer* ('59), and the movie that brought her the first of two Oscars, *BUtterfield 8* ('60). She had made the quantum leap to global fame; *Cleopatra* would take her to global legend.

Meanwhile Dick, son of a Welsh coal miner, was an Oxford student who got started on the stage in the '40s and gradually worked his way up the movie ranks in the '50s. At the cusp of the '60s, he was being hailed as one of Britain's brightest acting lights, having won a Tony nomination as Broadway's Best Actor in '58, a Golden Globe nomination for the film *Look Back in Anger* ('59), and a Tony Award in '61 for his King Arthur in *Camelot*. *The Longest Day* in '62 set him up for what would seem like the longest movie a year later.

In '63, *Cleopatra* was by far the most expensive movie ever made, costing 20th Century Fox three times what it cost to make what was previously the most expensive movie, *Ben-Hur* ('59). It was also the most publicized film to date and was promoted with a soundtrack album and lots of press releases. Unfortunately, by costing the most, being delayed the most, and raising expectations the most, *Cleopatra* also flopped the most, collapsing under the sheer weight of the hype and the bloated production.

Liz's health suffered during the filming—she caught double pneumonia, had an emergency tracheotomy, and at one point was pronounced dead. The movie did showcase her voluptuous figure, flawless face, and legendary violet eyes, and Dick escaped relatively unscathed with his powerful accent intact, but supposedly Liz herself rushed home and threw up the first time she sat through it. They emerged the world's most closely watched stars and soon teamed up again for several more films, especially the masterful *Who's Afraid of Virginia Woolf?* ('66), which brought Liz a second Oscar. Dick was more successful on his own—he got three Oscar nominations for his non-Liz '60s films, including *Becket* ('64) and *Anne of the Thousand Days* ('69).

Liz's post-'60s films commanded attention but not much respect from audiences or critics, and she ended up doing a lot of TV and documentaries as her film roles dwindled and her weight increased. With fewer and fewer movie appearances, her most glamorous roles in the '80s and '90s came in commercials for her perfumes, Passion and White Diamonds. She also made some kind of TV history when she appeared on four network shows on one night in '96, each show continuing a story line about her lost gems.

Yet no matter what she does in her private or public life, nothing has diminished her stature as a Hollywood goddess and one of the last links to Hollywood's Golden Age. When AFI announced the "50 Greatest Screen Legends" in June '99, Liz was seventh among the actresses, right behind Marilyn. *Playboy* came, saw, and concurred, and on its '99 list of the century's 100 sexiest stars she was again seventh, sandwiched between '60s icon Sophia Loren and '90s pool toy Pamela Anderson. And finally, at the turn of the millennium, she became Dame Elizabeth Taylor, a prestigious British title bestowed by one Queen Elizabeth to another.

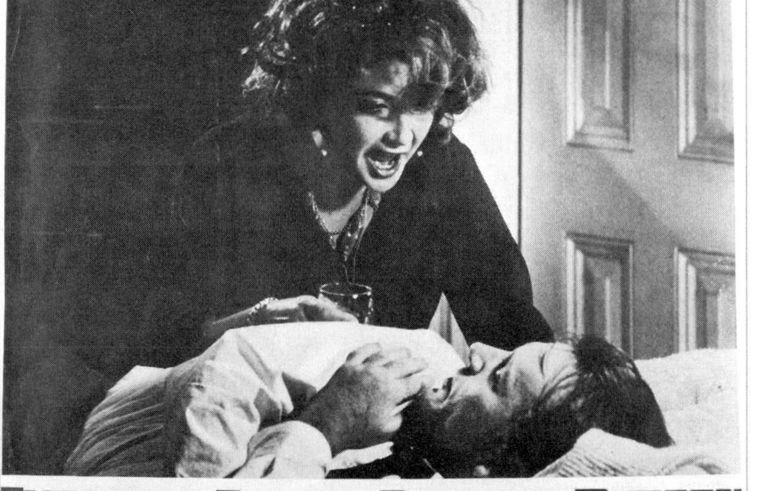

For Dick, the '70s brought one great role, *Equus* ('72), some bills-paying jobs like *Exorcist II* ('77), plus an attempt at a *Camelot* revival in the early '80s that was unfortunately interrupted by health problems. Liz and Dick did manage a reunion on stage with the play *Private Lives* in '83, and Dick had one last strong movie performance in him with *1984* ('84), but a cerebral hemorrhage finally took him that same year.

EVERYBODY LOVES SOMEBODY

Like you don't already know. That's the thing about Liz and Dick, their every move was played out in the press in the '60s. Both had been married before. At 18 Liz married her first husband, bad boy hotel heir Nicky Hilton, but they separated within a few months. Her next marriage was to English actor Michael Wilding in '52—he was 39, she was 20. Two kids later, they divorced in '56. A day after the divorce, Liz married swaggering producer Mike Todd, with Todd's best friend Eddie Fisher and his wife Debbie Reynolds in the wedding party. Liz had another child, and it looked like she had her true love at last, until tragedy struck. Because she was sick, Liz wasn't on Mike's plane *The Lucky Liz* when it crashed in New Mexico and killed him in '58. Six months later she took up with Eddie, who left wife Debbie in what was Hollywood's biggest scandal of the '50s. On the same day Eddie and Debbie were divorced in '59, Eddie and Liz got married.

While on their honeymoon in Europe she got a telegram inviting her to star in *Cleopatra*. At this time Richard Burton was already a husband and father. One story has it that when they first met on the Italian set, Dick showed up for the day's shooting with a hangover, Liz administered some much-needed coffee, an instant rapport was established, and combustible passions quickly ignited, even though Liz's husband Eddie was nearby. After Dick's divorce in late '63 they married in '64 with her pronouncement "this marriage will last forever." Drinking, brawling, and affairs led to several separations and finally a divorce in '74. Dick won her back a year later, they married in Botswana, and divorced for good in '76. He had two more marriages. She also had two more, bringing her total number of husbands to seven and marriages to eight.

MY BACK PAGES

When Liz was hired by MGM as a child, the studio arranged for everything throughout her adolescence, including her first "boyfriend"—football hero Glenn Davis—and a staged high school graduation with fake classmates and a fake diploma. . . . Liz wore a $10,000 Halston gown to the '72 Oscars, at the time the most expensive dress ever worn to that event, plus she was decked out with over a million-dollars worth of jewels she got from Dick. . . . As testament to her survival skills, she's bounced back from repeated illnesses and injuries and rehabs and broken bones and something like three-dozen surgeries overall. . . . She was an early and major AIDS fundraiser, efforts that brought her the Jean Hersholt Humanitarian Award in '93. . . . Dick was tied with Peter O'Toole for the most Oscar nominations (seven) with zero wins. . . . One last movie pairing Dick tried to make happen—the villainous pair in *Macbeth*.

Julie London

The smoky-voiced chanteuse was a sultry counterpoint to the decade's raucous rockers.

TAKIN' CARE OF BUSINESS

An actress and pin-up girl in the '40s and '50s, statuesque Julie London was known in the '60s for her smooth, sophisticated record albums. Born in Northern California to vaudeville performers with the last name Peck, Julie dropped out of high school at 15 and took a job as an elevator operator in L.A. Alan Ladd's wife spotted her and recommended her for a screen test, which led to early movie roles. She began recording in the mid-'50s, had an immediate hit with "Cry Me a River," and made a *Life* cover in '57. Julie was at her best singing sensual standards, as on the albums *The End of the World* ('63) and *All Through the Night* ('65), making the already-famous songs her own with a slow, intimate delivery. However, by '69 she was attempting Dylan and Doors songs on *Yummy, Yummy, Yummy* and seemed out of her element.

Julie ultimately crafted over three dozen albums and decorated most of the covers with sexy photos—today her records are known as much for the art as they are for the music. Throughout the '60s, she was also appearing onscreen, though the movies (*The Third Voice*, '60, *The George Raft Story*, '61) were minor. Dozens of TV appearances during the decade on everything from game shows to *Laugh-In* set her up for the TV career she enjoyed in the '70s as popular Nurse Dixie on *Emergency!*, a role that brought her a Golden Globe nomination. A stroke and health problems in the '90s preceded her death in 2000.

EVERYBODY LOVES SOMEBODY

Julie was married to actor Jack Webb from the late '40s into the mid-'50s. Webb, of course, was famous for the TV show

August 28, 1963—Dr. Martin Luther King, Jr. delivers his "I have a dream" speech at the Lincoln Memorial in Washington, D.C.
August 29, 1942—Sterling Morrison of the Velvet Underground is born. ☮ August 29, 1945—Sprinter Wyomia Tyus is born in Griffin, Georgia.
August 29, 1964—Walt Disney's *Mary Poppins* opens.

Dragnet. After their divorce Julie married composer/actor Bobby Troup, whose song "Route 66" was recorded by Nat "King" Cole, the Rolling Stones, and many others. Troup managed her music career and co-starred with her on *Emergency!*, the show produced, ironically enough, by Jack Webb. Julie had five kids, two with her first husband, three with her second.

MY BACK PAGES

In the '50s, Julie was recognized by *Billboard* magazine as the top female singer for three years in a row. . . . Fans will also recall Julie's vocals on early Marlboro TV commercials. . . . Besides *Emergency!* she and husband Bobby Troup appeared on several other shows together, including *Tattletales* in the '70s. . . . Julie thought the '69 album *Easy Does It* was her best record.

Claudine Longet

This lithe French import rendered breathy treatments of pop songs and was a popular screen presence.

TAKIN' CARE OF BUSINESS

Rarely asked to do more on-screen than look innocent and beautiful, Claudine Longet still made a memorable impression on audiences and today still commands a group of loyal fans. Blessed with a slender figure and a large-eyed, childlike beauty, Claudine got her start in '60 when she moved to Las Vegas and danced, appropriately enough for this Parisian, in the Folies Bergère. By '64 she was appearing on various TV shows often playing a young, naïve French waif. She was also on *The Andy Williams Show,* of course, plus numerous holiday specials that drew Super Bowl-like ratings.

On *Run For Your Life* in '66 she sang a song, which was impressive enough to get her a record deal with A & M Records, and soon she was on the charts with covers of gentle pop songs like the Beatles' "Here, There, and Everywhere." Her first album, *Claudine*, came out in '67, followed by four more in the next three years; none were huge sellers, and "Love Is Blue," one of her top hits off the '68 album of the same name, charted at only #71. But she picked great material to sing, she seduced listeners with soft, romantic whispering, and the records are now considered loungy collectibles.

In '68 she made her biggest movie splash as the life of *The Party*, an underrated Blake Edwards/Peter Sellers collaboration. Her song from that movie, "Nothing to Lose," was released in '68, and a TV movie, *Massacre Harbor*, followed a year later. After the '60s, Claudine did more TV, made one more movie, *How to Steal an Airplane* ('71), and recorded two more albums before retiring.

EVERYBODY LOVES SOMEBODY

Crooner Andy Williams claimed that he had seen Claudine when she was just a child roller-skating in Paris some 10 years before they got married. Later the story went that they met in '60 when he helped her one night after her car broke down in Vegas. When Claudine married Andy Williams in '61, she was about 20 years old and he was 34. They had three children in the '60s and then separated in '69. When they divorced in '75, Claudine got a multimillion-dollar property settlement.

In '76 Claudine made the front pages of national newspapers when she allegedly shot and killed her lover, a handsome and dashing Olympic skier named Spider Sabich, in

August 29, 1966—The Beatles perform their final stadium concert (San Francisco's Candlestick Park).
August 29, 1976—Actress Anissa Jones dies of a drug overdose at the age of 18. ☮ August 29, 1987—Actor Lee Marvin dies.
August 30, 1935—John Phillips of the Mamas and the Papas is born on Parris Island, South Carolina. ☮ August 30, 1943—Skier Jean-Claude Killy is born.

the Aspen, Colorado home that Claudine, her three kids, and Sabich shared. Supposedly he had mentioned to friends in the winter of '75 that he wanted to end the relationship, and he may have been trying to break up with her on the day he died. Claudine, who may have spent part of that day in a bar, was holding a pistol and, she claimed, it fired accidentally, hitting him once in the stomach. Claudine called the police in a panic, then rode with him in the ambulance, but Spider died on the way to the hospital.

Claudine spent that night with her neighbors, John and Annie Denver; her ex-, Andy Williams, flew to her side during these dark days. Claudine was charged, not with murder, but with reckless manslaughter, and during a four-day trial in January '77, her lawyer proved that the loaded gun could have gone off at any time without anyone actually pulling the trigger. The jury, after deliberating only four hours, found her guilty of only criminal negligence, a misdemeanor. Rumors swirled that she had kept a diary that would expose Aspen's seamy side, and also that she had tested positive for cocaine, but neither issue was allowed into the trial.

Throughout the ordeal she tearfully maintained that she and Sabich were deeply in love, and she's always stuck to her story that the gun had discharged accidentally. She spent just one month in jail, and the judge even let her choose when she would have to serve her time (between her sentencing and the 30 days in jail, Claudine vacationed in Mexico). In '86 Claudine married her defense attorney, and they now live in Aspen.

MY BACK PAGES

After the sensational trial, *Saturday Night Live* did a skit in which skiers came down a hill with gunfire going off and the announcement that one of them had been shot by Claudine Longet. . . . "Claudine" was a bootlegged Rolling Stones song that mocked her and the trial and ended with Mick commanding Keith to put his weapon down.

Jack Lord

Cool cop in a cool location.

TAKIN' CARE OF BUSINESS

Alongside Joe Mannix, Steve McGarrett stands as the coolest TV lawman of the late '60s (with both deferring to Steve McQueen in the movie *Bullitt*). McGarrett was played by Jack Lord, who was probably the tallest (at 6′ 2″) TV cop ever (and he might've had the best hair, too). Born John Ryan in New York, Jack served as a seaman in World War II, studied at the Actors Studio in the '50s, and was already working on Broadway when he got the role of C.I.A. agent Felix Leiter in Sean Connery's first Bond epic, *Dr. No* ('62). That year he also got his first starring series, the short-lived rodeo-themed *Stoney Burke*.

After many tough-guy appearances on other '60s series, Jack missed out on the Captain Kirk role in *Star Trek*, but in '68 he hooked *Hawaii Five-O*, an authentic new cop show set in (and named after) the fiftieth state. Glamorous locales, smart dialogue, and one of the best theme songs in history propelled the show to a dozen strong years, with a catch phrase—"Book 'em, Danno"—that endures still. A man of diverse talents, Jack was also a successful artist with museum-exhibited paintings.

EVERYBODY LOVES SOMEBODY

Jack had a wife in the '40s, with a son who died in an accident at 13. After divorcing, Jack was married again from the '50s until his death from heart failure in '98.

MY BACK PAGES

Wo Fat, the bad guy in the very first show, didn't get nabbed until the very last show. . . . The Ventures turned the show's theme song into a hit single. . . . Supposedly Traci Lords was such a fan as a teen, she chose her stage name in tribute and even named her cat Steve McGarrett.

August 30, 1947—Actress Peggy Lipton is born in New York. ☮ August 30, 1965—Bob Dylan's album *Highway 61 Revisited* is released.
August 30, 1967—*Point Blank* with Angie Dickinson opens. ☮ August 30, 1995—Velvet Underground guitarist Sterling Morrison dies.
August 31, 1928—Actor James Coburn is born. ☮ August 31, 1966—*The Patty Duke Show* concludes its three-season run.

Donna Loren

This talented, sweet-faced teen was a multidimensional star who excelled at the 3M's—music, movies, and modeling.

TAKIN' CARE OF BUSINESS

If you were anywhere in America during the '60s, you undoubtedly encountered the image or the voice of young Donna Loren. A talented child star from Boston, at 8 years old she sang on her first commercial, at 9 she cut her first record ("I Think It's Almost Christmas Time"), and at 10 she appeared on *The Mickey Mouse Club* TV show. Throughout her teens Donna continued making records until by the end of the '60s she'd released 18 pop singles, including "Honey Buggie," "The More I See Him," "Hands Off," "Muscle Bustle," and "So, Do the Zonk."

Donna was more than just a pretty voice, however; her pretty face took her to another level of popularity in '63 when she was chosen to be the first and only "Dr Pepper Girl." For the next five years she represented the soft-drink company on the radio, in a huge billboard campaign, in magazines, in calendars, on TV, and by making personal appearances around the country. As a model, she always looked great, and she always looked sincere—in her elegant white dress with long gloves, you really believed that she was the prettiest prom date you ever saw, and in jeans and a gingham shirt she looked like she was just about the cutest dang cowgirl who ever rode the range (recent photos of her put the grace in the phrase "aging gracefully").

Donna's wholesome image as a sweet, talented all-American girl made her a natural for the big screen, and from '64–'65 she got prominent roles in five popular bikini/beach movies, usually with cool songs to sing, too. During these years she was also a frequent presence on TV, especially as a featured vocalist every week on *Shindig* and as a regular on Milton Berle's mid-decade variety show. One of the most ubiquitous teens of the decade, she was even selected to write two monthly columns for *Movie Life* magazine in '66 and '67, one column giving personal advice and the other describing life in Hollywood.

After taking a career timeout during the '70s, in the '80s she tried a comeback as a singer with the country-flavored "Wishin' and Hopin'." The '90s saw a new limited-edition CD called *The Best of Donna Loren* and a new career in fashion. Even as a child Donna could sew, and in fact she designed and sewed most of the clothes she wore on stage as a young girl. Thus it was only fitting that Donna would reinvent herself as a fashion designer. Today she designs clothes under the ADASA Hawaii label and has her own boutique. She's been named one of Hawaii's top designers by *Honolulu* magazine, and her clothes were shown in a coffee-table book called *Hawaii: Heaven on Earth*. The career may be different from what she did in the '60s, but Donna Loren is still one of the most successful girls on the beach.

EVERYBODY LOVES SOMEBODY

Donna retired from show biz at the end of the '60s to devote herself to a marriage and a family. Happily married, she lives in Hawaii. Her son Joey Waronker plays drums for R.E.M., and her two beautiful daughters are following in Donna's footsteps in the music and fashion industries.

MY BACK PAGES

On the "Honey Buggie" single Donna's name is listed as Barbie Ames, and on "The More I See Him" her name is listed as Donna Dee. . . . Unlike Sophia Loren, who puts the emphasis on the –en in her last name, Donna's last name is pronounced to rhyme with foreign. . . . In case you thought we didn't know our punctuation, the official spelling of Dr Pepper has no period after the Dr. . . . Often the actresses in '60s beach movies played characters with unusual names like Sniffles, Animal, Lady Bug, and Sugar Kane, but not Donna—in three of the beach movies her character was also named Donna. . . . Donna was a real teenager in the beach movies, unlike some of the other "teens"—in *Beach Blanket Bingo*, Frankie was 26, Annette and Linda Evans were 24, and Jody "Bonehead" McCrea was 31.

Sophia Loren

This statuesque superstar made two movies a year through the '60s, picking up an Oscar along the way.

TAKIN' CARE OF BUSINESS

Many European actresses got famous in the '60s, but few have what Sophia Loren has: an Oscar. Far more than just a stereotypic sex symbol, Sophia earned a critical acclaim in the '60s that made her one of the most respected stars in the world. And one of the most popular, too, as verified by three Golden Globes as the World's Favorite Film Actress. Quite astonishing for a girl who had lived a true rags-to-riches story.

Living in poverty in an Italian town that was bombed in World War II, as a child Sofia Scicolone was nicknamed "the toothpick" because of her skinny, undernourished body. Debuting as a 15-year-old extra in '50, she filled out to become decorative scenery in dozens of films until *Gold of Naples* ('55) made her Italy's top box-office attraction. Her Hollywood breakthrough came at age 21 in her first two English-language films, the treasure-huntin' yarn *Boy on a Dolphin* and the war drama *The Pride and the Passion* (both in '57). Her critical breakthrough came at age 26 in Vittorio De Sica's *Two Women* ('61)—she was rewarded with a Best Actress Oscar, the first ever given to a woman in a foreign-language film.

Showing her range, she followed with some high-profile epics (*The Fall of the Roman Empire*, '64), some sexy comedies (*Marriage Italian Style*, '64, another Oscar nomination), adventure movies (the Gregory Peck spy thriller *Arabesque*, '66), and many more in the '60s. Throughout these years she was hailed as one of the world's sexiest stars, but the irony was that this glamorous bombshell with 38-24-38 measurements was most memorable when playing earthy working-class women.

But *Playboy* saw the riches beneath the rags—an August '60 pictorial lavished praise on her "unforgettably opulent figure," alliterating her as a "superlatively sensuous" and "classically curvaceous creature." In the '70s, Sophia crawled out of the crater left when *Man of La Mancha* ('72) bombed to make two dozen more movies that took her into the '90s and attracted a new generation of fans. After 50 years of perform-

September 1, 1966—The first Emma Peel episode of *The Avengers* airs in the U.S. ☮ September 2, 1940—Actress Beverly Sanders is born in Hollywood.
September 2, 1943—Singer Rosalind Ashford of Martha and the Vandellas is born in Detroit.
September 2, 1966—*The Farmer's Daughter* with Inger Stevens concludes its three-season run in primetime.

ing, she's received most of the lifetime-achievement honors available, including one at the Oscars in '91 "for a career rich with memorable performances that has added permanent luster to our art form." She's also written a cookbook and pitched her own eyewear and perfume. Sophia Loren—more than a film legend, a lifestyle.

EVERYBODY LOVES SOMEBODY

A smitten Cary Grant romantically wined and dined her as *The Pride and the Passion* was being filmed in Spain, even though he was already married. Sophia turned him down and instead married producer Carlo Ponti, whom she had met in the early '50s when he judged her in a beauty contest. However, five years after the wedding, with rumors of affairs on both sides and problems with the legality of the marriage in Italy, Sophia divorced Ponti in '62, then remarried him in France in '66. While she was linked to several prominent movie stars, she has emerged as a devoted wife and mother. Her sons have grown up to work in the arts (one as a classical conductor, the other as a filmmaker). Sophia and Carlo live in Europe; in 2006 they listed their 38-acre "retreat" near Thousand Oaks, California for $8.9 million.

MY BACK PAGES

In one of the most famous photos in Hollywood history, Sophia sat next to Jayne Mansfield at Romanoff's and stared incredulously as Jayne popped out of her low-cut top. . . . Sophia reportedly was going to play the love interest in Hitchcock's classic *North by Northwest*, but contractual problems kept her out and she was replaced by Eva Marie Saint. . . . Incredibly, Italy put her in jail in '82—Sophia served about half of her husband's 30-day sentence for tax evasion. . . . Sophia has said she still cuts and dyes her hair herself, and she's always maintained that she's never had any kind of cosmetic surgery. . . . On the *Playboy* list of the century's 100 sexiest stars, Sophia ranked sixth, one step ahead of Liz Taylor. . . . "I have no regrets," she once said, "regret only makes wrinkles."

The redheaded glamour girl and brown-eyed sweetheart booked a three-hour tour and got shipwrecked for three years.

TAKIN' CARE OF BUSINESS

What were the male castaways thinking? None of the three single guys on *Gilligan's Island*—not the Skipper, Professor, or Gilligan—ever made a serious play for the only two girls in town (or in this case, in jungle). And one of those girls had been in *Playboy*! In fact, New York-born Tina Blacker had a long, varied career before she was Tina Louise, famous castaway. "Debutante of the Year" in '53, she made lots of TV appearances in the '50s, worked on Broadway in *Two's Company* and in *Li'l Abner* as sexy Appassionata Von Climax, performed as a nightclub singer and even recorded an LP of Cole Porter songs in '57 called *Time for Tina*. Poised for stardom, she won a '59 Golden Globe as the Most Promising Newcomer. However, she was unhappy in the early '60s with the direction her Hollywood career was heading, so she moved to Italy in search of better roles in foreign films.

Eighteen months later she returned and in '64 became an island girl. That year, Sherwood Schwartz was creating *Gilligan's Island*, with one of the castaways to be modeled on Jayne Mansfield. When Jayne allegedly rejected the part, 30-year-old Tina got it, and eternal cult popularity was hers. *Gilligan's Island* ran from '64–'67 and has lived on ever since in reruns. The show raised far more questions than it ever answered: why would the Howells bring bags of cash? Why would everybody pack so many clothes for a short cruise? How come they could build a record player and a car but they couldn't fix a two-foot hole in the boat?

On the show Tina had a flair for comedy, occasionally sang, did a masterful Marilyn impression, and showed off a figure curvy enough to make her a featured femme in eight

September 2, 1966—*The Addams Family* with Carolyn Jones concludes its two-season run in primetime.
September 2, 1968—Jerry Lewis stages his third telethon for Muscular Dystrophy.
September 2, 1969—*Star Trek* with William Shatner concludes its three-season run in primetime.

Tina Louise

different issues of *Playboy* in the '60s. But later she told a journalist that she didn't even include the show on her résumé. She got more TV shows in the '70s (including a recurring role on *Dallas*) and beyond; she was also featured in almost two dozen post-'60s movies, usually of the unspectacular made-for-TV variety. In '97 Tina wrote a book about her childhood called *Sunday*, and she has worked to promote literacy in grade schools as a volunteer reading tutor on the island where she now resides, Manhattan. In 2001 another talent emerged—a New York gallery ran a one-woman exhibition of her paintings.

Like Tina, Reno-born Dawn Wells wasn't always a castaway. Miss Nevada and a Miss America contestant in '59, Dawn's early light was shining in lots of '50s and '60s TV shows. But not until that fateful trip on the *Minnow* did she become a star. Legend has it that when *Gilligan's Island* was being cast, Raquel Welch was one of the actresses who auditioned for the Mary Ann part (Mary Ann? Not Ginger?). Dawn, however, was the very personification of a naïve Kansas cutie, something akin to Dorothy in *The Wizard of Oz* but without the dog. Mary Ann was rarely at the center of the show's plots; in fact, she and the Professor weren't even mentioned in the original version of the theme song.

Though not the dazzler that Tina Louise's Ginger was on the show, Dawn's Mary Ann was always pretty, with a timeless country-girl appeal that still works today. Her clothes weren't always demure gingham, either; some of her best outfits on the show involved boots and a short skirt (yet another example of the castaways' bizarre packing strategy).

After the show's three-year run, Dawn returned a decade later to do the three related TV movies—*Rescue from* . . . ('78), *The Castaways on* . . . ('79), and *The Harlem Globetrotters on* . . . ('81)—plus the animated *Gilligan's Planet* in '82 (doing the voices of both Mary Ann and Ginger). Her screen résumé is fleshed out with minor movies and over 100 appearances on TV series and talk shows. She's also produced children's TV broadcasts, and late in the '90s she hosted her own fishing show called *Dawn Wells' Reel Adventures*.

Branching into other arenas, she's created her own line of clothes for the physically challenged (the Wishing Wells Collection, "special clothes for special people"). Now based in Idaho, she tours as a motivational speaker, teaches acting at the Dawn Wells Film Actors Boot Camp in Wyoming, and is an active supporter of wildlife causes. But Mary Ann is always close by: in '93 Dawn published *Mary Ann's "Gilligan's Island" Cookbook* (sprinkling recipes like Ginger's Snaps and Gilligan Stew with show anecdotes), and later she did a national commercial for Western Union in which she played Mary Ann and

September 2, 2001—Heart surgeon Christiaan Barnard dies. ☮ September 3, 1942—Al Jardine of the Beach Boys is born in Lima, Ohio.
September 3, 1966—"Sunshine Superman" by Donovan hits #1. ☮ September 3, 1969—Elvis Presley's *The Trouble with Girls* opens.
September 4, 1961—Ike and Tina Turner's "It's Gonna Work Out Fine" hits the charts.

Dawn Wells

revealed that she had married—ta da!—the Professor!

EVERYBODY LOVES SOMEBODY

Tina was married in '66 to Les Crane, a late-night talk-show host, and they had one daughter. The couple divorced in '70. Dawn's marriage ended in the mid-'60s.

MY BACK PAGES

According to the book *Inside Gilligan's Island,* when Tina was pitched the Ginger role, she was told that the show would be about her, with six others along as supporting players. . . . In the '78 TV movie *Return from Gilligan's Island* Ginger was played by Judith Baldwin—Tina said at the time that she wanted to break away from the role. . . . When the *Minnow* ran aground, Ginger was about to play Cleopatra in Broadway's *Pyramid for Two*. . . . Before she became an actress Dawn was training to be a ballerina. . . . Mary Ann supposedly had an Aunt Martha and Uncle George back home in Winfield, Kansas, and she usually did all the cooking on the island (coconut cream pie was a specialty, though who knows where the dairy products came from). . . . Mary Ann's last name on the show was Summers—other character names were Skipper Jonas Grumby, Thurston's wife Lovey Howell (some sources claim her first name was Eunice) plus science teacher Professor Roy Hinkley and Willie Gilligan (the first name was never used).

Lulu and Judy Geeson

This big-voiced Scot and cute British bird took the world "from crayons to perfume" in '67.

TAKIN' CARE OF BUSINESS

Born seven weeks apart, these two cute young actresses made their '60s splashes with the same hit movie, *To Sir, With Love* ('67). Born in Scotland, Lulu was a child star performing in public at age 9 and singing in clubs with a group called the Gleneagles while barely in her teens. Spotted by a talent scout, in '64 15-year-old Lulu (a peppy alternative to her given name, Marie Lawrie) and her renamed backup band, the Luvvers, made it into the Top 10 of the U.K. charts with a raucous remake of the Isley Brothers' "Shout." By '65 she was touring and recording as a solo act and also getting TV exposure.

Lulu

September 4, 1965—Marianne Faithfull's "Summer Nights" hits the charts.
September 4, 1967—Jerry Lewis stages his second Muscular Dystrophy telethon.
September 4, 1967—*Gilligan's Island* with Bob Denver concludes its three-season run in primetime.

The Lulupalooza phenomenon crossed the pond in '67 with *To Sir, With Love*. Not only did Lulu have a prominent role as a precocious London schoolgirl, but she sang the movie's lush theme too, pumping heartache into the provocative plea, "What can I give you in return?" The movie was a smash, the song quickly leaped to #1 in the U.S., and red-haired Lulu was a blazing star. She followed up with several more popular songs in the U.K., hosted her own BBC variety show, *It's Lulu*, and sang a song that hit number 007, the theme to the Bond flick *The Man with the Golden Gun* ('74).

Judy Geeson

More albums and U.K. hits followed into the 2000s, including a re-recording of "Shout" in '86 and the dancy "Independence" and "I'm Back for More" in '93. Expanding her skills, she wrote her autobiography in '85 and co-wrote Tina Turner's Grammy-nominated hit "I Don't Wanna Fight" in '94. Throughout the years Lulu has continued to make appearances in various screen and stage productions (especially a fun recurring role on the British comedy series *Absolutely Fabulous*).

The friendly young cutie who got Sidney Poitier out onto the dance floor in *To Sir, With Love* was Judy Geeson, an 18-year-old British actress who had been working her way up through British TV since '63. Tall, blonde, and leggy, she looked like the prototypical swingin' London girl and so played precocious girls in British movies for the next few years, especially in the fine *Three Into Two Won't Go* ('69). Smaller movie parts, lower-budget movies, and various TV roles carried her through the '80s; in the '90s she made two dozen appearances as snobby Maggie Conway on the popular sitcom *Mad About You*, and has kept busy into the 2000s with stage and TV work. Both Judy and Lulu reprised their roles (and still looked great doing it) for *To Sir, With Love 2* ('96).

EVERYBODY LOVES SOMEBODY

In '69 20-year-old Lulu married a Bee Gee, Maurice Gibb, with another Gibb brother, Robin, standing as the best man. Lulu divorced her Gibb in '74, married a hairdresser that same year, had a son in '78 and a divorce in '92. Judy was married for the second half of the '80s to longtime actor/TV director Kristoffer Tabori, the son of actress Viveca Lindfors and director Don Siegel.

MY BACK PAGES

On Lulu's *To Sir, With Love* album in '67, one of the arrangers was John Paul Jones, who would later play bass for Led Zeppelin. . . . In 2000 Lulu was awarded an O.B.E. (Order of the British Empire). . . . Judy's sister is British actress Sally Geeson, who appeared in numerous movies and shows in the '60s–'70s. . . . Judy is the proprietress of a charming antiques shop, Blanch & Co., near Beverly Hills.

Loretta Lynn

Straight-talkin', women-liberatin', song-writin' Loretta rose up from poverty to become one of the most influential singers of the '60s.

TAKIN' CARE OF BUSINESS

Loretta's impact on the '60s is not measured by her many musical accomplishments, but by her status as a symbol of women's rights. Loretta broke through social barriers so that women everywhere, from those who were strong and

September 5, 1939—Actor George Lazenby is born in Goulburn, Australia. ☮ September 5, 1940—Actress Raquel Welch is born in Chicago.
September 5, 1960—American sprinter Wilma Rudolph wins her second gold medal at the 1960 Olympics.
September 5, 1960—Annette Funicello's "Pineapple Princess" hits the charts.

independent to those who wanted to be strong and independent, could find something to admire about this simple country lady who fought through years of struggles to become one of the most successful women of the '60s.

It was easy to identify with Loretta: while pretty, she wasn't a staggering beauty, and while successful, she had real-life problems to deal with. And Loretta's message was even stronger because she didn't just sing those controversial songs, she wrote them. Thanks to Loretta's pioneering work in the '60s, great stars like Dolly Parton and Tanya Tucker were able to flourish in the '70s. In the '80s President George Bush summed up her impact succinctly: "Loretta is as close as you get to a household word in this country."

Born into a dirt-poor family, Loretta grew up in Kentucky's Appalachian Mountains in a tarpaper cabin. By her early teens she had taught herself guitar and was writing her own songs. Soon she had her own group, Loretta Lynn and the Trailblazers, and was playing in local towns. In '59 she and her husband Doolittle Lynn drove to California to try to land a record deal. Every studio turned them down until one producer helped her cut a record, "I'm a Honky Tonk Girl," which became a modest hit in '60 thanks to her relentless promotion: while her four kids stayed with her brother, Loretta and her husband drove around the country and pitched the song to small-town radio stations. Their determination paid off, and by '62 she had moved to Nashville, recorded a Top 10 hit ("Success"), and was being invited onto the Grand Ole Opry for 21 consecutive weeks by popular demand.

By the mid-'60s she was the "queen of the blue-collar blues," establishing herself as a musical force on a national level. Her biggest hits late in the decade included "You Ain't Woman Enough," "Don't Come Home A-Drinkin' (With Lovin' on Your Mind)," and "Fist City." Throughout these years she was touring by bus almost every day of the year, usually performing two shows a night. After the '60s, she enjoyed more success and became the household name George Bush mentioned.

In '70 her song "Coal Miner's Daughter" hit #1 on the country charts, Loretta became the first female millionaire in country music, and she bought a Tennessee mansion. She released more hit albums (*Home*, '75), teamed up with Conway Twitty for awhile, and in the middle of the decade she wrote and sang her most controversial songs, "The Pill" (a #1 hit but blacklisted at some radio stations) and "Rated X."

As Loretta's popularity swelled, she made the cover of *People* and *Newsweek* in the '70s, her autobiography, *Coal Miner's Daughter*, was a bestseller, and Sissy Spacek won an Oscar playing her in the movie. By this time Loretta had five dozen Top 20 singles and 15 #1 albums. She continued to record in the '80s and '90s, and *Still Woman Enough* in 2000 and the Grammy-winning *Van Lear Rose* (produced by Jack White of the White Stripes) in 2004 brought her a fifth decade of critical acclaim.

EVERYBODY LOVES SOMEBODY

At age 11 Loretta Webb met Doolittle Lynn, an older boy who married her when she was only 13. Within a year she was pregnant, and Doolittle left her for another girl for four months, but he came back in her seventh month of pregnancy. He then hitchhiked to Washington state, got a job on a farm there, and sent for Loretta, who arrived soon after by train. They lived on the farm, where Doolittle had set up a still and sold moonshine to the locals (he got the nickname "Mooney" because of it).

Loretta cleaned houses, picked strawberries, and cooked for the other farmhands. At age 18 she had four kids; at 29 she was a grandmother. In '64 she gave birth to twin girls who were raised by Doolittle while Loretta continued on her brutal touring schedule. Health problems resulted as Loretta succumbed to migraines and an addiction to prescribed pain pills. During her touring days she was hospitalized nine times for exhaustion. Her long relationship with Mooney ended with his death in '95.

MY BACK PAGES

One of her sisters is Crystal Gayle, who had her own monster hit in the '70s, "Don't It Make My Brown Eyes Blue". . . . In the '80s Loretta bought the town of Hurricane Mills, Tennessee, and opened it as a tourist attraction, complete with replicas of the coal mine where her father had worked and the tiny house where Loretta had grown up. . . . The White Stripes dedicated their blockbuster album *White Blood Cells* to Loretta. . . . Loretta's won tons of awards during her career, including 11 consecutive years as the Music City News #1 Female Artist, a #65 ranking on VH1's list of great rock women, and induction into the Country Music Hall of Fame in '88.

Sue Lyon

She was the luscious title character in *Lolita*, making her the very definition of tantalizingly precocious jailbait.

TAKIN' CARE OF BUSINESS

"How did they ever make a movie of *Lolita*?" That was the ad line used to publicize the controversial '62 movie in which Sue Lyon made her big-screen debut. First published in '55, Vladimir Nabokov's book had already been hailed as a literary masterpiece, but the book's love affair between a preteen and a middle-aged man was still scandalous and had caused the book to be temporarily banned in France—"I'm going to put off reading Lolita for six years," joked Groucho Marx, "I'm waiting until she turns 18."

A big-eyed blonde 16-year-old with a knowing smile, young Iowa-born Sue was a perfectly pouty nymphet, her alluring bikini action making her seem older and wiser than her years and less shocking than Nabokov's original prepubescent child. Sue's Lolita Haze perfectly captured the essence of a teen on the cusp between innocent adolescence and jaded adulthood, not too old to play with a hula hoop but already bored by her older lover's advances.

Her career off and running, Sue's sweet-but-seductive face landed on the August '62 cover of *Cosmo*, she won a Golden Globe in '63 as the Most Promising Newcomer, and soon she was whisked away to Mexico to shoot *The Night of the Iguana* with Hollywood heavyweights Richard Burton and Ava Gardner. In *The Flim-Flam Man* ('67), she was the cutest thing in blue jeans until nothing came between Brooke Shields and her Calvins a decade later. Unfortunately, as Sue matured starring roles came less frequently (*Evel Knievel*, '71), minor movies replaced the high-profile films she'd done as a teenager, and after a decade of unremarkable projects she left the screen for good in the mid-'80s.

EVERYBODY LOVES SOMEBODY

In '64 Sue married her longtime boyfriend Hampton Fancher III (an actor who later wrote the *Blade Runner* screenplay), but they divorced in '65. She had another one-year marriage from '70–'71, and another from '73–'74 when, according to legend, she married and divorced a convicted murderer who was serving a life sentence in prison. A fourth marriage, this one in '85, has endured and today Sue supposedly lives a quiet life in L.A.

MY BACK PAGES

In her early teen years, one of Sue's best friends, and the person who introduced her to the book *Lolita*, was young Michelle Phillips. . . . According to an article about her in *Movielife Yearbook* in '66, 20-year-old Sue was in a serious car accident that caused her "to realize she's in the wrong business" and briefly consider becoming a teacher.

Meredith MacRae

This strawberry-blonde beauty was a TV regular in the '60s.

TAKIN' CARE OF BUSINESS

Show biz was in Meredith MacRae's blood: Her father, Gordon MacRae, was the handsome singing star of movie musicals like *Carousel* and *Oklahoma!*; her mother, Sheila MacRae, starred in *The Sheila MacRae Show*; and her younger sis Heather played the cute preppy in the "giant runaway breast" segment of Woody Allen's *Everything You Always Wanted to Know About Sex*. Born in 1944 on a Texas army base and raised in Southern California, Meredith appeared in several of her dad's movies when she was a kid, and then as a UCLA student she turned up as a beach girl in several beach flicks.

On TV she was an appealing star on two of the decade's most popular comedies. On *My Three Sons*, Meredith played pretty Sally Ann Morrison, girlfriend and then wife to the eldest son, from '63–'65. She left the show when the son (Tim Considine) did, and both were written out with the explanation that they were moving away so he could take a teaching job. On *Petticoat Junction*, Jeannine Riley played Billie Jo from '63–'65, then blonde Gunilla Hutton was a new Billie Jo for the '65–'66 season, followed by Meredith as the third and longest-lasting Billie Jo from'66–'70. The show was an instant hit, generated merchandise about the characters, and spun off *Green Acres* in '65, which was set in the same town of Hooterville (in fact the owner of the general store was a regular on both shows).

After the '60s Meredith continued to work, most notably as an Emmy-winning host on the long-running talk show *Mid-Morning L.A.* A woman of diverse talents, she also performed nationwide in clubs and theatres, worked as a successful TV producer, had a successful beauty video called *The 15-Minute Acupressure Facelift*, was an acclaimed lecturer, and recorded over a dozen bestselling books on tape. Health issues hit her hard in the late '90s, and after undergoing three brain surgeries and a hip operation, Meredith died of a brain tumor in 2000. Because she loved scuba diving, her ashes were scattered at sea.

EVERYBODY LOVES SOMEBODY

In 1969 Meredith married actor Greg Mullavey, who was six years her senior and later the star of *Mary Hartman, Mary Hartman*. Their daughter, Allison, was born in '74. Meredith and Greg divorced in '92, and then in '95 she married the CEO of a Fortune 500 company.

September 7, 1923—Actor Peter Lawford is born in London. ☮ September 7, 1960—Sprinter Wilma Rudolph wins her third gold medal at the Olympics.
September 7, 1966—*The Dick Van Dyke Show* with Mary Tyler Moore concludes its five-season run in primetime.
September 7, 1967—*The Flying Nun* with Sally Field debuts. ☮ September 7, 1978—Keith Moon of the Who dies of an overdose in England.

MY BACK PAGES

Meredith cut two singles on her own during the '60s, plus she and the other *Petticoat Junction* girls made two records together and performed on *The Tonight Show*. . . . A tireless fundraiser, Meredith received many awards and commendations for her contributions to society and medical research.

The Mamas and the Papas

Friends, lovers, and spouses blended into one of the great hit-making groups of the decade.

TAKIN' CARE OF BUSINESS

Though the group only lasted from '65 to '68, the Mamas and the Papas had a significant impact on the history of rock 'n' roll, symbolizing the sophisticated folk-rock sound that was coming out of Southern California in the mid-'60s. Songs by the Mamas and the Papas were always well-crafted productions *à la* the Beatles, with intricate harmonies *à la* the Beach Boys, but ultimately they had a sound that was all their own. When the group was really cooking, the two-men-two-women lineup had a unique, timeless appeal that resulted in 13 hit singles and a place in the Rock and Roll Hall of Fame.

Born in Baltimore, Cass Elliot hit New York in '60 as an 18-year-old wannabe actress, but disappointments led her to try a singing career instead. Jobs in small Greenwich Village coffeehouses got her into a group, The Big Three, in '63, where she met Canadian folksinger Denny Doherty, who later left to join John Phillips's folk-rock band, the Journeymen. John was a tall South Carolina songwriter who'd been leading groups since the late '50s.

Cass went back to singing in small clubs until '65, when she met John and his wife Michelle at a party; when John, Denny, and Michelle took a vacation to the Virgin Islands, Cass followed and supported everyone with her credit card (as detailed later in the song "Creeque Alley"). When the money was gone, everyone went home, Cass to L.A., the others to New York. At Cass's invitation, by the fall of '65 all four were sharing an L.A. apartment and rehearsing as a group called the Inner Circle. Late in the year they changed their name to the Mamas and the Papas (taken from biker slang), they performed for producer Lou Adler, and in December the group's first album, *If You Can Believe Your Eyes and Ears*, introduced "Monday, Monday" and "California Dreamin'."

As a vocal quartet the group was matchless: John devised their complex sound and sang harmony; Denny sang male lead; and Cass's brassy, jazzy vocals blended perfectly with Michelle's sweet soprano. John was inspired by the group's interactions to write many of their hits, including "Go Where You Wanna Go," "Words of Love," and "I Saw Her Again." Quickly, the group was speeding down the rock 'n' roll highway—tours, huge celebrity parties, travel by Lear jet, impulsive exotic vacations, shopping sprees for cars paid with cash, and the obligatory drug excesses. In June of '67 they hit their peak when they coordinated, and were the closing act for, the prominent Monterey International Pop Festival, aligning themselves with other great '60s acts like Janis Joplin, Jimi Hendrix, and the Who. The ride ended quickly, however, as band tensions led to a break-up in '68.

Cass quickly scored a hit with her first solo single, "Dream a Little Dream of Me," she headlined Caesar's Palace in Las Vegas (a first for a rock star), and soon she was appearing on TV variety shows, doing comedy sketches, performing songs, and gaining popularity as a precocious, brilliant, funny interviewee and interviewer (she even hosted *The Tonight Show*). Her health was clearly suffering by '71, however—burdened with her 300+ pounds of weight, she was having trouble breathing and walking. Cass released several solo albums and in July '74 she performed at London's Palladium, but after a night of partying she died of a heart attack.

Michelle, meanwhile, was talented, beautiful, and well-connected, so after the group disbanded she established

September 8, 1925—Actor Peter Sellers is born in Hampshire, England.
September 8, 1932—Legendary singer Patsy Cline is born in Winchester, Virginia. ☮ September 8, 1937—Actress Virna Lisi is born in Italy.
September 8, 1960—*Let's Make Love* with Marilyn Monroe opens. ☮ September 8, 1963—*The Jetsons* concludes its one-season run in primetime.

a successful career in Hollywood. With her first major movie, *Dillinger* ('73), she was nominated for a Golden Globe as the Most Promising Newcomer, and a long list of movie credits and regular roles on prominent TV shows followed. Along the way she recorded a solo album and wrote an entertaining book about the group called *California Dreamin'*.

Denny has enjoyed a long, productive career that has included solo albums, many stage appearances (including a run on Broadway), and TV shows. John's post-'60s work came in fits and starts as serious drug and health problems overtook him. He wrote movie scores and a failed Broadway musical in the '70s, went to jail and rehab in the early '80s, wrote a candid, self-critical autobiography that detailed his debauched drug life, and toured into the '90s with various iterations of a new Mamas and Papas. Unfortunately, just as he was gaining momentum with a solo recording career, John died of heart failure in 2001.

EVERYBODY LOVES SOMEBODY

In '63 Cass married one of her bandmates in the Big Three so he could avoid the draft. Cass later fell for Denny and asked him to marry her. Instead he had an affair with Michelle that almost split the Mamas and the Papas apart. In August of '66 Cass announced that she was pregnant by an unidentified father (she joked that it was an "immaculate conception"), and a daughter arrived in '67. In '68 Cass had her marriage annulled and she careened through a wild life that included a brief marriage to a younger reporter in '71.

Michelle was a 17-year-old model in San Francisco who quickly fell for John in '61, and they married at the end of '62. The main speed bump during their marriage was the affair Michelle had with Denny—John, with Denny and Cass's support, expelled Michelle from the group in '66. Another singer, Jill Gibson, was brought in for several concert dates, a time Michelle later called "the most desperate, painful, hysterical months of my life." After Michelle begged to get back in, Jill was excused and the reformed Mamas and

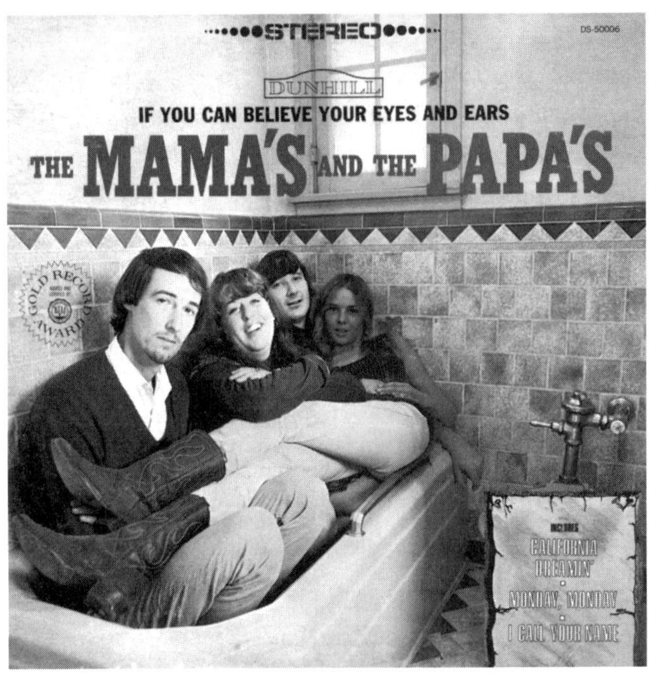

the Papas continued on for another year. In '68 Michelle had a daughter, but by the end of the year Michelle and John had broken up for good. Michelle then took up with actor Dennis Hopper, a relationship that culminated in a disturbing eight-day marriage in '70. During her Hollywood years she had relationships with several prominent stars; in the '80s she gave birth to one son and adopted another. Today, still living in L.A., she radiates happiness and looks more beautiful than ever.

Denny was married in the early '70s, with one child, and then remarried in the late '70s, with two more kids. Finally, before he met Michelle John had been married for five years and already had two kids, one of whom, Mackenzie, went on to a successful acting career (*One Day at a Time*). Chynna, his daughter with Michelle, later got famous with the '90s group Wilson Phillips. After Michelle, John remarried and had two more kids, with daughter Bijou growing up to become a model/actress/singer. After a dozen years this marriage, like the previous two, ended in divorce. John was married a fourth time from '95 until his death.

September 8, 1965—Actress Dorothy Dandridge dies at 41 in Hollywood.
September 8, 1965—*My Living Doll* with Julie Newmar concludes its one-season run in primetime.
September 8, 1966—*Star Trek* with William Shatner debuts. ☮ September 8, 1966—*That Girl* with Marlo Thomas debuts.

MY BACK PAGES

John told the story that Cass was unable to hit all the high notes he was writing in his songs until she accidentally banged her head on a pipe. . . . The night before she died, Cass called Michelle from London and cried with joy about her successful Palladium shows. . . . After Cass's death a cruel rumor circulated that she had choked on a ham sandwich, simply because a sandwich was found in her room, but the coroner clearly stated that a heart attack had killed her. . . . When Michelle and John were trying to name Chynna, Michelle suggested the name India, but John replied, "You might as well call it North Vietnam or China—ah, China, that's nice". . . . In '96, Denny was inducted into the Canadian Music Hall of Fame. . . . In a TV bio, Michelle fondly recalled the group's glory years: "Most wonderful things are not meant to last forever, they're special, they're unique. . . . And that's what the Mamas and the Papas were."

These two sluggers thrilled the sports world in '61.

TAKIN' CARE OF BUSINESS

Home runs are much more commonplace in the 21st century than they were in the '60s. Starting from 1901, it took baseball until '49 to accumulate nine seasons in which a major-league player hit 50 or more home runs; by contrast, there were nine 50-homer seasons just from '95–2005. When Mickey Mantle and Roger Maris were chasing the home run record in '61, only one player had ever hit 60 homers; nowadays, 60 seems much more attainable (60 is the new 50), and two players have even reached 70. That's why the M & M chase in '61 was so sensational—playing on the same team in the biggest city, they were climbing to Ruthian heights at a time when the Babe was still the ultimate slugger, and had been since he hit his 60 in '27.

Mickey was the popular favorite. As an Oklahoma high schooler he was a multi-sports star who suffered leg injuries that would trouble him the rest of his life. A switch-hitting shortstop in the minors, the Yankees called him up and in '52 put him in centerfield, anointing him as the heir apparent to the legendary Joe DiMaggio. Mickey didn't disappoint—he soon established himself as one of the game's fastest, strongest, greatest all-around players. He won the Triple Crown (a .353 average, 52 homers, 130 RBI) in '56, took three MVP trophies, set long-standing World Series records, and clubbed what many believe to be the longest home runs ever hit (one left Tiger Stadium and was estimated to have gone over 600 feet). And with a '61 contract of $75,000 a year, he was the highest-paid player in the game.

Meanwhile, Minnesota-born Roger was a baseball and football star at a North Dakota high school. He had a scholarship to play football at the University of Oklahoma, but he decided to play pro baseball instead, so he signed with the Cleveland Indians and made it to the majors in '57. In his third year he was an All-Star, and in his fourth year he was a Yankee, leading the league in RBI, finishing second in homers with 39 (one back of Mickey), winning a Gold Glove, and being named the A.L. MVP.

The '61 season didn't start out with any foreshadowing of the drama to come. By the end of April, Roger had just one homer, but four months later he was the first player ever to reach 50 before September, and Mickey was hot on his tail with 46. Crowds filled every stadium they played in, reporters hounded the pair, and America tensed for a dramatic finish. The race took its heaviest toll on Roger—often booed as he got closer and closer to the hallowed Babe, his hair started to fall out from the stress.

The sprint to October was interrupted when Mickey missed part of September and stalled at 54, his career high. Five days before the end of the season Roger tied the Babe at 60, and on the last day he passed him with a game-winning homer against the Red Sox. After the season Roger was again named the league's MVP. Injured for much of their remaining careers, both men continued to play for the Yanks for most of the decade.

Mickey, having moved from centerfield to first base in '67 because of his bum legs, finally retired in '69 with 536 home runs and numerous team records. Inducted into the Hall of Fame five years later in his first year of eligibility, the Mick became a top draw at autograph shows, and after several business failures his midtown Manhattan sports bar flourished.

Unfortunately, his years of drinking caught up with him in the '90s when serious health problems drove him into rehab. Despite having a liver transplant in '95, he died later that year and was eulogized by announcer Bob Costas as "a fragile hero to whom we had an emotional attachment so strong and lasting that it defied logic." To this day his signed memorabilia is among the bestselling in sports.

Roger's career with the Yankees ended when he was traded to the Cardinals before the '67 season; he retired at the end of '68 with 275 home runs, having played in five straight World Series with the Yankees in the '60s, plus two more with the Cards. After years of working as a beer distributor away from the spotlight, Roger died of cancer in '85, only 51 years old. He's never made the Hall.

EVERYBODY LOVES SOMEBODY

In '51 Mickey married an Oklahoma girl from his hometown. She and their four sons all had problems with alcohol at different times in their lives; two of his sons would die of illnesses before Mickey. Long known for his partying lifestyle, Mickey was separated from his wife in the '80s. Roger, meanwhile, was married to his high school sweetheart for almost 30 years right up until his death, and they had six kids.

MY BACK PAGES

Both players had their uniform numbers (Mickey's #7, Roger's #9) retired by the Yankees. . . . Both players appeared

League Leaders in Home Runs

National League		American League
	1960	
Ernie Banks (41)		Mickey Mantle (40)
	1961	
Orlando Cepeda (46)		Roger Maris (61)
	1962	
Willie Mays (49)		Harmon Killebrew (48)
	1963	
Hank Aaron, Willie McCovey (44)		Harmon Killebrew (45)
	1964	
Willie Mays (47)		Harmon Killebrew (49)
	1965	
Willie Mays (52)		Tony Conigliaro (32)
	1966	
Hank Aaron (44)		Frank Robinson (49)
	1967	
Hank Aaron (39)		Harmon Killebrew, Carl Yastrzemski (44)
	1968	
Willie McCovey (36)		Frank Howard (44)
	1969	
Willie McCovey (45)		Harmon Killebrew (49)

Harmon Killebrew

in two '62 movies—the baseball-themed family film *Safe at Home!* and the Cary Grant/Doris Day comedy *That Touch of Mink*. . . . Though drinking was a part of his baseball legacy (he's said to have homered while either drunk or hung over), Mickey later counseled others to not do what he did and lamented how great he might have been if he'd taken better care of himself. . . . Today the Mickey Mantle Foundation helps support organ donations. . . . Some critics disparaged Roger's record because he hit his 61 in 162 games, eight games more than Ruth. . . . Until Mark McGwire hit 70 homers in '98, Roger's record stood for 37 years, three years longer than Ruth's record.

Pete Maravich

A scoring machine, Pistol Pete was also basketball's super showman.

TAKIN' CARE OF BUSINESS

College basketball's purest scorer was born in Pennsylvania and was practicing trick moves and ball-handling as a child. After starring at high schools in North and South Carolina, in '66 he took his flamboyant game to Louisiana State University, where his dad, Press Maravich, was the coach. Pete was an immediate sensation on the freshman team (freshmen couldn't play varsity, unlike today) and poured in over 43 points per game.

For the next three years, Pete had the highest scoring average in the nation (over 44 points per game) and scored over 3,600 points for his career (all these impressive totals were compiled long before the three-point shot was in effect). He set NCAA records that still stand in almost every scoring category, but stats alone didn't endear him to fans—it was the way he played that made him a hoops legend.

With his long hair (for the time) flying and his baggy socks drooping around his low-top Converse All-Stars, Pete would drive fearlessly to the basket for a twisting lay-up; or he'd work his behind-the-back dribbles on top of the key for a deadly long-range bomb; or he'd make a quick through-the-legs pass to another driving teammate. Gunner, passer, dribbler, showman—Pete was the flashiest player on any court he ever played on.

As College Player of the Year in '70 he was a high draft pick by the NBA's Atlanta Hawks, where he played successfully (though sometimes injured, and only occasionally with his collegiate brilliance). He did make the All-Rookie team and several All-Star teams during his four years with the Hawks, but the team traded him to the New Orleans Jazz in '74. With the Jazz he enjoyed his finest pro seasons, finishing among the league's scoring leaders during the mid-'70s and being named a first-team All-Star in '76 and '77.

At decade's end, however, the slumping Jazz moved to Utah, Pete got waived as the team focused on younger stars, and he finished up his career with one season as a Boston Celtic. Seven years after he retired, Pete became the youngest player ever inducted into the Basketball Hall of Fame; a year later, Pete, only 40 years old, died of a heart attack while playing a pick-up basketball game.

September 9, 1961—Maria Beale Fletcher of North Carolina is crowned the 34th Miss America.
September 9, 1965—Sandy Koufax pitches a perfect game at Dodger Stadium.
September 9, 1966—*The Milton Berle Show* with Donna Loren debuts. ☮ September 9, 1967—Debra Barnes of Kansas is crowned the 40th Miss America.

EVERYBODY LOVES SOMEBODY

Pete was married in the mid-'70s and had two sons.

MY BACK PAGES

After he left the NBA Pete became a motivational speaker delivering messages about religion and family. . . . At LSU the 14,000-seat "Deaf Dome" is officially called the Pete Maravich Assembly Center.

Lee Marvin

The movies' toughest tough guy was the Oscar-winning star of several '60s classics.

TAKIN' CARE OF BUSINESS

Lee Marvin lived a life as tough as anything he played in the movies. A New York kid who was expelled from dozens of schools, he joined the Marines as a teenager and received a Purple Heart when he was wounded in battle in World War II. Back home, while working as a plumber at a community theatre in upstate New York, he got his first acting experience, which led him to Manhattan for acting classes and small stage roles. Bigger parts in successful Broadway dramas got him to Hollywood and some cool movies of the early '50s, especially as a biker challenging Marlon Brando in *The Wild One* ('53).

Later in the decade, after playing more movie bad guys, he got a juicy part as a detective in the *M Squad* series. Soon followed his remarkable run of movie heavies, hard cases, and action heroes—the vicious villain in *The Man Who Shot Liberty Valance* ('62), the rowdy vet who punched out John Wayne in *Donovan's Reef* ('63), the cold-blooded hitman in *The Killers* ('64), the dual roles in the Western comedy *Cat Ballou* ('65, bringing him an Oscar), the unintimidated leader of *The Dirty Dozen* ('67), and the icy assassin in *Point Blank* ('67).

Westerns, comedies, noir thrillers, war movies, Lee was believable in everything, always acting as if his fists were clenched, always with that steely stare and deep, growly voice (and prematurely white hair, too). Brave? He had to be to take on *Paint Your Wagon* ('69), the disastrous movie loosely based on a mildly successful '50s musical, but there he was brawling through the mud and croaking out songs (not sure who was braver in *Paint Your Wagon*: Lee, Clint Eastwood—who was making his singing debut—or the audience). More fistfights and guns filled his busy career into the late '80s, highlighted by *Prime Cut* ('72), *Emperor of the North* ('73), *The Big Red One* ('80), *Gorky Park* ('83), and a *Dirty Dozen* TV movie sequel, *The Next Mission* ('85). After he died of a heart attack at age 63, he was buried in Arlington National Cemetery.

EVERYBODY LOVES SOMEBODY

Lee was married twice, first from the early '50s into the mid-'60s, and then from the '70s until his death. In between was a relationship that became a tabloid sensation and a defining moment for future court battles. After he broke up with his live-in girlfriend, she sued him for financial support, saying

Oscars for Best Actor

1960–Burt Lancaster (*Elmer Gantry*)
1961–Maximilian Schell (*Judgement at Nuremberg*)
1962–Gregory Peck (*To Kill a Mockingbird*)
1963–Sidney Poitier (*Lilies of the Field*)
1964–Rex Harrison (*My Fair Lady*)
1965–Lee Marvin (*Cat Ballou*)
1966–Paul Scofield (*A Man for All Seasons*)
1967–Rod Steiger (*In the Heat of the Night*)
1968–Cliff Robertson (*Charly*)
1969–John Wayne (*True Grit*)

September 9, 1967—*Rowan and Martin's Laugh-In* debuts as a one-hour special.
September 10, 1929—Golfer Arnold Palmer is born in Youngstown, Pennsylvania.
September 10, 1934—Baseball star Roger Maris is born in Hibbing, Minnesota. ☮ September 10, 1939—John Lennon's ex-wife Cynthia Lennon is born.

that she'd given up her career for Lee. He denied any promises and fought her in court, and though she initially won the case, her award was only a small fraction of what she'd hoped for, a decision that Lee claimed was a victory for him. From then on the concept of "palimony" (a word newly coined for this case) for unmarried couples was forever established.

MY BACK PAGES

Supposedly Lee was named after a distant relative, General Robert E. Lee. . . . Part of Lee's acceptance speech when he won his Oscar: "Half of this probably belongs to a horse out there somewhere". . . . Lee was amazed when his *Paint Your Wagon* song "Wandering Star" became a million-selling hit in '69. . . . Two roles he's said to have turned down—the lead in *Patton* ('70), Quint in *Jaws* ('75).

Marcello Mastroianni and Federico Fellini

The Latin lover and master director spun movie magic in the early '60s.

TAKIN' CARE OF BUSINESS

As a young man in Italy during World War II, Marcello Mastroianni escaped from a Nazi prison camp and hid for the duration. After the war, he started working for a theatre company until he was discovered by film director Luchino Visconti, who made him a busy working actor through the '50s. But it was Federico Fellini who made Marcello an international star.

Federico had briefly tried to join the circus as a kid, then worked as a cartoonist and journalist before establishing himself in the mid-'50s as one of the world's most distinctive directors—by the time he teamed up with Marcello he'd already been nominated for several Oscars and two of his movies, *La Strada* ('54) and *Nights of Cabiria* ('57), had won Oscars as Best Foreign Film.

The haunting *La Dolce Vita* ('60) was Federico's visionary masterpiece, casting smart, soulful Marcello as a world-weary journalist on a dreamy search for meaning through Rome (his most famous encounter was with stunning Anita Ekberg as she splashed through the Trevi Fountain).

That the actor was representing the director seemed even more obvious in *8½* ('63), in which Marcello played a disillusioned, womanizing movie director who was again searching for meaning, again with Federico's signature dream-like images. They ultimately made four more movies together—*Roma* ('72), *City of Women* ('80), *Fred and Ginger* ('86), *Intervista* ('87)—none as influential as their classics of the early '60s, but all cementing their global reputations as admired filmmakers.

Marcello also made dozens of films for other directors and showed he was a subtle, charming actor who could effortlessly play comedy as well as drama. He was nominated for Best Actor for *Divorce Italian Style* ('61), *A Special Day* ('77), and *Dark Eyes* ('87). Federico got two more Best Director nominations for his post-'60s work—*Satyricon* ('70) and *Amarcord* ('73)—plus a writing nomination for *Casanova* ('76), and in '93 the Academy presented him with a special lifetime-achievement award in recognition of his long, accomplished career. Both men were born within four years of each other in the '20s, and they died within four years of each other in the '90s, Marcello from cancer, Federico from a heart attack.

EVERYBODY LOVES SOMEBODY

For over 45 years, Marcello was married to Italian actress Flora Carabella, with one child. Marcello and Flora were both in *Lunatics and Lovers* ('76). The French actress Chiara Mastroianni is the daughter of Marcello and Catherine Deneuve, his lover in the early '70s. Marcello was also in a serious relationship with actress Faye Dunaway. Federico was married for about 50 years, with a son who died in childhood.

September 10, 1948—Actress Judy Geeson is born in Sussex, England. ☮ September 10, 1960—Mickey Mantle hits his 600-foot HR. September 10, 1967—*The Mothers-in-Law* with Deborah Walley debuts. ☮ September 11, 1939—Singer Lola Falana is born in Camden, New Jersey. September 11, 1960—The Summer Olympics close in Rome, Italy.

MY BACK PAGES

While Marcello never won an Oscar, he was a big winner of many international film prizes, and in '65 the Golden Globes named him the World's Film Favorite. . . . He was paired with another Italian star, Sophia Loren, in over a dozen major films from the '50s–'90s, their best '60s pairing coming in Vittorio De Sica's *Marriage Italian Style* ('64). . . . *La Dolce Vita* is the movie that introduced *paparazzi* as the term for intrusive photographers. . . . There's long been speculation that the title of *8 ½* has sexual connotations, though cineastes also suggest that it represents the number of movies Federico had worked on up until then.

Peter Max

This immensely gifted (and immensely popular) artist provided the graphics for the Age of Aquarius.

TAKIN' CARE OF BUSINESS

In the late '60s, Peter Max's work was seen and his influence was felt everywhere and on everything—on dishes, sheets, clocks, posters, magazines, virtually anything, it seemed, that could show off his images—in media ranging from finger paint to oil, from charcoal to silk screen, from ceramic to video. Like Maxfield Parrish from decades before, he was a brilliant colorist creating gentle, dream-like pictures that were highly commercial and incredibly popular with all age groups. Even when he didn't work on something (the Beatles' wonderful animated film *Yellow Submarine,* for instance), it was assumed he did, that's how familiar his art was.

Peter was born in Germany and raised for 10 years in China, with stops in Tibet, South Africa, Israel and France before his family emigrated to America in '53. Informed by a range of early influences that included astronomy, comic books, classic movies, and modern photography, he studied

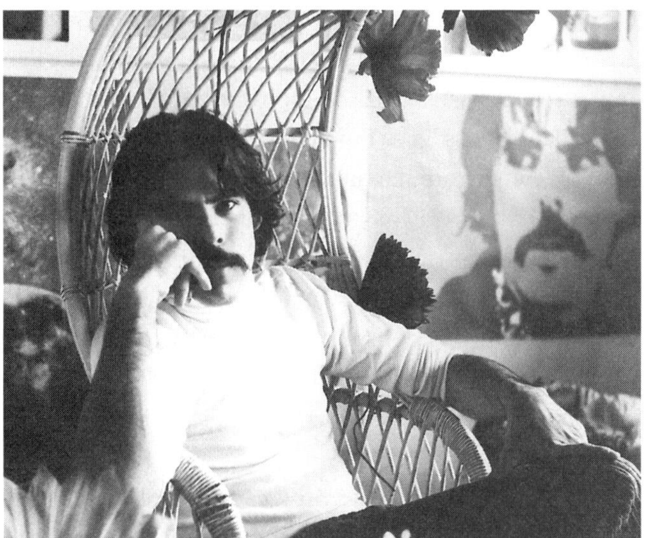

at several prestigious New York art schools, where his colorful, youthful ideas percolated. In the early '60s his graphic design for books and album covers brought him his first professional accolades, and in the mid-'60s his transcendent cosmic art brought fame and fortune.

Blending bright Day-Glo colors with sinuous lines and an innocent optimism perfect for an era blooming with joyous Flower Power, his graceful work suddenly adorned dozens of household items, wristwatches, billboards, silk stockings, key chains, tennis shoes, tea bags, and a *Life* magazine cover. Peter became a celebrity, his name became the shorthand definition of a style that everyone recognized, and ultimately something like a quarter-*billion* dollars worth of merchandise was sold. And while he didn't work directly with the Beatles, they knew his work, and he certainly inspired the artists who animated *Yellow Submarine* ('68), which holds up today as a beautiful tribute to his style and to the era he helped create.

Then, as quickly as he'd appeared, in '71 he walked away from his wildly successful commercial interests and withdrew to his studio, emerging only occasionally for special projects (the first 10-cent stamp among them). Able to pick and choose his commissions, he favored those that aided the environment and human rights: a Better World series of artworks, the enormous set for the Moscow Music Peace Festival in '89, posters for Bill Clinton's inauguration, stamps for the United Nations Earth Summit, among many, many others.

Famous around the world, in '89 he was given a section of the Berlin Wall to sculpt, and in '91 his one-man show at St. Petersberg's Hermitage Museum was the most attended show in Russia's history. Throughout, he's retained his positive outlook, his patriotism (many of his most recognizable works show the flag or the Statue of Liberty), and his boundless imagination (he still carries blank cards with him and draws constantly all day long).

Today his work is in the permanent collections of some of the world's most important museums, including New York's Museum of Modern Art; and Peter himself is as busy and as optimistic as ever, living in New York, overseeing an 80-person staff, supporting literally thousands of charities, still lean and still sporting the cool moustache that has made him the Beatle of the art world for over four decades now.

EVERYBODY LOVES SOMEBODY

Max has two grown kids, one a songwriter, the other a lawyer, from his first wife, a former beauty queen. In recent years he married a woman who's a professional ice skater.

MY BACK PAGES

More cool credits—Peter has been named the official artist for the Grammy Awards, the New Orleans Jazz Festival, the Woodstock Music Festival, the U.S. Open, World Cup USA, five Super Bowls, and the NHL All-Star Game. . . . He's also been credited with inventing the term "be-in" for a Central Park event and introducing tie-dyed clothes to the public. . . . Ambidextrous, Peter once created a painting using both hands simultaneously on Ed Sullivan's TV show. . . . For awhile Peter's car was a black Rolls-Royce decorated with psychedelic paint and decals.

Eugene McCarthy

The cerebral senator led a grass-roots presidential campaign that galvanized opposition to the Vietnam War.

TAKIN' CARE OF BUSINESS

A peaceable man in a turbulent time, Eugene McCarthy became a hero of young Americans in the late '60s when he spoke out against the ongoing Vietnam War. In his own youth, Eugene had studied literature and theology (at one time he seriously considered becoming a priest), and he had served with the Army Signal Corps during World War II. While teaching college economics in the late '40s he got elected to the House of Representatives from his home state of Minnesota; ten years later he won a Senate election that put him on the path to national prominence.

In the '60s Senator McCarthy was a strong supporter of liberal Democratic policies, especially in advocating civil rights and programs for the elderly. With more and more troops being sent to Vietnam, and no end to the war in sight, he loudly established his anti-war position and jumped into the '68 presidential race, even though nobody gave him a chance against President Johnson.

September 12, 1966—*Family Affair* with Anissa Jones debuts. ☮ September 12, 2003—Singer Johnny Cash dies at age 71 in Nashville, Tennessee. September 13, 1931—Actress Barbara Bain is born in Chicago. ☮ September 13, 1944—Actress Jacqueline Bisset is born in Surrey, England. September 13, 1959—Elvis and Priscilla meet in Germany. ☮ September 13, 1965—*The John Forsythe Show* with Peggy Lipton debuts.

Amazingly, the first primary in New Hampshire drew thousands of young people—"the children's crusade"—who recruited voters and won sympathy to Eugene's cause. Though he didn't win, he came close enough to show that LBJ was vulnerable on the Vietnam issue, and four days after the March primary another more prominent anti-war senator, Robert Kennedy, joined the race.

With anti-war talk heating up, LBJ astonished everybody by dropping out at the end of the month. RFK quickly picked up the anti-war torch and became the party's leading candidate; when he was assassinated in June of '68, Vice President Hubert Humphrey carried on as the new Democratic champion, but he was narrowly defeated by Richard Nixon that November.

Meanwhile Eugene left the Senate at the end of the decade, to be replaced by Humphrey. Eugene did make presidential runs in '72, '76, '88, and '92, but he was never the factor that he was in '68. In the '80s and '90s he lived in rural Virginia in an 18th-century farmhouse while writing books and poetry. He died in 2005 in a Georgetown retirement home.

EVERYBODY LOVES SOMEBODY

A North Dakota educator in the late '30s, Eugene got engaged to another teacher, whom he married after the war. They separated in '69 but never got divorced. He outlived one of his daughters, who died in 1990, and his wife, who died in 2001. When Eugene died, he left behind a son, two daughters, and six grandchildren.

MY BACK PAGES

Actor Kevin McCarthy (*Invasion of the Body Snatchers*, '56) and screenwriter/novelist Mary McCarthy (*The Group, '63*) were his cousins. . . . "Clean for Gene" was the mantra of young people when they cut their long hair, dressed up, and passed out leaflets promoting his '68 campaign. . . . David Frost asked him how his obituary should start: Eugene's laconic reply, "He died."

Patrick McGoohan

One of the great cult screen heroes, with memorable roles all decade long.

TAKIN' CARE OF BUSINESS

Handsome Patrick McGoohan was a worthy, dignified alternative to promiscuous, violent 007 in the screen spy wars of the '60s. Unlike Bond, Patrick's spies didn't carry guns and didn't chase skirts; unfortunately, Patrick's British spy shows underwhelmed America, where he's better remembered for some cool movies. Though most viewers figure that his elegant accent betrays a British birthplace, actually Patrick was born in New York, and he was raised in Ireland.

A busy stage actor in the '50s, he was a rising star of British TV when he got the lead in the new *Danger Man* spy series, a one-season wonder in its first incarnation. Branching out to movies, he starred in an acclaimed Disney TV adventure, *The Scarecrow of Romney Marsh* ('64), a stylish 18th-century Robin Hood-style story that had the bad luck to debut on the same night the Beatles set a ratings record on Ed Sullivan's show. American audiences might also remember Patrick in *The Three Lives of Thomasina* ('64), a successful Disney charmer.

Then, with the Bond movies thriving in theatres, in '64 his failed half-hour *Danger Man* series was resurrected as

a more action-oriented one-hour show (it was called *Secret Agent* in the States). Patrick's breakthrough as a cult icon came with a unique (but short-lived) spy series, *The Prisoner*, a surreal puzzler that he helped create, occasionally wrote and directed, and also starred in. The enigmatic show placed him as an unnamed agent who tried to escape from a strange prison in an unnamed location. Viewers have been debating it ever since, *TV Guide* ranked it seventh among the greatest cult shows ever, and several 21st-century directors have contemplated making modern movie versions.

For Patrick, a great movie followed his great show—he played the dapper secret agent on board the all-star sub in *Ice Station Zebra* ('68), Howard Hughes's favorite film and still a Cold War classic. Another two dozen screen roles took him into the '90s with popular hits (*Silver Streak*, '76, *Escape from Alcatraz*, '79), a big-time Oscar winner (*Braveheart*, '95), and a body of impressive TV movies that brought him two Emmy trophies.

EVERYBODY LOVES SOMEBODY

Maybe Patrick didn't want to play a womanizing secret agent because he wasn't a womanizing actor. Since '51 he's been married to the same woman, British stage actress Joan Drummond (supposedly they were married between that day's rehearsal and evening performance); for decades they've lived in L.A. They've got three daughters, one of whom, Catherine McGoohan, has appeared in a couple dozen movies and TV shows since the mid-'80s.

MY BACK PAGES

Fans of *The Prisoner* have found enough clues to fuel speculation that the hero was the same exact character who was in *Danger Man* (a rumor Patrick's denied). . . . Patrick voiced his character on *The Prisoner* for a 2000 episode of *The Simpsons*. . . . Two early roles he's said to have declined—Bond and the Saint. . . . Two recent roles he's said to have declined—Gandalf in *The Lord of the Rings* and Dumbledore in *Harry Potter*.

Denny McLain

One of the best baseball pitchers of the late '60s, who led a swingin' life until he ran into trouble.

TAKIN' CARE OF BUSINESS

In the late '60s, the flip side of the Dodgers' Sandy Koufax was Detroit Tigers' pitcher Denny McLain. If Sandy was a quiet artist, Denny was a brash, cocksure rebel. Denny did have notable accomplishments on the field: he's the only pitcher since Dizzy Dean in '34 to win 30 games (Denny won 31 in '68), he won the coveted Cy Young award two years in a row, and he made the cover of *Time* magazine under the headline "The Year of the Pitcher." Courting the spotlight, he also fashioned himself as a lounge organist who played Vegas and cut albums.

But amazingly, the most dominating American League pitcher of the late '60s bounced from team to team and was out of baseball by the early '70s, plagued by personal problems as much as by a fading fastball. Denny was suspended twice: once for consorting with gamblers and once

September 14, 1944—Entertainer Joey Heatherton is born in Rockville Center, New York.
September 14, 1960—*The Little Shop of Horrors* with Jack Nicholson opens. ☮ September 14, 1963—George Best debuts with Manchester United.
September 14, 1964—*Voyage to the Bottom of the Sea* with David Hedison debuts. ☮ September 14, 1964—*Wendy and Me* with Connie Stevens debuts.

for carrying a gun on the team plane. Later, he also did several stints in prison for drug possession, extortion, racketeering, and stealing millions of dollars from the pension fund of a company he co-owned. Struggling for cash, Denny became a golf hustler, used his plane to make $160,000 smuggling a fugitive across the border, and twice declared bankruptcy. The elegant Sandy Koufax seemed immortal; Denny McLain seemed all too human.

EVERYBODY LOVES SOMEBODY

Denny's best ally has always been his wife. The daughter of Hall of Fame player and manager Lou Boudreau, she met Denny when she was a teenager. They married in the '60s, she divorced him while he was in prison in the '90s, then they remarried in 2003. They have three kids (a fourth was killed in a car accident) and lots of grandchildren.

MY BACK PAGES

At the peak of his popularity Denny co-wrote the book *How to Play Better Baseball* with another star player who would have troubles—Pete Rose. . . . In baseball, Denny won big and lost big: three years after winning 31 games for the Tigers, he lost 22 games for the Senators.

Steve McQueen

Coolest guy of the '60s? The vote just might be unanimous.

TAKIN' CARE OF BUSINESS

His was a coolness that spanned decades and genres. Whether Steve McQueen was starring in a '50s horror flick, a classic '60s Western/war movie/cop thriller, or a '70s disaster epic, he was always the most watchable guy on the screen, at once handsome, physical, charming, sly, and

commanding. And he lived with as much gusto off-screen as he did on-screen.

Steve McQueen's life began with the first name Terence; born in Indiana, he was raised in Missouri by an uncle after his father left. Moving to L.A. with his mother, Steve started getting in trouble and was sent to a reform school for a few years before joining the Marines in '47, where he was credited with helping save some other men who had fallen into a lake. In the '50s he went to New York, started studying acting, and landed a role on Broadway that brought him decent movie parts in the late '50s, with *The Blob* ('58) his first lead. At the cusp of the '60s, Steve was the star of *Wanted: Dead or Alive*, a successful Western drama.

A screen-stealing turn as one of the magnificent *The Magnificent Seven* ('60) made him an action star and led to his glorious breakthrough, *The Great Escape* ('63).

September 14, 1965—*F Troop* with Ken Berry debuts. ☮ September 14, 1968—*The Archie Show* debuts.
September 14, 1968—Pitcher Denny McLain wins his 30th game of the season.
September 14, 1996—Actress Juliet Prowse dies in L.A. of cancer at 59. ☮ September 15, 1964—*Peyton Place* with Mia Farrow debuts.

Though others had more scenes and lines than Steve, he got top billing over a huge international cast of stars and clearly stole the movie. *The Great Escape* established Steve once and for all as a cool renegade hero: while the other military men worked in teams and wore uniforms, Steve cruised through on his own and wore a torn sweatshirt; while others fretted over a botched tunnel that missed the woods, he smiled; while others made their escape via commuter trains and rowboats, he tore up the Bavarian countryside on a motorcycle, doing all the riding (except for the final jump) himself.

Suddenly the hottest actor in town, he made two movies a year over the next three years, including a suspenseful poker drama (*The Cincinnati Kid,* '65) and another high-action Western (*Nevada Smith*, '66). The best of all these was *The Sand Pebbles* ('66), the epic that brought Steve his only Oscar nomination, plus a Golden Globe trophy as the World's Film Favorite. All of these movies were building up a screen image perfect for the '60s, that of an admirable loner who successfully challenged the establishment's orders. He perfected this persona in *Bullitt* ('68), playing the renegade cop who drove a Mustang GT fastback the way POW Hilts had ridden a German motorcycle five years earlier. The movie was a smash at the box office and stands as a classic of the genre (if you liked *The French Connection*, the *Dirty Harry* movies, or car-chase flicks, thank *Bullitt*).

Showing his versatility, that same year Steve donned a stylin' suit for the super-cool crime caper *The Thomas Crown Affair* ('68). In some ways Steve's last '60s movie was a complete departure from his previous work, though it still

30 Classic War Movies

19th-Century Wars

The Alamo ('60)
The Charge of the Light Brigade ('68)
Khartoum ('66)
Zulu ('64)

World War One

The Blue Max ('66)
Lawrence of Arabia ('62)

World War Two

633 Squadron ('64)
The Battle of Britain ('69)
The Battle of the Bulge ('65)
The Bridge at Remagen ('69)
The Devil's Brigade ('68)
The Dirty Dozen ('67)
The Great Escape ('63)
The Guns of Navarone ('61)
Hell in the Pacific ('68)
In Harm's Way ('65)
The Longest Day ('62)
None But the Brave ('65)
P.T. 109 ('63)
Tobruk ('67)
The Train ('65)
Von Ryan's Express ('65)
Where Eagles Dare ('68)

Cold War

Dr. Strangelove ('64)
Fail-Safe ('64)
Ice Station Zebra ('68)
The Manchurian Candidate ('62)
Seven Days in May ('64)
The Spy Who Came in from the Cold ('66)

Vietnam War

The Green Berets ('68)

September 15, 1965—*Lost in Space* with Marta Kristen debuts. ☮ September 15, 1965—*Gidget* with Sally Field debuts. September 15, 1965—*I Spy* with Bill Cosby and Robert Culp debuts. ☮ September 15, 1966—Andy Warhol's *Chelsea Girls* opens. September 15, 1967—The Who blow up the stage on *The Smothers Brothers*.

presented him as a charismatic rogue. *The Reivers* ('69) was an adorable, well-crafted period film set in the South, with a car that could go only 18 MPH and a race run by horses, not cars (Steve won another Golden Globe). Throughout the '60s Steve was pursuing car racing and motorcycles in his spare time, and he brought his need for speed to his '71 projects, *Le Mans* (which he also produced) and *On Any Sunday* (which he produced and appeared in for a fun motorcycle ride). His career would last only eight more films, among them several major hits—*The Getaway* ('72), *Papillon* ('73), *The Towering Inferno* ('74).

Personal problems and health issues plagued his '70s, when his hair got long and shaggy and he lost his athletic physique. Sadly, after trying every treatment possible (including surgery and alternative therapies), Steve McQueen died of cancer in '80. For decades after, his name and image have been invoked by anyone who wanted to convey coolness quickly—songwriters (especially Sheryl Crow with her 2002 hit "Steve McQueen"), filmmakers (*The Tao of Steve*, 2000), and, of course, car companies (Ford used his *Bullitt* image for new Mustang commercials in 2005).

EVERYBODY LOVES SOMEBODY

A noted Hollywood ladies' man, Steve was married three times. Throughout the '60s he was married to actress Neile Adams; they had two kids, one of whom, Chad McQueen, had small roles in many '80s and '90s movies. After a '72 divorce, Steve was married to actress Ali MacGraw, star of *Love Story* ('70), for five years. Steve married again in the last year of his life; his third wife, Barbara Minty, appeared in the 2005 documentary about Steve called, appropriately enough, *The Essence of Cool*.

MY BACK PAGES

In *The Great Escape*, Steve rode a motorcycle not only as the escaped POW, but also as one of the Nazis in pursuit. . . . Supposedly another icon of '60s cool, Sean Connery, was offered *The Thomas Crown Affair* and later regretted turning it down. . . . Steve himself was offered *Butch Cassidy and the Sundance Kid* ('68), and when he said no Robert Redford's career was made. . . . Steve really drove the Mustang in the *Bullitt* chase, hitting speeds over 115 MPH. . . . Once he was a success, Steve made appearances at his old reform school. . . . He never won an Oscar, but he did make it into the Motorcycle Hall of Fame in '92, which he might've preferred anyway.

The Men from U.N.C.L.E.

Robert Vaughn and David McCallum played two suave superagents.

TAKIN' CARE OF BUSINESS

With the Cold War at its most frigid, and with James Bond films setting records in theatres, in '64 the TV vets behind *Dr. Kildare* and other popular shows pulled together all the elements (with Ian Fleming's blessing) for a Bond-style TV series. *The Man from U.N.C.L.E.* had gadgets, wit, a S.P.E.C.T.R.E.-style evil empire called T.H.R.U.S.H., memorable villains, and handsome heroes with dynamic chemistry. Napoleon Solo and Illya Kuryakin were played by brainy New Yorker Robert Vaughn and blonde Scotsman David McCallum.

Robert had made hundreds of TV appearances before *U.N.C.L.E.*, he'd already been nominated for an Oscar (*The Young Philadelphians*, '59), and he'd been counted among *The Magnificent Seven* ('60); later he would play powerful (and often ruthless) men in *Bullitt* ('68), *The Towering Inferno* ('74), and many other movies and shows. Pre-*U.N.C.L.E.*, David had been in British films and *The Great Escape* ('63); post-*U.N.C.L.E.* he's enjoyed a long, steady career on the big and little screens. Supervising them on

September 16, 1963—*The Outer Limits* with Vic Perrin debuts. ☮ September 16, 1964—*Shindig!* debuts.
September 16, 1965—*Mona McCluskey* with Juliet Prowse debuts.
September 16, 1965—Entertainer Joey Heatherton debuts on her first *Dean Martin Show*.

U.N.C.L.E. was Leo G. Carroll, the man who steered Cary Grant across America in *North by Northwest* ('57).

So popular was the show, in the mid-'60s it spawned TV movies (really just re-edited TV episodes), lines of merchandise, and a spin-off, the one-season *The Girl from U.N.C.L.E.* with Stefanie Powers in '66. Unfortunately, what was clever and hip early became sillier and outdated later, and *The Man from U.N.C.L.E.* was cancelled after four seasons. It did get lots of award nominations, however, plus a TV reunion movie in '83 that featured ex-Avenger Patrick Macnee and ex-007 George Lazenby in the cast.

EVERYBODY LOVES SOMEBODY

Robert married actress Linda Staab in the mid-'70s and has two children. From the late '50s-early '60s David was married to actress Jill Ireland, who later married Charles Bronson; David remarried in the late '60s and has four kids.

MY BACK PAGES

Robert studied for his Ph.D. while still working in the late '60s-early '70s. . . . A trained musician, David released three LPs of original songs and covers in the late '60s. . . . The show's cool car—a custom gull-wing blue Piranha with flame throwers, rockets, lasers, and amphibious propellers. . . . U.N.C.L.E. stood for United Network Command for Law Enforcement, while T.H.R.U.S.H. was an acronym for Technological Hierarchy for the Removal of Undesirables and the Subjugation of Humanity (never given on the show, but explained in a novel). . . . Among the hundreds of guest stars were Jill Ireland, Leonard Nimoy, William Shatner, Sharon Tate, Vera Miles, Janet Leigh, Joan Collins, Nancy Sinatra, Sonny and Cher, Jack Lord, and Leslie Nielsen. . . . "The Man from A.U.N.T.I.E." (Association for Unbelievably Nauseating Television and Idiotic Entertainment) was the *Mad* magazine parody starring Napoleon Polo and Illya Nutcrackin.

Hayley Mills

A spunky Disney dynamo, Hayley moved from classic juvenile movies to more mature themes at decade's end.

TAKIN' CARE OF BUSINESS

Like Mia Farrow and Vanessa Redgrave, Hayley Mills was born into a show-biz family. She's the London-born daughter of Sir John Mills (star of Disney's *Swiss Family Robinson,* '61) and writer Mary Hayley Bell. Hayley's older sister is Juliet Mills, who was nanny Phoebe Figalilly on TV's *Nanny and the Professor* in the early '70s. The Mills family lived on an English farm, where 13-year-old Hayley was visited one day by Walt Disney himself.

Walt's wife Lillian had seen *Tiger Bay* ('59), Hayley's first starring (and award-winning) movie role, and recommended that Walt go meet Hayley before he cast his next film. He flew to England, was immediately smitten by the bright, charming girl, and quickly put her in *Pollyanna* ('60). The sunny hit brought her an honorary Oscar for Juvenile Performance and a Golden Globe as Most Promising Newcomer.

Things only got better for Hayley and Walt. They reteamed for *The Parent Trap* ('61), at the time his most successful film ever. She looked adorable—her sweet, open face was topped by a kicky 'do—and as an actress she was a natural charmer. So popular was Hayley, her recording of the movie's song, "Let's Get Together," raced up the music charts. *Whistle Down the Wind* ('61, based on her mother's book) and four more from Disney—*In Search of the Castaways* ('62), *Summer Magic* ('63), *The Moon-Spinners* ('64), and *That Darn Cat!* ('65)—established Hayley as the most popular young actress of the decade.

In her late teens she started to stretch into more mature roles. In '64 she gave a stirring performance as a disturbed girl in *The Chalk Garden,* and in '66 she played a mentally slow teen in *Gypsy Girl* (mom's script, dad's direc-

tion). The famous culmination of this gradual break from her Disney days was *The Family Way* ('66), in which she smoked, swore, drank, and even did a scene partially nude. But perhaps because she had been so endearing as a girl, audiences didn't want to accept that she (and they) were getting older.

Though she continued to work for the next 10 years, her momentum definitely slowed. Three *Parent Trap* TV movie sequels in the late '80s, plus shows like *Love Boat* and *Murder She Wrote,* typified her later screen roles. She did, however, continue to perform in plays, co-starring with her sister in the Noel Coward play *Fallen Angels,* and touring Australia and the U.S. in the '90s as the singing, dancing I in *The King and I.* She's emerged into the 21st century as a beautiful adult who still has the lively twinkle in her blue eyes that first made the world adore her over 40 years ago.

EVERYBODY LOVES SOMEBODY

Hayley's first crush was on Elvis, and she has said that she actually saw him driving his big Caddy in Hollywood in '62. Her first kiss, she claimed, came in *The Moon-Spinners* when she was 18. At 20 she met her future husband, Roy Boulting. He was the director of *The Family Way,* he was 33 years her senior, and he already had a wife and six kids (two of them older than Hayley). When they moved in together, her parents were outraged by the age difference, and movie magazines treated their pairing like a major international scandal. Everybody was bothered by the age difference, it seemed, except for the two people involved. They finally married in '71, had a son in '73, and divorced in '77. She then took up with actor Leigh Lawson and had his son, but she and Lawson split up in the mid-'80s (he went on to marry Twiggy). Later she had a relationship with the brother of Maxwell Caulfield, the actor who married her sister. She now lives in a 200-year-old cottage in Hampton, England.

MY BACK PAGES

When Hayley went to Hollywood for *Pollyanna,* Walt gave her a personal two-day tour of Disneyland. . . . During the filming of *The Parent Trap,* she shot up two inches, and all her costumes had to be altered. . . . She was considered for the lead in Kubrick's *Lolita* ('62) but she didn't pursue it because the sexy role didn't fit her squeaky-clean image. . . . In '98 Hayley was named an official Disney Legend.

Yvette Mimieux

This lithe beauty was a sci-fi sweetheart and bikini babe in several beloved films.

TAKIN' CARE OF BUSINESS

Born in Hollywood, Yvette Mimieux was modeling in L.A. when MGM signed her to a contract in '59 and promptly put her in some cool movies. The coolest was George Pal's Oscar-winning sci-fi sensation *The Time Machine* ('60), in which Yvette played a cute child-like girl from the year 800,000 A.D. who barely spoke and became Morlock bait. Then, still in '60, she co-starred with Connie Francis in the sweet beach classic *Where the Boys Are*. In '62 she was the princess in *The Wonderful World of the Brothers Grimm,* another of George Pal's Oscar-winning fantasy epics. For all of these films she was young, blonde, and pretty, her 107-pound, 34–21–35 figure perfect for any bikini or toga scene.

Another 10 films filled her '60s, highlighted by the dramatic *Toys in the Attic* ('63) with Dean Martin and Disney's *Monkeys, Go Home!* with Dean Jones ('67), plus she made two covers of *Life*. In the '70s Yvette recorded a hard-to-find album of poetry by Charles Baudelaire, with Indian music for accompaniment, and in '74 she both wrote and starred in her own TV movie, *Hit Lady*, in which she played a painter who was also an assassin. Always busy, her career in feature films (including Disney's *The Black Hole*, '79) gradually became a career in popular TV movies, one of which (*Obsessive Love*, '84) she wrote/produced/starred in. She also started doing instructional yoga videos and books in the late '90s, still looking great, as always.

EVERYBODY LOVES SOMEBODY

In '72 Yvette married Stanley Donen, the well-known director of such prominent movies as *Singin' in the Rain* ('51) and *Charade* ('63). After their mid-'80s divorce, Yvette married TV director Howard Ruby.

MY BACK PAGES

In *The Time Machine*, the year depicted for the arrival of civilization-destroying World War III was 1966. . . . In April 2003, Yvette was given an adoring full-page profile in *Vanity Fair*, which called her "the ultimate California beach bunny in *Where the Boys Are*. . . . With a knack for doing the right thing at the right time in the right outfit."

Peggy Moffitt

The top American model of the '60s was a startling innovator who didn't just wear fashions, she inspired them.

TAKIN' CARE OF BUSINESS

Jean Shrimpton and Twiggy got most of the fashion press during the '60s, a time when being British was the hippest thing you could be. But a less-heralded American, Peggy Moffitt, was wearing, and helping to shape, a fashion revolution. Peggy inspired the great Rudi Gernreich, who was to fashion what Stanley Kubrick was to movies: a daring innovator open to new technologies. If Mary Quant was the designer of the moment with her playful colors and sexy minis, Rudi Gernreich (1922–'85) was the designer of the future with his revealing clothes made out of clear plastic, his topless swimsuits, and his unisex designs.

He and Peggy met when he was designing for the Jax boutique in L.A. in the early '60s. He soon founded his own company in L.A. and began turning out fashions and

September 17, 1967—The Doors appear on Ed Sullivan's show. ☮ September 17, 1968—*Julia* with Diahann Carroll debuts.
September 17, 1968—*Good Morning World* with Julie Parrish concludes its one-season run in primetime.
September 17, 1989—TV announcer Jay Stewart commits suicide. ☮ September 18, 1939—Singer Frankie Avalon is born in Philadelphia.

furniture, unifying everything with his futuristic visions (and landing with Peggy on the cover of *Time* in '67). Gernreich's clothes were so daring and unconventional that on a couple of occasions the women who wore them in public were arrested.

Before meeting Gernreich, Peggy studied drama in New York in the early '50s and then returned home to L.A., where she got small movie parts for the rest of the decade. In the early '60s she was a model with the exclusive Nina Blanchard Agency, went to London mid-decade and played a model in Antonioni's startling *Blow-Up* ('66), and then became Gernreich's muse.

Tall and slender, she had the ideal model's figure, a fearless attitude towards nudity and fashion, and a witty approach to the runway. Her bold haircuts and strong, amazing make-up became styles by themselves: Vidal Sassoon shaped her short hair with precise geometric bangs cut right to her eyebrows, and her heavy eyeliner, neon eyelids, and long false eyelashes evoked theatrical face-painting. Gernreich changed the way women dressed; Peggy changed the way women looked.

EVERYBODY LOVES SOMEBODY

For over 40 years, Peggy has been married to photographer William Claxton; they live in Beverly Hills. His photo of Peggy is on the cover of the '58 jazz LP *Something For Both Ears*, one of her earliest photo shoots. Claxton began taking pictures of Rudi Gernreich's creations in '56 and continued all through the '60s. He and Peggy produced *The Rudi Gernreich Book* ('99), a chronicle of the fashion designer's life and work. William Claxton's photography book *Steve McQueen* was published by Taschen in 2004.

MY BACK PAGES

Peggy's dad Jack Moffitt was a screenwriter, listed as one of the writers on almost two dozen movies including Bogart's *Passage to Marseille* ('44) and Cary Grant's *Night and Day* ('46). . . . In '67 Rudi Gernreich appeared on an episode of *Batman* as the clothing designer to Julie Newmar's Catwoman. . . . In '75 Gernreich designed the striped uniforms for the TV show *Space: 1999* starring Martin Landau, and also in the '70s he designed the first thong bathing suit. . . . In 2003 Peggy teamed with the *Comme des Garçons* label to recreate Gernreich's designs.

The Monkees

An Emmy-winning TV show turned four unknowns into a formidable force in '60s music.

TAKIN' CARE OF BUSINESS

Aping the fast-paced hilarity of the Beatles' *Help!*, *The Monkees* enlivened TV airwaves for two years with wacky antics and well-crafted songs. Though dismissed by critics who found the plots chaotic and the slapstick silly, the show about a group of cute pop stars won an Emmy, was a ratings hit, and has endured for decades in syn-

dication. But it's the music—and the musical controversy—that most people remember.

Not only were the four musicians virtually unknown to the American public before the show debuted in '66, they were unknown to each other. Hundreds of young men responded to a *Variety* ad inviting auditions for the new show, with many recognizable names (Harry Nilsson, Stephen Stills, Paul Williams) getting turned away. Only one of the final four, Texan Mike Nesmith, was chosen from the pool of applicants. The rest came from inside contacts: Washington, D.C.'s Peter Tork was a Greenwich Village folkie recommended by Stills, L.A.'s Micky Dolenz was already a scene-stealing TV vet (*Circus Boy*) brought in by the producers, and Londoner Davy Jones, a '63 Tony nominee for playing the Artful Dodger in Broadway's *Oliver!*, was already under contract.

Mike had the strongest vision for the group's direction and became the spokesperson, both on and off the show. Peter was the best musician, skilled at a dozen instruments, though scripts often cast him as the fool singing goofy novelty songs ("Your Auntie Grizelda"). Micky, with the best rock voice and the most outgoing personality, sang lead on most of the up-tempo hits ("I'm a Believer," "Steppin' Stone," "Last Train to Clarksville") and inspired the most screen mayhem. Davy, the cutest, was the group's Paul McCartney, singing most of the love ballads ("I Wanna Be Free").

The group's fun-loving, parent-friendly image echoed the Beatles at their most innocent, an image reinforced by all the smiling merchandise that rolled off the assembly line (to see how closely they patterned themselves after the Beatles, compare the cover of *More of the Monkees*, '67, with *Rubber Soul*, '65). Unlike the Fab Four, the Pre-Fab Four didn't write their own material—nearly all the songs came from other people (including Neil Diamond and Carole King). But the music was polished, pleasing, and popular, resulting in consecutive #1 albums.

In '66 and '67, the group even performed live concerts, finally becoming in real life what they'd been portraying in sitcom life. However, stuffy critics became indignant when the Monkees themselves revealed the secret of their musical success—with only a few exceptions, the boys merely sang on the first two albums, and studio pros handled the instruments. (But why indignant? Nobody expected the Mod Squad to be catching actual criminals outside of their show,

A Dozen Late-'60s "Bubblegum" Hits

"98.6"–Keith

"Dizzy"–Tommy Roe

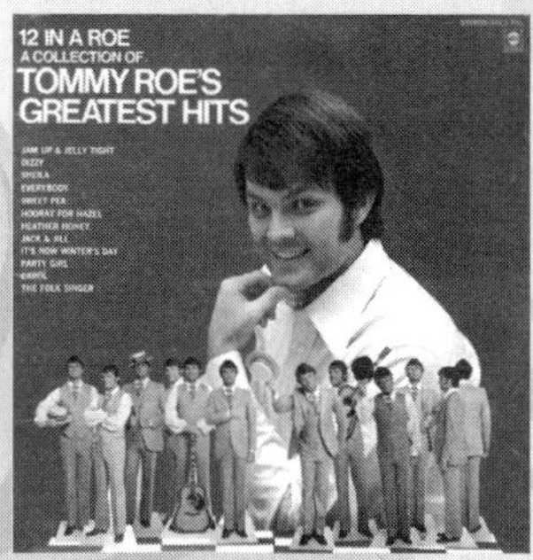

"Easy Come, Easy Go"–Bobby Sherman

"The Grooviest Girl In The World"–The Fun and Games

"I Think We're Alone Now"–Tommy James & The Shondells

"The Rain, the Park and Other Things"–The Cowsills

"Simon Says"–1910 Fruitgum Company

"Sugar Sugar"–The Archies

"Tracy"–The Cuff Links

"The Tra-La-La Song"–The Banana Splits

"Will You Be Staying After Sunday"–The Peppermint Rainbow

"Yummy Yummy Yummy"–Ohio Express

September 18, 1965—*Get Smart* with Barbara Feldon debuts. ☮ September 18, 1969—Singer Tiny Tim and Miss Vicky get engaged.
September 18, 1969—*Bob & Carol & Ted & Alice* with Dyan Cannon opens.
September 18, 1970—Guitarist Jimi Hendrix dies of an overdose at the age of 27. ☮ September 18, 2002—Athlete Bob Hayes dies.

but for some reason writers expected that the four actors playing a rock band really should be rock musicians.)

To prove themselves, the Monkees took over production of the third album, *Headquarters*, writing the songs, playing the instruments, generating another #1 hit LP. They also tried writing and directing a few TV episodes themselves, and with Jack Nicholson they concocted a surreal, little-seen movie, *Head* ('68). Unfortunately, audiences were starting to go bananas for harder music, the Monkees and the Beatles were simultaneously splintering (Peter and Mike both dropped out by 1971), and the mid-'70s would bring the end of the original Monkeemania.

Peter went on to work as a teacher and continued to make music. Mike wrote "Different Drum," a Linda Ronstadt hit, started the countrified First National Band (their biggest hit, "Joanne"), and with his video production company is often credited with making the first MTV-style music videos; he also produced several movies, including *Repo Man* ('84), and wrote several novels. Micky continued to make music and to work in TV, first as an actor and then as a director. Davy continued to act on-screen and onstage, plus he became post-Monkee what he'd been pre-Monkee—a jockey. In various iterations the group has toured on and off for three more decades, with an album from the complete quartet, *Justus*, in '96. In reruns or in concert, they still get affectionate receptions from fans happy to say "hey hey you're the Monkees."

EVERYBODY LOVES SOMEBODY

As with John Lennon's quiet marriage to Cynthia, the Monkees' private married lives were largely shielded from the public so as to make them seem more single for the teen girls in the audience. Mike was a married man for the entire run of the show, has now been married three times and has four kids. Peter was married briefly long before the show was conceived; he was then married twice more after the show ended, with three kids. Micky got married in '68 before the show ended (something he refused to hide) to a TV celebrity he met while he was with the band in England; they divorced in the mid-'70s. Micky has remarried twice more and has four kids. Davy married a month after the show was cancelled, has two divorces and four kids.

MY BACK PAGES

Mike inherited a sizable estate from his mother, the inventor of Liquid Paper. . . . Peter co-wrote the theme song used at the end of second-season shows. . . . In early episodes Micky wore a Beatle-style wig (the rowdy curls of season two were all his). . . . On the night of the Beatles' legendary American debut with Ed Sullivan, Davy was on the same show, performing with the cast of *Oliver!* . . . Among those making *Head* cameos: Annette Funicello, Sonny Liston, Teri Garr, Victor Mature, Frank Zappa, Toni Basil, Carol Doda, and Jack Nicholson. . . . The group is credited for accelerating one legendary rocker's career—they invited Jimi Hendrix to open for them on their '67 tour. . . . Just as the Beatles got to meet one of their idols, Elvis, the Monkees got to meet theirs—the Beatles threw a party for them when the Monkees played England in '67.

Sizzling superstar Marilyn defined Hollywood glamour and tragedy.

TAKIN' CARE OF BUSINESS

She's one of the few women known everywhere by a single name—say "Marilyn," and not only will everybody know whom you mean, they'll know something about her. Like Liz Taylor, who was probably the only other '60s actress to command truly global attention, Marilyn Monroe couldn't go to the mailbox without generating international headlines. Eternally photogenic, she made the cover of *Life*

September 19, 1928—Actor Adam West is born in Walla Walla, Washington. ☮ September 19, 1933—Actor David McCallum is born in Glasgow, Scotland. September 19, 1941—Singer Cass Elliot is born in Baltimore, Maryland. ☮ September 19, 1949—Model Twiggy is born in Neasdon, England. September 19, 1968—*Funny Girl* with Anne Francis opens. ☮ September 19, 1969—*Bracken's World* with Linda Harrison debuts.

magazine five times during the '60s, three times posthumously. However, her Hollywood career was tragically short, lasting little more than a decade. Raised in a foster home, Norma Jean Mortenson, then Norma Jean Baker, was a model and a bit player in movies in the '40s, a centerfold in the first issue of *Playboy* (December '53), and a star by '53. In '60, she was just coming off her best, most acclaimed movie, *Some Like It Hot* ('59). She finished only two more movies (*Let's Make Love*, '60, *The Misfits*, '61), and was fired from a third (*Something's Got to Give*, '62), but her popularity was undiminished—in early '62 she won the Golden Globe as the World's Film Favorite.

Later that year, after bouts with alcohol and pills, she died in her Brentwood bedroom of an overdose of 47 Nembutal and chloral hydrate pills at age 36. L.A.'s Chief Medical Examiner ruled it an accidental suicide, but her death is still shrouded in mystery and myth. Her plain but famous wall crypt, for decades decorated by Joe DiMaggio's fresh roses, is in the same Westwood, California cemetery where Natalie Wood is buried.

Tony Curtis, Marilyn Monroe, Jack Lemmon

In '99 she ranked high on several significant millennium lists: the American Film Institute ranked her sixth among screen legends, and *People* and *Playboy* named her the century's sexiest star. Her figure, of course, was legendary, the 37-23-35 measurements describing a geometry that has transcended any transitory notion of what's stylish or alluring.

Her assets were shown off to stunning effect on the famous spring night in '62 when she was stitched into a $12,000 rhinestone-encrusted handmade gown so she could sing the sultriest, breathiest version of "Happy Birthday" ever heard to President Kennedy at his Madison Square Garden "Birthday Salute." In '99 that dress was auctioned off for almost $1,300,000, the world's record for the highest auction price ever for a woman's garment. Fashions come and go, styles change hourly, but Marilyn, as that auction proved 37 years after her death, is eternal.

EVERYBODY LOVES SOMEBODY

During her life Marilyn had many relationships, some rumored, some factual, and all part of the legend that has made her one of the most discussed, most written about, most desired women in history. She was married and divorced three times: to factory worker James Dougherty from '42 to '45 when she was in her mid-teens, to baseball star Joe DiMaggio for ten months of '54, and to playwright Arthur Miller from '56 to '61.

Famous Hollywood and political names frequently come up in published discussions of her other relationships (though she claimed that her idea of a sexy man was Albert Einstein). In the early '60s it was DiMaggio who would rally to her support, emotionally and financially, and it was he who made the arrangements for, and cried throughout, her funeral.

MY BACK PAGES

Marilyn was the only actress of the early '60s to have her own production company. . . . *Something's Got to Give* would've included a famous nude swimming scene had it been completed (she'd been rehired and was set to resume filming when she died). . . . A gift from Frank Sinatra—a poodle named Jewel, who outlived her. . . . Quotable Marilyn: "I've been on

September 20, 1934—Actress Sophia Loren is born in Italy. ☮ September 20, 1963—*The Farmer's Daughter* with Inger Stevens debuts. September 20, 1968—*Hawaii Five-o* (the two-hour pilot movie) debuts. ☮ September 20, 1968—*The Name of the Game* with Tony Franciosa debuts. September 20, 1969—The Archies' "Sugar Sugar" hits #1. ☮ September 21, 1964—The 12-meter yacht *Constellation* wins the America's Cup for the U.S.

a calendar, but never on time". . . . Asked what she wore to bed, she replied "Chanel No. 5". . . . Asked what she had on when she posed for the *Playboy* photo, she answered "the radio". . . . And finally, a Marilyn for the ages: "I knew I belonged to the public and to the world, not because I was talented or even beautiful, but because I never had belonged to anything or anyone else."

Elizabeth Montgomery

A pretty blonde nose-twitcher, Elizabeth Montgomery worked a spell on audiences with *Bewitched*.

TAKIN' CARE OF BUSINESS

One of the queens of '60s TV, Elizabeth Montgomery reigned longer than any other '60s actress in a major show. Not only durable, she was one of the most talented TV stars—her magical performance on *Bewitched* brought her Best Actress Emmy nominations every year from '66–'70. Elizabeth was born in Hollywood to parents who were both actors. Her father, Robert, made over 50 movies in the '30s and '40s and was nominated for two Best Actor Oscars. Growing up in New York, Elizabeth attended private schools and began appearing on her dad's *Robert Montgomery Show,* which ran for seven years in the '50s.

She proved herself as a serious stage actress when her first Broadway play, *Late Love,* brought her a *Theatre World* award. Her performance in the '55 film *The Court-Martial of Billy Mitchell,* and roles on prominent TV dramas, also received strong critical acclaim. Her TV career in the '60s included a classic *Twilight Zone* episode as the last woman on Earth, and an episode of *The Untouchables* that brought her the first of nine Emmy nominations. *Bewitched* in '64 established her once and for all as a TV legend.

Working with her husband, producer William Asher,

Elizabeth helped conceive *Bewitched* and its main characters, Darrin and Samantha Stephens. In the show's first episode, the couple got married, but not 'til the honeymoon did he discover she was a witch. *Bewitched* quickly became ABC's biggest hit to date, ranking second overall in the '64 Nielsen ratings. Up to that time, most TV shows had positioned their female leads as nutty foils for their wiser, more stable husbands (think of Lucy Ricardo on *I Love Lucy*); *Bewitched* gave Samantha all the brains and power, making her a uniquely appealing heroine.

A surprising change came to the show in '69 that has forever brought bemused smiles to fans. From '64–'68 Sam's

September 21, 1969—"The Woody Allen Special" airs. ☮ September 21, 1974—Writer Jacqueline Susann dies of congestive heart failure in New York. September 22, 1943—Dancer Toni Basil is born in Philadelphia. ☮ September 22, 1964—*The Man from U.N.C.L.E.* with Robert Vaughn debuts. September 22, 1987—Comedian Dan Rowan dies of cancer in Florida. ☮ September 23, 1930—Singer Ray Charles is born.

husband Darrin was played by Dick York; from '69–'72 the role was played by Dick Sargent, with no explanation for the obvious switch (York's increasing back pain was the cause). Other changes included the introduction of a daughter, Tabitha (played by three sets of twins), and a son, Adam (again played by twins). Just as Barbara Eden did on *I Dream of Jeannie,* Elizabeth sometimes played a mischievous relative to juice the story a little. Introduced in episode 54, Sam's cousin Serena gave Elizabeth a chance to go a little wild with colorful miniskirts and peace signs inked onto her cheek; her portrayal was so good, many viewers didn't realize that Elizabeth was both Sam and Serena (the credits didn't help—they named Pandora Sparks as the actress playing Serena).

Ultimately, the show enchanted primetime audiences for almost a decade and conjured up 16 Emmy nominations (plus four Golden Globe nominations for Elizabeth). The magic didn't end until '72 when *Bewitched* went up against *All in the Family* on Saturday nights. Suddenly light fantasy/comedy seemed outdated, and the show floated over to rerunland. Elizabeth's post-Samantha work was dominated by two dozen acclaimed TV movies from the '70s to the '90s, three of which yielded Emmy nominations—*A Case of Rape* ('74), *The Legend of Lizzie Borden* ('75), and *The Awakening Land* ('78). She turned up on a few TV shows, did commercials, and also narrated the Oscar-winning documentary *The Panama Deception* ('92). Unfortunately, in '95 at the age of 62, Elizabeth died of cancer.

EVERYBODY LOVES SOMEBODY

Elizabeth married the stage manager on her father's show when she was 21, but they divorced within a year because he refused to leave New York when Hollywood beckoned to her. She then married actor Gig Young, who was 20 years her senior, but he became abusive as alcoholism overtook him and they divorced in '63.

William Asher, who was 14 years older than Elizabeth, was her next husband. He produced or directed many TV shows, notably *Bewitched*, plus five beach movies in the mid-'60s (Elizabeth made a cute cameo in *How to Stuff a Wild Bikini*). With Asher she had two sons and a daughter, all born before '70. Soon after the marriage split up in '74, she met actor Robert Foxworth, who co-starred with her in *Mrs. Sundance* ('74) and was in *Airport '77, Omen II* ('78), and many TV movies and shows. He and Elizabeth lived together for 19 years, married in '93, and were together until her death in '95.

MY BACK PAGES

Her two main hobbies—painting, and collecting antiques. . . . According to ABC press kits, Elizabeth created many of the outfits on the show and even designed a *Bewitched* line of coats. . . . During the '80s Elizabeth worked for various political causes, included AIDS research. . . . As for the longtime popularity of *Bewitched,* Elizabeth explained it this way to Nick at Nite: "It's not about cleaning the house with a magic wave . . . Or zapping up the toast . . . Or flying around the living room. It's about a very difficult relationship. And I think people pick up on this. They know there's something else going on besides the magic."

Keith Moon

The Who's chaotic drummer was the Clown Prince of rock, known as much for his impulsive stunts as he was for his explosive drumming style

TAKIN' CARE OF BUSINESS

Separating history from myth is one of the challenges for anyone who writes about Keith Moon's short but intense life. Given to spontaneous, youthful surges of anarchic energy, and unfettered by any sense of physical, legal, or behavioral limits, he was capable of almost anything.

September 23, 1938—Actress Romy Schneider is born in Vienna, Austria. ☮ September 23, 1962—ABC's first color TV series, *The Jetsons*, debuts. September 23, 1967—"To Sir with Love" by Lulu hits the charts. ☮ September 23, 1969—*Butch Cassidy and the Sundance Kid* with Katharine Ross opens. September 24, 1924—Actress Sheila MacRae is born in London. ☮ September 24, 1941—Photographer Linda Eastman is born in New York.

Was he the greatest rock drummer of the '60s? Many peers and critics have said so (he certainly played more frenetically than anyone else). Was he a cross-dresser? Not really, though many photos do show him in drag (they also show him nude and in wild costumes—clearly this was a man who liked to parade). Did Keith cause Pete Townshend's hearing loss? Pete said so, pinpointing the band's '68 appearance on *The Smothers Brothers* show (Keith ignited an explosive charge under his drums at the conclusion of "My Generation," unfortunately with Pete leaning in too close).

Did Keith run over himself with his own car? Very possibly; he owned dozens of expensive cars, hot rods, motorcycles, a tractor (which he took to the pub), and even a hovercraft, and he drove them all with reckless vehicle-crashing, property-destroying abandon despite rarely having a valid driver's license. Did Keith run over his own chauffeur with his Rolls-Royce? Well, sort of (Keith backed over him by accident, not realizing he'd fallen under the car; the poor man was killed and Keith was nailed for drunk driving). Did Keith drive his Lincoln into a hotel swimming pool? Yes, knocking out a front tooth in the process.

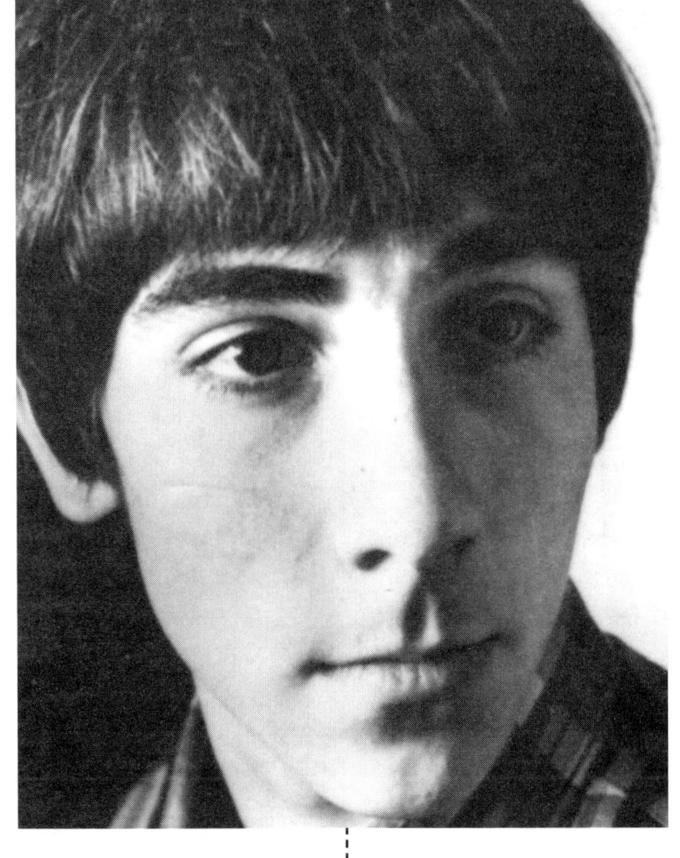

Did Keith get banned from hotels for starting fires, throwing cherry bombs, popping waterbeds, defenestrating TV's, chopping up furniture with axes, and nailing furniture to the ceiling? Yes, yes, yes, yes, yes and somehow yes (who brings a hammer and nails to a hotel?). Was he a devoted husband and father? He was definitely a husband and father, and he may have wanted to be devoted, but you don't get nicknamed Moon the Loon for staying home at night. Did he suffer for his crazy antics? Most definitely, breaking bones, his bank account, and his own heart along the way.

Born near London, Keith John Moon was a scene-stealer all through school. At age 12, his teachers wrote on his report card comments such as "goonery seems to come before everything" and "retarded artistically, idiotic in other respects." Not surprisingly, he left school three years later when he dropped his noisy bugle and took up the drums. A year later he was playing surf tunes with Britain's Beachcombers; a year after that, Keith auditioned for the Detours, who would become the legendary Who. Keith's brief audition lasted only as long as the drum kit did. "This was the man for us," acknowledged the group's guitarist, Pete Townshend, upon witnessing the carnage.

Keith was invited in as the youngest member, Who hits like "My Generation," "Magic Bus," and "Substitute" soon followed, and their reputation as the most vigorous, destructive live act in rock history quickly spread. By the end of the decade, when the Who rivaled the Stones and the Beatles for the title World's Greatest Rock Band, Keith was in heaven, and he happily told a fan mag that his only ambitions were "to stay young forever" and "to smash 100 drum kits." Unfortunately, such protracted buffoonery comes at a cost, which Keith paid in the '70s.

An undiscriminating drug and alcohol consumer, he became more of a distraction than a boon to the Who. In '73 he collapsed on stage at San Francisco's Cow Palace after taking a massive animal tranquilizer. There were speculations that his drumming was dubbed by studio musicians on some songs, while on others there were no drums at all. He dabbled in acting, landing small, scene-stealing parts (especially as debauched Uncle Ernie in *Tommy*, '75). *Two Sides of the Moon* was his attempt at a solo record, but it was more memorable for his full moon on the inside sleeve than for his feeble crooning. By the mid-'70s he was living in L.A., partying endlessly and surrendering his baby-faced cuteness to bearded bloat. Sadly, in '78 Keith died in his sleep from an unintentional overdose of prescription drugs, a casualty, like Janis and Jimi and Jim, of excess success.

EVERYBODY LOVES SOMEBODY

"There is no question at all but that Keith Moon only ever loves one woman in his life and that woman is Kim. The only real question is whether there is anyone else he treats worse than Kim." So wrote Keith's longtime chauffeur about the late Kim Kerrigan. A slim, beautiful blonde model who had lived in Malaysia and Africa as a child, Kim met Keith in '64. An oft-told story has it that she was dating both Rod Stewart and Keith simultaneously, and one night on a train the two men supposedly discovered they were both going to visit Kim. Kim herself dismissed this rumor as something Keith embellished, just because it was so entertaining.

Kim moved to London to be with Keith and often traveled with the band as it conquered the U.K. Pregnant in early '66, Kim (17) and Keith (19) married at a register's office; daughter Mandy was born that summer. Unfortunately, Kim's years with Keith were tumultuous, punctuated by his womanizing and irrational behavior. Keith spent little time with his daughter while he toured with the Who. At home, fights were many. A curious artifact Keith kept was a champagne bottle he'd thrown angrily at Kim, only to see it become embedded in the wall—he left it there and even framed the bottle.

Finally, in '73 Kim had enough and left with Mandy, getting a divorce in '75. His next major relationship was with a dead ringer for Kim. Kim married another rocker, keyboardist Ian McLagan of the Small Faces ("Itchycoo Park") in '78 and moved to the U.S. The McLagans moved to a 15-acre home on the Texas range in '94; still youthfully beautiful, Kim had her own skin-care business near Austin and lived in rural contentment until she tragically died in a 2006 car crash.

MY BACK PAGES

Only occasionally was Keith allowed to sing with the Who, usually to comic effect—the growly "Uncle Ernie" on *Tommy*, the hyper-accented "Bellboy" on *Quadrophenia*, the falsetto "Barbara Ann" in the film *The Kids Are Alright*. . . . The cover of *Who Are You*, the last Who album with Keith, showed him sitting in a chair stenciled with the words "Not to Be Taken Away"—he died a few weeks later in the same borrowed London flat where Mama Cass had died in '74. . . . Supposedly the Muppets' character Animal was based on Keith.

Jim Morrison

The Lizard King electrified the rock world with his complex lyrics and daring performances.

TAKIN' CARE OF BUSINESS

Jim Morrison's short, strange trip has been the subject of books, movies, and wild conjecture. Born in Florida into a military family, Jim had a mystical experience at age 13 that stayed with him throughout his life: on a driving trip through New Mexico, the family car slowly passed a roadside wreck, and Jim felt that one of the souls of the dead or dying

"landed" inside of him (he would refer to this charged moment in later writings).

Estranged from his parents (he'd later claim he was an orphan), the teen bounced through Florida colleges until he headed to California in '64 to try UCLA's film school. There he met keyboardist Ray Manzerek, who was impressed by Jim's mystical poetry, and soon a nascent band was formed with guitarist Robbie Krieger and drummer John Densmore. The Doors (the name came from a William Blake poem and an Aldous Huxley book) blended Jim's poetic lyrics with a hypnotic, distinctive rock sound that replaced the traditional bass guitar with electric keyboards. Jim's emotional vocals and sexually charged live performances drove the band to prominence in the late '60s.

Radio hits were consistent in their appealing inconsistency, ranging from the propulsive "Break on Through" to the radio-friendly "Hello, I Love You," from the rollicking "Love Her Madly" to the haunting "Riders on the Storm." The Doors made their name as rock rebels, however, with their long anthems, especially the landmark "Light My Fire" (with lyrics too risqué for Ed Sullivan, who tried unsuccessfully to change them for his show), the highly controversial "The End" (with lines about killing the father, sleeping with the mother), and the glorious epic "L.A. Woman" (their last hit).

Jim himself went through huge transformations in a relatively short time: after bursting onto the scene in '67 as a lean, erotic rock god in tight leather pants, by '69 he was a bloated, bearded, drug-saturated alcoholic stumbling through songs and getting arrested on a Miami stage for indecent exposure. In '71, after moving to Paris to regain control of his life (and escape the jail sentence waiting for him in America), 27-year-old Jim died under mysterious circumstances, officially of a heart attack, supposedly of a heroin overdose, and mythically in a staged event that brought him an ongoing life in seclusion.

EVERYBODY LOVES SOMEBODY

Pamela Courson was a red-haired pixie from Northern California who was the love of Jim's life: he called her his "cosmic mate," dedicated his self-published books of poetry to her, wrote songs to and about her, and left his entire estate to her in his will. They met in '65 when she was a 19-year-old art student at L.A. City College and he was a Door performing at a Sunset Strip nightclub. Love came quickly, but fidelity never did.

In '67 Jim moved into her apartment in the L.A. hills, but he was carousing and drinking so much the band had to get "babysitters" to watch over him and make sure he showed up to gigs. During these years, Pamela traveled with the band, attempted to run a short-lived fashion boutique that Jim bought her, and sampled all the drugs passing by. She also took his last name, though they were never legally married. Pamela and Jim both had affairs outside their relationship—his were usually with the legions of groupies who threw themselves at him, hers were often used as a way to get back at him. He had a relationship with the Viking-like singer from the Velvet Underground, Nico, and in '70 he even "married" another girlfriend, Patricia Kennealy, at a Wiccan wedding in which they drank each other's blood and performed rites of witchcraft.

With Jim in Paris, Pamela was the one who discovered him dead in the bathtub and called the police. After Jim's

September 26, 1962—*The Beverly Hillbillies* with Buddy Ebsen debuts. ☮ September 26, 1963—*Here's Edie* with Edie Adams debuts.
September 26, 1964—*Gilligan's Island* with Bob Denver debuts.
September 26, 1965—Queen Elizabeth decorates the Beatles with the Order of the British Empire. ☮ September 26, 1968—Andy Warhol's *Flesh* opens.

death, she became a reclusive heroin addict and more and more mentally unstable. She was telling friends that Jim was still alive right up to her own premature—but not surprising—death in her Hollywood apartment three years after his.

MY BACK PAGES

His favorite nickname—Mr. Mojo Risin' (an anagram of Jim Morrison). . . . The band's first LP, *The Doors*, was the first rock album touted on a Sunset Blvd. billboard. . . . In '70, Jim supposedly told friends that after the recent deaths of Jim Hendrix and Janis Joplin, "You're drinking with number three". . . . The night that Jim died in Paris, he and Pamela went to see a movie—*Death Valley*. . . . Reports say that Jim's will left nothing to his parents, but after Pamela died, his parents and her parents supposedly split the entire fortune. . . . Pamela wanted to be buried next to Jim in Paris's famous Pere-Lachaise cemetery, but due to legal complications she was cremated in Southern California instead. . . . Jim's graffiti-covered gravesite has long been one of Paris's most-visited tourist spots. . . . Val Kilmer played Jim and Meg Ryan played Pamela in Oliver Stone's *The Doors* ('91).

Janet Munro

A spirited Disney doll who starred in the blockbuster hit of '60.

TAKIN' CARE OF BUSINESS

Despite all the screen vets who starred in *Swiss Family Robinson* ('60)—names like Tommy Kirk, James MacArthur, John Mills, Dorothy McGuire, and Sessue Hayakawa—that great island adventure was stolen by cute, redheaded Janet Munro, who spent part of the movie masquerading as a teenage boy. It wasn't Janet's first Disney triumph—a year before she'd co-starred as Sean Connery's spirited love interest in the delightful *Darby O'Gill and the Little People*.

Born to a father who was a Scottish comedian, young Janet had helped entertain the troops before getting work on British television. "Miss English Television of '58" then hit the movies and won the Golden Globe as Most Promising Newcomer with her Disney debuts. Her move into more mature roles through the '60s started off well—*The Day the Earth Caught Fire* ('61) was a well-made sci-fi drama—but by the end of the '60s her career was clearly on the decline. Problems with alcohol made things worse, and finally her health failed her in '72 when she tragically died of heart disease at only 38 years old.

EVERYBODY LOVES SOMEBODY

Janet was married twice, both times to British actors. She and her second husband, Ian Hendry, had two daughters and were in the '68 drama *Cry Wolf* together before they divorced in '71.

MY BACK PAGES

Janet shared her Golden Globe with three other Promising Newcomers in '60—Angie Dickinson, Stella Stevens, and Tuesday Weld. . . . Earlier versions of *Swiss Family Robinson* didn't have Janet's character in them—in a '75 TV movie made by Irwin Allen, "Roberta" was played by young Helen Hunt.

Murph the Surf

The decade's most famous thief almost pulled off a daring heist.

TAKIN' CARE OF BUSINESS

Before he was a world-famous jewel thief, handsome Jack Murphy from L.A. was a surf star in Florida. He won championships in '62 and '63, appeared in surfing documentaries, and even had his own Florida surf shop while still in his mid-20s. When business turned bad, he turned to crime, beginning with small-time Miami cat burglaries. Then, he and a partner attempted the decade's most audacious heist.

After studying the caper movies *To Catch a Thief* and *Topkapi* for inspiration and ideas, the pair scaled the fences and walls of New York's famed American Museum of Natural History at night and slipped in through an open window. Upon discovering that the alarm for the world's largest sapphire, the 563-carat Star of India, wasn't working, they cut into the glass cases, scooped up the Star and two dozen other famous gems, and left the way they'd entered.

Back in Miami the police got tipped off and soon arrested the burglars, and most of the jewels (including the Star of India) were found in a bus locker. Jack got a three-year sentence at Rikers Island, of which he served two. But bigger problems were ahead. In '69 Jack was convicted of robbery and murder in Florida and was given a life sentence. He was paroled in '86, having taught himself to paint. Now a born-again Christian, he runs a prison ministry. And he still surfs.

EVERYBODY LOVES SOMEBODY

A sun-worshipping Miami playboy in the late '50s, Jack was married in the early '60s, though he was soon divorced. At the peak of his crime success he had homes in Hawaii, Manhattan, and L.A. He's been married with children since the late '80s—he met his wife in prison when she visited to film a documentary.

MY BACK PAGES

The '75 film *Murph the Surf* (also released as *Live a Little, Steal a Lot*) fictionalized his exploits—longtime TV actor Don Stroud played Jack. . . . Mined in Africa and donated to the museum by J.P. Morgan, the Star of India is an almost flawless dome-shaped gem the size of an egg, with a distinctive star pattern on each side. . . . In '96, Murph the Surf was inducted into a Surfing Hall of Fame on the East Coast. . . . Surfers know another Murph the Surf—that was the name of a cool little '60s cartoon character drawn by surfer/artist Rick Griffin for *Surfer* magazine.

Joe Namath

The playboy QB effected one of the biggest upsets in football history.

TAKIN' CARE OF BUSINESS

The closest pro football came to producing a rock star in the '60s was Joe William Namath, who burst into the spotlight in '65, was quickly a star attraction in the sport's biggest city, and played at the top of his game for the rest of the decade. A child of Hungarian immigrants, Joe hailed from a small town near Pittsburgh. In high school "the Hungarian Howitzer" starred in football, basketball, and base-

September 27, 1966—*Dinner at Eight* with Pamela Tiffin opens on Broadway. ☮ September 28, 1924—Actor Marcello Mastroianni is born in Italy. September 28, 1934—Actress Brigitte Bardot is born in Paris. ☮ September 28, 1934—Actress Janet Munro is born in Lancashire, England. September 28, 1960—Connie Francis's "My Heart Has a Mind of Its Own" hits #1. ☮ September 28, 1960—Ted Williams homers in his last at-bat.

ball, and upon graduating he had his choice of colleges and careers (several pro baseball teams offered him contracts).

Choosing Bear Bryant's University of Alabama football team, Joe was a two-time All-American for the Crimson Tide, though he suffered the knee injury in his senior season that would plague (and shorten) his pro career. Blessed with a rocket arm and an innate understanding of the game, he was praised by Bryant, not just as the greatest quarterback, but as "the greatest athlete" he'd ever coached.

After being named the Orange Bowl MVP in '65, Joe signed with the AFL's New York Jets for a record $427,000 per year (plus a new Lincoln). Instantly, he was the league's and the town's star attraction. He was Rookie of the Year, and he made the AFL All-Star team his first year (as well as in '67, '68, and '69). These were years when giants quarterbacked the gridiron—John Unitas, Bart Starr, Len Dawson—but only Joe passed for over 4,000 yards in a season. His long (by pro football standards) shaggy hair, rugged good looks, dashing white shoes, sideline fur coat, cocky attitude, and electrifying passes brought a new rebellious excitement to the game when crew-cutted Unitas and military-precise Starr were the establishment heroes.

Joe's greatest glory came in Super Bowl III, when he led the fledgling AFL to its first championship victory over an NFL titan. At the time the AFL was denigrated as an inferior league, and the Jets were 18-point underdogs to the powerful Baltimore Colts, who were led by their own MVP quarterback, Earl Morrall, and legendary defensive lineman Bubba Smith. The week of the game, however, Joe brashly guaranteed victory, and he delivered, 16-7, with a careful, controlled performance (he threw for only 206 yards) that won him the MVP trophy. The AFL was made legitimate, and Joe was the coolest athlete in America.

Capitalizing on his name and fame, endorsement deals poured in, including ads for appliances, shirts, Ovaltine, cologne, panty hose (amazingly, he was shown wearing them!), and, most famously, Norelco razors—in '69 he earned $10,000 for shaving off his Fu Manchu moustache in a commercial. Like George Best, England's young star footballer, Joe got into the bar business, but the league ordered him to abandon Bachelors III before his (and the game's) reputation could be tarnished by "undesirables." Joe refused and at 26 even retired briefly, but he was back in a Jets jersey the following summer, sans saloon.

10 Classic Quarterbacks

George Blanda–
Houston Oilers, AFL Player of the Year '61

Greg Cook–
Cincinnati Bengals, AFL Rookie of the Year '69

Roman Gabriel–L.A. Rams, NFL MVP '69

Jack Kemp–
Buffalo Bills, AFL Player of the Year '65

Daryl Lamonica–
Oakland Raiders, AFL Player of the Year '67

Earl Morrall–Baltimore Colts, NFL MVP '68

Bart Starr–Green Bay Packers, NFL MVP '66

Y.A. Tittle–New York Giants, NFL MVP '62

John Unitas–Baltimore Colts, NFL MVP '67

Norm Van Brocklin–
Philadelphia Eagles, NFL MVP '60

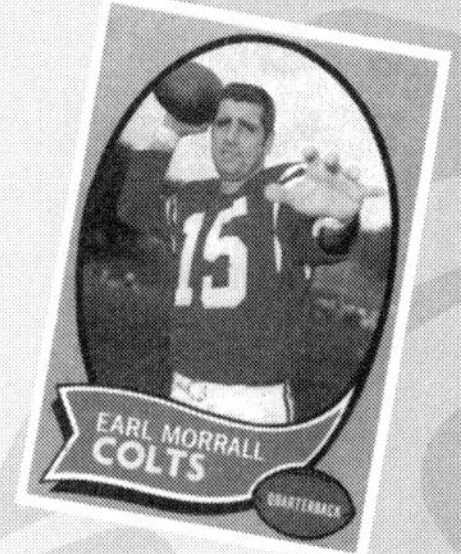

September 28, 1961—*Dr. Kildare* with Richard Chamberlain debuts. ☮ September 28, 1968—Janis Joplin's "Piece of My Heart" hits the charts.
September 29, 1912—Director Michelangelo Antonioni is born in Italy. ☮ September 29, 1931—Actress Anita Ekberg is born in Malm, Sweden.
September 29, 1960—*My Three Sons* with Fred MacMurray debuts.

The new decade brought a cheeky autobiography (*I Can't Wait Until Tomorrow, Because I Get Better Looking Everyday*) and a new side career when Hollywood came calling with several starring roles, starting with the Ann-Margret/biker flick *C.C. and Company*. Seven more years with the Jets brought continued fame but more knee problems and no championships, and in '77 Broadway Joe was waived by the Jets and acquired by the L.A. Rams, where he played inconsistently for a year before retiring. He left the game with stats that showed his perseverance—four different seasons he was too injured to play in half the games—and his fearlessness—he finished with far more interceptions (220) than touchdowns (173).

EVERYBODY LOVES SOMEBODY

"I like my Johnny Walker Red and my women blonde." That was Joe all over. He was charming, he drank, he loved women, he stayed out all night, he went home to a swingin' Manhattan bachelor pad, he lived a larger-than-life existence—as many have said before, he was football's Beatle. After completing many late-night passes, he finally settled down with marriage in '84 and two kids before his '99 divorce.

MY BACK PAGES

After he retired from football, Joe continued his show biz career with starring roles on stage, his own one-season TV series (*The Waverley Wonders* in '78), an announcing gig on *Monday Night Football* in '85, and many appearances on talk shows and sitcoms. . . . Joe's longtime problems with alcohol surfaced in 2003 when he made slurred comments to an ESPN reporter on live TV—after profusely apologizing, he later went through rehab successfully and explained that his social drinking had intensified during his pro football career as a way to obliterate physical pain. . . . Western Pennsylvania has been called "the cradle of quarterbacks" because six Hall of Famers have come from the area—Joe, Dan Marino, Joe Montana, Johnny Unitas, George Blanda, and Jim Kelly.

Paul Newman and Robert Redford

The "buddy movie"was reinvigorated when these two handsome, intelligent, dignified stars teamed up for a much-loved Western.

TAKIN' CARE OF BUSINESS

Newman and Redford may sound like a comedy act, but the ones really laughing were the studio executives, all the way to the bank. Paul Newman and Robert Redford both had successful Hollywood careers independent of each other before *Butch Cassidy and the Sundance Kid* shot them into the cinematic stratosphere.

Born in Cleveland, classically handsome, and with the bluest eyes this side of Frank Sinatra, by the late '60s Paul was a much-lauded veteran of stage and screen, having starred on Broadway in the '50s and gotten four Best Actor Oscar nominations for his dramatic work in *Cat on a Hot Tin Roof* ('58), *The Hustler* ('61), *Hud* ('63), and *Cool Hand Luke* ('67). The younger, blonder Santa Monica native Robert was an up-and-coming star with a growing résumé of acclaimed work, including a classic *Twilight Zone* episode in which he played Death, *Inside Daisy Clover* ('65) with Natalie Wood, and the Neil Simon charmer *Barefoot in the Park*, first on Broadway and then in the '67 film alongside Jane Fonda.

A year later, when Steve McQueen stepped away from the role of Sundance, Bob stepped in to play the reticent gunslinger, and Hollywood history was changed. *Butch Cassidy* went on to become a beloved blockbuster (the biggest box office ever for a Western), Oscar handed out multiple nominations and wins, both actors got "super" added to their star status, and everyone connected with the movie (including co-star Katharine Ross, director George Roy Hill, screenwriter William Goldman, singer B.J. Thomas, and Burt Bacharach, composer of the hit soundtrack album) saw their careers launched to new heights.

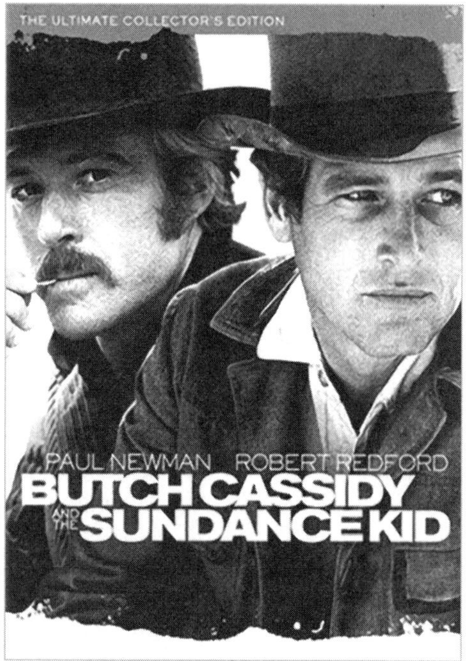

Reflecting the rebellious era, the movie upended conventions of traditional Westerns: the heroes were lovable bad guys; the gang leader had never shot anyone; the sheriff requested that he himself be gagged and tied; the school marm was young and voluptuous; half the movie was set in South, not North, America; and old-fashioned horses were giving way to newfangled bicycles.

Posed on posters like sexy male models, the two charming leads generated a chemistry that Hollywood has tried to replicate ever since. Previously, "buddy movies" were more like vaudeville acts (Hope and Crosby) or merely presented established comedy teams (Abbott and Costello, Martin and Lewis) in nutty settings; after *Butch Cassidy*, a long, steady wave of movies that teamed two attractive, sometimes mismatched rogues (among them Gene Wilder and Richard Pryor, Eddie Murphy and Nick Nolte, Mel Gibson and Danny Glover, Chris Farley and David Spade, Susan Sarandon and Geena Davis) swept into theatres in hopes of recapturing that Newman/Redford magic.

The pair reteamed for another classic Oscar-winning comedy, *The Sting*, in '73 (Bob got a Best Actor Oscar nomination), and then went on to legendary careers of their own, resulting in some of the most successful, most admired movies in history. Crowd-pleasers (Paul's *The Towering Inferno* in '74), powerful political thrillers (Bob's *All the President's Men* in '76), Best Actor Oscar-winners (Paul's *The Color of Money* in '86), and Best Director Oscar-winners (Bob's *Ordinary People* in '80) are only the most conspicuous products of their prodigious, enduring talents.

EVERYBODY LOVES SOMEBODY

The two world-famous matinee idols could have been two world-famous playboys in the full glare of the paparazzi, but instead they have led private lives that are indeed private and away from the Hollywood spotlight. In the '60s, both were in the early years of long marriages. Paul was first married in '49 and had three kids (one of whom died in '78) before his divorce nine years later; since '58 he's been married to actress Joanne Woodward, who won the Best Actress Oscar for *The Three Faces of Eve* ('57). Together they've had three daughters. Robert was married in '58, had four kids (one of whom died young), and has discreetly dated after his mid-'80s divorce.

MY BACK PAGES

Both actively campaigned for McCarthy in the late '60s. . . . In addition to his acting nominations in the '60s, Paul also got a Best Picture Oscar nod as co-producer (with his wife) of *Rachel, Rachel* ('68). . . . Just as successful as his movie career are his business and philanthropy careers—his Newman's Own line of salad dressings and sauces has generated over $100,000,000, all donated to charity. . . . For over 30 years he's indulged his long passion for race cars by driving competitively and/or owning race cars. . . . Robert was a college baseball player and a struggling painter in Paris before studying acting in New York. . . . Roles Robert is said to have been offered—George Segal's part in *Who's Afraid of Virginia Woolf?*, Ben in *The Graduate*, the male lead in *Rosemary's Baby*, Michael in *The Godfather*, and Paul Newman's Oscar-nominated lawyer in *The Verdict*. . . . The deeply committed con-

September 29, 1967—Writer Carson McCullers dies in New York of a cerebral hemorrhage at age 50. ☮ September 29, 1969—*Love, American Style* debuts.
September 30, 1924—Author Truman Capote is born in New Orleans, Louisiana.
September 30, 1931—Actress Angie Dickinson is born in Kulm, North Dakota.

Top-Grossing Movies by Year (Approximate U.S. Gross)

1960–*Swiss Family Robinson* ($20,000,000)
1961–*101 Dalmatians* ($14,000,000)
1962–*The Longest Day* ($40,000,000)
1963–*Cleopatra* ($48,000,000)
1964–*Mary Poppins* ($31,000,000)
1965–*The Sound of Music* ($80,000,000)
1966–*The Bible* ($35,000,000)
1967–*The Jungle Book* ($40,000,000)
1968–*Funny Girl* ($50,000,000)
1969–*Butch Cassidy and the Sundance Kid* ($90,000,000)

servationist has long fought for environmental issues. . . . *Butch Cassidy* inspired the names for two of their passions—Paul created the Hole in the Wall Gang Camp for sick children, and Robert founded the Sundance Institute for independent filmmakers.

Nichelle Nichols

This elegant, coolly professional actress was the starring female on *Star Trek*.

TAKIN' CARE OF BUSINESS

How's this for name-dropping: Duke Ellington hired her, Martin Luther King, Jr. advised her, and Whoopi Goldberg and an astronaut took inspiration from her. Though she was only a supporting character on a TV show, often with simple lines ("Hailing frequencies open"), Illinois-born Nichelle Nichols was the fulcrum for several important TV advances.

A successful singer who toured North America and Europe with Duke Ellington, Nichelle made her TV debut in '63. *The Lieutenant* was a short-lived cop drama, and Nichelle was on just one episode, but she planted a seed in the mind of the show's producer, Gene Roddenberry. In '66 that seed blossomed into a part on Roddenberry's new *Star Trek* series. The groundbreaking character Lieutenant Nyota Uhura (*uhuru* is the Swahili word for "freedom") made Nichelle the first African-American woman with a prominent role on a major network show. But it wasn't easy.

Subjected to occasional racial hostility on the set, she soon found out that she alone among the major characters didn't have a contract and was being paid on a daily basis. The studio, she discovered, was even withholding her fan mail! About to quit in the show's first season, she changed her mind after Dr. Martin Luther King personally praised her as "a wonderful role model." Much later, Whoopi Goldberg told her that Uhura was the character who made her want to be a star, and the first African-American woman in space, Dr. Mae Jemison, also credited Uhura as an inspiration. Her most controversial moment came in '68 when she and series star William Shatner shared what's said to be TV's first interracial kiss.

Her post-'60s career included lots of star trekkin': six *Star Trek* movies, voices for the *Star Trek* cartoon and video games, and appearances at fan conventions. Outside of the *Star Trek* universe, she has also lived long and prospered with performances on-screen, onstage, and in nightclubs. Nichelle wrote a frank and fascinating autobiography in '94 and a sci-fi novel in '95. An advocate of space travel, she's attended many NASA ceremonies and has helped the agency recruit minorities. Among her many international awards and honors, she was the first African-American actress to place handprints in front of Hollywood's Grauman's Chinese Theatre.

EVERYBODY LOVES SOMEBODY

Nichelle confessed in her autobiography that she and Gene Roddenberry had fallen in love in '63. Roddenberry wasn't boldly going where no man had gone before, however—in her teens she was married, divorced, and a mother. Nichelle remarried in '68, this time to a songwriter, but that marriage ended in divorce a few years later.

MY BACK PAGES

In her autobiography she described a tense confrontation between her father (a mayor) and Al Capone—and it was Capone who backed down! . . . Nichelle released an album in '67 called *Out of This World*, which included her interpretation of the *Star Trek* theme. . . . When Roddenberry died of cardiac arrest in '91, Nichelle sang two songs at the service.

Jack Nicholson

The '70s superstar was a hard-workin' '60s writer/actor.

TAKIN' CARE OF BUSINESS

Everybody knows Jack Nicholson's devilish eyebrows, impish grin, and impressive career highlights—*Chinatown* ('74), *One Flew Over the Cuckoo's Nest* ('75), *Terms of Endearment* ('83), *As Good As It Gets* ('92), and on and on for a dozen Oscar nominations in some of Hollywood's most important movies. But not everybody knows the '60s Nicholson who was not only stealing scenes as an actor, he was writing some pretty groovy movies too.

Dennis Hopper, Jack Nicholson, Peter Fonda

Roger Corman gave him his start in/as the *Cry Baby Killer* ('58), followed by notable roles in quickie flicks, including *The Wild Ride* ('60), the made-in-two-days *The Little Shop of Horrors* ('60), and the made-in-four-days *The Terror* ('63). Around this time he started working behind the camera as well as in front, getting producing, writing, and/or acting credits on little-seen films like *Thunder Island* ('63), *Ride in the Whirlwind* ('65) and *The Shooting* ('67).

Jumping into drug-influenced, youth-oriented movies, he played Stoney, a pony-tailed San Francisco hippie, in *Psych-Out* ('68), wearing flamboyant threads as he cranked out lead guitar for an acid rock band and introduced free love to naïve Susan Strasberg (his script was the basis for the movie). With the Monkees, he co-wrote and appeared in *Head* ('68), an abstract jaunt more fun to make than to watch.

Disappointed with his career direction, Jack was ready to quit acting for producing when he replaced Rip Torn as the drunken lawyer in *Easy Rider* ('69). Jack explained the world to the biker heroes ("What you represent to them is freedom"), got killed by Southern rednecks, and earned his first Oscar nomination. *Five Easy Pieces* a year later would confirm his rising stature as one of Hollywood's best actors, a promise fulfilled over the next 30+ years.

EVERYBODY LOVES SOMEBODY

Jack's childhood wasn't clarified for him until adulthood: he had been raised by his grandmother, and the woman he thought was his older sister was actually his mother. He himself has had one marriage, to actress Sandra Knight from '62–'68, with one child. He then had a child with actress Susan Anspach, three more kids with two different models, another out-of-wedlock child who claimed to be his daughter in 2005, and a long rela-

October 1, 1944—Model Mandy Rice-Davies is born. ☮ October 1, 1949—Photographer Annie Leibovitz is born in Westbury, Connecticut. October 1, 1961—Roger Maris hits homer #61, breaking Babe Ruth's record. ☮ October 1, 1963—*Lilies of the Field* with Sidney Poitier opens. October 1, 1964—The Rolling Stones make their first appearance on Ed Sullivan's show. ☮ October 1, 2003—Actress Julie Parrish dies in L.A. of cancer.

tionship with actress Anjelica Huston. His other relationships (with actress Lara Flynn Boyle, for instance) and his off-camera antics (the golf club incident with a car) are usually well-chronicled in magazines.

MY BACK PAGES

Jack's house is on Mulholland Drive above L.A., near Warren Beatty's home and Marlon Brando's former estate. . . . He also owns a house in Aspen, a prominent art collection, and Lakers season tickets. . . . Roles he's said to have turned down: Michael Corleone in *The Godfather*, Johnny Hooker in *The Sting*, Roy Neary in *Close Encounters*.

Chris Noel

Lovely Chris Noel walked away from a budding acting career to entertain the troops in Vietnam for the last half of the '60s.

TAKIN' CARE OF BUSINESS

In the late '60s, every American soldier knew Chris Noel. More accurately, they knew her marvelously tomboyish voice, which still cracks and soothes with the warmth of a summer afternoon. That voice, and her remarkable looks, made her a Hollywood star before she became a G.I. legend. A Florida beach girl, Chris Noel was modeling, winning beauty pageants, and cheerleading for the New York Giants while still a teen.

In '63, Hollywood scooped her up and debuted her all-American appeal in Steve McQueen's *Soldier in the Rain* ('63). *Beach Ball* ('65) was her breakthrough to stardom, giving her star billing and showcasing her bikinied image on the poster. Elvis's *Girl Happy* ('65) cast her as a pretty sidekick, and *Wild, Wild Winter* ('66) gave her another starring role in a teen movie. Throughout the decade Chris was guesting on dozens of popular TV shows, and she also graced a dozen magazine covers (blonde, green-eyed, brightly smiling Chris projected the perfect girl-next-door image—if, that is, you happened to be lucky enough to live next to a stunning starlet with 36-23-34 measurements).

The turning point, not just in her career but in her entire life, came when she toured a vets hospital in '65. The sight of the broken, mutilated casualties brought home the reality of what was happening in Vietnam. She asked to audition for the Armed Forces Network and in '66 began hosting her own hour-long radio show. "Hi luv," she'd say at the opening of *A Date with Chris*, and then would follow music, dedications, interviews, and Chris's own spontaneous chat. The show ran from '66 to March '71 and made her "the Voice of Vietnam," the cheery darling of war-weary G.I.'s everywhere. Thousands carried her picture with them into battle; thousands more wrote her loving, grateful, nostalgic letters.

That first year she taped the show in California, but by '67 she was actually in Vietnam for months at a time, voluntarily touring the bases and visiting the hospitals and flying into war zones too remote for Bob Hope's big showy productions. For four years she sang, autographed, joked, talked, comforted, and mothered the boys on those distant and dangerous front lines. Twice her helicopter was shot down, mortar fire sometimes exploded around her, and bullets whizzed past her more times than she could count.

Returning to Hollywood after the war, Chris put in some minor movie and TV appearances, but she was soon

October 2, 1959—*The Twilight Zone* with Rod Serling debuts. ☮ October 2, 1962—Johnny Carson hosts his first *Tonight Show* as the permanent host. October 2, 1965—*Repulsion* with Catherine Deneuve opens. ☮ October 3, 1960—Sam Cooke's "Chain Gang" hits #2. October 3, 1961—*The Dick Van Dyke Show* debuts. ☮ October 3, 1967—Singer Woody Guthrie dies at age 55.

suffering from the same post-war syndrome that was plaguing vets all across America. Migraines, flashbacks, depression, and rage were the symptoms of the emotional storm roiling deep within, to be treated with years of therapy. In '85 she was in *Cease Fire*, a riveting movie that exposed this trauma. Her own autobiography, *A Matter of Survival* ('87), was another attempt to exorcise the wounds of war.

To help others who also continued to suffer from memories of Vietnam, she traveled around the country to support veteran organizations and joined the boards of many Vietnam-related councils and groups. In the '80s, she organized the Women's Interaction Network to help women cope with the war's lingering fallout. Since '93 she's run the Vetsville Cease Fire House, a homeless shelter she founded for Florida's disenfranchised vets. Chris Noel, still tirelessly fighting the good fight and providing a beacon of hope for those who first heard her voice some 40 years ago.

EVERYBODY LOVES SOMEBODY

In '65, Chris was dating singer Jack Jones when she learned of the Armed Forces Network. While in Vietnam, she married a Green Beret captain in '68, but tragedy would end their life together before it could really begin. Upon returning home, and suffering from delayed-stress syndrome, her husband of eleven months committed suicide at Christmas in '69. Later remarried and divorced twice, she's happily married again and living in south Florida.

MY BACK PAGES

Chris's last name is pronounced with the accent on the second syllable, like "gazelle". . . . Chris was once the national champion in baton twirling. . . . Her album *Forgotten Man* was dedicated to vets everywhere, with profits going to vets groups. . . . Another collection of songs, *Nashville Impact*, came out in late '99. . . . Chris has been honored with tons of humanitarian awards, among them the Distinguished Vietnam Veteran award from the National Vietnam Veterans Network in '84.

Kim Novak

The glamorous '50s star was still a popular, busy actress in the '60s.

TAKIN' CARE OF BUSINESS

While other blonde bombshells of the '50s (especially Marilyn Monroe and Jayne Mansfield) struggled with their careers in the '60s, Kim Novak endured. Though her '60s films didn't match her great '50s work, audiences still loved her enough to vote her their favorite film star in a poll taken at the New York World's Fair in '64.

Kim was born in Chicago and was winning beauty contests in her mid-teens. Before she was discovered by the studios, she worked as a model and had to demo iceboxes as "Miss Deepfreeze of 1953." Once the studios got hold of her, they changed her first name from Marilyn to Kim and cast her as a buxom "lavender blonde" replacement for Rita Hayworth.

October 3, 1979—29-year-old Claudia Jennings, a popular *Playboy* Playmate in '69, dies in an auto accident on the Pacific Coast Highway in Malibu. October 3, 2004—Actress Janet Leigh dies in Beverly Hills at age 77. ☮ October 4, 1941—Actress Lori Saunders is born in Kansas City, Missouri. October 4, 1970—Singer Janis Joplin dies of a drug overdose at age 27.

Kim was decorative scenery in early '50s flicks until a run of popular movies, including *Picnic* ('56), *Pal Joey* ('57), and Hitchcock's masterful *Vertigo* ('58), made her a top star, with the trophies to prove it—a '55 Golden Globe as the Most Promising Newcomer and a '57 Golden Globe as the World's Film Favorite. In the '60s, her best work came in the first half of the decade: *Strangers When We Meet* with Kirk Douglas ('60), *The Notorious Landlady* with Jack Lemmon ('62), and Billy Wilder's *Kiss Me, Stupid* ('64). With her movies diminishing in frequency and significance in the late '60s, Kim soon semi-retired.

The '70s and '80s saw her in over a dozen lesser films and TV movies—the best were *The Mirror Crack'd* ('80) and the *Falcon Crest* TV series ('86). Kim came out of retirement for the '79 Oscars, attracting considerable attention with a plunging black gown that she called "the most fabulous dress of my career." At the turn of the century *Playboy* rightly remembered her as one of the sexiest stars ever, ranking her between #17 Betty Grable and #19 Ursula Andress.

EVERYBODY LOVES SOMEBODY

Kim was engaged twice before she left for Hollywood at age 20. Once in Tinsel Town, during the '50s her contract stipulated that she had to date certain "pretty boys" who were also under contract to advance everybody's careers. She was romantically linked with Cary Grant, playboy Aly Khan, and several Rat Packers.

Late in '57, studio head Harry Cohn was furious when word leaked of her affair with Sammy Davis, Jr. Terrified that rumors of the explosive relationship would ruin his top star's career, Cohn used his influence (and, according to legend, some hired thugs) to force the pair to break up. Sammy soon married someone else, and Kim got involved with a rich married man. Mid-decade she was married for a year to Richard Johnson, her co-star in *The Amorous Adventures of Moll Flanders* ('65). Married again in '76, she lives with her husband, a veterinarian, and raises animals in Oregon.

MY BACK PAGES

Racy photos taken when Kim was a teen were bought up by her studio once she became a star (though she said they were relatively "prudish" compared to modern films). . . . Kim has said that she was offered the Holly Golightly role in *Breakfast at Tiffany's* before it went to Audrey Hepburn. . . . Movie legend has it that Kim was the first choice to play Dean Wormer's drunken, promiscuous wife in *Animal House* (the role went to Verna Bloom). . . . It's hard to verify this, but many fans swear that Kim went braless in many of her films. . . . In '66 Kim survived a near-fatal car accident near Monterey, California. . . . What's more, she's had two of her homes destroyed by natural disasters, the first in the '60s, when her Bel-Air home was crushed in a mudslide, and the second in 2000, when a falling tree knocked over a power line, causing a fire that gutted her Oregon home. . . . Among the items she's lost in these devastations were an extensive art collection and the computer on which she was writing her autobiography.

Peter O'Toole and Omar Sharif

***Lawrence of Arabia* turned these two unknowns into international stars.**

TAKIN' CARE OF BUSINESS

On the American Film Institute's list of the hundred greatest films of all time, David Lean's majestic *Lawrence of Arabia* ('62) is the highest-ranked '60s film (it's #5, right between two '39 classics, *Gone with the Wind* and *The Wizard of Oz*). Maybe the ultimate "guys movie" (war, heroism, dashing leads, and not a single word spoken by a woman during its almost four-hour length), *Lawrence* made sensations out of its two 30-year-old stars, both of whom were unknown before the movie, both of whom

October 5, 1933—Actress Diane Cilento is born in Queensland, Australia. ☮ October 5, 1961—*Breakfast at Tiffany's* with Audrey Hepburn opens. October 5, 1962—*Dr. No* with Sean Connery opens in the U.K. ☮ October 5, 1962—Actress Sue Ane Langdon makes the cover of *Life*. October 5, 1965—Singer Johnny Cash is busted for drugs in El Paso. ☮ October 5, 1968—Steppenwolf's "Magic Carpet Ride" hits the charts.

got Oscar nominations from the movie, and both of whom had long successful careers after the movie.

Born in Ireland and raised in England, Peter O'Toole served in the Royal Navy before studying at the Royal Academy of Dramatic Arts in the '50s. Primarily a stage actor, he had only a couple of movies (including Disney's *Kidnapped*, '60) on his résumé before he got the part of British officer T.E. Lawrence. Hollywood legend says that Albert Finney was offered the role first but turned it down because of the long location shoot required, and that Katharine Hepburn was the one who pointed the producers to Peter.

It was the role he's still best known for and showed him at his most handsome and charismatic. His powerful voice and personality made him a perfect king, and, in fact, he got two Oscar nominations in the '60s for playing the same royal, Henry II, in two different movies, *Becket* ('64) and *The Lion in Winter* ('68).

Busy throughout the decade, he starred in an interesting range of movies, from a rascally comedy (*What's New, Pussycat?*, '65) to a seafaring drama (*Lord Jim*, '65), from a caper romance (*How to Steal a Million*, '66) to a sad, sensitive musical (*Goodbye Mr. Chips*, '69). The latter brought him a fourth Oscar nomination, to be followed in the '70s and '80s by three more—*The Ruling Class* ('72), *The Stunt Man* ('80), and *My Favorite Year* ('82)—but no Oscar wins, making him one of the most-nominated-but-still-winless actors in history.

Throughout these later decades he also starred in some high-profile bombs (especially *Man of La Mancha*, '72) and some undeniably lightweight movies, and for much of the '70s his life was complicated by health and alcohol problems. But in the '80s and '90s, he seemed to have regained his footing and was in dozens of movie and TV projects (best was the Oscar-winning *The Last Emperor*, '87). While no longer the lead in his films, he is still, as he's been for over 40 years now, one of the world's great movie stars and was thus awarded an honorary Oscar in 2003 for his career achievements.

Dark and pessimistic when Peter was blonde and optimistic, Omar Sharif made just as strong an impact in *Lawrence of Arabia* and was rewarded with a Best Supporting Actor nomination and a Golden Globe trophy as the Most Promising Newcomer. Born in Egypt and fluent in four languages, he'd already been in 20 Egyptian movies before making his English-language debut in *Lawrence*.

For the rest of the decade he averaged two movies a year, including another hit with Peter, the Nazi thriller *Night of the Generals* ('67). *Doctor Zhivago* ('65), of course, remains his best loved role; again working for David Lean, Omar was an intense, handsome match for beautiful Julie Christie in one of the most romantic epics ever made (ironically, Omar's part was supposedly offered to Peter first, who turned it down). *Funny Girl* ('68), *Mackenna's Gold* ('69), and the title role in *Che* ('69) rounded out his successful '60s; he's stayed busy with some 60 movies, documentaries, and other projects ever since (some of them prominent—*Funny Lady* in '75, *Hidalgo* in 2004—others not so much). He has even been in a couple more movies with Peter (*The Rainbow Thief* in '90, the Ted Danson *Gulliver's Travels* in '96). Like Peter, he has also overcome health problems, including a heart attack in the '90s, and emerged into the 21st century as a respected cinematic veteran.

EVERYBODY LOVES SOMEBODY

Both men were married throughout the '60s. For some 15 years, Peter was married to Welsh stage and screen actress Sian Phillips; of their two daughters, Kate has been in plays, movies, and TV shows through the '90s and 2000s. Peter also has a son from his girlfriend in the '80s. Omar's long marriage to Egyptian film legend Faten Hamama ended in divorce; his son, Tarek, is also an actor and made his debut as a child in *Doctor Zhivago*.

MY BACK PAGES

Both men are authors—Peter wrote his critically acclaimed memoirs, and Omar, a championship bridge

October 6, 1936—Actress Anna Quayle is born in London. ☮ October 6, 1942—Actress Britt Ekland is born in Stockholm, Sweden.
October 6, 1961—Actress Liz Taylor makes the cover of *Life*. ☮ October 6, 1963—*Tom Jones* with Albert Finney opens.
October 6, 1965—Sandy Koufax skips the World Series opener because it's Yom Kippur.

player, wrote several books of bridge strategy. . . . Omar also breeds race horses. . . . Having learned to ride a camel in *Lawrence of Arabia*, Peter rode one onto *Late Night with David Letterman* in '95.

Anita Pallenberg

This lanky actress provided liberated companionship to the Rolling Stones.

TAKIN' CARE OF BUSINESS

Born in Italy but living in England, Anita Pallenberg was a teen model who did some work for *Vogue* in the early '60s. As an actress, Anita made her biggest screen splash when she played the Black Queen in *Barbarella* ('68), followed later that same year by a minor role in the cult classic *Candy*. In '69, her sex scene with Mick Jagger in *Performance* seemed so real that many observers, including an outraged Keith Richards, assumed it was. Anita also has some claim to music fame: she sang "oo-oo" with the chorus on "Sympathy for the Devil," and she maintains that she co-wrote "Honky-Tonk Women" and "You Can't Always Get What You Want" with Keith (though she's not listed as one of the composers).

Anita Pallenberg, Mick Jagger

Whatever her role, she was a definite '60s scenemaker, an alluring blonde, and a fab dresser who was a worthy complement to the wildly flamboyant Stones. Pervasive drug abuse, unfortunately, marked her life with and after the group. By the end of the '70s, she'd lost her beauty and sleekness, almost becoming a poster girl for the wretched results of '60s excess. However, she turned herself around in the mid-'80s, kicked drugs, lost weight, and was able to establish once and for all a life apart from any Rolling Stones.

EVERYBODY LOVES SOMEBODY

Based on various biographies and histories, Anita apparently did everything and everyone during the '60s (some stories even put her in beds with Marianne Faithfull and Princess Margaret). Having met and quickly fallen for Brian Jones in '65, she left him in '67 after he beat her. She turned to Keith Richards for comfort, they were together all through the '70s, and they had a son and a daughter (another son died at 10 weeks in '76). "Loneliness and boredom," she said in the book *Rock Wives*, drove her to drugs and affairs while she was with Keith.

So reckless and incessant was her drug use, she reportedly was doing heroin in the months before her daughter was born and got arrested for hash possession in '77. Eventually Keith left her and married American model Patti Hansen in '83. Devastated, Anita said, "I thought I could never have another love in my life—where can you go after you've been in love with Keith Richards? What else is there? But it heals, it really does, you can actually get over a person." Supposedly she'll explain how to do that in the autobiography she's reportedly writing, which must have all the Stones very, very nervous.

MY BACK PAGES

It was Anita's idea for Brian to wear the uniform of a Nazi SS officer and stomp on a doll in an infamous photo he did for a German magazine. . . . Believing that she was a witch, Anita supposedly practiced black magic, one time stabbing a voodoo doll of Brian Jones and causing him to have stomach cramps. . . . In '79, a 17-year-old kid was found shot to death in the bed of Keith and Anita's upstate N.Y. home, but the couple wasn't implicated, just embarrassed, and they were cited only for illegal gun possession. . . . In a 2001 issue of *Mojo Collections* (a magazine devoted to vinyl LPs) Anita listed 10 songs from her home jukebox, among them Elvis's "Blue Moon," the Stones' "Satisfaction," Frank's "My Way," and Wagner's "Ride of the Valkyrie". . . . A movie about Brian Jones has been discussed for years, with Courtney Love the rumored choice to play Anita.

Arnold Palmer

The most exciting golfer of the '60s led the devoted Arnie's Army.

TAKIN' CARE OF BUSINESS

Many people who see Arnold Palmer today doing commercials know he's a famous golfer, but they don't appreciate how important he was to his sport in the '60s. An amateur from a small town in Pennsylvania (his dad was the golf pro at the local country club), he turned pro in the mid-'50s and within five years was golf's biggest money-winner.

But it's not just the flurry of victories (four Masters, a U.S. Open, and two British Opens from '58 to '64) that made his reputation. It was the man's style that endeared him to fans—his fierce will to win, his knack for making thrilling comebacks (especially his late charge at the Masters and U.S. Open in '60), his down-to-earth charm that made him seem like a regular guy (albeit an incredibly gifted regular guy). All these put him in command of the vast Arnie's Army and made him the decade's most recognizable and respected golfer.

A big reason for his success was TV—he started dominating just as golf was starting to be televised, so he ranks as the sport's first media superstar. Experts recognized his wide-ranging influence—the Associated Press crowned him Athlete of the Decade. Businesses did, too—he was quickly endorsing lines of clothing and equipment, and he soon branched out into his own companies.

Begun in the mid-'60s, Arnold Palmer Enterprises is now a far-flung empire that embraces golf course ownership (he led a group that bought Pebble Beach for over $800 million in '99), golf course design (over 200), car dealerships (still with one in his hometown), an aviation company, and, of course, the commercials for motor oil, cars, and more.

Name any sports-related award, chances are he's won it, including the Sportsman of the Year award from *Sports Illustrated* ('60), induction into several halls of fame, and even the Presidential Medal of Freedom. No longer playing competitively in major seniors tournaments (he didn't stop until 2005), he devotes much of his time helping charities and hospitals (he was honorary national chairman of the March of Dimes for two decades).

EVERYBODY LOVES SOMEBODY

In '54, Arnie proposed to his future wife Winnie four days after he met her, and he married her soon after that. Together they had two daughters and numerous grandchildren. After her death in '99, Arnie remarried in 2005.

MY BACK PAGES

Arnie first broke 100 at age 7. . . . In '67, he became the first golfer to amass $1,000,000 in career earnings. . . . Arnie appeared as himself in Bob Hope's *Call Me Bwana* ('63), and later he hosted *The Tonight Show*, swinging a real club instead of the make-believe club Johnny pretended to hold. . . . He's an experienced pilot with his own jet (and an airport named after him). . . . He helped found the Golf Channel in '95.

Masters Champions (with Winning Score and Margin of Victory)

1960–Arnold Palmer (282, 1)

1961–Gary Player (280, 1)

1962–Arnold Palmer (280, playoff)

1963–Jack Nicklaus (286, 1)

1964–Arnold Palmer (276, 6)

1965–Jack Nicklaus (271, 9)

1966–Jack Nicklaus (288, playoff)

1967–Gay Brewer (280, 1)

1968–Bob Goalby (277, 1)

1969–George Archer (281, 1)

Arnold Palmer, Gary Player

Barbara Parkins

Combining pretty innocence and sultry sexuality, beautiful Barbara had starring roles in two wildly popular screen soapers.

TAKIN' CARE OF BUSINESS

Barbara Parkins from Vancouver, British Columbia was the star of two of the most highly publicized projects of the '60s. As a child, Barbara had been given up for adoption, and then her adoptive father died when she was in grade school. At 16 Barbara and her mother moved to Hollywood, where she studied acting and started appearing as a nightclub singer and dancer. Barbara had already guested on several stalwart TV series in the early '60s before she moved into *Peyton Place* in '64.

Playing Betty Anderson on what was the first prime-time soap opera, Barbara was originally going to be killed off in a car wreck after the first six weeks, but she was such an audience favorite that eventually the show was built around her. She was a favorite with critics, too, and won an Emmy nomination in '66. Ultimately Barbara was the only major female star to stay with *Peyton Place* throughout its remarkable '64–'69 run. Barbara's impact on audiences was so strong that after *Peyton Place* was cancelled the show's producers planned to spin off her own TV series, to be called *The Girl from Peyton Place* (Ryan O'Neal, who played Betty's husband, refused to participate, putting the kibosh on those plans).

Meanwhile, Barbara was establishing herself as a film star, especially with the high-profile *Valley of the Dolls* ('67). Her character Anne was described as "the good girl with a million-dollar face and all the bad breaks—she took the green pills." Though it was savaged by critics, *Dolls* was successful with audiences, who have come to make the movie something of a cult classic. Jacqueline Susann, author of the bestselling novel on which the movie was based, long felt that Barbara was one of the only redeeming features of the film (it's usually assumed that the beautiful, sensible Barbara was playing a character modeled after Susann herself).

Barbara Parkins, Sharon Tate, Patty Duke

Playboy loved her and did several pictorials on her: the '67 pictorial was called "The Late Show" and featured four pages of Barbara modeling "turned-on sleepwear for the tuned-in male." After her busy '60s in Hollywood, she moved to England and there starred in several British productions, among them *The Mephisto Waltz* ('71), the Roger Moore adventure *Shout at the Devil* ('76), and several significant TV miniseries. By the early '80s, Barbara was back in Hollywood working on more TV movies, including *Peyton Place: The Next Generation* ('85), and in '91 she starred in a Canadian mystery series called *Scene of the Crime*.

EVERYBODY LOVES SOMEBODY

Ryan O'Neal once said of Barbara that she did "the wildest watusi in town." Rumors abounded in mid-'60s gossip mags that he and Barbara had an affair while they were both on *Peyton Place*, even though he was married at the time. Some sources go so far as to say that Barbara was the reason O'Neal got divorced. For most of the '70s Barbara lived in England, then at the end of the decade she moved to France, got married, and in the mid-'80s gave birth to a daughter.

MY BACK PAGES

Peyton Place was so popular that for awhile it was shown three times a week. . . . In the *Valley of the Dolls* book Anne ends up in New York spiraling into pill addiction, but in the movie she returns to her small New England town, wiser and happier and healthier after all her big-city adventures. . . . In '66 Barbara befriended her *Valley of the Dolls* co-star Sharon Tate, and when Sharon married director Roman Polanski in '68, Barbara was a bridesmaid at their London wedding.

Peter, Paul and Mary

These Greenwich Village folkies enjoyed a decade of hits.

TAKIN' CARE OF BUSINESS

Peter Yarrow, Paul Stookey, and Mary Travers combined to become one of the biggest, and most durable, vocal groups in music history. Not only did they popularize traditional folk music and actively promote social causes, they also propelled the career of a struggling young artist named Bob Dylan.

As a teenager in the mid-'50s, Mary Travers sang with the Song Swappers, a group that cut several folk and children's records and even performed at Carnegie Hall twice. In '58, Mary left to join the chorus of a short-lived Broadway musical, made occasional nightclub appearances in New York, and worked in ad agencies. Living in Greenwich Village, she met Noel Stookey, who had gone to Michigan State and come to New York to be a photographer, though he found work as a young emcee, comic, and musician. Joined in '61 by Peter Yarrow, a Cornell graduate who was teaching and playing in Greenwich Village, the group took the name Peter, Paul and Mary (to their ears Paul had a more euphonious sound than Noel), and started playing at Folk City and the Bitter End.

October 9, 1994—Mario Andretti drives his last professional race. ☮ October 10, 1933—Hairstylist Jay Sebring is born in Alabama. October 10, 1961—*Splendor in the Grass* with Natalie Wood opens. ☮ October 10, 1963—*From Russia with Love* with Sean Connery opens in the U.K. October 10, 1965—The Supremes appear on *The Ed Sullivan Show*. ☮ October 10, 1966—The Monkees' first album is released.

The group's first album hit #1 in '62, and for the rest of the decade they were a durable fixture on the national music scene with many memorable hits: "If I Had a Hammer" ('62), "Puff, the Magic Dragon" ('63), "Tell It on the Mountain" ('64), "I Dig Rock & Roll Music" ('67), and "Leavin' on a Jet Plane" ('69), among many others. Some of their most popular songs were Dylan compositions (especially "Blowin' in the Wind") at a time when he was still relatively unknown. Peter, Paul and Mary won two Grammy Awards in '62, another in '63, and in '66 *Playboy* named them the best vocal group for the third straight year (the Beatles came in second).

Their peak was probably late '63, when half of the country's six bestselling albums were theirs. Instantly and consistently a popular live act, they had an interesting, intelligent appeal, the two guys looking like kind professors, Mary with her long blonde hair (at a time when other girl singers were heavily made-up and wore kicky new hair styles). They delivered powerful messages and emotions with their heartfelt songs, plus they usually managed to inject some easy-going humor into the proceedings. What's more, the group's heart has always been in the right place: name the benefit, they probably appeared for it, including the famous '63 March on Washington in which Martin Luther King delivered his famous "I have a dream" speech.

Towards the end of the decade the group was writing more of its own material and developing a more sophisticated sound, but in a show of versatility they also won another Grammy for the Best Children's Album (*Peter, Paul and Mommy*, '69). In '70, the group took what it said was a "sabbatical" and everyone released solo albums. Mary also produced and starred in a TV series in the U.K.; Paul had a solo hit with "The Wedding Song" and established a multimedia company for different children's projects; and Peter co-wrote the '70s hit "Torn Between Two Lovers" and created several popular TV specials.

In the late '70s, the three reteamed for (naturally) a benefit concert, and they have continued touring and recording as a group ever since. In the '90s and 2000s, they did several well-received TV specials, recorded several children's albums, and played prestigious gigs at the Hollywood Bowl and Carnegie Hall. Today, despite Mary's battle with leukemia, they are still out there spreading a message of freedom and hope to appreciative brothers and sisters all over this land.

EVERYBODY LOVES SOMEBODY

In '71 Peter married Marybeth McCarthy, whose uncle was presidential candidate Senator Eugene McCarthy (Paul's "The Wedding Song" was written for the ceremony). Paul's been married since '63. Mary got married in '58 and had two daughters, one born in '60 and another in '66.

MY BACK PAGES

When Dylan went electric at the Newport Folk Festival in '65, Peter was the one who introduced him and later urged him to go back out and perform acoustic numbers. . . . Paul donated all the proceeds from "The Wedding Song" to charity. . . . One of Mary's good friends from the Greenwich Village days in the '60s is Judy Collins.

Wilson Pickett

One of music's great screamers, Wicked Pickett brought a ferocious intensity to '60s R & B.

TAKIN' CARE OF BUSINESS

The youngest of 11 children in a poor Alabama household, Wilson Pickett (like two other great '60s soul singers, Marvin Gaye and Otis Redding) was singing in church as a kid. As a teen he joined two vocal groups, the Violinaires and the Falcons, had a hit with "I Found a Love" in '62, and was then signed to a solo deal. He filled the mid-'60s with funkified hits, many that he co-wrote, all of which he delivered with raspy intensity, including "It's Too Late," "In the Midnight Hour," "Mustang Sally," "Land of 1000 Dances," and "Funky Broadway." Live he was no less intense, sometimes dropping to his knees to pour out raw screams.

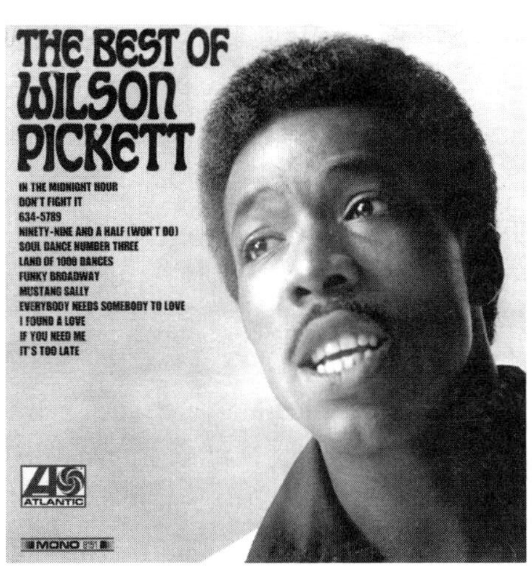

Classics kept coming into the '70s (the '71 album *Don't Knock My Love* produced five hit songs), and he even formed his own record label, Wicked. Wilson appeared in two movie musicals, *Sgt. Pepper's Lonely Hearts Club Band* ('78) and *Blues Brothers 2000* ('98), got a Grammy nomination in the '90s for the album *It's Harder Now,* and was inducted into the Rock and Roll Hall of Fame in '91. Still performing some four decades after he'd started, he died of a heart attack in early 2006.

EVERYBODY LOVES SOMEBODY

Problems with the law peppered his later years. In addition to getting arrested on alcohol- and drug-related charges, he was accused of assaulting his girlfriend in '91. Obituaries mentioned no wife, but two sons and two daughters survived him.

MY BACK PAGES

Wilson wrote "If You Need Me," a #2 hit for Solomon Burke in '63. . . . Wilson's career was celebrated in *The Commitments,* the '91 film about Irish musicians emulating their hero. . . . Wilson's songs have been recorded by dozens of rock groups, including Led Zeppelin, Van Halen, Creedence Clearwater Revival, and Bruce Springsteen.

Sylvia Plath

An intense poet who killed herself at age 30, Sylvia Plath is now recognized as a major 20th-century writer.

TAKIN' CARE OF BUSINESS

Sylvia Plath was perhaps the most famous female poet of her generation. Greater than her impact on the literary world, however, was her impact on young women of the '60s who identified with the turmoil she experienced as depression, isolation, and a fascination with death overtook her.

Sylvia displayed her talent early—a precocious straight-A student as a young girl in Massachusetts, she wrote her first poem at eight years old and won a scholarship to Smith College in '50. While there she kept a long, detailed journal and wrote over 400 poems. In '53, she won a short story contest in *Mademoiselle* magazine and worked in their New York offices as a "guest editor." However, during this time she also suffered severe depression, attempting suicide on one occasion via sleeping pills.

After graduating *summa cum laude* she won a Fulbright Fellowship to study in England at Cambridge, where she got her M.A. in '57 and married poet Ted Hughes. They lived in America and Sylvia taught at Smith for awhile, then they returned to England for good. In '60, 28-year-old Sylvia published *The Colossus*, her first book of poetry. Three years later came her autobiographical novel *The Bell Jar*, which presented a fictional character who endured what Sylvia herself had gone through—depression, suicide attempts, shock therapy, and recovery (the book was credited to her pseudonym, "Victoria Lucas").

Sadly, just as Sylvia was building toward a career as a literary superstar, in fact just as she was starting to do some BBC broadcasts and poetry readings, she killed herself in the middle of a hard winter in which her husband had left her for another woman, she was struggling with finances and chronic ill health, and her sanity was collapsing. After

October 11, 1967—The *Yoko Plus Me* art exhibition opens in London (the "me" is John Lennon).
October 11, 1968—Rowan and Martin make the cover of *Time.* ☮ October 12, 1942—Actress Daliah Lavi is born in Israel.
October 12, 1963—The Ronettes' "Be My Baby" hits #2. ☮ October 12, 1968—The Summer Olympics begin in Mexico City.

setting out milk and cookies for her children, she placed her head in a gas oven.

Ariel, her acclaimed book of poems, was published two years after her death, with more prose and poetry following in later decades (*The Collected Poems* earned her a Pulitzer Prize in '82). Unfortunately, Hughes burned the final volume of her journals, which covered the final seven months of her life. The remaining journals were published in April 2000 and shed light on her dark life, revealing her as a complex, moody woman whose days ran from occasional happiness to total despair.

EVERYBODY LOVES SOMEBODY

Supposedly when she met Ted Hughes at a Cambridge party in '56, she immediately and unhesitatingly bit him deeply on the cheek, drawing blood. The next day she wrote a poem about him, predicting that their relationship would be the end of her. They got married four months later. Unfortunately, their marriage was troubled, punctuated by affairs and repeated separations. They had two children, a daughter born in '60, and a son born in '62.

Hughes, who would later become England's Poet Laureate, is often portrayed as the villain when her life story is told—critics say he stifled her and then didn't do enough to memorialize her after her death. He said little about her in public for decades after she died, though supposedly he agonized about her in private, and he published a mournful collection of poems about her in '98, the same year he died.

MY BACK PAGES

Literary critics often name the death of her father, which came when Sylvia was only eight, as the root cause of the suffering that filled her life and her work. . . . One of the most bizarre entries in her journal concerns a weird out-of-body experience in '57, when "distant, stellar voices" studied her. . . . Sylvia Plath's grave in England was disfigured several times by her fans who removed the last name from the stone reading "Sylvia Plath Hughes," this as a way to protest his treatment of her. . . . *Sylvia*, a well-reviewed movie bio, came out in 2003 with Gwyneth Paltrow as the poet.

Playmates of the Year

All decade long goddesses cast come-hither looks from the pages of *Playboy*.

TAKIN' CARE OF BUSINESS

Of the 120 beautiful Playmates of the Month shown in *Playboy* during the decade, 10 were selected Playmates of the Year. We profile the three from '66–'68 as worthy representatives of them all.

Allison Parks

To get into *Playboy*, Allison Parks from the San Fernando Valley created for herself a new name (she was born Gloria Waldron), a new age (she said she was 22, not 24), and a new history (she wasn't single, she was a wife with two kids but figured the *Playboy* editors would like her a little less married). Allison quickly became one of the decade's most popular photographic sub-

October 12, 1972—*Lady Sings the Blues* with Diana Ross opens. ☮ October 12, 1999—Basketball star Wilt Chamberlain dies in L.A. of cardiac arrest. October 13, 1925—Comedian Lenny Bruce is born on Long Island, New York. ☮ October 13, 1941—Singer Paul Simon is born in Newark, New Jersey. October 13, 1942—Actress Pamela Tiffin is born in Oklahoma City, Oklahoma.

jects, both in and out of *Playboy*. She was Miss October in '65 then graced the cover of the magazine's December '65 and May '66 issues, the latter featuring her as the Playmate of the Year, a 5′ 6″ beauty with sparkling blue eyes.

Allison's *Playboy* prime came in those golden years when the girls actually smiled and nudity was more often suggested than flaunted. So wholesome-looking was Allison, she was even incorporated into America's space program: in '66 her photo went into space with the Gemini astronauts. Allison traveled extensively to promote *Playboy* and continued to appear in dozens of *Playboy* magazines, books, and videos over the years.

Away from *Playboy*, she did many TV commercials and print ads for everything from cosmetics to scuba diving equipment, trucks to TVs, and pools to appliances. She also landed some big- and small-screen roles at the end of the '60s, especially as a regular party guest on the '69 TV series *Playboy After Dark* (sometimes co-hosting the party alongside Hef). Family came first, however, so at the end of the decade Allison cut short her budding acting career in favor of more time at home. Later she ran a successful jewelry-design business with her daughter, worked for an investment company, and wrote a novel. Today she lives in the beautiful coastal town of Pacific Palisades and fills her active life with travel and writing.

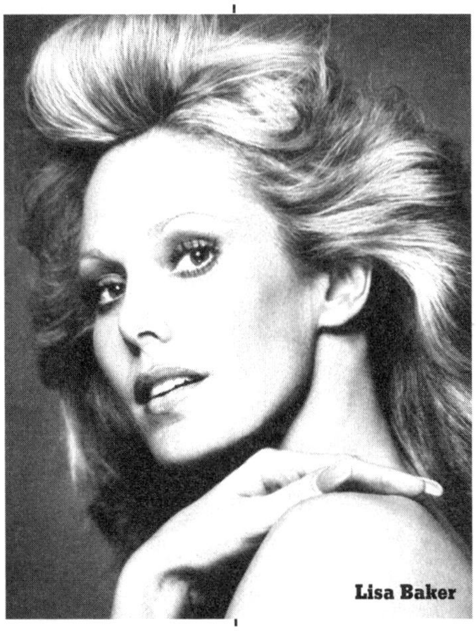
Lisa Baker

A Texas-born beauty from a large family, Lisa Baker was living in a small Oklahoma town when she was discovered by a photographer at a wedding in L.A. Soon she was in *Playboy*, first as a stunning green-eyed Miss November in '66, then as a 21-year-old Playmate of the Year for '67. The exposure also led to some appearances on *The Tonight Show*, but really she was working as a model and was still turning up in *Playboy* pictorials, calendars, and books (why not, with measurements of 35-23-35 on a long 5′ 8″ frame).

Blessed with a sweet, soft personality, she didn't have the huge ego and cutthroat attitude often necessary to make it in Hollywood, though she did appear in one movie, *Hot Summer in the City* ('76) along with several other Playmates. Lisa and her best friend, petite DeDe Lind, who was Playmate of the Month in August '67, have been attending autograph shows together for the last few years.

Appearing in seven issues of *Playboy* during the '60s, Angela Dorian was a voluptuous dark-haired Italian beauty who was born Victoria Vetri in San Francisco. Spotted by a Hollywood talent scout while attending Hollywood High in L.A., she was named Four Star Television's "Deb Star of 1962" and landed some minor film and TV work in the mid-'60s. Her big break came in '67 when the screen exposure led to *Playboy* exposure for her remarkable 36-21-35 figure.

Over the next 10 years she got more than a dozen plays in the magazine, with the touchdowns coming in September '67 as Playmate of the Month and the following spring when she was the Playmate of the Year for '68. For all of these *Playboy* appearances she was billed as Angela Dorian, a stage moniker playing on the name of the doomed Italian liner, the *Andrea Doria*.

In '68 more screen time came her way, notably a role as the belly-dancing Florence of Arabia on *Batman* and as a victim in *Rosemary's Baby* (in her scene with Mia Farrow, Mia offers curious dialogue that points out Angela's resemblance to Victoria Vetri!). A year later, after a successful screen test that was allegedly shot by budding director Francis Ford Coppola, filming began on *When Dinosaurs Ruled the Earth*, a stop-motion epic that attempted to jump on the

October 13, 1960—The Pittsburgh Pirates clinch the World Series over the Yankees.
October 13, 1962—*Who's Afraid of Virginia Woolf?* with Uta Hagen opens on Broadway. ☮ October 13, 1967—Celeste Yarnall appears on *Star Trek*.
October 14, 1964—*The Lively Set* with Pamela Tiffin opens. ☮ October 14, 1964—Martin Luther King, Jr. wins the Nobel Peace Prize.

bikini bandwagon of *One Million Years B.C.*

The '70s brought some "B" movies (one a real "bee" movie, '73's *Invasion of the Bee Girls*) plus some more TV appearances (including two guest shots on *The Tonight Show* billed as Angela Dorian on the first show and Victoria on the second). According to reports, in the '80s Victoria worked as a waitress in a popular watering hole near UCLA, hoping to save enough money to produce a movie.

EVERYBODY LOVES SOMEBODY

In the October '65 issue, *Playboy* said that for Allison "marriage will have to wait its turn." The truth was that she was already married and had been for over six years, with her first child born when she was 18. After getting divorced, she has been happily remarried for the last 30 years.

Lisa admits to a marriage and a divorce after the '60s, and she's occasionally returned to Hef's mansion for parties and events over the years. After living in Texas through the '80s and '90s, in 2000 Lisa moved to a Florida beach to drive the local boys wild as the hard-working, fun-loving girl next door (who just happens to be a former Playmate of the Year).

Details are sketchy about Victoria's personal life, but supposedly she was married in '67 and then two more times after that, with possibly one son born in '64. Sadly, there's a story that she was the victim of a brutal attack in her Hollywood home in '80, suffering a broken nose and broken ribs from two assailants who were never caught.

MY BACK PAGES

A month after Allison was named Playmate of the Year, her sister-in-law, Kelly Burke, was Miss June. . . . Allison was so well-known in her community, the post office would deliver mail addressed to "Allison Parks, Glendale, CA". . . . One of the dozens of gifts Allison received from *Playboy* for being Playmate of the Year was a package of flying lessons, which she used to get her pilot's license. . . . For being named Playmate of the Year, *Playboy* awarded Lisa gifts and merchandise totaling $12,000, plus a cash prize. . . . Among the many appearances Lisa made as Playmate of the Year was one at the Harvard Business School. . . . Victoria may have made a major career gaffe when she rejected the part of *Lolita* in Kubrick's famous '61 film, a break for young Sue Lyon. . . . Playmate lore: during one of the *Playboy* photo sessions, the hammock in which Victoria was reclining gave way and she suffered two broken ribs. . . . In '68 Victoria was filmed as a guest star in the pilot episode of *The Courtship of Eddie's Father*.

Playmates of the Year
(with Ages)

1960–Ellen Stratton (20)
1961–Linda Gamble (20)
1962–Christa Speck (19)
1963–June Cochran (20)
1964–Donna Michelle (17)
1965–Jo Collins (19)
1966–Allison Parks (22)
1967–Lisa Baker (21)
1968–Angela Dorian (22)
1969–Connie Kreski (20)

Sidney Poitier

This Oscar-winning actor broke new ground with his landmark movie performances.

TAKIN' CARE OF BUSINESS

The pioneering actor destined to be knighted Sir Sidney was born Sidney Poitier in Miami and raised in the Bahamas. After an Army stint and struggles in Harlem, Sidney started auditioning for, and landing, small roles in New York plays. In the '50s, his stagework got more and more prominent, culminating with a heralded Tony-nominated run on Broadway in *Raisin in the Sun* ('59). During the '50s he was also getting key roles in good films, notably *Blackboard Jungle* ('55), in which the 28-year-old actor played a high school student, and *The Defiant Ones* ('58), which brought him his first Oscar nomination.

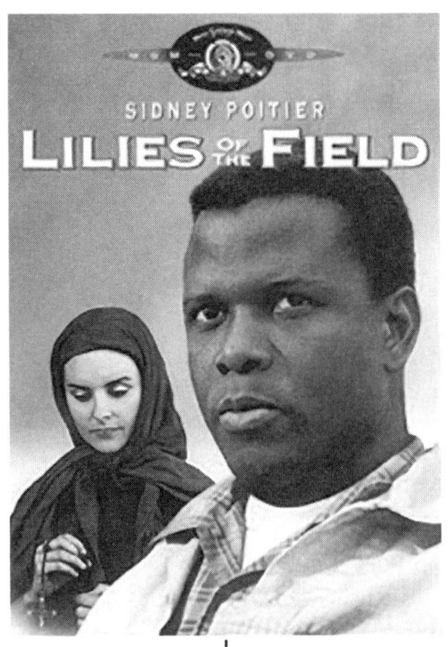

The '60s brought the beginning of his remarkable streak of popular, critically acclaimed movies: *All the Young Men* ('60), *Paris Blues* ('61), *Lilies of the Field* ('63), and *A Patch of Blue* ('65). At a time when the civil rights movement was building steam, Sidney's usually credited as being the first minority dramatic actor to gain wide acceptance by mainstream America, as evidenced by the Oscar he won as Best Actor for *Lilies of the Field* (the first Best Actor trophy won by an African-American).

In '67, he had one of the greatest years ever for an actor—lead roles in three wildly successful hits, including the Best Picture winner—*In the Heat of the Night*, *Guess Who's Coming to Dinner*, and *To Sir, With Love*. Always he was a handsome, dignified, intelligent star in these '60s movies, a real breakthrough compared to the stereotyped supporting roles many African-American actors before him had to play.

After the '60s, his long, busy career has been punctuated by hit movies—the *Heat* sequel *They Call Me MISTER Tibbs!* ('70), the comedy *Uptown Saturday Night* ('74), the Emmy-nominated *Separate But Equal* ('91)—and nine major directing credits. His varied talents have brought him international respect and recognition all along the way, highlighted by knighthood in '74 and Kennedy Center honors in '95. Appropriately enough, on the same night in 2002 when Denzel Washington and Halle Berry won Academy Awards, Sidney Poitier was given a special Oscar for lifetime achievement.

EVERYBODY LOVES SOMEBODY

Sidney was married from '50–'65, but during the latter half of that marriage he was in a relationship with actress Diahann Carroll, his co-star in two movies—*Porgy and Bess* ('59) and *Paris Blues* ('61). Since '76, he's been married to Canadian actress Joanna Shimkus, who made films in Europe and America throughout the '60s and early '70s. Sidney has a total of six kids from his two wives; three of his daughters have appeared in movies with him.

MY BACK PAGES

In '67, Sidney became the first African-American actor to put his prints into the cement outside Hollywood's Grauman's Chinese Theatre. . . . He won a Grammy in 2001 for his spoken-word album, *The Measure of a Man*, which was also the title of his "spiritual autobiography" in 2000. . . . Twenty years earlier he wrote an autobiography called *This Life*.

Stefanie Powers

Super Stefanie enjoyed a busy '60s, highlighted by a dazzling turn as secret agent April Dancer.

TAKIN' CARE OF BUSINESS

Born in Hollywood, Stefania Zofia Federkiewicz left school at age 15 for a dancing career. After literally running into and impressing director Blake Edwards in a hallway, she was soon signed by Columbia Pictures, taking acting classes, and getting early bit parts. She distinguished herself in Edwards's dramatic *Experiment in Terror* ('62) and got co-star billing in *Palm Springs Weekend* ('63). By '65, Stefanie was a full-fledged star getting beaten up by Tallulah Bankhead in the horror flick *Fanatic*, taking Lana Turner's hubby away in *Love Has Many Faces,* and landing lots of guest-star parts on prominent TV shows. In '66 Stefanie won the coveted role of British superspy April Dancer for the TV series *The Girl from U.N.C.L.E.* Spun off from the popular *The Man from U.N.C.L.E.*, Stefanie's show lasted only 29 episodes, perhaps overwhelmed by all the other spy shows (including *The Avengers* and *Get Smart*) on the air at the time. However, the show did generate enough of a cult following to warrant a half-dozen *Girl from U.N.C.L.E.* books and a bi-monthly magazine.

For Stefanie, several minor movies and lots of TV appearances followed her show's cancellation until her career took off again in the '70s, when she established herself as a talented, hard-working performer not afraid to tackle widely different roles, everything from popular Disney films (*The Boatniks*, '70 and *Herbie Rides Again*, '74) to Westerns (*The Magnificent Seven Ride!*, '72) and adventure movies (*Escape to Athena*, '79). One of her most powerful TV movies was *Family Secrets* ('84), which she starred in and co-wrote.

In '79 Stefanie hit pay dirt (and got multiple Emmy and Golden Globe nominations) when she teamed with Robert Wagner in the popular series *Hart to Hart* (in the '90s she and Wagner were in eight *Hart to Hart* TV movies and she appeared with him in the acclaimed play *Love Letters*). Instructional fitness videos, successful commercials, dozens of appearances on talk shows and in documentaries, a line of clothes, her own perfume (Rare Orchid), a fitness book called *Superlife!*, continued stagework—Stefanie Powers has tried and succeeded at just about everything in show biz there is to try and succeed at.

EVERYBODY LOVES SOMEBODY

For the second half of the '60s, Stefanie was married to actor Gary Lockwood, he of *2001: A Space Odyssey* fame. For most of the '70s, Stefanie was the intimate of William Holden, the classic star who was some 26 years her senior. Together they traveled the world, making repeated trips to China, Africa, and the South Pacific. After Holden died in '81, Stefanie created and steered the William Holden Wildlife Foundation to preserve the wildlife in Kenya (she made the cover of *People* magazine in '82 while holding a leopard). Stefanie was again married and divorced in the '90s.

MY BACK PAGES

Early in her career she was briefly billed as Taffy Paul. . . . Stefanie has said that she loves to smoke cigars and began when she was 14 (she was featured in *Cigar Aficionado* magazine in '97). . . . Stefanie's also worked and spoken for issues that help children, especially with efforts to control children's rage. . . . It's reported that she is fluent in as many as six languages, including French, Italian, Spanish, and German. . . . On the Hollywood Walk of Fame, Stefanie's star is right next to Marilyn Monroe's.

October 16, 1964—American swimmer Sharon Stouder sets a new Olympic record while winning the gold medal in the 100-meter butterfly at the Olympic Games in Tokyo.
October 16, 1964—Driver Craig Breedlove is the first man to drive 526 MPH.

The Presleys

In the '60s Elvis shifted his career from music to movies to music, while Priscilla was the King's Queen.

TAKIN' CARE OF BUSINESS

The '60s were an uneven decade for the King. The most influential musician of the '50s, Elvis Presley had already changed the look, sound, and feel of music forever and seemed incapable of making anything but a hit record (a huge Elvis fan named John Lennon later declared that "before Elvis, there was nothing"). But in '58, Elvis was inducted into the Army and then sent to Germany; when he emerged in '60, it was not to pick up his career as the world's dominant musician, it was to revive his budding career as a movie actor.

Certainly there were memorable musical performances in the early '60s (the teaming with Frank Sinatra on Frank's TV special, to name one), but most of the King's time and energy were given to Hollywood. The schedule was brutal—two or three movies annually, a total of 27 from '60 to '69. The characters usually had cool jobs—Navy frogman, boxing champ, race car driver, water-ski instructor, helicopter pilot—usually with cool names—Pacer Burton, Tulsa McLean, Lucky Jackson (plus a few, uh, distinctive names like Toby Kwimper, Jodie Tatum, and Walter Gulick).

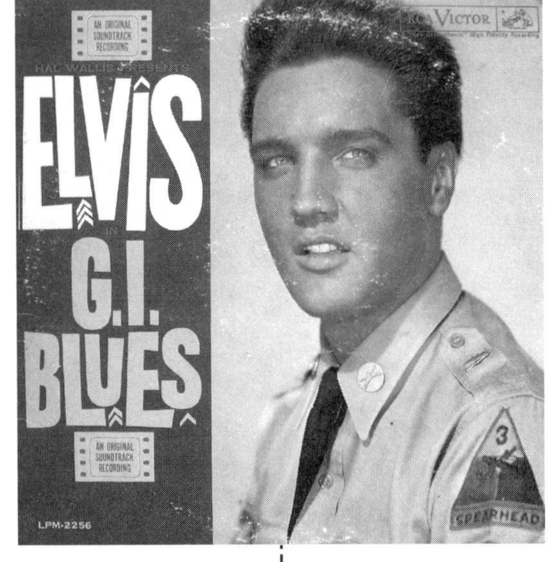

The results were mixed, swinging from highs like the romantic *Blue Hawaii* ('61) and the high-powered *Viva Las Vegas* ('64) to the lows of the slapstick *Kissin' Cousins* ('64) and the formulaic *Harum Scarum* ('65). Elvis looked like he was trying his best in only about half of the movies, and his lean rebel cool was gone midway through the decade. Even the one thing Elvis could do better than anyone—sing in front of an audience—was inconsistent, given the wide-ranging material he had to work with: for every instant classic like "Can't Help Falling in Love" there was an embarrassing "Ito Eats" elsewhere in the same movie (*Blue Hawaii*).

Fortunately, he recharged his career with an amazing rebound in '68—the legendary "comeback special" in which he wore the best outfit of his career (black leathers) and returned to his gospel and R & B roots. Soon followed sold-out concerts across the country and the last #1 hit he'd have in his lifetime, "Suspicious Minds." Sadly, the '70s brought the gradual, well-chronicled demise of his health as prescription drugs and weight problems took their toll. In '77 his was one of the most analyzed deaths in history and generated more where-were-you-when-you-heard conversations than any death since JFK's.

Meanwhile, Priscilla's job in the mid-late '60s was to be Mrs. Elvis. She was a teen living in Graceland in '63, married to E in '67, and by his side for most of the decade. Most of those years she had the biggest, tallest hair this side of the Supremes, dyed nice and black just the way Elvis liked it (he dyed his black, too). Her own Hollywood success didn't start until Elvis's life ended. First came a co-hosting job on *Those Amazing Animals* in '80, followed by five years on *Dallas*. Her comedic flair was shown off in the three *Naked Gun* movies ('88, '91, '94), while more TV roles (including frequent appearances on *Melrose Place*) continued to enhance her rep as a talented working actress. What's more, she published an enormous best-seller, *Elvis and Me* ('85), produced several Elvis-themed films, and came out with her own perfume (Moments).

October 16, 1969—The amazin' New York Mets win the World Series.
October 16, 1997—On the *Lost in Space* pilot episode, the date of the first adventure is said to be October 16, 1997.
October 17, 1926—Actress Beverly Garland is born in Santa Cruz, California. ☮ October 17, 1933—The Singing Nun, Jeanine Deckers, is born in Belgium.

Over the decades, the teenage prettiness matured into sophisticated beauty, acknowledged in the early '90s when *People* magazine named her one of the world's 50 most beautiful people. A savvy businesswoman, she steered Elvis Presley Enterprises into major profitability; deeply loyal to the King's memory, she has continually defended him and reminded the public of his generosity, his goodness, and his triumphs. As she wrote at the end of *Elvis and Me*, "He was, and remains, the greatest influence in my life."

EVERYBODY LOVES SOMEBODY

Take away her incredibly lucky break—being in Germany at exactly the right moment to meet Elvis—and she was just one of about a billion Elvis fans in the world. But there she was, 14-year-old Brooklyn-born Priscilla Beaulieu, daughter of a military man stationed in Germany, when who should show up in '59 but Private Elvis Presley, 24 years old and the hottest talent on the planet. Their courtship lasted eight years.

While they were in Germany, chaperones accompanied their dates, and Priscilla (who had never even been kissed) had to be home by 11 P.M. Returning stateside in the spring of '60, they stayed in contact while the King resumed his movie career in Hollywood. After a couple of years, she moved into Graceland (platonically) and then graduated from a Memphis high school in '63. Rumors of many casual affairs and several serious relationships trailed Elvis right up to the moment he got down on one knee, proposed to Priscilla, and handed over a 3.5 karat diamond engagement ring in '66.

Finally, in '67 21-year old Priscilla and 32-year-old Elvis married in Vegas. Exactly nine months later, Priscilla gave birth to Elvis's pride and joy, Lisa Marie, who decades later would have some high-profile relationships of her own. Infidelities and pressures would drive Priscilla and Elvis to divorce in '73; in the mid-'80s Priscilla found a new companion and gave birth to a son. But her legacy will always be as the King's official Queen, a title nobody else ever held.

MY BACK PAGES

Bracketing the decade were two important movie roles Elvis was offered but was advised to reject—Tony in *West Side Story* and Joe Buck in *Midnight Cowboy*. . . . In '61 the *Blue Hawaii* soundtrack topped the charts for five straight months, a record that stood until Fleetwood Mac's *Rumours* in '77. . . . Elvis's graduation present to Priscilla in '63: a new red Corvair. . . . Priscilla wrote in her book that in the mid-'60s she and Elvis experimented briefly with drugs, including LSD on one night in '65. . . . One of the most tantalizing meetings of the decade had to be the Beatles' '65 visit to Elvis's L.A. residence for an impromptu jam session. . . . A dozen years into his recording career, Elvis finally won a Grammy Award in '67 with his gospel album *How Great Thou Art*. . . . After the Vegas wedding ceremony, Priscilla and Elvis flew to Palm Springs in Frank Sinatra's private Lear jet, the *Christina*. . . . At the May 1st wedding reception in Vegas, the newlyweds danced to the first Elvis song she'd heard in Germany: "Love Me Tender."

Juliet Prowse

This long-limbed dancin' dazzler kicked up her heels in a half-dozen '60s movies.

TAKIN' CARE OF BUSINESS

Juliet Prowse's '60s debut caused an international ruckus, appropriate for this most international of stars. Born in Bombay and raised in South Africa, she was a ballet dancer brought to Hollywood for *Can-Can* ('60). The movie had a ring-a-ding cast (Frank Sinatra, Shirley MacLaine) and, of course, the leg-kicking, skirt-lifting, pulse-raising can-can dance itself. When Nikita Krushchev visited the set during rehearsals and saw the riotous dancing and revealing costumes, he was appalled. "Immoral," the Russian leader declared. Subsequent articles in the international press only

October 17, 1964—U.S. swimming sensation Donna de Varona sets an Olympic record in the 400-meter individual medley while winning the gold medal at the '64 Olympic Games in Tokyo.
October 17, 1966—*The Hollywood Squares* debuts. ☮ October 17, 1966—*Georgy Girl* with Lynn Redgrave opens.

brought more attention, and Juliet's career quickly picked up steam. "A most appealing newcomer," *Playboy* declared when it got a first look at Juliet in the movie (and, at close to six feet tall, maybe the tallest newcomer, too, with perhaps the best gams in the biz).

Soon she was starring opposite Elvis in *G.I. Blues* ('60), which showed off more of her dynamic dancing. The movie was a hit and Juliet went on to do more '60s movies and even get her own sitcom, the mid-decade one-season-wonder *Mona McCluskey*, in which she played a glamorous movie star trying to get by on her husband's limited salary. After the cancellation Juliet took her stunning stems to live stages, Vegas, and nightclubs, with the occasional TV special, commercial, or TV movie thrown in for fun. Sadly, in '96 Juliet died of pancreatic cancer at age 60.

EVERYBODY LOVES SOMEBODY

In the early '60s, you couldn't beat these royal references: Juliet was romantically linked to Elvis, then she was engaged to Frank Sinatra for five weeks in '62. Supposedly her relationship with the former was broken up by the latter in a Vegas dressing-room confrontation. Frank, though, decided not to marry her because she balked at relinquishing her career. Juliet did get married in '72 to a younger actor, but they divorced at decade's end.

MY BACK PAGES

Juliet performed at the JFK inaugural gala that Frank organized in '61, and she later played Frank's Cal-Neva Lodge in Tahoe. . . . In '87 Juliet was clawed by a leopard while preparing for the TV special "Circus of the Stars," but she gamely went on with the show—later the same cat scratched her again on *The Tonight Show*, sending her to the hospital for stitches. . . . During her lifetime she won numerous awards from dance and theatrical organizations, and one year she was named the Las Vegas Performer of the Year. . . . When she died, Juliet had been hosting Championship Ballroom Dancing on PBS for 13 years—her successor, Barbara Eden, hosted a tribute show to Juliet and called her "truly one of the greatest and best dancers of all time."

Mary Quant

If you ever wore a miniskirt, or admired someone who did, thank Mary Quant, who made the mini the decade's defining fashion statement.

TAKIN' CARE OF BUSINESS

Fab and fun, the flamboyant fashions of the '60s were the products of a determined revolution. In the '50s, young people had dressed in modified versions of their parents' conservative clothes: pop singers wore gowns or suits, girls wore gloves, and the most daring thing a guy could wear was a Brando-style T-shirt. But then came the '60s and a revolution not just in clothes, but in the people who created them.

A new breed of fashion designers, inspired by the energy in the streets, drawing on influences from Op and Pop

Art, invented styles that were more daring, more colorful, and more exciting than ever before. The revolution's catalyst was Mary Quant from Kent, England. She was the hippest designer in the hippest city in the world, the unrivaled Queen of Swingin' London perfectly in sync with the spirit of her times.

She started making her own clothes as a child; in her teens the clothes she created were designed for other teens, lots of sweaters and black tights. After graduating in '55 from Goldsmiths College of Art in London, 21-year-old Mary opened Bazaar, a stylish clothing shop in Chelsea. Catering to urban youth, she filled the shop (and a second one, opened in '57) with the exciting new clothes being worn by rock 'n' rollers—bell-bottoms, bright patterns, and especially, thigh-climbing skirts.

Her shop was an instant success and drew a celebrity crowd. She'd stay open late, and people would try on clothes out in the open. When she couldn't find the creative clothes she wanted, she designed them herself. And she wore them herself, too—unlike fashion designers of previous decades who were much older than their models, Mary was the same age and so wore what she created.

Some sources credit French designer Andre Courreges with actually inventing the miniskirt; perhaps, but Mary's definitely the one who brought the style to the masses by keeping prices affordable (J.C. Penney carried her designs as early as '62) and by keeping the look whimsical. Though she's best known for the mini, her legacy is more than a single garment—it's an entire style known as the "London Look," which by mid-decade meant clothes with simple lines, short/shorter/shortest skirts, bold colors, flat shoes, and strong, colorful eye make-up.

Brigitte Bardot and Nancy Sinatra were just two of her famous customers, and when George Harrison married model Pattie Boyd in '66, they were both wearing clothes designed by Mary Quant. Mary also designed the costumes for several popular films, including the Oscar-nominated *Georgy Girl* ('66) and Audrey Hepburn's *Two for the Road* ('67). Sparked by her design innovations, '60s fashions exploded in bursts of crazy new colors, prints, and fabrics.

Mary dropped another bombshell into the fashion world in '69—hot pants, which did for shorts what her minis did for skirts. Later, she brought her touch to hosiery, linens, and home furnishings. She also wrote several books, among them her autobiography, *Quant by Quant,* followed by books on make-up and beauty. Today her Colour Concepts boutiques, which showcase her color-saturated make-up, are located in world capitals like Paris, New York, and Tokyo. Mary is still working in London, with jewelry, umbrellas, bags, and socks among her latest creations. The '60s may be over, but the revolution lives on.

EVERYBODY LOVES SOMEBODY

When Mary opened Bazaar in '55, she had two partners. Mary married one of them and together they have one son.

MY BACK PAGES

When the Queen awarded Mary the Order of the British Empire (O.B.E.) in '66, Mary accepted while wearing a miniskirt. . . . Other prominent awards she's won include the Hall of Fame Award from the British Fashion Council in '69. . . . Two direct results of Mary's mini-revolution: the inventions of pantyhose and the maxi-coat (to keep suddenly exposed legs warm).

The Rat Pack

The decade's longest, swingin'est party was thrown nightly in Vegas by these talented entertainers.

TAKIN' CARE OF BUSINESS

any people with fond '60s memories will let you keep your Beatles and hippies and Woodstock if you'll just give them a ticket to the swingin'est party of the

October 18, 1964—At the Tokyo Olympics, swimmer Don Schollander wins his fourth gold medal.
October 18, 1967—*Far from the Madding Crowd* with Julie Christie opens.
October 18, 1968—Paul Newman and Joanne Woodward make the cover of *Life.* ☮ October 18, 2000—Actress and singer Julie London dies.

decade, the long raucous Summit convened by the Rat Pack in '60. All five charter members—Frank Sinatra, Dean Martin, Sammy Davis, Jr., Peter Lawford, and Joey Bishop—had pre-Pack careers, of course, ranging from legendary (Frank's) to nascent (Joey's).

Clockwise from left: Frank Sinatra, Dean Martin, Peter Lawford, Joey Bishop, Sammy Davis, Jr.

At the beginning of the '60s Frank was already a swaggering Oscar-winner (*From Here to Eternity*, '53) and the most acclaimed singer in American history; in the '50s he recorded some of his most heralded albums—the "concept" LPs for Capitol that were unified around either swingin' dance themes or melancholy ballads—creating a rich catalog of classic material that he drew upon for the rest of his performing career.

Ex-boxer Dean was fresh off his successful 11-year partnership with Jerry Lewis, which ended sourly in '57 after a long run of record-setting live performances and 16 wacky movies; he'd also gotten surprising praise for his recent role in the war drama *The Young Lions* ('58). Sammy's career had begun when he was a tap-dancing child in vaudeville and had progressed from nightclubs to TV to movies, punctuated by an Emmy nomination in '56 and a show-stopping turn as Sportin' Life in the '59 film *Porgy and Bess*.

Debonair British actor Peter Lawford had been appearing in movies since the '30s and was a busy contract player in MGM romantic comedies and musicals in the '40s and '50s. Finally, Bronx-born comic Joey Bishop had been a soldier in World War II (he was the only Rat Packer to go to war) and was working the nightclub circuit in the '50s, with occasional TV appearances and a couple of movies building him some momentum.

The original Rat Pack was a group of stars and friends—including Humphrey Bogart, Lauren Bacall, Frank, Judy Garland, and David Niven—who partied and traveled together in the early and mid-'50s. They had a name (the Holmby Hills Rat Pack, coined by Lauren), titles (she was Den Mother, Frank was Pack Master), even a Coat of Arms.

After Bogie's death in '57, after Frank and Dean had co-starred in the hit *Some Came Running* in '58, and after they'd both appeared together on stage at the Sands (the classy Vegas hotel Frank owned a piece of) in '59, Frank informally convened the new Pack with a new plan. He had in mind a film project, a Vegas caper called *Ocean's 11* that was originally discovered by Peter, with a great plan for filming—make the movie with his chums by day, perform and party at the Sands by night, everybody makes money, everybody has fun, everybody (the movie, the hotel, and Vegas itself) gets tons of free fabulous pub. Win-win-win-win-win.

All five Rat Packers, plus mascot Shirley MacLaine (who'd become a platonic pal when she was the female lead in *Some Came Running*) were on board. The filming, and the famous Sands shows, took place in early '60—both were mostly improvised, hours fluctuated wildly (most of the stars only worked on the movie a few hours a day), but everything

October 19, 1937—Artist Peter Max is born in Germany. ☮ October 19, 1959—*The Miracle Worker* with Patty Duke opens on Broadway.
October 19, 1966—The Simon and Garfunkel album *Parsley, Sage, Rosemary and Thyme* is released.
October 20, 1935—Baseball star Mickey Mantle is born in Oklahoma. ☮ October 20, 1938—Actress Dolores Hart is born in Chicago.

had style, from the impeccable tuxedos they wore to the impressive A-list movie stars and celebrity guests (including JFK) who came to the Sands.

The show included solos, group numbers, dances, impressions, prepared jokes, spontaneous jokes, off-color jokes, racial jokes, jokes yelled from off-stage, jokes at each other's expense, sight gags, lots of smoking and drinking onstage, and pretty much doing whatever they felt like doing because at that moment they were probably the most confident, most liberated entertainers in the world. Joey was the dour ringmaster who kept things moving, Peter tried to keep up with the three main stars, Sammy always got in a great crack after he'd been teased, Dean was the smoothest and most natural comedian, and Frank was, well, Frank, the leader they all followed (and whom only Dean dared rib).

Tickets (including dinner) were $5.95 and almost impossible to come by for the month or so that the Summit (Frank's term) officially convened (unofficial parties continued elsewhere after the show). There was a last Vegas show the night of the *Ocean's 11* premiere in August, then shows in other cities (especially Miami).

The movie turned out to be pretty lightweight—the "map" for the caper was more like a broadly illustrated napkin—but it got the mood right and included a couple of musical numbers (disappointingly, none were by Frank). More movies followed, again with numerals in the titles to emphasize the gang instead of a particular star: *Sergeants 3*, *4 for Texas* (Frank and Dean, no Sammy, Peter, or Joey), *Robin and the 7 Hoods* (no Peter or Joey). On his own Frank made well-received movies through the '60s (*The Manchurian Candidate*, '62, *Von Ryan's Express*, '65, *The Detective*, '68), he started up his own record label (Reprise), and despite the burgeoning rock revolution he stayed true to his ring-a-ding-ding roots with a steady stream of stylin' hits ("That's Life," the Grammy-winning "Strangers in the Night").

Dean had the biggest hit of his career in '64 with *Everybody Loves Somebody*, a long-running loosey-goosey variety show in '65, and the role of playboy secret agent Matt Helm in a string of spy spoofs at decade's end. Sammy had his biggest hit with "Candyman" in '68, plus a show of his own. Peter struggled to find himself through the '60s and became an aging hipster showing up for talk shows and game shows. Joey had his own sitcom from '61–'65 in which he played a talk-show host, then in '67 he started a futile two-year run as an actual talk show host going up against Johnny Carson. Later he frequently subbed for Johnny, and today he is the last surviving member of the group.

EVERYBODY LOVES SOMEBODY

Frank's romantic exploits are the stuff of legend—the early marriage, the many affairs, the exhilarating highs and devastating lows of the Ava Gardner relationship in the '50s, the fling with dancer Juliet Prowse in '62, the two-year, mid-decade marriage to young Mia Farrow, and the long final marriage to Zeppo's ex-, Barbara Marx. Son Frank Jr. has had a long show biz career as a singer and musical director; daughter Nancy, one of the first great solo women in rock music and a popular '60s actress, still records and performs; and daughter Tina has acted and worked behind the scenes.

Dean had three wives and three divorces. During the '60s he was married to the former Queen of the Orange Bowl, and one of his many kids was Dino of the '60s pop group Dino, Desi and Billy. Most of Sammy's '60s were spent in a controversial marriage with blonde actress May Britt. They had three kids (two of them adopted), but he was an absentee husband and father concentrating on his Broadway career, and the couple divorced in '68. In '70 he married a dancer who was with him until his death in '90. Peter, by way of marriage to Patricia Kennedy, was related to JFK in the early '60s (Frank called Peter the brother-in-Lawford). Three more marriages (one to the daughter of Dan "*Laugh-In*" Rowan) followed until in '84 he became the first Rat Packer to pass away. Joey's wife of almost 60 years died in '99; their son is actor/director Larry Bishop.

October 20, 1965—It's "Possum Day" in Beverly Hills as the city celebrates TV's *The Beverly Hillbillies.*
October 20, 1968—Jacqueline Kennedy marries Greek shipping magnate Aristotle Onassis on the island of Skorpios.
October 20, 1979—Herb Alpert's "Rise" hits #1. ☮ October 21, 1940—Actress Julie Parrish is born in Middlesboro, Kentucky.

MY BACK PAGES

One of the most intense times of Frank's life came in '63 when his son was kidnapped and held for ransom—almost a quarter-million dollars was paid to the kidnappers, who were caught and convicted. . . . Dean was related to a Beach Boy—Carl Wilson married his daughter. . . . Frank and Peter's friendship was interrupted for a few years in the early '60s, in part because Frank blamed Peter when he delivered the message that JFK wouldn't be staying at Frank's Palm Springs estate. . . . Frank was best man at Sammy's wedding with May Britt. . . . The co-host on Joey's talk show—Regis Philbin. . . . Joey's ranked #96 on Comedy Central's list of stand-up comedians. . . . At the end of *Ocean's 11* the cast walked past the Sands sign that listed the five stars. . . . Dean, Sammy, Frank, and Shirley reunited for the feeble *Cannonball Run II* ('84).

Otis Redding

One of the decade's most intense singers died tragically.

TAKIN' CARE OF BUSINESS

Otis Redding's brilliant legacy is even more impressive when you consider how few years—only four—he enjoyed as a star. At age 5 he was singing in a church choir in his home state of Georgia, and in his late teens he was singing on tour with Johnny Jenkins and the Pinetoppers. By '60 he'd sung on his first record, though nobody noticed. Two years later he got some attention with "These Arms of Mine," a ballad he both wrote and sang.

Going on tour with other popular R & B artists like Sam and Dave, Otis started building an international reputation with his earthy, soulful voice, his powerful, sexually charged concerts (captured on the live album *Otis Redding in Europe*, '67), and a string of mid-decade hits, including "I Can't Turn You Loose," "Mr. Pitiful," "Try a Little Tenderness," and "I've Been Loving You Too Long." His most famous song during this time was one made legendary by somebody else—Otis wrote and recorded "Respect" in '65, but Aretha Franklin made it an anthem in '67 (37 years later *Rolling Stone* ranked her version as the fifth-greatest rock song ever).

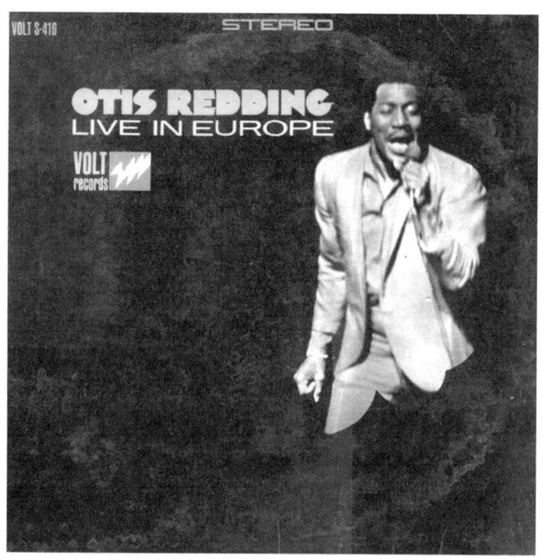

Otis's own superstardom seemed assured when he delivered an electrifying performance at the high-profile Monterey International Pop Festival in '67. Resting near San Francisco after his Monterey success, Otis sat on a Sausalito houseboat and penned what would be remembered as his signature song. In December, Otis recorded "(Sittin' on) the Dock of the Bay," a smooth, almost folk-rock tune that was very different from the intense workouts he'd previously performed.

"Dock of the Bay" would rise to #1 (his first and only #1) on both the R & B and pop charts in March of '68, would win two Grammy Awards, and sell over a million copies, but sadly Otis never lived to see it become a hit. Three days after finishing the record, Otis, like Buddy Holly and several other rock greats before him, died in a plane crash. Otis's plane crashed in Wisconsin and took most of his backup band too.

October 21, 1967—"To Sir with Love" by Lulu hits #1. ☮ October 21, 1984—Director François Truffaut dies in France of a brain tumor.
October 22, 1920—Timothy Leary is born. ☮ October 22, 1942—Actress Annette Funicello is born in Utica, New York.
October 22, 1943—Actress Catherine Deneuve is born in Paris. ☮ October 22, 1947—Actress Lee Meredith is born in River Edge, New Jersey.

After his death more of his unreleased songs—"The Happy Song (Dum Dum)," "Amen," "I've Got Dreams to Remember"—and anthology albums were released, most of them successful, all of them reminders of how brightly and briefly he'd flared above the music scene. As tributes to his lasting legacy, he was inducted into the Rock and Roll Hall of Fame in '89, and his image appeared on a postage stamp in '93.

EVERYBODY LOVES SOMEBODY

The book *Bill Graham Presents* offered recollections of Otis as the most sexually compelling singer anybody had ever seen, plus stories that he "left his mark" offstage with women wherever he went. Throughout most of the decade he was a married man with kids at home (two would go on to found an R & B group in the '80s).

MY BACK PAGES

Reversing the British Invasion, Otis's songs were huge in England, where his hits did almost as well as they did in the States. . . . Many of his songs (especially "Respect") have been used in popular movies, including *Top Gun* ('86), *Platoon* ('86), *Dirty Dancing* ('87), and *Forrest Gump* ('94). . . . Otis's body was recovered from the lake where the plane crashed—he was buried back home in Georgia, and in 2002 a memorial statue of him went on display in Macon.

The Redgraves

Vanessa and Lynn brought their famous family heritage to key '60s movies.

TAKIN' CARE OF BUSINESS

Vanessa and Lynn Redgrave weren't '60s superstars, but they were both highly respected actresses with lead roles in some of the decade's most memorable films. Both were born in London, both were in Best Picture Oscar-winners (Vanessa in *A Man for All Seasons,* '66, Lynn in *Tom Jones,* '63), both were cast in '66 as the vivacious Georgy in *Georgy Girl* (Vanessa left and was replaced by Lynn), and both were up for Best Actress Oscars in '67 (Vanessa for *Morgan!,* Lynn for *Georgy Girl,* but Liz Taylor won it). Both belong to the distinguished family of actors that includes their father Sir Michael Redgrave, their mother Rachel Kempson, their brother Corin Redgrave, Vanessa's daughters Natasha and Joely, and their niece Jemma Richardson.

Dignified and elegant, Vanessa was an actress with the Royal Shakespeare Company in the early '60s before making a sensational screen splash in '66 with three films: the cult classic *Morgan!* (her first Oscar nomination), as Anne Boleyn in the Oscar-dominator *A Man for All Seasons*, and in Michelangelo Antonioni's influential *Blow-Up*. Often starring in historical movies, in '67 she was a singing Guinevere in the majestic medieval musical *Camelot*, and in '68 she starred as a free-thinking 1920s dancer in *Isadora* (her second Oscar nomination).

Her subsequent career has been filled with interesting, challenging, sometimes eccentric projects, among them *Mary, Queen of Scots* ('71, her third Oscar nomination), *Murder on the Orient Express* ('74), *Julia* ('77, her first Oscar), *The Bostonians* ('84, another Oscar nomination), *Howard's End* ('92, yet one more Oscar nomination), and many more, with lots of prominent stagework filling the gaps between her films.

Inseparable from Vanessa's working career are her politics. She traveled to Cuba in '62 and supported Castro's revolution, in '67 she loudly protested America's bombing in North Vietnam, in '73 she joined the Socialist Labor League, and in '74 she raised funds for a Marxist school in Britain. When she won the Oscar in '77, she made a controversial political speech that was roundly chastised. She discussed her busy life and controversial stances in a poignant, articulate autobiography in '94. If the '60s were about revolution and fighting for important causes, then Vanessa Redgrave may be the most archetypal '60s actress of all.

Her younger sister's career hasn't been quite so dramatic, though it's been just as long and almost as acclaimed. After winning the Golden Globe as Most Promising Newcomer in '67, Lynn fulfilled that promise with another 70+ roles in a wide variety of projects, including an Emmy-nominated hospital administrator in the TV series *House Calls* and the Oscar-nominated housekeeper in *Gods and Monsters* ('98), plus steady stagework and some much-viewed Weight Watchers commercials. Talk about range—she was a royal for Woody Allen's *Everything You Wanted to Know About Sex* ('71), the lead hooker in *The Happy Hooker* ('75), and the lead teacher in the *Teacher's Only* TV series ('82). The Queen was watching and was impressed: in 2001 she awarded Lynn the prestigious O.B.E. (Order of British Empire).

EVERYBODY LOVES SOMEBODY

From '62 to '67, Vanessa was married to Tony Richardson, the Oscar-winning director of *Tom Jones* ('63) and the father of her two daughters. Richardson directed Vanessa in three movies, including *The Charge of the Light Brigade* ('68), which also had brother Corin, mother Rachel, and daughters Natasha and Joely. In the late '60s-early '70s, Vanessa had a relationship and a son with actor Franco Nero, her *Camelot* co-star; in '97 she said she was targeted by a fascist group because of her rumored relationship with an African-American actor. Meanwhile, Lynn was married in '67 to British actor John Clarke, who had been a child star on stage and on radio and then became Lynn's manager and the director of several of her stage shows. They had three kids before divorcing in 2000.

MY BACK PAGES

Lynn was nominated twice ('76 and '93) for Tony Awards, but Vanessa finally won it in 2003 for her celebrated performance in the Broadway classic *Long Day's Journey Into Night*. . . . The sisters teamed for a TV remake of *Whatever Happened to Baby Jane?* ('91) and *The White Countess* (2005, which also starred Vanessa's daughter Natasha).

Cathy Rigby

America's first Olympic gymnastic pixie, this sensational sprite soared to fame at the Mexico City Games.

TAKIN' CARE OF BUSINESS

Though she didn't win a medal at the '68 Olympics, Cathy Rigby's youthful all-American appeal and superlative skill brought unprecedented popularity to gymnastics. Cathy, a 15-year-old 90-pound Long Beach girl, finished fourth at the '68 Olympics with remarkable routines that riveted a global audience to their TV sets. She revolutionized the very nature of her sport—after her came other petite gymnasts, names like Korbut and Comaneci. Cathy's athletic career was studded with so many impressive accomplishments—she was the very first American woman to medal at the World Championships, for instance—that she made the *Wide World of Sports* list of the 25 most influential women athletes ever.

After competing in the '72 Games in Munich, Cathy trained with just as much dedication in a whole new arena—entertainment. By the late '70s she was ready, and the movies and musicals started to tumble in. One of her TV movies, *Perfect Body* ('97), struck close to home in telling the story of a female gymnast pressured to lose weight; in the interest of helping others, Cathy herself disclosed her own past eating disorders.

Her most spectacular roles have come on the stage, where's she proven herself to be a ticket-selling powerhouse. She made her musical debut as Dorothy in *The Wizard of Oz* and performed in *Annie Get Your Gun*, *Meet Me in St. Louis*, and *Paint Your Wagon*, among others. When she came to Broadway with *Peter Pan* in '91, she was nominated for a Tony Award and set box-office records. By now she's logged more

October 23, 1968—Elvis Presley's *Live a Little, Love a Little* opens.
October 23, 1968—U.S. swimmer Debbie Meyer breaks the Olympic record while winning the gold medal in the 800-meter freestyle event at the '68 Mexico City Olympics.

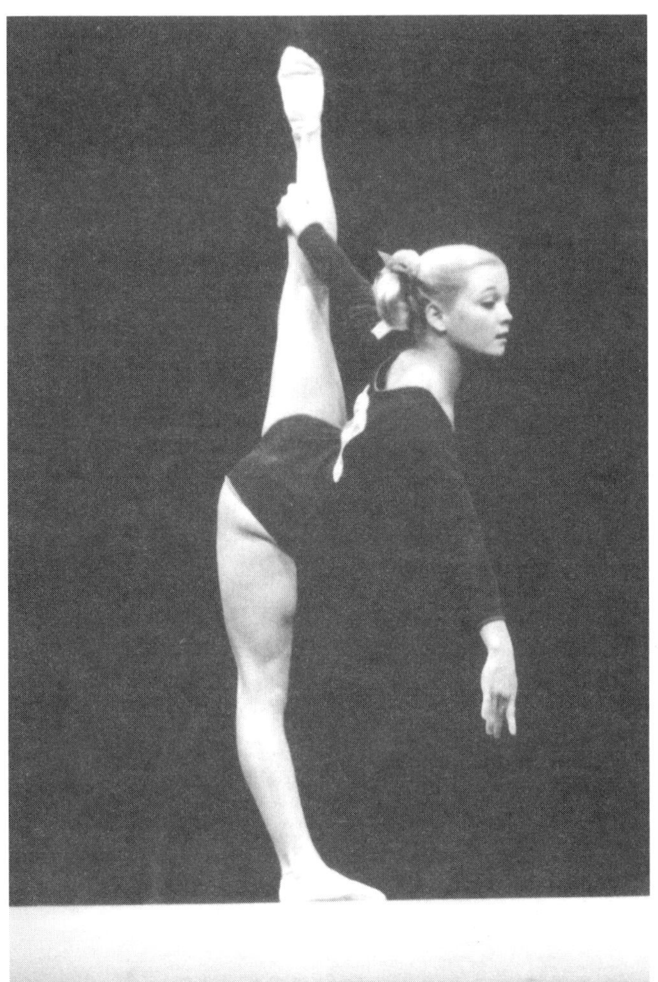

"frequent flyer" miles than any other actress who ever played Peter and has continued soaring into the 21st century.

When not performing on a Broadway stage, Cathy has headlined in Vegas (winning the George M. Cohan Award there for Best Specialty Act), she's done narration for various videos, and she's a national spokesperson for the Fast Track exercise machine. Maybe she didn't win the gold for gymnastics, but she's certainly won it for versatility.

EVERYBODY LOVES SOMEBODY

Thankfully, this Olympic hero had no awful scandals in the '60s. Cathy has married two Toms: the first, Tom Mason, from '72–'81, ended in divorce but brought her two sons; the second, Tom McCoy, from '82 onward, has brought her two daughters. Tom McCoy has teamed with Cathy to create McCoy/Rigby Entertainment, based in Southern California.

MY BACK PAGES

In '72, Cathy told *Sports Illustrated* that Olympic diving and gymnastics should be performed nude, for aesthetic reasons, and in fact she was nude in a hazy photo for *SI*. . . . She was Mother of the Year in '92. . . . She still devotes time to the Special Olympics, the Boy and Girl Scouts of America, the Will Rogers Institute, Mercy Corps International, and The National Center for the Prevention of Sudden Infant Death Syndrome.

Diana Rigg and Patrick Macnee

A slinky sophisticate as good with a gun as she is with a Shakespeare soliloquy, regal Diana was judo-choppin' Emma Peel alongside suave Patrick Macnee's John Steed on *The Avengers*.

TAKIN' CARE OF BUSINESS

Graceful, beautiful Diana Rigg is one of the most respected of all screen stars. Born in England, young Diana lived in India for six years before starting a theatre career. From '59 to '62 she was a rising star with the Royal Shakespeare Company, and then came Emma. *The Avengers,* the great English spy series starring Patrick Macnee as elegant John Steed, had been running with Honor Blackman as Steed's partner, Cathy Gale. When Honor left to make *Goldfinger*, Diana entered as Mrs. Emma Peel, Steed's new platonic partner (the "Mrs." referred to her husband, who had disappeared in South America).

With her saucy charm and liberated spirit, Emma was a rich, fascinating character, able to pick a lock, karate chop an enemy, and read both *Basic Nuclear Physics* (a book shown in Emma's home) and *Advanced Ventriloquism* (a book we saw her reading). It's a toss-up what looked better—Emma in a swingin' mod outfit or in her fightin' jumpsuit— but either way Diana's long, lean 5' 8" figure got her voted as the sexiest TV woman *ever* by *TV Guide* in '99; that same year *TV Guide* also listed Emma Peel #8 of TV's greatest characters (#3 Lucy Ricardo was the only other woman in the top 10).

After a three-year run as Emma, Diana briefly returned to the Royal Shakespeare Company, and then she Bonded in '69. *On Her Majesty's Secret Service* introduced Australian model George Lazenby as 007 and showed Bond marrying Diana's character (though the bride died on her wedding day). Diana is still hailed as perhaps the strongest, and the best, of the Bond women.

Her career continued, blending lighter projects—*The Hospital* ('72), a quickly cancelled TV series ('73), *The Great Muppet Caper* ('75), and hostess of the *Mystery* TV series in the '90s—with prestigious classics—the films *Julius Caesar* ('70) and *King Lear* ('84), the plays *Medea* ('94) and *Who's Afraid of Virginia Woolf?* ('97). She also compiled the text for *No Turn Unstoned: The Worst-Ever Theatrical Reviews* (including some written about her). Major awards punctuate her long career: five Emmy nominations (two wins for *The Avengers* and a win in '97 for *Rebecca*), a '72 Golden Globe nomination for *The Hospital*, a Tony Award in '94, and, most impressive of all, knighthood, bringing with it the exalted titles Dame Diana Rigg and Dame Commander of the British Empire.

Emma's ally on *The Avengers* was dapper and debonair John Wickham Gascone Berresford Steed, played by dapper and debonair Daniel Patrick Macnee. A Londoner born into an aristocratic family, Patrick got expelled from Eton for bookmaking and then served in the Royal Navy during World War II. He returned to London to pursue an acting career, and during the '50s he was in English and American films (including a part in the Christmas classic *Scrooge*, '51). He was also a pioneer on Canadian TV before riding Steed to glory.

Steed's conservative old-school mannerisms (symbolized by his bowler hat, Edwardian suits, and umbrella) perfectly balanced the youthful exuberance of his female partners (Cathy Gale wore leather, Emma wore tight, athletic clothes). The vehicles they drove also suited their personalities: Steed drove a vintage Bentley, Cathy rode a motorcycle, Emma whipped around in a blue Lotus Elan sports car, and Emma's successor, Tara King, drove a deep-red AC Cobra.

And unlike other TV cops and agents, Steed didn't chase women (he never even called Emma by her first name or kissed her on the cheek until her final episode), and he never had to resort to firearms, using guile and quickness to outfox and outclass the villains. After the series ended in '69, Patrick continued playing elegant, sophisticated gentlemen onstage, in movies, and on TV, including a Broadway run in *Sleuth* ('73), a prominent Sir in a Bond film, *A View to a Kill* ('85), and Steed once more in *The New Avengers* ('76). In the last decade he's become a popular reader for books on tape, and he's written books, too, a recent autobiography and an *Avengers* memoir adding to two novels he co-wrote in the '60s.

EVERYBODY LOVES SOMEBODY

Far too classy for scandals, Diana's generated no simmering '60s stories,

October 25, 1927—Actress Barbara Cook is born in Atlanta, Georgia. ☮ October 25, 1928—Actor Tony Franciosa is born in New York.
October 25, 1963—Yvette Mimieux makes the cover of *Life*. ☮ October 25, 1967—*Camelot* with Vanessa Redgrave opens.
October 25, 1968—American swimmer Pokey Watson sets a new Olympic record in the 100-meter backstroke at the Olympic Games in Mexico City.

which is just about right for our smart Emma. Later on Diana divorced two husbands, one in '76 after three years of marriage and the other in '90 after eight years and one daughter. Patrick's had three wives—two kids with the first, wife #2 was an actress whose character was killed on the first episode of *The Avengers*, and marriage since '88 to #3.

MY BACK PAGES

Playboy ranked Diana #75, ahead of supermodel Kathy Ireland, on its list of the century's sexiest stars. . . . Brigitte Bardot and Catherine Deneuve were serious contenders for Diana's role in her Bond movie. . . . In Diana's last episode of *The Avengers*, we glimpsed long-lost husband Peter Peel—his clothes were identical to Steed's, and in fact Patrick Macnee played the role in a long-distance shot. . . . Emma's replacement, who passed the departing Emma on the stairs up to Steed's flat, was Agent 69, Tara King, played by Canadian Linda Thorson—the show clearly implied that she and Steed had a physical relationship (the show was cancelled a year later).

The Rolling Stones

Rock's bad boys were a dark alternative to the sunny Beatles.

TAKIN' CARE OF BUSINESS

Maybe the bouncy Beatles were content to wanna hold your hand, but not the Rolling Stones. They brought a whole new surly attitude and dangerous style to '60s rock that has been emulated by strutting rockers ever since. Like the Beatles and the Who and many other British bands, the Stones were built on a bedrock of American blues, taking their early material, their guitar-based sound, their yowly vocals, and even their name from blues masters.

The group began with the brief childhood friendship of Londoners Mick Jagger and Keith Richards. Meeting again in the early '60s, they teamed up with versatile guitarist Brian Jones, and the three roomed together and started to play London clubs with other blues-minded musicians. With bassist Bill Wyman and drummer Charlie Watts the Stones' five-man lineup was in place by '63. Creative management and an outlaw image came courtesy of a visionary P.R. man, Andrew Loog Oldham, who intentionally wanted to contrast the Stones with the Beatles' innocent, safe appeal—parents could love the cheerful Beatles but not his sinister Stones.

Their first records in '63 and '64 were mostly written by other people (Chuck Berry, Buddy Holly, even Lennon and McCartney); not until '65 did Mick and Keith pen their own #1 hit, and when they did, it was a classic: "(I Can't Get No) Satisfaction," with the famous guitar riff that came to Keith in his sleep, has been widely heralded as one of the all-time great rock songs and an anthem for dissatisfied youth. Throughout these years the Stones were a thrilling live act, again decidedly different from the Beatles—when the smiling Fab Four played for Ed Sullivan on TV, they chatted amiably with Ed; when the Stones played, they snarled through

October 25, 1968—The Jimi Hendrix album *Electric Ladyland* is released.
October 25, 1991—Promoter Bill Graham dies in a helicopter accident near San Francisco.
October 26, 1933—Model Suzy Parker is born in San Antonio, Texas.

"Satisfaction" and Ed threatened to never invite them back (though he did anyway). Albums started to come quickly from the Stones, and Mick and Keith established themselves as prolific, ambitious composers: *Aftermath* ('66) included only their own songs and presented more sophisticated arrangements (vibes on "Under My Thumb"); *Between the Buttons* ('67) had a pop sound and introduced their most overtly sexual lyrics yet ("Let's Spend the Night Together"); *Flowers* ('67) was a repackaging of brilliant singles; *Their Satanic Majesties Request* ('67) was a psychedelic reply to the Beatles' landmark *Sgt. Pepper's* album (complete with colorful costumes).

Increasingly, the group was getting more eclectic with its music and more outrageous in its appearance, even going in drag for some photos. Watching were unamused authorities, who in '67 pinched Mick, Keith, and Brian in drug busts. The most seriously affected was Brian, who went into a personal and creative tailspin and was barely part of *Beggar's Banquet* ('68). Though he'd been a founding member, the frustrated group expelled him in '69; a month later he mysteriously drowned in his swimming pool. A free tribute concert was held in London, offering poetry readings and a new blues guitarist, young Mick Taylor, to a crowd of 300,000 people.

Powerful instant classics seemed to pour out of the band during the decade's last two years—"Sympathy for the Devil," "Jumpin' Jack Flash, "Street Fighting Man," "Gimme Shelter," "Honky Tonk Women," "You Can't Always Get What You Want," and more. The year ended with an apocalyptic album, *Let It Bleed*, and an apocalyptic event, the free concert at the Altamont Speedway some 50 miles east of San Francisco. Whereas that summer's Woodstock festival had celebrated love and peace, this winter concert, with security provided by the Hell's Angels, deteriorated into a grim nightmare of violence and death.

The Stones, shaken but unstoppable, leaped into the '70s with their own record label, a sexy new hit ("Brown Sugar"), and the ambitious double LP that many fans consider their masterpiece, *Exile on Main Street* ('72). Huge, and hugely successful, tours continued for the next decades as the group assumed the mantle of World's Greatest Rock Band from the defunct Beatles, validating the title with more hit albums (*Some Girls*, '78, *Tattoo You*, '81), more classic songs ("It's Only Rock and Roll"), and even some successful concert movies.

Despite personnel changes, and despite splintering off into various solo projects, the eternal Stones have kept rolling along into the 21st century with the ultimate accolades: in-

Stones' U.S. Top 10 Hits in the '60s

1964

"Time Is On My Side" (#6)

1965

"As Tears Go By" (#6)
"Get Off Of My Cloud" (#1)
"(I Can't Get No) Satisfaction" (#1)
"The Last Time" (#9)

1966

"Have You Seen Your Mother, Baby, Standing in the Shadow?" (#9)
"Mother's Little Helper" (#8)
"19th Nervous Breakdown" (#2)
"Paint It Black" (#1)

1967

"Ruby Tuesday" (#1)

1968

"Jumping Jack Flash" (#3)

1969

"Honky Tonk Women" (#1)

duction into the Rock and Roll Hall of Fame in '89 (their first year of eligibility), and knighthood for Sir Mick in 2002. For rock's original bad boys, that had to be satisfaction, indeed.

EVERYBODY LOVES SOMEBODY

In her autobiography, Marianne Faithfull speculated on the true love of Mick's life—Keith Richards. They've certainly been together the longest (even though they almost broke up for good in the '80s). While the group has been known for its debauchery and legions of groupies, all the band members have enjoyed long periods of married life. Mick's been married twice, to sultry Brazilian model Bianca Jagger for almost the entire '70s (when he was leading the kind of jet-set life chronicled in Carly Simon's "You're So Vain"), and then to tall Texas model Jerry Hall for almost the entire '90s. From these and other relationships he's got at least seven kids.

Brian fathered two children before he was 17 and then another one with the woman who would later marry Donovan. Before he died, Brian was in a serious relationship with model Anita Pallenberg—when he got abusive in '67, she ran to Keith, and they were together for over a dozen years, with three kids (one of whom died in infancy) and several long, harrowing drug addictions. Keith married New York model Patti Hansen in '83, with two more kids.

Insiders say the group's real ladies' man has always been quiet Bill, though he was married for virtually the entire '60s. His most discussed relationship came when he fell for a girl in her early teens—he was around 50 during their courtship. They married in the late '80s for about two years, and when Bill's son got engaged to the teen's mom, Bill's son was about to become Bill's father-in-law. Bill married again in the early '90s. Charlie, the steadiest Stone, has been married for over 40 years, with one daughter born in the '60s.

MY BACK PAGES

Not everybody was impressed by the Stones in the '60s—Dean Martin famously introduced them on the show *Hollywood Palace* with mocking grimaces. . . . Before Stanley Kubrick got involved with *A Clockwork Orange*, Mick hoped to make the movie with himself as Alex and the Stones as his gang. . . . Mick tried an acting career with two films in '70—*Ned Kelly* and *Performance*—and he later produced several films, including *Enigma* (2001). . . . Keith's mannerisms inspired Johnny Depp's pirate character in *Pirates of the Caribbean* (2003). . . . The band's first Grammy for Best Rock Album didn't come until '94 for *Voodoo Lounge*.

Katharine Ross

***The Graduate* girl was the love interest in two of the decade's biggest movies.**

TAKIN' CARE OF BUSINESS

Combining brains and beauty with sensitivity and subtle sexuality, Katharine Ross was an icon for young actresses of the late '60s. Her impact on Hollywood was swift and strong. Born in Hollywood, she started as a busy TV actress, often appearing in Western dramas.

After a couple of minor movies in the mid-'60s, she made a major breakthrough when she played Elaine, headstrong daughter to Anne Bancroft's Mrs. Robinson, in *The Graduate*. The sly comedy was one of the greatest movies of that or any decade, and Katharine was suddenly one of the hottest actresses of the year. The exposure brought her the '68 Golden Globe as the Most Promising Newcomer and an Oscar nomination as Best Supporting Actress.

Then in '68, when 20th Century Fox could've cast anyone it wanted for the high-profile *Butch Cassidy and the Sundance Kid,* the studio chose Katharine. Smart and sexy, she was a perfect match for the handsome, witty leads, Paul Newman and Robert Redford. And with her natural, youthful beauty, she made even a traditional farm dress look sexy, as evidenced by the long slow disrobing scene that made Sundance a hardened criminal indeed.

More Westerns (Redford's *Tell Them Willie Boy Is Here*, '69), other notable dramas (*The Stepford Wives*, '75), and a regular role on *The Colbys* ('85–'87) highlighted her ever-busy later decades. As testament to her career, when the American Film Institute ranked the 100 best American movies of all time, Katharine Ross had starred in two of them: *The Graduate* (#7) and *Butch Cassidy* (#50).

EVERYBODY LOVES SOMEBODY

With several marriages behind her, in '84 Katharine married actor Sam Elliott, the mustachioed star of *Mask* ('85) and *Tombstone* ('93). They met on the set of *Butch Cassidy*, where he had a small part as one of the card players in the sepia-toned opening sequence. Besides *Butch Cassidy*, he and Katharine have been in six movies together (one of which, *Conagher* in '91, they also co-wrote). Together they have a daughter and live in Malibu.

MY BACK PAGES

In *The Graduate*, Katharine played Anne's daughter, though the actresses were actually only ten years apart in age. . . . A photogenic pair, Katharine and Sam Elliott were on the cover of *Playgirl* in '79, billed as "Hollywood's Sexiest Couple."

Ed Roth

Big Daddy was the heart of Kustom Kulture.

TAKIN' CARE OF BUSINESS

For Ed Roth, cars weren't merely transportation, or even transportation you could enhance to go faster. They were works of art. Art, of course, is in the eye of the beholder, and the cars Big Daddy built in the '60s were considered bizarre monstrosities by his critics, and, uh, bizarre monstrosities by his fans. But no matter what you thought, you had to look.

Unlike the works from hot rodders, who built/refined/souped up cars for racing, or at least for driving, many of Ed's cars were more like museum pieces, one-of-a-kind attitudinal sculptures with bulbous glass and extravagant chrome that you wouldn't want in traffic. Cars like flying saucers, cars with engines and pipes bursting out of them, cars with two engines/swords for shifters/asymmetric headlights.

Ed had been building cars in his L.A. garage since he was a teen in the '40s. After serving in the Air Force he turned his imagination loose on a new material, Fiberglas. In the early '60s he supported his art by pinstriping and spraypainting other people's cars, then painting and selling T-shirts. Some of the latter sported a grotesquely exaggerated rodent, a Rat Fink, which eventually became plastic models, tattoos, posters, and record covers. The fink made it cool to be weird. Ed later turned his attention to other vehicles—motorcycles, go-karts, even a motorized barstool. He found religion, and museums eventually found him, lionizing him in the '90s as one of the pioneers of a uniquely American art form, the custom car.

EVERYBODY LOVES SOMEBODY

Before he got famous, Ed was already married with five sons. After the '60s he relocated to Utah, though he still continued to travel to car shows until a heart attack took him in 2001.

MY BACK PAGES

The show cars got names, including Outlaw, Mysterion, Beatnik Bandit, Rotar, Orbitron, Surfrite, Road Agent, Tweedy Pie, and Druid Princess. . . . Besides Rat Fink, other "family members" were Drag Nut, Mother's Worry, and Mr. Gasser. . . . In the '60s Ed also fronted a band, Mr. Gasser and the Weirdos, that recorded several albums.

October 29, 1945—Entertainer Melba Moore is born in New York. ☮ October 29, 1960—Muhammad Ali wins his first pro fight (beats Tunney Hunsaker).
October 29, 1964—Murph the Surf steals the Star of India from a New York museum.
October 29, 1995—Writer Terry Southern dies in New York of respiratory failure. ☮ October 30, 1939—Singer Grace Slick is born in Chicago.

Rowan and Martin

Dan and Dick steered TV's most frenzied show to classic status.

TAKIN' CARE OF BUSINESS

Surely more popular catch phrases came out of *Rowan and Martin's Laugh-In* than any other show: "Sock it to me," "Verrrry interesting," "Here come da judge," "You bet your sweet bippy," "Look that up in your Funk and Wagnall's," and "One ringy-dingy" all sprang from the decade's hippest comedy.

Laugh-In offered a set of loosely structured comedic bits—"The Cocktail Party," "Laugh-In Looks at the News," "The Flying Fickle Finger of Fate," "The Joke Wall"—and then poured rapid-fire jokes, ad-libs, bloopers, quick-cutting film footage, and cameos into them. It was psychedelic vaudeville: tattooed girls in bikinis danced, actors got doused with water, dirty old men hit on insulted old women, tricycle riders tipped over, the announcer seemed to be announcing a different show, and one comedian's prepared joke was interrupted by another's spontaneous lunacy.

Laugh-In wasn't just the funnest show to watch in the late '60s, it was the funnest show to be on, and as with *The Tonight Show* everyone from national politicians to movie legends to star athletes were eager to join in the merriment (indeed, the guest list reads like a who's who—Richard Nixon, John Wayne, Bing Crosby, Liberace, the Monkees, Joe Namath, Peter Sellers, Ringo, Wilt Chamberlain, Johnny Cash, Johnny Carson, Bobby Darin, Hugh Hefner, Diana Ross, Rod Serling, Truman Capote, Bob Hope, and on and on, often a half-dozen top stars per show).

The ringmasters of this mayhem were a comedy team that had been performing together since the '50s. Dan Rowan was born in Oklahoma and worked carnivals with his parents as a child entertainer; later he was a medal-winning pilot in World War II. Detroit's Dick Martin, who was actually slightly older than Dan, was a popular L.A. bartender before teaming with Dan. Their act, perfected in nightclubs and in Vegas, presented Dan as the dignified pipe-smoking straight man (clean-shaven at first, then mustachioed and bearded in later seasons) and Dick as the handsome girl-crazy nitwit.

The show started as a one-hour special in '67 and then replaced the tiring *The Man from U.N.C.L.E.* in early '68. An immediate hit, *Laugh-In* quickly topped the ratings and started claiming its annual Emmy nominations. As with *Saturday Night Live* in the '70s, many of the troupe's charter members—including Goldie Hawn, Judy Carne, and Henry Gibson—left the show to pursue solo careers, and though capable replacements—Lily Tomlin, Barbara Sharma, Richard Dawson—came aboard, the show lost steam and was all laughed-out in '73.

Dan and Dick attempted a movie, *The Maltese Bippy*, that tried too hard and entertained too little. Dan made some TV appearances in the '70s but mainly retired to Florida, where he died of cancer in '87. Dick has continued to appear on TV and in minor movies, plus he became a successful TV director in the '80s and '90s.

EVERYBODY LOVES SOMEBODY

Dan was married in the '40s, had three kids, divorced, then remarried in the '60s; one of his daughters was married to Peter Lawford for awhile. Dick was married several times; one of his wives was England's Dolly Read, a former *Playboy* Playmate (May, '66) who co-starred in *Beyond the Valley of the Dolls* ('70).

October 30, 1965—The Toys' "A Lover's Concerto" hits #2. ☮ October 30, 1965—Patty Duke's "Say Something Funny" hits the charts.
October 31, 1927—Actress Lee Grant is born in New York. ☮ October 31, 1944—Actress Sally Kirkland is born in New York.
October 31, 1964—Barbra Streisand's album *People* hits #1. ☮ October 31, 1964—The Supremes' "Baby Love" hits #1.

MY BACK PAGES

The Maltese Bippy wasn't the team's first film—they made a little-seen Western comedy, *Once Upon a Horse*, in '58. . . . The only performers to make it through the show's entire run were Dan, Dick, Ruth Buzzi, and announcer Gary Owens. . . . Specials honoring the *Laugh-In* legacy were ratings hits in the '90s.

Darrell Royal

Coach Royal built his football legacy in the country's footballin'est state.

TAKIN' CARE OF BUSINESS

Voted by '60s sportswriters as college football's coach of the decade, Darrell Royal is revered like a god in Texas, the most football-frenzied state. But Darrell was a Sooner, of all things, before he was a Longhorn. After serving in World War II, he played tailback, quarterback and defensive back at the University of Oklahoma (one of Texas's biggest rivals) in the late '40s, was named an All-American, and then went on to several coaching jobs, including stints in the Canadian Football League, at Mississippi State, and at the University of Washington.

In '56, the youthful 32-year-old Darrell took over a beleaguered Texas team that was coming off a 1-9 season and immediately led the Longhorns to the Sugar Bowl. His glory years came in the '60s with two undefeated national-championship teams in '63 and '69, culminating with a "game of the century" (the kind that seems to get played every couple of years). This one was against Arkansas and paired the country's #1 and #2 teams, a match-up so enticing that even President Nixon helicoptered in to watch. For once the game proved to be worthy of all the hype: Texas rallied from a two-touchdown deficit in the fourth quarter to pull out a thrilling 15-14 win, highlighted by a dramatic fourth-down 43-yard pass late in the game.

Another national title in '70, a total of 11 Southwestern Conference titles, and a legacy as an innovative coach both on the field (he introduced the wishbone offense) and off (he helped his players graduate by hiring the first academic counselor) established him as one of the game's true legends. He retired from coaching at only 52 years old, having won over 75% of his games with the Longhorns. In '83 he was elected to the College Football Hall of Fame, and in '96 Texas renamed its stadium after him. Today he still works for the university as a special assistant to the president and is treated like, well, Royalty everywhere he goes.

EVERYBODY LOVES SOMEBODY

Darrell and his wife Edith have been married for over 60 years. Their daughter was killed in a car accident in '73.

MY BACK PAGES

In his 23 years as a head coach, Darrell never had a losing season. . . . After introducing the wishbone in '68, over 100 rival coaches attended his practices in '69 to learn the offense. . . . Famous Texas friends—he and his wife were frequent guests of LBJ, in '91 Darrell helped pay off the tax debt of his pal Willie Nelson, and among those who appeared in the '99 documentary *The Story of Darrell Royal* were George W. Bush and Matthew McConaughey.

10 Legendary Coaches

Walter Alston–L.A. Dodgers baseball
Red Auerbach–Boston Celtics basketball
Toe Blake–Montreal Canadiens hockey
Paul "Bear" Bryant–
University of Alabama football
Woody Hayes–Ohio State football
Vince Lombardi–Green Bay Packers football
John McKay–USC football
Ara Parseghian–Notre Dame football
Casey Stengel–N.Y. Mets baseball
John Wooden–UCLA basketball

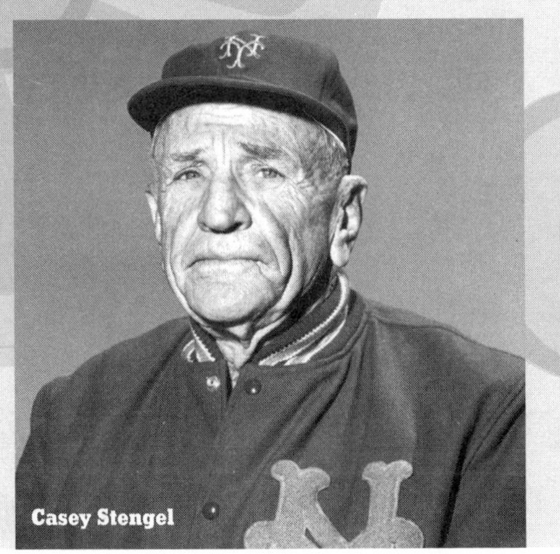
Casey Stengel

Wilma Rudolph

This pioneering American sprinter overcame formidable obstacles to become one of the greatest athletes of all time.

TAKIN' CARE OF BUSINESS

Wilma Rudolph's records—as the first American woman to win three gold medals in a single Olympiad—only begin to define her impact. She was born prematurely (only 4.5 pounds) into a poor Tennessee family, the twentieth of 22 children. As a child she suffered from polio, measles, mumps, scarlet fever, chicken pox, and double pneumonia. Wilma Rudolph was so sickly that many believed she would never walk, and she was so crippled that she didn't even go to school and was instead tutored at home while wearing a leg brace for four years.

However, physical therapy four times a day brought a gradual recovery, and as a high school sophomore she played varsity hoops, scoring 49 points in one game and eventually leading her team to the state championship. Also running track, she was invited to train at Tennessee State University and made the '56 Olympic team, but in Melbourne the only medal she won was a bronze with the relay team.

At the '60 Olympics in Rome, she won the 100-meter dash and the 200-meter dash, and she was the anchor on the winning 400-meter relay team. She won several national athlete-of-the-year trophies, was named America's top amateur athlete, and eventually was elected to the Black Sports Hall of Fame, the U.S. Track and Field Hall of Fame, the U.S. Olympic Hall of Fame and the National Women's Hall of Fame.

In '62 she left active competition to return to college to get her degree and become a teacher and track coach. Later she gave speeches at universities, and she also did some broadcasting. So popular was Wilma, she was honored with her hometown's first racially integrated parade, and in '97 Tennessee declared June 23rd as Wilma Rudolph Day. She died in

November 1, 1968—New York mayor John Lindsay makes the cover of *Time*. ☮ November 1, 1969—The Beatles' *Abbey Road* album hits #1. November 1, 1969—Elvis Presley's "Suspicious Minds" hits #1. ☮ November 2, 1942—Actress Stefanie Powers is born in Hollywood. November 2, 1964—*Where Love Has Gone* with Joey Heatherton opens.

her Nashville home of a brain tumor at age 54, her casket draped with the Olympic flag.

EVERYBODY LOVES SOMEBODY

In '63, Wilma married her high school sweetheart, and they had four children before eventually divorcing.

MY BACK PAGES

Her nicknames: Lady of Gold, the Black Pearl, and *La Gazelle Noire*. . . . The non-profit Wilma Rudolph Foundation helps underprivileged youth by providing free coaching and academic assistance. . . . Her bestselling autobiography, *Wilma*, became a TV movie in '75 with Cicely Tyson and Denzel Washington. . . . She was ranked #41 on ESPN's millennium list of the century's 50 greatest athletes.

Jim Ryun

This Kansas teen ran his way to stardom.

TAKIN' CARE OF BUSINESS

In an era that celebrated youth, teenage Jim Ryun was the world's fastest middle-distance runner in the mid-'60s. In '64, as a tall, crew-cutted junior at his Wichita high school, he became the first high school athlete to break the four-minute mile, an electrifying feat that got him onto the cover of *Sports Illustrated*; the following year, he beat the reigning Olympic champ in the mile and set the American high school record with a time so low (3:55.3) it wouldn't be beaten until the '90s.

During the '60s, Jim endured exhausting two-a-day workouts, but they gave him the famous finishing kick he was known for. Global glory came in '66 when the 19-year-old University of Kansas student set new world records in the mile (taking 2.3 seconds off the record) and half-mile; a year later he broke the mile record yet again with a time of 3:51.1, a record that stood into the mid-'70s. In '67 he was named America's best amateur athlete in any sport, and *Sports Illustrated* proclaimed him Sportsman of the Year.

Starting in '64 (when he was still in high school), Jim made three Olympic teams, winning a silver medal in '68 and missing a medal opportunity in '72 when he was boxed in during a qualifying heat, got tripped up and fell. Later he was a motivational speaker, set up a running camp, became the founder and president of a P.R. company, and has been elected many times as a Congressman from his home state of Kansas.

EVERYBODY LOVES SOMEBODY

Jim got married in '69; he and his wife still live in Kansas and have four children.

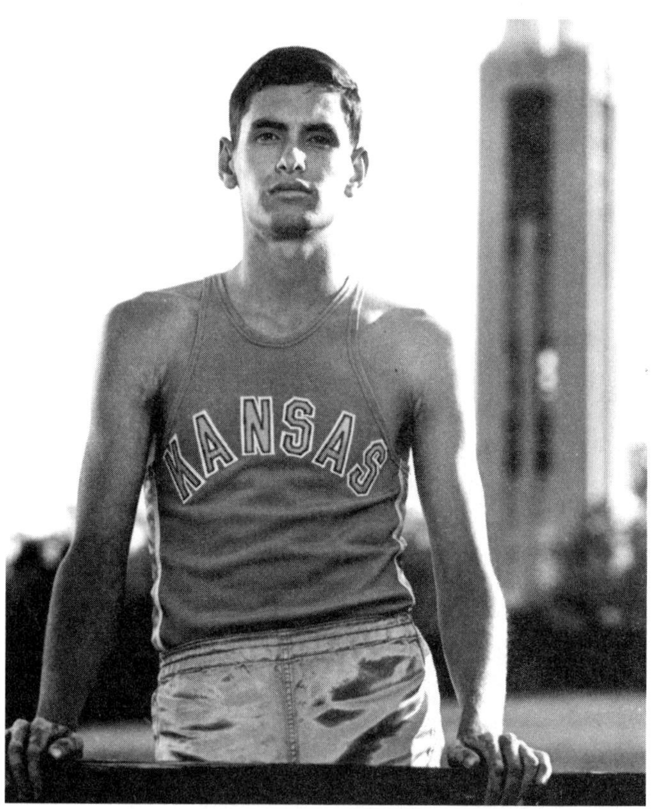

November 2, 1965—Model Jean Shrimpton creates a scandal when she wears a miniskirt, no stockings, no hat, and no gloves to the Melbourne Cup in Australia.
November 2, 1965—Craig Breedlove is the first man to drive 555 MPH. ☮ November 2, 1966—*Fahrenheit 451* with Julie Christie opens.

MY BACK PAGES

From '64–'72, Jim made one cover of *Newsweek* and seven covers of *Sports Illustrated*. . . . As of 2001, of the six fastest mile times ever recorded by a high schooler, Jim still had five of them. . . . Ever since his 3:51.1, no other American has held the world record in the mile.

The San Francisco Sound

Bands under this psychedelic umbrella—including the Dead and the Airplane—created events as much as they created music.

TAKIN' CARE OF BUSINESS

In the second half of the '60s, San Francisco was one of the two coolest cities in the world (and it welcomed curious ambassadors—including various Beatles—from London, the other coolest city). Inspired by the Beat poets of the '50s and Ken Kesey's LSD-fueled mid-decade happenings/parties/ festivals, for '66 and '67 San Francisco was the bohemian headquarters for the Love Generation, the Age of Aquarius, Flower Power, the hippies, and any other youth-oriented anti-establishment movement of the day.

The adventurous scene blossomed in January of '67 with the "Human Be-In" festival in the city's Golden Gate Park (local rock bands, 30,000 people), and that June it fully flowered two hours down the coast with the three-day Monterey International Pop Festival. What the world called the Summer of Love was more like the Couple Years of Love in San Francisco.

Propelling the scene forward was innovative new guitar-based music from unknown local bands that would soon become legendary. Leading the way was the Grateful Dead, the masters of the marathon cosmic jams that influenced every other San Francisco band. Formed in '65 as the Warlocks (and quickly renamed), the band was led by versatile guitar virtuoso Jerry Garcia and incorporated elements of jazz, rock, bluegrass, blues, and folk into their eclectic sound.

Unlike radio-friendly bands that churned out three-minute pop singles, the Dead performed long instrumental improvisations that made them a concert and festival favorite. They rarely made bestselling records ("Truckin'," a moderately successful '70 hit, remains their best-known song), but by the mid-'70s they were one of the world's most durable and successful touring acts, their shows drawing vast legions of loyal fans who followed them from venue to venue to create a joyous celebratory party that extended from the stage to the parking lot and lasted much longer than the concerts did. The Grateful Dead also helped centralize the San Francisco scene by sharing a flamboyant Victorian-style house in the Haight-Ashbury district near Golden Gate Park.

Prolific and adventurous, Jerry enjoyed numerous side projects after the '60s, releasing many solo albums and forming other bands so he could indulge his personal passions, even while the Dead continued to tour and record (he also inspired Ben & Jerry's "Cherry Garcia" ice cream). Unfortunately, the band's last decade was marred by drug problems and drug busts, though they were enjoying late success with one of their bestselling albums (*In the Dark*) and most popular hits ("Touch of Grey"). Jerry died in '95 at a drug-treatment clinic; the remaining members have continued, either solo or teamed up, to make music and play live.

San Francisco's other top '60s band was the Jefferson Airplane, the first local band to sign with a major record label. Jefferson Airplane soared in '67 with the release of two short-but-powerful radio hits, "White Rabbit" and "Somebody to Love," and a majestic album, *Surrealistic Pillow*, that became (along with *Sgt. Pepper's* and *The Doors*) one of the three seminal albums of the Summer of Love.

At its peak, Jefferson Airplane was both vital and popular, showing its psychedelic stuff at all three major rock fes-

November 2, 1966—Woody Allen's *What's Up, Tiger Lily?* opens. ☮ November 2, 1986—Paul Frees, the voice behind many popular '60s cartoons, dies.
November 3, 1924—Shirley Chisholm, the first black congresswoman and presidential candidate, is born in New York.
November 3, 1931—Actress Monica Vitti is born in Rome. ☮ November 3, 1948—Singer Lulu is born in Glasgow, Scotland.

tivals of the late '60s (Monterey in '67, then Woodstock and Altamont in '69). Pretty, dark-eyed Grace Slick was the band's vocalist and centerpiece, a former model who commanded attention with her riveting beauty and a fearless stage presence that made her capable of doing anything at any time, from lifting up her skirt to improvising monologues to dressing as a nun (quite a contrast to the more traditional styles of contemporaries like Petula Clark and Dionne Warwick).

Like the Dead, Jefferson Airplane also shared a Victorian house in San Francisco, "the Big House" of the early '70s, which was painted black and filled with bizarre furniture (including an unplugged electric chair). Unfortunately, Jefferson Airplane's flight was relatively short—within a few years the tensions among the band members and consecutive commercial failures brought the group crashing back to earth.

Renamed Jefferson Starship, the band released a huge hit, "Miracles" in '75, but by '78 Grace Slick had quit to make a couple of solo albums. She reboarded in the mid-'80s, and with another name, Starship, the group had enough fuel for a few more hits—especially "We Built This City" in '85—before Grace left the band for good in '88 to write her autobiography and create successful mixed-media art shows.

Presenting most of the concerts by these bands was a determined, innovative businessman, Bill Graham. Bill brought professionalism to what had been a chaotic concert scene, and in the '60s his Avalon Ballroom and Fillmore Auditorium (and later Winterland) were the city's most prominent music venues and would be the targets of most major touring acts. Bill was born Wolfgang Grajonca in Germany and as a kid made his way to America to escape the Reich. He earned a Bronze Star and Purple Heart in Korea and had early acting ambitions (that came to fruition late in his career with appearances in high-profile films like *Apocalypse Now* in '79 and *Bugsy* in '91).

But it was as an innovative, powerful concert impresario that he made his reputation. He championed important but unheralded artists, introduced new concert concepts (such as medical support for fans and his popular "Day on the Green" summer stadium shows), and he put on some of the most famous music events in history (the Band's "Last Waltz" and Live Aid). He was also a tireless fundraiser for numerous charities (many of the concerts he promoted were benefits). Bill Graham died in a helicopter accident in '91—a year later, he was inducted into the Rock and Roll Hall of Fame, where his fellow inductees now include both the Grateful Dead and the Jefferson Airplane.

10 More San Francisco Bands (and '60s Hits)

The Beau Brummels ("Laugh Laugh")

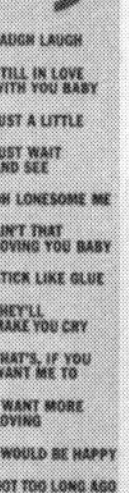

Big Brother and the Holding Company ("Piece of My Heart")

Blue Cheer ("Summertime Blues")

Country Joe and the Fish ("I Feel Like I'm Fixin' to Die Rag")

Creedence Clearwater Revival ("Suzie Q")

It's a Beautiful Day ("White Bird")

Moby Grape ("Omaha")

The Quicksilver Messenger Service ("Who Do You Love?")

Santana ("Evil Ways")

The Steve Miller Band ("Space Cowboy")

November 3, 1960—*The Unsinkable Molly Brown* with Tammy Grimes opens on Broadway.
November 3, 1962—The Crystals' "He's a Rebel" hits #1. ☮ November 4, 1913—Actor Gig Young is born in St. Cloud, Minnesota.
November 4, 1965—Driver Lee Breedlove sets the female land speed record (308.56 MPH) in Utah.

EVERYBODY LOVES SOMEBODY

Jerry was married twice. From '81 to '94 he was with "Mountain Girl," a well-known San Francisco scenemaker who had a child with Ken Kesey in the '60s. Jerry married again a year before he died. He left behind four daughters born between '63 and '87. Meanwhile, Grace Slick is admirably unapologetic about her affairs with: A. most drugs known to man; and B. most men known to drugs. She's written about her arrests, her stays in rehab, and her many lovers, which included most of Jefferson Airplane, Jim Morrison, and other rockers. And much of this happened while Grace was a married woman. Her cool last name came from "the boy next door" she married in '61; she left him mid-decade but they didn't divorce until the early '70s. In '71 she had a daughter, China, in '76 she married again, and in the mid-'90s she was living alone in Malibu. Finally, Bill was married to a staffer in his company, Bill Graham Presents, had two sons, and was later divorced.

MY BACK PAGES

The first San Francisco band with a national hit was Sopwith Camel ("Hello Hello"). . . . The mid-decade Charlatans had no hit records but were notable as a pioneering folk-rock band, one of the first to wear outrageous clothes (they dressed like Wild West outlaws), and also one of the first bands to use psychedelic posters to promote their shows.

Vidal Sassoon

Stylist to the stars.

TAKIN' CARE OF BUSINESS

Remember Judy Carne's boss bob on *Laugh-In*? How about Mia Farrow's shorn locks in *Rosemary's Baby*? These cuts were created by a celebrated hairstylist who worked on some of the most famous heads of the '60s. Vidal Sassoon was a Londoner who spent six of his childhood years in an orphanage, though both his parents were still alive (but split up). He was working in a salon in his early teens, and in the '50s he was cutting hair alongside London's top stylist, Raymond of Mayfair.

Vidal started his own London salon in the early '60s and within a few years was famous for reinventing the flapper's short bob haircut of the 1920s with a modern angular flair. Women loved the look because it was low-maintenance (wash 'n' wear hair, compared to the teased beehive sculptures of the late '50s-early '60s), and the fun little hair matched their fun little miniskirts. Suddenly Vidal was hanging out with rock stars, famous models, and celebrity friends like Roman Polanski and Sharon Tate right when England was at its swingin' peak. In '65 he opened his first eponymous salon in America, and later Paramount paid him $5,000 to fly in for a special *Rosemary's Baby* delivery—a short kicky 'do to replace Mia Farrow's long blonde hair (which he did with the press watching).

In the '70s he expanded his salons (there are now over two dozen salons, plus about a dozen academies) and he expanded his business by adding his own products that promoted healthy hair (in the TV commercials he himself described how hair was mostly protein). The '80s only got better—his own TV show (*Your New Day*), designation as the official hairstylist of the '84 Olympics in L.A., and books. By the mid-'90s over $400,000,000 of Vidal's products were selling annually. No longer cutting celebrity hair (and in fact no longer connected to the brand and salons that carry his name), he's still as stylish as ever, living in Beverly Hills, walking and swimming to overcome surgeries he's had in recent years.

EVERYBODY LOVES SOMEBODY

Vidal was married to beautiful actress Beverly Adams in '66; she was in numerous '60s beach movies and played Lovey Kravezit in Dino's *Murderer's Row* ('66). Before they divorced in the early '80s, Vidal and Beverly had four kids (one daughter, an actress, died in 2002, and two sons are both in show biz, one a producer, the other a TV director). Vidal met his fourth wife at the Proctor & Gamble headquarters, where she was working as a consultant; they were married in the early '90s and are still together.

MY BACK PAGES

From Vidal's commercials—"If you don't look good, we don't look good". . . . Vidal created the International Center for the Study of Anti-Semitism at the University of Jerusalem in '82.

Lalo Schifrin

Some of the decade's coolest theme songs came from this versatile composer.

TAKIN' CARE OF BUSINESS

Everyone knows the work, because Lalo Schifrin's compositions have been used for some of the coolest TV shows and movies in American history. The hip jazz in *Bullitt*? The Latin-influenced *Mission: Impossible* theme? The energetic music from *Cool Hand Luke* that was adopted by news stations in the late '60s? Thank Lalo.

His music career began with classical training in his native Argentina, where his father was the concertmaster of a philharmonic orchestra. In the early '50s, Lalo studied at the Paris Conservatory even while he was already getting work as a jazz pianist, composer, and arranger. Back in Buenos Aires he formed a band, was heard by Dizzy Gillespie, and in '58 was invited by the jazz titan to join him as a pianist/arranger.

Moving to America, in the early '60s Lalo started composing for Hollywood, and his career soared. During the decade his jazzy themes brought him a Grammy nomination for *The Man from U.N.C.L.E.* and a Grammy win for *Mission: Impossible*; Oscar nominations resulted from his music for

Cool Hand Luke ('67) and *The Fox* ('67). In addition to these highlights he also composed the music for *The Cincinnati Kid* ('65), *Bullitt* ('68), *Murderer's Row* ('68), *The Big Valley*, *Medical Center*, and many many others during the decade. After the '60s his career accelerated and diversified. He continued with movies and TV shows—*Kelly's Heroes* ('70), *Dirty Harry* ('71), *The Amityville Horror* ('79), *Rush Hour* ('98), *X-Men 3* (2006), *Night Gallery*, *Starsky and Hutch* and over *100* more (including many for Clint Eastwood)—but he also established himself as a force in classical music.

For five years he was musical director of the Paris Philharmonic, and for six years he was musical director of the Glendale Symphony. He's conducted all the great orchestras

November 5, 1963—*Palm Springs Weekend* with Connie Stevens opens.
November 5, 1965—The character Katy (played by Inger Stevens) marries her congressman on *The Farmer's Daughter*.
November 6, 1942—Model Jean Shrimpton is born in Buckinghamshire, England. ☮ November 6, 1946—Actress Sally Field is born in Pasadena, California.

around the world, composed over 60 classical works, and created the innovative "Jazz Meets the Symphony" concerts and recordings. By now he's won four Grammys (21 nominations) and been nominated for six Oscars, with lifetime-achievement recognition coming from several major music organizations.

EVERYBODY LOVES SOMEBODY

Lalo's been married for over 30 years. All three of his kids are in entertainment, one as a screenwriter, another as an art director, a third as a director.

20 Classic TV Themes and Composers

"The Addams Family"–Vic Mizzy, also did "Green Acres"

"The Andy Griffith Show"–Earle Hagen/Herbert Spencer, Hagen also did "The Dick Van Dyke Show," "That Girl," "Gomer Pyle USMC"

"The Avengers"–John Dankworth/Laurie Johnson, Johnson also scored Kubrick's *Dr. Strangelove*

"Batman"–Neal Hefti, also did "The Odd Couple"

"The Beverly Hillbillies"–Paul Henning, also the show's creator

"Bewitched"–Howard Greenfield/Jack Keller, their song replaced Sinatra's "Witchcraft"

"Bonanza"–Ray Evans/Jay Livingston, also wrote Bugs Bunny's "This Is It"

"Combat!"–Leonard Rosenman, also did "The Virginian," *Fantastic Voyage*

"Gilligan's Island"–Sherwood Schwartz/George Wyle, Schwartz was the show's creator

"Flight of the Bumblebee"–played by Al Hirt, *Green Hornet*

"Hawaii Five-O"–Morton Stevens, also did "Dr. Kildare," "The Wild, Wild West"

"I Dream of Jeannie"–Hugo Montenegro/Richard L. Weiss, lyrics never used on the show

"The Jetsons"–Joseph Barbera/William Hanna, the show's creators

"Lost in Space"–Johnny Williams, won Oscars with *Jaws, Star Wars*

"The Monkees"–Tommy Boyce/Bobby Hart, also wrote many Monkees' hits

"The Munsters"–Jack Marshall, also did "The Girl from U.N.C.L.E.," "The Debbie Reynolds Show"

"The Patty Duke Show"–Sid Ramin/Bob Wells, Ramin worked on *West Side Story*

"Spider-Man"–Ray Ellis/Bob Harris, Harris also wrote theme for Kubrick's *Lolita*

"Star Trek"–Alexander Courage, also did "Medical Center"

"The Tonight Show (Johnny's Theme)"–Paul Anka/Johnny Carson, Johnny added the drum part

November 6, 1964—Actress Shirley Eaton, painted gold, makes the cover of *Life*. ☮ November 6, 1968—Richard Nixon is elected president. November 7, 1943—Singer Joni Mitchell is born in Alberta, Canada. ☮ November 7, 1963—Carole Joan Crawford of Jamaica is crowned Miss World. November 7, 1963—*It's a Mad, Mad, Mad, Mad World* with Phil Silvers opens. ☮ November 7, 1980—Actor Steve McQueen dies in Mexico of cancer.

MY BACK PAGES

As a jazz musician he's worked with some of the giants—Count Basie, Dizzy Gillespie, Sarah Vaughan, Ella Fitzgerald, and Stan Getz. . . . Lalo wrote the "Grand Finale" for the Three Tenors concert in Italy in '90—that recording went on to become the biggest seller in the history of classical music. . . . He was also the arranger when the Three Tenors performed at Dodger Stadium in '94 and in Paris in '98. . . . Lalo also did the music for a holiday classic, "Christmas in Vienna," that's shown every year.

Jean Seberg

This talented but troubled actress built a serious film career in Europe before starring in American movies and FBI files.

TAKIN' CARE OF BUSINESS

American audiences didn't appreciate her the way French audiences did; in France, Jean Seberg was seen as someone who epitomized the independent, youthful style of cinema's New Wave. Jean wasn't French, though—she was born in Iowa. As a novice drama student, Jean outpaced 18,000 other actresses in a national talent search and won the short-haired lead in Otto Preminger's much-noticed *Saint Joan* ('57). The movie was not a box-office success, nor was her next big movie, *Bonjour Tristesse* ('58), again with Jean cast as a pretty French woman.

Moving to France, Jean became an international star with Godard's *Breathless* ('60); however, even though she continued to work in Hollywood throughout the '60s, the producers there didn't really seem to know how to use her to everyone's advantage. Her most significant Hollywood film was *Lilith* ('64), which brought her raves for her performance as a schizophrenic who seduces her therapist. *Paint Your Wagon* ('69) was a famous flop, best remembered for Clint Eastwood's singing, though Jean made a smart 'n' sexy frontier wife. Ironically, her most popular film would be the one with the lowest artistic aspirations, the overblown *Airport* ('71), a huge soapy success that somehow got nominated as Best Picture. She then returned to Europe and made some movies in Italy and France to mid-decade.

After a number of nervous breakdowns, Jean attempted suicide several times through the '70s and finally succeeded in '79 with a barbiturate overdose in her parked car. Her decomposing body wasn't found until a week after she died. At the time of her death, she was so consumed by paranoia she thought her fridge was watching her; her suicide note read, "I can't live any longer with my nerves." Rumors of her affiliation with the Black Panthers and the

November 8, 1922—Christiaan Barnard, who will perform the world's first heart transplant in '67, is born in South Africa.
November 8, 1960—Election Day, John F. Kennedy beats Richard Nixon in the closest race for the presidency up to that time.
November 8, 1965—*Days of Our Lives* debuts. ☮ November 8, 1966—Actor Ronald Reagan is elected governor of California.

attention from the FBI led to stories that she had been assassinated, though those were eventually dismissed. A year later, her ex-husband Romain Gary shot and killed himself.

EVERYBODY LOVES SOMEBODY

Jean had four husbands: the first in the late '50s; writer/director Romain Gary (who directed her in two movies) in '62 (with a son); director Dennis Berry in '72; and a restaurateur in the late '70s. The most controversial aspect of her life was her support of the Black Panthers, a group considered so dangerous that the FBI supposedly decided to try to ruin Jean. It's said that the FBI planted news stories saying the father of her still-unborn baby was a Black Panther, though Jean was married at the time. Incredibly, when her prematurely born baby died after two days in the summer of '70, Jean briefly displayed it in a glass casket to prove it was Caucasian.

MY BACK PAGES

Mary Beth Hurt, who later played Jean in the "fictional documentary" *From the Journals of Jean Seberg* ('95), is from Jean's hometown. . . . Jean was the subject of a documentary, *Jean Seberg: American Actress* ('95) and of a "musical tragedy" performed at London's British National Theatre.

Peter Sellers

The comic genius brought his accents to landmark movies.

TAKIN' CARE OF BUSINESS

"Minkey." Say that to a '60s fan, and they'll smile. Peter Sellers had that effect, and still does to this day, almost two decades after his death. The movies he made during the '60s still make audiences laugh, and think, and wonder—why didn't he ever win an Oscar? Born into a family of English vaudevillians, Peter had stage experience as an infant and dance training as a child. He served in the RAF during World War II and later hooked up with service pals (including Spike Milligan) for a live musical/comedy act. Radio's *Goon Show* and TV work (in which he often played multiple characters and did vocal impressions) led to Peter's first movie roles, highlighted by his scene-stealing turn as one of the criminal gang in *The Ladykillers* ('55).

The '60s brought him more and more movies (almost three a year) and bigger and bigger parts until by mid-decade he was a full-fledged star. Handsome, adept at accents, and a gifted physical comedian, he didn't so much star in movies as define them, especially when he worked with great directors like Stanley Kubrick and Blake Edwards. Kubrick let him bring some much-needed levity to the otherwise dark *Lolita* ('62), and in the classic *Dr. Strangelove* ('64) Peter ran amok as three vastly different characters (a frustrated President, a harried British officer, a mad German scientist—he would've played the determined pilot, too, if he hadn't taken ill). *Strangelove* brought him his first Best Actor Oscar nomination; Blake Edwards's *The Pink Panther* ('64) brought him the role that would last a lifetime.

As clumsy, dim-witted, but well-intentioned Inspector Clouseau, Peter was able to engage all his talents with one classic character. The first *Panther* movie was meant to be a showcase for superthief David Niven, but audiences so responded to Peter's Clouseau that the series was rebuilt around him. Three months later came *A Shot in the Dark*, another Clouseau comedy that actually was completed before *The Pink Panther* (but held until *Panther* succeeded). This gave Peter three monster hits in a six-month period, and his career as an international movie star was flying. In wigs, in costumes, in comedies galore—*What's New, Pussycat* ('65), *Casino Royale* ('67), *The Party* ('68), *I Love You, Alice B. Toklas* ('68).

The '70s, unfortunately, were a wildly uneven decade for him as he made a clinker for every gem. There were three more *Panther* movies (*Return of*, . . . *Strikes Again*, and *Re-*

venge of), but the true delight was *Being There* ('79). He'd been trying to get this quiet comedy made for a decade, and when he finally did, it brought him another Oscar nomination. His last movie, the forgettable *The Fiendish Plot of Dr. Fu Manchu*, was released after he died of a heart attack in '80. At his funeral, he had the song "In the Mood" played—he had always hated it, and so thought it would be a good in-joke for the mourners.

EVERYBODY LOVES SOMEBODY

Peter was married four times with sometimes tempestuous results. Wives one, two, and four (Anne Howe, Britt Ekland, Lynne Frederick) were actresses; wife three (Miranda Quarry) was a model. Britt was his wife from '64–'68 and his co-star in *After the Fox* ('66) and *The Bobo* ('67). Peter left three adult children when he died.

MY BACK PAGES

Dressed like a silent film star, Peter was the first man to make a *Playboy* cover—April '64. . . . He was named Commander of the British Empire in '66. . . . "Life is a state of mind" is the last line of *Being There* and the inscription on a plaque near the garden where his ashes were buried.

Rod Serling

Submitted for your approval, one of the decade's most influential writers.

TAKIN' CARE OF BUSINESS

Everybody's got a favorite episode—the one where Burgess Meredith just wants to read and he survives an H-bomb attack but he breaks his glasses; or the one where *To Serve Man* turns out to be a cookbook; or the one with the robot . . . the tiny spacecraft . . . the gremlin on the wing. And the music, who hasn't done that high-pitched "doo-doo-doo-doo, doo-doo-doo-doo"? And most of all, the narrator, the main writer, the brains behind it all—who can't acknowledge that Rod Serling was one of the most prolific geniuses of the '60s?

The New Yorker born on Christmas Day in '24 was an amateur boxer, a much-decorated paratrooper in World War II, a radio writer in the '40s, and one of the Midas men who effected TV's Golden Age. Dozens of his powerful dramas were produced in the '50s, many won Emmy Awards, and the classic *Requiem for a Heavyweight* was the first TV script to win the prestigious Peabody Award (later it also became a movie and a Broadway play).

In '59, frustrated by network alterations of his scripts, he launched his own show. *The Twilight Zone* lasted five years and presented 156 episodes, most of them written by Rod, all of them narrated by him (sometimes with cigarette in hand). More Emmy Awards and nominations came his way, as well as a lasting legacy—of wit and surprise, insight and imagination—that has endured, even increased, in reruns ever since.

The stories still impress, as does the remarkable guest list, a veritable who's who of future TV stars (Jack Klugman, Patrick Macnee, Anne Francis, Donna Douglas, William Shatner, Bob Crane, Elizabeth Montgomery, Peter Falk, Leonard Nimoy, Bill Bixby, Julie Newmar, Telly Savalas, just to name a few) and future Oscar winners (Sydney Pollack, Art Carney, Lee Marvin, Cliff Robertson, Robert Redford, Dennis Hopper, Robert Duvall, Martin Landau) and memorable favorites (Ida Lupino, Buster Keaton, Don Rickles, Burt Reynolds, Mickey Rooney).

Great TV? No, legendary TV, confirmed in 2004 when *TV Guide* named Rod the greatest sci-fi legend in TV history. But there's more. When the show was finally cancelled, Rod took his talents to the big screen to write some memorable movies, including *Seven Days in May* ('64) and the classic *Planet of the Apes* ('68). His final anthology series, *Night Gallery*, provided more creepy thrills from '69–'73. Rod then taught college classes before years of heavy smoking caught

November 9, 1965—A power failure blacks out much of the East Coast. ☮ November 9, 1967—The first issue of *Rolling Stone* is published.
November 10, 1925—Actor Richard Burton is born in Wales. ☮ November 10, 1969—Elvis Presley's *Change of Habit* opens.
November 10, 2001—Author Ken Kesey dies in Eugene, Oregon of cancer. ☮ November 11, 1922—Author Kurt Vonnegut is born in Indianapolis, Indiana.

up with him in '75. When he died of sudden heart failure, he was only 50 years old.

EVERYBODY LOVES SOMEBODY

Rod's marriage in '48 produced two kids and lasted until his death.

MY BACK PAGES

Brother Robert wrote the novel *The President's Plane Is Missing*, which became a TV movie in '73. . . . Though he seems now the obvious choice as narrator, the network wanted others, including Orson Welles, before settling on Rod. . . . He made three deadpan appearances on *Laugh-In*. . . . His script of *The Doomsday Flight* ('66) had a premise adapted by *Speed* 28 years later—pay the ransom, or a bomb will explode when the plane drops to a certain altitude. . . . In *Planet of the Apes*, Rod's been credited with adding the final Statue of Liberty scene. . . . *Night Gallery* gave Steven Spielberg his first job (directing movie legend Joan Crawford).

William Shatner

Not only did he boldly go where no man had gone before, William Shatner was an ubiquitous TV presence all through the '60s.

TAKIN' CARE OF BUSINESS

Has anybody had a career like William Shatner's? Consider: not only has it lasted for over five decades, it's actually *gained* momentum, and he's won two Emmy Awards in the 2000s while never even getting a nomination for his most famous role in the '60s.

Born in Canada, William graduated from McGill University and was a Shakespearean actor in the early '50s. He was doing Broadway and live TV in the late '50s before he started getting major films, among them the Oscar-winning *Judgment at Nuremberg* ('61). Though his was only a supporting role in that courtroom classic, already his good looks and precise diction were making him stand out, leading to appearances on some of the great TV dramas of the '60s—*Naked City*, *77 Sunset Strip*, *Thriller*, *The Outer Limits*, and of course *The Twilight Zone*, where he starred in one of that series' most famous episodes (in "Nightmare at 20,000 Feet" he was the only airline passenger to see a gremlin on the wing).

Star Trek took him from his 50+ TV appearances to one starring role, the one he'd forever be known for, in the second half of the '60s. After an earlier pilot episode starring Jeffrey Hunter got shot down by the networks, creator Gene Roddenberry tried again with William manning the helm. As Captain James Tiberius Kirk (a single father, born in Iowa in 2223, youngest captain in Starfleet), William played a charming, creative leader who roamed the galaxy, fought bizarre aliens, fired phasers, promoted peace, kissed beautiful women, wore velour, and occasionally waxed poetic.

Though it was nominated for two Emmy Awards as Outstanding Dramatic Series, the show was still underappre-

November 11, 1960—"The Eye of the Beholder" episode of *The Twilight Zone* with Donna Douglas debuts.
November 11, 1964—Elvis Presley's *Roustabout* opens. ☮ November 11, 1964—*Pajama Party* with Frankie Avalon opens.
November 11, 1968—John Lennon and Yoko Ono appear nude on the cover of their *Two Virgins* LP.

ciated in its day—it never finished a season higher than #52 in the ratings, was threatened several times with cancellation, and only lasted three seasons. However, later success in syndication gave the show and the characters new life. Ultimately, the original series spawned numerous spin-offs and movies, dozens of books and lots of merchandise, and it's now seen as a landmark of science fiction (in 2004 *TV Guide* named it the #1 cult TV show ever).

For William, the end of the '60s and the original *Star Trek* brought a slump to what had been a steadily rising career; throughout much of the '70s his roles diminished in stature and frequency (Kirk perhaps had stereotyped him). But when the *Enterprise* was revved up again in '79, so was he, with starring roles in six *Star Trek* movies into the '90s (he wrote and directed one, too).

He also stayed busy with his own TV series (*T.J. Hooker*), another 100 or so appearances on various shows (even the Academy Awards show recruited him), gigs as narrator for documentaries and specials, writing/producing/directing credits on his *TekWar* books and shows, popular behind-the-scenes memoirs called *Star Trek Memories* and *Star Trek Movie Memories* in the mid-'90s, long-running TV commercials, and fun, scene-stealing movie roles where he was often a good sport spoofing himself (*Airplane II*, '82, *Miss Congeniality*, 2000, *Dodge Ball*, 2004).

Okay, so his acting style pleases some people more than others (he was nominated for a Razzie Award as Worst Actor of the Century), and yes some of his co-stars have called him a prima donna, and sure he was the first celebrity targeted to be beaten up in *Fight Club* ('99), but you don't get to work as long as he has without being a versatile talent with widespread appeal. Prolific, professional, perennial—William Shatner has indeed lived long and prospered.

EVERYBODY LOVES SOMEBODY

William's been married four times. His first marriage began in '56 and ended in divorce in '69, with three daughters (two of whom appeared on *Star Trek*). In '73 he was married again, to an actress who'd been on several episodes of his *T.J. Hooker* series, until they divorced some two decades later. Tragically, his third wife drowned in their swimming pool in their second year of marriage. Since 2001, William's been married to a horse trainer, with a home in California and a horse farm in Kentucky.

MY BACK PAGES

His album *The Transformed Man* ('68) was a camp classic and included his overwrought, spoken-word versions of Dylan's "Mr. Tambourine Man" and the Beatles' "Lucy in the Sky with Diamonds". . . . William's second album, *Has Been*, came out in 2004 and teamed him with various rock stars. . . . By hosting numerous horse shows in Hollywood, he's raised millions of dollars for children's charities. . . . In 2006 his kidney stone sold for $25,000 in a charity auction.

Alan Shepard

America's first man in space.

TAKIN' CARE OF BUSINESS

A New Hampshire kid who graduated from Annapolis, Alan Shepard served in World War II and then became a test pilot primarily flying carrier-based jets. In '59 he was selected as one of the original seven astronauts for Project Mercury, and in '61 he was selected for the program's first flight. It wasn't much—an arc 116 miles high and 302 miles out into the Atlantic, only 15 minutes aloft with four minutes of weightlessness. But it was enough—he and *Freedom 7* both returned safely—and Alan was hailed a national hero, with parades and a White House visit and the eternal distinction of being America's first spaceman.

He would've commanded the first Gemini mission if not for an inner-ear disease; he would've been on the near-

The Mercury Seven (and '60s Flights)

Scott Carpenter–Three-orbit mission ('62)

Gordon Cooper–Set record for space time ('63); also *Gemini 5* ('65)

John Glenn–First American to orbit ('62)

Gus Grissom–Second American in space ('61); died in *Apollo 1* fire ('67)

Alan Shepard–First American in space ('61)

Wally Schirra–Six-orbit mission ('62); also *Gemini 6* ('65) and *Apollo 7* ('68)

Deke Slayton–No flights, worked on NASA staff

disastrous *Apollo 13* flight in '70 if not for being bumped to *Apollo 14*. Alan walked on the moon (and awkwardly executed several one-handed golf swings there) in '71. Retiring from NASA and the Navy in '74 as a Rear Admiral, he then served on several corporate boards and in '88 co-wrote *Moon Shot*, an acclaimed inside look at the space race (it became a TV miniseries in '94). His legacy of achievement and experience can be matched by only a few men in history.

EVERYBODY LOVES SOMEBODY

When he died of leukemia in '98, Alan left behind a wife he'd been married to for 53 years, plus two grown daughters.

MY BACK PAGES

When JFK issued his audacious challenge to land a man on the Moon by decade's end, Alan was the only American who had actually been in space. . . . "The only complaint I have was the flight wasn't long enough," he said upon returning from his historic '61 mission.

Jean Shrimpton

Stunning Jean was one of the most famous and influential models of the '60s.

TAKIN' CARE OF BUSINESS

Jean Shrimpton was the first international fashion goddess of the decade. Though her goal in the late '50s was to become a secretary, and though she didn't think much of her looks ("if you take off the make-up, I'm ugly," she once said), in '60 she enrolled in modeling school and within a year was on the cover of *British Vogue. Glamour* dubbed her Model of the Year in '63, and from then on her face and lanky 5′ 9″ figure graced all the popular magazines that didn't have Mechanix in the title. *Elle* named her "The Most Beautiful Girl in the World," *Newsweek* put her on its cover in '65, and she was the subject of a documentary called *The Face on The Cover.*

By mid-decade Jean was making the then-extravagant sum of $60 an hour and writing her first book, *My Story*. In '65 she made fashion history with a fashion scandal—she dared to wear a miniskirt to the toney opening-day ceremonies of the Melbourne Gold Cup in Australia. Mary Quant was already making minis in England, but Australian high society had never seen anything like them. Everyone was stunned by her amazing look, her scandalous attire landed her on front pages worldwide, and the miniskirt revolution was on its way.

Jean then established herself as perhaps the first true supermodel by inking a three-year deal to represent Yardley cosmetics and hair products on TV and in magazines. Her brief foray into movies—*Privilege* ('67)—was a box-office bust, so Jean continued her modeling career until about '72, though at the insistence of photographer David Bailey she did some hair-color ads a decade later. An autobiography came out in '90, but most of her post-'60s years have been spent out of the spotlight. She ran an antiques shop in the '70s and later

November 13, 1934—Charles Manson is born in Cincinnati, Ohio. ☮ November 13, 1938—Actress Jean Seberg is born in Marshalltown, Iowa. November 13, 1945—Actress Valerie Leon is born in London. ☮ November 13, 1960—Sammy Davis, Jr. marries Swedish actress May Britt. November 13, 1964—Driver Paula Murphy sets the women's land speed record of 226.37 MPH.

owned and operated a 300-year-old hotel in Penzance, England. Intentionally staying out of the public eye and away from the camera lens, she told *People* magazine in '99 that "it was great fun becoming famous, but I got tired of it."

EVERYBODY LOVES SOMEBODY

As one of the pre-eminent faces of the decade, Jean's ups and downs were followed in the press, especially her engagement to swingin' photog David Bailey and her subsequent affair with Bailey's pal, actor Terence Stamp. David got divorced in '63, and in early '64 he and Jean were engaged. That same year, however, Jean became attracted to Terence and was living with him in L.A. by the summer of '64, but by the summer of '67 Jean was living in New York with someone else. Jean eventually married a photographer and today they have one son.

MY BACK PAGES

Her nickname was "the Shrimp," a name she disliked. . . . Her younger sister is Chrissie Shrimpton, herself an actress/model and Mick Jagger's girlfriend in the early '60s before Marianne Faithfull swept him away. . . . Chrissie was supposedly the subject of the Stones' "19th Nervous Breakdown" and "Under My Thumb". . . . Jean was mentioned in the first line of a song by the Smithereens, "Behind the Wall of Sleep". . . . Colleagues have said that Jean was the most tireless of models, always punctual and professional. . . . She once said that she existed throughout her whole career owning only one evening dress.

Simon and Garfunkel

This intellectual duo created sophisticated and enduring folk/pop classics.

TAKIN' CARE OF BUSINESS

Before they were Simon and Garfunkel, Paul and Art were '50s high schoolers teamed as Tom and Jerry (Art was Tom). Their Everly Brothers-style act made it onto the *Billboard* charts in '57 with their first record, "Hey, Schoolgirl." Briefly splitting up to attend different colleges, they reteamed in the early '60s as a folk duo hitting the New York scene just as Joan Baez and Bob Dylan were reinventing traditional folk music as modern protest music. Paul's early compositions, and the pair's first album, *Wednesday Morning, 3 AM,* included a protest song, a Dylan song, traditional folk songs, and four Paul originals, among them a quiet version of "The Sound of Silence."

Still success eluded them, and again the duo split up, with Paul moving to England. While he was there, American radio stations began playing "The Sound of Silence"—smelling a hit, the record company, without Paul's knowledge, remade the original with a more urgent sound and rereleased it. By the end of '65 it topped the charts. A surprised Paul flew back to America for a reunion, and their new album in early '66 presented what are now affectionately

remembered as some of their most-cherished classics, all Paul originals—"April Come She Will," "Kathy's Song," "I Am a Rock," and more.

For the next couple of years the duo could do no wrong—Paul's delicate acoustic guitar, Art's angelic voice, and their perfect harmonies beautifully expressed the most intellectual, poetic aspects of the Age of Aquarius, with occasional forays into harder songs that still displayed sophisticated musicality. "Scarborough Fair/Canticle," "Homeward Bound," and "The 59th Street Bridge Song (Feelin' Groovy)" were the best known songs off the album *Parsley, Sage, Rosemary and Thyme*, which accurately posed the two on the cover as gentle minstrels. A year later *The Graduate* showcased some of their older songs plus "Mrs. Robinson," a new #1 hit composed for the movie (while they weren't even nominated for Oscars, Simon and Garfunkel did win Grammy Awards for *The Graduate*).

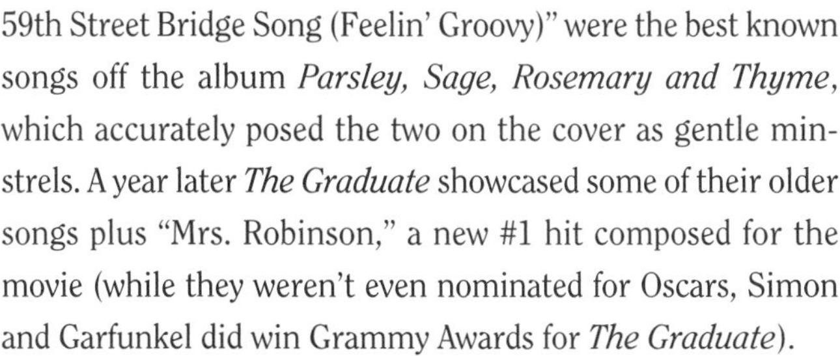

Bookends in '68 showed the team broadening its musical horizons with playful songs ("Punky's Dilemma"), more songs of alienation ("America"), hard-edged songs ("A Hazy Shade of Winter"), and even songs that weren't songs at all ("Voices of Old People"). By this time Paul and Art were broadening their career horizons, too. Art made his acting debut in *Catch-22* ('70), and Paul was poised to release solo albums. *Bridge Over Troubled Water* ('70) was their powerful Grammy-winning swan song; the title track hit #1, three other songs ("The Boxer," "El Condor Pasa," and "Cecilia") rode high on the charts, and "So Long, Frank Lloyd Wright" was Paul's farewell to Art.

Quickly, Paul broke out as a mature, articulate solo artist with albums (*Paul Simon*, '72, *There Goes Rhymin' Simon*, '73, *Still Crazy After All These Years*, '76, *Graceland*, '86) full of memorable hit songs ("Duncan," "Mother and Child Reunion," "Kodachrome," "50 Ways to Leave Your Lover," "You Can Call Me Al," and many more). Art made albums too, mostly lush and romantic, though they weren't as ambitious or as successful as Paul's.

Both worked onscreen—Paul with a role in *Annie Hall* ('77), as host of *Saturday Night Live*, and with his own movie, *One Trick Pony* ('80); Art in *Carnal Knowledge* ('71) plus several *Saturday Night Live* gigs. They did several benefit concerts together, recorded another hit song ("My Little Town"), and gave a massive free concert for a half-million people in Central Park ('81). More concerts followed through the '80s, '90s, and 2000s, induction into the Rock and Roll Hall of Fame came in '90, and their remarkable careers were capped with a lifetime-achievement award at the Grammys in 2003.

EVERYBODY LOVES SOMEBODY

Paul was married for the first half of the '70s, with one child (his wife, Peg, was named in the '72 song "Run That Body Down"). He then married actress Carrie Fisher for a year in the mid-'80s ("Crazy Love, Vol. II" on the *Graceland* LP is said to be about their split). In '92 Paul married singer Edie Brickell of the New Bohemians; they're still together and have three kids. Art was also married for the first years of the '70s; his girlfriend of the later '70s, who played the girlfriend of Paul's

November 14, 1969—On *Get Smart*, Agent 99 gives birth to twins. ☮ November 15, 1932—Singer Petula Clark is born in Surrey, England. November 15, 1934—Actress Joanna Barnes is born in Boston. ☮ November 15, 1956—Elvis Presley's first film, *Love Me Tender*, premieres in New York. November 15, 1964—Golfer Mickey Wright shoots a 62, the lowest score ever for a woman pro.

'60s Stars in the Rock and Roll Hall of Fame (with Year of Induction)

Animals ('94)
Hank Ballard ('90)
Band ('94)
Beach Boys ('88)
Beatles ('88)
Bobby "Blue" Bland ('92)
Booker T. and the M.G.'s ('92)
Buffalo Springfield ('97)
Byrds ('91)
Johnny Cash ('92)
Ray Charles ('86)
Sam Cooke ('86)
Cream ('93)
Creedence Clearwater Revival ('93)
Bobby Darin ('90)
Dells (2004)
Dion ('89)
Doors ('93)
Drifters ('88)
Bob Dylan ('88)
Duane Eddy ('94)
Four Seasons ('90)
Four Tops ('90)
Aretha Franklin ('87)
Marvin Gaye ('87)
Grateful Dead ('94)
Isley Brothers ('92)
Etta James ('93)
Jefferson Airplane ('96)
Jimi Hendrix Experience ('92)
Janis Joplin ('95)
Kinks ('90)
Brenda Lee (2002)
Lovin' Spoonful (2000)
Mamas and the Papas ('98)
Martha and the Vandellas ('94)
Roy Orbison ('87)
Wilson Pickett ('91)
Gene Pitney (2002)
Rascals ('97)
Otis Redding ('89)
Jimmy Reed ('91)
Righteous Brothers (2003)
Smokey Robinson ('87)
Rolling Stones ('89)
Sam and Dave ('92)
Del Shannon ('99)
Shirelles ('96)
Simon and Garfunkel ('90)
Percy Sledge (2005)
Dusty Springfield ('99)
Supremes ('88)
Temptations ('89)
Traffic (2004)
Ike and Tina Turner ('91)
Velvet Underground ('96)
Who ('90)
Jackie Wilson ('87)
Yardbirds ('92)
Frank Zappa ('95)

character in *Annie Hall,* killed herself in '79. Art married again in '88 and has a son.

MY BACK PAGES

Paul was set to be in *Catch-22* along with Art, but his part was cut before any of his scenes were shot. . . . Paul was inducted into the Rock and Roll Hall of Fame as a solo artist in 2001. . . . Before the pair reteamed in the early '60s, Art briefly attempted a solo career as Artie Garr, and Paul recorded as Jerry Landis and then as Tico in Tico and the Triumphs. . . . Art is known as a great walker and has crossed both Japan and America on foot. . . . His book of poetry, *Still Water,* was published in '89.

Nancy Sinatra

A stylin' songstress who scored major mid-'60s success with hit movies and hit songs.

TAKIN' CARE OF BUSINESS

The eldest child of Frank Sinatra, Nancy Sinatra established herself in the '60s as one of the decade's pre-eminent teen rebels. She was born in Jersey in '40, and by the end of '44 everybody knew her name because of her dad's song, "Nancy with the Laughin' Face." Nancy's first major showcases were on Frank's '59 and '60 TV shows. Within a few years she was appearing in teen-oriented movies like *Get*

Yourself a College Girl and *For Those Who Think Young* (both in '64), but her singing, while popular in other countries, was still mired in saccharine puddles of soft pop and novelty tunes.

A radical remake of her image mid-decade positioned her as a tough, no-nonsense alternative to gentle vocalists such as Annette Funicello and Shelley Fabares. In '66 she hit the top of the charts with her assertive anthem, "These Boots Are Made for Walkin'." "Summer Wine," "Sugar Town," and "Somethin' Stupid" (another #1) quickly followed, giving her a total of 10 Top 40 hits in a three-year period. Her voice wasn't the equal of classic divas like Janis Joplin, but she did convey the right attitude at a time when there was revolution in the air.

The hits fortified her movie career and brought starring roles alongside Peter Fonda in *The Wild Angels* ('66) and alongside Elvis in *Speedway* ('68). In the latter she belted out "Your Groovy Self," one of the few times an actress was allowed to solo in an Elvis movie. During this time she had her own innovative TV special, "Movin' with Nancy," which brought her a Golden Globe nomination as Best TV Star, and in '67 she joined a select group of vocalists who sang a theme song for a James Bond movie (*You Only Live Twice*).

In '67 and '68 she performed in Vietnam for the troops, and in '69 she headlined in Vegas (some kind of record was set during her stint, because her dad and brother were also performing in separate hotels at the same time). Nancy spent the next two decades concentrating on her family, with only sporadic recording. In the '90s she made a comeback that included a popular *Playboy* spread in May '95 at age 55. Late in the '90s she returned to the concert stage with a series of well-received concerts at some of the country's hippest venues, proving that she is still one of the most durable and popular stars to emerge from the '60s.

EVERYBODY LOVES SOMEBODY

In '60, 20-year-old Nancy married pop singer Tommy Sands, who would star with Annette in *Babes in Toyland* a year later. Nancy and Tommy divorced in '65. Later stories linked her with both Bobby Darin and Elvis. Whatever her brief relationship was with Elvis, it allegedly broke off when his wife, Priscilla Presley, announced she was pregnant. Nancy then threw Priscilla's baby shower. Early in the '70s Nancy remarried and gave birth to two girls. Meanwhile, resolutely and tenaciously loyal to her family, Nancy has written two books about her famous dad and worked hard to preserve his legacy and defend his reputation when she's felt it has been unfairly attacked.

MY BACK PAGES

Her dad's nickname for her—Chicken. . . . When she appeared on *The Man from U.N.C.L.E.* she played a character named Coco Cool and sang a duet—"Trouble"—with Illya Kuryakin, played by David McCallum. . . . In 2004 Nancy toured again in support of a well-received new album that featured collaborations with Bono and other admiring rock stars.

Nuns not cool?
Read on.

TAKIN' CARE OF BUSINESS

During the '60s two women—a nun who became a star, and a star who became a nun—snagged national attention. The nun-turned-star was born in Belgium in '33 as Jeanine Deckers. During World War II her family lived in France while her father joined the resistance, all returning to Belgium at war's end. In the '50s Jeanine took the name Sister Luc-Gabrielle and became a Dominican nun. After entertaining her convent with her charming guitar-backed songs, she paid a recording studio to cut a record she could give as gifts.

The Philips Record Company, knowing a good novelty

November 16, 1968—On *Get Smart*, Agents 99 and 86 get married.
November 16, 1971—Model Edie Sedgwick dies in Santa Barbara, California of a drug overdose.
November 17, 1943—Model Lauren Hutton is born in Charleston, South Carolina.

act when it heard one, signed her to a contract and recorded a bouncy religious song, "Dominique," that somehow captured worldwide attention and won a Grammy in '63. Sung partly in French, the song rode high at #1 on the American charts above the Kingsmen's "Louie Louie." Reluctantly taking the stage name Soeur Sourire ("Sister Smile"), she then did a knock-out rendition of "Dominique" for Ed Sullivan in '64. A year later MGM made a Debbie Reynolds musical about her, but soon the Singing Nun retired and returned to her order.

Then, in a surprising display of '60s independence, she quit the convent to resume her singing career, still religious but now decidedly modern. She changed her name again, and as Luc Dominique recorded *I Am Not a Star* in '67, a controversial LP with one song that praised the birth control pill, and another song with the words "Sister Sourire's dead." After the '60s, her life took some bizarre twists. Now wearing more contemporary clothes and even lipstick, she started using pills and occasionally smoking. Teaming with a woman who may have been her lover, she owned a school for autistic children, but in the '80s the Belgian government threatened to close it over unpaid back taxes (she had donated all her proceeds to the convent but was still held accountable for the taxes). In '85, she and her woman friend killed themselves with an overdose of tranquilizers.

Meanwhile teenage Dolores Hicks, later Dolores Hart, of Chicago landed the plum role of the sweet love interest in two of Elvis's early pre-Army movies, *Loving You* ('57, in which she sang two songs) and *King Creole* ('58). More late '50s movies and a Tony-nominated turn on Broadway were followed by a flurry of popular early '60s hits, especially the lead in the teen romp *Where the Boys Are* ('60) and the part of a sexy stew seeking romance in *Come Fly with Me* ('63). Then, on the brink of major Hollywood and financial success, with the studios touting her as a new Grace Kelly, in '63 she made a courageous career change: after taking a break at a Benedictine convent in Connecticut, 24-year-old Dolores Hart decided to join the Abbey of Regina Laudis for good. She's lived and worked at the over-300-acre abbey ever since, first as Sister Judith (a new name symbolic of her new life), then in '70 she took the vows to become Reverend Mother Dolores.

Jeanine Deckers

EVERYBODY LOVES SOMEBODY

In the '50s, Jeanine was briefly engaged but then decided to join the convent (the rumors were that she joined the order because her lover had jilted her). As for Dolores, at the time she abandoned Hollywood for the abbey, she was engaged to a businessman; they never married but have stayed close.

MY BACK PAGES

Jeanine attended art school as a child, and her watercolors were shown in her first album. . . . She never liked *The Singing Nun* film, which added fictional elements, including a male love interest played by Chad Everett. . . . She agreed with John Lennon's controversial statement that the Beatles were more well known in the modern world than Jesus: "I may not feel this is right," she said, "but it is certainly undeniable". . . . In 2001 Dominick Dunne, who'd known her 40 years earlier, ran into Dolores again and praised her still-youthful beauty in *Vanity Fair*. . . . In 2000 her abbey released a CD, *Women in Chant: Recordáre* on which Dolores sang with the choir and read a meditation. . . . Nuns (many of them singing) were depicted several times on-screen in the '60s, especially in *Lilies of the Field* ('63), *The Sound of Music* ('65), *The Flying Nun* ('67), *Where Angels Go, Trouble Follows* ('68) with Stella Stevens, and Elvis's *Change of Habit* ('69) with Mary Tyler Moore.

The Smothers Brothers

The pretty cool cabaret act became a very cool TV show.

TAKIN' CARE OF BUSINESS

Funny, folkie, and family-safe early in the '60s, the Smothers Brothers became delightfully satirical counterculture heroes late in the '60s. The brothers were born in New York City; their father died during World War II and the boys were raised by their mother in California. After playing with a folk group in the late '50s, the brothers split off in '59 and hit some hip San Francisco nightclubs as a musical/comedy act that consisted of folk songs (Dick on bass, Tom on guitar, nicely blended harmonies, matching conservative suits) and a jokey rivalry between a calm, smart brother (played by Dick), and his wacky nitwit sibling (Tom, though the disparity in their intelligences was just an act).

Popular live albums and successful appearances on TV variety shows that made "Mom always liked you best!" a well-known catch phrase led to their own '60s show. A one-season sitcom that reversed their birth positions, *The Smothers Brothers Show* ('65) offered Tom as the dead younger brother who came back as a bumbling angel to help older brother Dick, unfortunately with less-than-hilarious results.

In '67 the boys got their own variety show, and they began to make history. *The Smothers Brothers Comedy Hour* looked like a traditional variety show (dancers, orchestra, famous guests) but it courted controversy by openly joking about drugs, the Vietnam War, racial issues, politics, and even the very censors who were cutting material over the brothers' loud protests. Steve Martin and Rob Reiner were two of the anarchic writers, Pat Paulsen was the sonorous comic they pushed for President, and boisterous groups like the Who and Jefferson Airplane showed up to rock the TV studio (even the Beatles appeared by sending in early music videos).

Despite its successful three-year sprint, the show was ended by nervous executives while it was still in the top 10 of the TV ratings; after it was cancelled it won an Emmy for the writing. In the '70s and '80s, the boys made several attempts at a variety-show comeback—some of them bland, some of them inspired—but the spark and the audiences were gone, and none of the new attempts lasted or had the same impact of the '60s original. For a few years the act broke up, Dick became an avid race car driver, and Tom went solo as a deft "yo-yo man." Today the boys own and operate a California vineyard and still perform live.

EVERYBODY LOVES SOMEBODY

Both Tom and Dick got married in the '90s. Tom's got three kids, Dick's got six (his wife brought in an additional five).

MY BACK PAGES

Both brothers attended San Jose State, which later granted them honorary degrees. . . . The set-up of their '65 sitcom was

November 18, 1962—The Swiss Family Treehouse attraction opens in Disneyland.
November 18, 2002—Actor James Coburn dies in Beverly Hills of a heart attack.
November 18, 1966—Baseball star Sandy Koufax announces his retirement.

vaguely reminiscent of another '65 one-season wonder, *My Mother the Car*, and both fit right into the "fantasy" genre of mid-'60s sitcoms (*I Dream of Jeannie*, *Bewitched*, etc.). . . . One of the most memorable moments on the *Comedy Hour* came in '67 when the Who reached the climax of "My Generation"—not only did the group destroy its instruments, but drummer Keith Moon set off an alarmingly powerful explosive charge that permanently damaged guitarist Pete Townshend's hearing. . . . Other passions: golf and healthy cooking (Tom), cycling and yoga (Dick).

Elke Sommer

In the '60s, this busy blonde averaged almost four movies a year, including some stellar comedies.

TAKIN' CARE OF BUSINESS

Born into one of the oldest families in Germany, honey blonde Elke Schletz was discovered by director Vittorio De Sica while she vacationed in Italy. The teenager began modeling and making movies in Europe in the late '50s and came to Hollywood in the early '60s. After winning the '64 Golden Globe as the Most Promising Newcomer, she made movies nearly every year of the decade, and after mastering seven languages, she made movies in many different countries, including Germany, Italy, France, and England.

American audiences have often seen her as a beautiful innocent in comedies, especially in the '60s when she was in such nutty farces as Peter Sellers's *A Shot in the Dark* ('64) and Bob Hope's *Boy, Did I Get a Wrong Number!* ('66). In the Sellers movie her pretty face and sweet, come-hither smile made her the perfect alluring victim, and her glorious 36-22-36 figure made her the perfect nudist at the nudist camp. *Playboy* devoted splashy pictorials to her and later ranked her #31 (just ahead of another Teutonic temptress, Marlene Dietrich) among the century's sexiest stars.

Her post-'60s movies declined in prominence and number, though she did get starring roles in the adventure flick *Zeppelin* ('71), in the swashbuckler *The Prisoner of Zenda* ('79), and in the TV movie *Anastasia: The Mystery of Anna* ('86), among many others. Diversifying as a performer, she's enjoyed a long stage career, she's a great guest on international talk shows (thanks to those language skills), and in her movie-makin' prime she released a record album called

November 19, 1956—Actress Glynnis O'Connor is born in New York. ☮ November 19, 1966—The Supremes' "You Keep Me Hangin' On" hits #1. November 19, 1967—*Tony Rome* with Jill St. John opens. ☮ November 19, 1973—Keith Moon collapses in San Francisco onstage at the Cow Palace. November 20, 1925—Robert Kennedy is born in Brookline, Massachusetts. ☮ November 20, 1939—Comedian Dick Smothers is born in New York.

Elke Sommer: Love in Any Language ('65).

What's more, she's established herself as a serious painter. A budding artist even as a child, Elke had her first gallery exhibition in '65, and she has since had her work shown in over three dozen one-woman shows around the world. She even hosted the instructional PBS series *Painting with Elke*. In fact, she's claimed that she'd "rather be known as a painter who acts than as an actress who paints."

EVERYBODY LOVES SOMEBODY

Married from the early '60s-early '80s to journalist Joe Hyams, in '93 she married her current husband, hotelier Wolf Walther.

MY BACK PAGES

An avid race car driver, Elke hosted a syndicated TV show called *The World of Speed and Beauty*. . . . The L.A. house where Elke once lived is known to some as a site of strange paranormal activity. . . . Elke's sexiness was referred to by Krusty the Clown in an episode of *The Simpsons* in 2002.

Sonny and Cher

The brains and the beauty who comprised one of the decade's most popular singing acts.

TAKIN' CARE OF BUSINESS

When Sonny first sang a work-in-progress called "I Got You Babe" to her, Cher said it was "just another song." Three million record-buying fans disagreed, and the single soared to #1. The success was validation for Salvatore Philip Bono, a poor kid who had left Detroit for L.A. and quit high school in the '50s in hopes of breaking into the music biz. For years he held part-time jobs, among them delivery runs to music studios where he was able to hang around and learn from legends like Little Richard and producer Phil Spector.

Then came Cher, who wasn't always Cher. In '64, Cherilyn Sarkisian from El Centro, California began her singing career as Bonnie Jo Mason, releasing the obscure "Ringo, I Love You" and "Beatle Blues." When Sonny discovered the stunning big-voiced teen, he quickly reinvented himself as a producer/composer/performer. After several false starts and names (including Caesar and Cleo, hoping to capitalize on Liz and Dick's *Cleopatra*), they mined gold as Sonny and Cher in '65, following up "I Got You Babe" with other nuggets like "The Beat Goes On" and a dozen other Top 40 gems.

Though the material was pretty lightweight, it was elegantly crafted, and the pair became one of the most popular acts of the decade. Despite severe stage fright that almost kept her from performing, as the '60s progressed Cher became a more confident, passionate singer, and one of the most visually striking—long and lean, she dazzled with psychedelic colors and two of the widest bell-bottoms in town. Meanwhile Sonny, though over 30, was one of the era's quintessential pop stars, replete with long hair, fur vests, and too-cool attitude in photos.

After Sonny's failed solo album, *Inner Views*, and a failed self-written movie, *Good Times*, the good times were temporarily squelched at the end of the decade when the two seemed to lose touch with fans who were demanding music that was harder and louder. To reinvent themselves, they hocked the furniture in their Bel Air mansion and borrowed money so Sonny could write and produce *Chastity* ('69), hoping to launch Cher's movie career. When that didn't happen, Sonny once again recast the team, this time as a glamorous comedy couple.

Successful Vegas appearances led to the wildly popular Emmy-nominated *The Sonny and Cher Show* in the early '70s, with more #1 songs ("Dark Lady," "Half Breed") for Cher. Breaking away from Sonny mid-decade, Cher starred in her own Emmy-nominated show, *Cher*, in '75, followed by a flamboyant Vegas act and then yet another reinvention, this time as an accepted actress. Cher found

November 20, 1943—Actress Mie Hama is born in Tokyo, Japan. ☮ November 20, 1946—Actress Kaye Ballard is born in Cleveland, Ohio. November 20, 1964—*First Men in the Moon* with Martha Hyer opens. ☮ November 20, 1968—*Head*, co-written by Jack Nicholson, opens. November 21, 1937—Actress Marlo Thomas is born in Detroit. ☮ November 21, 1941—Actress Juliet Mills is born in London.

Broadway success in '82 with *Come Back to the 5 and Dime, Jimmy Dean, Jimmy Dean*, leading to a lengthy film career highlighted by her wonderful Oscar-winning performance in *Moonstruck* ('87).

She continued to branch out, going into the perfume business in '88 with her Uninhibited line and even doing some career-deflating infomercials in the early '90s. Resurrecting her career yet again, she had another hit album, *Believe*, in the late '90s and undertook a dazzling farewell tour in the 2000s that generated an estimated $200 million. After decades of Sonny and Cher success, Hollywood glamour, tabloid scandals, defeat, and triumph, she has reinvented herself one last time—as a mature, though playful, survivor able to laugh at herself and her mistakes while not making any apologies for who she was or is. "I answer to two people," she told an interviewer, "myself and God."

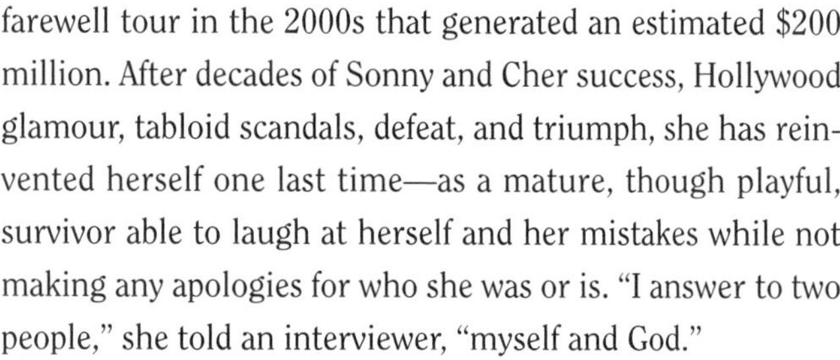

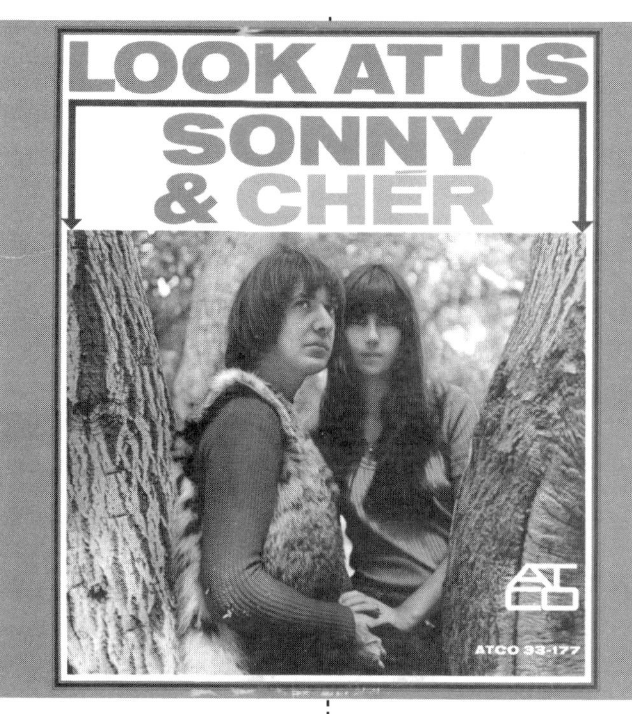

Sonny's life was quite different. After the break-up, Sonny, though still well-liked, was only getting offers for shows like *Fantasy Island*, so he quit in the '80s and became a successful restaurateur, first in West Hollywood and then in Palm Springs, where he was elected mayor in '88. Four years later he lost a Senate race, but in '94 he won a race for the House of Representatives and became a high-profile conservative Congressman. Sadly, Sonny was killed in a Tahoe skiing accident in '98. His death brought an outpouring of love and praise from all quarters, especially from Cher, who delivered an eloquent, heartfelt eulogy at his funeral and described him as "the most unforgettable character I've ever met."

EVERYBODY LOVES SOMEBODY

One of Cher's best talents—and what helped endear her to TV audiences—is her quick wit, usually sharpened by her deadpan delivery: "The trouble with some women is that they get all excited about nothing—and then marry him." But she wasn't quipping when she first set her eyeballs on Sonny. The year was '62; she was 16; he was 27, already with a wife and daughter (he later admitted fathering a son from an affair he had during the mid-'60s). Cher was still a teen when they unofficially married two years later in a bathroom. They officially married in '69 when their daughter Chastity was born. They stayed married into '75, at which point Cher's tabloid life began in earnest.

Within three days of her divorce, Cher married heroin-addled musician Gregg Allman in Vegas. After having his son she divorced Allman in '79 and was then linked with numerous younger entertainers. After the Cher split, Sonny married again in the early '80s, a union that lasted about three years. He had two more kids with his last wife, Mary Bono, a gymnast and fitness trainer who was with him from the mid-'80s until his death, and she was later elected to take his Congressional seat.

MY BACK PAGES

Cher's mother has been married three times to Cher's father. . . . Daughter Chastity is now a prominent activist in the lesbian community. . . . At the '86 Oscar ceremony, Cher wore a $12,000 Bob Mackie gown, at the time the most expensive

November 21, 1945—Actress Goldie Hawn is born in Washington, D.C. ☮ November 21, 1960—John and Jackie Kennedy make the cover of *Life*. November 21, 1962—Elvis Presley's *Girls! Girls! Girls!* opens. ☮ November 22, 1932—Actor Robert Vaughn is born in New York. November 22, 1943—Tennis ace Billie Jean King is born in Long Beach, California. ☮ November 22, 1961—*The George Raft Story* with Julie London opens.

dress ever worn to that event. . . . While she's always had music's biggest eyes and best cheekbones, she also admits to having had repeated plastic surgeries and at least six tattoos. . . . Of her own life, Cher told syndicated columnist Liz Smith: "I've always lived quietly. It's just that when I'm out, I am really out. People think I'm sort of a madwoman, but you know what? I'm really very boring". . . . Though Sonny stopped pursuing a full-time entertainment career once he got into politics, he did take occasional acting jobs, notably *Hairspray* in '88. . . . In the mid-'90s on David Letterman's *Late Night* show they had a moving, tearful reunion and sang "I Got You Babe" together for the first time in decades.

Terry Southern

The very definition of literary cool, Terry Southern hung out with everyone who was anyone and helped shape some of the decade's movie milestones.

TAKIN' CARE OF BUSINESS

Among the hipsters shown in the photo montage on the *Sgt. Pepper's* cover is one Terry Southern. Today his name might not ring a bell, but Southern's work sure does, loud and clear and cool. A sharply satirical writer who seemed to have had a hand in everything that was *with it* during the '60s, Terry wrote articles, essays, novels, and screenplays to lavish acclaim from peers like Hunter S. Thompson, Norman Mailer, Tom Wolfe, and Joseph Heller.

Born in Texas in the '20s, by the end of the '40s he had fought at the Battle of the Bulge and graduated from Northwestern as a philosophy major. From there he was off to Paris, studying at the Sorbonne and writing fiction (one piece was the first-ever short story published in *The Paris Review*). He hung with the Beat poets in Greenwich Village in the early '50s, then moved to Geneva and got his first novels, including *Candy* and *The Magic Christian*, published at the end of the decade.

Relocating to Connecticut, he took on writing assignments for *Esquire,* made a Stanley Kubrick connection via Peter Sellers, and got invited to make Kubrick's black comedy *Dr. Strangelove* even blacker and funnier—the result was an Oscar-nominated screenplay. Terry then contributed to the Steve McQueen gambling tale *The Cincinnati Kid* in '65, the frenzied *Casino Royale* in '67, and the surreal sci-fi Fondathon *Barbarella* in '68. Then came the movie version of Terry's *Candy*, a fascinating messcapade with a script by Buck Henry (*The Graduate*) and a rogue's gallery of scene-stealers including Marlon Brando, Richard Burton, and Ringo Starr.

In '69, Peter Fonda and Dennis Hopper brought Terry on-board to add coherence to their rambling motorcycle epic (he invented the *Easy Rider* title, created the basic outline with Fonda, and wrote much of the dialogue, though it's hard now to separate script from improv). Their joint effort (in all senses of those words) on the screenplay brought another Oscar nomination.

Along the way Terry wrote more books, helped turn

his novel *The Magic Christian* into a wild Peter Sellers movie for an end-of-the-decade release, and generally seemed to be in all the hip places at all the right times. The momentum of Terry's '60s dissipated in the '70s, unfortunately. He continued to write prolifically, but after the mixed reception to his bawdy novel *Blue Movie* in '70 his work didn't generate the buzz in Hollywood it once did.

He wrote dozens of screenplays that never became movies; he toured with the Stones as their authorized reporter; he contributed made-up letters to *National Lampoon*; he briefly joined the staff of *Saturday Night Live*; he and Harry Nilsson co-wrote a lame Whoopi Goldberg comedy, *The Telephone* ('88). But anything close to his '60s success eluded him. His last novel, *Texas Summer*, came out to lukewarm reviews in '92. Before he died from respiratory failure in '95, he'd been teaching screenwriting at NYU and Columbia.

EVERYBODY LOVES SOMEBODY

Terry got married in '56, separated a decade later, and divorced in '72, with one son (who later co-edited a Terry Southern anthology). From the early '50s onward, his was a partying, peripatetic life fueled by drink and drugs. Anyone hanging with the Stones in London was bound to be indulging in all the temptations of the time. In a Stones documentary he's even seen nosing around some powder and commenting on the price of cocaine.

MY BACK PAGES

On the *Sgt. Pepper's* cover, Terry stands next to Dylan Thomas, and he's the only one of the 62 people wearing shades. . . . Matching the crazy casting in *Candy, The Magic Christian* got appearances from John Lennon, Ringo, Raquel Welch, Roman Polanski, Christopher Lee, Richard Attenborough, Laurence Harvey, Spike Milligan, and Yul Brynner (plus Pythons John Cleese and Graham Chapman contributed to the script). . . . In *The Man Who Fell to Earth* with David Bowie, Terry was briefly on-screen playing a journalist.

Phil Spector

The legendary producer who created the influential Wall of Sound.

TAKIN' CARE OF BUSINESS

If the Beatles' George Martin ranks as the most important producer of the late '60s, Phil Spector has to be #1 for the early '60s. A versatile talent who could play, compose, arrange, and invent, he was so important that he was almost as famous as the groups he produced. Born Harvey Phillip Spector in the Bronx, Phil spent his teen years in L.A., where he was the multipurpose brains behind a smash-hit lullaby in '58, "To Know Him Is to Love Him" by the Teddy Bears (Phil was composer/player/singer, the title taken from the words on his father's headstone).

Moving back to New York in '60, Phil learned the biz under Leiber and Stoller, the music team responsible for many '50s golden oldies (including Elvis's "Hound Dog"). A year later Phil was in L.A. again, this time with his own label, Philles Records. Almost immediately he got on a hot streak that flooded the radio with songs he produced for Gene Pitney ("Every Breath I Take"), Ben E. King ("Spanish Harlem"), the Crystals ("Da Doo Ron Ron"), the Ronettes ("Be My Baby"), and others.

The "Wall of Sound" was his signature sonic contribution. Using advanced studio techniques and complex arrangements, he piled layers of voices, rock instruments, and orchestra instruments into dense two-minute, mono-

November 23, 1941—Actor Franco Nero is born in Italy. ☮ November 23, 1960—Elvis Presley's *G.I. Blues* opens.
November 23, 1962—Joan Baez makes the cover of *Time*. ☮ November 23, 1966—Elvis Presley's *Spinout* opens.
November 23, 2001—Baseball star Bo Belinsky dies in Las Vegas of cancer. ☮ November 24, 1921—New York mayor John Lindsay is born.

recorded symphonies that still carried sweet, simple teenage messages. His "Wrecking Crew" team of crack studio musicians featured all-star players and helped provide the soundtracks for many of these hits. Brian Wilson was a major fan of Phil's sound—the lead Beach Boy said that hearing "Be My Baby" on his car radio for the first time caused him to pull over immediately, and later he based his group's intricate vocal arrangements on careful analysis of Phil's records (he even occasionally borrowed Phil's Wrecking Crew).

In the mid-'60s Phil transplanted his Wall of Sound onto two other acts—the Righteous Brothers ("You've Lost That Lovin' Feeling") and Ike and Tina Turner ("River Deep, Mountain High"). When the British Invasion swept through the mid-'60s, Phil briefly retired, to be brought back to recording at decade's end by, ironically, the main British Invaders, the Beatles. Unable to complete their last album, tentatively called *Get Back*, the Beatles brought in Phil to rescue it, and the result was *Let It Be* (the heavenly choir Phil added to "The Long and Winding Road" was popular with fans but not with composer Paul McCartney).

As further testament to Phil's coolness, Elvis brought him in to produce the King's famous "comeback special" in '68; what's more, when Peter Fonda and Dennis Hopper were looking for someone to play the drug connection to kick-start their ultra-hip biker epic *Easy Rider*, Phil got the call. In the '70s and '80s Phil worked with Cher, Dusty Springfield and the Ramones, produced solo albums for John Lennon and Yoko Ono, and ultimately retreated into his Orange County mansion. There a tragic death by gunfire in 2003 exposed a sinister side of his eccentric private life, but his public music remains intact—*Rolling Stone* magazine ranked him #63 among the greatest rock artists ever, and the Rock and Roll Hall of Fame welcomed him in with an '89 induction.

EVERYBODY LOVES SOMEBODY

Phil married one of his protégés, Veronica Bennett (Ronnie of the Ronettes) in '68. After they broke up in '74, she sued him for the unpaid royalties on her hits and won over $2 million. Phil's got five kids, three of them adopted. Over the years, claims of domestic violence, tales of abuse by some of his children, and allegations of substance abuse have been aired in the media.

Girl Groups with Top-Three Pop Hits ('60–'65)

Angels–"My Boyfriend's Back" ('63)
Chiffons–"He's So Fine" ('63)
Crystals–"He's a Rebel" ('62), "Da Doo Ron Ron" ('63)
Dixie Cups–"Chapel of Love" ('64)
Martha and the Vandellas–"Dancing in the Street" ('64)
Marvelettes–"Please Mr. Postman" ('61)
Ronettes–"Be My Baby" ('63)
Shangri-Las–"Leader of the Pack" ('64)
Shirelles–"Will You Love Me Tomorrow" ('60), "Soldier Boy" ('62)
Supremes–"Where Did Our Love Go" ('64), "Come See About Me" ('64), "Stop! In the Name of Love" ('65), "Back in My Arms Again" ('65), "I Hear a Symphony" ('65)
Toys–"A Lover's Concerto" ('65)

MY BACK PAGES

Phil flew to England to meet the Beatles before they invaded America, and he was on the plane that brought them to the States for their first appearance with Ed Sullivan in '64. . . . Part of Phil's legacy is his reputation for sometimes bizarre, even violent behavior, and he's said to have pulled a gun in several recording sessions. . . . In addition to Brian Wilson, Bruce Springsteen has admitted to being heavily influenced by Phil's work (as heard on one of the Boss's biggest hits, "Born to Run").

November 24, 1960—Wilt Chamberlain pulls down a record 55 rebounds against the Celtics.
November 24, 1963—Lee Harvey Oswald, John F. Kennedy's alleged assassin, is shot in front of a live TV audience.
November 24, 1965—Elvis Presley's *Harum Scarum* opens. ☮ November 25, 1914—Baseball star Joe DiMaggio is born in Martinez, California.

Dusty Springfield

This blonde, husky-voiced pop-rocker charted big with numerous Top 10 hits.

TAKIN' CARE OF BUSINESS

Riding in on the British Invasion that swept across America in the mid-'60s, Dusty Springfield was one of the decade's most prominent singers. Born Mary Isabel Catherine Bernadette O'Brien in London, she started singing with folk groups as a teen. Changing her style to emulate the Motown sound she loved, Dusty hit the British charts in '63 with the peppy "I Only Want to Be with You," which jumped across the Atlantic concurrently with the first Beatles songs to become an American hit in '64. Three years of steady airplay followed, highlighted by "Wishin' and Hopin'" and "You Don't Have to Say You Love Me."

During the decade she toured, appeared on *Ready, Steady, Go!* and Ed Sullivan's show, and even hosted her own music-variety show on the BBC (among her guests were Jimi Hendrix, Tina Turner, and Woody Allen). Not one for wild costumes or mod fashions, she dressed glamorously in glitzy gowns when she was onstage, an attempt to morph from the ugly-duckling kid she thought she'd been into the beautiful entertainer she wanted to become. But it was her voice that people loved, a raw, intensely soulful sound that conveyed heartfelt emotions and unspoken vulnerability ("the Queen of Soul," some called her, and *Rolling Stone* magazine named her Britain's best pop singer *ever*).

Surprisingly, she never scored a #1 hit, but at decade's end she did release a landmark album, the soulful *Dusty in Memphis* with its classic "Son of a Preacher Man." Critics instantly hailed the album as her masterpiece. Sadly, at age 30, she had reached the pinnacle of her career, and she began a long, depressing slump. Her late-'70s attempt at a comeback got only a lukewarm reception, but she did have a few more milestones left in her: she sang with the Pet Shop Boys on "What Have I Done to Deserve This?," a #2 hit in '88; "Son of a Preacher Man" was on the *Pulp Fiction* soundtrack in '96; and she had two anthology albums released in the '90s.

After recording her last album, Dusty was diagnosed with breast cancer. She later told a London newspaper her reaction when got the news: "I shed about three tears in the hallway and then said, 'let's have lunch'." Five years later, she died in her home at age 59. Her death came a day before she was to be honored at Buckingham Palace and 11 days before her induction into the Rock and Roll Hall of Fame. Even the Queen of England said she was "saddened" by Dusty's demise.

EVERYBODY LOVES SOMEBODY

When the hits stopped coming in the early '70s, Dusty claimed she was "bored with Britain" and moved to L.A., dropping out of show biz for most of the decade. During the L.A. years Dusty lived alone and was the topic of wild rumors concerning her bisexuality, which she neither admitted nor denied. What she did admit to was a life of drugged debauchery, a prolonged depression, and an attempted suicide. After 15 years in California, Dusty moved to Amsterdam and then back to her homeland for the rest of her life.

MY BACK PAGES

The British press had a nickname for her—"the white Negress," because of her soulful style. . . . One of the early critics of apartheid, Dusty was deported from South Africa in '64 after performing for a racially mixed audience. . . . After she died, Elvis Costello, Lulu, and Neil Tennant (lead singer of the Pet Shop Boys) spoke at the service.

November 25, 1944—Actress Candy Darling is born on Long Island, New York.
November 25, 1960—Jackie Kennedy gives birth to her second child, son John Jr., in Washington, D.C.
November 25, 2005—Soccer star George Best dies in London of a chest infection.

Barbara Steele

The memorable menace in numerous '60s cult horror films.

TAKIN' CARE OF BUSINESS

Barbara Steele was one of those actresses you've seen, but you're not sure where. An English actress getting small roles in the '50s, she graduated to starring roles in two films a year during the '60s, most of them in the first half of the decade, and most of them Italian chillers. Highlights included *Black Sunday* and *The Pit and the Pendulum* (both in '61), two gothic greats that showed her off as a good screamer playing evil-yet-seductive characters (no less than director Tim Burton, who knows something about dark scary movies, declared *Black Sunday* his favorite horror film).

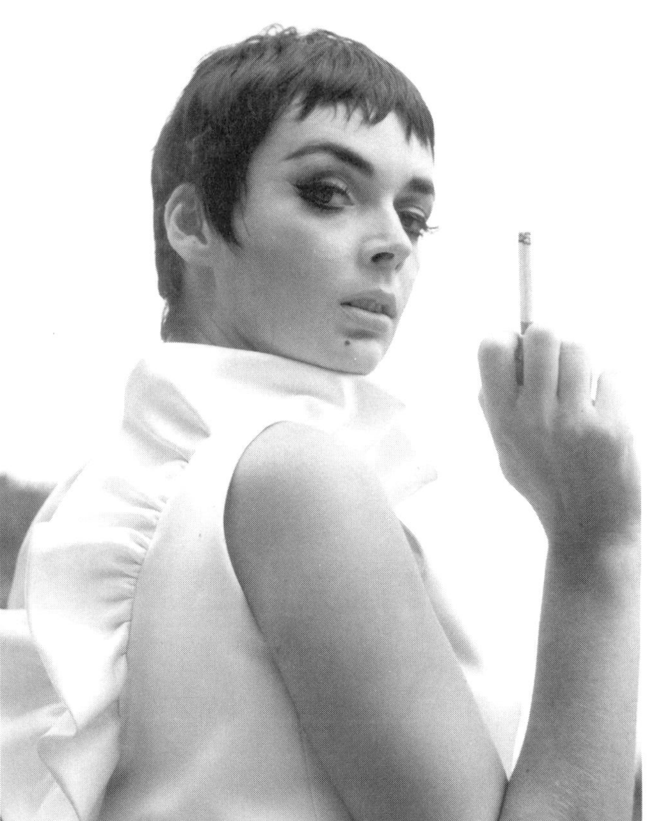

Slim and sinister, she always looked right in period costumes, and her small face/big eyes/raven-black hair gave her a fascinating, intense appeal that made you want to both approach and run. Working overseas, her voice was dubbed in a lot of her movies (including, for some reason, the English-language film *The Pit and the Pendulum*). More (and mostly lesser) horror movies followed through the '60s, plus she also appeared in Fellini's masterful *8½* ('63) and on several cool mid-decade TV shows like *I Spy* and *Secret Agent*.

Post-'60s screen roles included a sadistic lesbian warden in the bondage-heavy *Caged Heat* ('74), plus (naturally) more horror—David Cronenberg's creepy *Shivers* ('75), *Piranha* ('78), *Silent Scream* ('80), and the revived *Dark Shadows* TV series of the '90s. These years she was working behind the scenes, too, and had a producing credit for *The Winds of War* mini-series ('83) and a producing Emmy Award for *War and*

15 More Horror Hits

The Birds ('63)
Blood Feast ('63)
Brides of Dracula ('60)
The Curse of the Werewolf ('61)
The Devil Rides Out ('68)
Dracula, Prince of Darkness ('66)
The Evil of Frankenstein ('64)
The Fall of the House of Usher ('60)
Frankenstein Must Be Destroyed ('64)
The Gorgon ('64)
The Haunting ('63)
The Innocents ('61)
The Mask of the Red Death ('64)
Night of the Living Dead ('68)
Rosemary's Baby ('68)

Remembrance ('88). Today she's still got a large cult following and is fondly recalled as one of the original, and one of the great, screen scream queens.

EVERYBODY LOVES SOMEBODY

Barbara was married for about a decade (late '60s-late '70s) to James Poe, screenwriter on *Around the World in 80 Days* ('56) and *They Shoot Horses, Don't They?* ('69), with a son born in the early '70s. For *They Shoot Horses*, the part of the aging actress was written for Barbara, but ultimately it went to Susannah York.

MY BACK PAGES

In '66 the University of North Carolina Press published a book of poems by noted poet R.H.W. Dillard—the title was *The Day I Stopped Dreaming About Barbara Steele*. . . . Still one of the most nightmarish images of '60s cinema is Barbara's face in *Black Sunday* after it's been spiked full of holes. . . . Still scaring audiences, she helped produce the *Queer Eye for the Straight Guy* TV series in the 2000s.

Connie Stevens

Cute Cricket Blake on *Hawaiian Eye* was a TV, movie, and singing star who transformed herself from a mod '60s pixie into a successful business tycoon.

TAKIN' CARE OF BUSINESS

"An apple blossom with the wham of a bulldozer," according to gossip columnist Hedda Hopper; in the early '60s that "wham" brought Connie a hit series (*Hawaiian Eye*) classic teen movies (*Palm Spring Weekend*, '63), and even some hit songs ("Kookie, Kookie, Lend Me Your Comb" and "Sixteen Reasons"). In '61 and '63 *Photoplay* magazine named her the Most Popular Female Star, and throughout the early '60s she was a popular role model for teenage girls.

After *Hawaiian Eye* ended in '63, Connie was the Wendy of *Wendy and Me*, a '64 sitcom with George Burns as the "Me." She also continued making movies throughout the decade, won a *Theatre World* award for her starring role in Broadway's *Star-Spangled Girl* ('66), and toured Vietnam with Bob Hope's USO show in '69. Quite the versatile decade for a Brooklyn-born girl who spoke only Italian until she was 5 years old and who had started her career as a singer. As a teen she formed vocal groups—the first, in New York, was called the Foremost (the other singers later became the Lettermen), and the second, in Hollywood, was the Three Dubs (which she later jokingly called the Three Duds).

She started performing onstage and as a movie extra,

November 27, 1965—Herb Alpert's *Whipped Cream* album hits #1. ☮ November 28, 1963—*Who's Minding the Store* with Jerry Lewis opens.
November 28, 1964—The Shangri-Las' "Leader of the Pack" hits #1.
November 28, 1966—Truman Capote throws the decade's biggest party, the infamous, exclusive, legendary Black and White Ball at the Plaza Hotel.

then Jerry Lewis put her in his *Rock-a-Bye Baby* ('58). A Warner Bros. contract and *Hawaiian Eye* followed a year later. After her busy '60s, in the '70s Connie toured the country, playing nightclubs and hotel lounges coast to coast while still starring in popular movies and lots of hit TV shows. Then in '89 she mortgaged her house and jumped into the skin-care game.

Connie eventually remade herself as a powerful businesswoman, launching her own Forever Spring skin-care and make-up line, creating the Garden Sanctuary spas on the West Coast, and ultimately generating a net worth of over $100 million. Still working in entertainment, in recent years Connie produced, wrote, edited, and directed a documentary about Vietnam called *A Healing,* she recorded a Christmas album with her daughters, and she's continued to play occasional nightclub dates. Versatile, vivacious, very successful—and she still looks great, too.

EVERYBODY LOVES SOMEBODY

As a young starlet in the early '60s, Connie dated actor Glenn Ford and then Elvis, whom she later said was "a great kisser." In '63 she married actor James Stacey, but they broke up after three years. She started dating singer Eddie Fisher in '67 while she was in New York for *Star-Spangled Girl*. When they married, their daughter Joely was already four months old (Joely later became an actress and played Paige Clark on *Ellen*). With Fisher Connie had another daughter, Tricia Leigh, who's also a singer and an actress.

Connie and Eddie had a turbulent marriage that ended in divorce in '69. Connie asked for no alimony and single-handedly raised her daughters, even while she was touring and working in Hollywood. Today she's still single and enjoys an opulent home in the toney Holmby Hills neighborhood of L.A., plus houses in Puerta Vallarta, Las Vegas, New York, Palm Desert, and a 10-acre retreat in Jackson Hole, Wyoming.

MY BACK PAGES

Her parents were both jazz musicians, her brother was a drummer. . . . Part Mohican, Connie established the Windfeather Foundation to raise money for Native Americans. . . . She also hosts an annual Celebrity Ski Extravaganza in Wyoming that raises funds for the mentally and physically challenged. . . . In '94 Connie performed the voice of the mother of her daughter's character on *Ellen*. . . . Two of the awards she's won that she's proudest of are the Lady of Humanities Award from Shriners Hospital (the armed forces' highest honor for a citizen of the U.S.) and the Parent of the Year Award from the Cedar Sinai Medical Center Helping Hand. . . . She's also got a star on the Star Walk in Palm Springs, on Hollywood Blvd. and in the Brooklyn Botanical Gardens.

Stella Stevens

The decade's first *Playboy* Playmate made 15 movies during the '60s, including some of the decade's swingin'est.

TAKIN' CARE OF BUSINESS

Stella Stevens packed more living into her first quarter-century than most people do into a full lifetime. Married at 15, Mississippi-born Stella was a divorced single mother two years later. Then, in the first month of the first year of the '60s, 23-year-old Stella was a *Playboy* Playmate ("bella Stella," the magazine called her). The *Playboy* connection continued with later features in May '65 and January '68, and in '99 the magazine rated her #27 (right between Grace Kelly and Jane Fonda) among the century's 100 sexiest stars. But it was on the silver screen where her stunning beauty made its greatest impact.

After winning a Golden Globe as the Most Promising Newcomer for her debut as Appassionata von Climax in *Li'l Abner* ('59), she was one of the title females in Elvis's *Girls! Girls! Girls!* ('62). Stella then starred as wide-eyed Stella

November 29, 1932—Actress Diane Ladd is born in Meridian, Mississippi.
November 29, 1940—Denny Doherty of the Mamas and the Papas is born in Halifax, Canada.
November 29, 1981—Actress Natalie Wood drowns at age 43 off Catalina Island.

Purdy in Jerry Lewis's *The Nutty Professor* ('63), and she adeptly played it for laughs in Dino's *The Silencers* in '66. Her awesome screen appeal kept her busy all decade in a wide variety of roles, from college co-ed to scheming seductress to drug addict to even a nun in *Where Angels Go, Trouble Follows* ('68). In '70 she got one of her richest roles in the Sam Peckinpah Western *The Ballad of Cable Hogue*, and two years later she played the doomed curly-haired ex-hooker in *The Poseidon Adventure*.

She's worked ever since, building an amazing résumé that pushes her big- and small-screen appearances into triple digits. With four projects in '77, five in '79, five more in '90, four in '94, and on into the new millennium with a role on TV's *General Hospital*, the sheer number of her movies and TV shows, covering every year from '59 onward, is truly impressive.

As if all that weren't enough to keep a star busy, in the '90s she appeared as characters in computer games, she's done stagework, she's twice tried her hand at film directing, in '99 she co-wrote a novel called *Razzle Dazzle*, and she's working on her autobiography. She even launched her own fragrance company (appropriately enough, Stella's scents are called Sexy, with Gold Label for women and Black Label for men). Stars may come and go, centuries may pass, but Stella Stevens, it appears, is eternal.

EVERYBODY LOVES SOMEBODY

As Stella acted for him on the set of *The Nutty Professor*, a smitten Jerry Lewis wrote to her, "You are the reason men can't live without the pride and thrill of direction." Stella's the mother of actor/director/producer Andrew Stevens. Since '84, she has been living in Beverly Hills with a record producer who was formerly the lead guitarist for Alice Cooper and Meatloaf.

MY BACK PAGES

Her moniker at birth was Estelle Eggleston, which she changed to Stella Stevens at 18. . . . Before she hit it big, she attended Memphis State University. . . . After being named a *Playboy* Playmate in '60, Stella later provided the requisite Playmate data: her turn-ons included eating fresh strawberries for breakfast in bed; her hobbies were writing, reading, and collecting records; and her favorite sports were horseback riding and skin diving.

Jill St. John

This redheaded, hour-glassed knockout blazed across the big screen alongside some of the decade's most prominent leading men.

TAKIN' CARE OF BUSINESS

Jill St. John has lived, looked, and played like a true Hollywood star, even though she hasn't had a stellar movie career. But she's sure stolen some scenes in her time. Jill Oppenheim at birth, she was a stage actress at age 5, a movie

actress in '50s flicks as a teen, and a star in Irwin Allen's *The Lost World* ('60) at 20. High-profile movies filled her '60s, including Jerry Lewis's *Who's Minding the Store?* ('63), *The Liquidator* with Rod Taylor ('65), *Tony Rome* with Frank ('67), and *Eight on the Lam* with Bob Hope ('67).

Unappreciated by film critics, these credits and more (including a couple of TV movies, numerous TV specials, and *Batman* in '66) still didn't add up to Jill getting much respect as an actress. In fact, some sources say she was only brought into *Tony Rome* because she was Frank's girl (he did get parts in that movie for all his gang and several of his playmates). But with that stunning face, sexy red hair, and curvy 5' 7" figure, Jill was one of those actresses so dang attractive it didn't matter if she was a great actress or not. Sometimes there just for set decoration—in a slender bikini stuffed with big scoops of firm vanilla ice cream, or in a glamorous gown bedecked with jewels—her sex appeal resonated long after many of her movies were forgotten.

She does have the distinction of being the first American-born Bond Beauty—the sparkling role of Tiffany Case in the penultimate Connery Bond flick, *Diamonds Are Forever* ('71), showed her off at her sexiest and propelled her onward to many more screen appearances, including a half-dozen TV movies, regular cooking demos on *Good Morning America*, lots of Bob Hope specials, and even a *Seinfeld* in '97. A food columnist for the *USA Weekend* newspaper, she wrote *The Jill St. John Cookbook* in '87.

EVERYBODY LOVES SOMEBODY

She once said that "the longest period of celibacy for Jill St. John is the shortest distance between two lovers." In laymen's terms that translates into lots of husbands and lots of boyfriends. One of her husbands was playboy Lance Reventlow (the son of Woolworth heiress Barbara Hutton). She had some '60s hey-hey with Sinatra, and something undefined with Henry Kissinger. Of the latter, Jill found his intellect to be his most admirable feature and a good match for her own high I.Q., which is said to be 162.

Since '90 she's been married to Natalie Wood's ex-husband, Robert Wagner. She and Wagner worked together on the TV movie *How I Spent My Summer Vacation* in '66; they were reintroduced in '82, two months after Natalie tragically drowned off Catalina Island. They now have homes in

Aspen, Colorado, and Pacific Palisades, California, where Jill keeps a number of horses.

MY BACK PAGES

Jill, Natalie Wood, and Stefanie Powers all were in the same ballet class as kids. . . . Supposedly Jill beat out Raquel Welch, Faye Dunaway, and Jane Fonda for *Diamonds Are Forever*. . . . Since they married, Jill and Robert Wagner have been in several screen projects together, including the *Around the World in 80 Days* miniseries ('89), *The Player* ('92), and *Something to Believe In* ('98), and they've also toured in the play *Love Letters*.

The Supremes

The most commercially successful girl group of all time had an incredible run of '60s hits.

TAKIN' CARE OF BUSINESS

Glamorous and soulful, polished and urgent, the Supremes were record-setting record-makers whose across-the-board popularity rivaled that of any other great group—the Beatles, Stones, Beach Boys—of the '60s. Though there were many lineup variations over the years, the main three were Diana Ross, Mary Wilson, and Florence Ballard, all thin teenagers living in Detroit (Diana's hometown, Florence and Mary were from Mississippi).

They began as a quartet called the Primettes, got a new name and a contract from their local Motown Records label in '61, and soon lost Barbara Martin, their fourth singer, to retirement. Taking turns on lead vocals, the trio recorded with little acclaim and feeble sales for the next three years until "When the Lovelight Starts Shining Through His Eyes" became a Top 40 hit in late '63.

With Diana now singing lead, the girls began a remarkable streak in mid-'64 that produced five #1 hits in a row ("Where Did Our Love Go," "Baby Love," "Come See About Me," "Stop! In the Name of Love," and "Back in My Arms Again") in only 10 months. No other American group had ever enjoyed such consistent chart-topping success. Grammy nominations, groundbreaking TV appearances, a movie showcase (*Beach Ball*, '65), product endorsements, and international concerts fueled their popularity as rock's reigning pop princesses, a title abetted by their graceful moves, glamorous gowns, and high-styled wigs.

Ultimately, the group had a dozen massive hits in the mid-'60s, adding instant classics like "I Hear a Symphony," "You Keep Me Hangin' On," and "You Can't Hurry Love" to their repertoire, and to the public it seemed like the charismatic group could do no wrong. Internally, though, tensions were building. Diana was seen as the supreme Supreme, an impression confirmed by the '67 name change to Diana Ross and the Supremes. That same year Florence, troubled by the politics within the group, was replaced by one of Patti LaBelle's backup singers, Cindy Birdsong, and for some recording sessions unnamed Motown singers were being brought into the studio. The material was changing, too, taking on edgier topics with mixed results—"Love Child" was one of their last #1 hits, with many other releases not even making the Top 20.

Motown was already orchestrating Diana's move to a solo career, and in '70 she left the Supremes for good. She struck instant gold with her own Grammy-nominated #1 hit ("Ain't No Mountain High

December 1, 1935—Writer/director Woody Allen is born in Brooklyn, New York. ☮ December 1, 1960—Actress Sandra Dee marries singer Bobby Darin.
December 1, 1967—Model Peggy Moffitt and designer Rudi Gernreich make the cover of *Time*.
December 2, 1925—Actress Julie Harris is born in Grosse Point, Michigan. ☮ December 2, 1965—*That Darn Cat!* with Hayley Mills opens.

Enough") and a successful album (*Diana Ross*), and soon her new movie career brought her a Best Actress Oscar nomination for *Lady Sings the Blues* ('72). Solo success continued for the next two decades, with another half-dozen hit songs ("Touch Me in the Morning," '73) and more high-profile movie roles (*The Wiz*, '78).

Meanwhile the Diana-less Supremes soldiered on with Jean Terrell in Diana's place. Popularity gradually dwindled, more personnel changes ensued, and by '78 the Supremes had disbanded. Florence died of heart failure in '76, her post-Supremes years having been marred by serious financial problems and deep depression; Diana and Mary both wrote bestselling books about the glory days; and in '88 the group was inducted into the Rock and Roll Hall of Fame. Attempts at 21st-century reunions with Diana, Mary, and Cindy fell apart, and Diana's "Return to Love" concerts with two '70s Supremes were aborted mid-tour, but the group's stature as a '60s legend remains undiminished.

EVERYBODY LOVES SOMEBODY

Florence married a Motown chauffeur in '68 and gave birth to twins that year, with another child in '73. Mary was married and divorced, with two kids. Diana had a relationship with Smokey Robinson in the '60s and a daughter with Motown founder Berry Gordy, Jr. in '71; she was then married in the '70s (with two daughters) and then again for about 15 years (with two sons). In 2005 rumors put her in the company of actor Jon Voight.

MY BACK PAGES

Beach Ball showed the girls singing two beachy-keen numbers at a hot rod show, "Beach Ball" and "Surfer Boy". . . . Nearly all of the group's hits were written by the Motown trio of Brian and Eddie Holland and Lamont Dozier. . . . Diana has sung at most major American events, including a Super Bowl halftime show ('96) and a huge free concert in Central Park in '83. . . . The Broadway musical and Hollywood movie *Dreamgirls* loosely retells the story of the Supremes. . . . On VH1's list of great women in rock, the Supremes come in sixteenth, right behind Patti Smith.

Jacqueline Susann

The Queen of Pulp Fiction led a life as fascinating as anything she wrote about in her bestselling novels.

TAKIN' CARE OF BUSINESS

She is the only writer ever to have three novels in a row atop the *New York Times*' bestseller list; in the *Guinness Book of World Records, Valley of the Dolls* is tied with *Gone with the Wind* and *To Kill a Mockingbird* as the bestselling novels (over 20 million copies) of all time by a female writer; movies were made of her books, and movies were made of her life. In her wake came other female novelists who churned out popular potboilers (Danielle Steel, Jackie Collins), but Jacqueline Susann paved the way for all of them.

Born in Philly, Jacqueline showed writing talent as a child, but by high school she was a pill-popping party girl. Moving to New York to work as an actress, she got only bit parts and commercials. In the '40s she wrote a play that ran (briefly) on Broadway; in the early '50s she wrote a minor romance/science-fiction novel, *Yargo*. Later that decade she wrote, produced, and starred in commercials for late-night TV, and she also attempted an entertainment exposé she would've called *The Pink Dolls*.

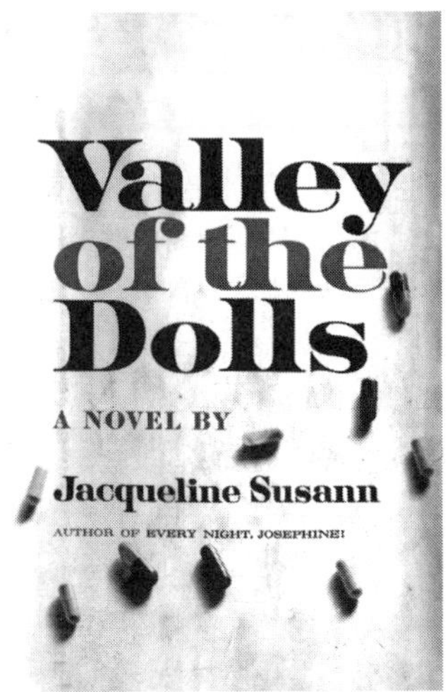

Depressed and taking pills, in '62 she began writing a simple, fun novel about her poodle, "a report from the other end of the leash," as it was billed; that same year she was diagnosed with cancer and dedicated herself to becoming a bestselling author. Eleven months later *Every Night, Josephine!* came out and was a popular hit. Buoyed by this success, for the next two years she worked all day every day, with a blackboard nearby for notes, on *Valley of the Dolls*, an inside look at the seamy side of show biz. When it was published in early '66, scholarly critics attacked it as a tawdry soap opera, but Jacqueline promoted the book extensively on TV and with book tours, and it rose to #1, where it stayed for the rest of the year.

Always glamorous with her Pucci clothes and sparkling jewelry, Jackie became a popular, outspoken guest on talk shows and also had a cameo in the *Valley of the Dolls* movie ('67). In '69 she published *The Love Machine*, which examined the passions and scandals in the world of TV. With more book tours, this time in a pink plane dubbed "the love machine," it too was a #1 bestseller for half a year. Her third bestseller, *Once Is Not Enough*, was published in early '74, and it also hit #1, an unprecedented trifecta in publishing history. Sadly, Jackie finally lost her long fight with cancer later that year.

EVERYBODY LOVES SOMEBODY

Jackie lived like a glamorous star, even before she was famous. She and her husband/agent, Irving Mansfield (whom she'd married in '39), resided in a ritzy hotel on Central Park South, and they filled the '60s with parties, travels, and celebrity friends. Jackie's two words of advice for brides: "room service," because she herself never cooked. With Irving she had more of a happy, successful partnership than a passionate, monogamous marriage; there were often rumors of her infidelities with famous men and women, and for awhile in the '40s she and Irving separated. In '46 they had a son, but after he was diagnosed as being autistic he was committed to an institution for the rest of his life.

MY BACK PAGES

Rumors suggested that the Helen character (played by Susan Hayward in the *Valley of the Dolls* movie) was modeled after Ethel Merman, Neely (Patty Duke) was Judy Garland or Betty Hutton, Jennifer (Sharon Tate) was Marilyn Monroe or Carole Landis, and Anne (Barbara Parkins) was Jacqueline herself. . . . There was also an '81 TV movie with Britt Ekland and Richard Dreyfuss, plus there was a *Valley of the Dolls* TV series in '94 with Sally Kirkland as Helen. . . . Like many other celebrities, Jacqueline claimed that she was supposed to be at Sharon Tate's house the night of the Manson murders. . . . In '69 Truman Capote cattily described Jacqueline on *The Tonight Show* as "a truck driver in drag"—she threatened to sue him and NBC, and he later apologized—to truck drivers everywhere. . . . The TV movie *Scandalous Me* in '98 starred Michele Lee as Jackie, and *Isn't She Great* in 2000 starred Bette Midler. . . . Jackie herself thought the '60s would be remembered for three things—Andy Warhol, the Beatles, and her.

Sharon Tate and Jay Sebring

The stunning beauty starred in a camp classic, and the handsome haircutting playboy lived fast and famously, but tragically both fell to the murdering Manson Family.

TAKIN' CARE OF BUSINESS

We'll never know how big a star Sharon Tate might've become. Born in Dallas as the daughter of an Army officer, Sharon was a well-traveled beauty-contest winner and prom queen at an American high school in Italy. Heading to Hollywood, she spent the '60s steadily building a screen career, first with TV commercials, then as a bank secretary on 14 mid-decade episodes of *The Beverly Hillbillies.*

December 4, 1942—Chris Hillman of the Byrds is born in L.A. ☮ December 4, 1943—Actress Patti Chandler is born in California.
December 4, 1944—Dennis Wilson of the Beach Boys is born in L.A. ☮ December 4, 1969—*A Boy Named Charlie Brown* opens.
December 5, 1934—Writer Joan Didion is born in Sacramento, California. ☮ December 5, 1963—*Charade* with Cary Grant opens.

Movies came calling, most notably the parts of doomed pill-popping Jennifer in *Valley of the Dolls* ('67) and the koo-koo accomplice for Dino's Matt Helm in *The Wrecking Crew* ('68). In both movies she showed why she was regarded as one of Hollywood's most beautiful actresses, said to have looked much younger than she really was (supposedly many people who met her thought she was in her mid-teens, not her mid-20s).

All taut lines and awesome curvage, she was capable of playing athletic roles (like the trampoline-bouncing sky-diver in *Don't Make Waves*, '67) and sexy roles (the naïve innkeeper's daughter in Roman Polanski's *The Fearless Vampire Killers*, '67). *Playboy* loved her, of course, publishing in March '67 a "Tate Gallery" of erotic photos taken by Polanski.

Then, on a hot summer night, in a rented Beverly Hills house, 26-year-old Sharon Tate was horribly butchered, a tragic, senseless killing engineered by the brutal Charles Manson and executed by his blindly allegiant, drug-ravaged followers. Sharon was eight-and-a-half months pregnant at the time. Her death, and the savage slayings of the four others at the house, will forever be remembered as one of the most awful, sadistic events in L.A. County history. And one of the grisliest: wearing only her undergarments, Sharon died with 16 knife wounds in her body and a rope around her neck, her blood used to write "Pig" on the door; at the other end of the rope, the end wrapped around his neck, was a shot, knifed Jay Sebring.

Four days later, Sharon was buried wearing a Pucci mini, with stars like Yul Brynner, Steve McQueen, Warren Beatty, Kirk Douglas, and Peter Sellers in attendance. A year later Manson's motivations were revealed—he hoped to start an apocalyptic race war by slaughtering rich white people. More celebrity murders would've followed: the Manson Family had a "death list" of Hollywood stars to be targeted, among them McQueen, Frank, Liz and Dick, and Tom Jones.

If Vidal Sassoon was the decade's most famous haircutter of celebrity women, Jay Sebring was the decade's most famous haircutter of celebrity men. Alabama-born Thomas Kummer grew up in Detroit, worked as a barber in the Navy, and went to Hollywood in the '50s with a sexy new name taken from the famous car race in Florida. His haircuts started to get attention, Kirk Douglas brought him in to do the styles on *Spartacus* at the end of the decade, and by the mid-'60s he had his own shop in West Hollywood with a list of devoted clients that included Paul Newman, Steve McQueen, Frank Sinatra, Peter Lawford, Warren Beatty, and George Peppard. Reputedly he also styled Jim Morrison's long, shaggy locks.

Playboy Jay tooled around town in custom clothes and expensive cars, threw huge parties, and lived in the Benedict Canyon mansion once owned by Jean Harlow. Late in the decade he recruited investors from among his famous clients and launched Sebring International to take his own hair products and salons global. Unfortunately, he happened to be visiting Sharon Tate and friends on the night when the Manson Family showed up at Sharon's canyon home. He was buried back home in Michigan four days later.

EVERYBODY LOVES SOMEBODY

"My whole life has been decided by fate," Sharon once said. "I've never planned anything that happened to me." Fate decided that she would have some famous boyfriends and an intense marriage. After a serious relationship with Jay Sebring, Sharon married director Roman Polanski in '68. In a December '71 *Playboy* interview, Polanski remembered her as "the sweetest, most innocent, lovable human being. . . . She just didn't have a bad bone in her body." When they married, the bride wore an off-white taffeta mini, the reception was held at London's Playboy Club, and the honeymoon was spent skiing in the Swiss Alps.

For Sharon and Roman, their life together was a whirlwind of travel and Hollywood parties. They counted among their friends Sean Connery, Peter Sellers, Rudolf Nureyev, Warren Beatty, Vidal Sassoon, and Rolling Stones Brian Jones and Keith Richards, all of whom attended their wedding reception. Oh, and one other famous person Sharon probably met during her life, though he wasn't famous at the time: Manson himself, who in March '69 came to her door and likely spoke to Sharon while looking for someone else. Meanwhile Jay married a model in '60 but they split up after three years. He met Sharon Tate in '65 and was engaged to her for a year before she hooked up with Polanski on the set of *The Fearless Vampire Killers*. Jay was living the playboy life until his tragic death.

MY BACK PAGES

After the murders, many celebrities claimed they had been invited to the house that night but weren't able to make it (investigators later dismissed these claims as either fiction or mistakes). . . . One of those claiming a near-miss was Steve McQueen, who said that he picked up another woman on the way to Sharon's and spent the night with her instead. . . . Polanski dedicated *Tess* ('79) to Sharon. . . . Jay appeared on *Batman* as a character named Mr. Oceanbring (a play on Sebring). . . . In '75, Warren Beatty loosely based *Shampoo*, about a playboy haircutter dreaming of his own salons, on Jay Sebring's celebrated '60s life.

Leigh Taylor-Young

The very embodiment of the '60s flower child, Leigh Taylor-Young was a Broadway, TV, and movie star in the '60s who passionately pursued spiritual enlightenment.

TAKIN' CARE OF BUSINESS

Leigh Taylor-Young has been a radiant presence in anything she's ever appeared in. Born in Washington, D.C., she was a theatre major at Northwestern until she dropped out in '64 to focus on acting. Moving to New York, at 21 Leigh was a Broadway star, and then in '66 she replaced Mia Farrow on the hit primetime soap *Peyton Place*.

Yet Leigh made her most lasting mark as the beautiful young hippie chick with the "groovy" brownies who led square Peter Sellers astray in the critically acclaimed film *I Love You, Alice B. Toklas* ('68). She was nominated for a Golden Globe as Most Promising Newcomer, made lots of magazine covers, and was photographed by Richard Avedon

December 6, 1972—Actress Janet Munro dies at the age of 38 in London of acute myocarditis.
December 7, 1936—Baseball star Bo Belinsky is born in New York.
December 7, 1963—"Dominique" by Soeur Sourire (Sister Smile) aka Jeanine Deckers hits #1.

for *Vogue*. In the early '70s she continued to make movies, including *The Adventurers* ('70) and the sci-fi thriller *Soylent Green* ('73), and a decade later she was a key witness in the popular *Jagged Edge* ('85). She was also a regular on *Dallas* and other shows (winning an Emmy in '94 for *Picket Fences*), she's starred in eight "movies of the week," and she's continually worked in theatre in world capitals.

Even more important than her career success, however, has been her quest for spiritual enlightenment, a quest that began in the late '60s and continues to this day. After finishing her work on *Soylent Green*, Leigh quit the biz and, taking Peter Sellers's advice, flew to an ashram on an island in the Indian Ocean. After two weeks there she went to another ashram in the Himalayas for two months, an experience she described as being physically tough but spiritually rewarding. She maintained her new lifestyle—white robes, health food, meditation—upon her return to L.A. and continued her spiritual studies.

In '73, upon the recommendation of actress Sally Kirkland, Leigh joined the Church of the Movement of Spiritual Inner Awareness. Since joining she's done the vocals for the church's *Search for Serenity* series of audio meditations and has become an ordained minister; still as youthfully beautiful as ever, she currently lives in L.A., continues to work regularly on TV, and practices a healthy regimen of meditation, diet, and exercise.

EVERYBODY LOVES SOMEBODY

Leigh's first love was actor Ryan O'Neal, her *Peyton Place* co-star. At age 22 she was pregnant with his child, though he was still married to actress Joanna Moore. Leigh and Ryan lived in the Benedict Canyon house that had formerly belonged to Bogie and Bacall. Ryan had her exercising all through her pregnancy, and in fact she played tennis the day her son was born in '67.

Two weeks later studio execs voided her *Peyton Place* contract, using their "act of God" clause to dismiss her because of her pregnancy. Her character was written out of the show with a story that she had gone insane and was in an institution. Leigh went on to *I Love You, Alice B. Toklas*, but ironically Leigh herself was the clean-living opposite of the groovy hippie girl in the movie. She and O'Neal split up in '71 after his affair with Barbra Streisand went public. In the spring of that year, Leigh and her son moved to Santa Fe. There she studied homeopathy and Chinese medicine, preludes to the deeply spiritual life to come.

MY BACK PAGES

Leigh's hyphenated name comes from her father, a State Department official, and her stepfather, a Detroit business exec. . . . In a '60s interview she said she took her first *Peyton Place* paycheck and went on a solo shopping trip to Geneva, Switzerland. . . . Publisher Alice B. Toklas died the same year Leigh's movie was filmed. . . . A great '60s moment: at the premiere of *I Love You, Alice B. Toklas*, Andy Warhol painted a butterfly on Leigh's thigh for photographers. . . . Leigh has represented the United Nations Environment Programme (UNEP) and spoken internationally on its behalf, she's been a goodwill ambassador for the U.N., she's been active with Ted Turner's Better World Society, Hands Across America and numerous charitable foundations, and she's hosted the Muscular Dystrophy Telethon.

Marlo Thomas

That Girl was a lively mod-dressin', kite-flyin', voice-crackin' star.

TAKIN' CARE OF BUSINESS

Marlo Thomas was a natural. And given her parentage, is it any surprise? She was born Margaret in Michigan, the daughter of entertainment legend Danny

December 7, 1967—Singer Otis Redding records his single "Dock of the Bay."
December 7, 1968—Marvin Gaye's "I Heard It Through the Grapevine" hits #1.
December 7, 1993—Actress Janet Margolin dies of ovarian cancer at age 50. ☮ December 8, 1925—Entertainer Sammy Davis, Jr. is born in New York.

Thomas. Though famous for *That Girl,* Marlo appeared on several other shows in the '50s and '60s, most notably as recurring character Stella Barnes on *The Joey Bishop Show,* and later she was the unmarried, pregnant title character taking up with Alan Alda in the soapy *Jenny* ('70), which brought her a Golden Globe nomination as the Most Promising Newcomer. But *That Girl* was the show that brought her the most '60s acclaim (a Golden Globe in '67 as Best Actress, and four Emmy nominations).

That Girl was something of a breakthrough in that it was about a modern single woman, thus paving the way for such other acclaimed shows as *Julia* and *The Mary Tyler Moore Show*. Produced by her powerful papa, and created by the former writers of *The Dick Van Dyke Show, That Girl* focused on young, wholesome, fashionably dressed, forward-thinking model/actress Ann Marie (Marie was her last name), who navigated the Big Apple with her patient boyfriend Donald (Ted Bessell). The zany gags often revolved around the zany gigs Ann would get to support herself while waiting for her big break, including one commercial where she dressed as a chicken and other temporary jobs as a meter maid and chef. Marlo, with her brunette flip, sunny smile, and pretty face, was the ultimate in kookie urban charm.

But more impressive than the jokes or the looks was the show's strong stance on women's rights, making Ann Marie perhaps primetime's first feminist. Ann Marie gave young, female viewers someone with whom they could identify—she was approximately their age, she wore their same hip clothes, and like her audience she juggled jobs, dates, and family obligations (all while staying warm-hearted, ambitious, and liberated). Viewers followed her romantic relationship from its beginning (passerby Donald rescued her from what he thought was a kidnapping) to matrimony (almost).

After *That Girl* became Cancelled Girl in '71, Ann Marie resurfaced two years later with Marlo doing the vocals for the animated TV special "That Girl in Wonderland," which put her in the roles of various fairy tale heroines. Marlo then shifted from her classy TV show to lots of classy TV movies and specials, including *It Happened One Christmas* ('77), *Nobody's Child* ('86, bringing her an acting Emmy), and *Held Hostage* ('91).

Generations of children have been influenced by her two remarkable multimedia children's projects: Marlo co-produced, performed in, and won an Emmy for the landmark children's special "Free to Be . . .You and Me" in '74 (also creating the classic children's book), and she won another Emmy for hosting "The Body Human: Facts for Girls" in '80. Other entertainment achievements include several starring roles on Broadway, and an episode of *Friends* that brought her another Emmy nomination in '96. Off-screen, she continues to support numerous social causes and charities, especially one, St. Jude's Children's Research Hospital, that was founded by her father. That Girl of the '60s is now That Woman of the 21st century, as energetic and idealistic and accomplished as ever.

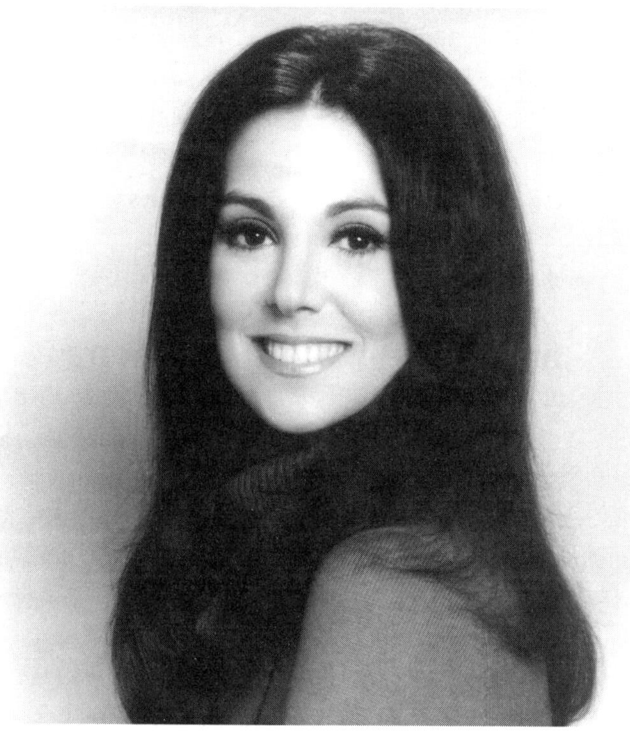

December 8, 1937—Actor James MacArthur is born in L.A. ☮ December 8, 1943—Jim Morrison of the Doors is born in Melbourne, Florida.
December 8, 1980—John Lennon is assassinated in front of New York's Dakota building by Mark David Chapman.
December 9, 1965—*A Charlie Brown Christmas* debuts. ☮ December 9, 1967—Lyndon Johnson's daughter Lynda gets married in the White House.

EVERYBODY LOVES SOMEBODY

She met talk-show host Phil Donahue on his show in '77; they married in '80 and have been one of the most durable show-biz couples ever since.

MY BACK PAGES

Her dad played a priest on a *That Girl* episode—when Ann Marie bumped into him she said, “”Excuse me, father,” to which he replied, “That's all right, my child”. . . . In season five Danny showed up in an episode with Milton Berle, both playing themselves, and Danny and Marlo performed a musical number. . . . Despite struggling to earn a living, Ann Marie managed to have nice Manhattan apartments, plus all the latest mod fashions. . . . She's one of the few actresses of the '60s immediately identified by her own theme song.

Pamela Tiffin

The beautiful star of several drive-in classics.

TAKIN' CARE OF BUSINESS

Pamela Tiffin Wonso of Oklahoma City is remembered as one of the most stunning young actresses of the '60s. After working as a New York model in her teens, Pamela's first screen appearance came in the steamy *Summer and Smoke* ('61). Billy Wilder then cast her as a wild young thing in his comedy *One, Two, Three* ('61), perhaps her best film and one that brought her Golden Globe nominations for Best Supporting Actress and Most Promising Newcomer. More movie roles came quickly, especially *Come Fly with Me* ('63), with Pamela as one of the mile hi-larious comedy's man-chasing stews.

Though she had aspirations for serious, sophisticated films, Pamela's youth and beauty seemed to make her better

suited for the lightweight movies aimed at the drive-in crowd—*The Lively Set*, *For Those Who Think Young*, and *The Pleasure Seekers* were three entertaining big-BIG-screen hits in '64. *Harper* ('66) teamed her with Paul Newman (and put her on top of a diving board in a well-filled polka-dot bikini for a sexy dance), and in '66 Pamela hit Broadway in a revival of *Dinner at Eight*, which brought her a *Theatre World* award as Most Promising Newcomer.

Anyone with her looks was going to be invited onto TV shows, of course, and thus she was a popular staple of TV talk shows, and a bright panelist on various game shows, during the decade. With her marriage ending at the end of the '60s, Pamela moved to Rome, went blonde, and made Italian movies into the next decade, with only a few intermittent screen appearances stateside peppering her late career.

December 9, 1969—Charles Manson is formally charged with the slaying of Sharon Tate and others.
December 10, 1960—*Swiss Family Robinson* with Janet Munro premieres.
December 10, 1964—The Nobel Peace Prize is awarded to Dr. Martin Luther King, Jr.

EVERYBODY LOVES SOMEBODY

In '62 20-year-old Pamela married Clay Felker, the prominent *Esquire* editor who later co-founded *New York* magazine. They divorced in '69. In '74, while living in Italy, Pamela married Edmondo Danon, son of the movie producer behind the wildly popular *La Cage aux Folles* ('78). With the birth of two daughters, Pamela basically retired from show biz. Both daughters are grown and pursuing acting careers, and Pamela now splits her time between homes in New York and Illinois.

MY BACK PAGES

The February '69 issue of *Playboy* included a sexy feature on her called "A Toast to Tiffin"—according to the little-read text Pamela is fluent in French, Italian, and Spanish. . . . Praised director Billy Wilder in *Playboy*, "Pamela is the greatest film discovery since Audrey Hepburn. She learns so quickly, I can't understand why she isn't on the Supreme Court bench". . . . In '82 Pamela co-hosted a televised Lincoln Center tribute to Wilder.

Tiny Tim

The decade's unlikeliest male pop star.

TAKIN' CARE OF BUSINESS

In the '60s, Tiny Tim became a household name (though his real name was Herbert Khaury). Fame came by virtue of his outrageous appearances on the hit TV show *Laugh-In* and his campy hit song, "Tiptoe Through the Tulips With Me," which successfully presented a gentle, humorous alternative to the acid rock of the time. His first album, *God Bless Tiny Tim,* was a smash, and the falsetto-singing, ukulele-strumming New Yorker earned and squandered almost $1,000,000 from '67 to '68. He was even successful enough to get published as a poet with a book called *Beautiful Thoughts.*

While it's easy to make fun of Tiny (and many people did), he had an encyclopedic knowledge of early 20th-century music, and in fact he wrote a loving, fact-laden article for *Playboy* about America's great crooners. Unfortunately, in the early '70s Tiny, distraught over his failing marriage, went on eating and drinking binges, and he started slipping into a bizarre fantasy world. With job offers coming less frequently, by the mid-'70s he was playing second-class motel lounges. Never in the best of shape, Tiny was a passenger in a bad car accident that laid him up for months. Later he played on cruise ships and was a frequent guest on Howard Stern's radio show, but sadly Tiny had a fatal heart attack in '96, collapsing on stage into the arms of his third wife.

EVERYBODY LOVES SOMEBODY

In the article he wrote for *Playboy*, Tiny disclosed his romantic technique—in a recording booth he'd cut a record in which he talked and sang to a girl, who'd then get the record as a gift. But that's not how he met his first wife. When Tiny first met a New Jersey teen named Vicki Budinger at a store where he was doing a signing, he was immediately smitten.

December 10, 1965—The Grateful Dead performs their first Fillmore concert. ☮ December 10, 1967—Singer Otis Redding dies in a plane crash. December 10, 1969—*They Shoot Horses, Don't They?* with Susannah York opens. ☮ December 10, 2005—Senator Eugene McCarthy dies in Virginia. December 11, 1912—Director Carlo Ponti is born in Italy. ☮ December 11, 1931—Actress Rita Moreno is born in Humacao, Puerto Rico.

After she disappeared, stories say he either placed an ad in the local papers or used press contacts to find her. Somehow they hooked up, and in September he announced their engagement on *The Tonight Show*.

Three months later Miss Vicki (18) and Tiny Tim (37) got married in front of Johnny's viewers in what was the first live televised wedding. The event (or Tiny himself) was such an object of curiosity that over 45 million viewers stayed up late to gape (there were no VCRs in those days). One of the shocks was how attractive dark-haired Miss Vicki was. Most people probably assumed she'd be as freakish as Tiny (he had a definite pear shape to his body and . . . umm, distinctive facial features). Instead she was a lithe, pretty young girl who made a fetching bride in white. Photos ran in global media, and today a clip of the ceremony is included in Carson's own "Best of . . ." collections.

After a two-week tropical honeymoon, Miss Vicki was soon pregnant, but that child was stillborn. Happily, she gave birth to a healthy girl in '71. But by this time Vicki felt constricted by Tiny; striking out on her own, she had portfolio photos taken at a local studio, paid for them with her wedding ring, and left with daughter Tulip while Tiny was touring. Later she worked as a go-go dancer, posed nude for *Qui* magazine in '75, finally divorced Tiny in '77, and was said to be running a New Age store in New Jersey in the '90s.

Post-Vicki, Tiny had two more marriages. The first one was to "Miss Jan" in '84 (he was 52, she was 34); they had a brief courtship and a secret marriage in Vegas, but unfortunately she wouldn't live with his mom and left him within weeks. Tiny's third marriage in '95 was to a 39-year-old Harvard graduate he called Miss Sue. The daughter of a rich industrialist, Miss Sue supported Tiny and helped him complete his last album, *Girl*, in '96.

MY BACK PAGES

The Tonight Show ceremony featured a seven-foot-tall cake and 10,000 tulips. . . . Among Tiny's eccentricities: he took up to six showers a day, he didn't use cloth towels (only paper towels), and he regularly wore Depends diapers. . . . Tiny was buried with his ukulele and six tulips in Minnesota (where Miss Sue was from). . . . In November 2002 newspapers reported that Miss Vicki was the girlfriend of a rabbi who had hired hit men to kill his previous wife.

François Truffaut

The influential director rode the crest of the French New Wave.

TAKIN' CARE OF BUSINESS

Steven Spielberg is among the many filmmakers who are admiring fans of François Truffaut's work. Born in Paris, François grew up unhappy and rebellious. Pursuing an early love of films, in his early 20s he was writing film criticism for an influential French movie magazine and was an outspoken champion of great directors such as Alfred Hitchcock, whom he regarded as cinematic artists expertly exercising control over every aspect of their films. This "auteur theory" would be the hallmark of New Wave cinema and François's own movies.

He began with short films and quickly found success with his first major feature—*The 400 Blows* ('59). This autobiographical story of a French child growing up with an abusive father was an Oscar-nominated art-house sensation in America. Not only directing but

December 11, 1939—Activist Tom Hayden is born in Detroit. ☮ December 11, 1943—Actress Donna Mills is born in Chicago.
December 11, 1944—Singer Brenda Lee is born in Lithonia, Georgia. ☮ December 11, 1949—Actress Teri Garr is born in Lakewood, Ohio.
December 11, 1961—Elvis Presley's *Blue Hawaii* album hits #1. ☮ December 11, 1964—Singer Sam Cooke is shot in L.A.

also writing and producing his films, he followed with a run of personal, complex, often romantic hits that established him as the most popular French director of the '60s: *Shoot the Piano Player* ('60), *Jules and Jim* ('62), the sci-fi drama *Fahrenheit 451* ('66), and *Mississippi Mermaid* ('69).

Alternating darker movies with light charmers, he made another dozen acclaimed films through the '70s and early '80s, especially *Two English Girls* ('71), *Day for Night* ('73, an Oscar as Best Foreign Film), *The Man Who Loved Women* ('77), and *The Last Metro* ('80, a major award-winner in France). A half-dozen of his films after *The 400 Blows*—*Love on the Run* ('62), *Love at Twenty* ('68), *Stolen Kisses* ('68), and *Bed and Board* ('70)—featured that original movie's child actor as he matured for the next two decades and pursued relationships. American audiences will recognize François as the lead alien-chasing scientist in Spielberg's *Close Encounters of the Third Kind* ('77). Having completed a Hitchcock-style thriller, *Confidentially Yours* ('83), and planning his next film, he died of a brain tumor in '84.

EVERYBODY LOVES SOMEBODY

François was married in '57 and had two kids by '61. After a '65 divorce, he had a relationship with Claude Jade, an actress some 16 years his junior who was in several of his '70s films. Later his longtime partner was an even younger actress, Fanny Ardant, who starred in two of his '80s movies. They had a daughter a year before François died.

MY BACK PAGES

A lifelong Hitchcock fan, François conducted a long interview with the director he considered "the master" and published it as a book in '67. . . . He also hired Hitchcock's favorite composer, Bernard Herrmann, on two films (one of them *Fahrenheit 451*). . . . *Stolen Kisses* and *The Last Metro* were both nominated for Oscars as Best Foreign Film, and François also had screenplay nominations for *The 400 Blows* and *Day for Night*.

Twiggy

Still the person most synonymous with "swingin' London" and fab Carnaby Street fashions, doe-eyed 90-pound Twiggy was the world's most famous model.

TAKIN' CARE OF BUSINESS

Twiggy's impact was instant and international. In her prime, her elfin face was on the cover of *Vogue* four times, and her name and image were merchandised on dolls (the Twiggy Barbie), Mattel purses, "Trimfit" hosiery, Yardley cosmetics ("for those great big Twiggy eyes"), and lunchboxes. She made records (the single "When I Think of You"/"Over and Over" in '67), she wrote (or authorized) an autobiography, and she owned her own boutique and hair salon. So newsworthy was she, in '67 ABC presented three separate "Twiggy in New York" TV specials, just to follow her around Manhattan.

Was there any face more perfect for the '60s? The press didn't think so. She was anointed by London's *Daily Express* as "the face of 1966," and again in '99 by *Time* magazine, which named her one of the 20th century's 20 most beautiful stars. Flashing with brightly colored eye-enlarging make-up (the secret: three pairs of false eyelashes above the eyes, penciled-in eyelashes below), and crowned by a distinctively short boyish haircut (it took eight hours to perfect the first time it was cut),

and with a spray of freckles across her nose, Twiggy's was a face that expressed both the boldness and the innocence of the age. Yet her remarkable face wasn't what made her so special and brought her the name.

With 31-22-32 measurements and barely 90 pounds on her 5′ 6″ frame, Twiggy in a lime-green mini and green tights represented a bold departure from the softer, rounder shapes of '50s and early-'60s models dressed in sophisticated Chanel suits. And then suddenly, all of 19 years old, having modeled for just four years, she retired in '69 to devote herself to acting. Proving there was genuine talent and intelligence behind the pixie image, her '70s were highlighted by *The Boy Friend* ('71, with two Golden Globes as Best Actress and Most Promising Newcomer), another autobiography, and two albums (*Twiggy* and *Please Get My Name Right*).

Continuing to distance herself from her modeling days, in the '80s she reinvented herself once again, this time as a tap-dancing, Gershwin-belting, Broadway-starring Tony-nominated musical sensation in *My One and Only* alongside towering tapboy Tommy Tune (her co-star in *The Boy Friend*). The '90s found her starring in an off-Broadway musical, publishing her autobiography (*Twiggy in Black and White*) in '97, and releasing more albums. She's achieved all this public exposure despite having stage fright. She's even gotten involved with modeling again, including an adorable, much-noticed turn in '98 for the opening of London's Fashion Week, and a stint as one of the judges on *America's Next Top Model*. And a glance at all the new young modeling waifs shows that she's still much imitated. Twiggy's no longer the model, but the Twiggy look is still the style.

EVERYBODY LOVES SOMEBODY

Leslie Hornby was born in a London suburb in '49, which meant she hit the '60s at only 11 and spent most of the decade as a minor. At 15 years old she met her manager/ boyfriend, who was 10 years her senior and married at the time. They promptly started seeing each other, and he began to steer (some would say control) her '60s career. They got engaged in '68, but Twiggy broke free in the '70s when she set her sights on the movies.

In '77 she married actor Michael Whitney, who was in her second movie, *W* ('74), and they had a daughter. In '83 Whitney died of a heart attack. Five years later she married respected English actor Leigh Lawson (who was formerly with Hayley Mills). Lawson directed Twiggy in *If Love Were All* in the late '90s, the off-Broadway musical that brought them both rave reviews. They now live in England.

MY BACK PAGES

Hoping to get publicity for its new car, in '65 the Ford Motor Company loaned Twiggy one of its first Mustangs to drive around. . . . Twiggy is partly responsible for discovering a popular singer of the late '60s—when she heard then-unknown Mary Hopkin sing on TV one night, Twiggy recommended Mary to Paul McCartney, who quickly signed her to the new Apple Records label and recorded Mary's one huge hit, "Those Were the Days," which knocked the Beatles' "Hey Jude" from the top of the British charts.

Roger Vadim

Roger directed and romanced some of the decade's sexiest stars.

TAKIN' CARE OF BUSINESS

Never considered a great director, Roger Vadim is still remembered as someone who loved, and lovingly showed, beautiful women. Born Roger Vladmir Pemiannikov, he worked as a stage actor in his hometown of Paris as a teen. In the late '40s he started working on film crews, and in the early '50s he appeared in several movies that introduced young Brigitte Bardot. After working on the screenplay for her *Joy of Living* ('55), Roger wrote and directed the movie that made Bardot an international sex symbol, *And God Created Woman* ('56). Ultimately, he made five more films with her, none of them regarded as classics.

In the '60s he made a movie a year, usually on erotic themes but always more sweet than vulgar. *Circle of Love* ('64) starred another young actress and future Mrs. Vadim, Jane Fonda. Roger and Jane's *Barbarella* ('68) was an English-language sci-fi send-up that today stands as one of the sillier relics of the psychedelic era. Trying too hard to be hip, the movie ended up being campy instead of sexy and laughable instead of being clever.

Roger continued to make movies for the next three decades, but interest in him declined as younger, more talented cinematic masters emerged. His attempt to remake *And God Created Woman* in '87 with Rebecca De Mornay was again racy but was too little, too late to revive his career. In his last decades he wrote several volumes of memoirs, one with the title that showed what he was best known for—*Bardot, Deneuve, Fonda*. Roger died of cancer in 2000 and is buried in St. Tropez.

EVERYBODY LOVES SOMEBODY

Roger knew sexy, both on the screen and in his private life. He was married to teen-queen Brigitte Bardot for half the '50s. From '58–'60 he was married to Annette Stroyberg, one of the stars of his *Les Liaisons Dangereuses* ('59). Roger then lived with actress Catherine Deneuve in the early '60s; she starred in his *Vice and Virtue* ('63). He married Jane Fonda, who was in four of his movies, in '65. After they broke up, Roger was married two more times to two more French women: wife #4 was a costume designer, and wife #5, Marie-Christine Barrault, was in *Cousin, cousine* ('75) and Woody Allen's *Stardust Memories* ('80). All these women, except for his first and last wife, had children with him; all these women, except for Catherine Deneuve, attended his funeral.

MY BACK PAGES

One of the images he's most known for is one of the first he ever put on film—an early scene in *And God Created Woman* of Bardot sensuously sunbathing. . . . Several of Roger's kids have worked in the movies—Nathalie, his daughter with Annette, has worked on film crews since the '80s; Christian, his son with Catherine, has been an actor since the '80s; Vanessa, his daughter with Jane, is a documentary filmmaker.

Mamie Van Doren

More than just a movie star, in the '60s Mamie Van Doren was a sexual icon on the level of the other famous "M's" she's usually compared to—Monroe and Mansfield.

TAKIN' CARE OF BUSINESS

Acting has been Mamie Van Doren's main career, but acting talent has never been her greatest claim to fame. As she wrote in her autobiography, "Fun, I believe, was where I excelled." After a childhood spent on a South Dakota farm, Joan Lucille Olander got her first job at 13 as an usherette at Hollywood's Pantages Theatre, and a year later she landed her first acting gig, a bit part on an early TV talk show. Soon she was winning local beauty pageants (at age 15 she was Miss Palm Springs), working as a band singer, and appearing in movies for Howard Hughes's RKO Studios. At 18 she posed for Alberto Vargas, and his glamorous "Varga Girl" rendition of her made the July '51 cover of *Esquire*. *Forbidden* in '53 got her a contract with Universal and the official name-change to Mamie Van Doren.

She made some rockin' records in the mid-'50s, did another dozen '50s movies including *High School Confidential* ('58), and became identified with the energetic rock and roll revolution. Her most memorable '60s movies came early in the decade, especially the campy but entertaining *Sex Kit-*

tens Go to College alongside Tuesday Weld, Conway Twitty, Brigitte Bardot's kid sister, and Vampira ('60).

Throughout the '60s, Mamie was in a dozen more movies, none of them award-winners. When the movie roles dried up, she hit Broadway in *Gentlemen Prefer Blondes*, performed in nightclubs and in Vegas showrooms, appeared in men's magazines, and even made two tours of Vietnam and Southeast Asia in '68 and '71 to entertain the troops. After the '60s, she's stayed in the spotlight and kept busy with constant projects, appearances, and a highly revealing autobiography called *Playing the Field* ('87). For over 40 years now she's been stealing the spotlight—always working, always visible, always being Mamie.

EVERYBODY LOVES SOMEBODY

There's no doubting Mamie's active lifestyle—she herself has talked and written about it at length in fascinating detail. Among the famous names she's been linked with are boxer Jack Dempsey, singers Eddie Fisher and Johnny Rivers, athletes Bo Belinsky and Joe Namath, cool guys Steve McQueen and Burt Reynolds, playboys Robert Evans and Nicky Hilton, stars Johnny Carson and Tony Curtis, and even Rock Hudson.

Even more impressive is the list of men Mamie rejected. According to her book, Mamie turned down Howard Hughes, Burt Lancaster, Warren Beatty, Frank Sinatra, James Dean, Cary Grant, Henry Kissinger, and Elvis. Mamie's got lots of stories about all of 'em: just to relate one, she wrote that Henry K. took her on a private tour of the White House in '73 and let Mamie sit in the president's Oval Office chair.

When she wasn't dating, Mamie was marrying, and by now she's had five husbands. At age 17 she eloped to Santa Barbara with a sportswear manufacturer who proved to be abusive, so she soon got out of the marriage. Two months pregnant in '55, she married bandleader Ray Anthony and in early '56 gave birth to her son; baseball player Lee Meyers was briefly her third husband, and businessman Ross McClintock was briefly her fourth. She also had a wild, high-profile engagement with baseball star Bo Belinsky in '63. For over 25 years now Mamie's been happily married and living in Newport Beach, California. Still the life of any party, Mamie's a regular guest at Hef's soirees at the Playboy Mansion.

MY BACK PAGES

At 17, Mamie used her Vegas showgirl money to buy her first car—the MG roadster formerly owned by Humphrey Bogart. . . . In '64, Mamie flew to Paris in search of dresses to wear in an upcoming Aqua Velva commercial—Coco Chanel herself met with Mamie and made the arrangements for Mamie's black dress. . . . Also in '64, Mamie was at the Whisky-a-Go-Go in L.A. when the Beatles were there, and a drunk George Harrison accidentally flung his drink on her (he was trying to throw it on some predatory journalists). . . . The *Playboy* ranking of the century's 100 sexiest stars put her at #29, right behind Jane Fonda.

December 14, 1946—Actress Patty Duke is born in Elmhurst, New York. ☮ December 14, 1946—Singer Jane Birkin is born in London. December 14, 1961—*Babes in Toyland* with Annette Funicello opens. ☮ December 14, 1967—*In Cold Blood* with John Forsythe opens. December 14, 1967—Singer Eartha Kitt debuts as Catwoman on *Batman*. ☮ December 14, 1969—*John and Mary* with Dustin Hoffman opens.

The Velvet Underground and Nico

The marvelously macabre Nico was the headlining chanteuse for the Velvet Underground.

TAKIN' CARE OF BUSINESS

Some songs written for or about Nico: "I'm Not Sayin'" (Gordon Lightfoot); "The Last Mile" (Jimmy Page); "I'll Be Your Mirror" (Lou Reed); "These Days" (Jackson Browne); "I'll Keep It With Mine" (Bob Dylan); "We Will Fall" (Iggy Pop). The inspiration for these songs was born Christa Päffgen in Germany just before the start of World War II. Raised by an aunt after her father died in the war, Nico moved to Paris at 16, where her striking, green-eyed beauty and magnificent height (about six feet) landed her modeling gigs for *Vogue* and an appearance as a nutty, deep-voiced girl in Fellini's *La Dolce Vita* ('60).

Hoping to reunite with Bob Dylan (whom she'd met in Paris), Nico made a mid-decade move to New York, where she soon fell in with artist Andy Warhol, manager of the dark, poetic Velvet Underground. Far ahead of their time, the Velvets would have profound influence on bands as disparate as R.E.M., the Sex Pistols, the Talking Heads, and U2. The group was comprised of guitarist/singer Lou Reed and classically trained Welsh musician John Cale (who had been performing together in various bands since '64), New York guitarist Sterling Morrison (Lou's college friend), and drummer Maureen "Moe" Tucker (who turned her bass drum on its side and played it with a mallet).

Their radical songs explored mature themes, and their innovative shows were part of Warhol's "Exploding Plastic Inevitable" multimedia presentations. Recognizing Nico as a compelling image (Andy described her as someone who looked like she came to America "right at the front of a Viking ship"), Warhol immediately grabbed her to be the band's headlining singer, though she could barely carry a tune and her flat voice sounded like a sonorous foghorn (perfect for the Velvets' hypnotic music).

In '67, the Velvet Underground released the eponymous record album that is now considered a rock landmark, though at the time it was deemed insignificant—*Rolling Stone* magazine didn't even review it, and its highest chart position was #171. Ultimately, however, it would be the foundation upon which the Velvets' lofty rep was built. Nico sang only three songs on the album and so, feeling under-utilized, she left the group in '68. Out on her own, her career never really took off, despite two impressive '60s albums—*Chelsea Girl* in '68 and *The Marble Index* (produced by John Cale) in '69.

For the next two decades she struggled to write bleak songs and perfect her minimalist sound, even as prolonged drug use took its toll. She made a half-dozen obscure foreign films in the '70s while living in Paris, released only a few, mostly impenetrable albums, and at age 49 died in a bicycling accident in Spain. The compilation CD *Nico: The Classic Years* was released in '98.

Meanwhile, the Velvets, recording without Nico, made only one more album, the harsh, experimental *White Light/White Heat* in '68, before John Cale left the group. *The Velvet Underground* in '69 was a gentler, more introspective album than any previously released; the fourth album, *Loaded*, in '70 delivered some of their best-known songs ("Sweet

December 14, 1985—Baseball star Roger Maris dies in Houston, Texas of cancer.
December 15, 1939—Singer Cindy Birdsong of the Supremes is born in Camden, New Jersey.
December 15, 1961—*One, Two, Three* with Pamela Tiffin opens. ☮ December 15, 1966—American icon Walt Disney dies of cancer at age 65.

Jane") and listed Maureen as the drummer though basically she was retired. Over the years live and unreleased material has emerged on bootlegs and compilations.

Lou maintained a successful, if occasionally bizarre, solo career through the '70s and '80s while also maintaining dangerous drug habits. He and John reunited in the late '80s to make *Songs for Drella*, a tribute album for the recently deceased Andy Warhol. The classic Velvet lineup of Reed/Cale/Morrison/Tucker toured and recorded again in the early '90s before breaking up for good. John has had a long, successful career as a record producer (including Patti Smith's breakthrough album). Singing and playing guitar, Maureen made several solo albums in the '80s. Sterling Morrison died of cancer in '95. A year later the group was inducted into the Rock and Roll Hall of Fame.

EVERYBODY LOVES SOMEBODY

In the early '60s, Nico lived with a filmmaker/nightclub owner and then had a child with a French actor (whose mother raised Nico's son). In '64 it's likely that Nico had relationships with Brian Jones and Bob Dylan, both of whom she met in Europe. While she was a Warhol Factory regular, Nico was probably having affairs with various musicians (including Lou Reed). In '67 she met Jim Morrison in L.A., and they had a brief, intense relationship (Nico rarely saw her son during any of these years).

John married fashion designer Betsey Johnson in '68 (*Vogue* ran photos of the wedding), but they split up in the early '70s. Sterling got married in the early '70s and had two kids. Maureen was pregnant when she left the group during the *Loaded* sessions. Lou, married in the '70s and '80s, has been with performance artist Laurie Anderson since the mid-'90s.

MY BACK PAGES

The band's name came from the title of a book by Michael Leigh, who exposed the seamy, depraved side of the swingin' '60s. . . . Andy captured the band in an experimental documentary called *The Velvet Underground and Nico* in '66 (Nico also appeared in his *Chelsea Girls* a year later). . . . Known for introducing bizarre elements into his compositions, John once wrote a piece for piano and axe. . . . Sterling had a Ph.D. in medieval studies and taught at a Texas college in the '80s. . . . Rock legend has it that Maureen's drums were stolen before a performance, so she retrieved some trash cans from outside and played those instead. . . . At the time of her death, Nico was working on an autobiography called *Moving Target*.

Andy Warhol

The Prince of Pop conquered the art world with his unique vision and style.

TAKIN' CARE OF BUSINESS

The most famous practitioner of Pop Art (some would say its inventor), Andy Warhol's successful '60s were the culmination of his early artistic pursuits. Born Andrew Warhola in Pittsburgh, he showed a talent for drawing as a kid and studied art at the Carnegie Institute of Technology in the '40s. Moving to New York, in the early '50s he built a reputation drawing ads and illustrations for fashion magazines (his shoes were especially famous), and throughout the '50s he participated in gallery and museum exhibitions in New York.

In the early '60s, Andy blurred the distinction between fine art and mass production by painting common American objects—comic books, soup cans, money, Coke bottles—and repeating their images over and over on single canvases to show that what was popular could make beautiful art, thus fusing Pop and Art into a single genre. In '62 he replaced the common objects with famous people—Marilyn Monroe, Elizabeth Taylor—to show that celebrities had become just as totally commercialized as anything bought in a store.

December 15, 1966—Hairstylist Jay Sebring appears on *Batman*. ☮ December 15, 1967—*Valley of the Dolls* with Barbara Parkins opens. December 15, 1967—Dr. Christiaan Barnard makes the cover of *Time*. ☮ December 16, 1939—Actress Liv Ullman is born in Tokyo, Japan. December 16, 1962—*Lawrence of Arabia* with Peter O'Toole opens. ☮ December 16, 1966—Jimi Hendrix's "Hey Joe" is released.

Soon he was not only showing mass-produced imagery, he was making it himself with a studio in midtown Manhattan, the Factory, where employees worked from tracings to churn out silkscreen prints under his supervision. Painted entirely in silver (floors, ceiling, phones, everything), the Factory also became the headquarters of a remarkable social scene, with parties and rock stars and fashion models drifting in and out (the actual location of the Factory changed several times). Around him Andy gathered his "superstars," hangers-on and wanna-bes who accompanied him out on the town and went to speaking engagements with him (sometimes for him, occasionally *as* him).

In the mid-'60s, Andy branched out into filmmaking with dozens of underground movies. Some were scandalous, others boring, most were totally improvised, virtually all were thoroughly confusing: to give one example, *Empire* in '64 was an eight-hour "point-and-shoot" epic showing the Empire State Building's exterior, the only "action" coming as the sunlight changed. *Chelsea Girls* ('66), which was really two movies shown side-by-side, was his most famous and successful of these experiments.

Branching out yet again, in '67 he added the singer Nico to the unknown Velvet Underground and produced one of the great rock albums of all time, the influential "banana" album with his peel-away yellow banana painting on the cover; *Rolling Stone* would later rank this debut as the thirteenth greatest rock album in history. During these years Andy affected the look (black clothes, conspicuous silver wigs) and mannerisms (a kind of innocent-yet-sly bemusement) that became his signature style. Andy's life almost ended in '68 when Valerie Solanis, a radical thinker and part-time employee at the Factory, shot him to try to eliminate his influence on her life. Barely surviving, he turned his attention from advancing his art to advancing his wealth.

In the '70s, he began doing lucrative commissions for high society, he founded a glamorous fashion magazine, *Interview*, and he produced the most mainstream of his movies (*Frankenstein*, '73, and *Dracula*, '74, made by Paul Morrissey). And there were successful books: in '77 *THE Philosophy of Andy Warhol* was his fun, fascinating collection of thoughts on art, sex, success, love, and more; three years later he produced *POPism*, his reflection on the '60s.

By night Andy was one of the regular celebrities hanging out at Studio 54, by day a beloved mentor to younger artists. When Andy died in '87 following a gall bladder operation, newspapers announced his sudden passing with front-page headlines, thousands turned out for the memorial mass held at St. Patrick's Cathedral, and throughout the world he was affectionately remembered as one of the most influential, and interesting, artists of the 20th century.

EVERYBODY LOVES SOMEBODY

Andy maintained a kind of detached voyeuristic asexuality in public, even as he was making his underground movies that occasionally qualified as gay pornography. One love affair of particular interest to '60s fans was discussed in Ultra Violet's book *Famous for 15 Minutes*: the long relationship between Andy and Truman Capote. After the two New Yorkers met in '51, Andy said he wrote to Truman daily for a year and that they were secretly engaged for 10 years, exchanging naked photographs instead of rings. Andy's illustrations of Truman's book *The Stories of Truman Capote* became the artist's first solo exhibit.

MY BACK PAGES

In '94 the Andy Warhol Museum opened in Pittsburgh, and in 2002 his self-portrait was used on the 37-cent stamp. . . . Andy's life was celebrated/shown/discussed many times in many media over the years, including a tribute album (*Songs for Drella*) by Lou Reed and John Cale, the films *I Shot Andy Warhol* ('96, Jared Harris as Andy) and *Basquiat* ('96, David Bowie as Andy), plus numerous documentaries and museum retrospectives. . . . An obsessive collector, Andy accumulated thousands of ordinary objects (cookie jars, for instance) that were auctioned off after he died.

Warhol Superstars

Andy's "in crowd" of superstars included the archetype of the "poor little rich girl" and a glamorous drag queen.

TAKIN' CARE OF BUSINESS

Hanging around Andy Warhol's Factory, either as employees working on his art and films or as hip revelers adding color and personality to his parties, were Andy's "superstars." This group of a couple dozen bohemians included a wild mix of artists, actors, performers, writers, and models, all of whom got at least their 15 minutes of fame. Two of the most famous superstars are profiled here.

Electric Edie Sedgwick blazed across Manhattan as a meteoric fashion model, a photogenic star of underground movies, and a world-famous scenemaker. An heiress to the vast Sedgwick fortune, 21-year-old Edie fled from her old-money New England heritage and chose instead a rebellious life in Manhattan. She hit town in '64 and was an instant sensation, quickly getting modeling jobs and recognition from *Vogue* magazine as a '65 "youthquaker."

Drawn to Andy's hip art crowd, she became a vibrant attraction at the celebrity-filled parties he threw in the Factory. From '65–'67 Andy put her in a number of his experimental underground films, including *Vinyl*, *Kitchen*, and *Chelsea Girls*, all of them bizarre but all of them showing Edie to be an eminently watchable actress with one of the '60s' defining looks. Hers was a striking, unforgettable beauty that blended optimism with tragedy, energetic youth with pained experience. *Vogue* gushed that Edie had "legs to swoon over," which she showed in black tights and Betsey Johnson fashions. Balancing her short bleached hair with long chandelier earrings, she summarized what it meant to be a hip New Yorker in the mid-'60s.

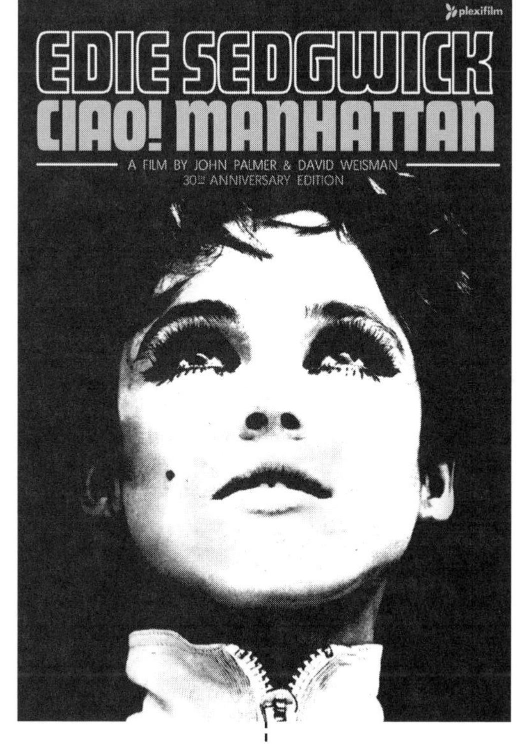

Sadly, her career ended almost as fast as it had started. Some say her affair with Bob Dylan caused Andy to lose interest in her, and he stopped using her in movies. With her modeling career wavering between inconsistent and nonexistent, Edie drifted away from the Factory family as drugs beckoned. Burned out, drugged out, and kicked out, she returned to Santa Barbara, her birthplace, where her career—and her life—unraveled completely as drugs took their toll.

Busted in '69, she was sentenced to five years of probation and was placed in the same hospital where she'd been born. While in the hospital she took lovers, and when granted leaves she continued her descent toward destruction by drinking, taking heavier doses of pills, and even doing heroin. She did manage to make one last movie, the chaotic, little-seen *Ciao! Manhattan*, but sadly, her glamour long gone and her health irrevocably broken by years of heavy smoking, drinking, and drug abuse, she died in '71 from what the coroner listed as a barbiturate overdose. A small country cemetery north of Santa Barbara is her final resting place, her grave marked by a modest rectangular stone that makes no reference to the glittery life she once knew.

Meanwhile, back in Manhattan, Candy Darling was another of Warhol's glamorous superstars. A man living and loving as a woman, Candy (born James Slattery in Long

December 18, 1943—Keith Richards of the Rolling Stones is born in Kent, England.
December 18, 1961—For the second year in a row the Associated Press names Wilma Rudolph the female athlete of the year.
December 18, 1964—Liz Taylor makes the cover of *Life*. ☮ December 18, 1966—Michelangelo Antonioni's *Blow-Up* opens.

Island) broke new ground as a gender-bending pioneer fearlessly rekindling memories of Hollywood's Golden Era. Candy evoked screen queens like Marilyn Monroe, covering his/her naturally brown hair with white-gold wigs and wearing bright red lipstick and a beauty mark. Andy Warhol described her in his book *POPism* as "the most striking drag queen I'd ever seen. On a good day, you couldn't believe she was a man."

In the mid-'60s, the transformed actress appeared in numerous off-off-Broadway plays; taken in by Warhol, Candy played a transvestite in his '68 film *Flesh* and became a fixture at Factory parties. In '69, Candy craved the lead role in *Myra Breckinridge*, believing her experience made her uniquely qualified to play the transvestite Myra (Raquel Welch got the part).

Candy's last big role came in Warhol's *Women in Revolt* ('72) alongside two more transvestite superstars, Jackie Curtis and Holly Woodlawn. Candy did another off-Broadway play and a low-budget slasher flick before dying of leukemia in '74, not yet 30 years old. Though Candy's family later destroyed many of Candy's private papers, two books of diaries and letters were published posthumously.

EVERYBODY LOVES SOMEBODY

Edie spent most of the decade partyin' with cool rock stars such as Bob Dylan and Lou Reed, all of whom gathered around Andy to indulge in the Factory's pleasures. Andy certainly took to her, though it's assumed to have been a purely platonic relationship. Her influence helped shaped rock history, too, as it's widely inferred that Dylan wrote "Just Like a Woman," and possibly "Like a Rolling Stone" and "Leopard-Skin Pill-Box Hat," about her. When Edie left New York for Santa Barbara in '70, she met another patient in the hospital where she was getting shock treatments. They were married in July of '71, but she died that fall.

New York was pretty sweet for Candy in the late '60s. According to Ultra Violet's *Famous for 15 Minutes*, at the *Flesh* premiere "the press went wild over Candy. In interviews she recited a long list of [fictional] films she was planning to appear in: . . . "*Beyond the Boys in the Band . . . Blonde on a Bummer, Sandwich a Trois*." Lou Reed's classic song, "Walk on the Wild Side," summarized her life: "Candy came from out on the island, in the back room she was everybody's darlin'," and you know the rest.

20 More Superstars

Paul America (born Paul Johnson)—actor
Brigid Berlin (AKA Brigid Polk)—actress/artist
Jackie Curtis (born John Holder, Jr.)—actor/actress
Joe Dallesandro (AKA "Little Joe")—actor
Eric Emerson—actor
Andrea Feldman (AKA Andrea Whips)—actress
Baby Jane Holzer (born Jane Brookenfeld)—actress
Naomi Levine—actress/director
Gerard Malanga—actor/poet
Taylor Mead—actor/director
Billy Name (born William Linich)—actor
Ivy Nicholson (born Irene Nicholson)—model/actress
Nico (born Christa Päffgen)—singer/actress
Ondine (born Robert Olivo)—actor
Jack Smith—actor/director
International Velvet (born Susan Bottomly)—actress
Ultra Violet (born Isabelle Dufresne)—actress/writer
Viva (born Janet Susan Mary Hoffman)—actress/writer
Holly Woodlawn (born Harold Danhackl)—actress
Mary Woronov—go-go dancer/actress

December 18, 1966—*The Family Way* with Hayley Mills opens. ☮ December 18, 1966—Dr Seuss's *How the Grinch Stole Christmas* airs for the first time. December 18, 1969—*On Her Majesty's Secret Service* with George Lazenby opens. December 19, 1946—Singer Marianne Faithfull is born in Hampstead, England. ☮ December 19, 1960—John and Jackie Kennedy make the cover of *Life*.

MY BACK PAGES

A reckless guest, Edie almost burned down the Chelsea Hotel single-handedly in '66. . . . The classic biography about her is Jean Stein's *Edie*—in it, her friends described her as being "very frail and vulnerable," "psychologically scattered," with "piles of clothes on every piece of furniture" and able to "keep everybody busy getting her things". . . . According to that book, at the end of her life Edie attended a Santa Barbara fashion show, where she watched the young models with rapt attention—afterwards, she told a designer, "I haven't seen clothes like this in so many years. I have been away". . . . Some of Candy's movies had surprising and bizarre cast lists: also in *Lady Liberty* were Sophia Loren, Danny DeVito and Susan Sarandon, while among those in *Women in Revolt* were actresses named Penny Arcade and Betty Blue. . . . Candy also inspired Lou Reed's '69 song "Candy Says". . . . *Factory Girl* (2006) starred Sienna Miller as Edie.

The silky-smooth singer who remains the best-ever interpreter of sophisticated, stylish Bacharach–David songs.

TAKIN' CARE OF BUSINESS

"I am a combination of my entire family," she said on an A&E biography about her. That New Jersey family included a father who promoted gospel records and a mother who managed a gospel group comprised of various aunts and uncles. As a child Dionne studied ballet and piano, then as a young teen she sang with the Gospelaires, a mid-'50s gospel-singing group that included her aunt, Cissy Houston, who was Whitney Houston's mother.

In '59, Dionne attended the Hartford College of Music in Connecticut and sang backup for other artists. In

'62, she quit school and moved to New York, where she was soon discovered by composer Burt Bacharach and lyricist Hal David. Dionne was a star from the moment she recorded her first Bacharach-David song, "Don't Make Me Over," in '62; it was an immediate hit on both the pop and R & B charts, making her one of the first black crossover artists. Not only did Bacharach and David write more songs for her, they produced her records, resulting in such timeless, elegant hits as "Do You Know the Way to San Jose?," "Walk On By," and "I Say a Little Prayer."

Though everybody had a go at singing them, including Petula Clark, Nancy Sinatra, and Aretha Franklin, Dionne's versions were the most popular, and during the decade the Bacharach-David-Warwick collaborations sold 12 million records, garnering an amazing 19 Top 40 hits. Dressed in glamorous gowns, Dionne sang on TV during these years, she sang the theme song for the movie *Valley of the Dolls* ('67), and she had the lead in a drama of the Old South, *Slaves* ('69). After the '60s, Dionne slumped as powerful soul music made Dionne's sophisticated pop seem irrelevant. Dionne did have one big hit in the '70s, the peppy "Then Came You" with the Spinners in '74. She continued to tour and at decade's end signed with Arista Records, where

December 19, 1961—*Pocketful of Miracles* with Ann-Margret opens. ☮ December 19, 1961—*Judgement at Nuremberg* with Spencer Tracy opens.
December 19, 1964—Marianne Faithfull's "As Tears Go By" hits #22. ☮ December 19, 1964—The Supremes' "Come See About Me" hits #1.
December 19, 1966—Nancy Sinatra's "Sugar Town" hits the charts. ☮ December 19, 1970—Judy Collins plays Carnegie Hall.

Barry Manilow wrote and produced her first Arista hit, "I'll Never Love This Way Again."

Dionne got some screen work in the '80s when she hosted *Solid Gold* for two years, plus she was in the Burt Reynolds flick *Rent-a-Cop* ('88). In '85 she reteamed with Bacharach for "That's What Friends Are For," donating the proceeds to AIDS research (and winning her fifth Grammy Award in '87). She's been releasing albums into the 21st century and now has over three-dozen albums on her résumé. And she's continued to be a major charity fundraiser with her Warwick Foundation, organizing benefit concerts and generating millions of dollars for AIDS research.

EVERYBODY LOVES SOMEBODY

In the mid-'60s, Dionne married actor/drummer Bill Elliott: "It was fashionable," said Dionne in a TV interview, "you're supposed to be a married lady, so I did." She and Elliott were divorced within a year; soon after, they remarried, "a case of can't do with, can't do without," she later explained. They had two sons but divorced a decade later. Dionne then had a long relationship with a Vegas club owner that ended in the early '90s.

MY BACK PAGES

Dionne was born Marie Dionne Warrick, but on her first record her last name was misspelled, and she kept the extra w. . . . One of her hits, "Alfie," had been recorded by 42 artists before she sang it, but her version outsold all the others. . . . Though not a psychic herself, Dionne's enormously successful infomercials for the "Psychic Friends Network" generated lots of attention—unfortunately none of the Psychic Friends foresaw the bankruptcy that would come in the late '90s. . . . Later in the '90s Dionne spoke out against the violence of "gangsta rap" and recorded a rap song with her family as a way to show that the music could be positive and poetic. . . . She wrote the autobiographical *My Point of View* in 2003. . . . VH1 ranked her #42, just ahead of Cher, on its list of great rock women.

Raquel Welch

This voluptuous beauty took a fantastic voyage from motherhood to international fame.

TAKIN' CARE OF BUSINESS

"My career started ass-backwards," she once joked. Forwards or backwards, by the mid-'60s Raquel Welch was one of the world's most famous actresses. As a teen Chicago-born Jo Raquel Tejada studied dance and was a curvy winner of numerous California beauty pageants. In '64, struggling as a divorced single mom with two kids, Raquel landed a job as the "billboard girl" on TV's *Hollywood Palace* variety show. Her stunning figure and photogenic appeal quickly led to auditions, a studio contract, bit parts on TV shows like *McHale's Navy,* and even a brief appearance in the first scene of Elvis's *Roustabout* ('64).

In '65 she shook 'n' shimmied while she sang "I'm Ready to Groove" in the beachy *A Swingin' Summer*. Then came her two back-to-back hits in '66 and '67: *Fantastic Voyage* was the landmark sci-fi film that put her in a clingy scuba suit; *One Million Years B.C.* was the landmark caveman film that put her in an animal-skin bikini. Suddenly the whole world knew who Raquel Welch was (or at least they knew her 5′ 6″, 118-pound frame and 37-22-35 measurements), and movie roles poured in. Her late-'60s highlights included starring roles in the spy flick *Fathom* ('67), Sinatra's *Tony Rome* sequel, *Lady in Cement* ('68), and the Jim Brown Western, *100 Rifles* ('69).

Her busy '70s began with the notoriously catastrophic *Myra Breckenridge* ('70), but she bounced back—and won a Golden Globe as Best Actress—with *The Three Musketeers* in '74 (when she made her acceptance speech she cried and said she'd been waiting for this "since one million years B.C."). Showing the wide range of her talent, throughout the '70s she headlined shows in Vegas and New York, in the '80s and '90s she starred in two big Broadway musicals,

December 19, 1996—Actor Marcello Mastroianni dies in Paris of cancer. ☮ December 19, 2000—New York mayor John Lindsay dies.
December 20, 1942—Athlete Bob Hayes is born. ☮ December 20, 1949—Pin-up girl Claudia Jennings is born in Minnesota.
December 20, 1952—Actress Brigitte Bardot marries director Roger Vadim. ☮ December 20, 1960—Elvis Presley's *Flaming Star* opens.

and she got rave reviews for acclaimed TV movies.

Ever diversifying, Raquel wrote a bestselling fitness book (stressing yoga and nutrition, not bodybuilding), she became a major activist for women's rights and health issues (meeting with President Ford in '74 at the White House), and she created her own lines of wigs and beauty products. Just to keep her hand in, she turned up on some pretty hip TV comedies of the '90s, especially a self-parodying cameo on 1990's *Seinfeld* episode called "The Summer of George" where, spoofing her rep, she beat up both Elaine and Kramer! At century's end her long reign as a cinematic beauty was recognized by *Playboy*, which placed her third, right between two other '60s icons named Mansfield and Bardot, on its millennium list of all-time sexiest stars.

EVERYBODY LOVES SOMEBODY

While her image in the '60s was that of a torrid sexpot, Raquel's private life seems to have been very different: "What I do on the screen is not to be equated with what I do in my private life," she once said. "Privately, I am understated and dislike any hoopla." She likes to be married, though. Raquel married James Welch, her high school sweetheart, in '59; they divorced in '64 after having two kids (one of them, Tahnee, is an actress in her own right). Late in the '60s she married publicist Patrick Curtis in Paris (he had played Olivia de Havilland's baby in *Gone With the Wind*), but they divorced five years later. In the early '70s she had a relationship with fashion designer Ron Talsky after he designed the dazzling dress she wore to the '71 Oscars. The '80s were spent married to a writer, then after a '90 divorce she married again in '99, this time to an L.A. restaurateur.

MY BACK PAGES

At times she's had the reputation for being difficult on the set, but when she sued the producers of *Cannery Row* ('82) for firing her because she was "unprofessional," Burt Reynolds testified on her behalf that she "was always on time, well prepared, and thoroughly professional," and she eventually won over $5 million. . . . Supposedly she came close to being a Bond girl—it's said that Raquel was signed to do *Thunderball*

('65), but 20th Century Fox got her out of her contract so she could star in *Fantastic Voyage*. . . . Allegedly Raquel also turned down one of the three starring roles in *Valley of the Dolls*. . . . Still stunning, in '97 Raquel made *Shape* magazine's list of the 10 sexiest women in the world.

Tuesday Weld

A beautiful but tragic figure whose youthful appeal brought her prominent movie parts and legions of loyal fans.

TAKIN' CARE OF BUSINESS

Tuesday Weld was born in New York as Susan Ker Weld and given the childhood nickname "Tu-Tu." Her father died when she was three years old, and she worked as a catalog model to help support her struggling family. Modeling led to TV commercials, then as a teen Tuesday became an understudy in Broadway's *The Dark at the Top of the Stairs* ('57). By decade's end she had appeared as a supporting actress in four films and as the delectable Thalia Menninger for a season of *The Many Loves of Dobie Gillis.*

Her momentum building rapidly, in '60 she shared the Golden Globe for Most Promising Newcomer with Angie Dickinson, Janet Munro, and Stella Stevens, and from '60–'61 she made seven movies. Projecting both vulnerable innocence and erotic allure, throughout the '60s she starred alongside some of the screen's biggest names, highlighted by *Wild in the Country* ('61) with Elvis and *The Cincinnati Kid* ('65) with Steve McQueen. She was in lots of good TV dramas, too, including *Route 66*, *The Fugitive*, and *Naked City*. Always a nubile young thang back then, her slender figure looked great in a simple dress—*Movie Life Yearbook* gave her stats as 5′ 3″ and 112 pounds, with a remarkable 36-19-35 figure—and she made an appealing cover girl for *Life* magazine in '63.

Her best screen moments came as the energetic sweetheart-turned-killer opposite Anthony Perkins in *Pretty Poison* ('68), something of a cult classic. Paired with Perkins once more, she got her second Golden Globe nomination for the gut-wrenching *Play It As It Lays* ('72). Post-'60s work was balanced between major and minor movies, the best being *Looking for Mr. Goodbar* ('77, with an Oscar nomination), *The Winter of Our Discontent* ('83, an Emmy nomination), *Once Upon a Time in America* ('84), and *Falling Down* ('93).

EVERYBODY LOVES SOMEBODY

Tuesday once said that she doesn't remember much of what she did, because "as a teenager, I was a wreck. I drank so much I can't remember anything." Distressingly, reports are that she was only 9 when she had her first nervous breakdown, was a serious drinker at 10, and had attempted suicide before she

December 21, 1946—Carl Wilson of the Beach Boys is born in L.A. ☮ December 21, 1960—Disney's *Swiss Family Robinson* with Janet Munro opens. December 21, 1962—*In Search of the Castaways* with Hayley Mills opens. ☮ December 21, 1966—*Grand Prix* with James Garner opens. December 21, 1966—*Star-Spangled Girl* with Connie Stevens opens. ☮ December 21, 1967—*The Graduate* with Dustin Hoffman opens.

turned 12. And all that was before she'd made her first movie. During the '60s and '70s, she reputedly was a hard-livin' lover of many '50s–'60s music and movie stars, plus there was a husband and a child in there. After getting pregnant by Dudley Moore, she married him and gave birth to his son in '76. Unfortunately, the marriage was rocky, and within two years Tuesday and Dudley were separated and living on opposite coasts. In the mid-'80s Tuesday married classical violinist Pinchas Zukerman, but that ended in the late '90s.

MY BACK PAGES

Collectors say that teenage Tuesday recorded a now-hard-to-find 45 of the song "Are You a Boy?". . . . When *Bonnie and Clyde* was first being discussed in the '60s, she was seriously considered for the role of Bonnie, as were Carol Lynley, Natalie Wood, and Shirley MacLaine, but they all lost out to Faye Dunaway. . . . Tuesday supposedly rejected leads in *Lolita* ('62), *Rosemary's Baby* ('68), *Bob & Carol & Ted & Alice* ('69), and *True Grit* ('70). . . . One of Tuesday's biggest fans was Steve McQueen, who said she was "the best actress I'd worked with up to that point". . . . She inspired the song "Tuesday Weld" by Walter Egan. . . . Rock star Alice Cooper used to say that the greatest turn-on he could imagine was Tuesday "in a dirty slip, drinking a can of beer."

The Who

Rock's most explosive live act also created one of the decade's most ambitious albums.

TAKIN' CARE OF BUSINESS

The Who were many things to many people—loud destructive hooligans to some, sensitive philosophical explorers to others, the only band that mattered to many. Nobody could deny that they were the decade's most energetic live band, or that they were versatile, artistic musicians who advanced the concept of what a rock album could be.

All born in London's working-class neighborhoods, art students Pete Townshend and John Entwistle joined Roger Daltrey's band, the Detours, in '62 and started playing local gigs. Pete and Roger were both guitarists early on, with John soon becoming the best bass player in Britain. With the addition of 17-year-old drummer Keith Moon in '64, and Roger's focus on lead vocals, the quartet's classic lineup was set, though not always friendly—fistfights punctuated their first couple of decades together.

As the Detours the group played "maximum R & B" covers, but as the Who Pete soon established himself as one of rock's most gifted and prolific composers, and the guiding force behind their image. Aligning themselves with the Mods—a mid-'60s youth movement defined by smart fashions, short hair, scooters, pills, and energetic music—the group wore Pop Art clothes (sometimes made of British flags) and scored some hits of teenage alienation: "I Can't Explain," "Substitute," and especially the anthemic "My Generation," still one of the most arresting records ever made (with one of rock's greatest lines—"hope I die before I get old").

The Who were also building a reputation as a fascinating, dynamic live act: John still and solid, fingers flying; Roger twirling his microphone, his voice as powerful as any in rock; wildman Keith playing drums like they were a lead instrument; and Pete, a leaping guitar virtuoso delivering the richest sonics this side of Jimi Hendrix. And then, incredibly, at the end of their shows they'd smash up all their equipment, emptying their pent-up frustrations and their bank accounts. Two live shows in '67 typified the Who on tour mid-decade: their American debut at the Monterey International Pop Festival, where they stunned the crowd with their destruction and raucous musicality, and an appearance on *The Smothers Brothers Comedy Hour*, where they stunned themselves with an unexpected explosion that caused Pete's permanent hearing problems.

But the Who did more than tour and record hit songs. Beginning with "A Quick One, While He's Away," a '66 rock medley about infidelity and forgiveness, the band was already experimenting with longer song forms. This "mini-opera" led first to a well-received concept album, *The Who Sell Out*, in '67, and then a full-blown double-album "rock opera," the groundbreaking *Tommy*, in '69. *Tommy* had an overture (also an "underture"), characters (all played by the band), a complex story, spiritual themes, hit songs ("Pinball Wizard," "See Me, Feel Me"), an avante-garde booklet of art—in short, it was totally different from virtually every other album of the '60s, most of which were thrown-together collections of disparate, teen-romance tunes sometimes recorded years apart.

So sophisticated, unified, and popular was *Tommy*, the Who did tours in which they played it straight through (including memorable shows at New York's Metropolitan Opera House in '70), and it would translate intact as a hit movie in '75 and hit Broadway musical in the '90s.

Subsequent decades would bring dramatic changes to the group. The much-heralded masterpiece, *Who's Next* in '71; a hugely ambitious two-record story of the Mods, *Quadrophenia*, in '73 (also a movie in '79); Keith and John's sudden deaths from drug-related problems in '76 and 2002; a '79 concert disaster in Cincinnati in which anxious fans outside the arena accidentally crushed 16 of their own to death; many successful solo albums by all the band's members; Pete's spiritual/alcoholic/literary pursuits; a successful documentary that anthologized their long history, *The Kids Are Alright* ('79); and always, the thoughtful, articulate albums and titanic tours in front of millions of fans around the world (sometime millions at the same time, as with Live Aid and Live 8).

Accolades have followed the Who every step of the way—seven albums in the Top 400 on the album list compiled by *Rolling Stone*; dozens of songs used for TV themes and national commercials; enshrinement in the Rock and Roll Hall of Fame the first year they were eligible; and a legacy that places them in the pantheon of the three greatest groups (alongside the Beatles and Stones) of the '60s.

EVERYBODY LOVES SOMEBODY

Groupies were a big part of the band's touring life, as documented in interviews they did and even in songs they recorded ("Trick of the Light," "It's Your Turn"). But all of them had wives at home. Roger was married and divorced in the '60s, married again in '71, has stayed married ever since, and now has a large family of kids. John was married in the late '60s and again in the late '80s, with one son. Pete was courting his wife through the mid-'60s, married her in '68, and they stayed together for three decades, with three kids. Moon the Loon

December 22, 1965—David Lean's *Doctor Zhivago* opens. ☮ December 22, 1969—Actress Marilyn Monroe makes the cover of *Life*.
December 22, 1969—Pete Maravich sets a single-game free-throw record (30 of 31) against Oregon State.
December 23, 1935—Football star Paul Hornung is born in Louisville, Kentucky. ☮ December 24, 1940—Actress Sharon Farrell is born in Sioux City, Iowa.

married his already-pregnant girlfriend in '66, but their tumultuous relationship ended in the early '70s; he was engaged at the time of his death.

MY BACK PAGES

Keith was the first one to wreck his instrument by accident (during his audition), Pete was first to smash an instrument deliberately. . . . For years the *Guinness Book of World Records* listed the Who as the loudest group ever. . . . Roger has been the most durable all-around entertainer, starring in movies, TV shows, and stage productions for over three decades now. . . . Rock legend has it that Keith gave Jimmy Page's new band its name in '69 by declaring that the group would go over "like a lead zeppelin". . . . John, "the Ox," often wrote sly songs on dark themes, including "Boris the Spider" and "My Wife," and he also played French horn on several songs. . . . One of rock's most eloquent stars, Pete worked for a publishing house in the mid-'80s and wrote a book of short stories, *Horse's Neck*, in '85.

This petite, dark beauty rode '50s success to '60s superstardom.

TAKIN' CARE OF BUSINESS

Natalie Wood was always a major star who looked and lived the part. Glamorously beautiful with great coloring, she was one of Hollywood's true beauties and one of the most popular queens of movie magazines. Born to Russian immigrants, she began her legendary career as Natasha Gurdin from San Francisco.

She was an adorable child star, most notably in the Christmas classic *Miracle on 34th Street* in '47. Without skipping a beat, her stardom continued through her teen years with two films per year during the '50s, including *Rebel Without a Cause* in '55 (her first Oscar nomination) and *The Searchers* in '56 (a Golden Globe as the Most Promising Newcomer). So busy and popular was Natalie that by the time she was 20 she'd already been in 30 movies.

Her '60s were filled with more hits that put her in romantic, comedic, dramatic, and musical roles, often as a sexy, strong-minded young woman. She starred in the classics *West Side Story* and *Splendor in the Grass* (both in '61, the latter bringing her a second Oscar nomination), *Gypsy* ('62), *Love with the Proper Stranger* in '63 (her third Oscar nomination),

December 24, 1964—Actress Pat Priest takes over for Beverly Owen as Marilyn on *The Munsters*.
December 24, 1984—Actor Peter Lawford dies of liver disease in L.A. ☮ December 25, 1924—Writer Rod Serling is born in Syracuse, New York.
December 25, 1963—*4 for Texas* with Frank Sinatra opens. ☮ December 25, 1963—*Captain Newman, M.D.* with Bobby Darin opens.

30 Non-Elvis Movie Musicals

Bells Are Ringing ('60)
Bye Bye Birdie ('63)
Camelot ('67)
Can-Can ('60)
Chitty Chitty Bang Bang ('68)
Doctor Dolittle ('67)
Finian's Rainbow ('68)
Flower Drum Song ('61)
Funny Girl ('68)
A Funny Thing Happened on the Way to the Forum ('66)
Goodbye, Mr. Chips ('69)
Gypsy ('62)
The Happiest Millionaire ('67)
A Hard Day's Night ('64)
Hello, Dolly! ('69)
Help! ('65)
How to Succeed in Business Without Really Trying ('67)
The Jungle Book ('67)
Mary Poppins ('64)
The Music Man ('62)
My Fair Lady ('64)
Oliver! ('68)
Paint Your Wagon ('69)
The Sound of Music ('65)
Star! ('68)
Sweet Charity ('69)
Thoroughly Modern Millie ('67)
The Umbrellas of Cherbourg ('64)
The Unsinkable Molly Brown ('64)
West Side Story ('61)

Sex and the Single Girl ('64), and *Inside Daisy Clover* and *The Great Race* (both in '65), all before she was 30.

After *Bob & Carol & Ted & Alice* ('69), the '70s and '80s saw a dwindling number, and a dwindling significance, of her films. Starring roles in Olivier's TV presentation of *Cat on a Hot Tin Roof* ('76) and *Brainstorm* ('83) stand as the best-known of the last works in a career that came to a sad, sudden end. Throughout her life, Natalie had an intense fear of water, and ironically, at the age of 43, she tragically drowned off Catalina Island. Today she's buried at Westwood Memorial Park in Westwood, California, the same cemetery where Marilyn Monroe is interred. And though she was a star who knew fame in every decade from the '40s to the '80s, her tombstone is a tribute to Natalie, the person: "Beloved daughter, sister, wife, mother & friend," with the words "More than love" an adoring coda to her memory.

EVERYBODY LOVES SOMEBODY

As a young actress Natalie supposedly dated much older actors. She also dated Elvis briefly: "Elvis was so square, we'd go . . . for hot fudge sundaes," she once said, "he didn't drink, he didn't swear, he didn't even smoke, it was like having the date that I never had in high school." She even flew to Memphis to meet the family, but the relationship didn't last. She was also linked with such luminaries as James Dean, Warren Beatty, Tab Hunter, Dennis Hopper, Robert Evans, Steve McQueen, Frank Sinatra, and pre-governor Jerry Brown. Supposedly the studio nudged Natalie into the relationship with Beatty while *Splendor in the Grass* was shooting, figuring the personal chemistry would help the picture; after they got together, Hollywood legend has it that they broke up when he left their restaurant table and departed with the hat-check girl.

Natalie had three marriages, but only two husbands. The first husband was suave Robert Wagner, whom she married in '57 (a formal wedding in Arizona) and divorced in '62. Late in the decade she was married to producer Richard Gregson for two years, and then in '72 she remarried Wagner (a more casual wedding in L.A.), who was her husband until her death. She had daughters with both Gregson and Wagner.

MY BACK PAGES

Early in her career she would wear six-inch high heels to add some loft to her 5′ 3″ height. . . . Bios refer to her slightly deformed left wrist, which she hid with bracelets, long sleeves, and proper camera angles. . . . Her sister is an awesomely constructed Bond girl, Lana Wood, who played Plenty O'Toole in *Diamonds Are Forever* ('71). . . . In *West Side Story* Natalie's singing was dubbed by Marni Nixon, who later dubbed Audrey Hepburn in *My Fair Lady* (but Natalie really did sing in *Gypsy*). . . . *Life* named her Screen Personality of the Year in '63. . . . Supposedly Warren Beatty begged her to co-star in *Bonnie and Clyde*, but she refused, not wanting to go on location in Texas for three months. . . . Natalie put in a cameo on Robert Wagner's *Hart to Hart* in '79; she and Wagner were also in *All the Fine Young Cannibals* ('62) and two TV movies together.

Celeste Yarnall

This blonde starlet was a celebrity spokesperson and memorable screen presence.

TAKIN' CARE OF BUSINESS

Born in Long Beach and given a name that derived from "celestial," Celeste Yarnall was barely out of high school when Rick and Ozzie Nelson spotted her in Hollywood. Impressed by her striking blonde beauty, they immediately cast her in *The Adventures of Ozzie and Harriet,* which soon led to an appearance as one of the students in Jerry Lewis's *The Nutty Professor* ('63). Small roles in more movies and shows quickly followed, and Celeste's career was off and running.

Her direction, though, was due east, because in '64 a nationwide search and 20 million votes in a public ballot brought her the title of "Miss Rheingold." The newly crowned spokesperson won $50,000, an Oleg Cassini wardrobe, cross-country tours, and appearances in ads and commercials for the beer company. After a year of touring and promoting, Celeste returned to Hollywood for a string of prominent TV shows, including *Land of the Giants*, *Bonanza*, *Bewitched*, *It Takes a Thief*, *Love American Style*, *Mannix*, and *Star Trek* (on the latter her character, Yeoman Martha Landon, had a famous relationship with Ensign Chekov in the popular episode "The Apple").

The King came calling in '68, when Celeste landed a memorable role in Elvis's *Live a Little, Love a Little*, spurn-

December 25, 1967—Paul McCartney of the Beatles and actress Jane Asher get engaged.
December 25, 1995—Dean Martin dies in Beverly Hills of cancer. ☮ December 26, 1940—Producer Phil Spector is born in New York.
December 26, 1965—*Funny Girl* with Barbra Streisand closes on Broadway.

Live-Action Science-Fiction/Fantasy TV Shows (with Years)

The Addams Family (1964–'66)
A for Andromeda (1961)
The Banana Splits Adventure Hour (1968–'70)
Batgirl (1967)
Batman (1966–'68)
Bewitched (1964–'72)
Captain Nice (1967)
Captain Scarlet and the Mysterons (1967)
Dark Shadows (1966–'71)
Doctor Who (1963–'89)
The Flying Nun (1967–'70)
Great Ghost Tales (1961)
The Green Hornet (1966–'67)
I Dream of Jeannie (1965–'70)
The Invaders (1967–'68)
It's About Time (1966–'67)
Journey to the Unknown (1968–'69)
Land of the Giants (1968–'70)
Legend of Death (1965)
Lost in Space (1965–'68)
Mr. Terrific (1967)
The Munsters (1964–'66)
My Favorite Martian (1963–'66)
My Living Doll (1964)
My Mother the Car (1965–'66)
One Step Beyond (1959–'61)
The Outer Limits (1963–'65)
Out of the Unknown (1965–'71)
The Prisoner (1967–'68)
The Second Hundred Years (1967)
The Smothers Brothers Show (1965–'66)
The Space Giants (1967)
Star Trek (1966–'69)
Strange Paradise (1969–'70)
Tarzan (1966–'69)
Thriller (1960–'62)
The Time Tunnel (1966–'67)
Twilight Zone (1959–'64)
Voyage to the Bottom of the Sea (1964–'68)
Way Out (1961)

ing his cinematic advances as he sang "A Little Less Conversation" to her astrology-obsessed character. A year later she was in another high-profile film, *Bob & Carol & Ted & Alice* ('69), and then in '71 she got star billing in two cult horror faves, *Beast of Blood* and *The Velvet Vampire*.

Throughout the '70s, Celeste continued to act, but she was also carving new career paths for herself. First she started her own commercial real estate business, then she became a successful talent manager. In the '90s she got a Ph.D. in nutrition, became a championship cat breeder, and began exploring alternative, holistic approaches to pet care. The results were her two popular books, *Natural Cat Care* and *Natural Dog Care*, a "how-to" video, and her own line of innovative pet products, Celestial Pets. Still living in Southern California, Celeste is constantly on the go with frequent speaking engagements, radio shows, occasional screen roles, and popular appearances at international fan conventions. The young '60s starlet is now the successful entrepreneuse for a new century.

EVERYBODY LOVES SOMEBODY

Celeste has been married twice. Her husband in the mid-'60s became her manager and helped make her a fixture in magazines and movies. In '70 Celeste gave birth to a daughter but soon after she was divorced. She was married again from '79 into the '90s.

MY BACK PAGES

Celeste was named a Deb Star in '67 at the Hollywood Stars of Tomorrow awards, the Foreign Press's Most Photogenic Beauty of the Year at the Cannes Film Festival in '68, and the Most Promising New Star of '68 by the National Association of Theater Owners. . . . In *Live a Little, Love a Little,* the movie's dog, Albert, was actually Elvis's own pet, Brutus. . . . Celeste was the last Miss Rheingold in a long line that dated back to the '40s.

December 26, 1966—*Time* magazine awards its Man of the Year cover to "The Younger Generation."
December 27, 1964—Jim Brown leads the Cleveland Browns to the NFL title, 27–0 over the Colts. ☮ December 27, 1968—*Apollo 8* orbits the moon.
December 28, 1933—Actress Nichelle Nichols is born in Robbins, Illinois. ☮ December 28, 1960—*Where the Boys Are* with Yvette Mimieux opens.

Susannah York

This versatile movie star filled the '60s with memorable roles in critically acclaimed hits.

TAKIN' CARE OF BUSINESS

Two of the movies in which Susannah was a main player won Oscars for Best Picture, something no other actress could say in the '60s. A Londoner who spent much of her childhood on a Scottish farm, Susannah won a scholarship to the Royal Academy of Dramatic Art at 17 and then began appearing in English films in the early '60s. In '63 she was the dignified blonde beauty who captured Albert Finney's heart in *Tom Jones*. Versatile and daring, she was a strong daughter in *A Man for All Seasons* ('66), generated considerable controversy with a lesbian sex scene in *The Killing of Sister George* ('68), and rounded off the decade with an Oscar nomination for *They Shoot Horses, Don't They?* ('69). She's now been in over 40 post-'60s film productions right up into the 21st century, including three *Superman* movies in '78, '80, and '87. She's done lots of impressive stagework continuing up to this day, performs voiceovers, appears in commercials in England, and has also narrated documentaries and audio books.

Oscars for Best Picture

1960–*The Apartment*

1961–*West Side Story*

1962–*Lawrence of Arabia*

1963–*Tom Jones*

1964–*My Fair Lady*

1965–*The Sound of Music*

1966–*A Man for All Seasons*

1967–*In the Heat of the Night*

1968–*Oliver!*

1969–*Midnight Cowboy*

EVERYBODY LOVES SOMEBODY

Throughout the '60s and into the mid-'70s, she was married to a British actor, with a son and a daughter.

MY BACK PAGES

Director John Huston called her one of the world's most brilliant actresses. . . . One of her acting techniques is to write in a journal about her character, exploring her character's personality and creating a history for her. . . . In the '70s Susannah wrote two beautiful children's books.

December 28, 1983—Dennis Wilson of the Beach Boys drowns in L.A. ☮ December 29, 1904—TV announcer Wendell Niles is born.
December 29, 1936—Actress Mary Tyler Moore is born in Brooklyn, New York.
December 29, 1937—Actress Barbara Steele is born in Birkenhead, England. ☮ December 29, 1965—*Thunderball* with Sean Connery opens.

Photo Credits

Don Adams and Barbara Feldon: *Get Smart* publicity photo, National Broadcasting Company (NBC), 1965

Lew Alcindor: Photo courtesy of ASUCLA Photography

Woody Allen: *Casino Royale* publicity photo, Columbia Pictures, 1967

Herb Alpert: Publicity photo, A&M Records

Ursula Andress: Cover of *Dr. No* soundtrack album, United Artists Records, 1962

Mario Andretti: Photo courtesy of the Indianapolis Motor Speedway

Ann-Margret: *Viva Las Vegas* publicity photo, Metro-Goldwyn-Mayer (MGM), 1964

Michelangelo Antonioni: Studio publicity photo, Metro-Goldwyn-Mayer (MGM)

Neil Armstrong: Photo courtesy of The Library of Congress/NASA

Jane Asher: Studio publicity photo, Paramount Pictures

Claudine Auger: Studio publicity photo, courtesy of glamourgirlsofthesilverscreen.com

Frankie Avalon: Cover of *Muscle Beach Party* album, United Artists Records, 1962

Burt Bacharach: Cover of *Burt Bacharach Plays His Hits* album, MFP Records, 1969

Joan Baez: Publicity photo, Vanguard Records

Carroll Baker: Photo courtesy of Carroll Baker

Lisa Baker: Photo courtesy of Lisa Baker

Anne Bancroft: Photo courtesy of Lisa Flood at Fannetastic.com

Brigitte Bardot: Studio publicity photo, courtesy of glamourgirlsofthesilverscreen.com

George Barris: Batmobile publicity photo, 20th Century Fox Television, 1966

Shirley Bassey: *Goldfinger* publicity photo, EMI Columbia Records, 1964

The Beach Boys: Cover of *Pet Sounds* album, Warner Bros. Records, 1972

The Beatles: Cover of *Introducing. . . . The Beatles* album, Vee-Jay Records, 1963

Warren Beatty and Faye Dunaway: *Bonnie and Clyde* publicity photo, Warner Brothers/Seven Arts, 1967

The Beau Brummels: Cover of *Introducing the Beau Brummels* album, Sundazed Records, 1965

Bo Belinsky: Photo courtesy of the L.A. Angels of Anaheim

Daniela Bianchi: Studio publicity photo, United Artists

Jacqueline Bisset: Studio publicity photo, courtesy of glamourgirlsofthesilverscreen.com

Honor Blackman: Studio publicity photo, courtesy of glamourgirlsofthesilverscreen.com

May Britt: Studio publicity photo, courtesy of glamourgirlsofthesilverscreen.com

Helen Gurley Brown: Photo courtesy of The Library of Congress/*World Telegram & Sun* photo by John Bottega

Jim Brown: Photo courtesy of the Syracuse University Athletics Department

Lenny Bruce: Cover of *The Sick Humor of Lenny Bruce* album, Demon Records Ltd., 1984

Truman Capote: Cover of *In Cold Blood* by Truman Capote, Modern Library Edition, Random House, Inc., 1992

Capucine: Studio publicity photo, courtesy of glamourgirlsofthesilverscreen.com

Johnny Carson: *The Tonight Show with Johnny Carson* publicity photo, Carson Productions, 1962

Johnny Cash: Cover of *I Walk the Line* album, Columbia Records, 1964

Chad and Jeremy: Cover of *The Best of Chad & Jeremy* album, Capitol Records, 1980

Wilt Chamberlain: Photo courtesy of the University of Kansas Athletics Department

Ray Charles: Publicity photo, ABC–Paramount Records

Julie Christie: Photo courtesy of the Tara Pollard Macia Collection

Dr. Eugenie Clark: Photo by Nina Foch, courtesy of Dr. Eugenie Clark

Petula Clark: Cover of *Downtown* album, Warner Bros. Records, 1964

Patsy Cline: Photo courtesy of Lisa Flood at Patsified.com

Judy Collins: Cover of *Wildflowers* album, Elektra Records, 1967

Sean Connery: Photo courtesy of Sir Sean Connery

Mike Connors: Photo courtesy of Celeste Yarnall

Sam Cooke: Cover of *Sam Cooke at the Copa* album, RCA Victor, 1964

Cool Screen Cars: *Bullitt* publicity photo, Warner Bros., 1968

Yvonne Craig: Photo courtesy of Yvonne Craig

Bobby Darin: Publicity photo, Capitol Records

Jeanine Deckers: Publicity photo, Philips Records

Catherine Deneuve: *Repulsion* publicity photo, Royal Films International, 1965

Pamela Des Barres: Photo courtesy of Pamela Des Barres

Jackie DeShannon: Cover of *For You* album, Liberty Records, 1967

Donna de Varona: Photo courtesy of ASUCLA Photography

Angie Dickinson: Photo courtesy of Angie Dickinson

Disneyland: Cover of *It's a Small World* album, Disneyland Records, 1964

Donovan: Cover of *Sunshine Superman* album, Epic Records, 1966

Donna Douglas: Studio publicity photo, courtesy of glamourgirlsofthesilverscreen.com

Bob Dylan: Cover of *Blonde on Blonde* album, Columbia Records, 1966

Shirley Eaton: Photo courtesy of Shirley Eaton

Anita Ekberg: Studio publicity photo, courtesy of glamourgirlsofthesilverscreen.com

Dolores Erickson: Cover of *Whipped Cream & Other Delights* album by Herb Alpert and the Tijuana Brass, A & M Records,1965

Marianne Faithfull: *Girl on a Motorcycle* publicity photo, Claridge Pictures, 1968

Mia Farrow: *Rosemary's Baby* publicity photo, Paramount Pictures, 1968

Sally Field: *The Flying Nun* publicity photo, American Broadcasting Company (ABC), 1967

Jane Fonda: *Barbarella* lobby poster, Paramount Pictures, 1968

Anne Francis: Studio publicity photo, courtesy of glamourgirlsofthesilverscreen.com

Aretha Franklin: Publicity photo, Atlantic Records

Al Fritz: Photo of Sting-Ray bike courtesy of Pacific Cycle, Inc.

Annette Funicello: Cover of *Beach Party* album, Buena Vista Records, 1963

Marvin Gaye: Cover of *What's Going On* album, Motown Records, 1971

Eunice Gayson: Studio publicity photo, courtesy of glamourgirlsofthesilverscreen.com

Judy Geeson: Photo courtesy of the Russ Lanier Collection

Bobbie Gentry: Cover of *Ode to Billie Joe* album, Capitol Records, 1967

Astrud Gilberto: Cover of *The Shadow of Your Smile* album, Verve Records, 1964

Curt Gowdy: Publicity photo, National Broadcasting Company (NBC Sports)

Vince Guaraldi: Photo courtesy of the Guaraldi family

Françoise Hardy: Cover of *Alone* album, Reprise Records, 1968

Linda Harrison: Photo courtesy of Linda Harrison

Susan Hart: Studio publicity photo, courtesy of glamourgirlsofthesilverscreen.com

Goldie Hawn: *Rowan & Martin's Laugh-In* publicity photo, National Broadcasting Company (NBC), 1968

Joey Heatherton: Studio publicity photo, courtesy of glamourgirlsofthesilverscreen.com

David Hedison: Photo courtesy of David Hedison

Tippi Hedren: Studio publicity photo, courtesy of glamourgirlsofthesilverscreen.com

December 29, 1967—"The Trouble with Tribbles" episode of *Star Trek* airs. ☮ December 30, 1920—Actor Jack Lord is born in New York.
December 30, 1929—Actress Barbara Nichols is born in Jamaica, New York.
December 30, 1935—Baseball star Sandy Koufax is born in Brooklyn, New York.

Joseph Heller: Cover of *Catch-22* by Joseph Heller, Everyman's Library Edition, Alfred A. Knopf, Inc., 1995

Anne Helm: Photo courtesy of Anne Helm

Jimi Hendrix: Publicity photo, MCA Records

Abbie Hoffman: Cover of *Steal This Book* by Abbie Hoffman, Pirate Editions, 1971

Dustin Hoffman: *The Graduate* publicity photo, Embassy Pictures, 1967

Paul Hornung: Photo courtesy of the College Football Hall of Fame, located in South Bend, Indiana

Ralph Houk: Baseball card by T.C.G., 1957

Olivia Hussey: *Romeo and Juliet* publicity photo, Paramount Pictures, 1968

Martha Hyer: Studio publicity photo, courtesy of glamourgirlsofthesilverscreen.com

Lee Iacocca: Photo of the author's 1966 Mustang by Sheryl Patton

I Spy: *I Spy* publicity photo, National Broadcasting Company (NBC), 1965

Fran Jeffries: Photo courtesy of Fran Jeffries

Carolyn Jones: *The Addams Family* publicity photo, ABC Television, 1964, courtesy of glamourgirlsofthesilverscreen.com

Tom Jones: Publicity photo, Decca Records

Janis Joplin: Cover of *Janis Joplin's Greatest Hits* album, Columbia Records, 1973

John and Jacqueline Kennedy: Photo by Cecil Stoughton, courtesy of the John F. Kennedy Presidential Library

Robert Kennedy: Photo by Cecil Stoughton, courtesy of the John F. Kennedy Presidential Library

Ken Kesey: Cover of *One Flew Over the Cuckoo's Nest* by Ken Kesey, A Signet Book, New American Library, 1963

Jean-Claude Killy: Photo courtesy of The Library of Congress

Harmon Killebrew: Photo courtesy of the Minnesota Twins

Martin Luther King: Photo courtesy of The Library of Congress

Sandy Koufax: Photo courtesy of the Los Angeles Dodgers

Marta Kristen: Photo courtesy of Marta Kristen

Stanley Kubrick: Studio publicity photo, Warner Bros.

Sue Ane Langdon: Photo courtesy of Sue Ane Langdon

Joi Lansing: Studio publicity photo, courtesy of glamourgirlsofthesilverscreen.com

Daliah Lavi: Studio publicity photo, Columbia Pictures

Linda Lawson: Photo courtesy of Linda Lawson

Janet Leigh: Studio publicity photo, courtesy of glamourgirlsofthesilverscreen.com

Richard Lester: *A Hard Day's Night* publicity photo, United Artists, 1964

John Lindsay: Photo courtesy of The Library of Congress/ *World Telegram & Sun* photo by Fred Palumbo

Liz and Dick: *Who's Afraid of Virginia Woolf?* lobby card, Warner Bros., 1966

Julie London: Publicity photo, Liberty Records

Claudine Longet: Cover of *Love Is Blue* album, A & M Records, 1968

Donna Loren: Photo courtesy of Donna Loren

Sophia Loren: *Boy on a Dolphin* publicity photo, 20th Century Fox, 1957

Tina Louise: Studio publicity photo, courtesy of glamourgirlsofthesilverscreen.com

Lulu: *To Sir, With Love* publicity photo, Columbia Pictures, 1967

Loretta Lynn: Cover of *Home* album, MCA Records, 1975

Sue Lyon: *Lolita* publicity photo, Metro-Goldwyn-Mayer (MGM), 1962

Meredith MacRae: Photo courtesy of Allison Mullavey

The Mamas and the Papas: Cover of *If You Can Believe Your Eyes and Ears* album, Dunhill Records, 1966

Pete Maravich: Photo courtesy of LSU Sports Information

Peter Max: Photo courtesy of Peter Max

Eugene McCarthy: Photo courtesy of The Library of Congress

Patrick McGoohan: *The Prisoner* publicity photo, CBS Television, 1967

Diane McBain: Studio publicity photo, courtesy of glamourgirlsofthesilverscreen.com

Denny McLain: Photo courtesy of the Detroit Tigers

Steve McQueen: *Bullitt* publicity photo, Warner Bros., 1968

Hayley Mills: Photo courtesy of the Russ Lanier Collection

Yvette Mimieux: Studio publicity photo, courtesy of glamourgirlsofthesilverscreen.com

The Monkees: Cover of *More of the Monkees* album, Colgems Records, 1967

Marilyn Monroe: *Some Like It Hot* publicity photo, United Artists, 1959

Elizabeth Montgomery: Studio publicity photo, courtesy of glamourgirlsofthesilverscreen.com

Keith Moon: Publicity photo, Track Records, 1967

Earl Morrall: Football card by T.C.G., 1970

Jim Morrison: Cover of *13* album by the Doors, Elektra Records, 1970

Janet Munro: Studio publicity photo, courtesy of glamourgirlsofthesilverscreen.com

Paul Newman and Robert Redford: Cover of *Butch Cassidy and the Sundance Kid* Collector's Edition DVD, 20th Century Fox, 2006

Julie Newmar: *Batman* publicity photo, 20th Century Fox Television, 1966

Jack Nicholson: *Easy Rider* publicity photo, Columbia Pictures, 1969

Chris Noel: Studio publicity photo, courtesy of glamourgirlsofthesilverscreen.com

Kim Novak: Studio publicity photo, courtesy of glamourgirlsofthesilverscreen.com

Anita Pallenberg: *Performance* publicity photo, Warner Bros., 1970

Arnold Palmer and Gary Player: Photo courtesy of Black Knight International

Luciana Paluzzi: Studio publicity photo, courtesy of glamourgirlsofthesilverscreen.com

Barbara Parkins: Cover of *Valley of the Dolls* soundtrack album, 20th Century Fox Records, 1967

Allison Parks: Photo courtesy of Allison Parks

Julie Parrish: Photo courtesy of Julie Parrish

Peter, Paul and Mary: Cover of *Moving* album, Warner Bros. Records, 1963

Michelle Phillips: Photo courtesy of Michelle Phillips

Wilson Pickett: Cover of *The Best of Wilson Pickett* album, Atlantic Records, 1967

Sidney Poitier: Cover of *Lilies of the Field* DVD, MGM, 2001

Stefanie Powers: *The Girl from U.N.C.L.E.* publicity photo, MGM Television, 1966

Elvis Presley: Cover of *G.I. Blues* soundtrack album, RCA Victor, 1960

Mary Quant: Photo courtesy of Mary Quant

The Rat Pack: *Ocean's 11* publicity photo, Warner Bros., 1960

Otis Redding: Cover of *Otis Redding Live in Europe* album, Volt Records, 1967

Cathy Rigby: Photo courtesy of Cathy Rigby

Diana Rigg: *The Avengers* publicity photo, ITV, 1965

Tommy Roe: Cover of *12 in a Roe* album, ABC Records, 1969

The Rolling Stones: Publicity photo, Decca Records

Rowan and Martin: *Rowan & Martin's Laugh-In* publicity photo, National Broadcasting Company (NBC), 1968

Darrell Royal: Photo courtesy of the College Football Hall of Fame, located in South Bend, Indiana

Jim Ryun: Photo courtesy of the University of Kansas Athletics Department

Lalo Schifrin: Photo courtesy of Lalo Schifrin

Janette Scott: Studio publicity photo, courtesy of glamourgirlsofthesilverscreen.com

December 30, 1937—Paul Stookey of Peter, Paul and Mary is born. ☮ December 30, 1942—Mike Nesmith of the Monkees is born in Houston, Texas. December 30, 1945—Davy Jones of the Monkees is born in London. ☮ December 30, 1963—*Let's Make A Deal* debuts. December 31, 1931—Singer Skeeter Davis is born in Dry Ridge, Kentucky. ☮ December 31, 1941—Actress Sarah Miles is born in Essex, England.

Jean Seberg: *Paint Your Wagon* publicity photo, Paramount Pictures, 1969, courtesy of glamourgirlsofthesilverscreen.com

Edie Sedgwick: Cover of *Ciao! Manhattan* DVD, Plexifilm, 2002

William Shatner: *Star Trek* publicity photo, National Broadcasting Company (NBC), 1966

Jean Shrimpton: Photo courtesy of the Tara Pollard Macia Collection

Simon and Garfunkel: Cover of *Bookends* album, Columbia Records, 1968

Simon and Garfunkel: Cover of *Wednesday Morning, 3 AM* album, Columbia Records, 1964

633 Squadron: Cover of *633 Squadron* soundtrack album, Sunset Records, 1964

Smothers Brothers: Photo courtesy of Knave Productions, Inc.

Elke Sommer: Studio publicity photo, courtesy of glamourgirlsofthesilverscreen.com

Sonny and Cher: Cover of *Look at Us* album, Atco, 1965

Terry Southern: Cover of *Sgt. Pepper's Lonely Hearts Club Band* album by the Beatles, Capitol Records, 1967

Phil Spector: *Easy Rider* publicity photo, Columbia Pictures, 1969

Dusty Springfield: Publicity photo, Philips Records

Terence Stamp: Photo courtesy of the Tara Pollard Macia Collection

Barbara Steele: Photo courtesy of the Russ Lanier Collection

Casey Stengel: Photo courtesy of Marc S. Levine/ New York Mets

Connie Stevens: Photo courtesy of Connie Stevens

Stella Stevens: Photo courtesy of Stella Stevens

Jill St. John: Studio publicity photo, courtesy of glamourgirlsofthesilverscreen.com

The Supremes: Publicity photo, Motown Records

Jacqueline Susann: Cover of *Valley of the Dolls* by Jacqueline Susann, Bernard Geis Associates, 1966

Sharon Tate: Studio publicity photo, 20th Century Fox

Leigh Taylor-Young: Photo courtesy of Leigh Taylor-Young

Marlo Thomas: Studio publicity photo, courtesy of glamourgirlsofthesilverscreen.com

Pamela Tiffin: Studio publicity photo, courtesy of glamourgirlsofthesilverscreen.com

Tiny Tim: Cover of *God Bless Tiny Tim* album, Reprise Records, 1968

Françoise Truffaut: Studio publicity photo, Universal Pictures

Twiggy: Publicity photo, Ember Records

Mamie Van Doren: Photo courtesy of Mamie Van Doren

The Velvet Underground: Publicity photo, Verve Records

Kurt Vonnegut: Publicity photo, Delacorte/Seymour Lawrence

Deborah Walley: Photo courtesy of Deborah Walley

Dionne Warwick: Publicity photo, Scepter Records

Raquel Welch: Studio publicity photo, courtesy of glamourgirlsofthesilverscreen.com

Tuesday Weld: Photo courtesy of the Russ Lanier Collection

Dawn Wells: *Gilligan's Island* publicity photo, CBS Television, 1964

The Who: Publicity photo, Track Records, 1965

Natalie Wood: Studio publicity photo, courtesy of glamourgirlsofthesilverscreen.com

Celeste Yarnall: Photo courtesy of Celeste Yarnall

Susannah York: *Sands of the Kalahari* publicity photo, Paramount Pictures, 1965, courtesy of glamourgirlsofthesilverscreen.com

The author and publisher have made every reasonable effort to contact all of the copyright holders in order to secure permission and provide appropriate credit. We regret any inadvertent errors or omissions that may have occurred, and anyone who for any reason has not been contacted is invited to write to the publisher so that a full acknowledgment may be made in subsequent editions.

The *Encycoolpedia*'s Encycoolpediast

This is the fifth book Chris Strodder has written since the turn of the millennium. The biographical compendium *Swingin' Chicks of the '60s* garnered widespread attention in 2000 and landed Chris on national TV (including the E! Channel and the A&E Network) and in prominent publications (*Playboy*, the *National Enquirer*, *USA Today*, the *L.A. Times*). Two diverse novels for Red Hen Press soon followed: *Lockerboy* (an adventure story for young adults) in 2002 and *The Wish Book* (a comic novel) in 2004. Red Hen Press also published *Stories Light and Dark*, a collection of short stories, in 2006. His first book, *A Sky for Henry*, was written for children and published in 1985. Chris lives in Mill Valley, California.

December 31, 1961—Football star Paul Hornung sets the record for points scored (19) in a title game.
December 31, 1962—Michelle and John Phillips of the Mamas and the Papas marry. ☮ December 31, 1962—*The Match Game* debuts.
December 31, 1970—Paul McCartney sues John, George, and Ringo in an effort to dissolve the Beatles.